From This World to the Next

A Handbook for Mourners

מגיד
MAGGID

RABBI GAVRIEL GOLDMAN

From This World to the Next

A HANDBOOK FOR MOURNERS

Eliyahu Weinstein Edition

Translated by Rabbi Gideon Weitzman and Liron Kranzler-Feldman

Maggid Books

From This World to the Next
A Handbook for Mourners

First English Edition, 2021

Maggid Books
An imprint of Koren Publishers Jerusalem Ltd.

POB 8531, New Milford, CT 06776-8531, USA
& POB 4044, Jerusalem 9104001, Israel
www.maggidbooks.com

Cover background artwork by freepik / kjpargeter

The publication of this book was made possible through
the generous support of The Jewish Book Trust.

ISBN 978-1-59264-496-4, *hardcover*

In memory of
Eliyahu Weinstein
of blessed memory

Eliyahu Weinstein was a fine, good-hearted and welcoming man. An enthusiastic Zionist, he and his wife left a comfortable life in the US in order to fulfill their dream of living in Eretz Yisrael.

They established their home in Kfar Adumim, a community of both religious and secular, who live together with love and mutual respect.

Eliyahu loved the Torah, and despite his advanced age, traveled daily to Ohr Somayach yeshiva to learn Torah.

The greatest joy Eliyahu had besides immigrating to Israel was to become the adoptive father of two little boys at age fifty-seven.

Eliyahu died in Jerusalem at the age of seventy-eight, and was buried in Kfar Adumim.

May his soul be bound up in the bond of life.

With loving memories

Ronald Asserson, London

רפאל צבי בן אלחנן דוד

For my dear parents

Dr. David Shlomo and Shifra Goldman

with love and respect.

May you be blessed with long and happy lives.

ב"ה

MORDECHAI ELIAHU
FORMER CHIEF RABBI OF ISRAEL & RICHON LEZION

מרדכי אליהו
הראשון לציון והרב הראשי לישראל לשעבר

15th Adar 1, 5765

I was presented with a large section of this book, which has been written by a treasured rabbi, a man who works industriously for the sake of Torah, Rabbi Gavriel Goldman.

Rabbi Goldman serves as the rabbi of Kfar Adumim and as a rabbinical counselor at the PUAH Institute.

Through his years of responding to questions posed to him, Rabbi Goldman came to recognize that there was a true need for a mourners' guidebook. Such a book would include advice and halakhot about the arrangements during the mourning period, as well as sections on: **Halakhot and Customs, Analysis and Thought, Guidance for Supporting the Bereaved, Wills and Inheritance, and a Key Concepts section.**

Through great efforts, the author has compiled the numerous halakhot that people encounter when mourning. He has included Ashkenazic customs, *nusaḥ Sepharad,* and *Edot HaMizraḥ* (Sephardic customs).

I have studied the book a little and have seen the significant work that Rabbi Goldman has invested in this comprehensive and useful text.

I was not able to study the whole book. I therefore asked the esteemed head of the PUAH Institute, Rabbi Menachem Burstein, to sit with the author and review it, so that his own insights, from his knowledge and experience, could inform this valuable and important book. He indeed reviewed it and approved it.

I bless the author with long life and that he should see great blessings from his notable efforts. We should merit to the resurrection of the dead when the Holy Creator wills it and that death shall vanish eternally and God shall dry the tears from all faces; and we will no longer suffer, Amen.

With blessings,
Mordechai Eliahu
Former Chief Rabbi of Israel and Rishon LeTziyon

Rabbi Zalman Nechemia Goldberg

Member of the Rabbinic High Court
Head of the *"Da'at Moshe"* Kollel – Sadigura

B"H
14th Shvat, 5765

I come to give my praise for an exceptional Torah scholar, Rabbi Gavriel Goldman, Rabbi of Kfar Adumim, who strove and toiled in Torah and merited to compose a work called *From This World to the Next,* a handbook for mourners. The book is a treasure trove in which one can find all the halakhot and customs. May God help us and fulfill the promise that "Death shall eternally vanish," and then this book will only be used for Torah study and its rewards.

Signed, in honor of Torah and those laboring on her behalf,

Zalman Nechemia Goldberg

ב"ה

OVADIA YOSSEF
RISHON LEZION
AND PRESIDENT OF TORAH SAGES COUNSIL

עובדיה יוסף
הראשון לציון
ונשיא מועצת חכמי התורה

Jerusalem
15th Adar 1, 5765

I was presented with sections of this book on mourning, *From This World to the Next,* which contains guidance for mourners. It is the work of an artisan, an esteemed, dear, and faithful person who seeks the good of his people, Rabbi Gavriel Goldman. He has written, provided insights, and gathered, like cut grain from the threshing floor, compiling new thoughts and explanations, arranged and orderly like apples of gold in settings of silver, each idea in its proper place. He is to be commended for his valuable and reliable work.

May it be God's will that he succeed in completing the work soon and that his wellsprings shall gush forth, in good health and with God's guidance, for many years to come. "May he be like a tree planted beside streams of water, which yields its fruit in season, whose foliage never fades, and whatever it produces thrives."

Ovadia Yossef

Rabbi Avigdor Nebenzahl

BS"D

Jerusalem

5765

To our brothers, the whole house of Israel, who study Torah and hold it dear,

I have seen Rabbi Gavriel Goldman's book, *From This World to the Next,* on matters of passing away from finite life to eternal life, in terms of halakha, customs, and theoretical perspectives. I found the book to possess an abundance of information and to be well-arranged. It can be of benefit in those painful hours when someone has died, God forbid, seeing as the index makes it easy to find each item in its place. Our hope is that death will soon be eternally erased. May the author merit to study Torah in peace and in health, and may his wellsprings flow forth until the land is filled with knowledge.

Avigdor Nebenzahl

ישיבת ברכת משה - מעלה אדומים

YESHIVAT BIRKAT MOSHE - MAALEH ADUMIM

BS"D

23 Iyar, 5765

My dear friend, our teacher, Rabbi Gavriel Goldman
Greetings and blessings,

Congratulations on your commendable work, your book on the laws of mourning, "From This World to the Next." In these times, we see clearly that the merit of the deceased protects the living since, sadly, many people's only connection to Judaism and to Torah and mitzvot is through the rituals of mourning, God forbid. On the other hand, the adherence to these laws demonstrates the strong force within Jewish souls, who are not willing to give up entirely on the laws of Torah and Jewish tradition; the faith in the eternality of the soul shines through the confusion of the prevailing secularism. This leaves room for hope that the light of Torah will overcome the darkness and, when the days of mourning have ended, a new light of living Torah will shine.

In order for this hope to be realized, our generation needs books on the laws of mourning that open a doorway to pure faith and to an understanding that all mitzvot lead to eternity. This requires accommodating to the emotional needs of mourners, which would not be satisfied by a stark presentation of the laws alone. I have no doubt that a book that is truly attuned to modern mourners has the power to create a positive transformation for many readers. I believe that your book shows clear indications of being able to meet this requirement.

May it be His will that you bring about the merits of others and a return from sin, and may the passage soon be fulfilled: "God shall wipe the tears away from all faces."

With blessings for the sake of Torah and her students,
Nahum Eliezer Rabinovitch

Contents

PART 3 – ANALYSIS AND THOUGHT

PART 4 – GUIDANCE FOR SUPPORTING THE BEREAVED

PART 5 – WILLS AND INHERITANCE

PART 6 – KEY CONCEPTS

PART 7 – SELECTED PRAYERS AND PASSAGES

Introduction

> *Before the silver cord snaps, and the golden bowl is shattered, and the pitcher is broken at the fountain, and the wheel falls shattered, into the pit. So the dust returns to the earth as it was, and the spirit returns to God who gave it.* (Eccl. 12:6–7)

This book is a guide for mourners. It is not a halakhic work in the usual sense; its primary goal is to guide mourners and those around them in coping with a relative's death. Following a relative's passing, mourners are left not only with sadness and pain, but also with confusion and questions.

Jewish law, in all its detail, provides a significant amount of support and answers – a response to the confusion and distress of the bereaved. However, over-involvement in the details can often distract a person from the guiding principles. Emphasizing the basic principles, rules, and explanations can lead to a better, deeper understanding of the halakhic details and enhanced fulfillment of the laws and customs. Approaching the bereavement process with this broader approach – which includes and integrates the detailed halakhot and customs – may also provide the mourners a degree of comfort and calm.

Through my job as Rabbi of Kfar Adumim, a town where religious and secular Jews live side by side, and as a member of the Binyamin Regional Council's burial society, *ḥevra kaddisha,* I have felt for some time that there is a need for a handbook for mourners. Such a book would not only present the halakha and halakhic rulings but would also explain the Jewish perspective and general halakhic principles in a simple and user-friendly way. There are many excellent halakhic works on this topic, written by the best of Torah scholars; however, often the simple reader who is not proficient in halakha is interested in understanding the reasons and the sources for the laws, but is unable to achieve this by reading the halakhic texts.

For this reason, the corpus of the halakhot of mourning is not addressed here in a scholarly manner. Rather, the book is intended to provide practical and halakhic guidance, food for thought, explanations and reasons for the laws and customs, and to motivate readers to become familiar with the concepts related to mourning. The book is intended not only for Torah-observant readers but for those who are non-observant, as well. Therefore, much of this book is dedicated to explanations and guidance.

In composing this book, the intention was to do so in a clear and accessible manner. In various places I included reasons for the laws, as well as some laws pertaining to particular Jewish subgroups. It is important to provide these, not only for those seeking more knowledge, but also so that the bereaved can be more intimately acquainted with the laws and customs; this may allow for a greater sense of understanding and awareness in their encounter with the rituals. It may also help them to grasp the meaning and the spirit of the halakha as it applies to marginal cases or those not discussed in this book.

For the most part, the book has been arranged in chronological order. The beginning of the book offers a practical guide for **Arrangements** leading up to the funeral and burial: Navigating practical and technical aspects, coordinating with the *ḥevra kaddisha*, and organizing the family for the funeral and for sitting shiva.

The main section of this book is the part on **Halakhot and Customs**. This section presents the halakhot together with introductions, explanations, and sources. The laws that are presented generally follow Rabbi Yosef Karo's *Shulḥan Arukh*, as well as the notes of Rabbi Moshe Isserlis (the Rema). Together with its commentaries, this work serves as the primary halakhic text adopted by the Jewish people. The *Shulḥan Arukh* was written five hundred years ago, and so in order to present contemporary halakhic decisions from the past few generations, as well as customs particular to Jerusalem, the halakhot have mostly been written in line with rulings by the following rabbis: For Ashkenazic customs, the halakhot largely follow Rabbi Yechiel Michel Tukachinsky's rulings from his book *Gesher HaḤayim*. For Sephardic customs, they follow the halakhic rulings of the late Sephardic Chief Rabbi Ovadia Yossef in his book *Yalkut Yosef* and those of the late Sephardic Chief Rabbi Mordekhai Eliahu in the book *Tzror HaḤayim*. Halakhic rulings are also brought from a variety of other books. This book is intended to try and provide answers for all subgroups and traditions. At the same time, it aims to present the laws clearly, without leaving too many things open-ended in undecided halakhic disagreements. With this in mind, some of the halakhic disagreements are discussed only in the footnotes.

This book is not a substitute for obtaining a halakhic ruling, especially when one is faced with a complex situation or question. In such cases, the issue should be discussed and clarified with a rabbi who is knowledgeable in the practical laws of mourning.

The book includes a part called **Analysis and Thought.** It includes discussions of: the various types of Kaddish and the mourner's relationship to Kaddish; perspectives on organ donation and organ donor cards; thoughts from the great rabbis – Maimonides, Rabbi Abraham Isaac Kook, and others – on death, the world to come, and the resurrection of the dead; and a section on purity and impurity and how they are related to death.

Because this book is also intended for people who are helping and supporting the bereaved, it includes a section titled **Guidance for Supporting the Bereaved**. It discusses: how to inform the deceased's family of a tragedy; how friends and relatives should conduct themselves while helping the bereaved; and psychological aspects of mourning. This section also gives special attention to the topic of bereaved children and their needs and feelings within the context of the bereaved family. These guidelines have been written by or with the input of professionals in the relevant fields. This section also includes information for *ḥevra kaddisha* volunteers: How to prepare in advance for conducting funerals and burials, organizational and technical aspects, and attending to the family. The section concludes with a chapter on memorialization.

In the part **Wills and Inheritance**, we have provided a preliminary outline for writing a will and inheritance order, with consideration of both the Jewish legal perspective and the secular legal perspective. Here too, the goal is to provide information and basic guidance about the various possibilities, but it should not substitute for a consultation with professionals in this field.

The **Key Concepts** part of this book is an important one. It is a sort of condensed encyclopedia on Jewish mourning that may be quite useful. People often seek to understand a particular concept and are not sure where to find information about it; sometimes people want to know a certain halakha but do not know where or in what context it would appear in a halakhic text. The listing of terms is arranged alphabetically and can make such situations easier.

The **Selected Prayers and Passages** part is a list of prayers said before one's death as well as prayers recited during mourning. In addition, it is customary to study Mishna during shiva, as Torah study serves as a great comfort to mourners. This part also provides a list of *mishnayot* to be learned.

* * *

> At the conclusion of blessings said in the Temple, they used to say: "Until this world." When the Sadducees perverted their ways and asserted that there was only one world, it was ordained that the response should be; "From this world to the next." (Mishna Berakhot 9)

The title of this book, *From This World to the Next,* expresses the deeply held Jewish belief in the eternal nature of the soul. The Jewish perspective views the world with awe and respect for its Creator, with an understanding that there are entire worlds beyond our human comprehension. It has gratitude to the Master of the universe for giving us the opportunity to contemplate and be in relationship with His phenomenal world through the Torah and the eternal life that He has placed within us. This book's title seeks to convey that when a person dies, he moves from his transient existence to the world of eternal life. The title also alludes to the book *Gesher HaḤayim* (lit. "Bridge of Life"), upon which much of this book is based. This is out of a sense of appreciation and admiration for that book and its author.

The beginning of the verse, "And God's kindness is from this world to the next"(Psalms 103:17) expresses gratitude for God's infinite kindness that is bestowed upon us. The continuation of the verse, "And His justice to the children's children," is a prayer that the Torah never depart from our children and our children's children.

* * *

ACKNOWLEDGMENTS

> Were our mouths filled with song like the sea, and our tongue full of joy like many waves, and our lips full of praise as the breadth of the heavens, and our eyes bright as the sun and the moon, and our hands spread out like the eagles of the sky, and our legs as swift as deer, we could still not suffice to thank You, God, and the God of our fathers, for one of the thousand thousands myriad goodnesses, miracles and wonders that You performed with our fathers and with us. (Shabbat morning prayer)

Were our mouths filled with song like the sea, we could not sufficiently thank the Creator for his kindness and goodness. I offer thanks to You for giving me the opportunity to learn and teach Torah and for giving me the courage to write this book about halakha and its guiding principles. I know that I am not worthy of the task, and I have therefore striven to show my work to those greater than I, in the hopes of producing something of value and integrity.

This is the place to thank the many wonderful individuals who have helped me immensely. Their words and comments had a significant impact on the book's form and content. Firstly, I would like to thank my teacher and rabbi, Rabbi Naḥum Eliezer Rabinovitch *zt"l*, who encouraged me to write and who graciously reviewed my imperfect manuscript, offering his invaluable, detailed comments. I will take this opportunity to express my gratitude to Rabbi Rabinovitch for the support and guidance he gave me for decades.

I am grateful to the late Chief Rabbi Ovadia Yossef, great teacher of Israel, for giving his letter of approbation for this book. I am also grateful to our great teacher, the late Chief Rabbi Mordechai Eliahu, for graciously supplying many oral and written answers to my questions and for his letter of approbation and blessing for this book. Thank you to the late Rabbi Zalman Nechemia Goldberg who agreed to review the book and gave his letter of approbation and blessing. My special thanks to Rabbi Avigdor Nebenzahl *shlita* who took the time to review the entire manuscript, offering his valuable comments and was gracious enough to sit with me numerous times and answer my questions. I thank Rabbi Nebenzahl for agreeing to have his comments included in the book. I thank Rabbi Yaakov Ariel *shlita* for allowing his article on organ donation to be included in the book.

A special thanks to Rabbi Yaakov Ruza *shlita*, rabbi of the Tel Aviv *ḥevra kaddisha* and expert in the halakhot and customs of mourning and burial, for meeting with me and answer my questions numerous times. I would also like to express my deep thanks to Chief Rabbi Yitzḥak Yosef *shlita* who reviewed the book and made important comments that have been incorporated into the book.

I thank Rabbi Shlomo Aviner *shlita* for allowing his article on organ donation to be included in the book. I would like to express thanks and appreciation to my friend Rabbi Yishai Buchris *shlita*, who agreed to write about the halakhic and Torah principles of inheritance and composing a will.

I have no words to express my thanks, appreciation, and respect for my friend and colleague, my teacher and rabbi, Rabbi Menachem Burstein, Head of the PUAH Institute. Rabbi Burstein invested many hours of his precious time, with unending patience, and read large sections of this book with me, word for word; he contributed dozens of comments on what was written. Thank you to my friend Rabbi Eliezer HaCohen Altshuler, rabbi of Susia and a rabbinic counselor at the PUAH Institute, who gave his input on the halakhot for *kohanim*. I also thank Tova Teper, secretary at the PUAH Institute, for all her help. I would like to express my gratitude to the librarian Binyamin Solomon *z"l*, who took the trouble to bring me books from the National Library of Israel; his passing was unexpected, may his memory be a blessing.

Thank you to my teachers and colleagues at the Maor Tuvia Yeshiva in Mitzpeh Yeriḥo. A special thank you to the *rosh yeshiva*, Rabbi

Thank you to my teachers and colleagues at the Maor Tuvia Yeshiva in Mitzpeh Yeriḥo. A special thank you to the *rosh yeshiva,* Rabbi Shabtai Sabato, who generously studied with me the sections of this book related to Kabbala, offering his insights and explanations. Heartfelt thanks to my friend Rabbi Chaim Greenspan, who gave his support and advice throughout the process of writing this book, as well as to my friend Rabbi Tzadok Elias. Thank you to my dear students Reuven Sasson, Eliezer Kenisberg, Refael Meyuchas, and David Kurtz for their tremendous help. I would like to express my heartfelt gratitude to the Maor Tuvia Yeshiva, where most of this book was written.

Thank you to my friends from Kfar Adumim: I want to first thank Ilan Greenfield; years ago, he approached me with a request to write a user-friendly guide on the subject of Jewish mourning, intended also for non-observant Jews, seeing that such a work was needed. I would like to express my thanks and deep appreciation to my friend Dr. Uzi Fuchs for his comments and advice, to Sarah Fuchs for her dedicated and precise language editing, and to my friend Dr. Zion Ukashy for his linguistic advice. Thank you to my beloved neighbors Elchanan and Dr. Vered Noam for their help, advice, and support. A special thanks to my friend and colleague Rabbi Yoel ben Harush for his guidance and assistance; to the psychologist Dr. Meir Perlov and the psychiatrist Dr. Forto ben Harush for the content they composed for this book; to the lawyer Yehuda Elram for his attention to the legal factors addressed in the book; and to Eyal ben Eliyahu and Aryeh Cohen for their assistance. I thank David Yehoshua and his brother Peter for their excellent work on the design and layout of the book. A special thank you to Justice Tzvi Tal who agreed to write a section about handling inheritance in accordance with an inheritance order or will, in consideration of both the Jewish and civil law perspectives.

A special thank you to my friend Rabbi Dr. Yehuda Brandes who read the first draft, made insightful comments, and opened up many new ways of thinking with regard to the book. Thank you to Chananya Shachor, the director of the Kehilat Yerushalayim *ḥevra kaddisha,* for his generous assistance in meeting with me and answering my questions. Thank you to Rabbi Nahum HaCohen Kook and to Rabbi Mordechai Vikhelder, both of whom helped with regard to the laws on autopsies, and to Michael Gutwein, coordinator of ZAKA's legal department, for agreeing to have their names and information appear in the book for those who might need them. A special thanks to Yehudit bar David for her important and sensitive contribution in writing about informing a family of a tragedy. Many thanks to the psychologist Nahi Alon and Prof. Haim Omer for allowing a chapter of their book to appear in this book. My deep thanks to Rabbi Shaul Farber and the ITIM organization, who provide support and assistance with Jewish lifecycle events. Thank you to Meir HaNegbi and to Yossi Munk from Milta Press for their participation and assistance.

A special note of thanks to Matthew Miller, Rabbi Reuven Ziegler, Ashirah Firszt, Ita Olesker, Caryn Meltz, Yedidya Naveh, and Alex Drucker of Maggid Books, for their thoughtfulness and professionalism in bringing this book to publication. I would also like to give a special thank you to the translators of this book, Rabbi Gideon Weitzman, and Liron Kranzler-Feldman, and to the editors, Liron Kranzler-Feldman and Rabbi Eli Clark.

Before concluding these acknowledgements, I would like to express my thanks, appreciation, and love for my first teachers at the Maaleh Adumim Yeshiva. Rabbi Yitzḥak Shilat *shlita* and Rabbi Haim Sabato *shlita* welcomed me into the yeshiva when I was a young man. Since then, the education and guidance they have given me have had a tremendous impact on me and my life, and for this I am truly grateful.

And the best for last: My deepest, most loving thanks to my wife, parents, and children for their patience, encouragement, and support along the way. May you all be blessed.

I pray that I have merited to understand the words of the halakhic authorities correctly and that I have not made any mistakes. Despite the great efforts invested in it, it is likely that this book contains things that require improvement or clarification. If a halakhic decision has been understood incorrectly, the responsibility is entirely my own, and I ask forgiveness from those whom I did not fully understand. I welcome feedback and insights; thank you in advance to anyone who sends me their comments on what is written in this book.

I hope and pray that no problems result from my work and that I may merit to be aligned with the truth of Torah.

Gavriel Goldman

Part 1

Arrangements

This section outlines the procedures involved in arranging for a relative's funeral and burial. It first presents the accepted practices in the State of Israel. Afterwards, we relate to the common practices in Jewish communities outside of Israel, particularly those in North America.

A RELATIVE HAS DIED – WHAT NEEDS TO BE DONE?

Finding out that a relative has died is extremely upsetting. It is natural to experience turbulent emotions and a sense of shock and confusion; this can lead one to turn inward. At the same time, the deceased's family members must immediately begin making arrangements for the funeral and burial. In Jewish law, caring for the deceased is an immediate imperative – so much so that there is a distinct halakhic category called ***aninut*** (intense mourning) during which the relatives are exempt from all mitzvot, so that they can dedicate themselves entirely to dealing with the deceased and his needs. In the following pages, we try to offer practical guidelines for this process.

Guidelines for Making Arrangements in Israel

SECTION 1: OFFICIAL DOCUMENTATION REQUIRED IN THE STATE OF ISRAEL

For official documentation, the following items are needed:

- A death certificate signed by a doctor
- The deceased's *teudat zehut* (identity card)

- A permit from the police (only if the person did not die in a hospital)
- A burial permit

Death certificate

If a person has died at home, a doctor must be summoned in order to declare the person's death and to prepare the death certificate. A death certificate signed by a doctor is an official document in the State of Israel. If the person died in a hospital, the certificate is issued by the hospital. Outside of the hospital, the certificate will generally be given by a doctor from Magen David Adom who declares the death, or by the family doctor.

In order to receive a burial permit, one needs **three copies of the death certificate**, as well as the deceased's ***teudat zehut*** **(identity card)**. If one does not have the identity card, one may try to obtain a burial permit without it.

The deceased cannot be buried without a burial permit.

Police certificate

In the case of an accident or suspicion of unnatural death, a document of **police authorization** must be obtained. This is a legal procedure; it is the police's responsibility to ascertain how the person died. The permit is usually given by the police after a relatively short inquiry, in order to proceed with the burial.

One copy of the death certificate is given to the police, and the family retains the other two.

Burial permit

The burial permit is issued by the **Regional Health Office**. If one needs to reach them outside of office hours, one can speak with the Health Ministry's **on-call doctor**. It is often possible and helpful to get help from the *ḥevra kaddisha*. In **public hospitals**, the burial permit is usually issued to the family in the hospital's **admittance office**, since public hospitals are under the jurisdiction of the Health Ministry. If the person has died outside of a hospital, the family will need to make arrangements to have the permit issued. In certain places, the ***ḥevra kaddisha*** takes care of obtaining of the burial permit.

In certain cases, the body must be taken to the Institute of Forensic Medicine. After releasing the body, the Institute will issue a burial permit. Generally, the family has the right to refuse an autopsy unless there is a court order to perform one.[1]

> *Death certificate*
> *The Health Ministry offices may have a form available to request the death certificate from the Ministry of Interior. This can be requested if one is already there in the offices. If so, the form should be filled out there, and the death certificate will be mailed to one's house. The death certificate usually must to be obtained from the Ministry of Interior. Note that the official death certificate is used for purposes of inheritance and estate and is not necessary for the burial.*

SECTION 2: COORDINATING WITH THE ḤEVRA KADDISHA AND/OR FUNERAL HOME

Burial location and time of funeral – standard procedures in Israel

A *ḥevra kaddisha* should be contacted to coordinate the **place of burial.** Relatives should be aware of the fact that there are different kinds of burial plots, for example, for different Jewish subgroups (e.g., Ashkenazic, Sephardic), for *kohanim,* etc. There are different prices for the various kinds of plots. The family should obtain information about the different types of graves, what they cost, how accessible they are, etc.; knowing the different possibilities and costs from the outset can help prevent misunderstandings.

The exact **time of the funeral** should be determined in close coordination with the *ḥevra kaddisha.* The main concern when setting the time for the funeral is the **honor of the deceased.** On the one hand, it is most respectful to the deceased for the body to be buried as soon as possible after death. On the other hand, it is an honor to the deceased

1. Rabbi Nebenzahl: One should make efforts to oppose an autopsy, or in the case of murder, to limit it as much as possible, even if the family is told that no damages will be awarded to them without an autopsy (e.g., in a car accident). See **Autopsy** in the Key Concepts section for practical advice on this matter.

if more people, especially close relatives, are able to attend the funeral to accompany the deceased to their final resting place.

One should take into consideration how much time will be necessary to inform people of the death and funeral, make arrangements, and allow for people, especially close family members, to arrive. If there are first-degree family members who are far way, the timing of the funeral will sometimes be set accordingly, in order to wait for them to arrive.[2]

There is a halakhic principle stating that one must try to avoid leaving the body overnight without a burial (see Key Concepts, **Leaving the Body Overnight** [***Halanat HaMet***]). In Jerusalem, it is customary to make special efforts to adhere to this. There are times when it is difficult to comply with this principle, especially if the death occurred in the late afternoon or evening. However, some families and some *ḥevra kaddisha*s are strict about this issue and prefer to hold by it even in such cases.

Another consideration when setting the time for the funeral is that, if the burial is completed before sunset, that day is counted as the first day of shiva (see Key Concepts, **Part of the Day Is Counted as a Whole Day**). This is another reason to try to complete the burial before sunset.[3]

One must also keep in mind that the *ḥevra kaddisha* needs time to prepare for the funeral and burial. It takes time to prepare the body, dig the grave (if they have taken on that task), and transport the body. In large towns or cities, there may be several funerals taking place on the same day. To ensure that the *ḥevra kaddisha* will have enough time to take care of all of the necessary preparations, the time of the burial and funeral should not be determined or announced before coordinating with them.

Paying for the burial – standard procedures in Israel

For residents of Israel, the cost of burial is generally paid by Bituah Leumi, the National Insurance Institute.

---

2. Rabbi Avigdor Nebenzahl: Rabbi Shlomo Zalman Auerbach did not permit delaying the burial for this purpose.
3. Rabbi Nebenzahl: It is sufficient if the grave has been closed and the mourners remove their shoes before sunset.

According to the directives of Bituah Leumi, burial in Israel is free of charge in the following cases:[4]

1. A resident of Israel who died in Israel and is buried in their place of residence
2. A resident of Israel who died abroad and is buried in their place of residence in Israel

Funding for the day of burial is transferred to the *ḥevra kaddisha* by Bituah Leumi.

According to Israeli law, the *ḥevra kaddisha* can charge a fee in the following cases:

1. When a plot has been purchased while a person was alive (according to the legal rates, which are different for different locations)
2. Burial in a special plot (a plot recognized as atypical by Bituah Leumi)
3. Burial in a closed cemetery (a cemetery that has been declared closed due to a limited number of burial plots)
4. If a resident of Israel died and the family wants to bury the deceased somewhere other than their place of residence
5. A Jew who is not a resident of Israel who is buried in Israel
6. Deviation from the regular driving route for the funeral
7. Special/embellished shrouds

Bituah Leumi covers the standard burial procedure: burial in the standard shrouds and a short route from the funeral home to the gravesite. The deceased's family is responsible for any special burial procedures, as well as the tombstone, funeral notices, and travel arrangements. The *ḥevra kaddisha* will usually transport the body free of charge on the day of the death; however, transportation after regular business hours,

4. This information is accurate to the best of the author's knowledge at the time of writing. It pertains to Israel. In Israel, in all cases, one should contact Bituah Leumi to check the burial rights. They can be contacted through their website, www.btl.gov.il, or at one's local branch.

transportation by private ambulance, or any other non-standard transportation will generally carry a fee.

A resident of Israel who has died abroad

A resident of Israel who falls under the jurisdiction of Bituah Leumi is entitled to burial free of charge in their place of residence – the place of residence written on their *teudat zehut* (identity card). It is the family's responsibility to arrange to fly the coffin to Israel and to transport it from the airport to the cemetery. Travel insurance usually covers the expense of transferring the body to Israel; this must be verified on a case by case basis.

If an Israeli resident dies in the U.S., a Jewish funeral chapel can be contacted; they will usually take care of the ritual purification and dressing of the body, travel arrangements, and coordination with the Israeli Consulate. International law in most places requires washing the body when transporting it from one country to another, and so the ritual purification will ordinarily take place outside of Israel; this is recommended. If the person dies in Europe, the local Israeli Consulate should be contacted to handle administrative concerns and the local Jewish community should be contacted to tend to the body.

In the case of someone who is not eligible for burial through Bituah Leumi (someone who is not a resident of Israel or who no longer resides in Israel), a family representative must first purchase a burial plot in Israel, obtain a permit from the *ḥevra kaddisha* that attests to this, and present this documentation to those dealing with the deceased outside of Israel. This allows the deceased to be brought to Israel.

A tourist who dies in Israel

If someone dies in Israel who is a Jewish non-resident, who does not hold Israeli citizenship, he is entitled to be buried in the city where he died. Halakhically, this person can be called a *met mitzva*,[5] whom it is

5. Rabbi Nebenzahl: If there are no relatives and no one is prepared to tend to the deceased. Nowadays, because there are *ḥevra kaddishas*, there are practically no cases of a *met mitzva*.

a mitzva to bury. Bituah Leumi accepts this halakhic stance and covers the cost of the burial.

Death subsidy for residents of Israel

If the deceased had been receiving one of the benefits listed below, a one-time grant is paid to the deceased's spouse at the time of death, or to the deceased's children if there is no spouse: senior benefits, benefits for surviving family members, general disability, low income, work-injury benefits (in accordance with the laws of Bituah Leumi). A request for this grant must be submitted at the branch of Bituah Leumi closest to the place of residence.

Guidelines for Outside of Israel, Particularly North America[6]

In most communities in North America, much of the technical and logistical aspects that follow the passing of a loved one are handled by funeral homes. Communities that have a sizable Jewish population almost always have a Jewish funeral home. One of the first things that should be done upon the passing of a loved one is to contact the local Jewish funeral home, inform them of the passing and ask them for information on the next steps that should be taken. Funeral homes can also help navigate the purchase of a burial plot in the local Jewish cemetery, if one had not been previously purchased for the deceased.

Most Jewish funeral homes have members of the *ḥevra kaddisha* who they work with, who will perform the ritual purification. One should also ask the funeral home to contact the local rabbi to officiate at the funeral and to deliver a eulogy.

While in Israel the *ḥevra kaddisha* is in charge of all aspects of the burial, outside of Israel, the community rabbi works together with the local (usually non-Jewish) authorities to ensure that the deceased receives a proper Jewish burial.

6. Thank you to Rabbi Avi Poupko and Rabbi Shai Finkelstein for their help in composing these guidelines.

In the process leading up to the funeral, the local community rabbi will usually give his personal attention to the bereaved family. (This is not the case in Israel with regard to the *ḥevra kaddisha*'s involvement.) The local community rabbi will be involved at the time of the burial and also during the week of shiva. The rabbi will usually be notified of the death, especially if it occurs in the daytime; if this has not occurred, then the funeral home will inform both the rabbi and the administrative director of the local synagogue. The rabbi will set a time to meet with the family; they will determine when the funeral will take place, in coordination with the funeral home and in accordance with the family's needs. The community rabbi will accompany the family during this time, sitting down with them and hearing from them about the deceased. The rabbi is the one who oversees the funeral, introducing the speakers and saying psalms and a eulogy. Furthermore, in many cases, the rabbi will come to the shiva house daily, especially if the family is not well-versed in the prayer-services, etc.

New immigrants to Israel should be aware of these differences and not become angry with the *ḥevra kaddisha* in Israel since they are operating according to the accepted standards in Israel. In Israel, the *ḥevra kaddisha*'s role finishes once the burial has ended.

SECTION 3: ARRANGEMENTS BY THE FAMILY FOR THE FUNERAL

Special coordination with the ḥevra kaddisha or funeral home

Apart from coordinating the **time and place** of the funeral with the *ḥevra kaddisha* as discussed above, other arrangements may be necessary: Some people take care to have the body **guarded** (see Sec. 5 "Caring for the Dying and the Deceased: Guarding the deceased") at all times and to have psalms recited beside it. If so, this must be organized. Friends can usually be asked to help with this.

If the family members want to say Kaddish at the burial but are not sure whether there will be a ***minyan*** present, this can be discussed with the *ḥevra kaddisha* to see if they can help.

The *ḥevra kaddisha* must be informed if the family is a family of *kohanim*. *Kohanim* are generally buried next to pathways so that relatives can visit the gravesite without becoming ritually impure by walking through other gravesites. The shrouds used for a deceased *kohen* are also different. See **Shrouds** in the Key Concepts section.

A **sound system** will sometimes be needed for the eulogies. One can check whether the cemetery has one. If it does not, a portable sound system can be brought. The sound system should be tested beforehand and someone capable should be given the task of operating it. If the funeral attendees include sick or elderly individuals, it may be relevant to ask if the gravesite is accessible by car or whether there is wheelchair access.

Funeral announcement

Once the time and place of the funeral have been determined in coordination with the *ḥevra kaddisha* or funeral home, friends and relatives of the deceased should be informed as soon as possible.

One should keep in mind that the *ḥevra kaddisha* may be working on a tight schedule; they cannot usually deviate from the agreed-upon time. Attendees can be told to try to arrive early so as to avoid the stress of waiting for latecomers.

The mourners themselves need not spend a lot of time calling people to inform them about the funeral. It is preferable to have a **designated individual from each circle of acquaintances** (different sides of the family, neighbors, co-workers, etc.) who is responsible for passing on the information to others.

In general, **it is a good idea to enlist friends for help** in the arrangements. Mourners are often greatly agitated. They may have trouble making decisions because of the intense or overwhelming emotions. Friends are in a natural position to help the family members make balanced and calm decisions. In most cases, they will be able to recognize the relatives' needs and be both respectful and empathetic. Enlisting their help can greatly ease the pressure on the relatives during this phase. The mourner's group of friends and community generally share in their grief, and they will often feel a desire to help out. Apart from the help itself, which can be very significant, the involvement of friends and community members can foster positive emotions in both the mourners and those helping them.

Death notices

Families that want to have a printed death notice should contact a printer who offers this service. One can also pay to have the notices hung up for a fee. Alternatively, the notices can be printed from a home computer and hung by friends.

The notice generally includes the **name of the deceased, the address for the shiva, and a list of the mourners.** If the notices are posted before to the funeral, the **place and time of the funeral** can be included. **Times of prayer services** in the shiva house can be added if they have already been decided. In Israel, the printers may have a standard text that can be used.

The family should keep several notices on hand to hang outside of the mourners' homes and at the house where shiva is taking place.

Preparing eulogies

The family should decide in advance which family members will deliver eulogies. Whoever is taking on this responsibility will need to dedicate time and thought to it. For this reason, the decision should be made as early as possible. Rabbis and public figures can be asked to say a few words during the funeral itself, since it is not always known ahead of time who will be present. However, where possible, it is best to decide ahead of time. If the rabbi delivering the eulogy did not know the deceased personally, it is appropriate to tell him about the deceased, including some of his or her good qualities. This should be done without exaggeration. It is best to designate **someone to coordinate the eulogies** and to be in contact with the *ḥevra kaddisha* about this. It may be that, during the funeral, friends or acquaintances will ask to speak. The family might appreciate this, but it is also possible that the family will not be pleased by it. One should be prepared for this, as well.

People at the funeral will be standing, often in cramped conditions or uncomfortable weather. Some may be elderly or frail, making it all the more difficult to stand for long periods of time. Some people may feel weak or heavy with emotion. Because of this, eulogies should **be kept brief** so as not to become burdensome. This should be mentioned politely, beforehand, to those preparing and delivering eulogies.

What to bring to the funeral

The funeral and burial take time and can be mentally and emotionally draining. It is important to prepare logistically and mentally for the event.

Bottles of water, tissues, sunglasses, *kippot* for men and head coverings for women, and **appropriate clothing** should all be brought. If there will be elderly or frail attendees, **folding chairs** should be brought. The family's period of mourning begins when the burial is over. It is marked symbolically with the mourners replacing their regular shoes with non-leather shoes or putting some dirt inside their regular shoes. If they plan to change into **non-leather shoes**, these should be brought to the funeral. The **mourners may change their clothing** before or in preparation for the funeral. In this context it should be noted that, in accordance with halakha, close relatives (parents, siblings, children, and spouse) will have a rip made in their clothing during the course of the funeral. The torn clothing is to be worn throughout the shiva,[7] while they sit on the ground or on a low chairs. They should therefore take a moment to consider which clothing will be best suited for wearing during the week of shiva, in terms of comfort and modesty when sitting low to the ground. Women who are having their garment ripped will, for modesty's sake, need to rejoin the torn sides immediately afterwards using **safety pins**. These should be brought to the funeral.

Mourners who plan to say Kaddish at the funeral but who are not practiced in saying it are advised to review the correct pronunciation of the Kaddish beforehand. A **clear, readable copy of the Kaddish** (in the appropriate *nusaḥ*) should be brought to the funeral, preferably with vowels for the Hebrew. Those who find it difficult to read Hebrew can use a transliterated text. The *ḥevra kaddisha* may have a copy for those who have not brought one. Nevertheless, if a mourner has not said Kaddish before, he should practice saying it so that he does not struggle with the text at the funeral.

The common Western custom of wearing black or dark clothing at the funeral is not the Jewish custom. (See Key Concepts, **Wearing Black.**)

---

7. Rabbi Nebenzahl: This is an obligation only for the children of the deceased.

Preparing the shiva house

After the funeral, mourners go to the place where they will be sitting shiva. The shiva location should be determined before the funeral. There is a halakhic preference that shiva be held in the deceased's home, but if necessary, or if it is more convenient for the mourners and those who will come to comfort them, shiva can take place elsewhere.

The following should be brought to the shiva house: **Memorial candles, benches and chairs** for the mourners and visitors, ***siddurim* and *kippot*** for prayer services in the house, copies of **Mishna passages** to give out, and **Psalms** for the shiva house and cemetery. A ***sefer Torah*** can be brought for the Torah reading during prayer services. This may be available from the local synagogue. If prayer services will be held in the house on Shabbat, then ***Ḥumash* books** should be brought. A **lectern** can also be brought for the prayer leader to use. Some communities have a set of "mourners' equipment" that is lent out.

The mourners' seats should be set up in advance. Usually, **low chairs** are used. It is important to think about how to arrange the seating in the house. If many visitors are expected, a **mourning tent** may be set up outside of the house to accommodate the large number of people. In such a case, **lighting** for the tent should be arranged.

The first meal that the mourners eat after the funeral is called the ***Seudat Havraah*** – the meal of condolence. It will be discussed later on, in the section on halakhot and customs. The meal is usually prepared by relatives or friends and is eaten in the house where shiva is taking place.

It is customary to serve light snacks and drinks to visitors.[8] There is a custom of visitors saying blessings over food and drink to bring merit to the departed soul. This is described in the Key Concepts, **Elevating of the Soul**. Those who have this custom must prepare **food and drinks**; they may prefer to use **disposable plates and cups**. It is also helpful to have a **hot-water urn for hot drinks.**

Sometimes a *tzedaka* box is put out in the shiva house, so that people can fulfill the mitzva of giving charity with the intention that it be a merit to the deceased's soul.

8. Rabbi Nebenzahl: This is not the custom among Ashkenazic Jews.

A family that is leaving their home in order to sit shiva should ask neighbors to keep an eye on the house. Unfortunately, there have been instances of burglars taking advantage of the family's absence in order to break in to the house during the funeral or shiva.

Summary of the "Arrangements" Stage:

- Obtaining death certificate and burial permit
- Coordination with the *ḥevra kaddisha* – setting the place and time of the funeral
- Moving the deceased (this is not always necessary and is usually done by the *ḥevra kaddisha*)
- Publicizing the death and preparing a death notice
- Preparation of eulogies
- Things to bring to the funeral
- Deciding where to sit shiva and preparing the house

Part 2

Halakhot and Customs

Halakha offers guidance for every step and stage of life. In the context of mourning, the detailed nature of halakhic guidance can have particular significance and value. Its specificity and structured nature can make things easier for bereaved families, who may find it hard in the initial phase to find ways to express their grief. Encountering the fixed, familiar rituals can offer mourners a sense of security in a time when they are likely to be grappling with difficult emotions and questions, as well as a sense of uncertainty about the future. In this sense, the familiar rituals may offer some relief.

The Jewish rituals can also foster a sense of belonging and connection – something that is critical during the mourning period. This is true both for the bereaved and for the community around them, who can empathize with and support them. Experiencing one's place within this established and recognizable framework provides a sense of support and security.

This perspective gives a certain layer of meaning to the halakhot and rituals of mourning. The very nature of the detailed instructions, the set rituals, and the familiar arrangements can free the mourners from the need to invest energy in planning their mourning process. It can allow them to concentrate on the mourning itself.

The following guidelines should be read with this perspective in mind. Mourners will have differing levels of stringency according to their individual sentiments and customs.

It is important to differentiate between halakhot and customs. We will try to both define and address the differences between the two.

The Halakhot and practices presented in this book generally follow the Ashkenazic tradition. Where Sephardic and Yemenite traditions are presented, the text identifies them as such.

Halakhot – Up until the Burial

SECTION 4: VISITING THE SICK (*BIKUR ḤOLIM*)[1]

> Rabbi Hama the son of Rabbi Hanina said: What does the verse "Go after God" mean? Can a person go after the Divine Presence? After all it says, "For God is a consuming fire"?! Rather, one should go after His attributes; the Holy One blessed be He visits the sick, as it says, "God appeared to him in Elonei Mamre." So too, you should visit the sick." (Sota 14a)

> These are the things, the fruit of which man eats in this world, while the principal remains for him in the world to come: ...Visiting the sick. (Shabbat 127a)

> It is a positive commandment of rabbinic origin to visit the sick... These are deeds of kindness that one carries out with his person that have no limit. Although all these mitzvot are of rabbinic origin, they are included in the Scriptural commandment: "Love your neighbor as yourself." That charge implies that whatever you would like other people to do for you, you should do for your comrade in the Torah and mitzvot. (Maimonides, *Mishneh Torah, Hilkhot Avel* 14:1)

1. It is not clear that halakhot about visiting the sick should be included in a book on the halakhot of mourning. We have chosen to do so in a concise manner. The halakhot are generally based on the book *Gesher HaḤayim*, which begins with these laws, as well as the *Shulḥan Arukh* (*Yoreh De'ah* 335 and onwards).

Guidance for visitors

1. It is a great mitzva to visit the sick.[2] This is alluded to in the verse, "And you shall inform them of the path that they should follow" (Ex. 18:20) – this is visiting the sick.[3] When visiting a sick person, the visitor should pray for the person, see what he needs, and offer assistance. This helps revive the sick person. The mitzva of visiting the sick is aimed at both the body and the soul: The body – through helping the sick with their needs (the meaning of the phrase "*bikur ḥolim*" (visiting the sick) also includes a "*bikur*" or examination of whether the sick person has all he needs and what he might still need), and the soul – through praying for him. Anyone who has visited the sick and did not pray for them did not fulfill this mitzva as it should be done.[4] A sick person's motivation to be healed is also very important. The person's willpower gives him hope and a chance to overcome the illness. Therefore, when visitors offer encouragement and mental or emotional support, these are meaningful and important ways of helping the sick person. If one helps to heal a sick person physically or mentally, one is also fulfilling the great mitzva of healing the sick.
2. One should be careful not to burden a sick person. If the person does not want assistance or company, then the visitor should only stay for a short time. The visitor should ask the sick person how he is feeling, say a prayer for him, and leave. If a short visit is also difficult for the sick person, the visitor should not enter the room at all. He should simply ask family members how the person is doing.
3. If there are two sick people, one poor and one rich, and many people are going to visit the rich person, one should go to visit

---

2. According to Maimonides, this is a rabbinic obligation; according to Rabbenu Yona (Berakhot, chapter 3) this is a commandment from the Torah. See *Yalkut Yosef* (1:1) who brings a number of reasons why no blessing is recited before performing this mitzva.
3. Bava Kamma 100a; Bava Metzia 30b.
4. Nahmanides, *Torah HaAdam* p. 17, quoted in the Bet Yosef and Rema 335:4.

the poor person; this is the meaning of the verse, "Happy is one who considers the poor" (Ps. 41:2).[5]

4. A person visiting the sick should not sit by the individual's head because the *Shekhina* (Divine Presence) is said to hover above a sick person's head. Also for this reason, if the sick person is lying on the ground, visitors should not sit on a chair above him. (See Key Concepts, **The *Shekhina* Is Above the Sick Person's Head.**) If the sick should need it, it is certainly permissible and a mitzva to sit by their head or feet or higher than them.[6] Nowadays, sick people usually lie in beds; one may sit next to them on a chair or bench.
5. Someone who is not a regular visitor in the sick individual's home should not come to visit him during the first three days of his illness. If, however, the person has suddenly fallen critically ill, such as in the case of an accident, one should come to visit immediately. If the visitor is close with the sick individual, he can come even during the first three days.
6. One who is terminally ill should be asked what he would like to have done regarding his affairs. For example, whether he borrowed something from someone, or someone borrowed something from him. This discussion should not make him afraid that he will die.[7] Such a discussion cannot be had with every person and not in all circumstances. On the other hand, it can be a relief for a sick individual to feel that his affairs are in order. Therefore, one should carefully weigh when to speak and when to keep silent about this – "The wise person has eyes in his head" (Eccl. 2:14).
7. Some have written that a person should arrange his will before he dies and that one should encourage him to do so. However, if this would distress the sick person or cause him to lose hope, then one should not raise the issue.[8]

---

5. *Gesher HaḤayim* 1:1,4; in the name of *Sefer Hasidim* (361).
6. *Gesher HaḤayim* 1:1,5.
7. *Shulḥan Arukh, Yoreh De'ah* 335:7.
8. *Nitei Gavriel,* vol. 1, 1:1–2.

What should a sick person be told about his illness?

8. Our attitude towards the sick is meant to encourage and support them. For this reason, if a sick person's relative has died, he should not be told about it if it will break his spirit.[9] Likewise, one should not describe the person's medical situation to him in an insensitive manner, lest he become depressed and lose hope. He can be told in a gentle, sensitive manner that his illness is serious and that he might increase his prayers and repentance. But one should not tell the sick person that there is no hope; one should always leave an opening for hope. This is because we can never have full certainty about the outcome of the illness and also to avoid causing the person distress and despair.[10]

Prayers for the sick

My son, take care to visit the sick person, for whoever visits him eases his illness. Try to help him return to his Maker, and pray for him, and then leave. Do not burden him with your visit, for the burden of his illness is enough. When you come in to the sick person, come in with gladness, for his heart and eyes are on all who come to visit him. (Will of Rabbi Eliezer HaGadol)[11]

9. When praying for a sick person in his presence, there is no need to mention his name, as when Moses prayed for Miriam saying, "Please God heal her, please" (Num. 12:13), without saying her name, and one may pray in a language other than Hebrew. When praying not in their presence, one should do so in Hebrew and mention the person's name.
10. In prayers for the sick, the person's name and mother's name are said.[12] If one does not know the mother's name, one can say

---

9. *Shulḥan Arukh, Yoreh De'ah* 337:1.
10. Based on *Peninei Halakha,* vol. 3, p. 262.
11. Brought at the end of *Pirkei DeRabbi Eliezer.*
12. When referring to the deceased, Ashkenazic Jews mention the individual's name and father's name and Sephardic Jews say the individual's name and mother's name. However, for one who is sick, all have the custom to say the individual's name and

the father's name.[13] If one does not know this either, one can say, "The son or daughter of Ḥava."[14] The Yemenite custom is to mention the father's name only.[15]

11. When praying for a sick individual, one should include him with all the other sick people of Israel. In this way, one's prayers are also for all others Jews who are sick. This is considered a merit for the sick person since he has caused people to pray for others who are also sick. As a general rule, the larger community has merits that exceed those of the individual and that is one reason why one should try to be a part of a community. This is especially important in times where someone is needing help and support.
12. On Shabbat, one adds: "It is the Sabbath, when one must not cry out, and recovery will come soon."
13. It is good to say these verses:

וְהֵסִיר ה' מִמְּךָ כָּל חֹלִי וְכָל מַדְוֵי מִצְרַיִם הָרָעִים אֲשֶׁר יָדַעְתָּ לֹא יְשִׂימָם
בָּךְ וּנְתָנָם בְּכָל שֹׂנְאֶיךָ.

The Lord will ward off from you all sickness; He will not bring upon you any of the dreadful diseases of Egypt, about which you know, but will inflict them upon all your enemies. (Deut. 7:15)

וַיֹּאמֶר אִם שָׁמוֹעַ תִּשְׁמַע לְקוֹל ה' אֱלֹהֶיךָ וְהַיָּשָׁר בְּעֵינָיו תַּעֲשֶׂה וְהַאֲזַנְתָּ
לְמִצְוֹתָיו וְשָׁמַרְתָּ כָּל חֻקָּיו, כָּל הַמַּחֲלָה אֲשֶׁר שַׂמְתִּי בְמִצְרַיִם לֹא אָשִׂים
עָלֶיךָ כִּי אֲנִי ה' רֹפְאֶךָ.

He said, "If you will heed the Lord your God diligently, doing what is upright in His sight, giving ear to His commandments and keeping all His laws, then I will not bring upon you any of

---

mother's name. The source for this is in the Zohar (*Lekh Lekha* 84): "Save the son of Your servant…remember the mother." *Gesher HaḤayim* 31: 2, 10.

13. Rabbi Nebenzahl: Some have the custom that one does not add the father's name or "son of Ḥava," rather to say "the son of Sarah." In the case of a sick person named Sarah, one can say "daughter of Rebecca."
14. *Yalkut Yosef* 1:20.
15. *Shulḥan Arukh HaMekutzar, Einei Yitzḥak, Yoreh De'ah*, vol 2, 175:4.

the diseases that I brought upon the Egyptians, for I the Lord am your healer." (Ex. 15:26)

בּוֹרֵא נִיב שְׂפָתָיִם שָׁלוֹם שָׁלוֹם לָרָחוֹק וְלַקָּרוֹב אָמַר ה׳ וּרְפָאתִיו.

Creating heartening, comforting words: It shall be well, well with the far and the near – said the Lord – and I will heal them. (Is. 57:19)

לֹא תְאֻנֶּה אֵלֶיךָ רָעָה וְנֶגַע, לֹא יִקְרַב בְּאָהֳלֶךָ. כִּי מַלְאָכָיו יְצַוֶּה לָּךְ לִשְׁמָרְךָ בְּכָל-דְּרָכֶיךָ.

No harm will befall you, no disease touch your tent. For He will order His angels to guard you wherever you go. (Ps. 91:10–11)

רְפָאֵנוּ ה׳ וְנֵרָפֵא, הוֹשִׁיעֵנוּ וְנִוָּשֵׁעָה, כִּי תְהִלָּתֵנוּ אָתָּה.

Heal us, O Lord, and let us be healed, save us, and let us be saved; for You are our glory. (From the *Amida* prayer, based on Jer. 17:14)

14. Psalms should be recited for the sick person's recovery. It is customary to recite the following 18 psalms: 2, 6, 13, 22, 25, 30, 32, 38, 69, 88, 102, 103, 107, 116, 118, 142, 143, 130. These 18 additional psalms can also be added: 9, 16, 17, 18, 23, 31, 33, 36, 39, 41, 49, 55, 56, 86, 89, 90, 91, 104.
15. Afterwards, one should say verses from Psalm 119 that spell out the sick person's name (see Key Concepts, ***Alpha Beita***), as well as the Hebrew verses that spell קרע שטן (meaning "rip up Satan") and the *Yehi Ratzon* (May it be Your will) prayer that is said for the sick.

Changing and adding a name

16. Many have the custom to "change" the name of a critically ill person by adding a new name. Changing the name expresses the hope and the prayer that what has been decreed for the sick individual shall be annulled. Since the Heavenly decree itself cannot always be changed, the person's name is changed so that the decree will no longer apply to that person. As it says in text used for changing the name, if there was a decree against the person called "X," this decree should not apply to this other

person, who is called a different, new name. When a name is added, prayers and psalms are recited in a *minyan*,[16] as is the *Mi Sheberakh* prayer, the Thirteen Attributes, and the *Yehi Ratzon* prayer for changing a name.

17. The name should be added to the beginning of the name,[17] e.g., if he was called Moshe and the name Refael is added, he should be called Refael Moshe.
18. If the person recovers from the illness, even a partial recovery, and the new name is used for thirty days after he recovers – then even if the person subsequently passes away, the new name is used from then on, forever. (This includes having it written on the tombstone and used at the memorial service or when learning or praying in memory of the deceased.) But if the new name was not used and the person did not recover within thirty days, then only the original name is used.

How to pray for a sick person who is suffering

On the day that Rabbi [Rabbi Yehuda HaNasi] died, the rabbis decreed a public fast and offered prayers for heavenly mercy. They furthermore announced that whoever said that Rabbi was dead would be stabbed with a sword.

Rabbi's handmaid ascended the roof and prayed: "The immortals desire Rabbi [to join them] and the mortals desire Rabbi [to remain with them]; may it be the will [of God] that the mortals may overpower the immortals." When, however, she saw how often he resorted to the privy, painfully taking off his tefillin and putting them on again, she prayed: "May it be the will [of the Almighty] that the immortals may overpower the mortals." As the rabbis incessantly continued their prayers for [heavenly] mercy she took up a jar and threw it down from the roof to the ground. [For a moment] they

16. Rabbi Nebenzahl: This is not essential and a name can be added even by one person.
17. *Gesher HaHayim* 1:3, 5.

ceased praying and the soul of Rabbi departed to its eternal rest. (Ketubot 104a)

19. If a sick person is suffering and there is no hope for his recovery, it is permissible and appropriate to pray that he die an easy death and that his suffering be ended.[18] One should not prolong the person's life in his suffering; but it is also prohibited to shorten his life. It is permissible and a mitzva to give the person painkillers to ease his suffering. These are the general rule. A more detailed discussion of this subject is beyond the scope of this book. Each case should be examined with gravity and sensitivity together with a halakhic authority.
20. One can pray that God do what is best for the sick person. It may be important for someone to suffer in order to be cleansed of any sin; we simply cannot know. Therefore, we offer this prayer, that God do what is best.

Can illness be beneficial?

Until Jacob there was no illness. Then Jacob came and prayed, and illness came into being, as it is written, "And one told Joseph, Behold, thy father is sick." (Bava Metzia 87a)

We generally pray that God should bless us with health and spare us from sickness or suffering. As the verse says: "The Lord will ward off from you all sickness" (Deut. 7:15). But of course human beings will, at times, experience hardship, suffering, and illness. When this happens, it is important to reflect upon whether there might be insights to glean or actions to take as a result of the crisis or hardship. Below is an excerpt from the book *Gesher HaḤayim* (1:4) on this subject. These ideas are based on the Talmud and the Midrash, which at first might

18. *Arukh HaShulḥan, Yoreh De'ah* 335:3; *Igrot Moshe, Ḥoshen Mishpat*, vol. 2, 73:1, based on the Talmud in Nedarim 40a that suggests that there are times when one should pray for the sick person to die. Even in such cases, it is inappropriate for family members to pray for the sick to die, lest an ulterior motive arise, for them to be eased of the burden of caring for the sick.

Rabbi Nebenzahl: And some disagree; in my opinion, it is good to pray that God should do what is best for them.

seem incomprehensible. How could it be that Jacob asked for there to be sickness in the world?!

> From the day the heavens and earth were created, no one sneezed and stayed alive, rather wherever one was walking, whether on the road or in the market, one would die. Until our forefather Jacob came and asked for mercy. He said before Him, "Master of the Universe, do not take my soul until I instruct my son," and he was answered, as it says: "And Joseph was told – Your father is ill" (*Yalkut Shimoni*, Job 927).[19]

The Holy One Blessed be He did a kindness for humans in having illness in the world, so that a person will not simply be walking in the marketplace and suddenly expire, as our forefather Jacob requested. A person can be awakened to repent and to arrange his affairs as a result of his illness. If illness is a divine kindness, then one should also strive to make a friend's illness into a kindness and a blessing and not just senseless suffering and sorrow.

When a person is going along on his way in the daily run of life, he distracts himself from the fact that all the living will eventually die. Even when he is reminded of this, the person thinks, "I have plenty of time...." He lives his life, seeing that others die and not him – why all the anxiety, he has plenty of time....

Most people do not settle their affairs, and they leave them unfinished. There are only a smart few who see the future clearly, who organize their affairs each year or every once in a while, whether in matters between man and his fellow or those between man and God. Whoever is not a fool will be roused to do this at the very least when he falls ill and before reaching a critical state, God forbid.

19. The Midrash concludes: "Therefore a person should give thanks when they sneeze and it changes from death to life, as it says: 'His sneezes flash forth light' (Job 41:10)." That is why, when someone sneezes, we say "Bless you" or "To your health!"

If someone does not even know how to ask when he is ill, you shall open [the conversation] for him and do a kindness to him by encouraging him to provide instructions regarding his affairs: (1) With regard to his property and what he would like done with it, (2) with regard to debts he may have or deposits he may have left with others, (3) with regard to charity he would like to give, (4) in order to do *Viduy* [ritual confession] and atonement.

One who assists the sick person in this should carefully and wisely weigh his words. If one is not able to do this, someone else should be found who is able to speak about such matters. (*Gesher HaḤayim* 1:4)

SECTION 5: CARING FOR THE DYING AND THE DECEASED

R. Eliezer said: Repent one day before your death. His disciples asked him: Does then one know on what day he will die? Then all the more reason that he should repent today, he replied, lest he die tomorrow, and thus his whole life is spent in repentance. And Solomon too said in his wisdom, "Let thy garments be always white; and let not thy head lack ointment." R. Yohanan b. Zakkai said: This may be compared to a king who summoned his servants to a banquet without appointing a time. The wise ones adorned themselves and sat at the door of the palace. ["For,"] said they, "is anything lacking in a royal palace?" The fools went about their work, saying, "Can there be a banquet without preparations?" Suddenly the king desired [the presence of] his servants; the wise entered adorned, while the fools entered soiled. The king rejoiced at the wise but was angry with the fools. "Those who adorned themselves for the banquet," ordered he, "let them sit, eat, and drink. But those who did not adorn themselves for the banquet, let them stand and watch." (Shabbat 153a)

The halakhic literature describes the final stages of dying in great detail. For the most part, its discussion is in the context of a time when people typically died gradually, at home – surrounded by relatives and in a relatively conscious state, with an awareness that the end was drawing near.

Today such situations are rare. Death usually occurs in a hospital, while the medical team attempts to delay the death, sometimes after resuscitation attempts during which the person is unconscious. That said, if the person is able to reach the exalted state that occurs in the moment the soul leaves the body – the moment of leaving this world – this is considered a merit for the deceased and his family. The following lines have been written for such situations.

When the end draws near

1. When the end is drawing near, the dying person may wash his hands and recite Psalm 29; some recite "*Nishmat Kol Ḥai*" ("Breath of All Life"), or "*Elohai Neshama*" ("My God, the Soul You Have Given Me"), or "*Ata Gibor LeOlam*" ("You, O Lord, are Mighty Forever") – all of these should be said without the concluding blessing.[20]
2. Some recite "*Pitum HaKetoret*" (the incense prayer) word by word, with careful attention to the meaning of the words.[21]
3. In the final hour, if possible, it is good for the ailing person to say the following verses:

   מִי אֵל כָּמוֹךָ נֹשֵׂא עָוֹן וְעֹבֵר עַל פֶּשַׁע לִשְׁאֵרִית נַחֲלָתוֹ לֹא הֶחֱזִיק לָעַד אַפּוֹ כִּי חָפֵץ חֶסֶד הוּא: יָשׁוּב יְרַחֲמֵנוּ יִכְבֹּשׁ עֲוֹנֹתֵינוּ וְתַשְׁלִיךְ בִּמְצֻלוֹת יָם כָּל חַטֹּאותָם (מיכה ז, יח–יט)

   Who is a God like You, forgiving iniquity and remitting transgression; Who has not maintained His wrath forever against the remnant of His own people, because He loves graciousness! He will take us back in love; He will cover up our iniquities, You will hurl all our sins into the depths of the sea. (Mic. 7:18–19)

   בְּיָדְךָ אַפְקִיד רוּחִי פָּדִיתָה אוֹתִי ה׳ אֵל אֱמֶת (תהלים לא, ו)

20. *Gesher HaḤayim* 2:1.
21. *Kuntras HaYeḥieli, Beit Olamim* 15. He writes that the reason for this is to spare the soul from fear and suffering through the Angel of Death, that he may die instead at the hands of the Angel of Mercy. Other reasons are discussed there, as well.

Into Your hand I entrust my spirit; You redeem me, O Lord, faithful God. (Ps. 31:6)

יְבָרֶכְךָ ה׳ וְיִשְׁמְרֶךָ, יָאֵר ה׳ פָּנָיו אֵלֶיךָ וִיחֻנֶּךָּ, יִשָּׂא ה׳ פָּנָיו אֵלֶיךָ וְיָשֵׂם לְךָ שָׁלוֹם. (במדבר ו, כד–כו)

The Lord bless you and protect you! The Lord deal kindly and graciously with you! The Lord bestow His favor upon you and grant you peace! (Num. 6:24–26)

לִישׁוּעָתְךָ קִוִּיתִי ה׳ (בראשית מט, ח)

I wait for Your deliverance, O Lord. (Gen. 49:18)

ה׳ אֵל אֱמֶת (תהלים לא, ו)

O Lord, faithful God. (Ps. 31:6)

מֹשֶׁה אֱמֶת וְתוֹרָתוֹ אֱמֶת.

Moshe is truth and his Torah is truth.

שְׁמַע יִשְׂרָאֵל ה׳ אֱלֹהֵינוּ ה׳ אֶחָד (דברים ו, ד)
בָּרוּךְ שֵׁם כְּבוֹד מַלְכוּתוֹ לְעוֹלָם וָעֶד.

Hear O Israel! The Lord our God, the Lord is One. (Deut. 6:4)
Blessed be the name of His glorious kingdom for ever and ever.

Ritual Confession (*Viduy*)

"For God has heeded the cry of the boy where he is" (Gen. 21:17) – on his own merit. The sick person's prayer for himself is better than all else. (Genesis Rabba 53:17)

Viduy – ritual confession – is part of the mitzva of repentance, *teshuva*. Being aware of one's sins is a necessary phase in understanding the need to improve one's actions. The *Viduy* is meant to be an authentic expression of feelings and not mere lip-service. It voices the profound human desire to be good, to be a person with integrity. The underlying belief here is that life is like a ladder on which a person strives to ascend and further his ethical and spiritual development. When a person is on his deathbed, with no ability to perform actions, the confession is a declaration of his intent for spiritual improvement.

4. It is a mitzva for the sick to recite a confession before they die. Great sensitivity is required in order to tell this to a sick person. It is therefore customary to tell the person that many have confessed and lived, and some did not confess and died. This should not be said in the presence of an unlearned person or in the presence of children, lest they start crying and it break the sick person's spirit.
5. The text of *Viduy*:[22]

מוֹדֶה אֲנִי לְפָנֶיךָ ה׳ אֱלֹהַי וֵאלֹהֵי אֲבוֹתַי שֶׁרְפוּאָתִי וּמִיתָתִי בְּיָדְךָ עַל כָּל הַחַיִּים וְצָרְכֵי הַחַיִּים שֶׁנָּתַתָּ לִי. יְהִי רָצוֹן מִלְּפָנֶיךָ שֶׁתְּרַפְּאֵנִי רְפוּאָה שְׁלֵמָה, וְאִם אָמוּת חַס וְשָׁלוֹם תְּהֵא מִיתָתִי כַּפָּרָה עַל כָּל חֲטָאִים וַעֲוֹנוֹת וּפְשָׁעִים שֶׁחָטָאתִי וְשֶׁעָוִיתִי וְשֶׁפָּשַׁעְתִּי לְפָנֶיךָ. וְתֵן חֶלְקִי בְּגַן עֵדֶן וְזַכֵּנִי לָעוֹלָם הַבָּא הַצָּפוּן לַצַּדִּיקִים. אֵל נָא רְפָא נָא לִי.

I acknowledge before You, Lord my God and the God of my fathers, that my recovery and my death are in Your hands. May it be Your will that You heal me with total recovery, but, if I die, may my death be an atonement for all the errors, iniquities, and willful sins that I have erred, sinned and transgressed before You, and may You grant my share in the Garden of Eden and grant me the merit to abide in the world to come which is vouchsafed for the righteous. Please God, heal me please.

One should also say:

אֲנִי מַאֲמִין בֶּאֱמוּנָה שְׁלֵמָה בַּה׳ אֱלֹהִים אֱמֶת וּשְׁמוֹ אֱמֶת וּבִשְׁלֹשָׁה עָשָׂר הָעִקָּרִים.

I believe with complete faith that God is the true God and His name is truth and in the Thirteen Attributes.

22. Nahmanides, *Torat HaAdam, Shaar HaMiḥush*, p. 47; *Shulḥan Arukh, Yoreh De'ah* 338:2.

The person then forgives everybody and asks forgiveness from everyone.

6. The text of the abbreviated form of confession is: "If I die, let my death atone for all my sins." One can say a lengthier confession and recite the text that is said on Yom Kippur, which appears in the High Holy Days prayer book.[23]
7. If the person cannot confess verbally, he should do so in his heart,[24] or another person may recite it on his behalf.
8. One may recite *Viduy* in a place that is not clean, but it should be said without mentioning God's name.[25]
9. It is good to give charity or set aside money for charity before reciting the *Viduy*.
10. *Viduy* may be recited on Shabbat and Yom Tov.[26]
11. Some recite the "*Yigdal*" prayer, which includes the Thirteen Principles of Faith. The reason for saying this can be explained as follows: It is written that when the soul leaves the body, Satan stands beside the person and says to them, "Reject the God of Israel." How can they escape from him? Through the Thirteen Principles of Faith and the verse, "Hear O Israel" – to accept upon themselves the yoke of Heaven and to declare the unity of God in the world. Suffering can sometimes cause a person to have sinful thoughts or doubts. The rectification for this is to strengthen one's faith; that is why the Principles of Faith are recited. The reason for reciting the verse, "Blessed is the Name of His glorious kingdom for eternity," is based on the Midrash brought in the Talmud (Pesaḥim 56b):

> "And Jacob called unto his sons and said: Gather yourselves together, that I may tell you [that which shall befall you in the end of days]." Jacob wished to reveal to his sons the "end

---

23. A longer version based on the Kabbala is found in *Kuntras HaYeḥieli, Beit Olamim, Sefer HaBikkurim*.
24. *Shulḥan Arukh, Yoreh De'ah* 338:1.
25. *Shemirat Shabbat Kehilkhata*, vol. 2, 64:1.
26. *Shemirat Shabbat Kehilkhata*, ibid. In the name of the *Be'er Heitev, Oraḥ Ḥayim* 288:3.

> of the days," at which point the *Shekhina* departed from him. Said he, "Perhaps, Heaven forfend! there is one unfit among my children, like Abraham, from whom there issued Ishmael, or like my father Isaac, from whom there issued Esau." [But] his sons answered him, "Hear O Israel, the Lord our God, the Lord is One: Just as there is only One in thy heart, so is there in our heart only One." In that moment, our father Jacob opened [his mouth] and exclaimed, "Blessed be the name of His glorious kingdom for ever and ever."

The acceptance of the yoke of Heaven is noted in the other verses, as well. Since the dying person cannot say the verses, someone else says them in his presence.

Some have written that one should help the sick person declare, while they are still lucid: If Satan should come, God forbid, at the last moment to draw me away and to transgress one of the Principles of Faith or one of God's commandments, even a rabbinic one, may my words be annulled and meaningless.[27] The liturgical poem *Adon Olam* ("Master of the Universe") should be recited, as well as *Ana BeKoaḥ* ("We Beg Thee with the Strength"), *Al Ken Nekaveh* ("We Therefore Hope").

12. If possible, the sick person should bless his children and family members before he dies. He should wash his hands, place both hands on the child's head. To sons, one says: יְשִׂמְךָ אֱלֹהִים כְּאֶפְרַיִם וְכִמְנַשֶּׁה, "May God make you like Ephrayim and like Menashe." To daughters, one says: יְשִׂימֵךְ אֱלֹהִים כְּשָׂרָה רִבְקָה רָחֵל וְלֵאָה, "May God make you like Sarah, Rebecca, Rachel, and Leah." Followed by:

    יְבָרֶכְךָ ה׳ וְיִשְׁמְרֶךָ: יָאֵר ה׳ פָּנָיו אֵלֶיךָ וִיחֻנֶּךָּ: יִשָּׂא ה׳ פָּנָיו אֵלֶיךָ וְיָשֵׂם לְךָ שָׁלוֹם.

    May the Lord bless you and watch over you. May the Lord cause His countenance to shine to you and favor you. May the Lord raise His countenance toward you and grant you peace.

---

27. *Nitei Gavriel*, vol. 1, 1:11. The source is *Rabbenu Yeruḥam* in the name of Maimonides.

וְנָחָה עָלָיו רוּחַ ה׳ רוּחַ חָכְמָה וּבִינָה רוּחַ עֵצָה וּגְבוּרָה רוּחַ דַּעַת וְיִרְאַת ה׳.
The spirit of the Lord shall alight upon him; A spirit of wisdom and insight, a spirit of counsel and valor, a spirit of devotion and reverence for the Lord.

After blessing each person, he should say *HaMalakh HaGo'el*: "The Angel who has redeemed me from all harm – Bless the lads. In them may my name be recalled and the names of my forefathers Abraham and Isaac, and may they be teeming multitudes upon the earth."[28] He can them instruct them on the importance of keeping God's ways and what he sees as important in life.

13. People should not cry or pray for a dying person in his presence; it might make him try to exert effort to somehow extend his life despite his suffering. For this reason, it is customary to send relatives out of the room while *Viduy* is being recited, lest they cry and it have a negative effect on the person. However, close relatives, especially the person's children, can remain beside him. It is good and appropriate for them to stand close to the dying person.

A person who is dying (*Goses*)

"*Goses*" is a halakhic term for a person who is critically ill, in the final stages of life. The halakhot about caring for a *goses* are extensive and complex. Only the main principles are presented here:

14. As long as there is hope that the sick person might live, he should be treated.
15. If a sick person is suffering, routine treatment, such as giving fluids, food, and oxygen, should continue. The person may not be taken off life-support machines in order to hasten his death. However, there is no obligation to administer extra treatment such as resuscitation if it will only extend the person's suffering, since one is not permitted to extend the suffering of another person.[29]

28. *Nitei Gavriel*, vol. 1, 1:13 and see also *Arukh HaShulḥan, Yoreh De'ah* 339:8.
29. *Nishmat Avraham*, vol. 4, 339:4.

16. Tranquilizers may be given in order to ease the person's pain, even if there is a chance that these medications might shorten his life. This is because it is not clear whether it will actually hasten the person's death, and we still have the obligation to ease their pain. It is also possible that the person may be able to handle the illness better if his pain is reduced.[30]
17. When a person is dying and can no longer be treated, he should not be moved from place to place; it is forbidden to hasten the person's death. However, if there is something that impedes the soul from leaving the body then it can be removed.[31] The sages likened a dying person to a flickering candle or lamp (*ner*), based on the verse, "The life-breath of man is the lamp of the Lord" (Prov. 20:27). Touching such a candle can extinguish it. Therefore, the sages forbid any touching that could hasten the person's death. Since this matter is very complex, delicate, and sensitive, from both a halakhic and practical standpoint, an expert halakhic authority should be consulted for specific cases.
18. Understandably, no preparations for the funeral and burial should be made prior to death.[32] It is permissible and commendable to privately study the laws related to death. This is not considered a bad omen for the sick person.
19. In the presence of the dying person, it is customary to say chapters from Psalms that are fitting for the mood of the hour.

The soul leaving the body

Our Rabbis taught: He who closes the eyes of a dying man at the point of death is a murderer. This may be compared to a lamp that is going out: If a man places his finger upon it, it is immediately extinguished (Shabbat 151b).

---

30. *Tzitz Eliezer*, vol. 13, 87.
31. *Shulḥan Arukh* and notes of the Rema, *Yoreh De'ah* 339. Much has been written about the distinction between hastening or causing death, which is forbidden, and removing an impediment, which is permitted. Much has also been written about artificially extending a person's life, which may cause the sick person great suffering. See the summary in *Encyclopedia Hilkhatit Refuit*, vol. 4, "*Noteh Lamut*," from p. 366.
32. *Shulḥan Arukh, Yoreh De'ah* 339:1.

20. At the point when the soul leaves, it is a mitzva to stand beside the dying person and not to leave the person alone.[33] It is preferable if ten Jews can be present. According to the Kabbala, they should not stand at the foot of the bed but along the sides of the bed.[34]

    In the hospital, relatives are sometimes sent out of the room when death is approaching. However, if the relatives would like to stay and it is not disruptive, they can request from the medical staff to do so.
21. In the dying moments, those standing nearby should take care to ensure that none of the person's limbs are sticking out from the bed. According to the Kabbala, no limb should leave the bed at the moment of death,[35] as it says for Jacob, "He drew his feet into the bed" (Gen. 49:33). If a limb was sticking out, it should not be touched but should be covered with a sheet.[36]
22. Those standing around the bed should meditate on *teshuva* and the thought, "What is man that You have been mindful of him" (Ps. 8). This is also to the merit of the dying person. According to the Kabbala, the moment of the soul leaving the body involves a divine revelation; the dying person sees the great light and yearns for it and then the soul departs. It is a merit for the deceased to have people standing nearby. It is also a merit for those standing beside him. The appropriate respect must be maintained, with an awareness of this lofty status.
23. Those present recite the verses:

    - שְׁמַע יִשְׂרָאֵל ה׳ אֱלֹהֵינוּ ה׳ אֶחָד
      Hear O Israel, the Lord our God, the Lord is One.
      Blessed be the name of His glorious kingdom for ever and ever. (Recited three times.)
    - בָּרוּךְ שֵׁם כְּבוֹד מַלְכוּתוֹ לְעוֹלָם וָעֶד

33. *Shulḥan Arukh, Yoreh De'ah* 339:4.
34. The reason is brought in the Key Concepts, **Angel of Death.**
35. *Maavar Yabok, Siftei Renanot,* 6.
36. *Kuntras HaYeḥieli, Beit Olamim* 15:12.

- The Lord is God. (Recited seven times.)
- The Lord reigns, the Lord has reigned, the Lord will reign for ever and ever.

24. It is customary to open the windows at the moment of death. This act symbolizes the soul's departure from the finite physical realm of the body and its passage into the infinite spiritual realm. The person had been confined to the physical world for his entire lifetime; opening the windows symbolizes his passage into the open air and the infinite heavens.

    In discussing where people should pray, the halakha specifies that one should pray in a house with windows. The windows symbolize the possibility of connecting with God, through prayer. Similarly, at the moment of death, we open the windows to symbolize that the soul is returning to and connecting with God.[37]

After the death

25. In the past, they would put a soft feather close to the person's nose to see whether the person was still breathing. Today, only a certified doctor may determine that death has occurred.
26. The original rule was that anyone present when the person dies, even someone who is not related, must perform *kriya,* i.e., tear their clothing.[38] However, over the past several generations, this halakha has changed and tearing of the clothing is not done at the moment of death. The reason being that there is a concern that people may avoid being present when someone dies to avoid having to rip their clothing. But if the person is left alone, the soul is considered to suffer when it leaves the body.[39] The Yemenite custom is that when the person dies, all who are present tear

37. Based on *Maavar Yabok, Siftei Tzedek* 26. He also brings other Kabbalistic reasons for this custom, having to do with banishing the evil spirits.
38. Moed Katan 25a; *Shulḥan Arukh, Yoreh De'ah* 340:5.
39. *Gesher HaḤayim* 4:9; in the name of *Shulḥan Gavoha.*

their clothing and recite the blessing "*Barukh Dayan HaEmet*" ("Blessed is the True Judge").[40]

27. The original rule was that the relatives should tear their clothing and recite the blessing, "*Barukh Dayan HaEmet*" ("Blessed is the True Judge") at the moment of death or when they hear that the person has died. Nowadays, however, this is done at the funeral (Ashkenazic custom) or after the burial (Sephardic custom). This is because, at the moment of death, the relatives are usually overcome with emotion and do not know what they are supposed to do. So they tear and make the blessing at the funeral, instead, when members of the *ḥevra kaddisha* can guide them. But if someone chooses to tear his clothing and say the blessing at the moment of death or upon hearing of the death – this is fine and in accordance with halakha.[41]
28. Non-relatives who are present at the moment of death recite the blessing "*Barukh Dayan HaEmet*" without saying God's name; they just say the words "*Barukh Dayan HaEmet.*"[42]
29. Two candles are lit beside the deceased's head; the custom according to the Kabbala is to light seven candles. In Judaism, the candle or lamp (*ner*) symbolizes the soul – "The life-breath of man is the lamp of the Lord" (Prov. 20:27). The sages used this image to honor the soul of the deceased. Light symbolizes several things in Scripture:

    - God as the source of light – "The Lord is my light and my help" (Ps. 27:1)
    - The presence of the *Shekhina* – "May the Lord make His face shine on you and be gracious to you" (Num. 6:25)
    - Light as equivalent to life – "Like babies who never saw the light" (Job 3:16)
    - The Torah – "The commandment is a lamp, and the Torah is a light" (Prov. 6:13)

---

40. *Shulḥan Arukh HaMekutzar Einei Yitzḥak, Yoreh De'ah* 176:5.
41. *Gesher HaḤayim* 4:6.
42. *Be'er Heitev, Oraḥ Ḥayim* 223:6; and see the *Mishna Berura* ad loc., who wrote that this is the common custom but that it not correct. In any event, if a Torah scholar or an important person dies and one feels sorrow at their passing one should make the blessing with God's name; *Gesher HaHayim* 3:1, 3.

All these images are the opposite of death and darkness. The sages called the soul, which is eternal, a candle or a lamp (*ner*) – "The soul which I placed in you is called a lamp."[43]

There is another resemblance between the two: The candle or lamp is comprised of the physical combustible material and the flame itself. The flame is the essence, the most important part of the candle, though it has no weight or mass. Similarly, humans possess the physical body, but their essence is the spiritual soul; it cannot be defined in physical terms, and it is the most significant part of man.

The light of the candle is drawn upwards, even though the combustible material comes from below it. One might say that the soul, similarly, is connected to the physical body but strives for lofty heights. When a person passes on to the next world, his spirit returns to God, to the higher worlds. The human candle returns to its source of light. (According to the Kabbala, there is additional significance to lighting candles next to someone who is dying. The reason is brought in the Key Concepts section, **Memorial (or Yahrzeit) Candle (*Ner Neshama*)**.

If a person dies at home

30. If a person has died at home, he should be left in the bed where he died for around twenty minutes. He should not be touched. This is because the person may still be in the category of *goses* (dying) and still be alive. One may not touch someone who is dying so as not to hasten his death, as explained above. That is why we wait for some time after the person has died.
31. After this, the deceased should be covered with a white sheet and placed on the floor. This is to prevent a bad odor from emanating from the body. It is best to place the body in a cool place, if possible.[44] Whenever the body needs to be moved, one should ask the deceased for forgiveness before doing so.

---

43. Shabbat 32a.
44. There is an additional reason according to the Kabbala: The deceased is placed on the floor, which cannot become impure, to prevent the forces of impurity from

32. The deceased's clothing is removed while he is covered with the sheet. Care is taken that at least the face and genitals remain covered at all times. A deceased man is handled by men and a deceased woman is handled by women. They shut the eyes and the mouth and straighten out the legs, bring them close together, with the feet pointing in the direction of the door.[45] The deceased's arms are placed on his chest. If those present cannot bring themselves to do this, they may wait for the *ḥevra kaddisha* to arrive and do it.
33. One should inform the local *ḥevra kaddisha* about the death right away, so they can begin arranging the funeral and burial as soon as possible.
34. Shabbat will be discussed in a later section.

Acceptance of God's Judgment (*Tziduk HaDin*)

35. After the face of the deceased[46] has been covered with a white cloth or sheet, the *Tziduk HaDin* (Acceptance of God's Judgment) is recited:

Blessed is the True Judge.

---

taking control of the deceased. This is preferable to leaving the deceased in the bed, which can become impure. Covering the body with a sheet is also done in order to hide the deceased from God's Attribute of Judgment, which has power only over that which can be seen (end of *Maavar Yabok, Siftei Tzedek* p. 112). Another reason is mentioned, as well (ibid., *Siftei Renanot* ch. 9): Everything strives to return to its source; that is its resting place. Therefore, the soul ascends heavenward from where it came, and the body returns to dust, for it is dust and will return to dust. In the *Kuntras HaYeḥieli* (*Beit Olamim* ch. 15) he adds that placing the body on the ground can be viewed as stoning, which can atone for him. In *Nitei Gavriel*, vol. 1 (5:3), he brings a reason in the name of *Sefer Zekhor LeAvraham* that this was the custom in the Land of Israel due to the sanctity of the ground, as it is written: "Your servants take delight in its stones" (Ps. 102:15).

45. Details and an explanation are brought in Key Concepts, **The Deceased's Feet in the Direction of the Door.**

46. Kabbalistic reason for this are brought in *Gesher HaḤayim* (3:1,1) and *in Maavar Yabok, Siftei Renanot*, ch. 9.

> The Lord has given and the Lord has taken. May the Name of the Lord be blessed. The Rock, His work is perfect, for all His ways are justice; a God of faithfulness and without iniquity, righteous and just is He. Your Vindicator shall march before you, the Presence of the Lord shall be your rear guard.
>
> Go on in peace and you shall rest and arise to your destiny at the end of days.

The *Tziduk HaDin* is not said on Shabbat and Yom Tov. "*Barukh Dayan HaEmet*" is said on Shabbat and Yom Tov.[47]

Respect for the dead

Since the deceased's body served as the vessel for containing the divine soul, it must be treated with respect.

The sages compared a Jewish person to a Torah scroll. Both the *sefer Torah* and the Jewish person have a connection to the Divine Presence. Therefore, one who is present when a Jew dies must tear his clothing, as if he were seeing a Torah scroll that was burnt.[48] The same way respect is given to a Torah scroll that can no longer be used, so too the body of a Jewish person is respected after the soul has left it and the person has passed on from this world. The custom is to also show respect for bones and limbs, and even for a small part of the corpse, since these are likened to a small piece of parchment from a Torah scroll.

There are many halakhot connected to showing respect for the dead – guarding the body, washing and dressing the body, the funeral and burial, and solemnity in the presence of the dead and in the cemetery.

36. One should not perform mundane activities in the presence of the deceased. One should not eat or drink in their presence, or smoke near them. One may not put on tefillin, say blessings, or learn

---

47. *Gesher HaḤayim* 3:1, 6.
48. Moed Katan 25a.

Torah within four cubits of the deceased or in the room that he is in. One should also not converse about mundane matters there.

37. It is permissible and appropriate to recite psalms to bring merit to the soul of the deceased. Some do not permit relatives in the pre-burial phase of mourning (*aninut*) to say psalms because there is a prohibition against learning Torah during *aninut*; some permit it.[49]
38. If the body will not be removed for some time because of an extended delay, it should be cooled down to prevent a foul odor, especially in summertime. Fans, air conditioning, or ice can be used. One is not permitted to violate Shabbat for this purpose; ice should be used.

Guarding the deceased

> It was taught, R. Shimon b. Eleazar said: A day-old infant, alive, need not be guarded from weasels or mice, but Og, king of Bashan, dead, needs guarding from weasels and mice. (Shabbat 151b)

There are several reasons for the custom of guarding the deceased: One is out of respect for the deceased; if left alone, it would appear as though the deceased had been abandoned and neglected like a disregarded vessel (Y. Berakhot ch. 3; Rema, *Yoreh De'ah* 373:5). The second reason for guarding the deceased is that the body is a holy sheath that has been emptied of the soul and, according to Kabbalistic texts, the spirits of impurity are then drawn to enter it. The texts compare it to a barrel that has been emptied of honey; bugs rush to go inside it. As the Zohar says (*Emor* 88b): "The whole time that the body is not buried ... an impure spirit rests upon it and contaminates that body."

These reasons are all the more true if the body is located somewhere where there is a risk of it being damaged or disrespected, such as a place where there are mice, rats, or dogs, a public place, or a place that

---

49. See in *Yalkut Yosef* (8:11) a case in which Rabbi Ovadia Yossef scolded an *onen* (one who is in the pre-burial phase of morning, *aninut*) who recited psalms by the bed of the deceased. However, in *Tzitz Eliezer* (vol. 5, *Ramat Raḥel* 46), he permits the *onen* to recite psalms.

    Rabbi Nebenzahl: Some permit reciting psalms for the deceased.

is at risk for catching fire. The body must be protected from damage and disrespect and should be brought to a safe location.

39. The deceased should be guarded until the burial or until it is transferred to the care of the *ḥevra kaddisha*.[50]
40. Someone who is guarding the body is considered to be involved in the mitzva of honoring the dead. Since someone who is involved in one mitzva is exempt from performing other mitzvot, this person is exempt from reciting *Shema* and prayers. If the time for reciting *Shema* is coming to an end, the person may leave the room to say *Shema* and then return; but one is not obligated to do so. If two people are guarding the body, one can remain with the deceased while the other goes to recite *Shema* and pray, and then they can switch.[51]
41. Those guarding the body should recite holy words – psalms and other prayers – to protect the deceased. They should not involve themselves in mundane matters.
42. Guarding is also required on Shabbat.[52]
43. Those guarding the body should not greet others nor respond to others who greet them.
44. One should not eat in the presence of the body. If the person needs to eat, he should do so in a separate place, or create a partition, or at the very least, turn away in order to eat.[53]
45. A *kohen* who must tend to his deceased relative is permitted to become ritually impure to guard the body. Some allow *kohanim*

50. If the people who are meant to replace the current guards are late to arrive, and those currently guarding the body need to leave because it will negatively affect their functioning the following day, they are allowed to leave the body. This should only be done after they have made reasonable efforts to locate their replacements (*Tzror HaḤayim* 40).
51. *Shulḥan Arukh, Yoreh De'ah* 403:9; *Tzror HaḤayim* 43.
52. Rema, *Shulḥan Arukh, Yoreh De'ah* 373:5; *Yalkut Yosef*, Introduction; *Tzror HaḤayim* 36.
53. *Shulḥan Arukh, Yoreh De'ah* 341:1; *Pitḥei Teshuva* ad loc. 2.

to do so even on Shabbat, despite the fact that one may not make arrangements for the burial on Shabbat.[54]

46. Those who come in contact with the dead, even indirect contact, must wash their hands afterwards.[55]
47. One may accept payment for guarding the body.[56]

Delaying the burial

> R. Yoḥanan said on the authority of R. Shimon b. Yoḥai: Whence is it inferred that whoever keeps his dead [unburied] overnight transgresses thereby a negative commandment? From the verse: "You must not let his corpse remain on the stake overnight, but must bury him the same day." (Deut. 21:23)
>
> If he [the relative] kept him overnight for his honor, so as to inform the [neighboring] towns of his death, or to bring professional women mourners for him, or to procure for him a coffin or a shroud, he does not transgress by doing so, for all that he does is only for the honor of the deceased. (Sanhedrin 46b–47a)

The commandment not to delay burial but to bury the person that same day is derived from the verse, "You must not let his corpse remain on the stake overnight, but must bury him the same day" (Deut. 21:23). Even though this verse refers to those who were liable to capital punishment, the rule was extrapolated from this verse to refer to all deceased individuals.

In addition to the negative commandment not to let the body lie overnight, there is a positive commandment to bury the dead on the day they died, before sunset. This commandment is derived from the second half of the verse: "But must bury him the same day."

---

54. *Gesher HaḤayim* 5:4, 3.
55. *Shulḥan Arukh, Oraḥ Ḥayim* 4:18. Some require that one wash three times on each hand, alternating from hand to hand (*Mishna Berura* ad loc.).
56. *Nitei Gavriel*, vol. 1, 10:10. In a note there, he wrote that it is permissible to receive payment even if the guarding was done on Shabbat.

The Talmud (Sanhedrin 47a) taught that the prohibition is only if the delay is degrading, as the verse described the corpse having been left hanging from the tree or stake. If, however, the burial is delayed for the sake of the deceased's honor, it is permitted; this is the halakha (*Shulḥan Arukh, Yoreh De'ah* 357:1).

In order to honor the deceased, it should not appear that the burial was delayed out of disrespect. Rashi explained (based on Sanhedrin 46b) that this would be a degradation of the Divine King, since man is made in God's image and the people of Israel are His children. It is compared to two brothers who resembled each other, and one became a king while the other was caught stealing and was hanged. Everyone who saw him said, "The king is hanging." So the king ordered that he be taken down. Some have linked this obligation to the verse, "Man does not understand honor; he is like the beasts that perish" (Ps. 49:21): Man, who is exalted and elevated beyond other creatures, should be buried immediately; otherwise he will be like an animal (Zohar, *Naso*). There is also a significant psychological benefit to this mitzva. The unburied body is a substantial burden for the family. There is psychological relief when the body has been brought to its resting place.

48. There is a positive commandment to bury the dead on the day they have died, before sunset. One is cautioned to bury the body promptly, unless the burial was delayed for the deceased's honor – to bring a coffin or shrouds, or so that relatives are able to attend.[57]
49. If the preparation of the body has been delayed, it is permissible to delay the burial so that the ritual purification can be done; this is considered honoring the deceased.[58] That said, the purification should be performed as promptly as possible.

---

57. See *Yalkut Yosef* 8:7: Even if the deceased left instructions to delay burial, they should still be buried immediately in order to prevent great suffering to the soul. In *Kol Bo al Aveilut* (p. 37, note 9) it is written that even if they delayed the burial so that all of the deceased's children could attend, it is not clear that this is for the deceased's honor.
58. *BeMar'eh HaBazak*, vol. 3, 62.

50. If the burial took place at night, before dawn, it is not seen as having delayed the burial.
51. If the deceased was placed in a coffin but not buried in the ground, this is considered a transgression of the commandment not to delay the burial.
52. Burial does not need to take place immediately for a gentile, a miscarried fetus, or limbs.[59]
53. A wicked person should also be buried promptly. The burial should not be delayed in order to degrade him, for the sake of atoning his sins or to save him from punishment. There is a Kabbalistic concept called *ḥibut hakever*, referring to the pain the soul suffers after death; the pain is thought to be eased if the person is buried close to Shabbat. So, if the person died on Thursday, people may want to bury the deceased close to Shabbat to save him from *ḥibut haKever*.[60]
54. In Jerusalem, burial is not delayed at all, even for the deceased's honor.[61] When someone dies in Jerusalem, the burial takes place right away.[62] Today, this is the custom in the Old City of Jerusalem,[63] but in the rest of the city, the general principle is followed – that delaying the burial is permitted if is for the sake of honoring the deceased.[64] Some have written that one should follow the stringency throughout Israel, as in Jerusalem.[65]

---

59. In *Gesher HaḤayim* (7:3, 2), he quotes from Naḥmanides, who brought a novel idea that in the Land of Israel there is another negative commandment: "You shall not defile your Land" (Deut. 21:23); and therefore, in Israel, gentiles should also be buried promptly.
60. *Yalkut Yosef* 8:8; and in the Responsa of the Radbaz, he wrote that this has no benefit.
61. Bava Kamma 82b.
62. Such is the tradition, but there is no reason for it – Rashi ad loc.
63. I.e., in the places where sacrifices could be eaten. The boundaries of the area are explained in the book *Ir HaKodesh VeHaMikdash* by Rabbi Tukachinsky, vol. 2, ch. 1, and in *Gesher HaḤayim* 7:3, 3.
64. Rabbi Nebenzahl: In the newer areas of Jerusalem, they also try to avoid delaying the burial; and when necessary, burials are even done late at night.
65. *Tzror HaḤayim* 46. This may be based on the aforementioned Naḥmanides interpretation, that in Israel there is an additional commandment: "You shall not defile your Land."

Restrictions on a *kohen*

55. In principle, a *kohen* may not enter a house where someone is dying.[66]
56. From the moment of death, a *kohen* who is not one of the seven close relatives (mother, father, sister, brother, son, daughter, spouse) may not be in the house until the body has been removed. (Laws about *kohanim* becoming ritually impure are discussed fully in Sec. 6, "Pre-Burial Phase of Mourning (*Aninut*)" from halakha 80.)
57. On Shabbat, it is appropriate for *kohanim* to be strict and avoid becoming impure, even for a close relative. There is a discussion as to whether the *kohen* is commanded to become impure for his relatives only for the purpose of burial or whether he may to do so even if it is not for the sake of burial. On Shabbat, when we cannot bury the dead, there is no purpose to the *kohanim* becoming impure (because they cannot deal with the burial on Shabbat). The halakhic authorities conclude that *kohanim* should be strict and not become impure. If there is a need for the *kohen* to guard his deceased relative, then he is permitted to do so since this has a purpose.[67]
58. On Shabbat, one can have gentiles remove the body from the house for the benefit of *kohanim* in the house since they may not remain in the house if there is a dead body there. Jews may remove the body only for the sake of a *kohen* who is sick. The dead body is considered *muktzeh* (an object forbidden for use on Shabbat); permission to move it is only given because of the barrier of the clothing on the body, which is not *muktzeh*.[68] Permission to remove the body is limited to carrying it to a place that is not a halakhic public domain.[69]

---

66. *Shulḥan Arukh, Yoreh De'ah* 370. However, there are halakhic authorities who are lenient and permit the *kohen* to enter the house as long as the person is alive. See *Beit Yosef* ad loc. and the Rema.
67. *Shulḥan Arukh* and Rema, *Yoreh De'ah* 373:5; *Shemirat Shabbat KeHilkhata*, vol. 2, 64:6.
68. Rabbi Nebenzahl: If the person was murdered, God forbid, he is buried in his clothing and then these clothing are also *muktzeh*. In this case, the only way to move the body is by placing something on it that is not *muktzeh* and moving it together with the body.
69. *Shemirat Shabbat KeHilkhata* ibid. 14. Only if the relatives want to the body to be moved.

One who was killed

Blood that comes out of the body at the moment of death is called *dam hanefesh* (life-blood), and it must be buried. If a person has been killed, it is likely that blood was absorbed into the his clothing and shoes. For this reason, the person is buried in that clothing instead of in shrouds. Because the ground that was near him when he died may also have soaked up some of the blood, that dirt is collected and buried together with the deceased.[70]

59. A person who has been killed is buried in his clothing and shoes, with the blood that was absorbed. The person is wrapped in a sheet called a *sovev* (from the word for encircling or surrounding), over the clothing.[71]
60. Anything that absorbed the blood of someone who was killed should be gathered up, as much as possible: clothes, sheets, and also dirt from the ground that absorbed the blood. These should all be buried together with the person.
61. If the person drowned, or was strangled, and did not bleed, then ritual purification is done in the usual manner and the deceased is dressed in the usual shrouds.
62. If a person was killed by non-Jews, even if he did not bleed, he is buried in his clothing. The halakhic authorities explain that this is done so that it will arouse God's anger and revenge.[72] Burying the deceased in his clothing expresses that this is a person who should not be buried in the usual manner, like everyone else; it express to Heaven that someone is being buried who should still be alive – someone who was murdered by gentiles, often simply because he was a Jew. It is a cry to God to redeem His people and to prevent any more desecration of His name. We ask God

---

70. *Siftei Kohen, Yoreh De'ah* 364:11. After the horrific terrorist attacks in Israel, members of ZAKA (a volunteer rescue organization) could be seen gathering every small piece of human flesh and anything splattered with blood, to be buried with those who were killed.
71. *Shulḥan Arukh, Yoreh De'ah* 364:4.
72. *Siftei Kohen, Shulḥan Arukh* 364:11; *Ḥokhmat Adam* 157:12.

to put an end to the reality in which Jews are murdered simply for being Jews.

63. If a person died several days after he suffered from sores that bled, there is no need to bury the person with this blood, since the obligation is to bury blood that exited the body at the moment of death, not before.[73]
64. For a woman who died in childbirth, the custom in Jerusalem is to dress her in shrouds. If her clothing absorbed blood, it is buried with her.[74]

Pouring out the water

65. There is a tradition to pour out uncovered water (in pots, vases, etc.) that was in the house of the deceased and in the surrounding vicinity.[75] The reasons for this are brought in the Key Concepts section, **Pouring Out the Water**. Water in bottles or closed vessels is not poured out. There is no need to pour out the water on Shabbat and Yom Tov. If necessary, the water can be used for washing or cleaning.[76]
66. Some have written that covered water should not be poured out; nor should water that was used for cooking; nor should water should be poured out on Shabbat – and that one can be lenient in this matter. Others write that nowadays this custom does not include the deceased's neighbors[77] and that even in the deceased's home we can be lenient – that it is sufficient to open the water faucet for a short while and let some water run out.[78]

---

73. Blood that came out after the person's death should be buried with them. See *Gesher HaḤayim* 11:5.
74. Rema, *Yoreh De'ah* 364:4; *Gesher HaḤayim* 11:6.
75. *Shulḥan Arukh, Yoreh De'ah* 339:5. This refers to the two houses closest to the house of the deceased (*Gesher HaḤayim* 3:3).
76. Some are of the opinion that pouring out the water includes hot water (*Gesher HaḤayim* 3:3, 10; *Yalkut Yosef* 6:6) while others permit the use of hot water (*Tzror HaḤayim* 296).
77. *Arukh HaShulḥan, Yoreh De'ah* 339:9.
78. *Har Tzvi, Yoreh De'ah* 261; *Yalkut Yosef* 6:3; *Ḥayim VeḤesed* 1:20.

Shabbat

Some of these laws about Shabbat appear elsewhere in the book, as well. They are presented here, together, for the reader's convenience.

67. One may violate Shabbat in order to save the life of a sick person. One is also allowed to violate Shabbat in order to extend someone's life, even for a short while.[79]
68. One should recite *Viduy* with a sick person who is about to die, even on Shabbat and Yom Tov.[80]
69. On Shabbat and Yom Tov, one does not do *kriya* (tearing one's clothes). It should be done after Shabbat or Yom Tov. But one may say the blessing, "*Dayan HaEmet.*"[81]
70. Needles and tubes may be removed from the body, without moving it. One can clean the deceased without wringing out the cloth or the cotton that is used to clean him.
71. The body should be moved to the floor even on Shabbat and the body should be kept cool.[82] However, Shabbat may not be violated for this. Shabbat may not be violated in order to call the *ḥevra kaddisha* or to remove the body.

---

79. *Shulḥan Arukh, Oraḥ Ḥayim* 329:4; *Bei'ur Halakha* ad loc., the paragraph staring with "*Eileh.*"

80. *Shemirat Shabbat KeHilkhata*, vol. 2, 64:1, in the name of the *Bei'ur Halakha, Oraḥ Ḥayim* 288:3.

81. *Gesher HaḤayim* 4:23. As mentioned earlier, the Ashkenazic custom is to recite this blessing at the funeral and the Sephardic custom is to do so at the end of the funeral; see also *Shemirat Shabbat KeHilkhata*, vol. 2, 64, note 7 (and also *Shulḥan Arukh, Yoreh De'ah* 339:3).

82. This is the conclusion of the *Gesher HaḤayim* (3:2, 3) after a discussion about moving the deceased on Shabbat; he also permits removing the clothing from the body for it not to become malodourous, both in summer and in wintertime. However, Rabbi Shlomo Zalman Auerbach wrote that if the body will not become malodourous, the clothing should not be removed on Shabbat (brought in *Lev Avraham*, vol. 2, p. 21; and *Encyclopedia Hilkhatit Refuit*, "Shabbat," vol. 11, p. 397). See also *Yalkut Yosef* (p. 4) in the introduction, where it is mentioned that some have the custom not to touch the deceased at all on Shabbat and Yom Tov. In *Nitei Gavriel* (vol. 1, 5:4) he mentions that the custom in Pressburg was not to place the body on the ground on Shabbat.

72. The water is not poured out on Shabbat or Saturday night.[83]
73. For the laws of *kohanim* on Shabbat, see the section above, "Restrictions on a *kohen*."

Informing relatives of the death

74. There is no obligation to inform relatives that someone has died, even if it is a parent. Describing the person who does inform them, the sages went so far as to bring the verse, "One who utters slander is a fool" (Prov. 10:18).[84] The rationale is that we should not cause people pain simply for the sake of telling them, if there is no purpose to it and the only result is that it causes them grief. Nowadays, it is obviously difficult to hide such information. It is usually best to inform the relatives so that they can prepare for the funeral and burial, and also so they do not find out in an undesirable way or if they would be angry not to have been told. Nowadays, it is customary to announce the death both to relatives and publicly. Sometimes this is even done outside with loudspeakers to inform people so they can come to the funeral and to comfort the mourners.
75. On Shabbat and Yom Tov, one should delay publicizing the information until nightfall, to the extent that this is possible. This is because no funeral preparations can be made and because one should avoid causing sorrow on Shabbat and Yom Tov. However, each case should be examined individually. One should consider whether the information will be passed on anyway over the course of the day.
76. Th information should be conveyed with maturity and sensitivity: "The speech of the wise is healing" (Prov. 12:18). See Sec. 62, "Informing a Family of a Tragedy."
77. If someone's parent has died, he should be informed so that he can say Kaddish.[85]
78. As long as the relatives are not informed about the death, they are not obligated in the laws of mourning. Therefore, even one

83. *Shemirat Shabbat KeHilkhata*, vol. 2, 64:7.
84. *Shulḥan Arukh, Yoreh De'ah* 402:12.
85. Rema, ad loc.

who knows of the death may invite the relatives to a wedding or other celebration.[86]

79. It is permissible to delay informing the relatives until close to the end of shiva, such that the relative will only sit for a short time before shiva is over. It is even permissible to delay informing the relatives until it becomes a "delayed report" ("*shmua reḥoka*"), where the person needs to sit only for a short amount of time, without sitting shiva or observing *shloshim* (the thirty-day mourning period). See later Sec. 49, "Receiving Notice of a Death," about a prompt report and delayed report. On the day before a holiday, the person should be told so that they can sit a short while before the holiday, and with this conclude the shiva.[87]
80. If the relatives ask after the deceased, one may not lie to them and say that they are still alive; but ambiguous language can be used, that could be understood in more than one way.
81. If the information could have detrimental medical repercussions, especially for a relative who is elderly or sick, one should weigh carefully whether it is worth telling that person about the death. Clearly, the information should only be withheld if this relative will not find out in another, more arbitrary manner, without being mentally prepared for it.

Autopsies

82. Generally, out of respect for the deceased[88] and the prohibition against deriving benefit from the dead, autopsies are not permitted.[89] It has already been mentioned that the sages likened a

86. *Shulḥan Arukh, Yoreh De'ah* 402:12. According to this, a man and wife may have marital relations even if one is a mourner, provided that he does not know about the death, even if the spouse does know. *Ḥidushei HaGershuni* ad loc., in the name of *Sefer Ḥasidim*, and also *Yalkut Yosef* 38:12 in the footnote.
87. *Yalkut Yosef* 19:3 and 30:38; *Nitei Gavriel*, vol. 1, 128:12.
88. Rabbi Nebenzahl: And due to the mitzva of burial.
89. Some have also written that this is included in the mitzva, "Love your neighbor as yourself" (*Amud HaYemini* 34). If an autopsy causes the burial to be delayed by a day, this also violates the prohibition of "You must not let his corpse remain" (Deut. 21:23).

Jewish person to a *sefer Torah*. Even if a Torah scroll has become unfit for use, it may not be cut up and destroyed; the same is true for a body, which was a vessel for the divine soul – it may not be destroyed or degraded.

83. Autopsies may not be done for educational purposes. The claim that autopsies done for medical training or research may be able to save future lives has been discussed extensively in the halakhic literature. Generally, this claim is accepted by halakhic authorities, since saving a life overrides the mitzvot;[90] but there are different approaches as to when this rule may be applied. Some accept this claim only in the following type of case: There are two people with the same illness and one of them dies; the doctors say that the other person may be saved if they perform an autopsy and learn about the disease (the halakhic term for this is "*ḥoleh lefaneinu,*" "a sick person at hand").[91] There are more lenient opinions that take into account that today, due to the immediate and ongoing communication between medical centers, the halakhic category of "*ḥoleh lefaneinu*" always applies, since learning something in one place can have immediate benefit to a sick person somewhere else.[92] Accordingly, the former Chief Rabbi of Israel Rabbi Herzog wrote:

> A board of three expert doctors should consist of: the head of the department in the specific hospital, a representative of the local rabbinate, and a representative of the family of the deceased. If they decide that there is a chance that the autopsy will shed light on the disease that caused the person to die… based on their written decision

---

90. Yoma 84b; *Noda BeYehuda*, vol. 2, *Yoreh De'ah* 210.

91. *Gesher HaḤayim* 5:6 brings these opinions and their reasons. See also *Igrot Moshe, Yoreh De'ah*, vol. 2, 151.

92. *Ḥazon Ish, Yoreh De'ah* 208:7. In "*Teḥumin*" (vol. 12, p. 382) a letter was published from Rabbi Yeḥiel Yaakov Weinberg to Rabbi Kalman Kahana, who was the Deputy Minister of Education at the time, discussing this issue. In his opinion, nowadays every case is considered "*ḥoleh lefaneinu,*" "a sick person at hand," since information is rapidly communicated between locations. This is a reason for leniency.

and signature, the autopsy may be performed, on the condition that they perform only essential procedures and that anything removed will be given to the *ḥevra kaddisha* afterwards for burial.[93]

84. Even according to stringent opinions, a small amount of blood may be drawn or other tissue removed in order to run tests.[94] These tests usually supply information that can preclude the need for an autopsy.
85. It is permissible to perform an autopsy on someone who was murdered in order to incriminate the murderer.[95]
86. If a person died as a result of medical malpractice, it is permissible to perform an autopsy in order to take legal action against the doctor and prevent future medical malpractice. This is on the condition that a representative of the family is present at the autopsy and will ensure that the entire body is brought for burial after the autopsy.[96]
87. Legally, the autopsy cannot be performed without the family's consent, or a court order. In all cases, a rabbi must be consulted.

    Due to the complexity and sensitive nature of this subject we have only presented some of the main points here. For more in-depth information on the subject, see the footnote.[97]

---

93. Letter of Rabbi Herzog from 4th Iyar 5714 (7th May 1954), published in *Pesakim VeKtavim* by Rabbi Herzog, vol. 5, 155.
94. *Igrot Moshe, Yoreh De'ah*, 4:152. At the end of the responsa.
95. *Tzitz Eliezer*, vol. 4, 14, 9.
96. An oral response from Rabbi Ovadia Yossef, as conveyed to me by his son, Israeli Chief Rabbi Yitzḥak Yosef. The case involved an autopsy that was to be performed in order to be able to collect a social security payment, but halakhic permission (a *heter*) was given in order to prevent further medical malpractice.
97. A broad summary appears in *Tzitz Eliezer*, vol. 4, 14; and in *Encyclopedia Hilkhatit Refuit*, vol. 4, "*Nituaḥ HaMet*"; in the *Kol Bo al Aveilut*, from p. 40 onwards; and in *Peninei Halakha*, vol. 3. Rabbi Kalman Kahana published a bibliographical review of articles on the topic of autopsies in halakha in *HaMaayan* (5727, 2:43–72 and in *Miluim*, 4:71–72).

Donating the body to science

88. Halakhically, there is no relevance to a person's instructions to donate his body and organs to science. The basic Jewish perspective is that a person does not own his body, rather that the body is on loan from the Creator for the span of one's lifetime. Therefore, it is forbidden for a person to harm his own body, commit suicide, or donate his body or organs to science.
89. Two issues can arise from such a request: One is a delay in burial, or even a lack of burial, for example if the person's skeleton will be placed in a museum. The second issue is the approval of an autopsy. With regard to non-burial, halakhic authorities have determined that even if a person gives instructions not to be buried, we disregard this,[98] since this is degrading for the family and for all Jews. Therefore, the person's desire to avoid burial or to delay it has no relevance.
90. However, if a person gave instructions to perform an autopsy and then to be buried, there are different opinions on this. Most authorities are of the opinion that a person is not permitted to degrade his own body since he was created in the image of God and may not degrade the body which houses the soul.[99] On the other hand, there are opinions that permit performing an autopsy on someone who agreed to it during his lifetime. Since the reason for the prohibition is to prevent degradation of the deceased, if the person agreed to it, it is not prohibited.[100] This was the position of the Israeli Chief Rabbinate under Rabbi Herzog[101] – that doctors can rely on the lenient opinion.
91. If a person donated his body to science and gave instructions not to be buried, the relatives do not need to observe the period of mourning. Because the person is considered to be "one who left the ways of the community" and rejected the

---

98. Maimonides, *Hilkhot Avel* 12:1.
99. *Ḥatam Sofer, Yoreh De'ah* 336; Rabbi Kook, *Daat Kohen* 199; *Igrot Moshe, Yoreh De'ah*, vol. 3, 140; *Yalkut Yosef* 14:14.
100. *Tzitz Eliezer*, vol. 4, 14.
101. *Encyclopedia Hilkhatit Refuit*, vol. 4, p. 537.

yoke of mitzvot, we do not mourn for him.[102] Some say that laws of mourning should be observed for a person who asked to donate his body to science, even though what the person did was improper from the perspective of Jewish law. If the person was a heretic who denied the resurrection of the dead, then one does not have to make efforts to bury him in a Jewish cemetery. And if the person gave these instructions out of a desire to assist humanity for the sake of saving lives, but during his lifetime did not renounce Judaism, it is a mitzva to bury the person in a Jewish cemetery.[103]

Organ donation

92. Donating organs from the deceased to save a life: In principle, donating organs is a great mitzva. There are halakhic limitations, however, both in principle and in practice. Since this is a complex issue, the subject cannot be covered here in its entirety. The Israeli Chief Rabbinate's official position on organ donation, as well as various practical opinions, are brought in Sec. 58, "Organ Donation and Transplants." (See also Key Concepts, **Benefit from the Dead.**)
93. If a person gave permission to donate his heart were he to become critically ill, and his heart was surgically removed for a transplant, the family should sit shiva for him. This is because his act was not done out of heresy or denying the resurrection and the soul's eternal nature.[104]

> When R. Yohanan finished the Book of Job, he used to say the following: The end of man is to die, and the end of a beast is to be slaughtered, and all are doomed to die. Happy is he who was brought up in the Torah and whose labor was in the Torah and who has given pleasure to his

102. Oral communication with Rabbi Ruza in the name of Rabbi Mordekhai Eliahu, based on *Shulḥan Arukh, Yoreh De'ah* 345:5.
103. *Yalkut Yosef* 14:13 and 49:2.
104. *Yalkut Yosef* 14:15.

> Creator and who grew up with a good name and departed the world with a good name; and of him Solomon said: "A good name is better than precious oil, and the day of death than the day of one's birth" (Eccl. 7:1). (Berakhot 17a)

> "A good name is better than precious oil, and the day of death than the day of one's birth" (Eccl. 7:1). When a person is born, everyone is happy; when a person dies, everyone cries. But this should not be the case. Rather, when a person is born, people should not be happy since they do not know how he will turn out and how he will act, whether he will be righteous or wicked, good or bad. When the person dies, the people should rejoice since he died with a good name and left the world in peace. It is like two boats sailing in the ocean, one leaving the port and one entering the port. With the one that leaves the port, everyone is happy, but with the one that enters the port none rejoice. One smart person was there and he said: I see the opposite. ...You find that when the righteous are born, no one notices, and when they die everyone feels it. When Moses was born, no one noticed, and when he died it was felt by all. (Ecclesiastes Rabba 7:4)

SECTION 6: PRE-BURIAL PHASE OF MOURNING (*ANINUT*)

> One whose dead [relative] lies before him is exempt from reciting the Shema and from the tefilla and from tefillin and from all the precepts laid down in the Torah. (Berakhot 17b)

> Rabbi Shimon b. Elazar said: Do not comfort your fellow when his dead [relative] is before him. (*Pirkei Avot* 4:20)

Aninut is the stage prior to the burial. The meaning of the word is sadness or deep sorrow.[105] *Aninut* is a time in which the mourner does nothing

105. As in "*ben oni*" (Gen. 35:18), which means "The son of my pain." And, "I have not eaten of it while in sorrow (*oni*)" (Deut. 26:14).

other than tend to the deceased and the burial. This is unlike *aveilut*, mourning, which is an extended period of time and involves a gradual, evolving process. *Aninut* represents the private sorrow of the heart,[106] as opposed to *aveilut*, which is made public through the mourner's actions and behavior.

During *aninut*, the relatives are exempt from all the positive mitzvot, out of respect for the deceased. It demonstrates that the *onen* (one who is in *aninut*) is completely focused on his grief over the relative's passing. It is also due to the practical need to deal with arrangements for the funeral and burial, as quickly and efficiently as possible.

Another reason for the exemption from mitzvot is brought in the Yerushalmi Talmud (Y. Berakhot 3:1): "As it is written, 'So that you may remember the day of your departure from the land of Egypt all the days of your life' (Deut. 16:3). And the sages taught – 'All the days of your life' – the days that you deal with life, and not the days that you deal with the dead."

The sages called an *onen* "one whose dead is before him," meaning that since the *onen* is able to care for the deceased, he is obligated to do so. It can be inferred from this reason that if someone is not able to care for the deceased, he is not considered an *onen*. This might be the case, for example, if the burial has been held up because of bureaucracy, or if the body has already been transferred to the *ḥevra kaddisha* who are going to bury the deceased in a different location.

When does *aninut* apply?

1. Someone who has lost one of the seven close relatives – father, mother, spouse, brother, sister, son, or daughter – is considered an *onen*. The status applies from the moment the relative died until the burial. The *onen* is exempt from all the positive commandments. As discussed in the introduction, the reason for this exemption is the need to deal with the deceased and the burial, and also out of respect for the deceased, so that it does not appear as if they were being ignored or forgotten.

106. *Aninut* is only in the heart – Sanhedrin 46b.

2. The laws of *aninut* apply to all seven close relatives, even to someone who is not actually handling the arrangements for the funeral and burial. Even if a father gave instructions that certain of his offspring should not be involved in preparations for the burial, they should follow his wishes, but *aninut* applies to all of them.[107]
3. The laws of *aninut* only apply if it is possible for the relatives to tend to the deceased and his needs. If they are not in the same place as the deceased, but can still make the necessary arrangements, they are still considered to have the status of *onen*. But if it is not possible for the relatives to deal with the deceased's needs, they are not considered to have the status of an *onen*. This will be explained further, below.
4. If the relatives cannot be involved in the arrangements, or if they have already finished caring for the deceased and have given the body over to the care of the *ḥevra kaddisha*,[108] *aninut* ceases to apply[109] to them; however, *aveilut* only begins after the burial is finished. Those who accompany the deceased to the burial continue the status of *aninut* until after the burial. See in the footnotes below: Some opinions hold that *aninut* still applies after the relatives have finalized the details of the funeral and burial with the *ḥevra kaddisha*, and the deceased is no longer their responsibility.[110]

---

107. *Tzror HaḤayim* 6; *Yalkut Yosef* 6:40.
108. The halakhic concept, **They Gave Him to the Pallbearers**, is explained in the Key Concepts section.
109. *Shulḥan Arukh, Yoreh De'ah* 341:3; *Gesher HaḤayim* 18:1, 4–6 and particularly note 1; *Gesher HaḤayim*, vol. 2, 15:9; *Kol Bo al Aveilut* p. 118; also see the next footnote.
110. *Pitḥei Teshuva* 21 on *Shulḥan Arukh, Yoreh De'ah* 341, in the name of the *Noda BeYehuda*; *Gesher HaḤayim* 18:2, 21. However in *Tzror HaḤayim* 6, he writes that in the Sephardic tradition, *aninut* continues until after the burial, even if the relatives are not involved with arranging the burial. He asserts that Ashkenazim should also practice *aninut* until after the burial. In *Yalkut Yosef* (7:1), as well, he writes that the *onen* is exempt from observing the positive commandments even if he concluded the arrangements with the *ḥevra kaddisha* and is no longer responsible for the burial. Rabbi Yitzḥak Yosef told me that since, in practice, even after one finishes the funeral arrangements, one still has to let people know about the funeral and handle other practical issues, the status of *aninut* continues. Rabbi Nebenzahl

5. Relatives who are accompanying a coffin to Israel have a status of *aninut* during the flight and should not eat meat until the burial. But relatives who remain outside of Israel begin *aveilut* as soon as the deceased leaves the country, unless they are continuing to handle funeral and burial arrangements; in that case, they continue to be in *aninut*.[111]
6. If there is a delay in the burial and, in the interim, there is no need to care for the deceased or arrange the funeral, for example if there is a delay of several days while waiting for the body to be brought Israel, the laws of *aninut* do not apply, even for those who will participate in the funeral.[112] Further details can be found in Sec. 47, "Delayed Burial," and see the Key Concepts term **Leader of the Household (*Gadol HaBayit*)**.
7. One should not inform someone of a relative's death while that person is in the middle of reciting the *Amida*. If this should occur, the person praying should not stop; he should complete the prayers. The same is true for someone reciting Grace After Meals. And if there is no urgency, it is appropriate not to inform relatives of the death until after they have prayed in the morning.[113]
8. If one's relative died in a different country and one does not intend to participate in the funeral, some say that *aveilut* should

---

appears to agree that someone who is still notifying people about the funeral continues *aninut*. But from the Yerushalmi Talmud brought in the *Noda BeYehuda* and also in the *Mishna Berura* 71:4, it appears that the law is that one ceases to be an onen from the time that the body is given over to the pallbearers because the care of the body is no longer his responsibility. To summarize: According to one approach, giving over the body completely annuls *aninut*. The other view is that the laws and status of *aninut* continue until after the burial. See more in *Kol Bo al Aveilut*, pp. 120–124, and in *Yesodei Halakha*, pp. 154–155, and in *Sefer Hilkhot Avel* 1:22.

111. *Igrot Moshe, Yoreh De'ah*, vol. 2, 170; *Yalkut Yosef*, 7:14.

112. Rema, *Yoreh De'ah* 341:3; *Gesher HaḤayim* 18:1, 4, and in vol. 2, p. 143, halakha 9. (However, Rabbi Yaakov Ruza told me that some have the custom, out of respect for the deceased, to continue with the *aninut* on the day of the death or the day of the burial. But if it is an extended period, they do not practice *aninut*. See also the previous footnote.)

113. *Yalkut Yosef* 7:6 and 27–28.

begin from the time of the burial, and some say that the laws of *aveilut* apply right away.[114]

9. If the body is held by the authorities and they are not allowing burial, then *aninut* does not apply since the deceased cannot be buried. However, the *aveilut* period does not begin either, because the family has not given up hope of burying the person. *Aninut* also does not apply in a situation where the relatives are detained such that they cannot be involved in the burial (such as a prisoner).[115]
10. There is no *aninut* and no *aveilut* for an infant who died within thirty days of birth.[116]
11. A child who became bar or bat mitzva during the time of *aninut* is obligated in the rules of *aninut*, from the time they become an adult.[117]

Laws of the *onen*

12. The *onen* must act with solemnity and be involved with the deceased and not behave frivolously.
13. The *onen* may not eat meat[118] or drink wine. In general, one should not sit down to eat in one's usual manner but should do

114. *Yalkut Yosef* 7:15; *Ḥayim VeḤesed* 3:13 brings the different opinions and concludes that one should be lenient in the case of the day before a holiday, so that the mourners can start sitting shiva before the holiday begins; the holiday will terminate the shiva. Rabbi Ruza told me in the name of Rabbi Shlomo Zalman Auerbach that mourning starts immediately, and this is the case not only when the deceased is in a different country, but even when they are in the same country.
115. *Shulḥan Arukh, Yoreh De'ah* 341:4; *Yalkut Yosef,* 7:12, another explanation appears later in the section on captives and missing persons in Sec. 50, "A Doubt Regarding Death.")
116. *Pitḥei Teshuva* 341:1; *Birkhei Yosef* in the name of Y. Yevamot ch. 11. In *Kol Bo al Aveilut,* p. 140, it says that whenever there is no mourning there is no *aninut* (except in the case of capital punishment by the *Beit Din*). See later, Sec. 16, "Who Mourns and for Whom?" halakhot 16–19, that if the birth was after a full-term pregnancy, mourning applies. And see the footnote there.
117. *Kol Bo al Aveilut,* p. 144, halakha 20.
118. Chicken is included in the prohibition, *Shulḥan Arukh, Orah Ḥayim* 551:10; *Yalkut Yosef* 7:7. And he wrote there that some say that other alcoholic beverages are not counted as "wine," but a person should be careful not to get drunk.

so more informally.[119] One may not participate in celebrations or have sexual relations. The same prohibitions that apply to mourners apply to the *onen*: not to wash,[120] shave, get a haircut, cut nails, do business, greet others, or learn Torah; these prohibitions will be explained later on.[121] The practical differences between the *onen* and the mourner are that the *onen* may wear regular shoes, unlike the mourner, and that the *onen* may not eat meat or drink wine, unlike the mourner. This is because it should not appear that the *onen* is ignoring his responsibility for the deceased.

14. Some have written that, before informing a person of a relative's death, one should tell the person that the relative is in critical condition, so that he can have a haircut, bathe, and change clothing before being informed of the death. Because as long as the *onen* does not know about the relative's death, he is permitted to cut his hair and bathe.[122]
15. The original rule required that the *onen* sit on the ground like the mourner, but the custom is to be lenient and allow sitting on regular chairs until after the burial. When involved in the

---

119. *Shulḥan Arukh, Yoreh De'ah* 341:1; *Gesher HaḤayim* 18:2, 3; according to the Bavli and Yerushalmi Talmud Berakhot, beginning of ch. 3.
120. But an *onen* may clean himself with a wet cloth (*Yalkut Yosef* 7:34).
121. According to Maimonides, however, the *onen* is not prohibited from bathing, doing laundry, cutting hair, or the other restricted practices of shiva. According to Naḥmanides, the *onen* is prohibited from all of these except for wearing regular shoes, which is permitted for the *onen* since he is involved in taking care of the deceased's needs. The *Shulḥan Arukh, Yoreh De'ah* 341, does not mention the customs of mourning in relation to the *onen* and so apparently follows Maimonides. But the Rema ad loc. brings the strict opinion, and the later authorities, both Ashkenazic (*Gesher HaḤayim* 18:2, 3) and Sephardic (*Yalkut Yosef* 7:34), were strict. See also *Kol Bo al Aveilut*, p. 150, describing the custom to be lenient regarding washing and haircutting prior to the burial, but that this was not accepted not in the Land of Israel. The Yemenite custom follows Maimonides (*Hilkhot Avel* 1:2), that the *onen* does not observe the prohibitions that apply to a mourner (*Shulḥan Arukh HaMekutzar Einei Yitzḥak, Yoreh De'ah* 178:5).
122. *Yalkut Yosef* 7:34.

preparations for the funeral and burial, one may sit in a regular chair.[123]

16. The *onen* is exempt from all the positive commandments, but is obligated in the negative commandments, even rabbinic obligations. Therefore, the *onen* is obligated to wash his hands without a blessing upon getting up in the morning and before eating bread and after going to the bathroom.
17. The *onen* is exempt from reciting the *Shema* and prayers, but he should say *Shema* and *HaMapil* before going to bed.[124] He should not make blessings, nor answer Amen.[125] The *onen* is not permitted to be strict with himself by praying or saying blessings, so as not to appear to be disrespecting the deceased.
18. Even though the *onen* is exempt from the mitzvot, it is customary to allow him to recite Kaddish before the burial[126] since this is part of honoring the deceased. The *onen* may go to synagogue for this purpose if someone else is able to handle the needs of the deceased.[127]
19. The *onen* is not counted for a quorum of three for reciting Grace After Meals (*zimmun*) nor for a quorum of ten (*minyan*), unless is it for him to recite Kaddish.[128]

---

123. *Maḥatzit HaShekel, Oraḥ Ḥayim* 551:8. In *Gesher HaḤayim* 18:5, he justifies the lenient custom to sit on regular chairs before the burial. See *Yalkut Yosef* 7:36. In *Tzror HaḤayim* 8, he writes that if it is difficult for the *onen* to sit on the ground, he can sit on a regular chair and that the Ashkenazic custom is to be lenient and sit on a regular chair.
124. *Hilkhot Avel* 1:10, in the name of Rabbi Shlomo Zalman Auerbach. In *Tzror HaḤayim* 21, he writes that they can recite the *Shema* for protection from danger, but it is preferable to have someone else recite it for them. The same is true of *Tefillat HaDerekh* (the Traveller's Prayer), since this is recited for protection (ibid. 24).
125. *Tzror HaḤayim*, p. 28 and *Yalkut Yosef* 7:3. And he adds that if the *onen* has handed over the body to the *ḥevra kaddisha* and they are taking care of all the arrangements for the burial, he can rely on the opinions that an *onen* is permitted to answer Amen.
126. *Gesher HaḤayim* 18:2, end of halakha 3. In *Tzror HaḤayim* 17, he writes that there is no obligation to recite Kaddish before the burial, but it is the custom in Jerusalem to recite Kaddish before the burial (ibid., Introduction to ch. 5).
127. *Nitei Gavriel*, vol. 1, 17:1.
128. *Gesher HaḤayim* 18:2, 3. In *Yalkut Yosef* 7:29, he only permits the *onen* to join a *minyan* to say Kaddish after the body has been given over to the *ḥevra kaddisha*.

20. The *onen* does not make the blessing that people say when visiting a cemetery, even if he has not been in a cemetery for thirty days. Before the burial, he cannot make the blessing because of his *onen* status, and afterwards he cannot make the blessing because he has already seen the graves and is exempt from saying it.[129] See Sec. 41, "Visiting the Gravesite," halakha 11.
21. The *onen* may not learn Torah besides for the laws of mourning but may say words of Torah in a eulogy since this is out of respect for the deceased.[130] Some forbid the *onen* from reciting psalms because he is not allowed to learn Torah and others permit it.[131]
22. The *onen* may give charity during the *aninut* period.
23. The *onen* wears tzitzit without reciting a blessing.[132]
24. An *onen* may wear regular shoes, since the removing of one's shoes is only done after the burial, when the laws of mourning commence. Some have written that since today there are comfortable non-leather shoes, there is no reason why the *onen* cannot wear these shoes to the funeral and thus already be in his non-leather shoes when the funeral is over.[133]
25. In specific circumstances, some permit the *onen* to sell his store or other business during the period of *aninut*, prior to the period of mourning. Before engaging in such a sale, one should ask a rabbi who is competent in this area. One is permitted to sell a business to one's spouse or children if they are not regular partners in the business.[134]
26. After the burial, the *onen* should complete any prayers that were not recited earlier, provided that they are still relevant for that

---

129. *Gesher HaḤayim* 18:2; 3; *Pnei Barukh* 5:14.
130. *Nitei Gavriel*, vol. 2, 21:2.
131. See *Yalkut Yosef* 8:11 for a case in which Rabbi Ovadia Yossef rebuked an *onen* who recited psalms next to the deceased; in *Tzror HaḤayim* 11 he also forbids it. But in Tzitz *Eliezer*, vol. 5, *Ramat Raḥel* 46 he permits the *onen* to recite psalms. Rabbi Nebenzahl: Some permit reciting psalms on behalf of the deceased.
132. *Minḥat Shlomo*, vol. 1, 91:25, 3; *Yalkut Yosef* 7:44; Rabbi Mordekhai Eliahu told me this, as well.
133. *Yalkut Yosef* 9:2
134. *Nitei Gavriel*, vol. 1, ch. 22

particular time. The *onen* may not recite prayers after their time has passed.[135] One may recite *Shema* with the blessings and pray Shaḥarit until a third of the day has passed, even until midday.[136] The *Musaf* prayer, blessings on the Torah, and the three "*SheLo Asani*" blessings may be recited at any point during the day, until the evening.[137] Some say that one must say the morning blessings as long as it is before sunset.[138] This is because the morning blessings relate to the general order of the world and are thus relevant at any point in the day.

27. Halakhot about washing clothing and bathing, as well as other laws relevant for both the *onen* and the mourner (*avel*), are explained later on in the halakhot of mourning.

The laws of tefillin

28. The *onen* may not wear tefillin on the day of his relative's death and the day of burial.[139] The reason for this is that the tefillin are called "*pe'er*," meaning a grand adornment; on this first day, the *onen* is deeply absorbed in his sadness and grief. While the tefillin represent freedom, honor, and beauty, the *onen* is steeped in pain sorrow. The sages also pointed out and discussed the contrast between the words "*pe'er*," grandness or adornment, and "*efer*,"

---

135. *Shulḥan Arukh, Yoreh De'ah* 341:2. However, if one had not yet prayed the relevant prayer before becoming an *onen*, e.g., if the relative died at night and one had not yet prayed Maariv – if the deceased was buried in the morning and then the person said Shaḥarit, he must also pray Maariv since he was obligated to do so before becoming an *onen*. But if he was not obligated to pray Maariv (e.g., if the relative died during the day), he does not need to make up the Maariv service. *Mishna Berura* 71:4. In *Yalkut Yosef* 7:30 he writes that it depends upon the *onen*: If he is able to concentrate, then he should pray. But in his prayer, he should stipulate that if he is not in fact obligated, his prayer should be accepted as a "voluntary prayer," *tefillat nedava*.

136. *Shulḥan Arukh, Oraḥ Ḥayim* 58:6; in the *Mishna Berura*, ad loc. 26, he writes that if one makes the blessings of *Keriat Shema* after the proper time, they are considered blessings said in vain. But the *Bei'ur Halakha* writes that if the delay was caused by circumstances outside his control – the custom is to be lenient to say the blessings up until midday. Regarding Shaḥarit, see *Shulḥan Arukh*, ad loc. 89:1.

137. *Mishna Berura* 71:4.

138. *Tzror HaḤayim* 31.

139. *Gesher HaḤayim* 18:4, 1–2.

dust or ashes, which contain the same letters in Hebrew but have opposite meanings. Tefillin are associated with magnificence and glory, as opposed to the *onen* who is represented by the ashes, as in the verse in Isaiah (61:3): "To provide for the mourners in Zion – To give them a crown of glory (*pe'er*) instead of ashes (*efer*), the festive ointment instead of mourning, a garment of splendor instead of a drooping spirit. They shall be called terebinths of victory, planted by the Lord for His glory."

29. If the burial is delayed for several days but there is a need to make burial arrangements during that time, *aninut* applies and one does not wear tefillin. But if it is not possible to deal with the deceased's needs, one is exempt from tefillin only on the day of burial. On the other days before burial, one is obligated in tefillin.[140]
30. On the day of the burial, if it is not the same day as the death, the custom in Jerusalem is that the mourner puts on tefillin privately without reciting the blessing.[141] But if the person died on Shabbat and is buried on Saturday night, the mourner does not wear tefillin on Sunday.

    The halakhot of tefillin for mourners are explained in the laws of mourning, Sec. 18, "Tefillin on the First Day."

Brit mila and *pidyon haben*

31. If the *onen* needs to circumcise his son, the burial should be performed first and the *brit mila* afterwards. If this is not possible, the circumcision should be done first and the *sandak* (the godfather) should make the blessing, "To bring him into the covenant of our forefather Abraham." This is the case even if a *brit mila* has been delayed; it should not be delayed further because of the *aninut*.[142]
32. In the case of *pidyon haben* (wherein a father has the mitzva to redeem his firstborn son from a *kohen* thirty days after the child is born), the burial should be performed first and then the *pidyon*.

---

140. *Gesher HaḤayim* 18:4, 3–4; *Minḥat Shlomo - Tanina* 95.
141. *Yalkut Yosef* 7:25, 25:1; *Tzror HaḤayim* 125; *Pnei Barukh* 18, note 8. Rabbi Nebenzahl: This is what Rabbi Shlomo Zalman Auerbach said to do, as well.
142. *Kitzur Shulḥan Arukh* 196:16.

But if the burial cannot be performed the same day, the *pidyon haben* should be delayed until after the burial.[143] The reason for the difference between circumcision and *pidyon haben* is that the obligation for *brit mila* falls both on the father and also upon all of the Jewish people; someone else can therefore say the blessing. However, *pidyon haben* is an obligation only on the father, and since he is an *onen*, he is exempt from the mitzva until after the burial.[144]

33. An *onen* who is a mohel should not perform circumcisions if there is another mohel available. If there is no other mohel, the burial should be performed first, if possible. If that is not possible, the body should be given over to the care of the *ḥevra kaddisha,* and then the mohel can perform the circumcision and make the blessing. If this is also not possible, then he should perform the circumcision, but the father of the boy or the *sandak* should recite the blessing.[145]
34. A *pidyon haben* should not be performed by a *kohen* who is an *onen*. If there is no other *kohen* available, the *kohen* who is an *onen* can redeem the child, but someone else should recite the blessing over the wine.

Weddings

35. A bride or groom is not bound by the laws of *aninut*. They are obligated in all mitzvot before the burial, and the groom puts on tefillin.[146] As explained later in Sec. 51, "A Bride and Groom."

143. *Gesher HaḤayim* 18:2, 17–18; and see *Shulḥan Arukh, Yoreh De'ah* 360.
144. Rabbi Nebenzahl: There is also a special obligation to perform a *brit mila* at the correct time, and this obligation cannot be fulfilled the next day.
145. *Nitei Gavriel*, vol. 1, 37:1.
146. *Gesher HaḤayim* 18:4, 12. Rabbi Nebenzahl: We need to understand the reason for this because *aninut* would generally apply even on a festival, if it is possible to bury the deceased. (*Gesher HaḤayim*, vol. 2, 15:3 brings a lengthy explanation of this point. The basic idea is that on a festival, everyone is equally obligated to honor the festival, and since they all have an obligation to bury the deceased, they all hold *aninut* status. But in the case of a groom, he alone is a groom, and the burial can be performed by other relatives. Therefore, he is not an *onen*. If there are no other relatives, it is considered a *met mitzva,* and the groom becomes an *onen*.)

36. If someone is in *aninut* and has a child getting married, if the *onen* is no longer responsible for tending to the deceased then he may participate in the wedding. But he should not participate in the dancing, nor eat with the guests.[147]

Shabbat

37. *Aninut* is suspended a short time before Shabbat[148] since at that time there is no possibility of burying the deceased. The *onen* can therefore pray Minḥa, the afternoon service. But if the *onen* is still involved with the needs of the deceased and the burial at that time, *aninut* still applies.[149]
38. The laws of *aninut* are not observed on Shabbat since the *onen* cannot be involved in the needs of the deceased and the burial on Shabbat.[150] One is permitted to eat meat and drink wine and is required to make blessings, pray, and perform all the other mitzvot. However, having marital relations is prohibited.[151]
39. If the *onen* does not live in the same location as the deceased, some permit marital relations on Shabbat, especially if it the couple's designated time for relations.[152]

---

147. *Nitei Gavriel*, vol. 2, 16:18. This is based on Maimonides' position that until the burial, the *onen* does not take on the prohibitions of the mourner. And even though the Rema (*Yoreh De'ah* 361:5) follows Nahmanides' view forbidding for the *onen* what is forbidden to the mourner, in pressing circumstances, we can be lenient in keeping with Maimonides' position.
148. Some hold that *aninut* is suspended only when Shabbat begins. Both opinions are brought in *Tzror HaḤayim* 13. In *Shemirat Shabbat KeHilkhata*, vol. 2, 64:22, he writes: Close to the beginning of Shabbat or the holiday, such that there is not time to perform the burial and *aninut* no longer applies.
149. *Nitei Gavriel*, vol. 1, 25:1.
150. Rabbi Nebenzahl: And if they are involved in the needs of the deceased, e.g., speaking to the *ḥevra kaddisha* about arrangements for the funeral, informing people about it, or speaking to those who will give eulogies – they are exempt from all mitzvot.
151. *Shulḥan Arukh, Yoreh De'ah* 341:1.
152. *Nitei Gavriel*, vol. 1, 25:8.

40. Regarding Shabbat meals and singing *zemirot*, the halakhot for the *onen* are similar to those of the mourner, as explained in Sec. 31, "Shabbat and Mourning: Shabbat meals."
41. The *onen* should not lead services nor read from the Torah, unless no one else can do so, or if he is the regular Torah-reader and were he to decline, it would be considered mourning in public, which is not allowed on Shabbat.[153]
42. On Shabbat, the *onen* may read the weekly Torah portion twice through, and once with *Targum*.[154]
43. A *kohen* in *aninut* should not make the priestly blessing in synagogue since he is not in a joyous state.
44. One may not ask a Jewish doctor to write a death notice on Shabbat or Yom Tov, but one may ask a gentile to do so.[155]

The conclusion of Shabbat

45. Some say that just before the end of Shabbat, the *onen* should recite the three paragraphs of *Shema* without a blessing.[156]
46. Some have written that the *onen* should pray Maariv just before the conclusion of Shabbat, before *aninut* applies.[157] However, in practice, halakhic authorities have written that one should not do so because at the time his obligation begins, he will be an *onen* and therefore exempt; he will only become obligated to pray after the burial.[158]

---

153. *Yalkut Yosef* 7:22.
154. *Tzror HaḤayim* 1.6
155. *Shemirat Shabbat KeHilkhata*, vol. 2, 64:29.
156. *Shulḥan Arukh, Oraḥ Ḥayim* 71:2; the conclusion of the *Mishna Berura* ad loc. 10; *Shemirat Shabbat KeHilkhata* ibid. 25.
157. *Turei Zahav, Oraḥ Ḥayim* 72:4; *Yalkut Yosef* 7:22. And see also *Kol Be al Aveilut*, p. 130.
158. *Mishna Berura* 71:10. According to his opinion, an *onen* should read the *Shema* before the end of Shabbat without the blessings but should not pray Maariv. *Gesher HaḤayim* 18:2, 9; the reason he gives is that the custom is not to pray Maariv before the end of Shabbat. Doing so earlier is an option for one who will be obligated to pray after Shabbat; but the *onen* will be exempt after Shabbat. In *Yalkut Yosef*, in the footnote, he brings the opinion of the *Shvut Yaakov* who wrote that if one prays Maariv before nightfall (*miBeod yom*), it is like a weekday for this person and the laws of *aninut* would apply and one would not be allowed to pray.

47. After Shabbat, the *onen* may eat without making Havdala, and he should make Havdala after the burial. This may be done until sunset on Tuesday.[159] The blessings over the candle and the fragrant spices are only said when Havdala is recited on Saturday night.
48. If the *onen* heard Havdala from another person and had the intention to fulfill his obligation, his obligation is fulfilled and he does not make Havdala after the burial since the *ḥevra kaddisha* are dealing with the deceased and the burial.[160]
49. When Havdala is recited after the burial, the opening verses are not recited; one begins Havdala with the blessings.
50. It is preferable for the *onen* to make Havdala on wine provided by a neighbor, similar to the practice at the meal of condolence (*seudat havraah*).
51. Even though an *onen* can perform activities prohibited on Shabbat before making Havdala, it is preferable that he say "*Barukh HaMavdil Bein Kodesh LeḤol*" ("Blessed is He who differentiates between holy and mundane") at the end of Shabbat, before doing these activities.[161]
52. If the *onen* prays Maariv on Motza'ei Shabbat after the burial, he should add "*Ata Ḥonantanu*." But if the burial is performed on Sunday or afterwards, the *onen* does not recite "*Ata Ḥonantanu*."

Holidays and other special days

Yom Tov and Ḥol HaMoed

53. The original rule was that if someone died on the first day of Yom Tov, he should be buried by gentiles; if someone died on the second day of a festival, then Jews should bury the deceased,

159. *Shulḥan Arukh, Yoreh De'ah* 341:2; *Siftei Cohen* 12; *Shemirat Shabbat KeHilkhata*, vol. 2, 64:25. However, some hold that one can only make Havdala with a blessing until the end of Sunday and after that Havdala should be recited without a blessing (*Ben Ish Ḥai*, 2nd Year, *Parashat Vayetzeh* 23; *Kaf HaḤayim, Oraḥ Ḥayim* 299:26).
160. *Yalkut Yosef* 7:23.
161. *Shemirat Shabbat Kehilkhata*, ibid. 26.

even on the second day of Rosh HaShana.[162] Nowadays, in Israel,[163] burial is not performed on Yom Tov, nor on the second day of Rosh HaShana, out of concern that the sanctity of the day might be violated. Because of this, there is no *aninut* on Yom Tov. The *onen* may eat meat, drink wine, and make Kiddush, including the blessing of *Shehekhiyanu*. In the rare event that the deceased is buried on Yom Tov, the laws of *aninut* apply if the *onen* is able to be involved with the needs of the deceased.

54. When Yom Tov ends, an *onen* may eat without making Havdala. He should make Havdala after the burial, any time until sunset on the following day.[164]
55. *Aninut* applies on Ḥol HaMoed (the intermediate days of the festivals) since one can tend to the deceased and perform the burial on Ḥol HaMoed.

Passover and counting the Omer

56. It is preferable for the *onen* to appoint someone else to perform *Bedikat Ḥametz* for him. If the other person lives in the same household, the person can recite the blessing; if not, the *onen* should hear the blessing from a person who is obligated to check for *ḥametz* in that person's house. This other person should have the intention to include the *onen*'s house in this blessing.[165] If there is no one available to do this, then the *onen* checks for himself without making

---

162. *Shulḥan Arukh, Oraḥ Ḥayim* 526:1–4; and the *Mishna Berura* (71:11) therefore wrote that an *onen* should not blow the shofar on Rosh HaShana. However, if he is not going to be involved in the burial until after the prayer services, he does not yet have the status of an *onen*. This also appears in *Gesher HaḤayim* 18:1, 11, and in *Shemirat Shabbat KeHilkhata*, vol. 2, 64:23; see also Responsa *Har Tzvi* (*Yoreh De'ah* 293) where he permits a non-Jew to drive the deceased to the burial on Yom Tov.
163. This is also the case in most places in the world, except in unusual circumstances. The local rabbi should be consulted.
164. *Mishna Berura* 299:16 in the name of Rabbi Akiva Eiger. *Yalkut Yosef* 7:58 wrote that if the burial is performed the day after Yom Tov, Havdala is not recited and the *onen* may eat without making Havdala.
165. *Gesher HaḤayim* 18:2, 13–14, wrote that the other person can make a blessing for checking the *onen*'s house. In *Yalkut Yosef* 7:71, however, he discussed at length why the other person cannot make the blessing.

a blessing. The *onen* is exempt from all positive commandments, but *Bedikat Hametz* helps people avoid transgressing the negative commandment of owning *ḥametz* on Passover. The negative commandments applies to an *onen*, and therefore it should be done. The *onen* can annul his *ḥametz* and sell it.

57. On Passover eve, an *onen* who is a firstborn should fast but should not participate in a *siyum* (a celebration for completing a unit of Torah, Mishna, or Talmud, including a festive meal). If the *onen* finds it difficult to fast, he is allowed to eat food other than bread.[166] Another possibility is for him to exempt himself from the fast by giving charity.
58. The *onen* is obligated in all the laws of the Seder night, including leaning.[167]
59. The *onen* may count the Omer without a blessing,[168] so as not to miss a day of counting, which would affect his being able to count the rest of the Omer.

Rosh HaShana and Yom Kippur

60. If an *onen* blew the Shofar to fulfill other people's obligation to hear Shofar – some say that he has fulfilled their obligation, even if he is burying his relative on Rosh HaShana.[169] And if the burial will take place after Rosh HaShana, he has certainly fulfilled their obligation.

---

166. *Nitei Gavriel*, vol. 1, 35:4. The reason for this is that the prohibition against eating is a negative commandment, which the *onen* is obligated to fulfill; but at the same time, he is prohibited from studying Torah and is thus exempt from the festive meal of the *siyum*. If it is difficult for the *onen* to fast, especially if he is involved in arranging the funeral and is immersed in his grief, he can rely on the opinions that say that the prohibition against eating on the Fast of the Firstborns is only to abstain from eating bread.
167. If the mitzva specifies that the food should be eaten while leaning, then if someone eats this food without leaning, he has not fulfilled his obligation; if the *onen* did not lean, he would not fulfill his obligation. The *Mishna Berura* 475:13 writes that the *onen* should lean in differently than he usually would and less than usual.
168. Rabbi Nebenzahl: If the burial takes place at night, the *onen* should count the Omer with a blessing after the burial.
169. *Yalkut Yosef* 7:59 in the name of the *Pri Megadim*.

61. The *onen* may not eat meat or drink wine on Erev Yom Kippur. But he can bathe and immerse in the *mikve* close to sunset, since *aninut* does not apply at that point.[170]
62. There is no *aninut* on Yom Kippur, since it is not possible to bury the deceased then.

Sukkot

63. On Erev Sukkot, if there is no one else who can build the *onen*'s sukka for him or who can buy and prepare the four species for him, then the *onen* may build the sukka himself and prepare the four species. But the funeral and burial may not be delayed because of this.[171]
64. The *onen* is obligated to eat in the sukka on the first night of Sukkot. Aside from this, he is exempt from the mitzva of sukka.[172] However, since burials do not take place on Yom Tov nowadays, *aninut* does not apply. Therefore, the person is obligated in the mitzva of sukka on Yom Tov.
65. An *onen* is exempt from sitting in the sukka on Ḥol HaMoed. Some write that the *onen* is obligated to fulfill the mitzva of sukka without saying the blessing "*Leshev BaSukka*" (the blessing for sitting in the Sukka), especially if the responsibility for the deceased has been passed on to the *ḥevra kaddisha*.
66. On Simḥat Torah, the *onen* can be called to the Torah and can participate in *hakafot*, but not in the dancing.[173]
67. If the *onen* was already chosen to be *Ḥatan Torah* or *Ḥatan Bereshit* (honors given to two people, one who receives the *aliya* for the last portion of the Torah reading and one who gets the *aliya* for the first portion, respectively) and a relative has died close to Yom Tov, he can still be the *Ḥatan*. This is to avoid public mourning on the holiday.[174] Some are of the opinion that the *onen* should go to

---

170. *Nitei Gavriel*, vol. 1, 31:6.
171. Ibid. 32:1–2.
172. Rabbi Nebenzahl: If they are involved in the needs of the deceased, e.g., guarding the body, they are exempt on the first night; the same is true for *Leil HaSeder*.
173. *Gesher HaḤayim* 23:3, 7.
174. *Yalkut Yosef* 22:23, 38:27.

a different synagogue so that someone else will be *Ḥatan* instead of him.[175]

Ḥanukka

68. It is preferable for someone in the household other than the *onen* to light the Ḥanukka candles and make the blessings. If the *onen* lives alone, he can light the candles without a blessing.[176]

Purim

69. *Aninut* does not apply in a place where the burial cannot take place on Purim.[177]
70. But if burial on Purim is possible, it is preferable to read the Megilla after the burial since *aninut* no longer applies then. However, if there will be no time to do so after the burial, someone should read the Megilla for the *onen* before the burial.[178]
71. If the members of the *ḥevra kaddisha* choose to delay the burial until after Megilla reading, the laws of *aninut* do not apply during that time and the *onen* should hear the Megilla then.[179]
72. An *onen* may eat meat and drink wine on Purim and make the blessings over them[180] because the positive commandment for the individual to mourn does not override the communal obligation to rejoice on Purim. However, the *onen* may not eat meat and drink wine on Purim night since it says, "The days of rejoicing and joy" (Est. 9:22)[181] – and not "the nights."

---

175. See *Pnei Barukh* 29:11. In *Nitei Gavriel*, vol. 1, 32:11, he wrote that a layperson should go to a different synagogue, but if it is the rabbi or another prominent person and he does not attend, this is considered public mourning; for that reason, he is allowed to attend and be called up as *Ḥatan*.
176. *Mishna Berura* 670 at the end; *Yalkut Yosef* 7:66.
177. *Shulḥan Arukh, Oraḥ Ḥayim* 696:7; *Mishna Berura* ad loc. 24; *Arukh HaShulḥan* ad loc. 11.
178. *Shulḥan Arukh, Oraḥ Ḥayim* 687:2; *Yalkut Yosef* 7:70.
179. *Mishna Berura* 71:11.
180. *Gesher HaḤayim* 18:2, 15. Rabbi Nebenzahl: This requires further consideration; why it is different from Ḥol HaMoed, when the *onen* is not permitted to eat meat and drink wine.
181. *Shulḥan Arukh, Oraḥ Ḥayim* 696:7; *Magen Avraham* ad loc.

73. On Purim day, the *onen* should give to the poor (*matanot laevionim*). The *onen* should send *mishloaḥ manot* without items that bring a lot of joy.[182]
74. *Aninut* applies on the 14th of Adar in Jerusalem and on the 15th of Adar, Shushan Purim, outside of Jerusalem.[183]

Fast days and Tisha B'Av

75. Those in *aninut* are obligated to fast on fast days. If the fast makes them feel weak and unable to deal with the burial and arrangements, they are exempt from fasting. If the deceased has been transferred to the care of the *ḥevra kaddisha*, the relatives are required to fast.[184]
76. Those in *aninut* should not leave the house at night to go to synagogue and should not read Lamentations, even though the burial will only take place during the day.[185]
77. An *onen* should wear non-leather shoes on Tisha B'Av.[186]

Scheduling the funeral

78. Scheduling the funeral is guided by the principle to honor the deceased. This involves avoiding any delay of the burial, but it also involves having the deceased's relatives present. Therefore, the funeral should not be delayed unless relatives need to come from far away and their presence would be an honor to the deceased. That said, it is not permissible for this to cause a great delay.
79. As mentioned above, the custom in Jerusalem is to bury the deceased on the day of the death, even in the absence of relatives. Some hold that this is proper practice in all the Land of Israel.[187]

---

182. *Piskei Teshuvot* 696:11.
183. *Shaar HaTziyun* 696:25.
184. *Yalkut Yosef* 7:78.
185. *Mishna Berura* 559:24.
186. *Yalkut Yosef* ibid. 79. *Minḥat Shlomo* (91:25, 8) wrote that if it is difficult to be dealing with arrangements for the burial without regular shoes, it is permissible to wear leather shoes. Nowadays, there are very comfortable non-leather shoes and these should be worn.
187. *Tzror HaḤayim* 46.

Restrictions on *kohanim*

80. Male *kohanim*, even those who are disqualified from serving in the Temple because of a physical disability, may not become impure from contact with a dead body. It is a mitzva to prevent even a child who is a *kohen* from becoming impure.[188]
81. This obligation means that a *kohen* may not touch a dead body, nor help with carrying the coffin. He may not stand on or pass over a grave or dead body, nor enter a building, i.e., be under the same roof where there is a grave or a dead body.[189] That is why a *kohen* may not visit the graves of *tzaddikim* (righteous people) – including the Tomb of the Patriarchs (Me'arat HaMakphela) and Rachel's Tomb.[190]
82. A *kohen* may not come within four cubits (about two meters) of a grave or a dead body.[191] Therefore, *kohanim* may not enter a cemetery. If it is possible for a *kohen* to stay more than four cubits away from the graves – for example, if the deceased is buried at the edge of the cemetery – then the *kohen* may enter the cemetery, with awareness of how far he is from the graves.[192] If there is a fence that is ten handbreadths (ninety-six cm) high, then he can come within four handbreadths (about forty cm)

---

188. *Shulḥan Arukh* 373:1.
189. *Shulḥan Arukh, Yoreh De'ah* 369. A *kohen* may enter a building that contains the dead body of a gentile but may not touch or carry the body. The *Shulḥan Arukh, Yoreh De'ah* (372:2) writes that the *kohen* should be stringent and not enter a building where there is a deceased gentile. *See Yalkut Yosef* 57:7. And see later in this section, halakha 94.
190. The *Tosafot*, Bava Metzia 114a–b, brings a midrash that says that the prophet Elijah buried Rabbi Akiva even though Elijah was a *kohen*. Based on this midrash, the authorities rule that a *kohen* is permitted to come into contact with the graves of the righteous. Nonetheless, in practice, the Responsa *Yaḥaveh Daat* (58) wrote that it is forbidden. In *Gesher HaḤayim* (6:3) he forbids it, as well. But see the book "*Taharat Sdei HaMakhpela*" by Rabbi Ido Elba whose opinion is that *kohanim* may enter the Tomb of the Patriarchs.

    Rabbi Nebenzahl: It is not clear whether it is forbidden to enter Rachel's Tomb since this grave was established before the Torah was given. (See Nazir 54a and *Tosafot*, Bava Batra 58a.)
191. *Shulḥan Arukh, Yoreh De'ah* 371:5. However, some permit coming even closer during the funeral; see *Siftei Cohen* ad loc. 18.
192. *Tzitz Eliezer*, vol. 4, 15; *Kol Bo al Aveilut*, p. 249.

of the grave or dead body.[193] A *kohen* who would like to visit relatives' graves should check whether the path to the grave is at least four cubits away from the graves, or if there is a fence between the graves and the path. He should check that there are no trees that overhang the graves and the path. Trees that become overgrown with time can be pruned back in order to allow access for *kohanim*. Some have written that if, on the anniversary of a relative's death (Yahrzeit), a *kohen* gets close enough to the grave to see it, it is as though he has visited the grave; this is considered commendable.[194]

83. Even a small piece of a dead body causes impurity. However, teeth, hairs, and fingernails from a dead body do not cause impurity.[195]
84. A *kohen* is permitted and commanded[196] to become impure for his seven close relatives – father, mother, wife (if he was halakhically permitted to marry her),[197] son or daughter, paternal brother and paternal sister who is single. For all of these, he may become impure, as long as their mother is Jewish.
85. A *kohen* who became impure for a relative may not become impure for other deceased people at the same time. Some allow him to become impure for other deceased people as long as he is tending to his own relative.[198]

---

193. *Shulchan Arukh* ibid. The distances written here (in centimeters) are according to the Ḥazon Ish, who was stringent about this because it is a Torah prohibition. He said that one handbreadth is equal to 9.6 centimeters. According to Rabbi Ḥayim Na'eh, however, a handbreadth is eight centimeters, in which case ten handbreadths is equal to eighty centimeters and four handbreadths is thirty-two centimeters.
194. *Ḥazon LaMoed* 27:4, in the name of *Dudaei HaSadeh*.
195. *Gesher HaḤayim* 6 explains, in detail, the halakhot about *kohanim* and the impurity of the dead body.
196. *Shulḥan Arukh, Yoreh De'ah* 373:3.
197. But he may not become impure for his divorced wife or his fiancée, nor can he become impure for a wife whom he was not halakhically permitted to marry. He may become impure for his mother even if she married against halakha; *Shulḥan Arukh, Yoreh De'ah* 373:4.
198. *Shulḥan Arukh* and Rema, *Yoreh De'ah* 373:7.

86. A *kohen* is required to become impure for a deceased person if no one else will bury him, even if the person is not his relative.[199] See the Key Concepts section for an explanation of ***Met Mitzva***.
87. The requirement of a *kohen* to become impure to take care of a *met mitzva* (a case of a deceased person whom no one else is caring for) applies even if there are gentiles who could bury the person.[200] Some do not allow this.[201]
88. A *kohen* may become impure for a *met mitzva* even if he could hire others to deal with the burial.[202]
89. A *kohen* may become impure for his deceased relative only if the body is intact.[203] He may become impure for a *met mitzva* even if the body was found not intact, as long as the head and most of the body were found.[204]
90. A *kohen* must mourn for the relatives for whom he can become impure and also for those relatives for whom he may not become impure – his maternal siblings or a married paternal sister, provided their mother was Jewish.[205]
91. According to some opinions, a *kohen* may become impure for his relatives even when he is not dealing with the body or burial, even on Shabbat when one cannot do these things. Others say that he may become impure only if it is necessary, and therefore not on Shabbat. All agree that it is a mitzva for the *kohen* to become

---

199. *Shulḥan Arukh, Yoreh De'ah* 374:1.
200. *Gesher HaḤayim* 6:7, 2; *Kol Bo al Aveilut*, p. 71.
201. *Arukh HaShulḥan, Yoreh De'ah* 374:3.
202. Rema, Yoreh De'ah 374:3; *Gesher HaḤayim* ibid.
203. If the person was missing a limb when he was alive – for example if his arm had been amputated – then the *kohen* is permitted to become impure when the person dies (*Shulḥan Arukh, Yoreh De'ah* 373:9, according to the opinion of the Rosh). A *kohen* may become impure if the deceased is missing an internal organ that cannot be seen externally (*Igrot Moshe, Yoreh De'ah*, vol. 1, 251; *Tzitz Eliezer*, vol. 9, 48). For example, if a woman had a hysterectomy, her sons who are priests can become impure for her (*Yalkut Yosef* 57:3). Some say that a person who was killed is considered an incomplete corpse and therefore a *kohen* should not become impure for this person; Rema, ibid.
204. *Shulḥan Arukh, Yoreh De'ah*374:2; *Kol Bo al Aveilut*, p. 71, in the name of the *Or Zarua*.
205. *Shulḥan Arukh, Yoreh De'ah* 374:4.

impure for his relative, even if there are others who can tend to the deceased.[206]

92. A *kohen* may become impure for the duration of the burial until the coffin is covered.[207] He may not become impure at other times, such as to visit the grave at the end of shiva, *shloshim*, or the first year. For this reason, it is customary to bury *kohanim* and their relatives on the periphery of the cemetery, to allow *kohanim* and their families to visit the grave.
93. The ashes of a dead person do not cause *tuma* (impurity). That is why *kohanim* are allowed to enter the Remembrance Hall in Yad VaShem.[208]
94. A *kohen* should not become ritually impure by coming into contact with a gentile's grave, even though some are lenient in this matter.[209]
95. The halakhot of impurity for a *kohen* are quite complex. They affect not only burials but also entering museums that house bones or skeletons; travelling on a train that passes over a cemetery;[210] and flying in an airplane that is carrying a dead body. In Israel, hospitals have restrictions on where *kohanim* can enter because of the presence of dead bodies. *Kohanim* should gather information about the situation and discuss it with a rabbi. Doctors and male nurses who are *kohanim* require special

206. *Shulḥan Arukh, Yoreh De'ah* 373:5; *Gesher HaḤayim* 6:5, 6.

207. According to the *Shulḥan Arukh, Yoreh De'ah* 373:7, even though the *kohen* can become impure for his relative, he may not become impure for another deceased person. According to the Rema (ad loc.), the prohibition against becoming impure for other deceased people begins when the burial of the *kohen*'s relative is completed.

208. Mishna Ohalot 2:2; *BeMar'eh HaBazak*, vol. 5, 102.

209. *Shulḥan Arukh, Yoreh De'ah* 375, 372:2; the lenient opinion is that of Maimonides (*Mishneh Torah, Hilkhot Tum'at Met* 1:13 and *Hilkhot Avel* 3:3). According to Maimonides, despite the fact that a gentile does not cause ritual impurity to a person under the same roof, it results from touching or carrying a gentile.

210. Rabbi Ovadia Yossef permits a *kohen* to travel on such a train for work since the train itself is a self-contained vessel, separating him from the impurity; *Yalkut Yosef* 57:4.

guidance in this area during their medical training and in their work in hospitals.[211]

96. With regard to places outside of Israel, the *Shulḥan Arukh* forbids a *kohen* from becoming impure by travelling to other countries. Later authorities have questioned whether this law applies today or whether it was applicable only when the laws of ritual purity and impurity were in effect in the Land of Israel.[212]

A broader discussion of ritual impurity and the conceptual connection between ritual impurity and death will be brought later on, in Sec. 61, "Ritual Purity and Impurity."

SECTION 7: ARRANGEMENTS FOR THE FUNERAL AND BURIAL

> These are the things the fruit of which man eats in this world, while the principal remains for him in the world to come, and they are… accompanying the dead. (Shabbat 127a)

A general description of the funeral rituals is presented here. Different places and communities may have different customs. The same is true for *ḥevra kaddisha*s in different places.

A list of preparations prior to the funeral appears above, in Sec. 3, "Arrangements by the Family for the Funeral."

---

211. A *kohen* is allowed to be a doctor – *Kol Be al Aveilut*, p. 19. The question of whether and how a *kohen* can study medicine even though it may involve contact with dead bodies, is a complex issue that cannot be covered in this book. An expert rabbi should be consulted. It is forbidden for a male nurse who is a *kohen* to become impure by coming into contact with a dead body. *Yalkut Yosef* 57:8–9; see also *Encyclopedia Hilkhatit Refuit*, vol. 3, "*Cohen*," p. 201.

212. *Shulḥan Arukh, Yoreh De'ah* 369. According to the *Siftei Cohen* and the *Turei Zahav* ad loc., nowadays *kohanim* do not become impure by visiting the Diaspora. However, in Responsa *Shvut Yaakov*, he wrote that this law does apply today (brought in *Pitḥei Teshuva* ibid.). *Shulḥan Arukh, Yoreh De'ah* 372:1 writes that this is forbidden but that one is permitted to leave Israel in order to get married or learn Torah. Rabbi Shlomo Zalman Auerbach wrote that one should avoid leaving Israel except for the special cases brought in the *Shulḥan Arukh* – for the purpose of getting married or studying Torah, etc. (*Yesodei Halakha*, p. 175).

Ritual Purification (*Tahara*)

> All the requirements of the dead may be done; he may be anointed with oil and washed. (Mishna Shabbat 151a)
>
> Rabbi Jeremiah instructed before he died: Dress me in white shrouds, and place shoes on my feet and my staff in my hand, and lay me down on my side so that I will be ready to awake and stand when the Messiah comes. (Y. Kilayim 9:3)
>
> I strongly request that the preparations of my body are done slowly; that I am cleansed between my fingers and toes, that my head is covered and combed with a comb like the living, and my fingernails and toenails cut, so that I will arrive pure and clean to my rest; as I went every Shabbat to synagogue after washing, cutting nails, and checking myself – thus they should do to me for my eternal rest. (Will of Rabbi Eliezer ben Rabbi Shmuel, grandfather of the Maharil [213])

The *ḥevra kaddisha* generally takes care of the *tahara* (purification) of the deceased before the burial. *Tahara* includes washing the body and dressing it in shrouds before the burial. For men, this process is done by men. For women it is done by women. *Tahara* is performed with great respect for the deceased – respect for the soul, which is a part of the Divine, and respect for the body that has served as a sanctuary for the soul.

The ceremony of *tahara* takes place in the funeral home in a designated room. During the ceremony, various verses related to washing and purification are recited, for example: "I will sprinkle clean water upon you, and you shall be clean. I will cleanse you from all your uncleanness and from all your fetishes" (Ezek. 36:25). The reason for reciting these verses is twofold: Firstly, because the verses relate to the purification ceremony, and second, because reciting the verses prevents those involved in the *tahara* from engaging in idle chatter and mundane matters. This is out of respect for the deceased.

The main part of *tahara* is the pouring of nine *kabin* (around twenty liters) of water over the body. Some have the custom to immerse

213. *Sefer Devarim Neḥmadim*, Husiatyn 5662 (1902) quoted in *Kol Bo al Aveilut*, p. 86.

the body of a deceased male in a *mikve*. They do this after washing the body, before dressing him in shrouds. In the Key Concepts section, see ***Tahara*** for greater detail.

After being washed, the body is dressed in simple white shrouds. One can request to purchase linen shrouds. The preference for linen is explained in Key Concepts, **Shrouds**. After the *tahara*, the body is not left in the purification room but is moved to the entrance where it will be taken out for burial.[214] There is a custom to wrap a man in a tallit for the duration of the funeral, but he should not buried in the tallit.[215] An explanation and further details are brought in Key Concepts, **Tzitzit on the Burial Shrouds**. An overview of the shrouds and the dressing of the deceased is brought in Key Concepts, **Shrouds**.

1. One should not participate in nor attend one's father's *tahara* out of respect for him. Nor should one participate in the *tahara* of one's father-in-law, stepfather, or sister's husband. But a father may be present at his son's or son-in-law's *tahara*.[216]
2. Students of a deceased rabbi who know how to perform *tahara* are permitted to take part in the rabbi's *tahara* if the *ḥevra kaddisha* allows them. If they do not know how to perform *tahara*, they should not enter the room where *tahara* is being performed.[217]
3. If a person died of an infectious disease, *tahara* should still be performed on the condition that the members of the *ḥevra kaddisha* take great care to maintain sterile conditions to avoid infection. They should wear gloves and consult with a doctor. They should also get the necessary vaccinations. If there is no way to take the required precautions, the burial should be performed without *tahara*.[218]

---

214. *Gesher HaḤayim* 12:1; *Pnei Barukh* 4:13.
215. In the *Tur* and *Shulḥan Arukh, Yoreh De'ah* 531 there is a discussion as to whether the tallit used for the deceased should be kosher or unfit for use.
216. *Gesher HaḤayim* 12:2, 4.
217. *Gesher HaḤayim* ibid.
218. *BeMar'eh HaBazak*, vol. 2, p. 135.

Identification of the deceased

4. When the *tahara* is finished, it is customary for the *ḥevra kaddisha* to summon the deceased's child or other relative so that he or she can identify the body. Identification is imperative in order to prevent mistakes, God forbid, which have occurred on occasion.
5. The deceased's face is not uncovered unless necessary.[219]

Closing the deceased's eyes

Alexander of Macedon returned from a place in Africa. On his journey, he sat beside a spring and ate bread and salted fish. When the fish were being washed, they gave off a sweet odor. He said: This shows that this well comes from the Garden of Eden. He followed the water until he came to the door of the Garden of Eden. He cried out, "Open the door for me." They replied, "This is the gate of the Lord, [the righteous shall enter into it]." He replied: "I too am a king; I am also of some account, give me something." They gave him an eyeball. He went and weighed all his silver and gold against it, and it was not equal to it. He said to the rabbis: "How is this?" They replied: "It is the eyeball of a human being, which is never satisfied" (Prov. 27:20). (Tamid 32b)

6. The deceased's son or daughter puts a small amount of earth on the father's or mother's eyes and closes them. When putting the earth on the eyes, one recites the following verses: "For dust you are and to dust you shall return" (Gen. 3:19); "And Joseph's hand will close your eyes" (Gen. 46:4). The source for closing the deceased's eyes appears in the Zohar (*Shelaḥ* 169): In the higher world, people can only see after their eyes have been shut from this world. In another place in the Zohar (*Vayeḥi* 226) it is written that one can only see God's glory after one has died, not when one is alive; for this reason, those nearby must close the deceased's eyes.

219. *Kol Bo al Aveilut* p. 36, halakha 10, based on Moed Katan 27a and Horayot 13b.

Tearing one's clothing and the "*Dayan HaEmet*" blessing

7. It is customary to perform *kriya,* the ritual tearing of one's clothing, before the funeral begins, if it has not been done at the time of death. Although the original law was to do *kriya* at the time of death, the Ashkenazic custom is to do it before the funeral,[220] and the Sephardic custom is to do it after the funeral.
8. The relatives tear their clothing and recite: "*Barukh ata Adonai, Eloheinu Melekh haolam, Dayan HaEmet,*" "Blessed are You, Lord our God, King of the universe, the True Judge."
9. It is customary for each of the relatives to make the blessing separately. However, if one of them is not able to make the blessing, another relative can make the blessing with the intention of including the other person in it.[221]

A detailed explanation of the laws of *kriya* is brought later on, Sec. 8, "Tearing of Garments (*Kriya*)."

Explanation of the "*Dayan HaEmet*" blessing

Our sages[222] said that a person must say a blessing over the bad just as one says a blessing over the good. A person should accept the bad and the good in equal measure. This is a difficult statement to accept and internalize, and it requires explanation. Rav Kook, in his Siddur, *Olat Raaya,*[223] relates to this in his characteristically poetic language:

> Elimination of emotion, to the point where one cannot distinguish between good and evil, and one does not value the individual self at all, is not the highest level of a soul; this is not the correct approach for a lofty person. Rather, the intelligent person should become familiar with good and evil – the beauty of life's good and the harm of evil's void, including in one's own life; and one should assign them their appropriate value.

---

220. *Gesher HaḤayim* 4:6.
221. *Gesher HaḤayim* 4:7; *Yalkut Yosef* 9:8.
222. Mishna Berakhot 9:5.
223. Vol. 1, p. 403.

That is to say, the principle of making a blessing over the bad as we do over the good, should not cause a person to blur the differences between good and evil, or between joy and sadness. On the contrary, the intelligent person must distinguish between and know the value of good and beauty, in contrast with evil and its lacking.

The question may still be asked, however: How can a person make a blessing over the bad with the same feeling as a blessing over the good?

> One should know that the Divine good and the complete justness of Higher Providence are infinitely beyond this; one should give oneself over to it with all of one's heart and soul. Therefore, with all of a person's knowledge of and feelings towards life and its value, he should happily accept everything that is given to him from God's love and through His ways, which are filled with justice and integrity. And although the blessings over events must be in attunement with the emotions that the soul experiences at the time – and they are certainly different when there is good versus when there is evil – the perfect wisdom will rise above and hold all of these with justice and deliberation, to accept them with joy.

That is to say, a person must know that the Divine good and the justice of the Higher Providence are infinitely greater than limited human perception and emotion. One can arrive at this understanding from a place of love for God and a recognition that all of God's works are just and merciful. This is what enables a person to be thankful for the bad things, out of acceptance and even joy – as if one were blessing the good.

Breaking clay

10. Before the funeral begins, as the body is brought out, there is a custom to break an earthenware vessel and say, "The trap has broken and we escaped" (Ps. 124:7).[224] Breaking is symbolic of the pain of death (similar to breaking a glass at a wedding

224. *Gesher HaḤayim* 12:4, 1; in *Kuntras HaYeḥieli, Beit Olamim*, ch. 9 he brings another reason for the breaking of the clay.

in memory of the destruction of Jerusalem). The broken clay represents the breaking of the body through death. The body can be likened to the clay that has been broken and now has no substance. A clay pot that becomes impure is purified by being broken; so too, death atones for one's sins. When the verse is recited, "The trap has broken and we escaped," it symbolizes the wish that nothing bad should happen to the family, as if to transfer the family's heartbreak to the broken clay – that the clay will break and the family shall continue to enjoy a good and long life. (This is similar to the *Kapparot* done on Erev Yom Kippur in which one says, "This chicken shall die and we shall go on to a good and long life and to peace.")

11. There is a Kabbalistic custom to blow the shofar when the deceased is taken out to be buried; and some blow the shofar after the recitation of Kaddish during the funeral.[225]

Descendants walking behind the coffin

12. The custom in Jerusalem, based on the Kabbala, is that the descendants of a man who has died (his sons, daughters, grandchildren, and great-grandchildren) do not walk behind the coffin (but his wife, sons-in-law, and daughters-in-law are permitted to). Some hold that the descendants do not even come to the cemetery. If the descendants want to be present at the burial, they can walk to the graveside ahead of the body, to deliver and hear eulogies. By doing so, they walk in front of the coffin rather than behind it. The custom is explained further in Key Concepts, **Ban *(Ḥerem)* – "His Seed Will Not Follow Him."** If family members are going to follow this custom, they ask the deceased for forgiveness before the funeral. At the end of the funeral, a member of the *ḥevra kaddisha* or the local rabbi asks again for his forgiveness. If this practice is done, it should be in consultation with the *ḥevra kaddisha*.

225. *Kuntras HaYeḥieli, Beit Olamim* 15:41. The Zohar (*Vayek'hel* 196) explains that this is in order to protect him from evil spirits.

13. Although it is halakhically permitted, some have the custom that pregnant women do not attend funerals. However, the emotional strain and potentially crowded environment may be taken into account, in terms of whether it might have a detrimental effect on her health.[226]
14. There is a Kabbalistic custom, based on the Ari (R. Isaac Luria), that women who are menstruating should not enter the cemetery before they have immersed in the *mikve*. Some opinions are lenient about this during the seven clean days.[227] If the woman is a relative of the deceased and would therefore be embarrassed by her absence at the funeral, she may go even if she is menstruating.[228] An explanation of this is brought in the Key Concepts section, **Women – Attending a Funeral and Going to the Cemetery**.
15. A person may go to the funeral of someone he disliked. There is no need to worry that it might seem like he is happy in his enemy's demise because, no matter what, everyone shares the same fate in the end.[229]

Eulogies

Sarah died in Kiryat Arba – now Hebron – in the land of Canaan; and Abraham proceeded to mourn for Sarah and to bewail her. (Gen. 23:2)

The deceased's keys and notebooks are hung on the coffin out of grief; and when Shmuel HaKatan died, they hung his keys and books on his coffin since he had no sons, and Rabban Gamliel and Rabbi Elazar eulogized him, and said – For such a person it is good to cry and good to mourn. When kings die, their crowns are left for their sons, rich people die and leave their wealth for their children, Shmuel HaKatan took all worldly joys and departed. (Smaḥot 8:7)

---

226. *Nitei Gavriel*, vol. 1, 67:7.
227. *Yalkut Yosef* 10:24.
228. *Tzror HaḤayim* 55. According to the Kabbala, it is preferable for women not to go to the cemetery at all, *Darkei Tahara*, p. 57.
229. *Siftei Cohen, Shulḥan Arukh, Yoreh De'ah* 344:1.

Funerals in general, and eulogies in particular, can cause people to reflect on the meaning of life. They may be inspired to think about how they could be better today than they were yesterday, and how they could be even better tomorrow than they are today. Our sages considered the thoughts and awakenings that arise in this context to be a merit to the deceased.

16. It is a mitzva to eulogize the deceased in a fitting manner and to praise them for the good deeds they did in their lifetime. One may emphasize the deceased's good qualities, but one should refrain from exaggeration. Anyone who exaggerates performs a disservice to himself and to the deceased.[230]
17. The sages debated whether eulogies are for the honor of the living or for the honor of the deceased. They concluded that eulogies are for the honor of the deceased. Therefore, if the deceased gave instructions not to eulogize him, we comply with these instructions.[231] If a great Torah scholar gave instructions not to eulogize him, but some people have decided to eulogize him in order to awake people to look inward and repent – they may do so, but they should limit their praises of the deceased.[232] (See Key Concepts, **Eulogy** and **Honor of the Living, Honor of the Deceased.**)
18. One should not bring a coffin into a synagogue in order to eulogize the deceased there, unless the deceased was a truly righteous person and exceptional Torah scholar.[233]
19. There are certain days on which eulogies are not delivered: After midday on Erev Shabbat or Erev Yom Tov;[234] Rosh Ḥodesh; Ḥol

230. *Shulchan Arukh, Yoreh De'ah* 344:1.
231. Ibid. 343:10.
232. *Pitḥei Teshuva* 344:1; and see *Yalkut Yosef* 10:6 and the footnote there.
233. *Shulḥan Arukh, Yoreh De'ah* 344:20; Although the *Shulḥan Arukh* wrote (ibid. 19) that students would eulogize Torah scholars and their wives in the synagogue and the beit midrash, the custom is not to do so, unless it is one of the great scholars of the generation (*Gesher HaḤayim* 13:2). *Nitei Gavriel* (vol. 1, 51:17) writes that the coffin of the city's rabbi may be brought into the synagogue to eulogize him; but it is not customary to bring his wife's coffin into the synagogue.
234. Rabbi Nebenzahl: This is not so straightforward, in my opinion. In response to a question that I asked him, Rabbi Auerbach told me that, although it is customary

HaMoed; the day following one of the three festivals (*isru ḥag*); the days between Yom Kippur and Sukkot; Ḥanukka; Purim and Shushan Purim; throughout the month of Nissan; *Pesaḥ Sheni* (the 14th of Iyar); Lag BaOmer; and the first twelve days of Sivan.[235] On these days, one may say words of Torah and parting words that do not cause people to cry.[236] A Torah scholar may be eulogized in the presence of his body on these days, but not on Ḥol HaMoed.[237]

20. One may deliver a eulogy on Motza'ei Shabbat, but it is customary to keep eulogies brief before midnight.[238]
21. One should try not to burden those attending the funeral by delivering excessively long eulogies. Attendees may be standing up, they may be elderly or frail, and there may be inclement weather. It is appropriate to prepare a list of those who will deliver eulogies, and to designate someone to coordinate this with the *ḥevra kaddisha*. Some people have the eulogies at the beginning of the funeral, and some do them after the burial.

Acceptance of God's Judgment (*Tziduk HaDin*)[239]

There was a story about Rabbi Meir who was sitting and expounding in the study hall on Shabbat afternoon, when two of his sons

---

not to deliver eulogies, it may actually be preferable to give eulogies because it is a mitzva to eulogize the deceased; the eulogies should, however, be kept brief. For the rabbinic holidays described in *Megillat Taanit*, the rabbis instructed not to deliver eulogies because they needed to strengthen their authority at that time. But they did not forbid eulogizing during *deOraita* (biblically ordained) holidays, such as Erev Shabbat or Erev Yom Tov. In another answer, Rabbi Auerbach said that there is no halakhic distinction between a eulogy and parting words.

235. *Shulḥan Arukh, Oraḥ Ḥayim* 429:2; *Tzror HaḤayim* 60.
236. *Tzror HaḤayim* 59; *Nitei Gavriel*, vol. 1, 52:4; this is what I was told by the "Kehilat Yerushalayim" *ḥevra kaddisha*. Rabbi Nebenzahl: And some disagree with this (see Rabbi Nebenzahl's previous note in the footnotes above).
237. *Bei'ur Halakha* 547; *Gesher HaḤayim* 13:10; *Pnei Barukh* 3:10. However, in *Yalkut Yosef* 11:5, he permits eulogies for a Torah scholar even on Ḥol HaMoed.
238. *Nitei Gavriel*, vol. 1, 52:14.
239. The custom in Israel is that the *Tziduk HaDin* is recited twice – once at the beginning of the funeral when the *Dayan HaEmet* blessing is said and again after the burial. The reason for this is that there were different customs: Some had the custom to

> died. What did their mother do? She placed both of them on the bed and spread a sheet over them. At the end of Shabbat, Rabbi Meir came home from the study hall. He said to her, "Where are my two sons?" She said, "They went to the study hall." He said to her, "I scanned the study hall and I did not see them." They gave him the cup of Havdala and he separated [the days of the week with the closure of Shabbat]. He repeated and said, "Where are my two sons?" She said, "They went elsewhere and they are coming now." She placed food in front of him and he ate and blessed. After he blessed, she said to him, "I have a question to ask you." He said to her, "Say your question." She said to him, "Rabbi, before today, a man came and deposited something with me, and now he is coming to take it. Should we return it to him or not?" He said, "My daughter, one who has a deposit with him must return it to its owner." She said to him, "Were it not for your consent, I would not have given it to him." What did she do? She grabbed his hand, brought him up to that room, had him approach the bed and took off the sheet from upon them. When he saw both of them dead and laying upon the bed, he began to cry and say, "My sons, my sons, my teachers, my teachers – my sons in the way of the world, my teachers in that they would enlighten my eyes with their Torah." At that time, she said to Rabbi Meir, "Rabbi, is this not what I told you – do I not need to return the deposit to its Owner?" He said, "'The Lord has given and the Lord has taken; may the name of the Lord be blessed'" (Job 1:21). (*Midrash Mishlei* 31)

Tziduk HaDin should not be understood as a de facto justification of a divine decree that we cannot change. It is an expression of acceptance: We receive our souls from God, as a deposit, and they will eventually be returned to their Owner. While the soul is in a person's possession, his task is to make use of it in the best way possible.

---

recite it before the burial and some said it after the burial. For this reason, it is customary in Israel to say it both before and after the burial, *Gesher HaḤayim* vol. 2, 24:4. The longer version is recited after the burial.

"Akkavya ben Mehalalel said: Look at three things and you will not come to sin; know where you came from, and where you are going, and before whom you will give reckoning. Where you came from – from a malodorous drop; and where you are going – to the place of dust and worms; and before whom you will give reckoning – before the King of Kings, the Holy One blessed be He" (*Pirkei Avot* 3:1). Rabbi Levi said: Akkavya deduced them all from one word: "Remember *Borekha*" (Eccles. 12:1). The word *Borekha* [your Creator], could be read *Be'erkha* [your well], *Borkha* [your pit], or *Borekha* [your Creator]. Your well – the place from which you came; your pit – the place to which you are going; your Creator – before whom you will give reckoning. (Y. Sota 2:2)

22. At the beginning of the funeral, the prayer-leader says:

עֲקַבְיָא בֶן מַהֲלַלְאֵל אוֹמֵר: הִסְתַּכֵּל בִּשְׁלשָׁה דְבָרִים וְאֵין אַתָּה בָא לִידֵי עֲבֵרָה. דַּע, מֵאַיִן בָּאתָ וּלְאָן אַתָּה הוֹלֵךְ וְלִפְנֵי מִי אַתָּה עָתִיד לִתֵּן דִּין וְחֶשְׁבּוֹן. מֵאַיִן בָּאתָ - מִטִּפָּה סְרוּחָה, וּלְאָן אַתָּה הוֹלֵךְ - לִמְקוֹם עָפָר רִמָּה וְתוֹלֵעָה, וְלִפְנֵי מִי אַתָּה עָתִיד לִתֵּן דִּין וְחֶשְׁבּוֹן - לִפְנֵי מֶלֶךְ מַלְכֵי הַמְּלָכִים הַקָּדוֹשׁ בָּרוּךְ הוּא. (פרקי אבות ג, א)

Akkavya ben Mehalalel said: Look at three things and you will not come to sin; know where you came from, and where you are going, and before whom you will give reckoning. Where you came from – from a malodorous drop; and where you are going – to the place of dust and worms; and before whom you will give reckoning – before the King of Kings, the Holy One blessed be He. (*Pirkei Avot* 3:1)

הוּא הָיָה אוֹמֵר: הַיִּלּוֹדִים לָמוּת, וְהַמֵּתִים לְהֵחָיוֹת, וְהַחַיִּים לִדּוֹן. לֵידַע לְהוֹדִיעַ וּלְהִוָּדַע, שֶׁהוּא אֵל, הוּא הַיּוֹצֵר, הוּא הַבּוֹרֵא, הוּא הַמֵּבִין, הוּא הַדַּיָּן, הוּא עֵד, הוּא בַּעַל דִּין, וְהוּא עָתִיד לָדוּן. בָּרוּךְ הוּא שֶׁאֵין לְפָנָיו לֹא עַוְלָה וְלֹא שִׁכְחָה, וְלֹא מַשּׂוֹא פָנִים וְלֹא מִקַּח שׁוֹחַד. וְדַע שֶׁהַכֹּל לְפִי הַחֶשְׁבּוֹן וְאַל יַבְטִיחֲךָ יִצְרְךָ שֶׁהַשְּׁאוֹל בֵּית מָנוֹס לָךְ. שֶׁעַל כָּרְחֲךָ אַתָּה נוֹלָד, וְעַל כָּרְחֲךָ אַתָּה חַי, וְעַל כָּרְחֲךָ אַתָּה מֵת, וְעַל כָּרְחֲךָ אַתָּה עָתִיד לִתֵּן דִּין וְחֶשְׁבּוֹן לִפְנֵי מֶלֶךְ מַלְכֵי הַמְּלָכִים הַקָּדוֹשׁ בָּרוּךְ הוּא. (פרקי אבות ד, כט)

He used to say: The born [are destined] to die, the dead to be brought to life, and the living to be judged; [it is therefore for them] to know and to make known so that it become known that He is God, He the Fashioner, He the Creator, He the Discerner, He the Judge, He the Witness, He the Complainant, and that He is of a certainty to judge. Blessed be He, before Whom there is no unrighteousness, not forgetting, not respect of persons, not raking of bribes, for all is His. And know that all is according to the reckoning. And let not thy [evil] inclination assure thee that the grave is a place of refuge for thee. For without thy will you were fashioned, without thy will you were born, without thy will you live, without thy will you die, and without thy will you are certain to give an account and reckoning before the King of the Kings, Blessed be He. (*Pirkei Avot* 4:29)

Afterwards, the prayer-leader recites the *Tziduk HaDin* verses:

גְּדֹל הָעֵצָה וְרַב הָעֲלִילִיָּה אֲשֶׁר עֵינֶיךָ פְקֻחוֹת עַל כָּל דַּרְכֵי בְּנֵי אָדָם לָתֵת לְאִישׁ כִּדְרָכָיו וְכִפְרִי מַעֲלָלָיו: (ירמיהו לב, יט)

Wondrous in purpose and mighty in deed, whose eyes observe all the ways of men, so as to repay every man according to his ways, and with the proper fruit of his deeds! (Jer. 32:19)

לְהַגִּיד כִּי יָשָׁר ה׳ צוּרִי וְלֹא עַוְלָתָה בּוֹ: (תהלים צב, טז)

Attesting that the Lord is upright, my Rock, in whom there is no wrong. (Ps. 92:16)

ה׳ נָתַן וַה׳ לָקָח יְהִי שֵׁם ה׳ מְבֹרָךְ: (איוב א, כא)

The Lord has given and the Lord has taken. May the Name of the Lord be blessed. (Job 1:21)

He concludes with the verse:

וְהוּא רַחוּם יְכַפֵּר עָוֹן וְלֹא יַשְׁחִית וְהִרְבָּה לְהָשִׁיב אַפּוֹ וְלֹא יָעִיר כָּל חֲמָתוֹ (תהלים עח, לח)

But He, being merciful, forgave iniquity and would not destroy; He restrained His wrath time and again and did not give full vent to His fury. (Ps. 78:38)

23. *Tziduk HaDin* is not recited on Erev Shabbat or Erev Yom Tov after midday,[240] nor on days when *Taḥanun* is omitted. The custom in Jerusalem is not to say *Tziduk HaDin* on the day before one of the days when *Taḥanun* is omitted (e.g., Erev Rosh Ḥodesh). The Ashkenazic custom is not to recite *Tziduk HaDin* at night. The Sephardic custom is to recite on all days and at night.[241] Sephardic groups who follow the *Ben Ish Ḥai* do not recite *Tziduk HaDin* at night.[242]
24. The mourners say Kaddish. See Sec. 13, "Laws of Reciting Kaddish." Kaddish is brought with translation and transliteration, along with explanations, in Sec. 57, "Kaddish."
25. Mourners who are not proficient in reciting Kaddish should review it beforehand so as not to stumble over the words.
26. Even a young boy (over the age of six) who understands to Whom the blessing is being made, should say Kaddish at the funeral. An adult should stand beside him and say the Kaddish together with him, word for word.[243]

Ashkenazic nusaḥ:

יִתְגַּדַּל וְיִתְקַדַּשׁ שְׁמֵהּ רַבָּא. בְּעָלְמָא דִּי בְרָא כִרְעוּתֵהּ, וְיַמְלִיךְ מַלְכוּתֵהּ,
[וְיַצְמַח פֻּרְקָנֵהּ, וִיקָרֵב מְשִׁיחֵהּ]. בְּחַיֵּיכוֹן וּבְיוֹמֵיכוֹן וּבְחַיֵּי דְכָל בֵּית
יִשְׂרָאֵל, בַּעֲגָלָא וּבִזְמַן קָרִיב, וְאִמְרוּ אָמֵן. יְהֵא שְׁמֵהּ רַבָּא מְבָרַךְ לְעָלַם
וּלְעָלְמֵי עָלְמַיָּא. יִתְבָּרַךְ וְיִשְׁתַּבַּח וְיִתְפָּאַר וְיִתְרוֹמַם וְיִתְנַשֵּׂא וְיִתְהַדָּר
וְיִתְעַלֶּה וְיִתְהַלָּל שְׁמֵהּ דְּקֻדְשָׁא, בְּרִיךְ הוּא. לְעֵלָּא מִן כָּל בִּרְכָתָא וְשִׁירָתָא,
תֻּשְׁבְּחָתָא וְנֶחֱמָתָא, דַּאֲמִירָן בְּעָלְמָא, וְאִמְרוּ אָמֵן. יְהֵא שְׁלָמָא רַבָּא

240. Rema, *Yoreh De'ah* 401:6.
241. *Shulḥan Arukh, Yoreh De'ah* 401:6; Rema, *Oraḥ Ḥayim* 429:2; *Kaf HaḤayim* ad loc. 30; *Siftei Cohen* 376:3; *Gesher HaḤayim* 16:6, 2; *Yalkut Yosef* 29:18; *Pnei Barukh* 5:18 in the name of the *Sdei Ḥemed, Aveilut* 212; *Nitei Gavriel*, vol. 1, 78:9.
242. Written communication from Rabbi Mordechai Eliahu.
243. *Yalkut Yosef* 10:18.

מִן שְׁמַיָּא, וְחַיִּים עָלֵינוּ וְעַל כָּל יִשְׂרָאֵל, וְאִמְרוּ אָמֵן. עוֹשֶׂה שָׁלוֹם
בִּמְרוֹמָיו, הוּא יַעֲשֶׂה שָׁלוֹם עָלֵינוּ וְעַל כָּל יִשְׂרָאֵל, וְאִמְרוּ אָמֵן.

Yitgadal, veyitkadash shemeh raba. (Cong: *Amen.*) *Be'alema di vera khiruteh, beyamlikh malkhuteh, beḥayyeikhon, uvyomeikhon, uvḥayyei dekhol beit Yisrael, baagala uvizman kariv, veimru Amen.* (Cong: *Amen.* All: *Yeheh shemeh raba mevarakh lealam ulalemei alemaya.*) *Yitbarakh veyishtabaḥ veyitpaar veyitromam veyitnaseh veyithadar veyitaleh veyithallal shemeh dekudsha, berikh hu.* (Cong: *Berikh hu.*) *Le'ela min kol birkhata veshirata, tushbeḥata veneḥemata daamiran be'alema, veimru, Amen.* (Cong: *Amen.*) *Yeheh shelama raba min shemaya veḥayyim (tovim) aleinu ve'al kol Yisrael, ve'imru Amen.* (Cong.: *Amen.*) *Oseh shalom bimromav, hu yaaseh shalom aleinu, ve'al kol Yisrael, ve'imru Amen.* (Cong: *Amen.*)

Magnified and sanctified may His great name be, in the world He created by His will. May He establish His kingdom in your lifetime and in your days, and in the lifetime of all the house of Israel, swiftly and soon – and say: Amen. (All: May His great name be blessed for ever and all time.) Blessed and praised, glorified and exalted, raised and honored, uplifted and lauded be the name of the Holy One, blessed be He, beyond any blessing, song, praise and consolation uttered in the world – and say: Amen. May there be great peace from heaven, and good lives for us and all Israel – and say: Amen. May He who makes peace in His high places, make peace for us and all Israel – and say: Amen.

Sephardic nusaḥ:

יִתְגַּדַּל וְיִתְקַדַּשׁ שְׁמֵהּ רַבָּא. בְּעָלְמָא דִּי בְרָא כִרְעוּתֵהּ, וְיַמְלִיךְ
מַלְכוּתֵהּ, וְיַצְמַח פֻּרְקָנֵהּ, וִיקָרֵב מְשִׁיחֵהּ. בְּחַיֵּיכוֹן וּבְיוֹמֵיכוֹן וּבְחַיֵּי
דְכָל בֵּית יִשְׂרָאֵל, בַּעֲגָלָא וּבִזְמַן קָרִיב, וְאִמְרוּ אָמֵן. יְהֵא שְׁמֵהּ רַבָּא
מְבָרַךְ לְעָלַם וּלְעָלְמֵי עָלְמַיָּא. יִתְבָּרַךְ וְיִשְׁתַּבַּח וְיִתְפָּאַר וְיִתְרוֹמַם
וְיִתְנַשֵּׂא וְיִתְהַדָּר וְיִתְעַלֶּה וְיִתְהַלָּל שְׁמֵהּ דְּקֻדְשָׁא, בְּרִיךְ הוּא. לְעֵלָּא מִן
כָּל בִּרְכָתָא וְשִׁירָתָא, תֻּשְׁבְּחָתָא וְנֶחָמָתָא, דַּאֲמִירָן בְּעָלְמָא, וְאִמְרוּ אָמֵן
[יש המוסיפים בנוסח זה: תִּתְכְּלֵי חַרְבָּא וְכַפְנָא וּמוֹתָנָא וּמַרְעִין בִּישִׁין
יְעַדֵּי מִנַּנָא וּמִנְּכוֹן וּמֵעַל עַמֵּיהּ יִשְׂרָאֵל וְאִמְרוּ אָמֵן]. יְהֵא שְׁלָמָא רַבָּא

מִן שְׁמַיָּא, חַיִּים וְשָׂבָע וִישׁוּעָה וְנֶחָמָה וְשֵׁיזָבָא וּרְפוּאָה וּגְאֻלָּה וּסְלִיחָה
וְכַפָּרָה וְרֵיוַח וְהַצָּלָה, לָנוּ וּלְכָל עַמּוֹ יִשְׂרָאֵל וְאִמְרוּ אָמֵן. עוֹשֶׂה שָׁלוֹם
בִּמְרוֹמָיו, הוּא בְּרַחֲמָיו יַעֲשֶׂה שָׁלוֹם עָלֵינוּ וְעַל כָּל יִשְׂרָאֵל, וְאִמְרוּ אָמֵן.

Yitgadal, veyitkadash shemeh raba. (Cong: *Amen.*) *Be'alema di vera khir'uteh, beyamlikh malkhuteh, veyatzmah purkaneh vikarev meshiheh* (Cong: *Amen.*) *behayyeikhon, uvyomeikhon, uvḥayyei dekhol beit Yisrael, baagala uvizman kariv, ve'imru Amen.* (Cong: *Amen.* All: *Yeheh shemeh raba mevarakh lealam ulalemei alemaya.*) *Yitbarakh veyishtabaḥ veyitpa'ar veyitromam veyitnaseh veyitdar veyitaleh veyithallal shemeh dekudsha, berikh hu.* (Cong: *Amen.*) *Le'ela min kol birkhata veshirata, tushbeḥata veneḥemata daamiran be'alema, ve'imru, Amen.* (Cong: *Amen.*) [Some add: *Titkelei, ḥarba vekafna vemotana umarin bishin ye'adei minnana, uminkhon ume'al amei Yisrael ve'imru Amen.*] *Yeheh shelama raba min shemaya ḥayyim vesava vishuah veneḥama vesheizava urefuah ugeulla useliḥah vekhaparah fereivaḥ vehatzalah, lanu, ulekhol amo Yisrael, ve'imru Amen.* (Cong.: *Amen.*) *Oseh shalom bimromav, hu beraḥamav yaaseh shalom aleinu, ve'al kol Yisrael, ve'imru Amen.* (Cong.: *Amen.*)

Magnified and sanctified may His great name be, in the world He created by His will. May He establish His kingdom in your lifetime and in your days, and in the lifetime of all the house of Israel, swiftly and soon – and say: Amen. (All: May His great name be blessed for ever and all time.) Blessed and praised, glorified and exalted, raised and honored, uplifted and lauded be the name of the Holy One, blessed be He, beyond any blessing, song, praise and consolation uttered in the world – and say: Amen. May there be great peace from heaven, life and help, salvation and consolation, refuge and healing, redemption, forgiveness and atonement, relief and salvation, for us and for all His people Israel; and say: Amen. May He who makes peace in His high places, make peace for us and all Israel – and say: Amen.

The funeral

Rabbi Judah and Rav said: Whoever sees a corpse [on the way to burial] and does not accompany it comes under the head of

"He that mocketh the poor blasphemeth his Maker" (Prov. 17:5). And if he accompanies it, what is his reward? R. Assi says: To him apply the texts, "He that is gracious unto the poor lendeth unto the Lord" (ibid. 19:17), and "He that is gracious unto the needy honoreth Him." (ibid 14:31). (Berakhot 18a)

27. It is a mitzva to escort the deceased. This is included in the commandment, "Love your neighbor as yourself." One should escort the deceased at least four cubits (about two meters).
28. Even in a place where the deceased does not need to be escorted, one must stand up in his presence.[244]
29. One should interrupt Torah study in order to escort the deceased. But if the deceased has all their needs met, then Torah study is not interrupted, on the condition that ten men are there so the mourners can recite of the Kaddish. In the deceased was someone who taught Torah, even if there are already thousands escorting him, Torah study is interrupted in order to allow students to escort him.[245]
30. It is customary that someone who wishes to escort the coffin for the minimum distance – four cubits – should wait until he can no longer see the coffin before he returns to his own affairs.[246]
31. One should not greet others during the funeral; this applies in the cemetery near the grave, as well.[247] The Yemenite custom is that one who meets a friend at the funeral says, "You shall be saved from all sorrow," and the friend answers in kind.[248]
32. When the pallbearers gather to carry the body, the custom is to say, "When the Tabernacle is to set out, the Levites shall take it down, and when the Tabernacle is to be pitched, the Levites

244. *Shulḥan Arukh, Yoreh De'ah* 361:4. The commentators there explain that one should also stand before those who are involved in handling the body.
245. *Shulḥan Arukh, Yoreh De'ah* 361:1.
246. *Yalkut Yosef* 10:2, in the name of the *Ḥizkuni, Parashat Shoftim* (Deut. 21:7): "And our eyes did not see." It is deduced from here that a person who escorts the body should wait until he can no longer see the coffin.
247. *Gesher HaḤayim* 14:1, 16.
248. *Shulḥan Arukh HaMekutzar, Einei Yitzḥak, Yoreh De'ah* 180:2; *Be'er LeḤai Roi* 45.

shall set it up" (Num. 1:52); "When the Ark was to set out, Moses would say: Advance O Lord! May Your enemies be scattered, and may Your foes flee before You!" (ibid. 10:35).[249] These verses are about the Tabernacle and the Ark of the Covenant. Just as the Divine Presence resided in the physical Ark and the Tabernacle, a Jewish person's physical body holds the soul – a part of the Divine – within it. Like the Ark, the Divine Presence resided in the body. A Jewish person is also compared to a *sefer Torah*, before which we recite the verse, "When the Ark was to set out." Like the Torah, a Jewish person should represent the epitome of positive and correct behavior.

33. Certain Kabbalists wrote in their wills that only one who had immersed in a *mikve* should carry their coffin. Some people hold by this custom for the funerals of outstanding Torah scholars.[250]
34. A Torah scroll should not be placed on the coffin of a Torah scholar. If the deceased authored books, however, these can be placed on the coffin to honor their author.[251]
35. The custom is for the coffin to be carried with the body's feet pointing forwards. The reason is brought in the Key Concepts section, **The Deceased's Feet in the Direction of the Door**. The Yemenite custom is to carry the body with the head first.[252]
36. During the funeral procession, Psalm 91 – "O you who dwell in the shelter of the Most High" – is recited. This psalm describes how God protects man from his enemies and from evil spirits. Kabbalistic texts write that when the soul leaves the body, the deceased is in a state where they need protection from impure forces and destructive angels. People say psalms for the protection of the deceased, especially in the time between the death and the burial. Psalm 91, in particular, conveys this protection.

249. *Maavar Yabok, "Siftei Renanot"* 15.
250. Rabbi Yaakov Ruza told me that this is the Kabbalistic custom.
251. *Shulḥan Arukh, Yoreh De'ah* 353:2; *Yalkut Yosef* 10:21.
252. *Shulḥan Arukh HaMekutzar, Einei Yitzḥak, Yoreh De'ah* 179:6.

> O you who dwell in the shelter of the Most High and abide in the protection of Shaddai – I say of the Lord, my refuge and stronghold, my God in whom I trust, that He will save you from the fowler's trap, from the destructive plague. He will cover you with His wings; you will find refuge under them; His fidelity is an encircling shield. You need not fear the terror by night, or the arrow that flies by day, the plague that stalks in the darkness, or the scourge that ravages at noon. A thousand may fall at your left side, ten thousand at your right, but it shall not reach you. You will see it with your eyes, you will witness the punishment of the wicked. Because you took the Lord – my refuge, the Most High – as your haven, no harm will befall you, no disease touch your tent. For He will order His angels to guard you wherever you go. They will carry you in their hands lest you hurt your foot on a stone. You will tread on cubs and vipers; you will trample lions and asps. Because he is devoted to Me I will deliver him; I will keep him safe, for he knows My name. When he calls on Me, I will answer him; I will be with him in distress; I will rescue him and make him honored; I will let him live to a ripe old age and show him My salvation. (The Hebrew text of Psalm 91 can be found on page 99.)

For a woman, one adds "Woman of Valor" (Prov. 31):

> A woman of valor who can find? She is far more precious than jewels. The heart of her husband trusts in her, and he shall lack no fortune. She does him good, and not harm, all the days of her life. She seeks wool and linen and works with willing hands. She is like the ships of the merchant; she brings her sustenance from afar. She rises while it is yet night and provides food for her household and portions for her maiden. She considers a field and buys it; with the fruit of her hands she plants a vineyard. She girds herself with strength and makes her arms strong. She perceives that her merchandise is profitable. Her lamp does not go out at night. She puts her hands to the distaff, and her hands hold the spindle. She opens her hand to the poor and reaches

out her hands to the needy. She is not afraid of snow for her household, for her entire household is clothed in scarlet. She makes bed coverings for herself; her clothing is fine linen and purple. Her husband is known in the gates when he sits among the elders of the land. She makes linen garments and sells them; she delivers sashes to the merchant. Strength and dignity are her clothing, and she smilingly awaits her last day. She opens her mouth with wisdom, and the teaching of kindness is on her tongue. She anticipates the needs of her household and does not eat the bread of idleness. Her children rise up and celebrate her; and her husband, he praises her, "Many women have done excellently, but you surpass them all." Charm is deceitful, and beauty is vain, but a woman who fears the Lord is to be praised. Give her of the fruit of her hands, and let her works praise her in the gates.

37. Some recite Song of Songs during the funeral. The custom is based on the Kabbala.
38. Some have a custom to stop the procession when passing a synagogue and to recite the following: the mishna "Akkavya ben Mehalalel says" and two verses of the *Tziduk HaDin*: "The Rock, His work is perfect, for all His ways are justice; a God of faithfulness and without iniquity, righteous and just is He," and "Wondrous in purpose and mighty in deed, whose eyes observe all the ways of men, so as to repay every man according to his ways, and with the proper fruit of his deeds!" Afterwards, the sons or other relatives recite Kaddish. (See Key Concepts, ***Maamad and Moshav*** [*Standing and Sitting*].) If the body is in a vehicle when they stop for this purpose, the vehicle's back door should be opened during the recitation.
39. The coffin of an exceptionally wise and brilliant person should be taken into the beit midrash where that person taught, and the eulogies should be said there.[253]

---

253. *Shulḥan Arukh, Yoreh De'ah* 344:20. See also *Responsa Yabia Omer*, vol. 9, *Yoreh De'ah* 46.

The burial

Joseph merited burying his father, and none of his brothers were greater than he, as it says: "And Joseph went up (to Israel) to bury his father... and chariots and cavalry went up with him." Who among us was greater than Joseph, that only Moses was permitted to attend to him? Moses merited [carrying] Joseph's bones [to Israel], and none of Israel is greater than him, as it says, "And Moses took the bones of Joseph with him." Who among us was greater than Moses, that only God merited dealing with him, as it says, "And He buried him in the valley." (Mishna Sota 1:9)

Burial is esteemed for two reasons: It is appropriate to appreciate someone from whom one benefited, as the Torah teaches, "You shall not abhor an Egyptian, for you were a stranger in his land" (Deut. 23:8). Likewise, the body should not be despised after the soul has dwelled within it. Indeed, if you see a person whose house was destroyed, you will feel sorry for him and your heart will ache for him if it has become a latrine. Such is the difficulty for the soul in seeing the body being degraded. And about this, they said, "Maggots are as excruciating to the dead as the stab of a needle to the flesh of the living." This comparison describes the reality of the difficulty. That is why burial is so important, as well as all the respect shown to the deceased, like the esteem shown to holy items which are stored away. The deceased's relatives also find comfort in this honoring... And the second reason, which is a stronger reason, is that it is necessary for our belief in the resurrection of the dead. For if we were to dispose of the body like a dead animal, people would think that we are like beasts; they would not accept the belief in the resurrection, as they can when they see the burial – that we build a house for them, dress them in clothing, and bury them with their family and forefathers since they will eventually rise up together with their family. And to uphold this essential belief, the Torah writes in relation to burial, "And I will lie down with my fathers"(Gen. 47:30). (*Kol Bo al Aveilut* 114)

40. Efforts should be made to have the burial during the day and not at night. If necessary, however, the burial may take place at night.

For example, if having the burial at night would prevent the body from sitting overnight, this should be done.[254]

41. In some places, the member of the *ḥevra kaddisha* who lowers the body into the ground removes his shoes.[255] The body is lowered into the ground feet-first and is laid on its back, facing upwards.[256] The feet should be pointing towards Jerusalem. Inside the grave, the member of the *ḥevra kaddisha* unties the temporary knots of the shrouds, straightens the limbs of the body, and opens the closed fingers. They cover the body with slabs of stone, starting at the head.[257] No blessing is recited upon burying the dead since gentiles may also bury the dead.[258]

When the body is lowered into the ground, it is customary to recite the Thirteen Attributes of Mercy:

The Lord! The Lord! A God compassionate and gracious, slow to anger, abounding in kindness and faithfulness, extending kindness to the thousandth generation, forgiving iniquity, transgression, and sin. (Ex. 34:6–7)

But He, being merciful, forgave iniquity and would not destroy; He restrained His wrath time and again and did not give full vent to His fury. (Ps. 78:38)

Death and burial are considered atonement for one's sins. At the end of the song of *Haazinu* (Deut. 32:43) it is written, "*Vekhiper admato – amo,*" "Atonement for the soil of his people"; death and

254. *Kol Bo al Aveilut*, p. 188–189.
255. *Gesher HaḤayim* 15:2, 1.
256. *Shulḥan Arukh, Yoreh De'ah* 362:2. Some derived this from the verse, "Then Abraham rose from beside his dead" (Gen. 23:3) – *Menaḥem Aveilim* 5:20, in the name of Rabbi Ḥayim ben Atar.
257. *Gesher HaḤayim* 16:5, 1.
258. In Menaḥot 42a it says: "Any mitzva that is appropriate for gentiles, Jews do not need to make a blessing." Rashi explains: "Because we cannot say 'who has commanded us,' since a gentile can also do so." And in the case of burial, a Jew can be buried by a gentile if needed; *Kol Bo al Aveilut*, p. 173.

burial are themselves atonement. This is why the Attributes of Mercy are recited at the burial.[259]

42. It is a mitzva to take part in the funeral by carrying the coffin or helping to cover the body in the grave with dirt. The relatives should also participate in covering the body.
43. When covering the body, the spade should not be handed directly from one person to another. It should be laid on the ground or placed in the mound of earth. The next person picks it up himself. This is done so that one person does not pass pain to another person.[260]
44. The dimensions of the grave are explained in the chapter on cemeteries, Sec. 45, "Laws Relating to the Cemetery: Dimensions of and distance between graves."

The custom to encircle the deceased

45. The custom to encircle the deceased before the burial is practiced by the Hasidim, the Yemenite community, and in Jerusalem. This practice is based on Kabbalistic ideas. It is explained in Key Concepts, ***Hakafot***.
46. Some people have the custom to turn the bier three times after the burial. The reason for this custom is that the word "*mitah*," meaning burial bier, has the same numerical value as the word "*Din*," judgment; turning the coffin symbolizes transforming the judgment into mercy and the eulogy to celebration, as alluded to in the verse, "You turned my lament into dancing" (Ps. 30:12).[261]

Tziduk HaDin

47. After the burial, *Tziduk HaDin* is said again (but only on days when *Taḥanun* is recited; not on Erev Shabbat or Erev Rosh

259. Some have written that, when burying the deceased, those doing the burying should have the following intention: The spiritual impurity that intervened with the dead through the sin of Adam shall be consumed in the ground, and the deceased shall remain cleansed (*Ḥazon LaMoed* 10:6, in the name of the Ari).
260. *Maavar Yabok, Sefat Emet* 27.
261. *Ḥokhmat Adam* 158:31; *Gesher HaḤayim* 15:2, 3; *Pnei Barukh* 5:21; *Shulḥan Arukh HaMekutzar, Einei Yitzḥak, Yoreh De'ah* 180:17.

Ḥodesh after midday, nor when the burial is at night. As mentioned above, some Sephardic communities say it at night):

הַצּוּר תָּמִים פָּעֳלוֹ כִּי כָל דְּרָכָיו מִשְׁפָּט, אֵל אֱמוּנָה וְאֵין עָוֶל צַדִּיק וְיָשָׁר הוּא. הַצּוּר תָּמִים בְּכָל פֹּעַל, מִי יֹאמַר לוֹ מַה תִּפְעָל, הַשַּׁלִּיט בְּמַטָּה וּבְמַעַל, מֵמִית וּמְחַיֶּה, מוֹרִיד שְׁאוֹל וַיָּעַל. הַצּוּר תָּמִים בְּכָל מַעֲשֶׂה, מִי יֹאמַר לוֹ מַה תַּעֲשֶׂה, הָאוֹמֵר וְעֹשֶׂה, חֶסֶד חִנָּם לָנוּ תַעֲשֶׂה, וּבִזְכוּת הַנֶּעֱקַד כְּשֶׂה, הַקְשִׁיבָה וַעֲשֵׂה. צַדִּיק בְּכָל דְּרָכָיו הַצּוּר תָּמִים, אֶרֶךְ אַפַּיִם וּמָלֵא רַחֲמִים, חֲמָל נָא וְחוּס נָא עַל אָבוֹת וּבָנִים, כִּי לְךָ, אָדוֹן, הַסְּלִיחוֹת וְהָרַחֲמִים. צַדִּיק אַתָּה ה׳ לְהָמִית וּלְהַחֲיוֹת, אֲשֶׁר בְּיָדְךָ פִּקְדוֹן כָּל רוּחוֹת, חָלִילָה לְּךָ זִכְרוֹנֵנוּ לִמְחוֹת, וְיִהְיוּ נָא עֵינֶיךָ בְּרַחֲמִים עָלֵינוּ פְקוּחוֹת, כִּי לְךָ, אָדוֹן, הָרַחֲמִים וְהַסְּלִיחוֹת. אָדָם אִם בֶּן שָׁנָה יִחְיֶה, אוֹ אֶלֶף שָׁנִים יִחְיֶה, מַה יִּתְרוֹן לוֹ, כְּלֹא הָיָה יִהְיֶה, בָּרוּךְ דַּיַּן הָאֱמֶת, מֵמִית וּמְחַיֶּה. בָּרוּךְ הוּא, כִּי אֱמֶת דִּינוֹ, וּמְשׁוֹטֵט הַכֹּל בְּעֵינוֹ, וּמְשַׁלֵּם לְאָדָם חֶשְׁבּוֹנוֹ וְדִינוֹ, וְהַכֹּל לִשְׁמוֹ הוֹדָיָה יִתֵּנוּ. יָדַעְנוּ ה׳ כִּי צֶדֶק מִשְׁפָּטֶךָ, תִּצְדַּק בְּדָבְרֶךָ וְתִזְכֶּה בְּשָׁפְטֶךָ, וְאֵין לְהַרְהֵר אַחַר מִדַּת שָׁפְטֶךָ, צַדִּיק אַתָּה ה׳, וְיָשָׁר מִשְׁפָּטֶיךָ. דַּיַּן הָאֱמֶת, שֹׁפֵט צֶדֶק וֶאֱמֶת, בָּרוּךְ דַּיַּן הָאֱמֶת, כִּי כָל מִשְׁפָּטָיו צֶדֶק וֶאֱמֶת. נֶפֶשׁ כָּל חַי בְּיָדֶךָ, צֶדֶק מָלְאָה יְמִינְךָ וְיָדֶךָ, רַחֵם עַל פְּלֵיטַת צֹאן יָדֶיךָ, וְתֹאמַר לַמַּלְאָךְ הֶרֶף יָדֶךָ.

The Rock, His work is perfect, for all His ways are just; a God of faithfulness and without iniquity, righteous and just is He. The Rock, perfect in all His works. Who can say to Him "What have You done?" He rules below and above, He brings death and restores life, brings down to the grave and raises up from there. The Rock, perfect in all His deeds. Who can say to Him, "What do You do?" You who says and fulfills, do undeserved kindness with us, and in the merit of him [Isaac] who was bound [on the altar] like a lamb, hearken and grant our request. Righteous One in all His ways, O Rock who is perfect, slow to anger and abundant in mercy, take pity and spare both parents and children, for to You, O Lord, pertain forgiveness and mercy. Righteous are You, Lord, to bring death and to restore life, for in Your hands are entrusted all spirits. Far be it from You to erase our memory. Look towards us with mercy, for Yours, O Lord, are mercy and forgiveness. A man, whether he be a year old, or whether he lives a thousand years, what does it profit him? For is it not as if he has never been? Blessed be the True Judge, who brings death and restores life. Blessed be He, for His judgment is true, as He scans everything with His eye, and He rewards man according to his account and his judgment. Let all give praise to His name. We know, Lord, that Your judgment is right. You are righteous when You speak and pure when You judge, and none shall question Your judgments. Righteous are You, Lord, and Your judgments are just. You are the True Judge, who judges with righteousness and truth. Blessed is the True Judge, for all of His judgments are righteous and true. The soul of every living creature is in Your hand, righteousness fills Your right and left hand. Have mercy on the remnant of the flock under Your hand, and say to the angel of death, "Hold back your hand!"

(Some have the custom to skip the first verse and to begin here):

גְּדֹל הָעֵצָה וְרַב הָעֲלִילִיָּה, אֲשֶׁר עֵינֶיךָ פְּקֻוּחוֹת עַל כָּל דַּרְכֵי בְּנֵי אָדָם, לָתֵת לְאִישׁ כִּדְרָכָיו וְכִפְרִי מַעֲלָלָיו. לְהַגִּיד כִּי יָשָׁר ה׳, צוּרִי וְלֹא עַוְלָתָה בּוֹ. ה׳ נָתַן, וַה׳ לָקָח, יְהִי שֵׁם ה׳ מְבֹורָךְ. וְהוּא רַחוּם יְכַפֵּר עָוֹן וְלֹא יַשְׁחִית, וְהִרְבָּה לְהָשִׁיב אַפּוֹ, וְלֹא יָעִיר כָּל חֲמָתוֹ.

You are great in counsel and mighty in action, Your eyes are watching all the ways of man, to give man according to his ways and according to the fruit of his deeds. To say that the Lord is Just; He is my Strength, and there is no injustice in Him. The Lord has given and the Lord has taken. May the Name of the Lord be blessed. He, being compassionate, pardons iniquity, and does not destroy; time and again He turns away His anger and does not arouse all His wrath.

The *Tziduk HaDin* customary in Sephardic communities:

צַדִּיק אַתָּה ה׳, וְיָשָׁר מִשְׁפָּטֶיךָ, צַדִּיק ה׳ בְּכָל דְּרָכָיו, וְחָסִיד בְּכָל מַעֲשָׂיו. צִדְקָתְךָ צֶדֶק לְעוֹלָם, וְתוֹרָתְךָ אֱמֶת. מִשְׁפְּטֵי ה׳ אֱמֶת, צָדְקוּ יַחְדָּו. בַּאֲשֶׁר דְּבַר מֶלֶךְ שִׁלְטוֹן, וּמִי יֹאמַר לוֹ מַה תַּעֲשֶׂה. וְהוּא בְאֶחָד וּמִי יְשִׁיבֶנּוּ, וְנַפְשׁוֹ אִוְּתָה וַיָּעַשׂ. קָטֹן וְגָדוֹל שָׁם הוּא, וְעֶבֶד חָפְשִׁי מֵאֲדֹנָיו. הֵן בַּעֲבָדָיו

לֹא יַאֲמִין, וּבְמַלְאָכָיו יָשִׂים תָּהֳלָה. אַף כִּי אֱנוֹשׁ רִמָּה, וּבֶן אָדָם תּוֹלֵעָה. הַצּוּר תָּמִים פָּעֳלוֹ כִּי כָל דְּרָכָיו מִשְׁפָּט, אֵל אֱמוּנָה וְאֵין עָוֶל צַדִּיק וְיָשָׁר הוּא. דַּיָּן הָאֱמֶת, שֹׁפֵט צֶדֶק וֶאֱמֶת, בָּרוּךְ דַּיַּן הָאֱמֶת, כִּי כָל מִשְׁפָּטָיו צֶדֶק וֶאֱמֶת. בִּלַּע הַמָּוֶת לָנֶצַח, וּמָחָה ה׳ אֱלֹהִים דִּמְעָה מֵעַל כָּל פָּנִים, וְחֶרְפַּת עַמּוֹ יָסִיר מֵעַל כָּל הָאָרֶץ כִּי ה׳ דִּבֵּר. יִחְיוּ מֵתֶיךָ נְבֵלָתִי יְקוּמוּן, הָקִיצוּ וְרַנְּנוּ שֹׁכְנֵי עָפָר כִּי טַל אוֹרֹת טַלֶּךָ, וָאָרֶץ רְפָאִים תַּפִּיל. וְהוּא רַחוּם יְכַפֵּר עָוֹן וְלֹא יַשְׁחִית, וְהִרְבָּה לְהָשִׁיב אַפּוֹ, וְלֹא יָעִיר כָּל חֲמָתוֹ. ה׳ הוֹשִׁיעָה, הַמֶּלֶךְ יַעֲנֵנוּ בְיוֹם קָרְאֵנוּ.

Righteous are You, Lord, and Your judgments are fair. The Lord is righteous in all His ways, and kind in all His deeds. Your righteousness is eternal and Your law is truth. The judgments of the Lord are true; they are all righteous. For the word of the king is supreme, and who can tell Him what to do? He is single-minded, who can sway Him? His soul desired – and so He did. The small and the great are there, and the slave is free from his master. Behold, His servants He does not trust and His angels he charges with frivolity. How much less a mortal – (that) maggot, and the son of man – (that) worm! The Rock, His work is perfect, for all His ways are justice; God of faithfulness and without iniquity, righteous and fair is He. True Judge judging with righteousness and truth. Blessed be the True Judge, for all of His judgments are righteous and true. May He swallow up death forever and may the Almighty God wipe away tears from every face and the scorn of His people He will remove from all the earth, because the Lord said so. Your dead will live [again]; my corpses will arise. Awake and sing, dwellers of dust! For the dew of light [is] Your dew, and the earth will give forth the dead. And He is merciful, atones for sin and does not destroy, frequently withdraws His anger and does not arouse all His rage. Save, Lord! The King will answer us when we call.

The Great Kaddish – *Kaddish HaGadol*

48. After *Tziduk HaDin,* a special Kaddish called "*Kaddish HaGadol,*" the Great Kaddish, is recited.[262] See Sec. 57, "Kaddish."

---

262. *Shulḥan Arukh, Yoreh De'ah* 376:4.

49. On days when *Tziduk HaDin* is omitted, *Kaddish HaGadol* is also omitted. Instead, Psalm 16 ("A *mikhtam* of David") is recited, followed by the Mourner's Kaddish.[263]

A *mikhtam* of David. Protect me, O God, for I seek refuge in You. I say to the Lord, "You are my Lord, my benefactor; there is none above You." As to the holy and mighty ones that are in the land, my whole desire concerning them is that those who espouse another [god] may have many sorrows! I will have no part of their bloody libations; their names will not pass my lips. The Lord is my allotted share and portion; You control my fate. Delightful country has fallen to my lot; lovely indeed is my estate. I bless the Lord who has guided me; my conscience admonishes me at night. I am ever mindful of the Lord's presence; He is at my right hand; I shall never be shaken. So my heart rejoices, my whole being exults, and my body rests secure. For You will not abandon me to Sheol or let Your faithful one see the pit. You will teach me the path of life. In Your presence is perfect joy; delights are ever in Your right hand.

El Maleh Raḥamim

50. "*El Maleh Raḥamim*" is recited at the end of the funeral:

אֵל מָלֵא רַחֲמִים שׁוֹכֵן בַּמְּרוֹמִים הַמְצֵא מְנוּחָה נְכוֹנָה עַל כַּנְפֵי הַשְּׁכִינָה בְּמַעֲלוֹת קְדוֹשִׁים וּטְהוֹרִים כְּזֹהַר הָרָקִיעַ מַזְהִירִים לְנִשְׁמַת (פלוני/ת בן/בת פלוני/ת) שֶׁהָלַךְ / שֶׁהָלְכָה לְעוֹלָמוֹ/ה. בַּעֲבוּר שֶׁמִּשְׁפַּחְתּוֹ/ה נוֹדֶבֶת בְּעַד הַזְכָּרַת נִשְׁמָתוֹ/ה בְּגַן עֵדֶן תְּהֵא מְנוּחָתוֹ/ה לָכֵן בַּעַל הָרַחֲמִים יַסְתִּירֶהוּ/ה בְּסֵתֶר כְּנָפָיו לְעוֹלָמִים, וְיִצְרוֹר בִּצְרוֹר הַחַיִּים אֶת נִשְׁמָתוֹ/ה ה׳ הוּא נַחֲלָתוֹ/ה וְיָנוּחַ/וְתָנוּחַ בְּשָׁלוֹם עַל מִשְׁכָּבוֹ/ה וְנֹאמַר אָמֵן.

O God, full of compassion, who dwells on high, grant true rest upon the wings of the *Shekhina* (Divine Presence), in the exalted spheres of the holy and pure, who shine as the resplendence of the firmament, to the soul of (mention his/her Hebrew name and that of his father/her mother) who has gone to his/her [supernal]

---

263. *Gesher HaḤayim* 16:6, 4.

world, for charity has been donated in remembrance of his/her soul; may his/her place of rest be in the Garden of Eden. Therefore, may the all-merciful One shelter him/her with the cover of His wings forever, and bind his/her soul in the bond of life. The Lord is his/her heritage; may s/he rest in his/her resting-place in peace; and let us say: Amen.

The Sephardic custom is to recite the *Hashkava*:
For a Torah scholar and a righteous person, the following is said:

And wisdom, where can it be found? And where is the place of understanding? Praiseworthy is the man, who found wisdom, and the man, who will derive understanding. How abundant is Your goodness that You have stored for those who fear You, that You have done for those who trust in You before the sons of men! How precious is Your kindness, O God! And the children of men take refuge in the shadow of Your wings. They are brimming from the nourishment of Your house and from the stream of Your delights You give them to drink. A good name is better than good oil and the day of death than the day of birth. At the end, when all has been considered: Fear God and keep His commandments for this is the essence of man. Let the devout rejoice in glory, they will sing joyously upon their beds.

Asking forgiveness

Afterwards, we ask the deceased for forgiveness. A member of the *ḥevra kaddisha* recites:

In the name of the *ḥevra kaddisha,* in the name of the friends who have dealt with you, in the name of your family and friends, I ask you for forgiveness if we have harmed you in any way during the purification process or in carrying the coffin or setting the grave. Forgive us, for it was a mistake. Everything we did was in your honor and in accordance with to the customs of the *ḥevra kaddisha.* We release you from membership to any societies or groups. Go in peace, rest in peace, and rise up in the end of days.

Be a good advocate on behalf of your family and friends, and life and peace shall be for us and all of Israel forever.

The beginning of *aveilut*

Weep ye for the mourners, not for what is lost: He found him rest; it is we who are left distressed. (Moed Katan 25b)

In the transition from *aninut* to mourning, the attention shifts from the deceased to the mourners.

51. After the conclusion of the burial, the mourners change into cloth or rubber shoes, or they place a bit of earth inside their regular shoes. This act symbolizes that, from that point onward, the laws of mourning apply.[264]
52. On Friday afternoon close to Shabbat: If the mourner intended to begin *aveilut*, even if he did not do an act of mourning (removing his shoes, sitting on the ground, being comforted by others), Friday is still counted as the first day of shiva. However, if there was no time to perform any such act or if the person did not have the intention to begin mourning, then Shabbat is counted as the first day of shiva.[265]
53. The seven days of mourning begin when the grave is covered. Therefore, one should try to complete the burial while it is still daytime so that the day of the burial may be considered a day of shiva. If the burial was completed immediately after sunset (up to thirteen minutes after sunset,[266] and some say up to seventeen minutes after sunset[267]), this is still considered part of the day for

264. *Shulḥan Arukh, Yoreh De'ah* 376:4.
265. *Gilyon Maharsha* and *Pitḥei Teshuva, Yoreh De'ah* 375:1; *Gesher HaḤayim* 21:12, 4; *Pnei Barukh* 8, note 3; and see later, Sec. 31, "Shabbat and mourning."
266. *Tzror HaḤayim* 75. Since all the laws of *aveilut* are rabbinic commandments, one may be lenient.
267. *Gesher HaḤayim* 19:4, 1; *Pnei Barukh* 8:10. *Yalkut Yosef* 15:2 writes that even if the burial was eighteen minutes after sunset, that day is counted since this is still considered daytime according to some opinions; however, we may not rely on Rabbenu Tam's opinion, according to which the day ends seventy-two minutes

the purpose of counting the days of shiva. But if one has already prayed Maariv, even if it was still daytime, that day is not counted for the *aveilut*; shiva begins the following day.[268]

54. Nowadays, graves are covered with stone slabs before being covered with earth, and so this is considered the closing of the grave. *Aveilut* begins from that point.[269]

55. A relative who is not present at the funeral nevertheless begins the shiva at the end of the burial, like the rest of the relatives. But if the relative does not know when the funeral is, or if the funeral has been delayed by a day, he can begin sitting shiva immediately.[270] See Sec. 47, "Delayed Burial." Some have written that if the body is being transported to Israel, those who are not accompanying the body begin shiva immediately, even if they do know when the burial will be because the funeral is taking place far away from them.[271]

Standing in rows

56. The men attending the funeral form two lines; the male mourners remove their shoes or put some earth inside of them and walk between the two rows. Those standing in the lines say, "May God comfort you among the other mourners of Zion and Jerusalem and may you have no more sorrow." The Sephardic custom is to say, "May you be comforted from Heaven."

---

after sunset. This is because Rabbenu Tam's opinion is not the accepted custom in Israel and the principle that mourning follows the most lenient opinion does not apply where the prevailing custom rejects that opinion.

268. *Shulḥan Arukh, Yoreh De'ah* 375:11 and 404:11. The *Turei Zahav* wrote that the reason is because this would be two conflicting lenient opinions: If a person prayed Maariv, then halakhically it is the next day for him and therefore it cannot be considered the previous day for shiva.

269. *Yalkut Yosef* 15:1.

270. *Shulḥan Arukh, Yoreh De'ah* 375:2; *Gesher HaḤayim* 19:4, 8; *Tzror HaḤayim* 75.

271. *Igrot Moshe, Yoreh De'ah*, vol. 2, 170. See also *Kol Bo al Aveilut*, p. 269. Rabbi Nebenzahl: But if the person is maintaining contact by phone and the like and is given instructions about how to publicize the details of the funeral and whom to inform, etc., then *aninut* still applies.

57. It is customary to form rows only for male mourners[272] out of a concern for modesty, even in the cemetery. But in a place where women would like to form lines for female mourners, and the local rabbi permits it, two lines of women may be formed to comfort the female mourners.[273]
58. The custom of forming rows is also practiced on Rosh Ḥodesh, Ḥanukka, Purim, and Ḥol HaMoed.[274]

Washing hands

59. When a person leaves the cemetery, he should wash his hands – three times each on alternating hands – in order to remove the impure spirit from the cemetery.[275] It is customary not to dry one's hands (although it is permitted).[276] It symbolizes that one is not quick to wash away the impressions from the funeral and the memory of the deceased. It also signifies the difficulty of parting from the deceased and that one is still focused on mourning.[277] It is customary not to enter a home before washing one's hands.[278]
60. This hand-washing does not require a washing cup.[279]
61. If a washing cup is used, it is customary not to hand it from one person to the other so as not to pass on suffering to another person. It should be placed on the ground or in the basin, and each person can pick it up for himself. Some also wash their face and say, "He will destroy death forever. May the Almighty God wipe away tears from every face" (Is. 25:8).
62. Some have the custom to pull up some dirt and grass and toss it behind them[280] and say, "He is mindful that we are dust"

---

272. *Gesher HaḤayim* 16:7, 4; he explains that it was not customary for women to accompany the deceased to the cemetery.
273. *BeMar'eh HaBazak*, vol. 5, 93.
274. *Gesher HaḤayim* 16:7, 2.
275. Rema, *Yoreh De'ah* 376:4.
276. *Yalkut Yosef* 10:26. Rabbi Nebenzahl: Rabbi Shlomo Zalman Auerbach taught that a person may dry his hands if he washed them a fourth time.
277. *Maavar Yabok, "Siftei Renanot"* 19.
278. Ibid. end of ch. 20; *Yalkut Yosef* ibid.
279. *Tzror HaḤayim* 58.
280. *Shulḥan Arukh, Yoreh De'ah* 376:4.

(Ps. 103:14); "Let men sprout up in towns like country grass" (Ps. 72:16). This is a demonstration of faith in the resurrection of the dead: Water represents the beginning of creation, dust represents death and the end of life, and grass represents the resurrection since grass is swallowed up into the ground and then sprouts and grows again. Like in the verse: "Let men sprout up in towns like country grass" (Ps. 72:16).[281] Naḥmanides[282] wrote that this is an allusion to the purification performed with water, ashes, and hyssop (referring to the ashes of the Red Heifer, which was combined with hyssop and mixed with spring water). And that therefore we wash our hands with water and throw dust and grass. Tossing the dust upward symbolizes sadness and mourning, as it says about Job's friends who, "Threw dust into the air onto their heads" (Job 2:12). Some have written that throwing it upwards expresses the idea that in the resurrection, the body will arise much purer that it is in its current physical state.[283] Another explanation for this custom is that is shows that the deceased has left behind the need for the physical sustenance that feeds the animal soul, symbolized by grass, and has been elevated to sanctified bread that feeds the soul.[284]

Returning from the funeral

63. Some have the custom to use a different route on the way back from the funeral than the one they used on the way there.[285] This was done to avoid meeting women who are escorting the deceased. (See Key Concepts, **Women – Attending a Funeral and Going to the Cemetery.**) If a person is returning from the cemetery when it is not the time of the funeral, he can use the same route.

281. *Maḥzor Vitri*, p. 247; *Tur, Yoreh De'ah* 376.
282. *Torat HaAdam*, p. 156.
283. *Maavar Yabok, "Siftei Renanot"* 20; *Menaḥem Aveilim – "Met."*
284. *Taamei HaMinhagim U'Mekorei HaDinim*, p. 440: 1029.
285. *Gesher HaḤayim* 14:1, 20; *Tzror HaḤayim* 57.

Burial for babies and miscarriages

Burying a baby is a traumatic experience for a family. All deaths are difficult, but losing a baby is especially so. It feels unnatural because of the baby's tender age, and the fact that parents must bury their child, which is the opposite of the natural order of things. It can also raise theological questions about the death of a person who has not committed any sin.

We cannot know God's calculations: "For My plans are not your plans, nor are My ways your ways – declares the Lord. But as the heavens are high above the earth, so are My ways high above your ways and My plans above your plans" (Is. 55:8–9). We believe in the Master of the Universe, that all His ways are true and just. Therefore, even the short life of a newborn baby has significance and meaning; every arrival of a soul in this world holds merit for the parents and for the deceased. There are hidden mysteries about souls and the transfiguration of souls that we are incapable of understanding. A soul may have come into the world to do a brief *tikkun*, a rectification, returning to its source when the task was completed.

Particularly because of the psychological difficulty involved in burying a baby, Jewish tradition emphasizes a return to normalcy. Halakha – as much as it stresses the importance of honoring the deceased and the family's pain and suffering – favors life over death. Situations of pathological over-attachment to the deceased can disrupt and damage the continuation of normative life. Therefore, when there is a deceased infant who must be buried, the goal is to ease the attachment of the parents and family members to the deceased. This is done to try and limit the painful memories and experiences and to facilitate, as much as possible, a return to a natural and normal life.

(For that reason, babies less than thirty-days old were traditionally buried by the *ḥevra kaddisha* without the parents and family present. However, the parents are permitted to attend if they wish. The burial is performed in a special plot, where the grave is unmarked. But the family is permitted to erect a marker, provided the cemetery does not object. It is not customary to visit the grave. This is to emphasize the need for life to go on.)

64. A baby more than thirty-days old receives a standard burial and the attendees form two lines and recite *Tziduk HaDin* and Kaddish, and *aveilut* is observed.

65. There is an obligation to bury an infant that died in the first thirty days of life, even though the customs of *aveilut* are not required to be observed.[286]
66. A miscarried fetus that had formed discrete limbs should be buried in the ground. This is because of the prohibition against deriving any benefit from the body; and out of a concern for ritual impurity for *kohanim*; and because the body is expected to arise during the resurrection. For this reason, the fetus is given a name before the burial.
67. Some have determined whether burial is necessary in terms of fetal development: Burial is performed for a fetus after five months, when the fetus is fully formed; for a miscarriage that occurred in the first three months of pregnancy, the fetus does not need to be buried.[287]
68. A male fetus or a male infant who died after birth but before being circumcised, is circumcised without a blessing. This is done in the purification room prior to the burial, in order to avoid the indignity of being buried with the foreskin.[288] The baby is given a name in order to be remembered and brought to life during the resurrection.[289] A female infant who died before being named is also given a name before the burial.[290]
69. It is not customary to bury the placenta.[291]

Burial of body parts and limbs

Four made oaths, three asked inappropriately and God answered them appropriately, and one asked inappropriately and God answered him inappropriately. And they were: Eliezer the servant of Abraham, Caleb, Saul, and Yiftaḥ… Yiftaḥ's limbs detached from him and were buried in many different places, as it says, "Then Yiftaḥ the Gileadite *died* and he was *buried* in

286. *Shulḥan Arukh, Yoreh De'ah* 353:4, 374:8.
287. *Nitei Gavriel*, vol. 1, 135:32–33.
288. *Prisha* on *Beit Yosef, Yoreh De'ah* 263:5.
289. *Shulḥan Arukh, Yoreh De'ah* 263:5, 353:6.
290. *Gesher HaḤayim* 16:3, 2.
291. Ibid. 3.

the towns of Gilead" (Judges 12:7). It does not say in the town of Gilad but in the towns of Gilad. This teaches us that a limb detached here and was buried in that spot, and another limb detached in another place and was buried there (Leviticus Rabba 37).

70. Human limbs should be buried. Here too, this is to avoid deriving benefit from the dead and out of the concern for ritual impurity. Furthermore, Judaism compares a person's body to a *sefer Torah*. The Torah scroll is a vessel with which to receive the divine message from God to the Jewish people, and therefore we honor the *sefer Torah* and treat it with sanctity. Likewise, the body is a vessel for the divine soul and should therefore be honored. The same way that each letter and parchment of the Torah has sanctity even though it is only one part of the scroll, each limb of the body has sanctity.[292]

    Thus, a limb that was amputated in an operation or severed in an accident should be buried. The custom is to wash and clean the limb, wrap it in linen cloth, and bury it. If the limb belonged to a person who is alive and who has a designated burial plot, the limb should be buried in that plot where the person will eventually be buried.[293]

    See more in the Key Concepts section – **Burial of Limbs.**

    When burying a limb or a fetus, the grave does not need to be very deep and the shape of the grave is less important.[294]

Today, some hospitals have a system for removing miscarried fetuses or limbs. If the hospital has a rabbi, one can check with him. If there is no hospital rabbi, one should speak with the *ḥevra kaddisha*, who have burial arrangements for these cases.

292. See *Maavar Yabok, "Siftei Renanot"* 25. And see *Yalkut Yosef* 45:9, where he writes that according to the letter of the law there is no obligation to bury a limb or a fetus but that it is correct to do so.
293. *Gesher HaḤayim* 16:2, 2.
294. Ibid. 5:3.

Flowers on the grave

71. The halakha does not favor placing flowers on the grave, but one who does should not be prevented from doing so.[295] Some halakhic authorities oppose this custom because of a concern that it imitates gentile practices.[296] However, it seems that, strictly speaking, it is permitted, because the prohibition against adopting gentile customs only applies to a practice that breaks the boundaries of modesty or is without reason;[297] Since placing flowers on the grave shows respect for the deceased, it is not forbidden.

    Another reason not to prohibit this custom is that there is an early tradition mentioned in the Talmud and the halakhic literature[298] in which people placed myrtle branches on the coffin. Hence, we should not stop someone who places flowers on a grave.[299]

Cremation

72. Cremating the dead is strictly prohibited; one who does so fails to fulfill the commandment to bury the dead. It causes significant problems and is a degradation of the deceased.[300] Failure to bury the dead is considered a curse in the Bible (e.g., Jer. 8:2; 14:16; 16:4, 6). Cremation is considered a sin: "For three transgressions of Moab, for four, I will not revoke it: Because he burned the bones of the king of Edom to lime" (Amos 2:1).
73. We do not comply with the request of someone who gave instructions to cremate his body. If the body was cremated, the ashes are

295. Rabbi Nebenzahl: The Ashkenazic custom is to be stringent not to place flowers on the grave.
296. E.g., *Tzror HaḤayim* 5; *Shulḥan Arukh HaMekutzar, Einei Yitzḥak, Yoreh De'ah* 194:6.
297. Rema, *Shulḥan Arukh, Yoreh De'ah* 178:1.
298. Nidda 37a, Rashi ad loc; *Shulḥan Arukh, Oraḥ Ḥayim* 526:7.
299. *Kol Bo al Aveilut*, p. 59; *Responsa Yabia Omer*, vol. 3, *Yoreh De'ah* 24; *Tzror HaḤayim* ibid.; *She'eilat Shlomo*, vol. 6, 101.
300. Cremation is more egregious than being buried among gentiles. Thus, in a place where they cremate the dead, it is preferable to be buried in a non-Jewish cemetery. This was taught to me by Rabbi Moredechai Eliyahu.

not buried in a Jewish cemetery. This is because a person who, during his lifetime, did not want the mitzva and virtue of burial and who rejected the concept of the resurrection, will not be atoned for by his burial when it comes time for the resurrection – God's image has left this person and the ashes have no sanctity.[301]

74. For someone who was burned in an accident, the ashes are buried in the ground, even though there is no mitzva to bury ashes and they do not cause impurity.[302]

    The reasons for burying these ashes are as follows:

    - So as not to derive benefit from the dead body
    - The ashes of those who were burned are likened to the ashes of the holy sacrifices, and must be buried as *geniza*.
    - The indestructible *luz* bone remains in these ashes. The *luz* bone contains the eternality from which a person will come back to life at the time of the resurrection.

75. The ashes may be buried in the ground in a receptacle, but it is better to bury them directly in the ground.
76. There is no obligation to escort the ashes or to perform a funeral, nor to erect a tombstone. The comforters do not stand in two lines, and the Mourner's blessing is not recited.
77. *Aveilut* begins from the time that the deceased was burned and not from when the ashes were buried.[303]

For further discussion, see Sec. 5, "Donating the Body to Science."

SECTION 8: TEARING OF GARMENTS (*KRIYA*)

And Jacob tore his clothing and girded himself with sackcloth and mourned his son for many days. (Gen. 37:34)

301. *Gesher HaḤayim* 16:9. But if the person was cremated due to a lack of knowledge because this was the custom where he lived, some rule leniently to permit his ashes to be buried; he is likened to a wayward children. (This answer was communicated to me orally by Rabbi Yaakov Ruza, in the name of Rabbi Mordekhai Eliahu.)

302. Mishna Ohalot 2:2.

303. *Gesher HaḤayim* 16:8.

Tearing a garment is a sign of pain and mourning, as we learn from Jacob, who tore his clothing when he thought that his son Joseph had did. Tearing one's clothing is also presented as a sign of mourning several times in the Tanakh – David for Saul and Jonathan, David for Avner, David upon hearing the news that Abshalom killed all his sons, Elisha upon Elijah's death, Job for his sons. There are many other examples of this practice as a symbol of sadness and upon receiving bad news – Joshua and Caleb during the episode of the spies, Yiftaḥ for his daughter.

The tearing symbolizes the mourners' pain and heartbreak. The prophet even had to rebuke the people, "Rend your hearts rather than your garments" (Joel 2:13). Tearing serves as a tangible expression of the mourners' strong emotions during the fraught time between the death and the burial. The *kriya* can bring up or increase painful feelings with overwhelming intensity. Therefore, even in the context of all the funeral rituals, doing *kriya* is considered an especially difficult moment. On the other hand, this act can also serve as an outlet, a way to vent emotions that should not be denied or held in. These two aspects are also expressed among commentators. Some wrote that tearing the clothing comes to awaken sorrow, while others wrote the opposite – that *kriya* serves to distract the mourner somewhat from the loss of his relative by having his thoughts turn to the loss of the garment.[304] We can integrate these two understandings and say that mourners have a need to express their sadness and to mourn through action; tearing the clothing is a tangible, symbolic expression. It both awakens sadness and allows mourners to release their painful emotions.

Kriya is derived from the commandment that Aaron and his sons were given on the day of the Tabernacle's dedication. On that occasion, Aaron's two sons Nadav and Avihu died. Aaron and his other sons received instructions not to act as mourners: "Do not rend your clothes" (Lev. 10:6). The sages deduced from this verse that, under normal circumstances, mourners are commanded to tear their clothing (Moed Katan 24a; Maimonides' *Mishneh Torah, Hilkhot Avel* 8:1; *Shulḥan Arukh, Yoreh De'ah* 340).

304. *Gesher HaḤayim* 4:1.

The sages are very strict about *kriya*, even though it is a rabbinic obligation (Naḥmanides, *Torat HaAdam* 63; *Beit Yosef*, 340).

Who does *kriya* and for whom?

1. Anyone who loses one of the seven types of close relatives – father, mother, spouse, brother, sister, son, or daughter – is obligated in *kriya*.
2. Both men and women have the obligation to do *kriya*.
3. A person must do *kriya* for his rabbi, i.e., the rabbi from whom he has learned the most.[305]
4. Despite our legitimate grief, *kriya* is not done for an infant who died within thirty days of birth, nor is the *Dayan HaEmet* blessing said, nor is shiva observed.[306] The reason for this is that an infant is only considered viable once thirty days have passed. Prior to this, the infant is not considered viable, and *kriya* and *aveilut* are not observed for an infant who was not viable.
5. Infants suffering from birth defects or placed in an incubator are discussed in Sec. 16, "Who Mourns and for Whom."
6. For a child whose relative has died, someone else performs *kriya* for the child. This is done out of a sense of grief, to intensify the expression of sorrow and mourning and not because of a halakhic obligation since children are not obligated in mourning. Children who have reached the age of maturity are discussed in Sec. 52, "One Who Did Not Observe Mourning."
7. A sick person whose relative dies is not informed and others do not do *kriya* for him, so that the person does not suffer distress.[307] See Sec. 4, "Guidance for Supporting the Bereaved: What should a sick person be told about his illness?"
8. If a sick person discovers that his relative has died: If the person is clear-headed but unable to perform *kriya* due to the illness, then he is exempt from performing *kriya* afterwards, unless he recovers

305. *Shulḥan Arukh, Yoreh De'ah* 340:7–8.
306. *Shulḥan Arukh, Yoreh De'ah* 374:8; *kriya* is only performed for those people for whom one is obligated to sit shiva, ibid. 340:1.
307. *Shulḥan Arukh, Yoreh De'ah* 337:1.

during the shiva. But if the sick person is not clear-headed, then when he recuperates, he is obligated to perform *kriya* within the *shloshim* because it is still a time of sorrow for him.[308] Some say that in any case the person is obligated to perform *kriya* when he gets better.[309]

9. A bride and groom do not perform *kriya* even though they recite the blessing, "*Dayan HaEmet*." This will be explained later in Sec. 51, "A Bride and Groom."
10. An adopted child can perform *kriya* for his adopted parents but is not obligated to do so. Some have written that the adopted child should not recite the blessing. But one can rely on the opinions that the blessing should be recited since the blessing is not on tearing the clothing but for the sad news.[310]
11. Some have written that a person is obligated to perform *kriya* for a stepfather who raised and supported him since he has been financially supported and educated by the stepfather.[311]

    Regarding performing *kriya* if one is present at the moment of death of someone who is not one's relative, see Sec. 5, "Caring for the Dying and the Deceased," halakha 26.

When and where is *kriya* performed?

12. According to the original practice, *kriya* was performed at the moment of death or when the person was informed of the death. However, it is generally customary to tear the garments at the beginning of the funeral. The Sephardic custom is to tear the

308. *Turei Zahav, Yoreh De'ah* 396:1.
309. *Siftei Cohen*, ad loc.
310. With regard to someone who is not a relative but who wants to do *kriya*, e.g., a son- or daughter-in-law, the halakhic problem is one of needlessly destroying the clothing; however, since the law is that one should perform *kriya* for a good, reliable person – if the deceased fits this category, then it is permissible to perform *kriya* for them (this was told to me by Rabbi Yaakov Ruza). Rabbi Yaakov Ariel wrote that it is not forbidden to perform *kriya* and that it is not considered to be needlessly destroying the garment because the person rends the garment out of true and deep sorrow (*Darka Shel HaYahadut BeMavet U'BeAveilut*, p. 360).
311. Rabbi Shlomo Min HaHar, brought in *Yesodei Halakha*, p. 187. According to this, an adopted child must perform *kriya* for the adoptive parents.

garments in the cemetery after the burial or in the mourner's home.[312] See below regarding Shabbat and Yom Tov.

13. The original law was that *kriya* was also performed in the following situations: upon hearing bad news, upon hearing blasphemy, for a *sefer Torah* that was burnt, and upon seeing the ruined cities of Judea, Jerusalem, and the destroyed Temple.[313]

How *kriya* is performed

14. One may change into simple clothing before the *kriya*.[314] One should take into consideration that this is usually the clothing that will be worn throughout the shiva.
15. *Kriya* should be performed while standing. This is derived from what King David did when he heard of the death of his sons: "At this, David stood and rent his garment" (II Sam. 13:31). In the Yerushalmi Talmud it is derived from Job, about whom it says, "And Job stood up and tore his cloak" (Job 1:20).
16. If one did *kriya* while sitting down, one should stand up and tear the garment again without reciting the blessing. A sick person or an invalid who cannot stand may lean on something[315] during the *kriya*; if this is not possible, the person may do *kriya* while sitting.

---

312. In *Gesher HaḤayim* 4:6, he presents several reasons why *kriya* is delayed: (1) Since not everyone is proficient in the laws of *kriya*, it is delayed until the members of the *ḥevra kaddisha* are present to guide the mourners. (2) Most often, someone else starts the tear on the garment and the mourner completes the tearing; therefore, it is delayed until people other than the relatives are present and can help them. (3) The beginning of the funeral is a time when the grief is intensified and when all of the mourners gather together, and it is therefore appropriate to do the *kriya* together before the funeral.
313. Moed Katan 26a; Maimonides, *Mishneh Torah, Hilkhot Avel* 9:2; *Shulḥan Arukh, Oraḥ Ḥayim* 561; *Yoreh De'ah* 340:36–38.
314. *Gesher HaḤayim* 4:1; *Gilyon Maharsha* on *Shulḥan Arukh, Yoreh De'ah* 340:9. In *Responsa Har Tzvi* 263, he writes that one should not change clothing before *kriya* for one's parents. But in *Ḥazon LaMoed* 6:8 he writes that one may change clothing before doing *kriya* even for one's parents. In *Tzror HaḤayim* 33, he writes that one should really do *kriya* on the clothing that one is wearing, but the custom is to be lenient and to change out of expensive clothing into less valuable ones.
315. *Yalkut Yosef* 9:4; *Tzror HaḤayim* 63; *Pnei Barukh* 1:8. See also *Shulḥan Arukh, Oraḥ Ḥayim* 94:6 and *Mishna Berura* 141:4.

17. *Kriya* is done on the front of the clothing, at the collar.[316]
18. The mourner recites the *Dayan HaEmet* blessing – "*Barukh ata Adonai, Eloheinu Melekh haolam, Dayan HaEmet*," "Blessed are You, King of the Universe, the True Judge" – and makes a tear that is eight to ten centimeters long, from the top of the garment downwards. The Yemenite custom is to tear across (and not down) the garment.[317] For an explanation of the blessing see Sec. 7, "Arrangements for the Funeral and Burial," after halakha 9, "Explanation of the '*Dayan HaEmet*' blessing."
19. The custom is that another person begins the tear by making a small cut in the mourner's garment with a knife or scissors.[318] There is greater anguish if someone else tears the clothing while the mourner remains silent; this is also a sign of accepting God's judgment, a type of *Tziduk HaDin*.[319] The Yemenite custom is that no one else should perform *kriya* for the mourner or begin the tear; the mourner does it alone.[320]
20. For help with the tearing, a man should tear for a man and a woman for a woman.
21. A woman who performs *kriya* should do so in a dignified way and should immediately close up the tear with a safety pin. If it will not be possible to close the tear, the *kriya* should be delayed until later.[321]
22. One who performed *kriya* on a borrowed garment has not fulfilled the obligation.[322]

A description of the various types of garments that are torn is brought in the following section.

---

316. *Shulḥan Arukh, Yoreh De'ah* 340:2. The reason is based on the Kabbala, as quoted in *Maavar Yabok, "Siftei Renanot,"* 9.
317. *Shulḥan Arukh HaMekutzar, Einei Yitzḥak, Yoreh De'ah* 177:2; *Be'er LeḤai Roi* 26, in the name of *Nefesh Kol Ḥai* and the Rabbis of Yemen.
318. In most books, it says to use a knife, but Rabbi Mordekhai Eliahu told me that there is no difference between a knife and scissors; this is also written in *Shulḥan Arukh HaMekutzar, Einei Yitzḥak, Yoreh De'ah* 177:6.
319. *Ḥidushim U'Biurim Yad Ephrayim, Hilkhot Kriya*, 2.
320. *Be'er LeḤai Roi* 16.
321. *Tzror HaḤayim* 61.
322. *Ḥazon LaMoed* 6:7, from *Siftei Cohen, Yoreh De'ah* 340:50.

Kriya for a parent, as opposed to other relatives

23. For most relatives, a person does *kriya* on the right-hand side, but for one's parents, it is done on the left-hand side, by the heart. If the wrong side was torn by mistake, the person has still fulfilled the obligation.[323]
24. For most relatives, one performs *kriya* privately, but for parents, one performs *kriya* in front of others.[324] A woman always does *kriya* in private. The Yemenite custom is to perform *kriya* at the moment of the death or upon hearing of the death, even if no one else is present.[325]
25. For most relatives, one may perform *kriya* by hand or with a knife; for parents, *kriya* is done only by hand. However, the tear in the collar can be started with a knife and then completed by hand.
26. For most relatives, just one garment is torn; for one's parents, one rips the layers of clothing until the heart is uncovered. One should not tear tzitzit or an undershirt,[326] nor pajamas or a robe.[327] Coats and sweaters are not torn.[328] There are different customs with regard to a suit jacket: The Sephardic custom is not to tear a suit jacket.[329] There are different opinions about the Ashkenazic custom, and for that reason some have written that one should not wear a suit jacket at the time of *kriya*.[330] The principle is that one must tear a garment that is usually worn[331] and not an outer garment worn to protect one from the rain or cold, or something worn for special occasions. And so, it also depends on what each person typically wears. Someone who generally wears a suit jacket or outer garment should tear it; this is the Ashkenazic custom.

---

323. *Ḥokhmat Adam* 152:6; *Pnei Barukh* 1:12.
324. *Shulḥan Arukh, Yoreh De'ah* 340:13.
325. *Be'er LeḤai Roi* 25.
326. Maimonides, *Mishneh Torah, Hilkhot Avel* 8:3. But in *Tzror HaḤayim* 64, he writes that one should tear one's undershirt.
327. *Yalkut Yosef* 9:19; *Moed LeKol Ḥai* 11:16 in the name of Rabbi Shlomo Fisher.
328. *Yalkut Yosef* 9:16.
329. *Shulḥan Arukh, Yoreh De'ah* 340:10.
330. *Gesher HaḤayim* 4:14.
331. *Turei Zahav, Yoreh De'ah* 340:5.

Kriya for several relatives

27. Someone who lost two relatives at once or who heard of their passing at the same time, performs *kriya* once for both of them.
28. If one did *kriya* for one relative and during the shiva found out about another relative's passing, one makes a new tear for the second relative. If the person only found out about the second relative after the end of shiva for the first relative, he can rip the original tear a bit further.
29. For a parent, one always tears until the heart is uncovered; it is not enough to add to an existing tear.[332]

A mistaken *kriya*

30. If a person was mistakenly informed that his parent died and performed *kriya*, but it was actually his child who died, or if his parent had actually been alive at the time of *kriya* and only died later, *kriya* must be done again.[333]

Changing out of the torn garment

31. For most relatives, one can change one's garment during the shiva if necessary; *kriya* does not need to be done again. For a parent, however, if someone changed his clothes during shiva, he must tear the garment that he put on.[334]

Shabbat and holidays

32. *Kriya* is not performed on Shabbat or holidays. If one mistakenly did *kriya* on Shabbat, even though it was a violation of Shabbat, he has fulfilled the obligation of *kriya*.[335]
33. There are different customs regarding Ḥol HaMoed. In a place where there is no clear custom, one should do *kriya* for all relatives during Ḥol HaMoed.[336] The custom in Jerusalem is to do

---

332. *Shulḥan Arukh, Yoreh De'ah* 340:21–22.
333. Ibid. 24–25 and if one heard the correct information right away, *kriya* does not need to be done again.
334. Ibid. 14.
335. Ibid. 28, 31.
336. Rema, *Oraḥ Ḥayim* 547:6, *Yoreh De'ah* 340:31.

kriya on Ḥol HaMoed for one's parents, but to delay *kriya* for other relatives and do it after the holiday, when *aveilut* begins.[337]

34. When *kriya* is delayed until after the holiday, the *Dayan HaEmet* blessing is recited immediately, even on Shabbat or a holiday. One should not wait until mourning begins to say the blessing since the blessing is said not for the mourning, but upon hearing the bad news.[338]
35. After performing *kriya* on Ḥol HaMoed, the torn clothing should be removed since public mourning is not allowed on holidays. After the holiday, one puts on the torn clothing again to avoid needing to tear another garment.
36. Residents of Israel who travelled abroad, even if they intend to return to Israel, follow the Diaspora custom regarding Yom Tov since *kriya* is a public act. Jews from the Diaspora who came to Israel and intend to return to the Diaspora, follow the Diaspora custom about the second day of the holiday for *kriya* and mourning.[339]

One who did not perform *kriya* or recite the *Dayan HaEmet* blessing

37. If a mourner did not perform *kriya* at the correct time, he can do so at any point during the shiva; after the shiva, it should not be done.[340] If the person was ill or incapable of performing *kriya,* he should do it after the shiva.[341] For the case of a person who only heard of a relative's death after the shiva, see Sec. 49, "Receiving Notice of a Death."
38. A person may perform *kriya* for one's parents at any time.[342]

---

337. *Yalkut Yosef* 9:25. And if they were buried on the holiday by gentiles, the *kriya* is delayed – since one does not tear on a holiday – until after the holiday. *Mishna Berura* 547:11; *Gesher HaḤayim* 4:23, note 5.
338. *Gesher HaḤayim* 4:26.
339. *Nitei Gavriel,* vol. 1, 61:11.
340. *Shulḥan Arukh, Yoreh De'ah* 396:1.
341. *Siftei Cohen* ad loc. 1, and see above in this section, halakha 8.
342. *Shulḥan Arukh, Yoreh De'ah* 340:18, 396:1.

39. The Ashkenazic custom is to recite the *Dayan HaEmet* blessing only within the first three days of the shiva.[343] The Sephardic custom is to make the blessing only on the first day of the shiva.
40. Even someone who refuses to perform *kriya* may make the blessing *Dayan HaEmet*.[344]

Mending the tear

A time for ripping and a time for sewing. (Eccl. 3:7)

41. When mourning a relative other than a parent, it is permissible to mend the tear after the shiva using a pin or by sewing the tear unevenly; after the *shloshim* it may be sewn up properly. For one's parents, the garment can be pinned together or sewn unevenly only after the *shloshim*, but it may never be sewn up properly.[345]
42. Nowadays, it is not common to mend the garments. People generally discard the clothing after the shiva.

In the House of Mourning

It is better to go to a house of mourning than to a house of feasting; for that is the end of every man, and the living should take it to heart. (Eccl. 7:2)

SECTION 9: MEAL OF CONDOLENCE (*SEUDAT HAVRAAH*)

The meal of condolence is the first meal that mourners are served when they return from the funeral. The Tanakh mentions that the people brought a meal to King David after Avner ben Ner was killed (II Sam. 3:35). From the case of the prophet Ezekiel, who was told not to mourn when his wife died, the sages derived that it is forbidden for mourners to eat their own food on the first day. Ezekiel was told, "Do not eat the bread of comforters" (Ezek. 24:17), i.e., that he should not eat the comforting meal. Ezekiel was an exception to the rule, and thus it teaches that a mourner usually eats a meal brought by other people (Moed Katan

343. *Gesher HaḤayim* 4:26 based on the *Ḥida*.
344. *Yalkut Yosef* 9:11.
345. *Shulḥan Arukh, Yoreh De'ah* 340:15.

27b). In the Book of Hosea (9:4), "bread of *onim*" is mentioned, which according to some interpretations refers to mourners' bread, eaten in grief and sorrow.

This is a time when the mourners are too upset to eat, distraught over the relative's death. We therefore emphasize their most basic need – eating – at the beginning of the mourning. Another aspect of the meal of condolence is that the mourners' community participates in preparing it. The meal is an opportunity for community members to offer a type of condolence. Some have given another reason for this meal, one that implies the opposite: Our sages said that whoever eats from the table of others', his world is darkened; this is the situation of the mourner.

When is this meal eaten?

1. When the mourners return from the cemetery, neighbors or relatives who are not mourning are obligated to feed the mourners. This meal is called "*Seudat Havraah*," the meal of condolence.[346]
2. If the neighbors did not bring food for a meal, the mourners may eat their own food. In general, the meal of condolence is not a true obligation. But the first meal on the day of the burial should be of food brought by others. The mourner may refrain from eating on the first day until the evening and then eat his own food.[347]

---

346. *Shulḥan Arukh, Yoreh De'ah* 378. The Yemenite custom is that mourners hold a large meal on the last day of the shiva and invite all those who came throughout the shiva. They call this meal "*seudat havraah*." It is also their custom that guests bring food and drink throughout the shiva and eat together with the mourners (*Shulḥan Arukh HaMekutzar, Einei Yitzḥak, Yoreh De'ah* 194:3, 187:11; *Halikhot Teiman, Minhagei Kevura VeAveilut*, p. 332. Rabbi Kapaḥ writes there that due to high costs and people's limited resources, visitors stopped coming to comfort the mourners because they could not afford to bring food. The rabbis therefore instructed that the amount of food brought to mourners should be reduced, but this regulation had only limited success; and nowadays costs have become high again.)
347. *Shulḥan Arukh, Yoreh De'ah* 378:3.

3. If the burial was at night, the mourners are fed that night. If no meal was brought that night, one may be brought the following day.[348]
4. If the burial was at twilight (*bein hashemashot*), the night is considered the second day of the shiva and there is no meal of condolence. See Sec. 7, "Arrangements for the Funeral and Burial," halakha 51, for a definition of twilight.
5. On Erev Shabbat or Yom Tov, about two and a half hours before candle lighting, no meal of condolence is served out of deference to Shabbat. The mourners wait until the evening meal.[349]
6. If the meal is delayed, mourners may drink their own coffee or tea in the meantime.

What is eaten?

> "Once when Jacob was cooking a stew, Esau came in from the open field, famished" (Gen. 25:29). It has been taught that that was the day on which Abraham our father died, and Jacob our father made a broth of lentils to comfort his father Isaac. Why was it of lentils? – In the West [in Israel, which is West of Babylon] they say in the name of Rabba b. Mari: Just as the lentil has no mouth, so the mourner has no mouth [for speech]. Others say: Just as the lentil is round, so mourning comes around to all the denizens of this world. (Bava Batra 16b)

7. The meal of condolence must include bread.[350] The custom is to eat bread or crackers with hard-boiled eggs or lentils, which are

348. *Pitḥei Teshuva, Yoreh De'ah* 378:2, in the name of the *Noda BeYehuda*.
349. *Shulḥan Arukh, Yoreh De'ah* 378:5; *Gesher HaḤayim* 20:2, 11. However in *Tzror HaḤayim* 71–72 he writes that nowadays, one may eat a meal of coffee and cake without bread. If the mourners did not manage to eat before Shabbat, they can eat the meal of condolence after Shabbat. In *Yalkut Yosef* 13:9 he writes that if they did not eat before Shabbat, there is no need to eat the meal after Shabbat; this is also the opinion of the *Shemirat Shabbat KeHilkhata* (vol. 2 68:1), following the Rema, *Yoreh De'ah* 378:11. In *Yalkut Yosef* he adds that if the burial was on Erev Yom Tov, the meal of condolence is served after Yom Tov since that is when the shiva and mourning commence.
350. Bread or cake – *Gesher HaḤayim* 20:2, 4. And in *Yalkut Yosef* 13:4 he writes that they should wash their hands and eat bread.

considered mourners' food.[351] Round foods symbolize the circle of life and mourning. Round foods also have no "mouth," like the mourner has no "mouth," sitting silently in his sadness and grief. The eggs should be peeled in advance so that the mourner does not appear ravenous. Some have the custom to drink wine at the meal of condolence, as it says in the verse, "Give strong drink to the hapless and wine to the embittered" (Prov. 31:6).[352]

How is the meal served?

> Formerly, they were wont to bring [provisions] to the house of mourning, the rich in silver and gold baskets and the poor in baskets of peeled willow twigs, and the poor felt shamed. They therefore instituted that all should bring [provisions] in baskets of peeled willow twigs out of deference to the poor. Our rabbis taught: Formerly, they were wont to serve drinks in a house of mourning, the rich in white glass vessels and the poor in colored glass, and the poor felt shamed: they instituted therefore that all should serve drinks in colored glass, out of deference to the poor. (Moed Katan 27b)

8. Someone other than the mourner should cut the bread and place a slice of bread in the mourner's hand. This is derived from the verse in Lamentations (1:17), "Zion spread her hands," which is understood to be an allusion to the slice of bread given into the mourner's hand. (For non-mourners, one places the bread in front of them, not into their hand.)
9. Men serve the male mourners and women serve the female mourners. When there are men and women who are mourning in the same room, one need not be stringent about this.[353]

---

351. *Shulḥan Arukh, Yoreh De'ah* 378:9.
352. "Rabbi Ḥanan said: Wine was created to comfort the mourners, as it says, "Give strong drink to the hapless and wine to the embittered'" (Sanhedrin 70a). *Yalkut HaḤayim VeHaShalom*, p. 37 and 53.
353. *Arukh HaShulḥan, Yoreh De'ah* 378:3; *Gesher HaḤayim* 20:2, 7; *Yalkut Yosef* 12:2.

10. A husband should not feed his wife food that belongs to him. Since a husband is obligated to provide his wife with sustenance, his food is considered to belonging to her, as well.

Grace after Meals

11. At the meal of condolence, the mourner does not join the quorum of ten men to recite Grace after Meals. It is preferable that there not be three sitting together, to avoid being obligated to say a *zimmun* before Grace after Meals.[354] At all other meals eaten during the shiva, the mourner does participate in the *zimmun*.
12. There is a special version of Grace after Meals for the house of mourning. See Sec. 10, "Customs in the House of Mourning: Grace after Meals."

On Ḥol HaMoed and Purim

13. On Ḥol HaMoed and Purim, the meal of condolence is eaten while sitting on regular chairs. Coffee and cake, etc., are eaten instead of eggs and lentils.
14. Some write that the custom in Jerusalem is that, during Ḥol HaMoed, the meal of condolence is only served to those mourning a parent. Some write that this is the custom on Purim, as well.[355]
15. If someone's relative died before a festival, and he did not mourn for them before the festival began: According to the Sephardic custom, the meal of condolence is served when the person starts sitting shiva, after the festival. According to the Ashkenazic custom, the meal of condolence is not served at all in such a case.[356]

---

354. *Siftei Cohen, Yoreh De'ah* 379:6; *Gesher HaḤayim*, vol. 2, 18:1. However, in *Yalkut Yosef* (13:15) he writes that the mourners join to make a *zimmun*, according to a straightforward understanding of the *Shulḥan Arukh*, ibid.

355. *Yalkut Yosef* 13:10. And in *Pnei Barukh* 28:11 and *Shemirat Shabbat KeHilkhata* (vol. 2, 65:4) they mention this custom in relation to Ḥol HaMoed. However, according to *Gesher HaḤayim* (20:2, 10), a meal should be served on Ḥol HaMoed to someone mourning any relative, with coffee and cake and not eggs and lentils. In *Gesher HaḤayim* he mentions this custom in the name of *Sefer Mizbeaḥ Adama*, but he writes that the custom is not clear and that we have no source for it.

356. *Tzror HaḤayim* 73.

SECTION 10: CUSTOMS IN THE HOUSE OF MOURNING

Where should shiva take place?

1. Mourners usually sit shiva in the deceased's home. It is a mitzva to hold prayer services with a *minyan* in the house. See Sec. 12, "Prayers in the House of Mourning."
2. Sometimes, if many people will be coming to comfort the mourners, too many for the house to accommodate, some people have the custom to sit shiva in the synagogue. This custom, however, seems to be improper since one generally should not enter a synagogue for one's own comfort (e.g., to escape the heat or rain outside); eulogies should also not to be said in a synagogue, nor should one should not eat or drink there. Still, if someone has this custom, others should not protest or argue with them. It is preferable to conduct oneself pleasantly and peacefully.[357] If the mourners sit in a classroom or hallway in the synagogue, this appears to be permitted.

Memorial candle

3. It is customary to have a memorial candle lit in the house of mourning from the time of the death through the end of the shiva, according to the verse, "The life-breath of man is the lamp of the Lord" (Prov. 20:27). Some insist on lighting with olive oil. Otherwise, a wax candle may be used. In the synagogue, an electric *ner neshama* is sufficient, to avoid making a mess. The connection between the candle and the deceased is explained in Key Concepts, **Memorial (or Yahrzeit) Candle (*Ner Neshama*)**.

Chairs, mirrors, and pictures

4. It is customary to cover mirrors in the house of mourning, especially if prayer services are held there. There is no need to cover pictures, except if the people praying in the house are facing them, in which case the pictures should be covered up. The basic

---

357. *Yalkut Yosef* 29:2.

reason for this practice is that prayer services are usually held in a shiva house, and one may not pray in front of a mirror, lest it appear that one is bowing to one's own reflection.[358] Another reason for covering the mirrors is that mirrors are generally used to help people beautify themselves and their body; in the house of mourning, they are mourning for the deceased's body that will decay and decompose. The two notions are at odds with one another.[359]

Blessings to bring merit to the soul

5. The Sephardic custom is to serve food and drink to the comforters, so they can recite blessings over the food and bring merit to the deceased's soul.[360] This is not an obligation. The food should be kept to a minimum, so as not to be a burden to the mourners and since the main purpose is to make the blessing and not the eating itself.

An explanation of the concept **Elevating the Soul** is brought in the Key Concepts section.

Grace after meals

6. There is a special version of Grace after Meals that is said in the house of mourning. During the *zimmun*, the version is as follows: "*Nevarekh Menaḥem aveilim she'akhalnu mishelo,*" "We will bless the Comforter of mourners from whom we have eaten." The reply is: "*Barukh Menaḥem aveilim she'akhalnu mishelo ubetuvo ḥayinu,*" "Blessed is the Comforter of mourners from whom we have eaten and from whose goodness we have eaten."
7. In the third blessing, the following is added:

---

358. Ibid. 28:6; and he adds in the footnote another reason based on the Kabbala.
359. Similar to Rabbi Elazar's statement about Rabbi Yoḥanan's beauty: "This beauty that is going to rot in the earth" (Berakhot 5b). "The mirror is made for beauty, and lest the mourner forget and adorn himself in the mirror. Or lest the mourner see his face and be shocked at how dreadful he looks" (*Or LaAvel*, p. 126, from *Minhagei Eretz Yisrael*).
360. Rabbi Nebenzahl: The Ashkenazic custom is not to eat in the house of mourning.

God, comfort those who mourn for Jerusalem and the mourners who are now mourning here. Comfort them from their mourning and gladden them from their sorrow, as it says: "As a mother comforts her son, so I will comfort you. You shall find comfort in Jerusalem." Blessed are You, God, who comforts Zion by building Jerusalem.[361]

The connection between people's individual mourning and the national mourning over the destruction of the Temple and Jerusalem appears in a number of places. This is evoked in the words we say to the mourners: "May God comfort you among the other mourners of Zion and Jerusalem." An explanation of this appears below, in Sec. 11, "Comforting the Mourners."

8. The Sephardic and Yemenite tradition is to add the following in the fourth blessing:

   The King who is alive is good and does good, the true God, the true Judge, who judges justly and takes souls in justice, controls His world to do His will, for all His ways are just and we are His people and His servants, and we must praise and bless Him for all, may He who repairs breaches repair this breach for us and for this mourner, for life and for peace.[362]

   They then continue, "*Hu gamleinu*," etc. The contemporary Ashkenazic custom is not to recite this addition.[363]

9. Other people that are eating with the mourners should also recite this version of Grace after Meals.[364]

---

361. If someone concludes the blessing with, "*Menaḥem aveilim beBoneh Yerushalayim*," others should not protest, *Yalkut Yosef* 13:17.
362. *Tur Shulḥan Arukh, Yoreh De'ah* 379, based on Berakhot 46b.
363. *Gesher HaḤayim* 20:2, 13; *Tzror HaḤayim*, p. 69.
364. *Tzror HaḤayim* 129.

10. These additions should not be said on Shabbat if there are other people in the house because public mourning is prohibited on Shabbat.
11. The mourner may lead the Grace after Meals and may say the *zimmun* over a glass of wine and drink from it, but he should not drink a large amount of wine.[365]
12. The custom in some places is that the mourner leads the *zimmun* for a full twelve months following the death, as a merit for the deceased. The basic explanation for this parallels that of Kaddish: In Kaddish, the mourner calls to others to bless and praise God. In the *zimmun*, as well, the summoner calls to the people around him to bless God. When a mourner is able to overcome his pain and praise the Creator, this increases merit for the deceased.[366]

The mourners' conduct

13. Mourners do not need to stand up for others, even for an important person.[367] But mourners should stand in the presence of a *sefer Torah*.
14. If the mourner stands up, he should not be told to sit down since this sounds as though he is being told to sit and wallow in his grief.[368]
15. It is forbidden to harm oneself, or to cut one's skin or pull out one's hair, out of grief over the deceased. The source for this prohibition is the Torah's commandment, "You shall not gash yourselves or shave the front of your heads because of the deceased" (Deut. 14:1); "Gashing" refers to cutting the skin out of sorrow over the death, which is a gentile practice. Part

365. *Shulḥan Arukh, Yoreh De'ah* 378:8.

366. *Mishna Berura* 210:1; *Pitḥei Teshuva* 375:3; *Kol Bo al Aveilut*, p. 378. I heard the reason from Rabbi Yaakov Ruza.

367. Rema, *Yoreh De'ah* 376:1. In *Yalkut Yosef* 21:6, he brings four reasons for this exemption: because the mourners are involved in their own sadness; because this is not an exaltation since the mourner is wallowing in the dust; since the mourner is compared to a king who sits at the head of the table (Ketubot 69b); and to prevent a situation where someone might say to the mourner, "Sit down." This is to be avoided, as explained in the next law. But according to his conclusion, the mourner is permitted to stand before a Torah scholar or the elderly.

368. Rema, *Yoreh De'ah* 376:2

of accepting God's divine plan is expressing sadness within the accepted framework and avoiding excessive behavior that could cause harm. (See Key Concepts, **You Shall Not Gash**.)

Those who are occupied with the funeral speeches ... they stand up and say the tefilla and the mourner stands up and accepts God's judgment and says: Sovereign of the universe, I have sinned much before Thee and Thou didst not punish me one thousandth part. May it be Thy will, O Lord our God, to close up our breaches and the breaches of all Thy people the house of Israel in mercy! Abaye said: A man should not speak thus, since R. Shimon b. Lakish said, and so it was taught in the name of R. Jose: A man should never speak in such a way as to give an opening to Satan. (Berakhot 19a)

When R. Samuel b. Judah lost a daughter, the Rabbis said to Ulla: Let us go in and console him. But he answered them: What have I to do with the consolation of the Babylonians, which is [almost tantamount to] blasphemy? For they say, "What could have been done," which implies that, were it possible to do anything, they would have done it. (Bava Kamma 38a)

16. A person should not say, "I have not been punished enough" (i.e., I deserve more severe punishment because of my bad deeds) or the like, so as not to invite more misfortune. One should also not say "What could have been done?" because it sounds like heresy.[369] The Jewish faith instructs us to accept God's judgment, that all of His judgments are just and correct even when we cannot understand them.

Taking items from the house of mourning

17. Some have the custom not to take anything from the house of mourning throughout the week of shiva since the evil spirit resides there. Others do not follow this since there is no source for the custom.[370]

---

369. Rema ibid.
370. *Kol Bo al Aveilut*, p. 262; *Yalkut Yosef* 28:8; *Pnei Barukh* 10:6.

SECTION 11: COMFORTING THE MOURNERS

I decided their course and presided over them. I lived like a king among his troops, like one who consoles mourners. (Job 29:25)

R. Hama son of R. Hanina further said: What means the text: "Ye shall walk after the Lord your God"? Is it, then, possible for a human being to walk after the *Shekhina*; for has it not been said: "For the Lord thy God is a devouring fire"?! But [the meaning is] to walk after the attributes of the Holy One, blessed be He… The Holy One, blessed be He, comforted mourners, for it is written: "And it came to pass after the death of Abraham, that God blessed Isaac his son," so do thou also comfort mourners. (Sota 14a)

When Rabbi Yohanan b. Zakkai's son died, his students came to comfort him. Rabbi Eliezer came in and sat before him and said to him: Rabbi, would you like me to say something? He replied: Say. He said to him: Adam had a son who died and he was comforted. How do we know that he was comforted? As it is written, "Adam knew his wife again" (Gen. 4:25), so you should also be comforted. He said: It is not only that I am upset myself, but you had to remind me of Adam's sorrow?!

Rabbi Joshua came in and said: Rabbi, do you want me to say something? He replied: Say. He said: Job had sons and daughters and they all died and he was comforted, so you should also be comforted. How do we know that Job was comforted? As it says, "The Lord has given and the Lord has taken; may the name of the Lord be blessed" (Job 1:21). He said: It is not enough that I am sad for myself and you had to remind me of Job's sorrow?!

Rabbi Yossi came in and sat before him, he said: Rabbi, would you like me to say something? He replied: Say. He said: King David had a son who died and he was comforted, so you should also be comforted. How do we know that he was comforted? As it says, "David consoled his wife Bathsheba; he went to her and lay with her. She bore a son and called him Solomon. The Lord favored him" (II Sam. 12:24). So you should also be comforted. He said: It is not enough that I am sad for myself but you remind me of King David's sorrow?!

> Rabbi Elazar ben Arakh went in. When Rabbi Yohanan b. Zakkai saw him, he said to his servant, take the vessel and go after me to the bathhouse since he is a great person and I cannot stand before him. He came and sat before him and said: I will give you a parable – it is similar to a person to whom the king gave a deposit. Each day he cried and said, Woe to me when will I be able to get out of this deposit in peace. You too, Rabbi, you had a son who studied Torah, Prophets, Writings, Mishna, halakhot and aggadot, and died without sin, you should be comforted that you have returned the deposit complete. He said: Rabbi Elazar, my son, you have comforted me in the way that people comfort. (*Avot DeRabbi Natan* 14)

The mitzva of comforting mourners begins in the cemetery after the grave has been closed. The comforters stand in two rows and say the words of condolence as the mourners pass between them. This mitzva continues when the comforters pay a visit at the shiva house.

This is a social mitzva that involves sharing in the mourners' grief. The mourners' suffering can be alleviated both by the fact that the visitors show up, demonstrating their care and empathy for the mourners, and by the respectful reflection and discussion about the deceased.

The communal and social participation that revolves around the house of mourning provides a support system for mourners. It can be of great help in getting through the mourning period. Through the demonstrations of support, mourners understand that they have not been neglected and do not need to face their sorrow alone. This is crucial, particularly in times of tragedy. When people come to comfort the mourners, the social status barriers are removed; prominent individuals comfort ordinary ones and vice versa. Often, even mourners who find the condolence calls burdensome at the time, later discover that the memory of these visits gives them a sense of satisfaction and respect.

The social support also addresses practical needs. In some communities, those offering condolences also bring food and help with the housework or shopping, especially if the house is full of visitors; they may help care for children, do errands, and make other necessary arrangements that the mourners are not able to take care of themselves.

The community also benefits from helping mourners, fostering a sense of fulfillment and unity.[371]

A further discussion of comforting the mourners is brought in Sec. 66, "The Forgotten Wisdom of Consolation."

How does one offer condolences?

> I note how they fare and will heal them. I will guide them and mete out solace to them, and to the mourners among them. (Is. 57:18)

> The important part of consolation is that the living should take heart, that this deceased person merited the good set aside for the righteous and has been taken from the dark world to the eternal light. (*Kli Yakar* on Gen. 37:35)

Mourners are not always emotionally available for friendly conversation. Often, the heaviness of their emotions makes them feel that spontaneous conversation is not possible. For this reason, visitors should wait for the mourner to open the conversation first. This shows the mourner's desire to connect in conversation with the comforter. Even a sigh or other indication from the mourner can be a sufficient opening for the comforter to begin speaking.

1. Comforting mourners is a great mitzva and is considered an act of loving-kindness to both the living and the deceased.[372]
2. The comforters are not permitted to initiate conversation until the mourner opens the conversation first.[373] This is derived from Job's friends who came to comfort him: "They sat with him on the ground seven days and seven nights. None spoke a word to him for they saw how very great was his suffering.

371. Based on *Sefer Ketz HaḤayim*, p. 213.
372. Therefore, comforting mourners takes precedence over visiting the sick in a case when one cannot do both. But if one can do both, then visiting the sick comes first since, through it, one revives the sick (Rema, *Yoreh De'ah* 335, and *Siftei Cohen* ad loc.).
373. *Shulḥan Arukh, Yoreh De'ah* 376:1.

Afterward, Job began to speak." (Job 2:13–3:1).[374] Silence can be a very meaningful expression of empathy, where words cannot adequately express the deep emotions that people are feeling. If the comforters see that the mourner is unable to speak, they should speak first, with positive statements about the deceased.[375]

3. Comforters do not greet the mourner by saying, "Hello," nor should they say, "Goodbye." The traditional Hebrew greeting "Shalom" comes from the word "*shleimut*," which means wholeness. One cannot say "Shalom" to the mourner since this person is experiencing grief, not peace or wholeness. See Sec. 24, "Greeting People."
4. Mourner sit on low chairs or stools, not regular chairs. The comforters sit on regular chairs. This expression of sadness also appears in the above verse about Job and his companions: "They sat with him on the ground." Indeed, the original practice was that the comforters would also sit on the ground, as described in the verse. However, if the mourner prefers, the comforters can sit on regular chairs. The contemporary custom is for the comforters not to sit on the ground since we assume that the mourner prefers this.[376] A further explanation is presented in Sec. 28, "Sitting on a Chair."
5. Comforters should be careful not to burden the mourners, especially if there is a large number of people coming to comfort them from morning until night. One should be sensitive about when to come and how long to stay. If the visitors are burdensome to the mourner, they should not stay.[377] Condolence calls provide support and encouragement but can be tiring, especially if there are many visitors, coming all day long and into the evening. Mourners are permitted to go rest occasionally and take turns receiving the

---

374. Moed Katan 25b.

375. *Yalkut Yosef* 26:6. A responsum of Rabbi Waldenberg, who relates that the *Ḥazon Ish* would begin to speak when he saw that the mourner found it difficult to speak, whether out of distress or out of awe and respect (*Kuntras Ohel Ḥana* at the end of *Pnei Barukh*, p. 472).

376. *Drisha* on the *Tur, Yoreh De'ah* 387, brought in *Siftei Cohen* ad loc.

377. *Shulḥan Arukh, Yoreh De'ah* 376:1.

comforters. There is a delicate balance between honoring those who have made the effort to come and allowing mourners to take breaks, which is necessary for their physical and mental well-being.

6. When the comforters depart from the mourners, they recite a special formula. The Sephardic custom is to say, "*Min haShamayim tenuḥamu*," "From heaven may you be comforted." The Yemenite custom is to say, "*Tenuḥamu min hashamayim*," "May you be comforted from heaven," when entering and leaving the house. The Ashkenazic custom is to say these words upon leaving the mourners: "*HaMakom*[378] *yenaḥem etḥem betokh shaar avlei Zion veYerushalayim* (*velo tosifu ledaava od*)," "May God comfort you among the other mourners of Zion and Jerusalem (and may you have no more sorrow[379]).[380] And the mourners can reply, "Amen."

   There is an enduring connection between the individual Jewish person and the collective. At the height of a bride and groom's personal joy, we declare, "If I forget you, O Jerusalem, let my right hand wither" (Ps. 137:5) and break a glass to remember the destruction of the Temple. In this way, we weave our personal journey into the larger, national narrative. During the individual's mourning, we remember Jerusalem as well.

   A deep symbolic principle is expressed in this connection between the individual dimension and the national one. Every personal building block, such as the *ḥuppa* and *kiddushin* at a wedding, is seen as a building block in the realization of the national home – the redemption and ingathering of the exiles. This is why the sages said that anyone who causes the bride and groom to

---

378. "*HaMakom*," literally "The Place," is a name for God; but "The Place" could also be explained as the spiritual place where the deceased is now, in the higher world, the spiritual level that the deceased has been able to reach through his good deeds and acts. This place is a source of comfort for mourners (based on *Yalkut Yosef* 26, note 3).
379. This phrase appears in parentheses because Rabbi Nebenzahl has commented that there is no source for it.
380. It is good to say the traditional Jewish words of comfort that include the mention of God. Since some comforters do not know the exact words of the formula, some have the words written out in the shiva house so that the comforters can read it.

rejoice, it is as though he has restored one of the ruins of Jerusalem. The Talmud[381] based this idea on the verses in Jeremiah:[382]

> Thus said the Lord: Again there shall be heard in this place, which you say is ruined, without man or beast – in the towns of Judah and the streets of Jerusalem that are desolate, without man, without inhabitants, without beast – the sound of mirth and gladness, the voice of bridegroom and bride, the voice of those who cry, "Give thanks to the Lord of Hosts, for the Lord is good, for His kindness is everlasting!" as they bring thanksgiving offerings to the House of the Lord. For I will restore the fortunes of the land as of old – said the Lord.

Our sages, guided by this verse, connect the individual building with the national building.

This connection is not only a part of joyous times but is part of times of mourning. Every individual's destruction is part of the national destruction, and therefore the mourner is comforted – "May God comfort you among the other mourners of Zion and Jerusalem." The connection is perpetual, in times of sorrow and joy.

This even more pronounced when someone has died because of their Jewish identity, whether killed in battle or murdered in an act of terror. In such circumstances, the mourning is felt not only in the personal-familial context, but in a national context, as well.

7. According to halakha, one does not fulfill the obligation to comfort a mourner by doing so over the phone or with a letter or electronic message. However, if one is unable to visit in-person, it is clearly preferable to express one's condolences in one of those ways.[383]

---

381. Berakhot 6a.
382. 33:10–11.
383. *Tzror HaḤayim* 145; *Yalkut Yosef* (26:9) writes that if the comforting is to show respect for the deceased then it cannot be done over the telephone, but if it is to show respect for the living then it can be. Therefore, if one cannot attend the shiva, one should at least offer comfort over the phone.

8. A person should not go to comfort a person he greatly dislikes, so that it does not appear as if he has come to gloat in the other's sorrow.[384] On the other hand, every case should be considered individually. Sometimes, if a third party has properly prepared the mourner and has checked whether the mourner is comfortable to have that person come, it is a gesture that can bring the two together. This is a delicate and complex question that requires careful thought.
9. Comforting non-Jewish mourners is done *mipnei darkei shalom*, because of the ways of peace.[385] (See Key Concepts, ***Darkei Shalom*** [**Ways of Peace**].)
10. Sometimes families write, "Please abstain from condolence calls." This causes great confusion since, on the one hand, friends want to respect the family's wishes and do not want to impose. But on the other hand, for most people, receiving condolences during mourning is essential and can be truly helpful in overcoming the pain and grief – in beginning to return to a normal routine and avoiding becoming excessively overwhelmed by the mourning. It could also be said that, often, those who write not to visit are those needing comforting the most; their inability to come to terms with their loss is expressed by the inability to host comforters, and when visitors do come, the visit will likely be positive and meaningful for the mourners. Mourners sometimes make this announcement in order to screen out visitors who are less close to them and to see who comes despite this. One can try to clarify the situation by asking those close to the mourners if it is alright to come in spite of the request. It is also possible that after a few days have passed, the mourners will change their mind, in which case it is then imperative to go and visit them and to fulfill the mitzva of comforting the mourners. One can also try to pay an informal visit to the mourners after the shiva is over, to offer strength and support. Another option is to write a letter to the mourners expressing one's empathy, respect, and support.

---

384. Rema, *Yoreh De'ah* 335:2.
385. *Shulḥan Arukh, Yoreh De'ah* 367:1.

When to comfort

11. Some have the custom not to visit mourners in the first three days;[386] others are not strict about this. The reason for this practice is that the first few days are the height of the grief and, as the sages taught us, "Do not appease your friend when he is angry and do not comfort him when his deceased is before him" (Avot 4:23). While it is true that the deceased is no longer physically with the mourners, some people wait for three days to pass. Those are the days of the most intense emotions, when the mourners face their grief and sorrow, surrounded only by relatives and very close friends.

    Every case is different; the nature of the relationship between the comforter and the mourner is very significant here. Some mourners need support and comfort specifically during the most difficult time, especially from close friends and relatives.

12. The custom is not to comfort on Shabbat and Yom Tov. However, when necessary, it is permitted to visit the mourners in order to soothe them with words of comfort.[387] On Shabbat, one says, "It is the Sabbath when one must not comfort, and comfort will come soon."

13. One who did not comfort the mourner during the shiva can come during the first thirty days and, for someone mourning a parent, for the whole first year. After this time, one should not offer condolences, but may simply say, "*Titnaḥem,*" "May you be comforted."[388] When a person meets someone whom they failed to visit during the shiva, he might be inclined to apologize for not coming. Instead, one can say a few words of comfort and, through this, fulfill the mitzva of comforting the mourner.

---

386. *Gesher HaḤayim* 20:5, 5. Rabbi Nebenzahl: Rabbi Shlomo Zalman Auerbach said that there is no source for this; even those who do not come to comfort them should come to prayer services.

387. *Shulḥan Arukh, Oraḥ Ḥayim* 287, based on the Talmud (Shabbat 12b): "It was [only] with difficulty that comforting mourners and visiting the sick was permitted on the Sabbath." *Yalkut Yosef* 26:2.

    Rabbi Nebenzahl: The custom is that, on Shabbat, only those who are close come to comfort the mourner.

388. *Shulḥan Arukh, Yoreh De'ah* 385:2.

Advice for those being comforted

It is a good practice to have a notebook available in which visitors can write down words of comfort and memories. Some families keep letters and other messages, or announcements and newspaper obituaries, as mementos. Some like to record the stories and memories that friends and family share in their visits. This is often not something that people think to do during the shiva; it may occur to them only afterwards, and they may try to recall what was said. Friends can be helpful in this area, as a way of supporting the mourners.

> When Resh Lakish's son died, they went to the house of mourning to comfort him. Rabbi Hiya bar Abba said to his orator: Rise [and] say something with regard to the praise of the Holy One, blessed be He. He spoke and said: The God, who is great in the abundance of His greatness, mighty and strong in the multitude of awe-inspiring deeds, who reviveth the dead with His word, who does great things that are unsearchable and wondrous works without number. Blessed art thou, O Lord, who revivest the dead.
>
> He then said to him: Rise [and] say something with regard to the mourners. He spoke and said: Our brethren, who are worn out, who are crushed by this bereavement, set your heart to consider this: This it is [that] stands for ever, it is a path from the six days of creation. Many have drunk, many will drink, as the drinking of the first ones, so will be that of the last ones. Our brethren, the Lord of consolation comfort you. Blessed be He who comforteth the mourners.
>
> He [then] said to him: Rise [and] say something with regard to the comforters of the mourners. He spoke and said: Our brethren, bestowers of loving-kindnesses, sons of bestowers of loving-kindnesses, who hold fast to the covenant of Abraham our father. Our brethren, may the Lord of recompense pay you your reward. Blessed art Thou who payest the recompense.
>
> He [then] said unto him: Rise [and] say something with regard to the whole of Israel. He spoke and said: Master of the worlds, redeem and save, deliver [and] help Thy people Israel from pestilence, and from the sword, and from plundering, and from the

blast, and from the mildew, and from all kinds of calamities that [may] break forth and come into the world. Before we call, mayest Thou answer, Blessed art Thou who stayest the plague. (Ketubot 8b)

SECTION 12: PRAYERS IN THE HOUSE OF MOURNING

The practice of holding prayer services in the house of mourning is based on Rabbi Judah who said (Shabbat 152a–b): "A deceased person who has no comforters, ten people come and sit in his place for all seven days of mourning." Later in that section, the Talmud tells of a man who lived near Rabbi Judah who died, and no one came to offer condolences. Rabbi Judah gathered ten men and they sat in his place. After the seven days had passed, the deceased appeared to Rabbi Judah in a dream and said, "Thy mind be at rest, for thou hast set my mind at rest." In *Maavar Yabok*[389] he writes that he must have gathered ten men to pray. The simple reason for conducting services in the house is that the mourner does not leave the house during the shiva.

Rules

1. It is a mitzva to pray in a *minyan* in the house where the deceased died; this is considered an act of loving-kindness to the deceased and to the mourners. If this is not possible, for example if the deceased died in the hospital, it is customary to hold services in the house where the mourners are sitting shiva.
2. It is a mitzva to gather a *minyan* in the place where the mourners are sitting shiva so that they can pray with a *minyan* and say Kaddish without having to leave the house.
3. If it not possible to have a *minyan* in the deceased's home, it is preferable to sit shiva in a different location where it is possible to have a *minyan.*[390]
4. The custom nowadays is that, if there is no *minyan* in the house on weekdays, the mourners go to the synagogue[391] to pray with a *minyan* and say Kaddish.[392]

---

389. *Atar Anan HaKetoret,* ch. 1.
390. *Tzror HaḤayim* 79.
391. Rabbi Nebenzahl: They should go in a private manner, with someone to guard them.
392. *Yalkut Yosef* 29:3 in the name of the Ritva (Moed Katan 23a).

5. Some say that in very small communities in which having a *minyan* in the mourner's house would cause the communal *minyan* to be cancelled, they should not hold the *minyan* in the mourner's house.[393] Others are of the opinion that, even in this case, it is preferable to hold services in the mourner's house.[394]
6. The mourner is counted in the quorum of ten for the *minyan* even on the first day of shiva, despite the fact that he does not wear tefillin.

Halakhic details for prayer leaders

The Priestly Blessing (*Birkat Kohanim*)

7. In Israel, the custom is for the Priestly Blessing to be recited in synagogue every day. According to Ashkenazic custom, *kohanim* do not recite the blessing in the house of mourning because the *kohen* must make the blessing with joy, and the house of mourning is a place of sadness and grief. The *kohanim* should step outside before the leader begins the "*Retzeh*" ("Look with favor") blessing.[395]
8. According to Sephardic custom, *kohanim* do recite the Priestly Blessing in the house of mourning, but mourners themselves do not make the blessing.[396]
9. In Jerusalem, there is a custom that even the mourner himself, if he is a *kohen*, makes the Priestly Blessing, whether on a weekday or on Shabbat. This is especially appropriate if there are no other *kohanim* present to make the blessing, or if there is only one other present since some hold the opinion that the mitzva is only fulfilled when two *kohanim* make the blessing.[397]

---

393. *Tzror HaḤayim* 148.
394. *Ḥayim VeḤesed* 10:18, in the name of Rabbi David Pardo.
395. *Bei'ur Halakha* on *Shulḥan Arukh, Oraḥ Ḥayim* 128:43. However, the *Gesher HaḤayim* (20:3, 5) writes that they should step out before "*HaTov Shimkha*" (i.e., before the *kohanim* are called).
396. *Yalkut Yosef* 29:8.
397. *Gesher HaḤayim* ibid.; *Tzror HaḤayim* 151; *Shemirat Shabbat KeHilkhata*, vol. 2, 65:31.

Taḥanun

10. *Taḥanun* (Supplication) is not recited in the house of mourning, even if the mourners are not participating in the service.[398] Shiva is compared to the seven days of the festivals, as the verse states "I will turn your festivals into mourning" (Amos 8:10); just as *Taḥanun* is omitted on holidays, it is omitted in the house of mourning.[399] Another reason is to refrain from invoking the Attribute of Judgment in the house of mourning:[400] Some portions of the prayer service are associated with loving-kindness, such as praises of God and requests for divine compassion. *Taḥanun*, on the other hand, involves the confession of one's sins, which can be humbling. Most of the time, this is an important process that leads a person to introspection and to improving his ways. But mourners are already struggling and in low spirits; *Taḥanun* should not be said to arouse a further, excessive sense of lowliness.
11. If the mourner attends synagogue during the shiva, the congregation recites *Taḥanun*, but the mourner does not.[401] If the mourner is leading prayers in the synagogue, the entire congregation omits *Taḥanun*.[402]
12. In the house of mourning, one does not say "*El Erekh Apayim*" ("God is merciful"), or "*LaMenatze'aḥ Mizmor LeDavid, yaanakha Hashem beYom tzara*" ("A Psalm of song to David, God will answer you on the day of suffering"), or the verse "*VeAni zot Briti*" ("And Me, this is My covenant"). This is because of the reason mentioned above, that one should not call down the Attribute of Judgment in a house of mourning. The reason that "*Zot Briti*" is not recited is that it should not appear that one is making a covenant for pain and sadness. Another reason is that the mourner is forbidden to study Torah, which is called the covenant.[403] On

398. *Tzror HaḤayim* 154.
399. *Beit Yosef, Oraḥ Ḥayim* 131, (4).
400. *Mishna Berura* ad loc. 20.
401. *Mishna Berura* ibid.
402. *Gesher HaḤayim* 20:3, 11; *Tzror HaḤayim* 155.
403. *Maavar Yabok, "Atar Anan HaKetoret,"* ch. 1.

Shabbat, however, these should be recited because it would otherwise this would be considered public mourning on Shabbat. But the mourners themselves should omit it.[404]

13. The *Yehi Ratzon* ("May it be Your will") prayer is recited after the Torah reading.

Torah reading

14. It is permissible to bring a *sefer Torah* into the house of mourning in order to read from it. Some synagogues lend out a Torah for this purpose; one should ask the rabbi or other person in charge. On should prepare a suitable spot for the Torah beforehand, where it can be brought before the Torah reading and returned afterwards. The place for the *sefer Torah* should be higher than ten handbreadths (eighty to ninety-six cm); it is preferable to bring it in a portable Ark, which may be available from the local synagogue.
15. The Torah may be brought to the shiva house on the day of the Torah reading; it should remain there for a day or two.[405] It is customary to make sure that the Torah is read from at least three times.[406] People should conduct themselves respectfully and appropriately in the room where the Torah is being kept.
16. It is customary that if there is no *sefer Torah* in the shiva house, people go to the synagogue after the prayer service to read from the Torah. But the mourner is not permitted to do so.[407]

---

404. *Yalkut Yosef* 29:17.
405. Rema, *Oraḥ Ḥayim* 135:14; *Mishna Berura* ad loc.; *Yalkut Yosef* 29:12 permits it to be brought on the same day.
406. *Arukh HaShulḥan, Oraḥ Ḥayim* 135:32; *Pnei Barukh* 10:24. In the *Kuntras Ohel Ḥanna* at the end of *Pnei Barukh*, p. 465, Rabbi Horowitz writes that one need not be stringent to read it three times. But one should take care to act with the proper respect for the Torah. In *Tzror HaḤayim* 152, he does not require that the Torah be read three times, but his opinion is that the Torah must be accompanied by ten men when it is moved from place to place.
407. *Yalkut Yosef* 29:13; and he adds that a person who cannot do this, for example someone who is hurrying to go to work, is not obligated to hear the Torah reading.

Additions to the prayers

17. The custom is to say "*Titkabel Tzlot'hon*" ("Accept our prayers"), etc., in the house of mourning, even when the mourner is leading the service.[408]
18. There is a custom to read Psalm 49 at the end of Shaḥarit and at the end of Maariv (some people's custom is to do this for Shaḥarit and Minḥa). This psalm is about man's fate after death and the attempt to reach eternal life. The poet compares a wealthy person, who rests upon his riches and praises his own strength and who thinks that his wealth will help him after death, to a person who believes and trusts in God; this is someone who does not fear death but who offers his thanks and blessings to God.

For the leader of the Korahites, a psalm. Hear this, all you peoples; give ear, all inhabitants of the world, men of all estates, rich and poor alike. My mouth utters wisdom, my speech is full of insight. I will turn my attention to a theme, set forth my lesson to the music of a lyre. In times of trouble, why should I fear the encompassing evil of those who would supplant me – men who trust in their riches, who glory in their great wealth? Ah, it cannot redeem a man, or pay his ransom to God; the price of life is too high; and so one ceases to be, forever. Shall he live eternally, and never see the grave? For one sees that the wise die, that the foolish and ignorant both perish, leaving their wealth to others. Their grave is their eternal home, the dwelling-place for all generations of those once famous on earth. Man does not abide in honor; he is like the beasts that perish. Such is the fate of those who are self-confident, the end of those pleased with their own talk. Selah. Sheeplike they head for Sheol, with Death as their shepherd. The upright shall rule over them at daybreak, and their form shall waste away in Sheol till its nobility be gone. But God will redeem my life from the clutches of Sheol, for He will take

408. *Gesher HaḤayim* 20:3, 7; *Yalkut Yosef* 29:11; *Pnei Barukh* 10:23. There are opinions that say that if the mourner leads the prayers, he should not say "*Titkabel*."

me. Selah. Do not be afraid when a man becomes rich, when his household goods increase; for when he dies he can take none of it along; his goods cannot follow him down. Though he congratulates himself in his lifetime – "They must admit that you did well by yourself" – yet he must join the company of his ancestors, who will never see daylight again. Man does not understand honor; he is like the beasts that perish.

19. On days when *Taḥanun* is omitted, Psalm 16 is recited instead. This psalm expresses man's trust in God, even after death. It includes joyful expressions such as, "Therefore my heart is glad" and "You will fill me with joy." The tone of these phrases parallels that of festive days on which *Taḥanun* is omitted.

A *mikhtam* of David. Protect me, O God, for I seek refuge in You. I say to the Lord, "You are my Lord, my benefactor; there is none above You." As to the holy and mighty ones that are in the land, my whole desire concerning them is that those who espouse another [god] may have many sorrows! I will have no part of their bloody libations; their names will not pass my lips. The Lord is my allotted share and portion; You control my fate. Delightful country has fallen to my lot; lovely indeed is my estate. I bless the Lord who has guided me; my conscience admonishes me at night. I am ever mindful of the Lord's presence; He is at my right hand; I shall never be shaken. So my heart rejoices, my whole being exults, and my body rests secure. For You will not abandon me to Sheol or let Your faithful one see the pit. You will teach me the path of life. In Your presence is perfect joy; delights are ever in Your right hand.

20. There is a Sephardic custom to recite *Tziduk HaDin* and *Hashkava* after Shaḥarit on days when *Taḥanun* is said; some also say it after Minḥa, before sunset. Some recite *Tziduk HaDin* even on days when *Taḥanun* is omitted. Each place should follow its own custom.[409]

---

409. *Siddur Kol Eliyahu*, p. 940.

21. It is customary to study Mishna in the house of mourning during the week of shiva, to bring merit to the deceased's soul. This is usually done between Minḥa and Maariv. It is customary to learn selections of Mishna that begin with the letters of the deceased's name. (See Key Concepts, ***Alpha Beita.***) Some people also learn four mishnas from Tractate Mikvaot (ch. 7:4–7) that spell out the word *Neshama* (soul). The mourner recites the Rabbis' Kaddish, found in Sec. 57, "Kaddish." Some congregations lend out books for using during shiva that include the passages of Mishna and the halakhot of mourning. Any section of Mishna may be learned for the sake of bringing merit to the soul of the deceased.
22. Any Torah study can be dedicated to bringing merit to the deceased's soul. It is customary for rabbis and Torah scholars who visit the house of mourning to say a few words of Torah for the merit of the soul.

Shabbat and holidays

In Israel, prayer services are never held in the shiva house on Shabbat because public mourning is not permitted on Shabbat; the mourners may go to synagogue.[410] However, we present the laws here for use in places where it is customary to have services on Shabbat in the shiva house. Halakhot about mourners going to synagogue are brought in Sec. 31 "Shabbat and Mourning."

23. *Kabbalat Shabbat* is recited in the house of mourning. Some have the custom that mourners themselves should begin the service at "*Mizmor LeYom HaShabbat*" ("A song for the Sabbath day").[411]
24. The Leader's Blessing at the end of the Friday night service should not be recited in the house of mourning.[412] Some say that the custom in Jerusalem is to recite it.[413]

410. *Darka Shel HaYahadut BeMavet U'BeAveilut,* note on p. 357 in the name of Rabbi Yaakov Ariel.
411. *Gesher HaḤayim* 20:3, 9; *Pnei Barukh* 23:6; *Shemirat Shabbat KeHilkhata,* vol. 2, 65:13.
412. *Shulḥan Arukh, Oraḥ Ḥayim* 268:10.
413. *Yalkut Yosef* 29:16.

25. After the Torah reading in the shiva house, the deceased is recalled in "*El Maleh Raḥamim*." This is done even on a Shabbat when *Birkat HaḤodesh* (blessing over the New Moon) is recited, when names of other deceased individuals are not mentioned.[414]
26. "*Av HaRaḥamim*" is said during Shaḥarit; at Minḥa, "*Tzidkatkha Tzedek*" is recited.[415] Some do not say "*VeAni Tefilati*" at Minḥa.
27. On Shabbat, Ḥol HaMoed, and Purim, the special psalms that are usually recited in the house of mourning are not recited.[416] On Motza'ei Shabbat after Maariv, Psalm 16 is recited.
28. After Shabbat, the mourner says "*Hamavdil bein kodesh leḥol*," "Who distinguishes between the holy and the mundane," and removes his shoes; he may then lead the service.[417] Some have the custom that the mourner removes his shoes only after Maariv.[418]
29. The Ashkenazic custom is not to recite Hallel in the house of mourning on Rosh Ḥodesh. This is because Hallel is about thanking God for a particular time, as it says: "This is the day the Lord has made; we will rejoice and be glad in it." Mourners are in a time when it is inappropriate for them to recite Hallel. Another reason is because of the verse, "For the dead cannot praise God." We want to avoid it appearing to be a mockery of the dead, who cannot recite Hallel. Non-mourners who attend praying in the house of mourning should recite Hallel afterwards, preferably in a synagogue.[419] The Sephardic custom is to recite Hallel in the house of mourning on Rosh Ḥodesh, except for the mourners themselves, who omit it.[420]

---

414. *Magen Avraham, Oraḥ Ḥayim* 284:7.
415. *Shemirat Shabbat KeHilkhata* ibid. 16.
416. Ad loc. 18.
417. Rema, *Oraḥ Ḥayim* 553:2; *Gesher HaḤayim* 20:3, 9; *Shemirat Shabbat KeHilkhata* ibid. 33.
418. *Yalkut Yosef* 34:8.
419. *Tzror HaḤayim* 150.
420. *Yalkut Yosef* 29:14. He adds that the custom in Jerusalem, if they are praying in the place where the person died, is for the others to go to a different room to recite Hallel and to then come back and complete the prayers. But if the person died in a hospital or in a different place, they do not need to go out.

30. If Rosh Ḥodesh falls out on the last day of shiva, then, after the Reader's Repetition, people can say the words of condolence to the mourner and he can conclude his mourning. The mourner can then say Hallel in the usual manner.[421]
31. Hallel is not recited on Ḥanukka in the house of mourning, but non-mourners should recite Hallel afterwards at home.[422] Some say that Hallel should be recited in the house of mourning, except by the mourners themselves,[423] and some even say that the mourners should recite Hallel.[424] The reason there are different rules for Rosh Ḥodesh and Ḥanukka is that reciting Hallel on Rosh Ḥodesh is a custom, whereas halakha requires that one say Hallel on Ḥanukka.
32. During the Ten Days of Repentance, "*Avinu Malkeinu*" ("Our Father, our King") should be recited even though *Taḥanun* is omitted. *Seliḥot* are recited but are shortened: The passages from "*Zekhor Raḥameikha*" until "*Shema Koleinu*" are omitted, and only the first three verses of *Shema Koleinu* are recited.[425]

Rules for the mourners

33. A mourner who is a *kohen* should not make the Priestly Blessing during shiva, neither on Shabbat nor during the week. He should leave the room before the blessing.[426] Some say that on Shabbat he should recite the blessing in order not to engage in public mourning.[427] As mentioned above, in halakha 9, the custom in Jerusalem is that *kohanim* in mourning make the blessing even during the week of shiva.
34. The mourner is not called to the Torah even if he is a *kohen* or Levite and there are no other *kohanim* or Levites present.[428] A

421. *Yalkut Yosef* ibid.
422. *Magen Avraham, Oraḥ Ḥayim* 131:10.
423. *Mishna Berura* 683; *Shaarei Teshuva* ad loc.; *Gesher HaḤayim* (20:3, 7) brings opinions that the mourner should also recite it afterwards.
424. *Yalkut Yosef* 29:14.
425. *Gesher HaḤayim* 20:3, 4.
426. *Shulḥan Arukh, Oraḥ Ḥayim* 128:43.
427. *Yalkut Yosef* 29:8.
428. *Shulḥan Arukh, Yoreh De'ah* 384:2.

kohen in mourning need not leave the room to avoid being called up, even if no other *kohanim* are present.[429] If he is inadvertently called to the Torah, the mourner should not accept the *aliya*.

35. The mourner may remove the Torah and return it to the Ark and may lift and wrap the Torah (*hagbaha* and *gelila*). If the mourner lifts the Torah, he can hold the Torah while seated on a regular chair.
36. The mourner may recite the *HaGomel* blessing and may also recite *Sheheḥiyanu* over a new fruit, if the fruit will not be available after the shiva. This is also true of the blessing, "*HaTov VeHameitiv*."[430]
37. The mourner should not say *Kiddush Levana* (Sanctification of the Moon) if it will still be possible to say it after the shiva. *Kiddush Levana* comes to express the joy of renewal in creation; this is in conflict with the mourner's feelings. Therefore, if possible, one should wait until after the shiva to sanctify the new moon. If the time for reciting *Kiddush Levana* will have passed by the time shiva is over, the mourner is permitted to leave the house and make the blessing but should recite only the blessing and not "*Shalom Aleikhem*" and the other additions.[431] Some permit others to say "*Shalom Aleikhem*" to the mourner during *Kiddush Levana*.[432]

The mourner as prayer-leader

38. The custom for Ashkenazic Jews and for some Sephardic groups is that one who is mourning his father or mother leads the prayers for the entire year of mourning. Someone who is mourning for other relatives can lead the prayers but is not required to do so.[433]

---

429. *Yalkut Yosef* 22:18.
430. *Kol Bo al Aveilut*, p. 281; *Yalkut Yosef* 38:10.
431. *Mishna Berura* 426:11; *Shemirat Shabbat KeHilkhata*, vol. 2, 65:36.
432. *Yalkut Yosef* 23:7; *Tzror HaḤayim* 149.
433. *Shulchan Arukh, Yoreh De'ah* 384:3; *Gesher HaḤayim* 20:3, 2; *Yalkut Yosef* 29:4, 31:6; *Pnei Barukh* 10:19. In *Tzror HaḤayim*, p. 75 and paragraph 215, he writes that the Sephardic custom is that someone who is mourning his parents does not lead the prayers unless there is no one else who can lead, as per the simple understanding of the *Shulḥan Arukh*.

39. According to Ashkenazic custom, it is preferable for one who is mourning his mother or father to lead the prayers.[434] If the person is unable to lead the whole morning prayer service, he can lead the prayers from "*Ashrei*" following the *Amida* to the end of the service.[435]
40. There is no halakhic obligation for the mourner to lead the prayers. Therefore, if it is difficult for him to concentrate when he is leading the service, or if he does not know how, he is not required to do so. But it is considered a great virtue to do it if he is able.[436]
41. Mourners say the Mourner's Kaddish whether or not they are leading the service.
42. If several brothers are sitting shiva together, there is no need to arrange for separate services so that each of them can lead. Instead, they should take turns leading. If two mourners are praying in the same synagogue, it is permissible to split up into two *minyanim* to allow both of them to lead the prayers but only if this is done amicably and respectfully.[437] In a house of morning, it is permissible to divide the *minyan* to allow two different mourners to lead services.[438]
43. Mourners do not need to go to a different synagogue in order to find a place where they can lead services. They should continue to attend their regular place of worship and lead services whenever possible. However, on the Yahrzeit, one should find a synagogue where one can lead the service. If, in order to lead the prayers at a particular synagogue, the mourner will need to pray so quickly that it will detract from his concentration, it is preferable for him not to lead and to pray more slowly.[439]

---

434. Rema, *Yoreh De'ah* 376:4.
435. *Gesher HaḤayim* 30:8, 3.
436. Based on *Tzror HaḤayim* 215.
437. *Yalkut Yosef* 31:7–8 in the name of Rabbi Shlomo Zalman Auerbach (*Halikhot Shlomo, Tefilla* p. 223 and p. 60).
438. *Tzror HaḤayim* 153.
439. *Hilkhot Avel*, ch. 3, p. 238, in the name of Rabbi Shlomo Zalman Auerbach.

44. In the Ashkenazic custom, when choosing a prayer leader, priority is given to a mourner during shiva. A mourner within the first thirty days of mourning is given priority over a mourner within the first year of mourning. Someone observing a Yahrzeit takes precedence over someone within the first year of mourning.[440] One who regularly prays in the synagogue takes precedence over a guest in the synagogue, even if the guest would have priority according to the above-mentioned rules (e.g., a mourner who is a regular there and who is within the first year takes precedence over a guest who is within the first thirty days).

45. Someone who prays according to one custom (*nusaḥ*) and is leading services in a synagogue that uses a different *nusaḥ* should say the silent *Amida* in his regular *nusaḥ* but should recite the Reader's Repetition according to the synagogue's *nusaḥ* of the synagogue. Some disagree with this.[441] If one goes to an unfamiliar synagogue, one should find out what *nusaḥ* and siddur are used and what their policy is about having a prayer-leader who normally prays with a different *nusaḥ*. If there is a local custom that is halakhically sound, it should be followed.

46. One should be particularly careful not to cause arguments or disputes about Kaddish or leading services. Such arguments are a desecration of God's name; the purpose of prayer and Kaddish is the opposite, to sanctify and bring honor to God's name.

47. The Ashkenazic custom is that one does not lead services on Shabbat and Yom Tov during the first year of mourning, although halakhically it is permitted.[442] This will be discussed in Sec. 39, "The Mourner as Prayer-Leader on Holidays." But he should say the Mourner's Kaddish. According to the Sephardic custom, a mourner may lead the prayers on Shabbat and Yom Tov.[443]

---

440. *Gesher HaḤayim* 30:10. And it seems that someone observing a Yahrzeit comes before someone within the *shloshim*. *Tzror HaḤayim* 216.

441. *Pnei Barukh* 35:3 in the name of *Responsa Shoel U'Meshiv* and the *Netziv*. In *Igrot Moshe* (*Oraḥ Ḥayim*, vol. 2, 29) he writes that the leader should recite the same *nusaḥ* silently and out loud, see the footnote in the *Pnei Barukh* ad loc.

442. Rema, *Yoreh De'ah* 376:4.

443. *Tzror HaḤayim* 215.

48. The custom is that the mourner leads services on Motza'ei Shabbat, a time when, according to tradition, souls return to hell after a respite on Shabbat. Thus, when a son prays and sanctifies God's name publicly, it can redeem his parent's soul from hell.
49. Some say that the mourner should try to always lead Maariv since it is said that the night is the time when Divine judgment dominates.[444] Some say that one should not lead all three prayer services each day and that leading one is sufficient; if so, it is preferable to lead Maariv for the above-mentioned reason.[445]
50. Some have the custom for the mourner to be called up to read the *maftir* during the year of mourning[446] if he knows how to read it properly. But one should take care not to allow arguments about this; if this custom would lead to arguments, it is better for the mourner not read.[447]

SECTION 13: LAWS OF RECITING KADDISH

Chapter 57, "Kaddish," discusses the text of Kaddish and translations, as well as a discussion of the different types of Kaddish, when each one is recited, and the relationship between mourning and Kaddish,. The laws of Kaddish are detailed in the *Shulḥan Arukh,* mostly in *Oraḥ Ḥayim,* 55–56. The following section presents the laws connected to the Kaddish recited by mourners.

Kaddish is not a prayer for the dead, nor does it come to commemorate their memory. Rather, it comes to praise and elevate the Creator's holy and great name in the world. It is a part of the regular prayer services. However, the mourners' recitation of Kaddish gives great comfort and merit to the soul of the deceased. For this reason, mourners, and especially those who have lost a parent, are encouraged to say

444. *Kitzur Shulḥan Arukh* 26:1.
445. The Admor of Munkatz in the book *Nishmat Yisrael* p. 573, quoted in *Otzarot HaTorah,* vol. 2, *Minhagei Aveilut,* p. 1026.
446. Rema, *Yoreh De'ah* 376:4; *Tzror HaḤayim,* p. 88:5 and 215. In *Shemirat Shabbat KeHilkhata* (vol. 2, 65, note 137) he explains that the blessings of the *haftara* contain a type of *Tziduk HaDin.* Rabbi Nebenzahl: And he causes the congregation to answer Amen.
447. *Yalkut Yosef* 40:37–38.

Kaddish DeRabbanan (the Rabbis' Kaddish), which is said after a session of Torah study in order to add merit to the deceased (as discussed further in Sec. 57, "Kaddish." For the Hebrew text, see pages 94–95).

How many times is Kaddish recited and when?

1. Every congregation and individual should hear Kaddish at least seven times a day.[448] The Ari and other Kabbalists were of the opinion that one must hear Kaddish twelve times a day. The custom nowadays is for Kaddish to be said thirteen times each day.[449]
2. One should not recite Kaddish more times than provided by the halakha.[450]
3. Mourners say *Kaddish DeRabbanan* in the beginning of Shaḥarit after "*Rabbi Yishmael omer*." In *nusaḥ* Ashkenaz, an extra Kaddish is added after "*Mizmor shir ḥannukat haBayit leDavid*." At the end of the morning prayers, Kaddish is said after *Shir Shel Yom*, and *Kaddish DeRabbanan* is said after "*Ein Keloheinu*" and "*Pitum HaKetoret*." The Ashkenazic custom adds an additional Kaddish after *Aleinu*.
4. At Minḥa and Maariv, Sephardim say Kaddish before *Aleinu* and Ashkenazim say it after *Aleinu*. Ashkenazic Jews who pray *nusaḥ Sepharad* add Kaddish in Maariv before *Aleinu*. Some Sephardic groups add the Half Kaddish after *Aleinu*.
5. In places where the Song of Songs is recited before Shabbat, the mourner recites Kaddish after it.
6. Mourners say Kaddish after *Kabbalat Shabbat*. Sephardim and those who pray with *nusaḥ Sepharad* add *Kaddish DeRabbanan* after "*BaMeh Madlikin*."

---

448. *Beit Yosef, Oraḥ Ḥayim* 55, in the name of the *Agur* and *Shibolei HaLeket*.
449. *Gesher HaḤayim* 30:7, 1.
450. In the *Arukh HaShulḥan* (*Oraḥ Ḥayim* 55:3) he writes: "Many people think that it is a mitzva to recite Kaddish many times; they are mistaken, and I call this 'The sacred stones are scattered at the head of every street' (Lam. 4:1); they should not use the scepter of the King of Kings more than He allowed, and one who does more degrades the honor of the holy."

7. On Rosh Ḥodesh, Kaddish is said after "*Barkhi Nafshi,*" and on Shabbat and Yom Tov, after "*Anim Zemirot.*" The Mourner's Kaddish is recited after *Kiddush Levana.*

   This section does not detail the recitation of Kaddish on all of the various holidays because there are many different customs. Each person should follow the custom of his *nusaḥ* as it appears in the siddur or *maḥzor* and according to the custom of the synagogue where he is praying.
8. If the mourner is the last person called up to the Torah during Shaḥarit, he says the Half Kaddish after the Torah reading. No Kaddish is recited after Torah reading at Minḥa. According to the halakha, he can also recite Kaddish if he was not called to the Torah.[451]
9. A mourner can recite Kaddish in the middle of *Pesukei DeZimra* if he will not be able to find a *minyan* later at which to recite Kaddish.[452]
10. If the mourner cannot lead the whole prayer service, he may lead the end of the prayers, from *Ashrei* (before "*Uva LeTziyon*"), and recite *Kaddish Titkabel.* In this case, he should take care to recite, "*Vekara zeh el zeh ve'amar*" out loud so that the congregation will answer "*kadosh, kadosh, kadosh.*" He should also say aloud, "*Vaeshma aḥaray raash gadol*" and the congregation will answer, "*Barukh kevod Adonai mimkomo.*"[453]
11. If the mourner came late to synagogue and has no time to pray before the congregation reaches "*Uva LeTziyon,*" he can lead the prayers and recite "*Uva LeTziyon*" with the congregation and say *Kaddish Titkabel* afterwards[454] in the manner explained above.
12. A mourner who came to the synagogue as the previous *minyan* was concluding its service may recite Kaddish with them, even

451. *Gesher HaḤayim* 30:8, 2. In *Tzror HaḤayim* (276) he writes that this is the Sephardic custom. But, as noted, the custom also appears in *Gesher HaḤayim.*

452. *Pnei Barukh* 34:19, in the name of his father who wrote this based on the *Orḥot Ḥayim.*

453. *Gesher Ḥayim* 30:8, 3.

454. *Pnei Barukh* ibid. in the name of the *Paḥad Yitzḥak.*

though he did not pray with them, and then say it again at the next *minyan* where he is going to pray.[455]

13. Mourners recite *Kaddish DeRabbanan* after studying a portion of Aggada. After Torah study, it is customary to recite the mishna that begins, "*Rabbi Ḥananya ben Akashya omer,*" and then to say *Kaddish DeRabbanan.*[456]
14. Ideally, *Kaddish DeRabbanan* is recited after Torah study in which ten men participated.[457] It can still be recited if fewer than ten were present during the study, but a full complement arrives in time for the Kaddish.[458]

Selected laws of Kaddish

15. Kaddish is only said in the presence of a *minyan*. If ten were present when Kaddish began and some left in the middle, as long as six remain (most of the *minyan*), the Kaddish can be completed. That said, it is considered a sin to leave, and to those who left, we apply the verse, "Those who leave God shall be consumed" (Is. 1:28). But if a minimum of ten remains, then it is permitted to leave.[459] If one of the ten people is still praying and cannot reply to the Kaddish, he is still counted in the *minyan*.[460]
16. A mourner who usually prays slowly must speed up his prayer in order to recite Kaddish.[461]
17. Kaddish should be recited loudly and audibly. If one has a sore throat and is having trouble speaking, one can still say the Kaddish; it is preferable to recite it quietly along with others who are reciting it at the normal volume.[462]
18. Kaddish is said while standing up. One should stand with one's feet together like in the *Amida*.

---

455. *BeMar'eh HaBazak*, vol. 4, 117 in the name of the *Ḥelkat Yaakov*.
456. Sota 49a.
457. *Magen Avraham, Oraḥ Ḥayim* 234.
458. *Turei Zahav, Oraḥ Ḥayim* 55:3; *Gesher HaḤayim* 30:8, 11.
459. *Shulḥan Arukh* and Rema, *Oraḥ Ḥayim* 55:1–2.
460. *Shulḥan Arukh, Oraḥ Ḥayim* 55:6.
461. *Tzror HaḤayim* 278.
462. *Yalkut Yosef* 30:14.

19. At the end of the Kaddish, one should take three steps back before saying, *"Oseh shalom biMromav,"* "He who makes peace in the heavens." It should not be said while one is walking backwards.[463] Stepping back at the end of Kaddish is similar to the way a student takes leave of his rabbi in a respectful manner – only after taking a few steps back while facing his rabbi does the student turn and walk away. This is the same reason for stepping backwards at the conclusion of the *Amida*.
20. Mourners can practice reciting Kaddish at home in order to be able to say it properly, especially the *Kaddish DeRabbanan*, which is more difficult to say.[464]
21. If no one attending the service knows how to recite Kaddish in the original Aramaic, then one of them can lead the service and say Kaddish in another language.[465] In practice, however, even those who cannot read Hebrew can still recite Kaddish in Aramaic by reading a transliteration.

Who recites Kaddish and for whom?

22. The primary value of Kaddish is when a child says it for a parent.[466] If a person dies and leaves no sons, then a son-in-law or a grandson who has been given permission by his parents can say Kaddish. If there are no children or grandchildren, then the deceased's father can recite Kaddish, or, if the father is no longer living, a brother or other relative can say it. If there is no relative to say Kaddish, another person may do so. It is preferable that this person be paid.[467] This is both because payment enhances the sense of obligation and because it is an extra merit for the deceased and the family that they are investing effort and resources for the sake of the deceased. If the person who will

463. *Shulḥan Arukh, Oraḥ Ḥayim* 56:5.
464. In *Igrot Moshe* (*Oraḥ Ḥayim*, vol. 2, 56) he writes that an adult who needs to learn how to recite blessings may practice using God's name so as not to make mistakes, and it is reasonable to assume that this applies to Kaddish, as well.
465. *Mishna Berura* 55:1 in the name of *Dvar Shmuel.*
466. Rema, *Yoreh De'ah* 376:4.
467. *Beit Yosef* 403; *Gesher HaḤayim* 30:8, 7; *Yalkut Yosef* 30:19, 22.

recite the Kaddish is poor, then this is also considered an act of charity. However, if there the deceased had sons, the sons are obligated to make the effort to say Kaddish themselves and not to pay someone else to say it for them.

23. A person reciting Kaddish for a fee should say, before praying in the morning, that all the Kaddish prayers he will say that day shall be "*Le'ilui nishmat ploni ben ploni*" ("For the merit of the soul of X, the son of Y"), meaning that, although Kaddish is for God's glory, the merits of its recitation will be for this specific deceased person.

    Some[468] suggest that he should say:

    May it be Your will, our God, the God of our forefathers, that You should be merciful with Your great mercy on the soul of (X, the son of Y). And for the Kaddish prayers that I said, I am Your servant on this day, erase all of the accusers and evil forces, and advocates should give good counsel on the deceased's soul, and peace should accompany him, and he should dwell in comfort and peace, tranquility and security. And Your kindness shall overcome the attribute of justice and the hard judgments shall be sweetened through the supernal wonder which is great loving-kindness and complete mercy.

    May the utterances of my mouth and the thoughts of my heart be acceptable before You, God, my rock and my salvation.

24. It is customary in many places that people whose parents are living do not recite the Mourner's Kaddish. But if someone receives permission from his parents to say it, he may do so.

25. A parent whose son or daughter has died is not obligated to recite Kaddish. But if one feels compelled to do so, one can say Kaddish, especially if the child died young or left no children of their own to say Kaddish; the parent can say Kaddish for a full

---

468. As brought in *Sefer HaKaddish*, p. 166, in the name of *Kaf HaḤayim* (*Oraḥ Ḥayim* 55:2). I did not find this text in the *Kaf HaḤayim*, but rather that he should say that it is *LeIlui nishmat ploni, vayehi noam*, etc. (ad loc. 30).

twelve months. The same is true for siblings, if one's parents have given their permission.[469]

26. The deceased's brothers can say Kaddish together with the deceased's sons. The deceased's father and brothers can both say Kaddish if the father allows it.[470]
27. Since it is a mitzva for a son to recite Kaddish to bring merit to his mother's soul, a father should not prevent his son from reciting Kaddish for his mother. If the father nevertheless refuses to permit his son to say Kaddish, then the son should obey; but he can lead the prayer service and recite the Kaddish as prayer-leader.[471] He can also increase his Torah study for the merit of his mother's soul.
28. If a person's wife died, he is not obligated to recite Kaddish, but is allowed to do so. If she died without sons to recite Kaddish for her, it is appropriate for the husband to recite Kaddish for her for twelve months.[472]
29. If a person has died leaving only daughters, then a son-in-law or grandson can recite Kaddish for the deceased, if their parents give permission. The family should make sure that one person has taken on the responsibility of saying Kaddish regularly.[473]
30. A child over the age of six should be taught to say the Mourner's Kaddish for his parent if he is mature enough to know Whom he is praising.[474] If it is not certain whether the child understands Whom he is praising, he should wait to say Kaddish until he is nine years old. A child under the age of thirteen is not eligible to lead the prayer service, nor to recite the Kaddish that is recited

469. *Yalkut Yosef* 30:35, 37.
470. *Tzror HaḤayim* 272–273.
471. Rema, *Yoreh De'ah* 376:4. And in *Yalkut Yosef* (41:1) he writes that the person should comply with his father's wish on the matter only if the father is concerned for his own life; but if the father told him not to recite Kaddish for the mother because he was angry with her, the son should not listen to the father since this is like telling one's son not to observe the Torah, in which case the son is not required to listen to him. See ibid. for details.
472. *Yalkut Yosef* 30:36.
473. *Tzror HaḤayim* 270.
474. *Yalkut Yosef* 30:18.

by the prayer-leader. See Sec. 52, "One Who Did Not Observe Mourning," for the laws regarding a child who has reached the age of mitzvot.

31. The Kaddish can be said for more than one individual.[475] Therefore, if there is no relative to say Kaddish for a person, one can ask someone who is already saying Kaddish for another individual to have the additional intention to bring merit to the soul of the first person.
32. Since Kaddish can be recited for several different people, if someone is being paid to recite Kaddish for one person and then one of his relatives dies, he may recite Kaddish for both of them.[476]
33. Some say that if a person is being paid to say Kaddish for several people, he can designate one Kaddish per day for each deceased person. In such a case, he should tell the relatives that he will say Kaddish for their deceased relative at least once a day. Indeed, in earlier times when they divided up the Kaddish among different mourners, a mourner would sometimes say Kaddish only once a day.[477]
34. If a person will be travelling to a place where he will not be able to recite Kaddish, as long as there are other brothers saying Kaddish, that is sufficient. If he is the only one saying Kaddish, then he should pay someone else to recite Kaddish instead of him.[478]
35. Kaddish can be said for a child and may also be said for a baby; but Kaddish is not said for a baby who died within the first thirty days after the birth. Likewise, the family does not sit shiva because an infant in the first thirty days of life is not considered viable, discussed further in Sec. 16, "Who Mourns and for Whom: Death of an infant."
36. An adopted child can and should say Kaddish for his adoptive parents.[479]

---

475. Rema, *Yoreh De'ah* 376:4; *Gesher HaḤayim* 30:8, 8.
476. *Yalkut Yosef* 30:23 and he adds that the person may continue to receive payment for the first deceased person.
477. *Igrot Moshe, Yoreh De'ah*, vol. 1, 254.
478. *Tzror HaḤayim* 277.
479. *Yalkut Yosef* 30:24.

37. A convert can and should say Kaddish for his gentile parents and it is proper to do so.[480] Although the obligation to recite Kaddish is only for a Jew who has died, since Kaddish is essentially the glorification and praise of God, there is no prohibition against saying it for a non-Jew. This is also an expression of the child's gratitude and recognition of the good his parents did for him, bringing him into the world. Likewise, one can say Kaddish for non-Jews who saved Jews during the Holocaust.[481]
38. Kaddish is said even if the deceased was an unrepentant sinner and committed suicide,[482] since even a sinful parent can be redeemed through his son's actions. The son of a sinful person is still obligated to honor his parent (as Maimonides teaches in *Mishneh Torah, Hilkhot Mamrim* 6:11).
39. Kaddish should not be said for an apostate. But if the person was killed by non-Jews, Kaddish should be said.[483]
40. A *mamzer* (child of a prohibited relationship) can say Kaddish for his parent and should continue saying it during the twelfth month of the year of mourning.[484]
41. One should say Kaddish even for a person who gave instructions not to say Kaddish after his death.[485]

---

480. *Nitei Gavriel*, vol. 2, 40:20 in the name of *Responsa Zkan Aharon*.
481. Ibid. 25–26.
482. *Gesher HaḤayim* 30:8, 10. In the book *BeMar'eh HaBazak* (vol. 5, 92) it is written that Kaddish should be said for someone who asked to be cremated, even though cremation is strictly forbidden.
483. Rema, *Yoreh De'ah* 376. The reason is written in the *Darkei Moshe*, that his death atones for him. In *Nitei Gavriel* (vol. 2, 40:4) he writes that Kaddish should be recited for an apostate in order to atone for his sins and save him from descending into hell.
484. *Nitei Gavriel*, vol. 2 49:11, in the name of *Responsa Divrei Sofrim*. The reason is that he is still obligated to respect his parents. And because his birth was due to what is considered a sin, he should say Kaddish through the twelfth month to atone for his parents.
485. *Yalkut Yosef* 41:3. Although in the *Pitḥei Teshuva* (*Yoreh De'ah* 344:1) he brings an opinion that one should follow the deceased's instructions, since the reason to say Kaddish is to sanctify God's name in the world, a person cannot prevent this and thus Kaddish should be said (see *Pnei Barukh* 34:6).

42. Kaddish can also be said if there is some doubt as to whether the person has died. However, if the person was married, Mourner's Kaddish should not be recited until the Rabbinic Court permits his wife to remarry. In cases of doubt, we are not allowed to mourn or recite Kaddish, lest it be brought as evidence that the person has definitely died and lead the wife to mistakenly remarry based on this. See a later section on captives and missing persons, in Sec. 50, "A Doubt Regarding Death."
43. If the deceased left behind only a daughter under the age of twelve, some permit her to recite Kaddish in the synagogue. Some permit this only in a *minyan* in a private home,[486] and some do not allow it under any circumstances.[487] Some permit women to recite Kaddish in the synagogue along with a man.

Recitation of Kaddish by several mourners at the same time

44. When there are several mourners saying Kaddish praying together, there are three approaches that people commonly take – one is ideal, one is fine, and one is very undesirable.

    The ideal practice is to assign the different Kaddishes in the service to the different mourners such that each Kaddish is said by only one mourner. Halakhic authorities have developed rules of priority for dividing up the Kaddishes among the mourners.[488] Under this system, one may not "snatch" a Kaddish from someone else, since the sages wrote that if someone says a Kaddish that was assigned to someone else, the recitation does not provide merit to the person for whom it was said, but for the person that it was meant to said for. Moreover, everyone

486. *Gesher HaHayim* 30:8, 5 brings sources from the *Be'er Heitev, Orah Hayim* 132, and *Responsa Havot Yair* as mentioned in the *Pithei Teshuva, Yoreh De'ah* 376:3, and from *Sdei Hemed, Aveilut* 160. *Sefer Or LaAvel* (p. 148) brings the *Mishpetei Uziel, Orah Hayim*, 1st ed., 12, and Rabbi Henkin, *Pardes* 38, pamphlet 6:45.
487. *Yalkut Yosef* 30:21.
488. As explained in the previous chapter about the order of choosing a prayer-leader (halakha 45). For more details, see Rema, *Yoreh De'ah* 376:4; *Bei'ur Halakha, Orah Hayim* 132; *Kitzur Shulhan Arukh* 26; *Gesher HaHayim* 30:10.

should know that one Kaddish can be said for several people and therefore there is no need for disagreements over the recitation of Kaddish.[489]

The acceptable approach is for all the mourners to say Kaddish together, word for word, in such a way that the congregation can answer Amen together.[490]

The worst practice is when the mourners each say Kaddish at their own pace, causing confusion in the congregation and in the other people saying Kaddish. They miss the point of the Kaddish, which is to praise God's name in His world.

Therefore, either the Kaddishes should be divided up or the mourners should say it together, slowly and audibly. In some synagogues, the mourners all stand together in one place to say Kaddish together at the same pace.[491]

45. A Sephardic mourner praying in an Ashkenazic *minyan* (or vice versa) should not change his usual custom if he is the only person saying Kaddish. However, if he says it together with Ashkenazic mourners, he can shorten the "*Yehe shlama*" in accordance with the Ashkenazic custom so that they all finish Kaddish together.[492]

    In practice, it is customary for everyone to say Kaddish according to their own *nusaḥ* and to pause and wait for those saying a longer version. Specifically, Ashkenazic mourners should wait for those who say, at the beginning of the Kaddish, "*Veyitzmaḥ purkanei veyikarev meshiḥei,*" which is included in the Sephardic *nusaḥ* and *nusaḥ Sepharad*. At the end, they should wait while those doing the Sephardic *nusaḥ* say the longer version of "*Yehe shlama raba.*"

46. When several mourners say the Kaddish at the same time and one person is saying it faster than the others, if someone

---

489. *Gesher HaḤayim* 30:10, 15.

490. In *Gesher HaḤayim* (ibid. 12) and in *Yalkut Yosef* (30:13) they wrote that this is the Sephardic custom.

491. *Gesher HaḤayim* 30:10, 12; *She'eilat Shlomo*, vol. 5, 75.

492. *Yalkut Yosef* 30:57.

answered Amen to one person and another mourner finished a second later, the Amen counts for both. But if more than a second has passed, the person should answer Amen again.[493]

47. When Kaddish is recited in the house of mourning, other people are allowed to recite Kaddish together with the mourners.

The period for saying Kaddish

48. The Ashkenazic custom is to say Kaddish for a parent for eleven months[494] from the date of burial; this rule applies even in a leap year. Some Ashkenazim say Kaddish for twelve months less one week.[495] The Sephardic custom is to say Kaddish for eleven months and then stop for one week and then resume saying it until the end of the twelfth month.[496] The reason that Kaddish is said for less than twelve months relates to the sages' teaching, "The wicked are judged in hell for twelve months."[497] Reciting Kaddish is intended to provide merit for the deceased's soul and to save them from being sent to hell; but since it is disrespectful to assume that one's parent was wicked, Kaddish is recited for less than twelve months. However, Kaddish is recited for a full twelve months for someone who committed suicide. See Sec. 54, "Suicide."

49. If a parent gave instructions to recite Kaddish for a full twelve months, this should be followed.[498] The reason for not saying Kaddish for the whole twelve-month period is to show respect for the parent; so if the parent requested that Kaddish be recited for twelve months, complying with this request shows honor to the parent.

---

493. *Gesher HaḤayim* ibid. 14; *Yalkut Yosef* 30:15.

494. Rema, *Yoreh De'ah* 376:4. The last day of reciting Kaddish is a month and one day before the one-year anniversary, e.g., if the person died on the 8th of Ḥeshvan then the last day is the 7th of Tishrei, or the 7th of Elul in a leap year; *Gesher HaḤayim* 32:13.

495. *Gesher HaḤayim* 30:9, 3.

496. *Yalkut Yosef* 30:5; *Tzror HaḤayim* 263.

497. Rashi, Kiddushin 31b, s.v. "*Mikan va'elekh.*"

498. *Gesher HaḤayim* 30:9, 6.

50. After the end of the first year, the son may continue saying Kaddish but it is preferable to do so only once a week, and he should say beforehand "*Bli neder*" ("without making a vow") to make it clear that he is not obligating himself to say it.[499]
51. The eleven months are calculated from the day of the burial, like most other customs of mourning. The Yahrzeit is calculated from the day of the death.[500]
52. The *Kaddish DeRabbanan* (Rabbis' Kaddish) is said for twelve months. This Kaddish can be recited by someone whose parents are living.[501] This is because there is a halakhic obligation to recite Kaddish after Torah study, which applies even in the absence of a mourner.
53. Relatives of the deceased who are not the person's children say Kaddish for thirty days.[502] But if the deceased died without children to say it for him, then relatives say Kaddish for twelve months, even though they observe the laws of mourning for only thirty days.[503] In this case, they can say Kaddish for twelve months and not eleven since the reason to stop early is to show respect to one's parents, and this does not apply to other relatives. Some have the custom to stop reciting Kaddish after eleven months for any relative.[504]
54. If a mourner is saying Kaddish for a parent and within the year becomes obligated to say it for another relative – according to the Sephardic custom, the person stops at the beginning of the

499. *Tzror HaḤayim* 267; *Yalkut Yosef* 39:4.
500. *Gesher HaḤayim* 30:9, 10.
501. Maimonides *Seder Tefilot kol HaShana*, end of *Sefer Ahava*: "*Kaddish DeRabbanan* – ten or more Jews who study the Oral Law, Midrash, or Aggada, when they finish one of them, they say Kaddish… which is called the *Kaddish DeRabbanan*." Maimonides' *nusaḥ* of this text is different than what is currently called *Kaddish DeRabbanan*; it is what we call "The Great Kaddish," as explained in Sec. 57, "Kaddish."
502. Rabbi Nebenzahl: The other relatives do not say Kaddish and, in this matter, they are like non-relatives. If they want to say Kaddish then they can lead the prayers or recite the *Kaddish DeRabbanan*.
503. *Tzror HaḤayim* 265 and 273.
504. *Gesher HaḤayim* 30:9, 4.

twelfth month for one week and then continues to say Kaddish afterwards.[505] Some say that he should not stop leading the prayers and saying Kaddish for even one day since also it overlaps with the period of mourning for the other person.[506] Some say that the Ashkenazic custom is to stop only on the first and last day of the twelfth month. Some say that the mourner should ask or hire someone else to recite Kaddish in his stead for this month.[507]

55. If a person hears of a parent's death a long time after the parent died, the obligation is to say Kaddish for eleven months after the burial. If the person was informed during the twelfth month, he should say it for the whole month except for the last day. If the person was informed after twelve months, he should not say Kaddish.[508]

Intentions during Kaddish

56. One should remember that the primary purpose of saying Kaddish is to praise and elevate God's name in the world, not any other purpose. This praise of God is a merit to the deceased for whom it is recited.
57. One should say Kaddish correctly and with intention. It should be read from the siddur without skipping words and with correct pronunciation.
58. The highest form of merit for the deceased is for their children to learn Torah. Therefore, mourners should increase their Torah study, try to participate in daily Torah classes, and use their spare time to involve themselves in Torah study, each according to his own ability.[509]

---

505. *Tzror HaḤayim* 264.
506. *Yalkut Yosef* 30:8. He wrote that this is brought in *Halikhot Shlomo* (*Tefilla*, p. 225) in the name of Rabbi Shlomo Zalman Auerbach.
507. *Gesher HaḤayim* 30:9, 8; *Tzror HaḤayim* ibid.
508. *Gesher HaḤayim* 30:9, 5; *Pnei Barukh* 34:4–5. However, in *Kol Bo al Aveilut* (p. 378) he writes that the person should say Kaddish.
509. *Yalkut Yosef* 30:11.

Introduction to the Laws of Mourning (*Aveilut*)

> A person should initially be enriched with the details, in order to give his soul the freedom and ability to view things through comprehensive examinations; that is the pleasure of one's spirit, which strives to expand the river of higher comprehension.
>
> Once a person has reached a suitable level of having acquired the details, the spirit formulates general rules, which are above all the details. When these are complete, the values of this higher understanding hover over each and every detail with a piercing comprehension, drawing from the higher understanding and enriching the multitude of details, in the plethora of their hues.
>
> Then comes the greatness of man, which demands that his actions not be rote, but that each action and custom, each service and mitzva, each feeling and idea, all Torah and prayers be illuminated with the hidden, universal light; this light is stored in the higher soul before it becomes actualized. (Rabbi Abraham Isaac Kook, *Orot HaKodesh*, vol. 1, *Ḥokhmat HaKodesh* 38)

The halakha guides a person at every step and juncture of life, down to the most minute detail. The study of these details can lead one to understand how, all together, they form lofty values and principles. A deeper understanding of the principles can illuminate the details in a new and higher light; this causes spiritually enrichment, furthering a new relationship to the details out of a renewed understanding of how they influence the bigger picture.

SECTION 14: A CONCEPTUAL UNDERSTANDING OF THE PROCESS OF MOURNING

Beyond the study of the halakhot of mourning, there is great importance to understanding its broader process. The objective here is to show that mourning is a gradual process. It starts with the beginning of mourning, the most difficult time, and evolves all the way through to the return to normal, mundane life, to the degree possible. The process of mourning is individual and varies from person to person; that said, there is a process that is common to most people.

We can use a simple graphic model:

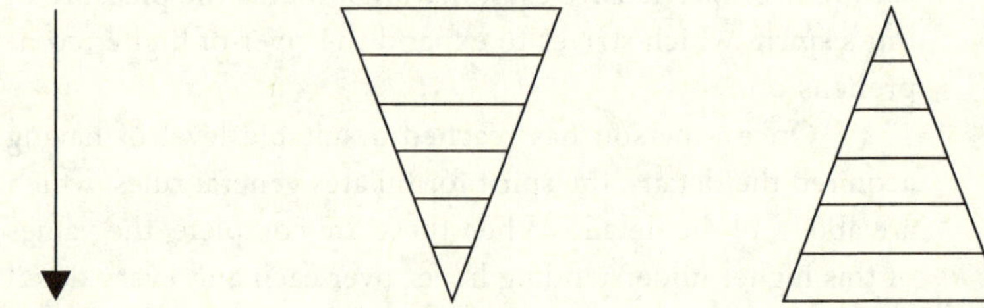

"Old mourning" is mourning for the destruction of the Temple and Jerusalem. "New mourning" refers to mourning for a relative who has died. Both processes are gradual, but they proceed in opposite directions.

The illustration above symbolizes these processes. The base of the triangle represents normal daily life, absent of special events or emotions. The tip of the triangle represents the most intense spiritual and emotional state, the height of the process. In old mourning, the process moves from the mundane to the height of emotion; in new mourning, it moves from the height of emotion to the mundane.

With old mourning, there is a desire to help a person move into the experience of feeling mourning, loss, and sorrow for the destruction of the Temple and Jerusalem. People tend to be involved in their everyday needs and concerns, without thinking about or feeling the sorrow over the destruction.

To avoid having people reach Tisha B'Av in a state where they are disengaged from feeling sorrow over the destruction of the Temple, the sages established a gradual increase in the intensity of mourning: The time of the Three Weeks, beginning with *Shiva Asar BeTammuz,* involves halakhic restrictions that become more severe as the time passes – from the beginning of Av, to the week of Tisha B'Av, and increasing on Erev Tisha B'Av. The culmination, on a halakhic and emotional level, is the day of Tisha B'Av itself. This process is designed so that people can reach Tisha B'Av after a gradual process that has prepared them halakhically and emotionally for mourning the destruction, which our sages wanted to emphasize.

The halakhot of new mourning embody the opposite process: They begin with the pain and suffering, which are most intense immediately following the death and are often accompanied by strong feelings of frustration, shock, and anger. On a halakhic level, as well, the most severe rules and restrictions apply to the beginning of this process.

Aninut is not part of the model described. The *onen,* whose deceased is "lying before him," unburied, is exempt from observing any mitzva. This is done out of respect for the deceased and also to allow the relatives to make arrangements for the funeral. During *aninut,* the process of mourning has not yet begun and therefore we do not yet comfort the mourners. The halakhic and emotional process of comforting the mourners begins only after the burial.

The guidance provided here aims to help foster an inner process of gradual evolution, from the initial shock towards an acceptance of the new situation. This is especially relevant in a case where someone has died young or has died suddenly, where difficult reactions may develop that require professional support. However, even in situations where a beloved relative has passed away at an advanced age and with minimal suffering, there are strong emotions and a need for guidance and support.

The five stages of mourning

Mourning can be divided into five stages that differ in terms of their laws and severity:[510]

1. The first day of mourning; this is a Torah obligation:[511] Mourners do not put on tefillin, even after the burial, and do not eat their own food for the first meal.

510. *Gesher HaḤayim* 21:1 and vol. 2, ch. 28.

511. However, the *Shulḥan Arukh* (*Yoreh De'ah* 398) brings an opinion that mourning is *DeRabbanan.* This is significant in determining for whom one mourns, which is explained in Ch. 16, "Who Mourns and for Whom?"

2. The first three days: These are called three days of crying, during which the mourning is most severe.[512]
3. The first seven days of mourning (i.e., an additional four days to these three) are known as the shiva (meaning "seven"), with fixed laws of mourning.[513]
4. The thirty days: In this period, only certain laws of mourning are observed.[514]
5. Twelve months: These are only observed for a parent – not a year, but twelve months.

Today, in practice, the most relevant concepts are shiva, *shloshim* (the thirty-day period), and the twelve months: In particular, shiva is associated with what is colloquially known as "sitting shiva"; the *shloshim* is associated with restrictions on shaving and haircuts; and the twelve months is observed when a parent has died. A survey of the above-mentioned periods describes a complete process that is structured and gradual and is intended to help mourners return to a state of normalcy.

New mourning can be likened to an occurrence of a sudden, painful physical injury that causes damage to the body. The initial treatment for this injury is a big and cumbersome bandage; over time, this is replaced by a smaller bandage, and then an even more minimal one. Likewise, the halakhic intensity around mourning is aligned with the emotional intensity and decreases with time. It should be stressed, however, that even when this process is over – when all of the bandages have been removed – a scar remains. Even after the long process of mourning,

512. For example, the mourners may not work, should not greet someone who has greeted them, and does not leave the house. It is written in Y. Moed Katan that during the first three days, the soul hovers over the body and considers returning to it, but since it sees that its face has changed, the soul departs.

513. I.e., the prohibitions against working and business transactions, bathing, anointing with oil, haircuts, laundry, learning Torah, greeting others, joyous activities, marriage, wearing leather shoes, marital relations, and sitting on a regular chair.

514. I.e., haircuts, ironing cloth, marriage, joyous activities, and travelling for business to another country.

which attempts to return a person to his normal life and to the state he was in before having lost a loved one, an emotional scar remains. The person will never completely return to his former state. But, the same way that proper treatment for physical injuries is extremely beneficial, the proper process of mourning can be of significant help in guiding mourners back to their routine. Self-awareness around the emotional process contributes to its success.

The sages related to this same process in a Midrash describing how the attribute of Divine Judgment hovers over the mourners, conveying a message that there is a need for them to be extra cautious and protective of themselves. The midrash also describes the gradual process of returning to the normal state:

> For the entire seven days, a sword is drawn; up to the thirty days it is loose; after twelve months, it returns to its scabbard. What is this like? Like an arch of stones, if one is removed, they all shake.[515]

Another version of this text reads:

> The [first] three days, the mourner should perceive as if there is a sword resting between his shoulders; from three to seven [days] as though it is across from him in a corner, from seven to thirty [days] as though it passes before him in the marketplace;[516] and for the first year, the Attribute of Judgment is spread before the family, and if a baby boy is born – the entire family is healed.[517]

Not only the mourning family, but the community surrounding the deceased, have a responsibility to conduct themselves with caution and gravity. The community ought to gain a new perspective on life following the death, as often occurs following the death of a close

515. Y. Moed Katan 3:3.
516. Moed Katan 27b.
517. Y. Moed Katan 3:7; *Shulḥan Arukh, Yoreh De'ah* 394:4.

friend. One's perspective and priorities may change and one may learn to appreciate things more; one may learn that many things in life are not a given, even the fact that we are alive. Simple things like health, family, and livelihood take on a new light. These thoughts and contemplations are likely to make us see the people with whom we share our lives with more love and appreciation. Thoughts of repentance can also surface – are we truly living our lives in accordance with our values and beliefs? Are we dedicating the proper amount of time, and relating authentically and correctly, to the people and principles that are important to us?

The sages expressed the need for such contemplation in a succinct sentence: "If one of the group dies, the whole group shall be concerned."[518] This is not meant to suggest a demoralizing or paralyzing anxiety, but rather a need for reflection that can lead people to renewal and productivity.

Excessive mourning

Despite great sadness over a death, the Jewish perspective maintains that one should not suffer and bewail the deceased more than the sages determined. In this context, the Talmud brings the following harrowing tale:

> Rab Judah said, as citing Rab: Whoever indulges in grief to excess over his dead will weep for another. There was a certain woman that lived in the neighborhood of R. Huna; she had seven sons, one of whom died [and] she wept for him rather excessively. R. Huna sent [word] to her: Act not thus. She heeded him not [and] he sent to her: If you heed my word it is well; but if not, are you anxious to make provisions for the others? He [the next son] died and they all died. In the end he said to her: Are you fumbling with provisions for yourself? And she died.[519]

518. Shabbat 106a; *Shulḥan Arukh, Yoreh De'ah* 394:5.
519. Moed Katan 27b.

A suitable, gradual timeline was set out by the sages, in accordance with the emotional process that mourners face:

> [Our rabbis taught]: "Weep ye not for the dead, neither bemoan him."[520] [That is], "Weep not for the dead" [that is] in excess, "neither bemoan him" – beyond measure. How is that [applied]? – Three days for weeping and seven for lamenting and thirty [to refrain] from cutting the hair and [donning] pressed clothes; hereafter, the Holy One, blessed be He, says, "Ye are not more compassionate towards him [the departed] than I."[521]

This was also established as the halakha:

> One should not grieve excessively for the dead, and whosoever grieves excessively for him, will weep for another [dead], save that three days [are designated] for weeping, seven for lamenting, thirty [to abstain from] cutting the hair and wearing pressed garments.[522]

When a person is too sorrowful, it can appear to be a defiance and insult towards Heaven. Faith in the eternality of the soul can give comfort and help to alleviate one's pain;[523] since the soul is not lost but has transitioned into a spiritual realm.

At the same time, the sages require people to mourn the death of their relatives. It would be cruel not to do so[524] since the end of life is a cause for sadness and reckoning:

> Whoever does not mourn as our sages instructed, this is cruel, rather one should fear and worry and examine one's actions and repent.[525]

---

520. Jer. 22:10.
521. Moed Katan, ibid.
522. *Shulḥan Arukh, Yoreh De'ah* 394:1.
523. Naḥmanides on the Torah, Deut. 14:1.
524. Maimonides, *Laws of Mourning* 13:12.
525. *Shulḥan Arukh, Yoreh De'ah* 394:6.

Whoever sheds a tear for a good person, God counts him and places him in His treasure storage.[526]

One who cries and mourns and sheds a tear for one's relatives and for a good person – this is the way of the righteous, the prophets, and people of action, and it indicates the purity of one's soul and one's subservience before God.[527]

Whenever a calamity befalls man, he should repent and mend his ways. This does not mean that one should blame oneself for what happened, but that one should delve deeper into the substance of one's life.[528]

The rabbis taught that when the Temple was destroyed, many people stopped eating meat and drinking wine. R. Joshua b. Ḥananya said to them: My children, why? They said: Can we eat meat that was offered on the altar and is now destroyed?! Can we drink wine that was poured on the altar and is now destroyed?! He said to them: If so we should not eat bread since the meal offering is no longer. They replied: We can eat fruit. He said: We should not eat fruit since the first fruits are no longer brought. They replied: There are other fruits. He said: We should not drink water since the water libations are no longer. They were silent. He said to them: My sons, let me say to you, to not mourn at all is impossible since the decree was made; but we cannot mourn too much, since we cannot make a communal decree unless most of the people are able to withstand it. Rather, this is what the sages said: When a person paints their house, they should leave a small part, a cubit by a cubit, opposite the entrance. A person makes all that they need for a meal and leaves a small part… a woman wears her jewelry and leaves some aside, as it says "If I forget you, O Jerusalem, let my right hand wither; let my tongue stick to my palate if I cease to think of you, if I do not keep Jerusalem in memory even at my happiest hour" (Ps. 137:5).[529]

526. Shabbat 105b.
527. *Responsa Radbaz*, vol. 3, 555.
528. *Responsa She'eilat Shlomo*, vol. 7, p. 236
529. Bava Batra 60b.

SECTION 15: THE SOURCES FOR MOURNING

> The word of the Lord came to me: O mortal, I am about to take away the delight of your eyes from you through pestilence; but you shall not lament or weep or let your tears flow. Moan softly; observe no mourning for the dead: Put on your turban and put your sandals on your feet; do not cover over your upper lip, and do not eat the bread of comforters: In the evening my wife died, and in the morning, I did as I had been commanded. (Ezek. 24:15–18)

It is a basic human need to have customs of mourning for the bereaved, both from an emotional and a societal standpoint. Humans have had customs of mourning since ancient times. The sources and meanings behind Jewish customs of mourning will be discussed here.

The source

There is an allusion to the seven days of mourning in the Torah, as it says about Joseph: "And he observed a mourning period of seven days for his father" (Gen. 50:10). Another verse – "And on the seventh day the waters of the flood came upon the earth" (Gen. 7:10) – was interpreted as referring to seven days of mourning for the righteous man Metushelaḥ; during these days, God waited and did not bring the flood, teaching us that eulogizing the righteous delays calamities.[530] Another allusion is found in the verse, "I will turn your festivals into mourning" (Amos 8:10) – as the festival lasts for seven days, so too mourning last for seven days.[531] The Midrash[532] explained the verse, "You shall not go outside the entrance of the Tent of Meeting for seven days," (Lev. 8:33) as follows: Moses told Aaron and his sons to mourn for seven days, until it no longer reaches you.[533]

530. Sanhedrin 108b.
531. Moed Katan 20a.
532. *Tanḥuma, Parashat Shemini.*
533. *Otzar Dinim U'Minhagim, Aveilut,* p. 4.

Even though the law of mourning from the Torah is only for one day,[534] Moses established seven days of mourning.[535] One might say that Moses gave halakhic validity to the ancient custom that existed from the time of our forefathers and even beforehand.

Many of the laws of mourning are deduced from the verses in Ezekiel that are quoted above. Ezekiel was told that his wife would die and he was instructed not to mourn. From the details he was told about how *not* to mourn, our sages found sources for the laws of mourning, as will be explained below.

The reason for mourning

Some have written that the purpose of mourning is to stir people to repent and introspect, and to counter the mistaken idea that human death is like that of animals.[536] Some have written that the reason for practicing mourning is to stress the importance of every human life – a unique life of free will and choice. It distinguishes the death of an animal's death, which is a monetary loss, from the death of a human, which is a loss of the essence of creation.[537]

The main reason to cease one's work and occupations for a week is to honor the deceased and remember them. The living will take note that this is man's end and will examine their own actions. Were a person to go about his regular activities, he would fail to remember the

534. Maimonides (*Mishneh Torah, Hilkhot Avel* 1:1) derives from Aaron's words "If I eat the sin offering today will it be acceptable before God?" (Lev. 10:19), that a person is obligated to mourn for a relative for the whole day, even after the burial, and it is forbidden to eat sacrifices the entire day. In *Sefer HaMitzvot* (*Positive Commandments* 37), Maimonides writes that it is a positive commandment for *kohanim* to become impure for their relatives and to mourn for them as others; he deduced this from the verse, "For her he may defile himself" (Lev. 21:3).

According to Maimonides, Naḥmanides, and the *Geonim*, the principle of mourning is from the Torah. But Rabbenu Tam, Rabbenu Yitzḥak, and the Rosh are of the opinion that mourning is a rabbinic commandment and not from the Torah. See *Tur, Yoreh De'ah* 398.

535. Y. Ketubot 1:1.

536. *Sefer HaḤinukh* 264.

537. *Gesher HaḤayim* 19:2.

deceased and the grief. For this reason, the Torah permitted *kohanim* to become impure in order to care for their deceased relatives and to mourn for them.[538]

SECTION 16: WHO MOURNS AND FOR WHOM?

Mourning is observed for the seven relatives mentioned in the following verses:

> The Lord said to Moses: Speak to the *kohanim*, the sons of Aaron, and say to them: None shall defile himself for any [dead] person among his kin, except for the relatives that are closest to him: his mother, his father, his son, his daughter, and his brother; also for a virgin sister, close to him because she has not married, for her he may defile himself. (Lev. 21:1–3)

Rules regarding the seven relatives

1. In the passage of the Torah that discusses priestly laws (Lev. 21), we learn about the seven relatives for whom even a *kohen* must become impure, to tend to the burial and to mourn. They are: a man for his wife,[539] a woman for her husband, father and mother, son and daughter, paternal brother and sister – if she is unmarried. The sages expanded the obligation to mourn to include maternal siblings and a married sister, even though a *kohen* may not become impure for them.[540]

   One does not observe the laws of mourning for a grandparent or a grandchild, nor for uncles, aunts, nephews, and nieces.

---

538. *Yalkut Yitzḥak*, Mitzva 264, brought in *Otzar Dinim U'Minhagim*, ibid.
539. According to the Talmud: "Except his relatives" – his relatives refers to his wife. But in the Torah it is written, "A husband should not become impure" (an apparent contradiction to the previous source). How is this possible? He becomes impure for his legitimate wife and does not become impure for his illegitimate wife (Yevamot 22b).
540. *Shulḥan Arukh, Yoreh De'ah* 374:4. This is opinion of Naḥmanides (*Torat HaAdam* p. 213), but according to Maimonides (*Mishneh Torah, Hilkhot Avel* 2:1), a husband's mourning for his wife, and a woman for her husband, is a rabbinic commandment. Rabbi Nebenzahl: Some say that all mourning is rabbinic.

In the word *"AVeL"* (mourner), the sages found an allusion to the different relatives for whom one mourns:

Aleph – *Av* (father), *Em* (mother), *Aḥ* (brother), *Aḥot* (sister), *Isha* (wife)
Bet – *Ben* (son), *Bat* (daughter), *Baal* (husband)
Lamed – the numerical value is thirty, corresponding to thirty days of mourning.
Although the period of mourning for a parent is twelve months.

2. One who never met his or her parent is nevertheless obligated to mourn when informed of the parent's passing.

   The laws pertaining to an adopted child will be discussed below.
3. One must mourn for one's siblings or children, provided they were Jewish.[541]
4. Children who are under the age of bar or bat mitzva are not obligated to mourn, but the custom is for them to tear their garments (*kriya*). The Yemenite custom is that a child who has reached the age of education does observe the laws of mourning.[542]

   Sec. 52, "One Who Did Not Observe Mourning," addresses the case of children who reach the age of bar or bat mitzva during the period of mourning.
5. Someone whose relative died but who did not learn of the death is not obligated to mourn. Hence, one is permitted to invite the person to a wedding or other celebration.[543]

Mourning for a spouse

It is taught in a baraita: A man dies only to his wife and a woman dies only to her husband. A man dies only to his wife, as it is

---

541. *Avel Rabati* 4:17; *Shulḥan Arukh* ibid.
542. *Shulḥan Arukh HaMekutzar, Einei Yitzḥak, Yoreh De'ah* 186:13; *Be'er LeḤai Roi* 6–7.
543. *Shulḥan Arukh, Yoreh De'ah* 402:12; and a couple can have relations if one of them is a mourner but does not know about it, even though the spouse knows. *Ḥidushei HaGershuni,* ad loc. in the name of *Sefer Ḥasidim,* and also in *Yalkut Yosef* 38:13, in the footnote.

stated: "And Elimeleh, Naomi's husband, died" (Ruth 1:3). And a woman dies only to her husband, as it is stated in Jacob's parting words to Joseph: "And as for me, when I came from Paddan, Rachel died on me" (Gen. 48:7). (Sanhedrin 22b)

6. A man mourns for his wife if they were married in accordance with halakha, but not for a fiancée or for a wife he married in violation of halakha.[544]
7. A couple who began the process of getting divorced are still considered married and should mourn for each other.[545] Some say that they do not mourn for each other.[546]
8. If a woman's husband died and there was no body to bury – if she subsequently remarried and then the first husband's body was recovered and buried, she does not observe the rules of mourning for him since her second marriage annulled the first relationship.[547]
9. If a person died childless and the widow dies while waiting for her brother-in-law to perform *ḥalitza*, the brother-in-law is legally obligated to tend to her burial and mourn for her.[548] However, some hold that he does not need to mourn, especially in Israel, where the accepted custom is to be lenient in this case.[549]

People other than the seven relatives

10. One mourns for one's rabbinic mentor for one day.[550]

544. *Shulḥan Arukh, Yoreh De'ah* 374:4.
545. *Tzror HaḤayim* 3; *Yalkut Yosef* 14:20; *Kol Bo al Aveilut*, p. 314 (although on p. 315 he brings opinions and proofs that one should not observe the laws of mourning).
546. Notes of Rabbi Akiva Eiger on *Shulḥan Arukh, Yoreh De'ah* 374, s.v. "*VeNesuah*" in the name of the *Yam Shel Shlomo*; *Gesher HaḤayim* 6:5, 4; *Yalkut Yosef* 14:20; *Nitei Gavriel*, vol. 1, 126:2–3; *Pnei Barukh* 9:4 brings both opinions.
547. *Yalkut Yosef* 14:19, in the name of the *Ḥatam Sofer*.
548. *Shulḥan Arukh, Yoreh De'ah* 373:4, in the name of the Rashba.
549. *Yalkut Yosef* 14:4. *Pnei Barukh* 9:3 brings both opinions.
550. Moed Katan 25b; Maimonides 9:12; *Shulḥan Arukh, Yoreh De'ah* 374:10

11. An adopted child is not, according to halakha, obligated to mourn for his adoptive parents. However, one should express sadness over their death and it is appropriate to recite Kaddish, especially if the parent has no other children to say it.[551] Some say that a person who was adopted should be encouraged to observe the laws of mourning for his adoptive parents out of gratitude; but he is not excused from the obligation to learn Torah.[552]
12. A relative who is not one of the seven relatives but who feels the need to mourn may observe some of the laws of mourning.[553] However, they are not permitted to sit shiva and observe all the prohibitions of mourning.[554] They can also say Kaddish if their parents agree to it.[555]
13. There is a halakhic principle: "Anyone for whom one is obligated to mourn, one shares in his mourning."[556] (See Key Concepts, **Whomever He Mourns For, He Also Mourns With**.) This means that if one of a person's seven relatives is in mourning, the person should observe the laws of mourning out of respect for that relative, when in their presence. For example, if one's grandchild died, even though one is not obligated to mourn for the grandchild, one still tears one's garment and observes the laws of mourning in the presence of one's child who has lost a son or daughter. However, when one is not in the presence the relative who is mourning, one does not mourn. A man observes the laws of mourning when his wife is sitting shiva for

---

551. *Yalkut Yosef* 14:18 and 30:24.
552. *BeMar'eh HaBazak*, vol. 5, 91, in the name of Rabbi Sternbokh (*Teshuvot VeHanhagot*, vol. 3, 374) and *Nishmat Avraham*, vol. 5, p. 141.
553. Rema, *Yoreh De'ah* 374:6.
554. *Pitḥei Teshuva* ad loc. 7.
555. *Tzror HaḤayim* 2; *Pnei Barukh* 9:1. *Yalkut Yosef* (14:3) wrote that the accepted Sephardic custom is that the son-in-law joins in the prayers, Torah study, and memorials to merit to the soul of his father-in-law; and if his parent-in-law did not have a son, he can recite Kaddish if his parents' consent.
556. Moed Katan 20b. It was established as the halakha in Maimonides' *Hilkhot Avel* 2:4–5; Naḥmanides, *Torat HaAdam* 141–44; *Shulḥan Arukh, Yoreh De'ah* 374:6.

her parents out of respect for his parents-in-law, but not for her other relatives. Likewise, a wife should observe mourning in the presence of her husband who is sitting shiva for his parents, but not for other relatives.

The Rema[557] writes that the contemporary custom is to be lenient in engaging in this type of mourning (for the relative of one's relative). Currently, the custom is not to observe this; anyone who acts strictly in this matter nowadays is considered to be acting bizarrely. That said, the relatives of the deceased do observe some level of mourning in the first week, i.e., until after the first Shabbat: They do not wash or change their clothing as they would on a regular Shabbat and do not attend festive meals.[558] If one wants to be strict and mourn for someone that he is not obligated to mourn for, he or she is permitted to do so. In these matters, the usual custom should be followed.[559] Some have written that we do not observe this type of mourning nowadays.[560]

Converts

14. A convert who converted together with his relatives is, according to the law, not obligated to mourn, based on the principle that one who converts is like a newborn child. Because of this, one is not considered to be halakhically related to one's biological relatives.[561] Still, the custom is to be strict and mourn for them. In any event, one is not prohibited from studying Torah during the mourning period, and one should not recite "*Dayan HaEmet*" upon hearing of the biological relative's death.[562]

---

557. *Shulḥan Arukh* ibid.
558. *Bayit Ḥadash*, ad loc., brought in the *Siftei Cohen* and the *Turei Zahav*.
559. *Siftei Cohen*, ad loc. 7.
560. *Pnei Barukh* 9, note 26, in the name of Rabbi Tzvi Pesaḥ Frank, although it is not clear to him whether this was not the custom in Jerusalem only, or everywhere.
561. *Shulḥan Arukh, Yoreh De'ah* 374:5.
562. *Tzror HaḤayim* 5. Rabbi Nebenzahl: In my opinion, if he is suffering, he can make the blessing.

15. A gentile who took upon himself to become Jewish, but who died before immersing in a *mikve* and completing the conversion process, should be eulogized and buried as a Jew.[563]

Death of an infant

16. Parents are not required to mourn for a baby who has died within thirty days of being born. But they are permitted to mourn voluntarily if they wish. If it is established that the infant was born full-term, after nine full months of pregnancy, then the parents are required to mourn, even if the baby only lived for one day.[564]
17. If there are twins of whom one died within thirty days and the other died after thirty days, the relatives do not mourn for the first baby, but are obligated to mourn for the second because the second infant was considered viable.[565]
18. If a baby was born at full-term and lived for more than thirty days but was on a respirator, the relatives are required to observe the laws of mourning since the baby was considered viable.[566] If a baby was born with a life-threatening birth defect, the halakhic

563. *Kol Bo al Aveilut*, p. 190. Rabbi Nebenzahl: In my opinion, this requires further consideration, since, until they have immersed in the *mikve*, they are not Jewish.
564. *Shulḥan Arukh, Yoreh De'ah* 374:8. And the Tosafot wrote (Yevamot 36b) that even if the infant died from falling off the roof or was consumed by a lion (i.e., died in an accident), the parents do not mourn since until an infant has lived for thirty days, and if we do not know for certain that the infant was born after nine complete months, we are lenient and do not require that mourning be observed. Naḥmanides (Moed Katan 20a) wrote that even according to the opinions that the first day of mourning is from the Torah, the parent is still exempt from mourning since there is a doubt as to whether the child was viable, and the person does not have the same anguish and sorrow for them and therefore does not mourn. This is brought in *Pnei Barukh* 9, note 11, and Rabbi Ruza told me the same (he referred to the book *Zikhron Meir* on mourning, which brings different opinions regarding this) and added that they do not observe *aninut* or *kriya* for a child who died in an accident within thirty days after birth. However, today's practice has changed, and it is permitted to perform *kriya* and mourn for a child who dies even within the first thirty days. See the book *KaḤalom Yauf.* Today's practice has changed and there are some couples that prefer to mourn for their babies that died within thirty days after birth. See *KeḤalom Ya'uf* by Rabbi Avraham Stav.
565. *Yalkut Yosef* 14:6.
566. Ibid. 7.

name for this is "*treifa*," and died after thirty days, mourning is observed, despite the fact that the baby's life was extended artificially.[567] Some say not to mourn in this case.[568]

19. If an infant was born prematurely and was in an incubator for more than a month and then died, some say that we count thirty days from the birth and therefore the laws of mourning are required to be observed. Others say that the laws of mourning are not obligatory since it was clear from the beginning that the baby was not viable. The halakha follows this opinion.[569] In any case, the parents are permitted to observe all of the mourning customs for the baby.

Mourning a non-observant Jew

20. Nowadays, we observe the regular laws of mourning for relatives who did not keep Shabbat or the other commandments of the Torah.[570]
21. The laws of *aninut, kriya,* and mourning are not observed for a well-known heretic who has abandoned Jewish practices and has no connection with Judaism. The relatives do not change their clothing, nor do they show signs of sadness or respect for the deceased. However, they should ensure that the deceased is buried in a Jewish cemetery, but preferably on the side.[571]
22. Relatives do not need to observe the laws of mourning if the deceased donated their body to science and gave instructions not

567. Rabbi Nebenzahl: Rabbi Shlomo Zalman Auerbach said that mourning is observed for a *treifa*, as well, if the infant lived for more than thirty days after coming out of the incubator.
568. *Tzror HaḤayim* 4.
569. The debate is brought in *Yalkut Yosef* 14:8. In the footnote, he discusses the explanations for counting from the birth, since the incubator is considered a medical device that aids the baby and is not a continuation of the pregnancy. Rabbi Ovadia Yossef himself is of the opinion that one should not mourn in such a case, since it was clear that the baby was not viable; and this is the opinion of the *Shevet HaLevi* and *Nitei Gavriel* (vol. 1, 126:5). Rabbi Nebenzahl: And that was the opinion of Rabbi Shlomo Zalman Auerbach.
570. *Yalkut Yosef* 14:16, since they are considered wayward children and not heretics against God.
571. *Gesher HaḤayim* 25:4, 1.

to be buried, since the person is in the category of those who left the community and have abandoned all commandments.[572] Some say that the relatives should still observe the laws of mourning.[573]

23. For a person who married a gentile and died without repenting, the relatives should not sit shiva as usual; they should sit only for one hour.[574] Nevertheless, the person should be buried in a Jewish cemetery, and the relatives are responsible for arranging the burial.[575]
24. An apostate should not be buried in a Jewish grave. This is explained in Sec. 45," An Apostate."

SECTION 17: CALCULATING THE DAYS OF MOURNING

Aveilut, mourning, begins immediately after the burial. Hence the shiva, *shloshim*, and twelve-month period of mourning for a parent are all counted from the time of the burial, not the day of the death.

The first day of mourning lasts from the burial until the evening. The governing principle is that part of a day spent in mourning is counted as a whole day. Therefore, if the burial was close to sunset, but the mourners managed to remove their shoes prior to sunset, that is counted as a complete first day of mourning. (As mentioned above, the day of burial is counted as one of the seven days of mourning even if the burial was 13.5 minutes after sunset, and some say even seventeen minutes after sunset.)

This principle also applies at the end of shiva and at the end of *shloshim*.[576] The shiva concludes on the morning of the seventh day, and the *shloshim* on the morning of the thirtieth day. The rule does not apply to the end of the twelve months. The reason is explained in the Key Concepts section, **Part of the Day Is Counted as a Whole Day.**

---

572. Rabbi Ruza told me this in the name of Rabbi Mordekhai Eliahu, based on *Shulḥan Arukh, Yoreh De'ah* 345:5.
573. *Yalkut Yosef* 14:13.
574. *Yalkut Yosef* ibid. 12. Rabbi Yaakov Ariel taught that the relatives should not mourn or say Kaddish for them since they have left the Jewish people (in *Darka Shel HaYahadut BeMavet U'BeAveilut*, p. 358).
575. *BeMar'eh HaBazak*, vol. 3, 65.
576. *Shulḥan Arukh, Yoreh De'ah* 395:1.

Mourning during the Shiva

SECTION 18: TEFILLIN ON THE FIRST DAY

The prohibition against wearing tefillin on the first day of *aveilut* is derived from the prophet Ezekiel who was told, "Wear your splendor upon you" (24:17). This is understood as a specific, one-time instruction to Ezekiel, teaching us that other mourners may not wear tefillin (called "splendor").[577] There are several explanations for this: Out of respect for the tefillin, because the mourner is sunk in pain and anguish that does not befit the splendor of tefillin.[578] Another reason is that when one glorifies oneself by wearing tefillin, it appears that one is not mourning,[579] i.e., because the tefillin represent freedom, glory, and beauty, and these are the opposite of the pain and sorrow of mourning. Our sages related to the difference between "*pe'er*" (splendor) and "*efer*" (ashes), which are comprised of the same letters but have opposite meanings. Tefillin are splendor, unlike mourning which is symbolized by ashes. This is seen in the verse in Isaiah (61:3): "To provide for the mourners in Zion – To give them splendor instead of ashes, the festive ointment instead of mourning, A garment of splendor instead of a drooping spirit." Some say that the reason for the prohibition is because the mourner cannot concentrate on the mitzva of tefillin in the beginning of the mourning period since he is immersed in his grief, and one may not wear tefillin without concentration.[580]

1. The mourner is prohibited from wearing tefillin on the first day of shiva.[581]
2. The first day is the day of the burial, even if this is not the day of the death, because this is the first day of *aveilut*.

577. Moed Katan 15a.
578. Rashi, Ketubot 6b.
579. Rashi, Sukka 25a.
580. *Melo HaRoim*, brought in the *Encyclopedia Talmudit, Aveilut*, note 93.
581. *Shulḥan Arukh, Oraḥ Ḥayim* 38:5.

3. The custom in Jerusalem is that if the burial does not take place on the day the person died, the mourner does put on tefillin, but in private, without making the blessing.[582]
4. If the burial takes place at night, the mourner does not wear tefillin the following morning. If the burial was at twilight (within 13.5 minutes after sunset), then the mourner does wear tefillin the following morning, with the blessing.[583]
5. If the deceased died on Shabbat and the burial takes place on Motza'ei Shabbat, the mourner does not wear tefillin on Sunday.[584]
6. If the burial took place on Ḥol HaMoed, the mourner wears tefillin on the first day after the festival since he has already been comforted during the holiday and his sadness has dissipated somewhat.[585] Where tefillin is worn on Ḥol HaMoed, the mourner wears tefillin from the second day of mourning.
7. When someone is informed of a relative's death within thirty days of the death (known as a "prompt report," "*shmua krova*"), that day is considered like the day of the burial; he does not wear tefillin that day. If he was wearing tefillin when he heard the news, he must remove them. If he heard the news at night, he should not wear tefillin the following morning.[586]
8. If one did not begin observing the laws of mourning on the correct day, whether by mistake or on purpose, he should put on tefillin in his usual manner on the first day of mourning.[587]

---

582. *Yalkut Yosef* 25:1; and, similarly, in *Tzror HaḤayim* 125; *Pnei Barukh* 12, note 8, in the name of Rabbi Shlomo Zalman Auerbach (this is also the opinion of the Maharitatz without any connection to the custom in Jerusalem; this is quoted in *Be'er Heitev, Shulḥan Arukh, Oraḥ Ḥayim* 38:4).

    Rabbi Nebenzahl: And one removes the tefillin immediately after putting them on.

583. *Yalkut Yosef* 25:3; in *Pnei Barukh* (12:6) he writes that one should not make the blessing.
584. Rabbi Nebenzahl: I believe that some disagree and are of the opinion that, in this case, one should put on tefillin in private on the first day and then remove them immediately.
585. *Yalkut Yosef* 42:17.
586. *Turei Zahav, Yoreh De'ah* 402:1 in the name of Maimonides; *Gesher HaḤayim* 18:4, 8.
587. *Kol Bo al Aveilut*, p. 275; *Moed LeKol Ḥai* 17:6–7.

9. If one is informed of a relative's death more than thirty days after the death ("delayed report," "*shmua reḥoka*") one may put on tefillin that day. If the news causes him to cry, he should immediately remove his tefillin.
10. A mourner who has the custom of wearing the tefillin of Rabbenu Tam should wear them during the shiva, as well.[588]
11. The mourner wears a tallit on the first day of mourning.[589]

SECTION 19: THE PROHIBITION AGAINST DOING WORK

Some of the halakhot of mourning concern the prohibition against doing work, which is not the same as the prohibitions on Shabbat and Yom Tov. Rather, it refers to going to work and conducting business during the shiva; work that entails a loss, however, is permitted. This will be explained below. The aim is to disrupt the normal routine that the mourners are accustomed to. It creates a pause, freeing up the mourners to think about the deceased, about the meaning of life, and about one's own life in particular. This pause is an essential part of the emotional process of consolation (as explained above in Sec. 14, "A Conceptual Understanding of the Process of Mourning.")

The prohibition against working is deduced from the verse, "I will turn your festivals into mourning" (Amos 8:10). Our sages learned from the comparison that, just as it is forbidden to work on the seven days of the festival, it is forbidden to do work during the seven days of mourning.[590]

Work to prevent a loss

1. As a rule, work should not be done during the shiva, i.e., mourners do not go to work during that time. Others, including non-Jews, should not do the mourners' work for them.[591]
2. Nevertheless, there is consideration for the damages that could be incurred by the mourners as a result of not working. Therefore, if there is a concern that losses will be incurred ("*Davar haaved*"), it is

588. *Yalkut Yosef* 25:5.
589. *Darkei Moshe, Yoreh De'ah* 388:1 in the name of the Mordekhai.
590. Moed Katan 20a, 21b; *Shulḥan Arukh, Yoreh De'ah* 380.
591. *Shulḥan Arukh* ibid.; *Yalkut Yosef* 16:5.

possible for others to do work on behalf of the mourner during the first three days,[592] and after three days,[593] the mourner can do work himself. If the work cannot be done by others, and in the case of a significant potential loss, some are lenient and allow the mourner to do the work himself, in private, during the first three days.[594]

3. A loss ("*Davar haaved*") is defined as a risk of economic loss, not merely a diminished profit. If there is a special opportunity to make a profit (e.g., at the end of a season or before holidays), it is permitted for someone else to buy and sell for the mourner.
4. Preventing a loss applies not only to a loss for the mourner, but also to damage that could be caused to others.
5. The mourner may handle matters of accounting if it essential to prevent a loss. If necessary, one can check one's account balance and pay bills over the phone or online.[595]
6. A debt may be collected if one is concerned that one will not be able to collect it after the shiva.[596]
7. If the mourner employs others and pays them, this is considered a loss; the employees are allowed to continue working.[597]

Partners

8. In the case of business partners, one of whom is sitting shiva, the partners' business or shop should be closed for seven days; the other partner may do work from his home or in private. Nowadays, especially in cases where this would cause a monetary loss, the

---

592. According to the Rema (*Shulḥan Arukh, Yoreh De'ah* 393:1), part of the third day is regarded as the whole day. *Yalkut Yosef* (16:3) and *Pnei Barukh* (13:2) bring contrary opinions, requiring that three complete days pass before doing work, and this is the decision in *Yalkut Yosef.*

593. In *Tzror HaḤayim* 86, he writes that the mourner can join important business meetings that are held in his house if it is considered something that would incur a loss. According to him, the Ashkenazic custom is to be strict during the first three days and therefore the meeting should be pushed off to after three days, but the Sephardic custom does not distinguish between the first three days and the rest of shiva.

594. Rema, *Yoreh De'ah* 380:5.

595. *Arukh HaShulḥan, Yoreh De'ah* 380:10; *Tzror HaḤayim* 87.

596. *Shulḥan Arukh, Yoreh De'ah* 380:8.

597. *Gesher HaḤayim* 21:2, 3, in the name of *Arukh HaShulḥan.*

custom is to be lenient and to allow the partner to resume business activities after the first three days.[598] According to some opinions, he can do so immediately if there would be a monetary loss.[599]

9. The best option is for the mourner to sell his share for halakhic purposes while in the *aninut* period. It can be sold to the partner or another person for the days of the shiva, so that the mourner removes himself from the business. If possible, this sale should be done even prior to the death. In this case, a sign should be hung at the shop's entrance, notifying that it has been sold and is now run by another person. It is best to consult a rabbi for guidance in the specific case.[600]
10. If the partners have two stores, and each one runs one of the shops and they share the profits, then the other partner can open his store on the first day of mourning.[601]
11. If a business partner dies, the death terminates the partnership and the surviving partner can open the business as usual.[602] Out of respect and sensitivity to the family of the deceased, this should be discussed with them.

Non-employee work, or work for the purpose of a mitzva or communal need

12. If the mourner gave work to non-employees before becoming a mourner, and it is not obvious that the work they perform is for the benefit of the mourner, then the contractor can do the work in his own home; he may not do it in the mourner's home.

---

598. *Gesher HaḤayim* ibid. 7.
599. *Tzror HaḤayim* 90–91.
600. *Gesher HaḤayim* 21:2, 14; *Kol Bo al Aveilut*, p. 324; *Yalkut Yosef* 16:4. Rabbi Ruza told me that if the mourner did not manage to sell his business before the death, it can be sold during the period of *aninut* since it is seldom permitted after the beginning of mourning. However, if the needs of the community would be served by the sale, then it can be sold on the morning of the third day since part of the day is counted as a whole day.
601. *Gesher HaḤayim* 21:2, 8.
602. Ibid. 10, based on *Shulḥan Arukh, Ḥoshen Mishpat* 176:19.

13. A mourner who is a taxi driver may rent out his taxi to another driver and receive a percentage of the earnings.[603]
14. The mourner may do any work for the purpose of a mitzva or for the needs of the community. Thus, one is permitted to fix a Torah scroll if another one is not available and no other scribe can do it. The same is true with regard to a doctor, mohel, or a ritual slaughterer, when there is no one else available. It is permissible for the mourner to leave the house if necessary and to receive reimbursement for one's expenses.[604]
15. If there is one shop in a small town that serves the community's needs, this constitutes another reason to allow it to remain open. As explained above, by selling the shop to someone else.
16. The mourner is permitted to receive a salary for the work days that were missed during the period of mourning since the prohibition is against working, not against receiving a salary.
17. It is permissible to check the price of a tombstone because it is important to act quickly on arranging for the tombstone.[605]

Housework

18. The mourner may do necessary housework, such as preparing food, arranging the house, and washing the floors.[606] Regarding washing clothes and ironing, see Sec. 26, "Laundry and New Clothes."
19. During the shiva, one should not sew, knit, or mend clothing.

SECTION 20: WASHING AND APPLYING LOTIONS AND MAKEUP

Refraining from washing and applying lotions is a sign of mourning that appears in the Tanakh. Yoav, David's army general, said to the clever woman from Tekoa, "Pretend you are in mourning; put on mourning

603. In the *Shulḥan Arukh, Yoreh De'ah* 380:15, he brings opinions that permit and opinions that prohibit, but since today the custom is to hire out taxis, it is permitted. *Yalkut Yosef* 16:22.

604. *Yalkut Yosef* 16:19–20.

605. *Tzror HaḤayim* 88.

606. *Shulḥan Arukh, Yoreh De'ah* 380:22.

clothes and do not anoint yourself with oil; and act like a woman who has grieved a long time over a departed one" (II Sam. 14:2). Washing and applying oil or lotions is refreshing and renews the body. The deceased's body will decompose and return to dust, and so mourners, in thinking of the deceased, should not be involved in taking care of and renewing their own body.

1. The mourner may not bathe his entire body in hot or cold water but may wash parts of the body in cold water. Lukewarm water is permitted since it is not as enjoyable as hot water.[607]
2. Brushing teeth is permitted.
3. The prohibition is against washing for pleasure, and one is therefore permitted to wash oneself to remove dirt. One who is fastidious and will suffer greatly if he does not bathe is permitted to wash, even in hot water, in private. This rule does not apply to one who merely claims that he is fastidious.[608] A post-partum woman or a sick person is permitted to bathe if he or she (or a physician) believes that washing will contribute to his or her recovery.[609] If the need to wash is not pressing, then they should not wash on the first day.
4. Some permit one who regularly goes to the *mikve* on Fridays to go to the *mikve* during the shiva, provided that he is immersing quickly and privately in cold water, when no one else is in the *mikve*, because this is not washing for pleasure.[610]
5. A woman may wash in order to perform a *hefsek tahara* but she should not go to the *mikve* during shiva.[611] If she did go to the *mikve*, she does not need to immerse again after the shiva.[612]
6. If a woman's husband is in mourning, she may go to the *mikve* as usual even though they are not permitted to engage in marital relations.

---

607. *Piskei Teshuvot* 551:48, in the name of the *Shaarim HaMetzuyanim BeHalakha.*
608. *Shulḥan Arukh, Yoreh De'ah* 381:3.
609. *Gesher HaḤayim* 21:3, 1.
610. *Nitei Gavriel,* vol. 1, 105:2, and 114:7.
611. *Shulḥan Arukh, Yoreh De'ah* 381:5.
612. *Kol Bo al Aveilut,* p. 295.

7. If one has to sit shiva for two different relatives over two consecutive weeks, one may bathe one's entire body in cold water at the end of the first shiva.[613]
8. Rubbing lotion on the body for pleasure is forbidden. It is permitted for medical or hygienic purposes, and so one a moisturizing or medicated cream can be applied. One may also use unscented deodorant.
9. A woman who is in mourning should not use makeup during shiva, but a bride in the first thirty days after her wedding, or a girl of marriageable age, may use makeup during the shiva.[614]

SECTION 21: WEARING LEATHER SHOES

The prohibition against wearing leather shoes is derived from Ezekiel the prophet who was instructed not to observe the laws of mourning and was told, "Put your sandals on your feet" (Ezek. 24:17). The context indicates that it is forbidden for mourners to wear sandals. Walking barefoot symbolizes mourning and sadness: "David meanwhile went up the slope of the [Mount of] Olives, weeping as he went; his head was covered and he walked barefoot" (II Sam. 15:30, when he escaped from his son Abshalom).

> And He said: Do not come closer. Remove your sandals from your feet, for the place on which you stand is holy ground. (Exodus 3:5)
>
> He said "Shal," "remove," from the word "Shlila," negative, be careful to negate from him the physical which is represented by shoes, because the physical cleaves to the body like the shoes stick to the foot. (Rabbenu Bahya, ad loc.)

613. *Shulḥan Arukh, Yoreh De'ah* 381:4, and in the *Arukh HaShulḥan* (ad loc. 7) he adds that, after the *shloshim* for the first period of mourning, one can bathe in hot water.

614. *Shulḥan Arukh, Yoreh De'ah* 381:6. The reason is that many visitors will be coming during the shiva, and so she needs to look nice. But she should be careful not to overdo the makeup since it is still a time of mourning.

In the Kabbala, shoes represent connection, both in the sense of them being the meeting point between man and the earth, the physical world, and also that the act of putting on shoes ("*ne'ila*"), involves tying, binding, and closing them up. In the Book of Ruth (4:7), we learn that giving a shoe symbolizes agreement: "Now this was formerly done in Israel in cases of redemption or exchange: to validate any transaction, one man would take off his sandal and hand it to the other. Such was the practice in Israel." During the *ḥalitza* ceremony, when a brother refuses to marry his deceased brother's wife, he does the opposite – he removes his shoe, which demonstrates a sort of protest against connecting himself with her. "Remove your sandals," the instruction given to Moses, also indicates a process of detachment. In that moment, Moses is asked to detach from the physical, to transition to the spiritual level of prophecy. Removing the shoe symbolizes this detachment; it is the opposite of wearing shoes or giving a shoe, which are symbols of connection.

The deceased has been detached from life and has been removed from the world. According to the idea above, death and disconnection are also expressed by the relatives who walk barefoot, without shoes.

1. Mourners may not wear leather shoes. They may wear rubber, cloth, wooden, or plastic shoes. Some permit wearing non-leather sandals even if the straps are made from leather.[615] According to the Kabbala, the mourner should not walk barefoot and should therefore wear socks, or stockings, or non-leather shoes.[616] Some say that because the land in Israel is holy, the mourner can walk barefoot.[617]
2. As mentioned above, mourners remove their leather shoes immediately after the burial. In some cases, at the end of the funeral, the mourners remove their regular shoes and put in a little bit of soil. They wear these shoes until they begin sitting shiva. Some bring non-leather shoes to the cemetery, changing into them after the funeral.

---

615. *Gesher HaḤayim* 21:4, 1; *Yalkut Yosef* 20:2.
616. *Tzror HaḤayim* 114.
617. *Yalkut Yosef* 20:4.

3. A post-partum woman within thirty days after giving birth, or a sick person, is permitted to wear leather shoes if necessary. Also, if someone must walk outside for an urgent reason and it is difficult to do it without leather shoes, he is allowed to wear leather shoes. This certainly applies where walking barefoot would be dangerous. However, today there are perfectly good shoes made from non-leather material, so mourners should make every effort not to wear leather shoes. If they still need to wear leather shoes, they should place some soil inside them and remove the shoes as soon as possible.
4. At a *brit mila* or *pidyon haben*, the parents may wear leather shoes,[618] though some authorities are strict and do not permit this.[619]
5. One may buy non-leather shoes for the shiva if one does not own any, provided that someone else wears the shoes first for a short while.[620]
6. One may polish one's shoes during shiva.[621]
7. Mourners say the blessing *She'asah li kol tzarki* ("Who fulfilled all my needs for me"), even though they do not wear shoes.[622]
8. There is no public mourning on Shabbat, so mourners wear leather shoes on Shabbat. The same is true for Ḥol HaMoed and Purim. Regarding using the deceased's shoes, see Key Concepts, **Property of the Deceased**.

SECTION 22: TORAH STUDY

The prohibition against Torah study during mourning is derived from the prophet Ezekiel who was told, "Moan softly" (24:17). In Y. Moed Katan

---

618. *Gesher HaḤayim* 21:8, 8.
619. *Yalkut Yosef* 20:7; *Tzror HaḤayim* 123.
620. *Yalkut Yosef* 20:3; *Moed LeKol Ḥai* 17:50, in the name of *Yikra DeḤai* and *Nitei Gavriel.* Rabbi Nebenzahl: It is a question whether this brings joy, since the non-leather shoes themselves remind a person of the mourning and sadness. Thus, it may not be necessary for someone else to wear them first.
621. *Yalkut Yosef* 17:13; *Tzror HaḤayim* 85.
622. *Mishna Berura* 554:31 regarding Tisha B'Av. Rabbi Nebenzahl: Some do not do say the blessing on Tisha B'Av and Yom Kippur, when everyone refrains from wearing leather shoes.

(3:5), they derived it from what was said to Job (2:13): "None spoke a word to him" – even words of Torah. There are some exceptions to the prohibition against Torah study, as explained below.

1. A mourner may not be called up to the Torah or study Torah during the shiva since learning Torah gladdens the heart, as the verse states: "The precepts of the Lord are just, rejoicing the heart" (Ps. 19:9). Torah study might also distract a person from his mourning.
2. The prohibition against Torah during mourning applies to both men and women.
3. Mourners should also refrain from studying secular subjects, so as not to become distracted from the mourning.[623]
4. Mourners are permitted to study Torah texts that do not bring joy, such as the Book of Job, the prophecies in the Book of Jeremiah about the destruction of Jerusalem and the Temple, and the laws of mourning. This is limited to learning the texts on a basic level. It does not include delving deeply into the text, which brings joy. Some permit the study of ethics (*mussar*) and *Pirkei Avot*.[624]
5. Mourners can and should study the practical halakhot of mourning. Therefore, during shiva, mourners should still say the blessing for Torah study.
6. Although halakha prohibits even non-mourners from saying words of Torah in the house of mourning,[625] it is customary to be lenient about this, to allow them to say words of Torah, especially if they dedicate it to the merit of the deceased's soul.[626] The Yemenite custom is to limit Torah in the house of mourning to subjects related to mourning (except for the recitation of psalms or the Zohar).[627]

623. *Arukh HaShulḥan, Yoreh De'ah* 384:9.
624. *Yalkut Yosef* 22:2, 5
625. *Shulḥan Arukh, Yoreh De'ah* 378:7, from Moed Katan 23a.
626. *Yalkut Yosef* 22:12.
627. *Hilkhot Teiman, Minhagei Kevura VeAveilut.*

7. It is permitted to recite psalms that are not joyous; any of the psalms may be recited when there is a need, whether in prayer or for inspiration.[628]
8. The mourner may recite the sections of Torah study that are part of Shaḥarit,[629] but should not recite the Sacrifices (*Korbanot*) section or *Pitum HaKetoret*.[630] Some have the custom that mourners do say these sections.[631]
9. If there is someone who has a well-established reputation for diligence in Torah study, some permit this person to study Torah as usual[632] because preventing him from studying Torah will cause him great sorrow.
10. A Torah scholar who answers halakhic questions and teaches others is permitted to do these things during the mourning period if people need him.[633] The source for this is in the Talmud (Moed Katan 21a): "The sages taught: These are the activities that a mourner is prohibited from engaging in… He is prohibited from reading in the Torah, and in the Prophets, and in the Writings, and from studying in the Mishna, in the Midrash, and in the halakhot, and in the Talmud, and in the *aggadot*. But if the public needs him to teach them these things, he need not refrain from doing so. There was an incident that the son of Rabbi Yossi died in Tzippori, and Rabbi Yossi entered the study hall and expounded there for the entire day." Some concluded that one who teaches Torah to children may

628. *Yalkut Yosef* 22:6. Rabbi Nebenzahl: This is not so straightforward, since reciting psalms is also Torah study. When we recite psalms for the sick, we consider it to be like Torah study, and we ask that it be a merit for the sick.
629. *Shulḥan Arukh, Oraḥ Ḥayim* 554:4; *Mishna Berura* ad loc. 7 and 554:1, note 17.
630. Rema, *Oraḥ Ḥayim* 559:4.
631. *Yalkut Yosef* 29:7.
632. *Yalkut Yosef* 22:13 in the name of Y. Moed Katan, ch. 3.
633. *Shulḥan Arukh* and Rema, *Yoreh De'ah* 384:1. And see *Yalkut Yosef* 22:14 in the footnote, that this is how Rabbi Ovadia Yossef himself acted when his father died; he taught his regular class on Motza'ei Shabbat to five hundred people on the subject of the halakhot of mourning.

therefore teach them while in mourning, since this constitutes being needed by the people.[634]

11. If a school teacher is sitting shiva and an urgent educational question arises regarding the teacher's class, the teacher may be consulted. However, the teacher may not grade students' tests or prepare classes during the shiva.[635]
12. For a detailed discussion on Shabbat, see Sec. 31, "Shabbat and Mourning," halakhot 21–22.

SECTION 23: MARITAL RELATIONS

The prohibition against marital relations is derived from David, as it says: "David consoled his wife Bathsheba; he went to her and lay with her" (II Sam. 12:24). This implies that before this, when they were mourning for their son, they were forbidden to have relations.

1. During shiva, mourners are forbidden to have marital relations; other expressions of intimacy are permitted. Nonetheless, it is appropriate to refrain from kissing and hugging, and not to sleep in the same bed.[636] The Targum to Ecclesiastes refers to this in the verse, "A time to embrace and a time to refrain from embracing" – "A choice time to hug his wife and a time to refrain from hugging during the seven days of mourning."[637] Other forms of contact are permitted.[638]
2. If the time to immerse in the *mikve* falls out while a woman is sitting shiva, she does not immerse. If her husband is ill and she

---

634. *Siftei Cohen* and *Turei Zahav, Yoreh De'ah* 384:1. And it seems that this should apply only when no other teacher can be found, *Yalkut Yosef* 22:29. Today, there are many Torah teachers and therefore it need not be permitted. But in the case of a teacher who is one of a kind, it is permitted. And thus Rabbi Ovadia Yossef himself taught his class publicly, since he was unique (see the previous note). But even he chose to teach the halakhot of mourning.
635. *Tzror HaḤayim* 89.
636. *Shulḥan Arukh* and Rema, *Yoreh De'ah* 383:1.
637. Brought in *Ḥidushei Rabbi Akiva Eiger* in the *Shulḥan Arukh* ad loc.
638. *Darkei Tahara*, p. 114.

is the only person who can care for him, she may immerse for the sole purpose of taking care of him.[639]

3. A woman may immerse in the *mikve* if her husband is sitting shiva, but they may not engage in marital relations.
4. The prohibition against marital relations applies on Shabbat, as well.
5. Marital relations on the seventh day and the night preceding it are addressed in Sec. 31, "When the Shiva Ends," and in Key Concepts, **Part of the Day Is Counted as a Whole Day.**

SECTION 24: GREETING PEOPLE

The prohibition against greeting people during mourning is derived from the prophet Ezekiel who was told to "moan softly." "Shalom," the Hebrew word used for greeting others, shares its root with the word "*Shleimut*," "wholeness." The mourners are not whole; they have lost someone dear to them. Therefore, others do not greet them with "Shalom" and they do not greet others with "Shalom." This is the reason that the door of the shiva house is sometimes left open, to prevent someone from greeting the mourners when entering the house.

> Our sages took care to teach that a person should bless another with "Shalom" any time he meets a friend or neighbor or other person. But they wisely understood that this polite behavior is inappropriate in the state of mourning during the shiva, when the mourner is lamenting the loss of a loved one. They thus forbade the visitor from blessing the mourner with "Shalom" and exempted the mourner from greeting those who come to comfort them. For it seems absurd to ask a mourner who has just lost a loved one, "Hello, how are you feeling?" This should not be seen as rejecting social norms or polite habits; on the contrary – it comes to demonstrate the comforters' understanding and sensitivity towards the mourners' painful state.[640]

1. The mourner may not greet people.

---

639. *Yalkut Yosef* 18:10.

640. *Darka Shel HaYahadut BeMavet U'BeAveilut*, p. 123.

2. The *halakha* prohibits saying the word "Shalom," which is one of God's names. Thus, some permit saying "Good morning," etc., without saying the word "Shalom."[641] others do not allow it.[642] One is permitted to bow one's head instead of saying a greeting.
3. Likewise, a phone conversation should not end with the word "Shalom." A different phrase should be used ("See you soon," "All the best," etc.) or words of comfort.
4. During the first three days, a mourner should not greet others, nor reply when others greet him. The mourner may explain to the other person that he is in mourning. During the rest of the shiva, one should not greet others but may reply quietly to their greetings. From the end of the shiva to the end of the *shloshim*, a mourner may greet others, but others should not greet him, and they should certainly not engage in long chats or boisterous conversation.[643]
5. Mourners may give or receive blessings. One may wish a mourner "Mazal Tov" on a festive occasion.
6. One may shake a mourner's hand.[644] Some prohibit this because shaking hands constitutes a kind of greeting.[645] But all agree that if someone extend their hand to the mourner, the mourner can shake it.
7. The mourner should not recite *Kiddush Levana* during the shiva if it would still be possible to do so after the end of the shiva. If he would no longer be able to say *Kiddush Levana* after the shiva, then he may leave his house and recite the prayer, but only the blessing and not "*Shalom Aleiḥem*" or the other additions.[646] Some

641. *Be'er Heitev* 385:2; *Yalkut Yosef* 23:1, 8; *Tzror HaḤayim* 185; *Yesodei Halakha*, p. 188 in the name of Rabbi Shlomo Min HaHar.
642. *Gesher HaḤayim* 21:7, 5; he wrote not to say "Good morning," but permitted other types of greetings.
643. *Shulḥan Arukh, Yoreh De'ah* 385:1.
644. *Pnei Barukh* 16:14, according to *Responsa Har Tzvi* 290; *Yalkut Yosef* 23:11.
645. *Tzror HaḤayim* 92.
646. *Mishna Berura* 426:11; *Shemirat Shabbat KeHilkhata*, vol. 2, 65:36.

permit others to say *Shalom Aleiḥem* to the mourner in *Kiddush Levana.*[647]

8. The mourner may wish "Shabbat Shalom" to others since there is no public mourning on Shabbat. In some places, it is customary to refrain from greeting the mourner with "Shabbat Shalom," and in other places it is not.[648]
9. Mourners do not participate in festive activities during the mourning period. Details are brought later, see Sec. 33, "Mourning During the *Shloshim*: Visiting friends."
10. Gifts should not be given to the mourner since giving gifts is a form of greeting.[649] The rabbis equated sending a gift with saying "Shalom" – both are a way of inquiring after the person. The laws of *mishloaḥ manot* are described later, see Sec. 38, "The Laws of Mourning on Jewish Holidays," halakhot 17–19.

SECTION 25: CELEBRATIONS AND WEDDINGS

1. The mourner should refrain from feeling joy during the shiva. This includes activities that are likely to make him happy, such as holding or playing with a baby.[650] Parents are permitted to take care of their children.
2. In a house of mourning, the person making Havdala at the end of Shabbat skips the introductory verses, which are verses expressing joy. He begins the Havdala from the blessing over the wine.
3. Mourners should not make a *Sheheḥiyanu* blessing over a new fruit during the shiva, unless the fruit will not be available when the shiva is over. However, at a *brit mila* or *pidyon haben,* the

647. *Yalkut Yosef* 23:7.

648. *Tzror HaḤayim* 160; *Shemirat Shabbat KeHilkhata* ibid. 12. In *Gesher HaḤayim* (21:12, 2) he writes that some people are strict and refrain from greeting the mourner on Shabbat during the first thirty days of mourning and some are careful to avoid meeting the mourner so that it not appear to be public mourning on Shabbat. In *Yalkut Yosef* (23:6) he writes that one says "Shabbat Shalom" to the mourner, in accordance with Maimonides' opinion, since this is considered public. This is the custom in Jerusalem.

649. Rema, *Yoreh De'ah* 385:3; *Tzror HaḤayim* 211.

650. *Shulḥan Arukh, Yoreh De'ah* 391:1.

baby's father may make the *Sheheḥiyanu* blessing, even during the shiva. We refrain from saying *Sheheḥiyanu* when it is about the joy of renewal, but it can be recited to celebrate a mitzva that has a set time like a *brit, pidyon haben,* or lighting Ḥanukka candles.

4. The baby's parents may wear festive clothing and shoes at the *brit* or *pidyon haben.*[651] Some do not permit them to wear leather shoes.[652]
5. A father can be called to the Torah on the day of his son's *brit mila;* some advise that he should try to avoid being called up.[653]
6. A father may arrange and participate in a festive meal in his home on the day of his son's *brit mila,* even during the shiva.[654] If there is not enough space in the house, it can be held in the synagogue or elsewhere.
7. If the *brit* was delayed for medical reasons and the reason ceases to apply during shiva, the *brit* should not be postponed due to the mourning.[655]
8. Grandparents who are mourning can attend their grandson's *brit* but should not participate in the meal.[656] See the footnote.
9. After the *brit mila* or *pidyon haben,* the rules of mourning again apply to the mourner.
10. A mourner can serve as mohel or *sandak* during the shiva, and a *kohen* in mourning may redeem his first-born son. Although he is permitted to leave the house for this purpose, he may not wear

651. *Gesher HaḤayim* 21:8, 8.
652. Rabbi Ovadia Yossef in *Responsa Yabia Omer,* vol. 9, *Yoreh De'ah* 42; *Yalkut Yosef* 20:7; *Tzror HaḤayim* (123) writes that the baby's father can wear un-ironed Shabbat clothes but may not wear leather shoes or participate in the meal.
653. *Gesher HaḤayim* 21:8, 8; *Nitei Gavriel* (vol. 2, 24:4) writes that he cannot be called to the Torah.
654. Rema, *Yoreh De'ah* 391:2; *Gesher HaḤayim* 21:8, 6. As mentioned above, the *Tzror HaḤayim* (123) does not permit the mourner to join the meal for the *brit mila* during the shiva.
655. *Yalkut Yosef* 38:22.
656. *Tzror HaḤayim* 124. Rabbi Nebenzahl: It may be that they can participate in the meal according to Rabbi Shlomo Zalman Auerbach. (In answer to a question I put to him, Rabbi Nebenzahl told me that in practice, one can be lenient and allow grandparents to participate in the meal since it is a festive day for them.)

Shabbat clothes or leather shoes and see the footnote, below.[657] Someone who is mourning for a parent is not allowed to change his torn clothing, but those mourning other relatives may change their clothing. The mourner may not leave the house to go to a *brit* in order to receive the honor of escorting the baby to the *brit* (known as the "kvatter").[658] The reason for the distinction is that serving as mohel, *sandak*, or the *kohen* who redeems the child is a mitzva; if the mourner is needed to fulfill the mitzva, he is permitted to leave his house.[659] But escorting the baby to the *brit* is not considered a mitzva, so the mourner is not allowed to leave the house for this purpose. But if the *brit* is in the mourner's house, the mourner can be the kvatter.

11. A boy who becomes bar mitzva while his parents are sitting shiva should be called to the Torah and begin putting on tefillin at the correct time. If there is no Torah scroll in the house of mourning, the parents may go to the synagogue for the service in the boy's honor. But the festive meal should be delayed until after the shiva.[660]
12. Parents of a bride or groom who are sitting shiva are permitted to attend the *ḥuppa* and the wedding, even on the first day of shiva, but they may not participate in the meal or eat there.[661] Only the parents are allowed to go, and not other relatives. The mourner may wear Shabbat clothing. Regarding new clothing, see the next section.
13. A mourner should not go to weddings for the duration of the *shloshim*.

---

657. *Birkei Yosef* 391:1, quoted in *Pnei Barukh* 20:6; *Yalkut Yosef* 38:23. Rabbi Nebenzahl: The law is the same here as it is concerning the child's father, where some allow and some prohibit him to wear leather shoes.
658. *Pnei Barukh* 20:7 in the name of *Sdei Ḥemed*.
659. Rema, *Yoreh De'ah* 393:3.
660. *Moed LeKol Ḥai* 17:121 in the name of *Zikhron Yitzḥak* and *Nitei Gavriel*.
661. *Responsa Igrot Moshe, Yoreh De'ah*, vol. 2, 169. This is because it would be very distressing for them to be absent from their child's *ḥuppa*; but the permission is only given for the parents. In *Yalkut Yosef* (38:17) he writes that after the *ḥuppa*, the parents should return home for the rest of the shiva. Rabbi Yaakov Ruza told me that they may participate in the rest of the wedding but should eat at a side table, not at the table reserved for the parents.

14. Engagement parties ("vort")[662] may be held during the shiva, without a party or a celebration, simply to ensure that the engagement remains intact.
15. For the laws concerning a bride or groom in *aveilut*, see Sec. 51, "A Bride and Groom."

SECTION 26: LAUNDRY AND NEW CLOTHES

The prohibition against laundering clothing is derived from the verse, "Yoav sent to Tekoa and brought a clever woman from there. He said to her, 'Pretend you are in mourning; put on mourning clothes and don't anoint yourself with oil; and act like a woman who has grieved a long time over a departed one.'" (II Sam. 14:2). The implication is that the "mourning clothes" were inferior to other clothing (Moed Katan 15b).

Laundering clothes

1. Mourners may not wash their clothing during the shiva, and they may not wear freshly washed clothing.
2. When necessary, mourners may change underwear and socks during the shiva, as well as dirty clothing if it is bothering them,[663] since the prohibition is against putting on clean clothes for pleasure.
3. When mourning a parent, one should wear the same torn clothing for the entire shiva. If a mourner changes his shirt, he should tear the new one. One does not need to tear the new piece of clothing for other relatives.[664]
4. A woman in mourning may wear clean clothing during her seven clean days, even during the shiva.

---

662. Today, this usually implies declaring a match in such a way that does not carry halakhic significance but that gives public validity to the decision to get married. Engagements as were practiced in Talmudic times were permitted even on the day of death. Nowadays, the halakhic engagement, along with the marriage, is performed at the *ḥuppa*, and so there is usually no practical significance for this. (*Shulḥan Arukh* and Rema, *Yoreh De'ah* 392:1.)
663. *Arukh HaShulḥan, Yoreh De'ah* 389:7; *Gesher HaḤayim* 21:10, 1 in the name of *Pitḥei Teshuva* 389:2; *Tzror HaḤayim* 119.
664. *Tzror HaḤayim* ibid.

5. If something that the mourner is wearing becomes soiled, the dirt can be washed out with water.
6. If someone left a garment at the cleaners and then became a mourner, the cleaner is permitted to clean the garment.[665]
7. The clothing of small children may be washed even if the child is in mourning for a parent.[666]
8. Parents who are mourning should not wash their children's clothing.
9. The family members of a mourner who are not mourners themselves may launder their clothes and wear freshly laundered clothing.
10. The Sephardic custom is to observe the prohibition against laundering clothing only during the shiva.[667] The Ashkenazic custom is to refrain from wearing freshly-laundered clothing until the end of the *shloshim,* unless the garment was already worn by someone else or laid on the ground so that it is no longer completely clean.[668] Since mourning still applies during the *shloshim,* a freshly washed garment should only be worn if one symbolically soils the garment.[669]

New clothing

11. New clothing should not be purchased or worn by mourners. If necessary, a new piece of clothing can be worn after someone else has worn it for two or three days.[670]

---

665. *Shulḥan Arukh, Yoreh De'ah* 389:4.
666. Ibid. 2.
667. Ibid. 1.
668. Rema, *Yoreh De'ah* 389:1. In *Pnei Barukh* (18, note 18), in the name of *HaKerem Shlomo,* he writes that this is the case even if it was placed on the ground or if it gets creased. Also in *Nitei Gavriel,* vol. 2, 10:5. And in *Shulḥan Arukh HaMekutzar, Einei Yitzḥak, Yoreh De'ah* 109:5 it is permitted if the clothing became somewhat dirty on the ground.
669. Rabbi Nebenzahl: I believe that Rabbi Shlomo Zalman Auerbach was strict in this matter.
670. *Gesher HaḤayim* 21:10, 3.

12. New dishes or furniture can be bought only after the *shloshim*, though some permit it after the shiva.[671]
13. The house can be painted even during the *shloshim*.[672]
14. Laws concerning Shabbat are explained in Sec. 31, "Shabbat and Mourning."

SECTION 27: HAIRCUTTING, SHAVING, AND CUTTING NAILS

The prohibition against haircutting is derived from the instruction given to Aaron's children, "Do not let your hair become unkempt" (Lev. 10:6); the context implies that other mourners are forbidden from cutting their hair and must let it grow unkempt (Moed Katan 14b).

Letting one's hair grow and the prohibition against shaving and haircutting are signs of mourning. They convey a certain disregard of physical appearance, a principle that is repeated in several forms in the halakhot of mourning. We pay less attention to the physical body, which will eventually waste away, and focus on the eternal soul. This is also true of how we relate to the deceased: The body has been buried and is no longer with us. Instead, we are interested in focusing on and emphasizing the spiritual part of the person.

Haircutting and shaving

1. A mourner may not shave or get a haircut until the end of the *shloshim*. If a festival falls out in the middle of the shiva, the prohibition of haircutting remains in effect. For a parent, see later, page ???.
2. One may trim a moustache that interferes with eating, even during the shiva.[673]
3. One may comb one's hair during the shiva, even if hairs are pulled out as a result.[674] A woman may shave or cut her hair before going to the *mikve*.

---

671. This is what Rabbi Nebenzahl told me, because there is stringency regarding clothing but not other items.
672. *Yalkut Yosef* 17:14; *Pnei Barukh* 18:12.
673. *Shulḥan Arukh, Yoreh De'ah* 390:1.
674. *Yalkut Yosef* 37:2; the *Tzror HaḤayim* (112) writes that it is permitted to comb one's hair, but it is customary for men not to comb their hair.

4. With regard to cutting hair after the shiva, see Sec. 33, "Mourning during the Shloshim: Haircutting and shaving."

Fingernails

5. Fingernails should not be cut until the end of the *shloshim*, but if they are trimmed in an unusual manner, e.g., with one's hands, teeth, or a knife, it is permitted even during the shiva. One can make a small cut in the nail with nail-scissors and then remove the nail with one's teeth, etc.[675]
6. A broken or cracked nail that is bothersome may be cut.

SECTION 28: SITTING ON A CHAIR

The prohibition against sitting on a chair is derived from the verse in Job (2:13), "They sat with him on the ground." It may also be derived from King David: "At this, David rent his garment and lay down on the ground" (II Sam. 13:31).

1. During the shiva, mourners sit on the ground[676] or on a low chair that is not more than three handbreadths high.[677] An elderly or sick person may sit on a regular chair;[678] some say that women should also sit on regular chairs if sitting on a low chair would be immodest.[679]
2. The mourner does not need to sit other than when people come to comfort him. The rest of the time, the mourners can stand and walk around the house.
3. If the mourner goes to synagogue, he may sit on a regular chair.[680]

---

675. *Yalkut Yosef* 37:8.
676. *Yalkut Yosef* (21:1) wrote that we should allow sitting on tiled floors, despite the Kabbalistic warning not to sit on the ground for fear of evil spirits. However, it is preferable to have a piece of clothing or material separate the person from the ground.
677. According to the *Ben Ish Ḥai,* it is preferable that it should be no higher than one handbreadth (*Tzror HaḤayim,* p. 60).
678. *Tzror HaḤayim* 102.
679. *She'eilat Shlomo,* vol. 1, p. 410.
680. *Yalkut Yosef* 21:3.

4. Even though according to the original halakha, mourners should sleep on low mattresses or on the floor, the custom is to allow sleeping in a bed because people are averse to sleeping on the floor and it can make them unwell.[681]
5. How visitors should sit is addressed in Sec. 11, "Comforting the Mourners," halakha 4.

SECTION 29: LEAVING THE HOUSE

The sages taught: During the first week after his bereavement, the mourner may not go out of the entrance of his house. During the second week, he may go out, but he may not sit in his usual place in the synagogue. During the third week, he may sit in his usual place, but he may not speak. During the fourth week, he is like any other person. (Moed Katan 23a)

1. As a general rule, the mourner does not leave his home for the entirety of the shiva, especially during the first three days. The reason is that the mourner should not mix with other people and become distracted from his mourning. Mourners have no need to leave the house since they are not allowed to work or take trips.[682]
2. Mourners should not go out even for something that is a mitzva, such as a *brit mila*, a wedding, or a funeral.[683] They may attend a funeral after the first three days of shiva.[684]
3. It is customary that mourners do not leave their house to comfort other mourners. Although in the Talmud, it appears that after three days the mourner can go to a house of mourning,

---

681. *Gesher HaḤayim* 20:5, 11; *Yalkut Yosef* 21:5. But in the *Pitḥei Teshuva* (*Yoreh De'ah* 387:2) he brings a strict opinion that does not permit the mourner to sleep in a bed; in *Tzror HaḤayim* (p. 60) it says that the mourner should sleep on a low bed and not in his usual way.
682. *Arukh HaShulḥan* (*Yoreh De'ah* 393:1–4) stresses that this is not forbidden and therefore we can be lenient if necessary.
683. *Gesher HaḤayim* 21:13, 4, based on the Rema, *Yoreh De'ah* 393:1.
684. *Shulḥan Arukh, Yoreh De'ah* 393:1. Although the *Tzror HaḤayim* (99) writes that this is the Sephardic custom only, the *Gesher HaḤayim* (21:13, 4) also wrote that this is the custom, just that the mourner should walk for only four cubits and at some distance from the rest of the people escorting the coffin.

and he should sit with the mourners, not among the other comforters. Nowadays, it is not customary to leave for this purpose.[685]

4. Mourners are permitted to leave their house for a mitzva where they need to physically be present, such as circumcising one's son or attending the funeral of a close relative, or for some other significant reason such as a monetary loss, or to accompany one's wife if she is giving birth. But something that is not urgent, such as a routine doctor's appointment, should be postponed to a later date.[686]
5. If a mourner does not feel well, some say that it is preferable to bring a doctor to the house, even though it may be expensive.[687]
6. If necessary, the mourner may leave the house of mourning and return to his own home to sleep at night.[688] On Friday, the mourner may return home for Shabbat.[689]
7. A woman sitting shiva may go home to care for her children if they need her, but it should be done in a discreet manner.[690]
8. Some allow the mourner to move to a different location in the middle of the shiva to allow visitors to come and offer condolences without having to travel great distances.[691]
9. Even when a mourner is permitted to leave the house, it should be done in a discreet manner, preferably at night or in such a way that he will not run into people. The mourner should be accompanied by someone else (see Key Concepts, **Guarding the Mourner**).
10. Prayer services are held in the house of mourning so that the mourner does not need to leave the house to pray and recite

---

685. *Gesher HaḤayim* 21:13, 1, in a footnote. Although the *Shulḥan Arukh, Yoreh De'ah* 393:1 writes like the Talmud that the mourner can leave after three days, the Rema wrote that this is not the custom and that it is better not to go.
686. *Tzror HaḤayim* 98.
687. Ibid. 97.
688. *Kol Bo al Aveilut*, p. 262; and in *Tzror HaḤayim* (93) he permitted it when absolutely necessary, e.g., if there is no space or if it is very noisy in the house of mourning.
689. *Yalkut Yosef* 33:1–3; *Tzror HaḤayim* 95.
690. *Tzror HaḤayim* 94.
691. *Tzror HaḤayim* 96; *She'eilat Shlomo*, vol. 5, 72. Rabbi Nebenzahl: Rabbi Shlomo Zalman Auerbach was opposed to this.

Kaddish. If there is no *minyan* in the house, the mourner may go to a nearby synagogue. If the synagogue is far away, then after three days have passed, the mourner may leave the house discreetly to go to services. If the mourner would need to pass through a crowd of people in order to do so, he should instead stay home.[692] Some permit the mourner to leave the house in any case in order to pray and recite Kaddish.[693]

11. It is customary for mourners to go to synagogue on Shabbat.

SECTION 30: CHANGING ONE'S SEAT IN SYNAGOGUE

Solomon saw that the observance of loving-kindness was great before the Holy One, blessed be He. When he built the Temple, he erected two gates, one for the bridegrooms and the other for the mourners and the excommunicated. On Sabbaths, the Israelites went and sat between those two gates; and they knew that anyone who entered through the gate of the bridegrooms was a bridegroom, and they said to him, "May He who dwells in this house cause thee to rejoice with sons and daughters." If one entered through the gate of the mourners with his upper lip covered, then they knew that he was a mourner, and they would say to him, "May He who dwells in this house comfort thee."

When the Temple was destroyed, the sages instituted (the rule) that the bridegrooms and mourners should go to the synagogues and to the houses of study. The men of the place see the bridegroom and rejoice with him; and they see the mourner and sit with him upon the earth, so that all the Israelites may discharge their duty in the service of loving-kindness. With reference to them, he says: Blessed art Thou, who giveth a good reward to those who show loving-kindness. (*Midrash Pirkei DeRabbi Eliezer*, ch. 17)

---

692. *Gesher HaḤayim* 21:13, 6.
693. *Responsa Tzitz Eliezer*, vol. 5, *Even HaEzer* 57:8.

1. The mourner changes his usual seat in the synagogue[694] for the duration of the *shloshim*. According to the Ashkenazic custom, someone mourning a parent changes his seat for the entire twelve months. This can be seen as a symbolic, temporary exile, where the mourner leaves his safe, familiar, habitual place, and moves somewhere else. It is considered an additional sign of mourning. The mourner behaves differently in order to express his sadness and to draw attention to the fact that he is in mourning. The source for this is the mishna (Middot 2:2) that describes how mourners go in the direction opposite to the rest of the people:

   All who would enter the Temple Mount entered toward the right and would encircle it and exit through the left. Aside for one to which something has occurred [that he is a mourner], that he would encircle it towards the left.

   > "Why are you encircling towards the left?"
   > "Because I am a mourner."
   > "He who rests in this house should comfort you."

2. The mourner's new seat in the synagogue should be at least four cubits (forearm's length) away from the old one; if this is not possible, a smaller change is acceptable.[695] Some permit a smaller change if it is obvious that the person has changed seats because he is a mourner.[696]
3. The person should not move to a seat that is considered more important.[697]
4. There is no public mourning on Shabbat. Because of this, the Sephardic and Yemenite custom is not to change seats on

694. In the synagogue but not in one's own home, *Gesher HaḤayim* 22:3; *Tzror HaḤayim* (p. 69) wrote that the mourner should change his seat at home, as well.
695. *Gesher HaḤayim* ibid.
696. *Responsa Tzitz Eliezer*, vol. 5; *Even Yaakov* 58:2. Also in *Nitei Gavriel* (vol. 2, 12:9) he wrote in the name of the *Maharam Shik* that one need not move four cubits; the idea is simply to change one's usual seat.
697. *Nitei Gavriel* ibid. in the name of *Maharam Shik*.

Shabbat, while the Ashkenazic custom is to do so only during the *shloshim*.[698]

5. A son may sit in his father's seat after he dies because we assume that the father would have consented and that it demonstrates respect towards the father to have his son sit in his seat after his death (some opinions disagree).[699]
6. The rabbi of a community, whose change of seat would be keenly felt, does not need to change his seat on Shabbat.[700] And some say that this is also true for the *gabbai* or other important persons.[701]
7. Someone who changes his seat due to mourning may continue to sit in his new seat after the mourning period is over.
8. The Yemenite custom is that no one should sit in the deceased's seat for thirty days or three months. Some have the custom that, if the deceased was a prominent person, no one should sit in his seat for twelve months.[702]

SECTION 31: SHABBAT AND MOURNING

Rabbi Yossi ben Ḥalafta would praise Rabbi Meir before the people of Tzippori, that he was a holy and humble man. Once, Rabbi Meir saw mourners on Shabbat and asked after their welfare. They asked Rabbi Yossi, "Is this the person that you praised so much?" He said to them "What did he do?" They told him. Rabbi Yossi said to them, "Do you want to know of his greatness?

698. *Gesher HaḤayim* ibid., according to the *Shulḥan Arukh* and the Rema, *Yoreh De'ah* 393:4. And in *Shemirat Shabbat KeHilkhata* (vol. 2, 65:24) he wrote that the person should change his seat for twelve months, and it also appears in *Tzror HaḤayim* (161) that this is the Ashkenazic custom. The Yemenite custom appears in *Be'er LeḤai Roi* 135, from the books *Anaf Etz Avot* and *Nefesh Kol Ḥai*.
699. *Responsa Tzitz Eliezer*, vol. 15, 41:2; *Yalkut Yosef* 21:10.
700. *Responsa Tzitz Eliezer*, vol. 5, *Even HaEzer* 58:6. In *Nitei Gavriel* (vol. 2, 12:12) he brings an opinion that he should change his seat slightly so that the congregation will learn from him.
701. *BeMar'eh HaBazak*, vol. 3, 67.
702. *Shulḥan Arukh HaMekutzar, Einei Yitzḥak, Yoreh De'ah* 193:5.

> He came to inform us that there is no mourning on Shabbat, as it says: 'It is the blessing of the Lord that enriches, and no sadness can increase it' (Prov. 10:22). 'The blessing of the Lord that enriches' – this is the blessing of Shabbat, and 'No sadness can increase it' – this is mourning (which is not practiced on Shabbat)." (Y. Moed Katan 3:5)

Shabbat is described with the language of delight – "And call the Sabbath a delight" (Is. 58:13) – unlike the festivals, which are defined as a time for joy – "You shall rejoice in your festival…you shall have nothing but joy" (Deut. 16:14–15). This different terminology is significant in the context of mourning.

The holidays are a break from regular routine – a joyful disruption that either breaks up the mourning process or delays it. Holidays and mourning cannot coexist, and so there is no mourning on holidays. When holidays fall out in a time of is mourning, the mourning is either stopped or postponed, as will be explained below.

Shabbat, on the other hand, is the pinnacle of the week – a pause and a time to rise above the other six days. But because it is part of the normal weekly routine, it does not have the same degree of divergence from everyday life that the holidays do. Thus, mourning continues on Shabbat, but only in private.

General rules

1. Shabbat does not curtail the mourning, and it is counted as one of the days of the shiva. Since the seven days of shiva will always include one Shabbat, if Shabbat curtailed the mourning, seven days of shiva would never occur. Furthermore, some of the laws of mourning are observed on Shabbat.[703]
2. If the burial was on Friday and the mourners observed the mourning customs, however briefly, then Friday is counted as one of the days of shiva and the shiva ends the following

703. *Shulḥan Arukh, Yoreh De'ah* 400:1.

Thursday. But if they did not observe any mourning practices before Shabbat, then Shabbat is counted as the first day of shiva and the shiva ends the following Friday. Because laws of mourning are observed in private on Shabbat, it is counted as one of the days of shiva, as described above.

3. If a mourner did not attend the funeral but knew that it was taking place on Friday, if he intended to begin mourning before nightfall, he can count Friday as the first day of the shiva even if he did not actually observe any mourning practices. If he did not know when the burial was but, out of uncertainty, removed his shoes while it was still daytime on Friday, then Friday is counted as the first day of the shiva.[704]
4. Mourning is not observed publicly on Shabbat, but it is observed privately. This includes the prohibitions on marital relations and bathing. Mourners are permitted to wash their hands, face, and feet in preparation for Shabbat. It was mentioned above that washing for pleasure is forbidden, but if the mourner was sweaty or particularly fastidious about personal hygiene, he may bathe quickly in cold or warm water.
5. Mourners wear leather shoes, change their undergarments,[705] and wear Shabbat clothes in honor of Shabbat.

When to get up from sitting on Friday

6. On Friday, the mourner should get up from sitting an hour and a quarter before sunset.[706] Some are lenient and allow the mourner to get up two and a half hours before, based on the time of praying *Minḥa Ketana*. Some require the mourner to wait until close to the time for candle lighting.[707]

---

704. *Gesher HaḤayim* ibid.; *Gilyon Maharsha* and *Pitḥei Teshuva, Yoreh De'ah* 375:1.
705. *Gilyon Maharsha* ibid.; and in *Yalkut Yosef* (34:2) he writes that the mourner should not change undergarments.
706. *Gesher HaḤayim* 21:12, 3.
707. *Yalkut Yosef* 34:1. And this is the Yemenite custom, *Be'er LeḤai Roi* 157 in the name of *Beit Moed* and *Nefesh Kol Ḥai*. Rabbi Nebenzahl: This was Rabbi Shlomo Zalman Auerbach's opinion.

Candle lighting

7. A woman who lights a number of candles based on the number of people in the household should continue to light the same number of candles after the person's death.[708]

In the synagogue

If Shabbat prayer services are being held in the house of mourning, see Sec. 12, "Prayers in the House of Mourning."

8. Mourners go to the synagogue and sit on regular chairs. According to the Sephardic and Yemenite custom, the mourner does not change his place on Shabbat. The Ashkenazic custom is to do so until the end of the *shloshim*.[709]
9. The original custom in Ashkenazic communities was to greet mourners on Friday night before saying the psalm, "*Mizmor Shir LeYom HaShabbat.*" The congregation said, "Go out to the mourner." This saying was meant to comfort the mourners and served as a reminder that public mourning is suspended, beginning at *Kabbalat Shabbat*. In practice, this should only be said where the recitation of the psalm, "*Mizmor Shir LeYom HaShabbat*" is being said before nightfall. In many communities, Shabbat comes in well before this; therefore, many communities do not continue this custom so as not to practice public mourning on Shabbat.[710]
10. Some say that mourners should omit the psalms of *Kabbalat Shabbat* and *BaMeh Madlikin*. Others say that mourners recite *Kabbalat Shabbat* as usual.[711]

---

708. *Tzror HaḤayim* 292.
709. *Gesher HaḤayim* 22:3, based on *Shulḥan Arukh, Yoreh De'ah* 393:4. In *Shemirat Shabbat KeHilkhata* (vol. 2, 65:24), he writes that the mourner should change his place for twelve months. The Yemenite custom is brought in *Be'er LeḤai Roi* 135 from the book *Anaf Etz Avot* and *Nefesh Kol Ḥai*.
710. *Turei Zahav, Oraḥ Ḥayim* 526:1.
711. *Gesher HaḤayim* 20:3, 9; *Shemirat Shabbat KeHilkhata*, vol. 2, 65:13; *Tzror HaḤayim* 162. And in *Yalkut Yosef* (29:15) and *Nitei Gavriel* (vol. 1, 115:5) they write that the

11. In Israel, *kohanim* who are in mourning go up to say the Priestly Blessing on Shabbat.[712] Some say he should not do so on Shabbat. If there is no other *kohen*, or there is only one other *kohen*, then the mourner should go up and make the blessing.[713]
12. The mourner is not called up to the Torah unless he is the only *kohen* or Levite, or if he was called up by mistake,[714] or if he is a groom within the first seven days of marriage.[715] Some say that a person may be called to the Torah if he is observing a Yahrzeit.[716]
13. If a mourner's wife gave birth to a son and their custom was that the father is called up to the Torah on Shabbat, this is allowed, to avoid engaging in public mourning. Some have written that there can be singing for the father, but less than usual.[717]
14. A mourner who is the regular Torah reader may read on Shabbat during the shiva.[718]
15. If a mourner's seventh day of shiva falls out on Shabbat, the Ashkenazic custom is that he may be called to the Torah during Minḥa but not during Shaḥarit. According to the Sephardic custom, some follow the custom of Hebron in which, before "*Barukh SheAmar*," the prayer leader comes to the mourner and recites the verses that mark the end of mourning, "*Lo yavo od shimshekh*" ("Your sun shall set no more"), etc. and thus the

---

mourner should say it as usual. *Nitei Gavriel* writes that one who usually recites Song of Songs before Shabbat can do so after having accepted Shabbat.

712. *Yalkut Yosef* 29:8; *Tzror HaḤayim* 165.
713. *Gesher HaḤayim* 20:3, 5.
714. *Shulḥan Arukh, Yoreh De'ah* 400:1.
715. *Pnei Barukh* 23:27 in the name of *Sdei Ḥemed*. In a place where the custom is to call the groom up for a special portion, they should still do it, the same as with any other groom.
716. *Pnei Barukh* ibid. 25, he writes that he should not go up in such a case. But some do permit it.
717. *Chayim VeḤesed* 13:27.
718. *Responsa Yabia Omer*, vol. 9, 45. However, some prefer that he not read and advise that he should even go to a different synagogue, *Pnei Barukh* 23:23.

mourner concludes shiva; and he can then be called to the Torah, even in Shaḥarit.[719]

16. The *El Maleh Raḥamim* prayer is said after the Torah reading, even if the Shabbat when they are blessing the new moon (i.e., it is a Shabbat when *El Maleh Raḥamim* is usually omitted).[720] Some of these laws have been explained above in Sec. 12, "Prayers in the House of Mourning: Shabbat and holidays."
17. The mourner may lift and wrap the Torah (*hagbaha* and *gelila*) and return the Torah to the Ark.
18. A *Mi Sheberakh* prayer may be recited for the mourner.[721] If the mourner is the *gabbai*, he may call people up and make the *Mi Sheberakh* prayer for them as usual.
19. Mourners may wish others "Shabbat Shalom" on Shabbat since there is no public mourning on Shabbat. There are different customs about whether one should say "Shabbat Shalom" to the mourner. It is said in some places and not in others.[722]

Shabbat meals

20. Mourners recite "*Shalom Aleikhem*" on Friday night, bless their children, and sing *zemirot* as usual, even if there are no other people in the house except for the mourners.[723] Some have the

---

719. *Tzror HaḤayim* 164; *Yalkut Yosef* 34:7.
720. *Magen Avraham, Oraḥ Ḥayim* 284:7.
721. *Gesher HaḤayim* 21:7, 7; *Shemirat Shabbat KeHilkhata*, vol. 2, 65, note 51.
722. *Tzror HaḤayim* 160; *Shemirat Shabbat KeHilkhata*, ibid. 12; in *Gesher HaḤayim* (21:12, 2) he wrote that some are strict during the *shloshim* not to say "Shabbat Shalom" to the mourner. Some are careful to avoid meeting the mourner so that it should not appear to be public mourning on Shabbat. *Yalkut Yosef* (23:6) writes that one should say "Shabbat Shalom" to a mourner following Maimonides' opinion since this is considered something public. This is the custom in Jerusalem.
723. *Kol Bo Aveilut*, p. 281; *Shemirat Shabbat KeHilkhata* ibid. 215; *Tzror HaḤayim* 166; *Yalkut Yosef* 22:10. (My friend Rabbi Shmuel Kedar told me that the source for permitting the mourner to sing *zemirot* at the Shabbat table is *Shibolei Leket*, where he writes to sing *zemirot* in the context of *Pesukei DeZimra* and not as *zemirot*. Since *zemirot* at the Shabbat table are joyous and not a mitzva, it appears that they should not be sung on Shabbat.)

custom not to recite *"Shalom Aleikhem"* and not to bless the children on Shabbat during the shiva.[724]

Torah study

21. Mourners may not study Torah on Shabbat. But if their usual practice is to read the weekly portion twice with the *Targum,* they are permitted to do so.[725] Some permit any regular Torah study that a person usually does on Shabbat.[726]
22. The mourner should not recite *Pirkei Avot* after Minḥa nor *Barkhi Nafshi.* Some permit the study of *Pirkei Avot,* even during the week, if it fosters ethical behavior in the person and engenders fear of Heaven.[727]

After Shabbat

23. After Shabbat, the mourner says *"Barukh hamavdil bein kodesh leḥol,"* removes his shoes, and leads the Maariv prayer.[728] Some write that the mourner should remove his shoes after Maariv.[729]
24. The mourner skips the opening verses in Havdala and begins with the blessings. Some have written that the Ashkenazic custom is to omit the blessing over the spices.[730] The blessing over the spices was instituted because, on Shabbat, one is endowed with an extra soul, elevating the person and makes him glad; the extra soul departs on Motza'ei Shabbat and the person is left feeling

---

724. *Gesher HaḤayim* 21:12, 1; *Pnei Barukh* 23:11–12.
725. *Shulḥan Arukh, Yoreh De'ah* 400:1, *Gesher HaḤayim* 21:12, 1; *Yalkut Yosef* 22:8. But *Tzror HaḤayim* (168) writes that the Sephardic custom is not to read it and that they should catch up on their learning after the shiva.
726. *Arukh HaShulḥan, Yoreh De'ah* 400:6 and 384:3–5. This is based on Y. Moed Katan, that if one strongly desires to learn Torah one may do so. Rabbi Nebenzahl: Not everyone who attends a Torah class strongly desires to learn Torah (is *"lahut"*). One who strongly desires Torah (a *lahut*) refers to one who never wastes time away from Torah study.
727. *Yalkut Yosef* 22:5.
728. Rema, *Oraḥ Ḥayim* 553:2; *Gesher HaḤayim* 20:3, 9.
729. *Yalkut Yosef* 34:8.
730. *Tzror HaḤayim* 170.

sad. The sages established the practice of smelling spices in order to lift people's spirits at the end of Shabbat.

The mourner, however, is occupied with his grief. Even on Shabbat, when there are no external expressions of mourning, the mourner is still without joy in his heart and without the extra soul. And so some say that mourners should omit the blessing over the spices because they do not experience sadness at the departure of Shabbat. The accepted custom is that mourners do make the blessing over the fragrant spices[731] since each person does indeed receive an extra soul due to the special nature of Shabbat, no matter his mental or emotional state.

25. If the shiva ends on Shabbat morning, it is clear that the mourner does not need to sit shiva on Saturday night.

Mourning after the Shiva

SECTION 32: WHEN THE SHIVA ENDS

1. The Sephardic custom is to arrange a meal and Torah study for the merit of the deceased's soul on the night before the seventh day of shiva. Mourners are permitted to leave their house in order to go to the synagogue to hear words of Torah; they may sit on regular chairs.[732] If the last day of shiva is Shabbat, then this is done on Thursday night.
2. After the morning service on the morning of the seventh day, the mourners sit for a short time and have other comfort them. Then the others say to them, "Stand up." The Sephardic custom is to say the verse, "Your sun shall set no more, your moon no more withdraw; for the Lord shall be a light to you forever, and your days of mourning shall be ended" (Is. 60:20); and also the verse, "As a mother comforts her son, so I will comfort you; you shall find comfort in Jerusalem" (ibid. 66:13).
3. After the mourners get up from shiva, they are permitted to do those things that were forbidden to them during the shiva

---

731. *Gesher HaḤayim* 20:3, 10; *Yalkut Yosef* 26:14; *Pnei Barukh* 23:35.
732. *Yalkut Yosef* 35:8.

(besides for shaving, haircutting, and celebration, as will be explained in the next chapter). They may change their torn clothing. The principle is that part of the day is counted as a whole day; and, just as this applies to the beginning of the shiva, it applies to the end of the shiva. At the beginning of shiva, if the burial was close to sunset but the mourners managed to observe mourning however briefly, it is considered the first day of shiva. Similarly, at the end of shiva, even if they sit for a few minutes, it is counted as a full day of sitting shiva.[733] Therefore, if they started the shiva on Sunday before sunset, the mourning ends on Shabbat morning.

4. Some say that if there is a pressing need, the night before the seventh day can also be counted as a whole day.[734]
5. Regarding marital relations, part of the day is counted as a whole day. But some say it is forbidden until nightfall of the seventh day.[735]
6. If no one comes to comfort the mourners, or if it is Shabbat, when people do not come to comfort – then the mourning ends when it would have been possible for people to come and comfort, i.e., shortly after the end of the morning service, or the time when people usually leave the synagogue. The Sephardic custom is that mourning ends on the seventh day after sunrise.
7. If the seventh day falls out on Shabbat, some have the custom not to be called up to the Torah in the morning, only at Minḥa. But if someone did have an *aliya* in the morning, he can rely on the lenient opinions that allow it. See the previous chapter, in

---

733. *Shulḥan Arukh, Yoreh De'ah* 395:1.
734. Naḥmanides, *Torat HaAdam*, p. 215, quoted in the *Tur, Yoreh De'ah* 395. The *Shulḥan Arukh* disagrees with Naḥmanides and agrees with the Maharam of Rotenburg that at least part of the day must first pass; but in extenuating circumstances, we can rely on the lenient opinion. This is explained more fully in the Key Concepts section, **Part of the Day Is Counted as a Whole Day**. The *Gesher HaḤayim* (21:14, 3) writes that one can be lenient in private matters on the night before the seventh day, but the *Tzror HaḤayim* (169) does not permit this since mourning still applies.
735. *Turei Zahav, Oraḥ Ḥayim* 555, and in *Yoreh De'ah* 402:5; *Arukh HaShulḥan, Yoreh De'ah* 395:3; *Shemirat Shabbat KeHilkhata*, vol. 2, 65:10. A couple should not have relations during the day unless it is necessary and only in a darkened room, see *Shulḥan Arukh, Oraḥ Ḥayim* 240:11 and *Even HaEzer* 25:5.

the section, "In the synagogue," about the custom of Hebron, see Sec. 31, "Shabbat and Mourning," halakha 15.

8. It is important to complete shiva in the deceased's home, where shiva was held. If the need arises, it is permitted to complete the shiva in one's own home. For example, if the seventh day is Shabbat and the mourners want to return home on Friday to be with their families, they may do so.[736]
9. It is customary to visit the grave on the seventh day.[737] See later for the prayers said in the cemetery, Sec. 41, "Visiting the Gravesite: The memorial service in the cemetery." The mourners may eat and change their clothing before going to the cemetery.[738]
10. If the seventh day is on Shabbat, mourners go to visit the grave on Sunday. However, if there are mourners who sat shiva in Israel but live elsewhere and they want to return home on Sunday, they may go to visit the grave on Friday.[739] The halakhot of going to visit the grave are discussed Sec. 41, "Visiting the Gravesite."
11. The Yemenite custom is that, when a mourner is called up to the Torah for the first time after finishing shiva, then after saying the last blessing, he adds: "I give thanks to You, O Lord! Although You were wrathful with me, Your wrath has turned back and You comfort me" (Is. 12:1).[740]
12. The halakhot of setting a tombstone are discussed in Sec. 44, "The Tombstone."

SECTION 33: MOURNING DURING THE SHLOSHIM

And the Israelites bewailed Moses in the steppes of Moab for thirty days. The period of wailing and mourning for Moses came to an end. (Deut. 34:8)

According to rabbinic law, a mourner should observe some of the mourning customs throughout thirty days. From

736. *Tzror HaḤayim* 77.
737. Rabbi Nebenzahl: Some do not go to visit the grave.
738. *Yalkut Yosef* 35:5.
739. *Yalkut Yosef* 35:3.
740. *Shulḥan Arukh HaMekutzar, Einei Yitzḥak, Yoreh De'ah* 194:2.

> what biblical passage have the sages derived the number of thirty days? It is written: "She shall mourn her father and mother for a full month" (Deut. 21:13). Hence, a mourner ought to grieve throughout thirty days. (Maimonides, *Hilkhot Avel* 6:1)

Some of the following halakhot repeat what has already been written, but for the reader's convenience, we have grouped the laws into those observed during the *shloshim* and those observed during the twelve-month mourning period. This chapter mostly presents the principles that apply to the *shloshim*; details that do not appear here are likely to be found in an earlier section. For the case of a holiday that falls out during the *shloshim*, additional details are brought in Sec. 35, "Holidays and Festivals."

1. After the shiva, twenty-three days remain until the end of the *shloshim*, the thirty-day mourning period. Some of the laws of mourning are observed during this time.[741]
2. The principle of "part of the day is counted as a whole day" is applicable to the thirtieth day.
3. The *shloshim* are calculated from the day of the burial, not the day of the death.

Haircutting and shaving

4. Mourners should not shave or cut their hair during the *shloshim*.
5. The Sephardic custom is that a woman is permitted to get a haircut after the shiva. According to the Ashkenazic custom, the prohibition on haircutting applies to both men and women.[742]

---

741. Naḥmanides (*Torah HaAdam*, p. 145) brings a section from the Yerushalmi Talmud that derives this from the verse, "Do not let your hair become unkempt" (Lev. 10:6), and a comparison to the nazarite – "The hair of his head being left to grow untrimmed" (Num. 6:5); the standard period of nazarite status (for a "*stam nazir*") is thirty days. This does not appear in our version of the Yerushalmi Talmud.
742. *Shulḥan Arukh, Yoreh De'ah* 390:5. Some make a distinction between coloring and styling one's hair in a salon, which is forbidden during the *shloshim*, and washing and arranging hair which can be permitted during the *shloshim* (*Darka Shel HaYahadut BeMavet U'BeAveilut*, p. 128).

6. If one is mourning for a parent, then this prohibition continues to apply after the *shloshim* until a friend criticizes the mourner's appearance. The idea is that the mourner's hair has become unruly and a friend feels the need to urge him to get a haircut and shave. This is explained in the next chapter.
7. A bride or groom may get a haircut during the *shloshim* even if he or she is mourning a parent.
8. If the *sandak*, mohel, or baby's father is within the *shloshim*, he may not get a haircut on the day of the *brit*. Some permit a haircut for the baby's father.[743]
9. If one needs to shave or cut one's hair for the sake of others, then this is allowed after the shiva. This could apply, for example, to a doctor or someone in a public role, where it would be unacceptable for the person to be unshaven. In this case, one should get a haircut in a private manner.[744]
10. The mourner may not shave during the *shloshim*. However, some are lenient and permit shaving during the *shloshim* for a festive event.[745]
11. Some say that there is room for leniency with shaving because not shaving makes the mourner unkempt and uncomfortable. These opinions hold that one can shave after two or three weeks.[746]
12. One can shave or get a haircut for a medical need, e.g., if one has lice.[747]

---

743. *Yalkut Yosef* 37:7.
744. *Responsa Divrei Aharon, Yoreh De'ah* 44.
745. *BeMar'eh HaBazak*, vol. 5, 94.
746. *Kol Bo al Aveilut* p. 352, based on the reasoning of the *Noda BeYehuda* (141, *Oraḥ Ḥayim*, 14), that since people tend to shave their beards nowadays, they already look disheveled after a couple of weeks, and therefore the appearance of the mourner is deserving of criticism. But he only permits shaving after thirty days, even if the mourner's appearance is deserving of criticism before then. The *Ḥatam Sofer* relied on the *Noda BeYehuda* with regard to a case where a person had consecutive periods of mourning within the *shloshim*.
747. *Nitei Gavriel*, vol. 2, 3:13.

13. If the mourner needs to hide the news of the death from a relative who is ill out of concern that it will worsen his health, he may shave and get a haircut for this purpose.[748]
14. If the *shloshim* ends on Shabbat, some permit the mourner to shave and get a haircut on Friday, (except when mourning for a parent), and some do not permit it.[749]
15. If a holiday falls out during the *shloshim*, the mourner (other than for a parent) may shave and get a haircut on the day before the holiday begins, since the holiday overrides the prohibition against shaving and haircutting.
16. If the *shloshim* ends on the day before a holiday, even one who is mourning for a parent may shave and get a haircut after his appearance has been criticized by a friend.[750] Some permit one who is mourning for a parent to get a haircut on the day before a holiday, even if the holiday occurs on the thirtieth day, and even without one's appearance being criticized.[751] See Sec. 37, "Calculating the *Shloshim* when a Holiday Cancels Shiva: If shiva ended before the holiday."
17. If the last day of *shloshim* falls out between *Shiva Asar BeTammuz* and the week in which Tisha B'Av falls out, the mourner is allowed to shave.[752] But if it ends during the week in which Tisha B'Av falls out, the beard can be trimmed with a blade, not with scissors.[753]
18. If the *shloshim* ends between the first of Iyar and Lag BaOmer, the mourner may shave and cut his hair. Some do not permit this.[754]

---

748. *Nitei Gavriel* ibid. 17.
749. *Shemirat Shabbat KeHilkhata*, vol. 2, 65:43.
750. *Yalkut Yosef* 37:3. And he wrote that in this type of case, Ashkenazic people can also be lenient, even in places where the custom is to wait until the thirty-first day.
751. *Tzror HaHayim* 180.
752. *Mishna Berura* 551:87. But some permit it only up until Rosh Ḥodesh Av, and the *Shaar Tziyun* wrote to be lenient in a case of genuine need.
753. *Shulḥan Arukh, Oraḥ Ḥayim* 551:15.
754. *Pnei Barukh* 19:18, see the sources there.

Cutting nails

19. Nails should not be cut with regular nail-scissors. They may be cut in an unconventional way – with a knife, with one's fingers or teeth, or, according to some, using a nail file.[755] One can start the cut with nail-scissors and tear off the nail by hand.[756]
20. After the first seven days, a woman may have her nails cut by another woman to prepare for going to the *mikve*. If there is no one available to help her, she may cut her own nails.[757]
21. If the thirtieth day is on Shabbat, the mourner may cut his nails on Friday, even if one is mourning for a parent.[758]
22. If the person's fingernails are long, they can be cut in honor of Shabbat.[759]
23. A bride and groom may cut their nails during the *shloshim*, even if they are mourning for a parent.

Bathing

24. Bathing is permitted after the shiva. The Ashkenazic custom is not to bathe for pleasure during the *shloshim*, e.g., going to a swimming pool, but one is permitted to bathe in hot water[760] for cleanliness and certainly for medical reasons.[761] Some say that the Ashkenazic custom in Israel is to allow bathing after the shiva, especially in summertime.[762]
25. A woman goes to the *mikve* according to her regular schedule. She may bathe and prepare for the *mikve* as she normally does.
26. A married woman may bathe normally as needed, so as not to become unattractive to her husband.[763]

---

755. *Tzror HaḤayim* 174; *Moed LeKol Ḥai* 21:20 in the name of *Rav Pealim*.
756. *Yalkut Yosef* 37:8; *Pnei Barukh* 19:5 in the name of *Responsa Shvut Yaakov*.
757. *Shulḥan Arukh, Yoreh De'ah* 390:7. *Tzror HaḤayim* (175) permits her to cut her nails as usual before the *mikve*.
758. *Yalkut Yosef* 37:9.
759. *Gesher HaḤayim* 21:11, 9; *Shemirat Shabbat KeHilkhata*, vol. 2, 65:44.
760. *Gesher HaḤayim* 22:1, 7; *Nitei Gavriel*, vol. 2, 8:2. In *Shemirat Shabbat KeHilkhata* (ibid. 42) he is lenient and allows washing in cold water in honor of Shabbat.
761. *Arukh HaShulḥan, Yoreh De'ah* 381:5.
762. *Tzror HaḤayim* 172.
763. *Shulḥan Arukh, Yoreh De'ah* 381:6.

New and laundered clothing

27. According to the Sephardic custom, mourners can wear freshly laundered clothing after the shiva, but not white garments. According to the Ashkenazic custom, another person should wear the laundered garments before the mourner wears them. Some place the clothes on the ground so that they are not fresh from the laundry, and then the mourner is permitted to wear them.[764]
28. New clothing should not be purchased or worn unless someone else wears them first.[765] Some apply this rule only to a starched white garment, and allow all other new clothing.[766]
29. New underwear and socks may be worn since they are not important garments.

New items

30. A mourner may purchase an electrical appliance or new furniture when necessary, if it is difficult to wait until after the *shloshim*.[767]

Greetings and changing one's seat in synagogue

31. According to the original law, one should not greet mourners during the *shloshim*, but mourners may greet others. However, in practice, the custom is to be lenient like the Rema's opinion[768] since modern-day greetings (e.g., "How are you?" or "How are things?") do not qualify as greetings for halakhic purposes.[769] There is an additional basis for leniency if the mourner might

---

764. *Gesher HaḤayim* 22:1, 3; *Tzror HaḤayim* 173 (but he wrote that this is not a good custom). *Yalkut Yosef* 17:5. Rabbi Nebenzahl: Rabbi Shlomo Zalman Auerbach did not permit this.
765. *Gesher HaḤayim* 21:10, 3.
766. *Yalkut Yosef* 38:3.
767. *Yalkut Yosef* ibid. 4.
768. Rema, *Yoreh De'ah* 385:1.
769. Rabbi Nebenzahl: It is certainly permissible to say, "How are things?"; this is said even in the shiva house. The restriction is only on saying "Shalom."

not know the law and would be offended if he met a friend who did not say "Good morning," "How are you?," etc.[770]

32. One should not give the mourner a gift during the *shloshim* since giving a gift is viewed as a greeting in the halakha.[771] Details regarding the twelve months are brought later. See section, "The Twelve-Month Mourning Period," halakhot 8–9.
33. The Sephardic custom is for the mourner to change his seat in the synagogue during the *shloshim*. The Ashkenazic custom is to change one's seat in the synagogue for the entire year of mourning for a parent.[772]

Celebrations

A mourner who is getting married

34. As a general rule, a wedding should not be scheduled for a time during a bride's or groom's *shloshim*.[773] But if the date for the wedding was set before the relative died, it should not be delayed because of this, even if it was their parent who died. The mourner may get a haircut and shave on the wedding day and during the first seven days after the wedding.[774] One may buy whatever is needed for the wedding. The bride or groom can celebrate as usual at the wedding, with dancing and music.[775]
35. It is permissible to get married after the *shloshim*, even if the bride or groom is mourning for a parent. A man who does not yet have both a son and daughter, and so has not yet fulfilled the the mitzva of procreation, can get married even during the *shloshim*.[776]

---

770. *Tzror HaḤayim* 185. (I have adjusted the phrasing based on Rabbi Nebenzahl's comment.)
771. Rema, *Yoreh De'ah* 385:3; *Tzror HaḤayim* 211.
772. *Shulḥan Arukh* and Rema, *Yoreh De'ah* 393:2; *Tzror HaḤayim* 214; *Yalkut Yosef* 38:5.
773. See *Gesher HaḤayim* 21:9, note 10. In *Nitei Gavriel* (vol. 2, 15:4) he permits setting the wedding date for the day before the thirtieth day.
774. *Yalkut Yosef* 37:6.
775. *Tzror HaḤayim* 182; *Yalkut Yosef* 38:15.
776. *Shulḥan Arukh, Yoreh De'ah* 392:2. But even if someone has not yet fulfilled the mitzva of procreation, it is best that the wedding not be scheduled during the *shloshim* since some only permit it after the *shloshim*. *Tur, Yoreh De'ah* 392.

36. One may remarry his ex-wife during the *shloshim,* but without a festive meal.[777]
37. If a man's wife died, he should not remarry until a cycle of three festivals (Pesaḥ, Shavuot, Sukkot) has passed. The reason is that the joy of the festivals will help ease the pain from the loss of his first wife. If he badly needs help managing his household (for example, if he has small children), he may get engaged immediately and marry after the shiva; but he should only consummate the marriage after the *shloshim.* One who has not fulfilled the obligation of procreation (see paragraph 35) can marry and consummate the marriage immediately after the shiva.[778] Today many authorities are lenient with men who have lost their wives and allow them to remarry after the *shloshim.*[779]
38. A woman may remarry three months after her husband's death. This law does not relate to the rules of mourning but is intended to make sure that we can identify whether the child was fathered by the first husband or the second husband. This law also applies to a woman who has gotten divorced.[780] If she has a newborn baby, she should not get married until the baby is twenty-four months old.[781]
39. Strictly speaking, singles may agree to marry during the shiva, without a party or celebration, for the sake of preserving the relationship.

Participation in weddings and celebrations

40. The mourner may not celebrate during the *shloshim.* For someone mourning a parent, this applies for twelve months. Therefore, during this time, mourners should not attend festive occasions or parties, etc.

---

777. *Arukh HaShulḥan, Yoreh De'ah* 392:1. This is because it is not a joyous occasion since it is permitted even during Ḥol HaMoed, and therefore does not fall under the prohibition on holding a celebration during a festival.
778. *Shulḥan Arukh, Yoreh De'ah* 392:2.
779. Rema ad loc.; *Yalkut Yosef* 38:14. Rabbi Nebenzahl: This is not customary, unless he needs someone to take care of him.
780. *Shulḥan Arukh, Even HaEzer* 13:1.
781. Ibid. 13.

41. A mourner may attend a *ḥuppa* but may not participate in the wedding meal. The joy of a wedding is at odds with the mourner's sadness. Refraining from participating in celebrations is one of the symbols of mourning. This can sometimes cause the bride and groom to be sad that their relatives are not able to participate in the celebration, and therefore if the need arises, some say that a mourner in the *shloshim* or twelve-month period for a parent, may serve at the wedding meal (like a waiter) and eat at a side table.[782] In this way, the mourner can attend the wedding. The mourner may not participate in the dancing. This applies to relatives of the bride and groom.[783] In the case of the bride or groom's siblings, this is permitted even during the *shloshim* for one's parents. If the mourners are the parents of the bride or groom, they may participate even if they are not "servers" at the meal, and they may lead their child to the *ḥuppa*;[784] but they should not dance during the *shloshim*.[785]

There are other circumstances in which we can be lenient when necessary:

- If it is crucial for the mourner to participate in the wedding, e.g., if the mourner's absence would diminish the bride and groom's joy and cause them anguish.[786]
- A grandparent can participate in a grandchild's wedding, even during the *shloshim* for a parent.[787]

---

782. Rema, *Yoreh De'ah* 391:3; *Arukh HaShulḥan* ad loc. 13. In *Tzror HaḤayim* (192) he claims that this is not effective advice today, especially if done only symbolically. Rabbi Nebenzahl: And this was Rabbi Shlomo Zalman Auerbach's opinion.

783. *Gesher HaḤayim* (21:8, 11) only permits this for the relatives. But *Nitei Gavriel* (vol. 2, 20:4) makes no distinction between relatives and others, and if they serve the guests as required, then it is permitted for everyone.

784. *Gesher HaḤayim* 21:8, 11.

785. *Tzror HaḤayim* 183.

786. *Arukh HaShulḥan, Yoreh De'ah* 391:5.

787. *Arukh HaShulḥan,* ibid. 10, he brings the lenient opinions that permits joining a meal that is a mitzva, with the limitation only applying to participating in a festive meal that is not a mitzva. The *Arukh HaShulḥan* writes that we can rely on the lenient opinions when necessary since the halakha follows the lenient opinion in the laws on mourning.

- If the mourner is needed as the tenth man in a *minyan* for the wedding or *Sheva Berakhot,* or to be the "new face" at a *Sheva Berakhot* meal.[788]
- The meal for the *Sheva Berakhot* can be held in the mourner's house if no other venue is available.[789]
- Some permit the mourner to host a meal for *Sheva Berakhot* in his house; others do not.[790]
- Even though mourners may not participate in a *Sheva Berakhot* meal outside of their home, relatives whose absence would be felt (such as the bride or groom's siblings) are permitted to participate on Shabbat so that it not appear to be public mourning.[791]

In these cases, the mourner should not participate in the dancing and should eat at a side table. If the *Sheva Berakhot* is held in the mourner's home, musical instruments should not be played.

42. One may send a wedding invitation to a mourner even if one knows that the mourner will not be able to attend.

Bar mitzva

43. Mourners during the *shloshim* may hold a bar mitzva for their son and wear Shabbat clothes and participate in the meal, but they should not participate in the meal as usual; rather, they should serve the other guests.[792] There should be no music. Some do permit having music.[793]

---

788. *Gesher HaḤayim* 21:8, 7; *Pnei Barukh* 20:21. Rabbi Nebenzahl: But the mourner may not recite one of the *Sheva Berakhot.*
789. According to Rabbi Nebenzahl's instructions.
790. Rema, *Yoreh De'ah* 391:2 is strict and in *Pnei Barukh* (20, note 30) he writes that he heard from some major rabbis to be lenient.
791. *Gesher HaḤayim* 21:8, 12; *Pnei Barukh* 20:16.
792. *Kol Bo al Aveilut,* p. 360.
793. This was the practical advice given to me by Rabbi Nebenzahl. He said that the parents can join in the meal since it is for a festive day for them, and in any case, since they are the hosts, they can also serve the guests.

Celebratory meal after a mitzva is performed (Seudat mitzva)

44. A mourner may participate in events that are a mitzva where no music is being played, such as a *brit mila, pidyon haben,* or celebration of a couple's engagement. They should not participate in the meal[794] but may have the refreshments. Some permit joining the meal and, when necessary, we can rely on these opinions.[795] But if there is live music and dancing, one should not attend.[796]
45. At meals were there is live music, such as at a bar mitzva, the mourner can come during the speeches, wish the family congratulations, and leave. One can attend the reception since, at that point, the atmosphere of celebration has not yet begun.[797]
46. The mourner should not participate in a meal for a *siyum* (a celebratory meal upon finishing any unit of Torah study) unless the mourner himself has completed the learning. The mourner may participate if he does not eat.[798] If light refreshments are served, this is not considered to be a meal.[799] If the *siyum* is in honor of the deceased, the mourner can participate even if he did not complete the Torah study himself.

---

794. Rema, *Yoreh De'ah* 391:2; *Gesher HaḤayim* 21:8, 1; *Pnei Barukh* 20:23; *Tzror HaḤayim* 191. In paragraph 195 he is strict about grandparents participating in a *brit mila* for a grandchild and the festive meal. Even those who are strict would permit participating in a *brit mila* on Shabbat, or a *shalom zakhor,* or a meal for the *Ḥatan Torah,* etc., if their absence would be noticeable, since it would appear to be public mourning (ibid. 196–197). The *sandak* and the mohel may join the meal after shiva for their relatives, and after the *shloshim* if mourning for a parent, *Gesher HaḤayim* 21:8, 10; *Pnei Barukh* 20:14.
795. *Arukh HaShulḥan, Yoreh De'ah* 391:10; *Yalkut Yosef* 38:7. However, in ibid. 25 he writes that many are strict and do not permit participating in a meal, and he wrote not to participate in *Sheva Berakhot.*
796. Rabbi Nebenzahl: This requires further consideration (similar to Rabbi Nebenzahl's guidance in the footnotes above). (His approach is to be lenient in allowing a mourner to participate in a *seudat mitzva* after the shiva even if there is music, but the mourners may not sing and dance.)
797. *Responsa She'eilat Shlomo,* vol. 5, 74.
798. *Nitei Gavriel,* vol. 2, 29:1.
799. *Magen Avraham* 551:10.

47. At meals where a mourner may not participate, the mourner is considered to be eating separately if a table has been set up on the side specifically for him.[800]

Guests on Shabbat

48. On Shabbat and Yom Tov, mourners are allowed to invite guests for a meal, and to be hosted by friends.
49. It is permissible to participate in a *kiddush* at the synagogue after services on Shabbat morning.
50. The mourner can go to a *shalom zakhor* or an *oneg Shabbat* even if words of Torah will be said and Shabbat songs will be sung. Some only permit this if the mourner's absence would be noticeable, so as avoid demonstrating public mourning on Shabbat.[801]
51. The mourner can go to a *Sheva Berakhot* solely to wish "Mazal Tov" to the celebrants, provided that he does not eat there or stay for the dancing.
52. The mourner can participate in a *Seuda Shelishit* even if it continues after nightfall.

Visiting friends

53. According to the Ashkenazic custom, social gatherings are forbidden, and therefore mourners should not invite friends over for a meal during the *shloshim* or the twelve-month period for a parent.[802] If the mourner receives an invitation from friends, some permit him to attend[803] and others do not.[804]
54. Those who need emotional support from their friends may invite them for a meal.[805]
55. A visit from friends is not considered a social gathering.

---

800. *Tzror HaḤayim* 193.
801. *Tzror HaḤayim* 196. In *Shemirat Shabbat KeHilkhata* (vol. 2, 65:65) he brings both the strict and the lenient opinions. *Tal LeBrakha,* vol. 2, 106.
802. Rema, *Yoreh De'ah* 391:2.
803. *Tzror HaḤayim* 184 and 200; *Responsa She'eilat Shlomo,* vol. 5, 74.
804. *Pnei Barukh* 31:14; Responsa from Rabbi Shlomo Zalman Auerbach in *Ohel Hanna* (ibid., p. 459).
805. *Tzror HaḤayim* 200.

56. On Shabbat, one may have guests and may go to others for a meal, as mentioned above.
57. According to the Sephardic custom, there is no limitation on social gatherings that are not a festive occasion.[806]

Parties, conferences, and ceremonies

58. Celebratory parties are forbidden. Kindergarten or school parties that have serious content are permitted.
59. One may participate in a professional conference and attend the meals since this is part of the conference and is done for work purposes.[807]
60. Mourners with children in the army may attend the various army ceremonies since they are attending out of love for their child and not for the entertainment.[808]

Trips

61. A family hike is permitted, but a trip to a fair or amusement park is forbidden. Similarly, going to a quiet restaurant is permitted, but going to a busy public place is forbidden.[809]
62. One may take a trip for reasons of health, family, study, or rest, but not for pleasure.[810]
63. Tour guides or teachers who need to go on trips as part of their work are permitted to do so.[811]

Music

64. The mourner's family does not need to stop listening to music because of the mourner. The same is true for one's co-workers, roommates, or fellow passengers in a car. Mourners do not need to cover their ears, but they should try not to enjoy the music and

806. *Ḥida, Birkei Yosef,* quoted in *Yalkut Yosef* 38:24.
807. *Tzror HaḤayim* 203.
808. Ibid. 202.
809. Ibid. 205; *Responsa She'eilat Shlomo,* vol. 5, 73.
810. *Tzror HaḤayim* 199.
811. Ibid. 205.

should not purposely go to a place where they will hear music.[812] The mourner can listen to music while driving in order to stay awake.[813]

65. A music student or teacher can listen to and teach music after the shiva, provided that it is for the sake of continuing one's studies or profession.[814]

SECTION 34: THE TWELVE-MONTH MOURNING PERIOD

Rav said: A dead person is only forgotten from the heart after twelve months have elapsed. (Berakhot 58b)

When one's mother or father has died, one is considered a mourner for twelve months, out of respect for one's parents. Even after death, the obligation to honor one's parents continues. The child's mourning is connected to the honor and respect that one is obligated to show towards one's parents during their lifetime. This chapter discusses the obligation of mourning; it does not address the obligation to recite Kaddish for eleven months, or the Ashkenazic custom to lead prayers. These have been discussed above.

Some of the laws of the *shloshim* continue to be observed after the *shloshim* have ended:

Haircuts

1. Someone who is mourning for a parent may not get a haircut after the end of the *shloshim* until a friend has admonished him that he needs a haircut.[815] The mourner's spouse or child may tell him to get a haircut; the mourner may invite them to tell him.[816]
2. The admonition about one's appearance is only relevant after the *shloshim*. If no one criticizes his appearance, the mourner

---

812. Ibid. 208; *Responsa She'eilat Shlomo*, vol. 5, 74.

813. *Tzror HaḤayim* 207. Rabbi Yitzḥak Yosef – But it is better not to listen to music, rather to listen to a lecture, etc. One can be lenient only when there is no other choice and there is a concern that the driver might fall asleep.

814. I heard this from Rabbi Mordekhai Eliahu, and it appears that the reason is since such music does not cause joy and can therefore be permitted.

815. *Shulḥan Arukh, Yoreh De'ah* 390:4.

816. *Yalkut Yosef* 37:1; *Tzror HaḤayim* 176.

may wait the *shiur geara*, which is the time when he would be reasonably admonished, and can then shave and get a haircut.[817] Some require that a person actually tell him to shave.[818]

3. The *shiur geara* is thirty days for shaving.[819] For haircutting, it is three months since the last haircut; some are stringent to wait three months from the beginning of *aveilut*.[820] Some wait for the entire twelve months.[821] According to the Sephardic custom, it is enough to wait for two months.[822] Some have permitted mourners, both Ashkenazic and Sephardic, to get a haircut after thirty-one days if the mourner's appearance was criticized.[823]

New clothes and items

4. New clothes should not be bought after the *shloshim* until the next festival and until a friend criticizes the mourner's appearance. The Ashkenazic custom is to refrain from buying new clothing for twelve months.[824] Clothes that must be bought (e.g., if the mourner's clothes were worn out, or if one wants a new garment for the holiday) can be purchased and worn, and the mourner can say the *Sheheḥiyanu* blessing,. A woman who is in mourning may buy new clothing if she feels that she has nothing to wear.[825] The limitations only apply to expensive garments; simple clothing, such as pants and the like, are permitted. If

---

817. *Gesher HaḤayim* 22:2, 1.
818. *Tzror HaḤayim* 178.
819. Responsa of the *Ḥatam Sofer*, quoted in the *Pitḥei Teshuva* in the *Shulḥan Arukh, Yoreh De'ah* 390:4; and see above, in the previous section, the laws of shaving during the *shloshim*. Rabbi Nebenzahl: This requires further consideration (regarding thirty days for shaving.)
820. *Gesher HaḤayim* 21:11, 3.
821. Rema, *Yoreh De'ah* 390:4.
822. *Yalkut Yosef* 37:4.
823. *Tzror HaḤayim* 176, but he requires an actual rebuke and says that it is not enough for the time to pass.
824. *Shulḥan Arukh* and Rema, *Yoreh De'ah* 389:3, 5.
825. *Tzror HaḤayim* 209.

someone else wears the piece of clothing for a short while, then even expensive garments can be worn.[826]

5. If necessary, new shoes may be bought after the *shloshim*.[827]
6. A tallit or another piece of clothing for a mitzva may be bought, since these are not bought for pleasure.
7. The mourner may not buy luxury items but is permitted to buy products that are truly needed. For example, one can trade in one's car for a new one that is safer or more spacious if it is needed to transport one's family.[828]
8. The mourner may buy a gift and give it to the intended recipient, but one should avoid giving items that bring joy. Other items may be given, even though the experience of receiving a gift in inherently joyful.[829]
9. One should not give a mourner a gift since giving gifts is halakhically equated with saying "Shalom."[830] However, if the mourner is getting married during the twelve months, one may give the person a wedding gift. A groom may send a gift to his bride even if she is in mourning.[831] A husband can and should buy his wife a gift in honor of Yom Tov in order to enhance the peace in their home.
10. The mourner may renovate his house during the twelve months of mourning if the renovations are necessary – building, flooring, etc. Redecorating for its own sake is not permitted.[832]
11. It is permissible to move to a new house, if necessary. One can also host a meal, without music, to dedicate the new home.[833]

---

826. *Arukh HaShulḥan, Yoreh De'ah* 389:11.
827. *Nitei Gavriel*, vol. 2, 10:17.
828. *Tzror HaḤayim* 210. Rabbi Nebenzahl: According to the original law, unnecessary items should not be prohibited, but one should limit one's purchases.
829. *Shulhan Arukh, Oraḥ Ḥayim* 696:6, and *Magen Avraham* ad loc.
830. Rema, *Yoreh De'ah* 385:3; *Tzror HaḤayim* 211.
831. *Yalkut Yosef* 23:17–18.
832. *Tzror HaḤayim* 112. Rabbi Nebenzahl: It appears to me that one can be lenient. (See Rabbi Nebenzahl's previous note, above.)
833. *Yalkut Yosef* 38:4; *Ḥayim VeḤesed* 14:12 in the name of *Responsa Imrei Yatziv* by the Rabbi of Sanz.

12. A mourner may plant trees in his garden.[834]

Celebrations

13. Participation in celebrations, parties, and trips was discussed in the previous chapter on the laws of mourning during the *shloshim*.
14. The mourner may participate in a bar mitzva meal if there is no musical ensemble and no dancing.[835]
15. Mourners may not participate in a wedding but may attend the *ḥuppa* if it is held in a different location than the wedding celebration. They can also partake of the wedding dinner if they serve at the meal.[836]
16. Mourners may participate in their son's or daughter's wedding and in the *Sheva Berakhot*. The siblings of the bride and the groom may also participate if their absence would upset the bride or groom.[837]
17. A wedding should not be postponed due to the parents being in the twelve-month mourning period; on the contrary, the wedding should be held as soon as possible.[838]
18. It is preferable for a person who is in mourning not to join their spouse if they are attending a wedding. However, if the peace in their home would be adversely affected by this, they may go together.[839]
19. A rabbi may perform a *ḥuppa* within the year of his mourning, but he is not permitted to participate in the meal, nor in the dancing and rejoicing after the *ḥuppa*.[840]
20. If parents instructed their children not to avoid celebrations during the year after their death, the children may follow the

---

834. *Tzror HaḤayim* 213.
835. Responsa of Rabbi Shlomo Zalman Auerbach in *Kuntras Ohel Ḥanna* at the end of *Pnei Barukh*, p. 429.
836. *Gesher HaḤayim* 22:2, 6.
837. *Tzror HaḤayim* 187–189.
838. *Yalkut Yosef* 38:18.
839. *Igrot Moshe, Yoreh De'ah*, vol. 1, 255.
840. *Tzror HaḤayim* 190; see also *Yalkut Yosef* 38:21.

parents' instruction after the *shloshim*.[841] Since mourning for an entire year is specific to parents, if the parents relinquished this honor, their wish should be followed. (See Key Concepts, the **Mitzva to Fulfill the Deceased's Wishes.**) They should let it be known that this was the parent's wish, so that it does not appear as though they are doing something wrong.

21. A mourner may invite guests for Shabbat.[842] Mourners may be hosted by others on Shabbat if they have been invited.[843]
22. A mourner may participate in a class reunion on Shabbat during the year of mourning.
23. A student may participate in sports activities and school trips but should not participate in singing, dancing, or celebrations.[844]

Changing one's seat

24. The Ashkenazic custom is for a mourner to change his seat in the synagogue for the twelve months; but on Shabbat, after the *shloshim* have ended, one does not change seats.[845]

Defining the period of mourning

25. The mourning period for a parent is defined as twelve months. Therefore, even during a leap year, mourning lasts for twelve months.
26. The twelve months are counted from the day of the burial.[846] There are some opinions that say it is from the day of the death.[847] The principle of "part of the day is counted as a whole day" is not employed for the twelve-month period; one counts

841. *Siftei Cohen, Yoreh De'ah* 344:9; *Yalkut Yosef* 41:3.
842. Rabbi Nebenzahl: I disagree with this, unless they are people who need a place for Shabbat, and the same applies to being invited for Shabbat.
843. *Tzror HaḤayim* 201.
844. *Tzror HaḤayim* 204.
845. *Gesher HaḤayim* 22:3.
846. *Mishna Berura* 568:8, following the opinion of the *Siftei Cohen* and *Masaat Binyamin*; *Yalkut Yosef* 40:4.
847. *Tzror HaḤayim* 88 (following the opinion of the *Turei Zahav*).

until the end of the last day of the twelve months.[848] The reason for this difference is that for shiva and *shloshim,* we count a certain number of days and can thus apply the rule that part of the day is counted as a whole day. For the twelve-month period, however, we count months, and thus the rule is not applicable.[849]

27. The Ashkenazic custom is to observe some of the laws of mourning on the first Yahrzeit as well as on future Yahrzeits.[850]
28. It is customary that when mentioning one's mother's or father's name during the first twelve- month period, the mourner says, "*Hareini kaparat mishkavo/mishkava,*" "I am the atonement for him/her." And when the mourner mentions the parent in writing, he also writes this phrase using the acronym "HK'M". The reason and explanation for this custom can be found in Key Concepts, ***Hareini Kaparat Mishkavo/Mishkava.*** After twelve months, one says "*Zikhronam livrakha,*" "May their memory be a blessing."[851] The mourner may say "*Zikhronam livrakha*" during the twelve months as well, but after twelve months one should not say "*Hareini kaparat mishkavo/mishkava.*" This is because the wicked are said to be judged in hell for only twelve months.[852]
29. There is a set time for mourning, and our sages disapproved of one who offers condolences after twelve months:

Rabbi Meir said: One who finds another in mourning after twelve months and speaks to him words of consolation, to what may this situation be likened? To a person who broke his leg and it healed, and afterward a physician found him and said to him: Come to me, for I will break it a second time and then I will heal it, so that

848. *Shulḥan Arukh, Yoreh De'ah* 395:3.
849. *Turei Zahav* ad loc. 2 in the name of the *Terumat HaDeshen.*
850. Rema, *Yoreh De'ah* 395:3 and end of 391.
851. *Shulḥan Arukh, Yoreh De'ah* 240:9.
852. *Siftei Cohen* ad loc. 13; *Yalkut Yosef* (39:4) writes that one can be stringent and say it even after twelve months.

you may know how good my medicines are and how well they work. (Moed Katan 21b)

Mourning on Jewish Holidays

SECTION 35: HOLIDAYS AND FESTIVALS – ENDING THE MOURNING PERIOD IF MOURNING PRACTICES WERE OBSERVED BEFORE THE HOLIDAY

This chapter discusses mourners who buried a relative shortly before the onset of a holiday and observed some of the laws of mourning, even if only briefly.[853]

Our sages said: "The coffin yields before a bride" (Ketubot 17a). They wanted to illustrate a principle and did so by giving the example of a funeral procession that is coming down a road from one direction at the same time that a bride and her entourage are coming from the other direction, on the same road. The two processions must not intermingle because it would be inappropriate to have the two emotional extremes confront each other – the depths of pain and sorrow on the one hand, and the height of joy on the other. One of these processions must step aside and let the other pass, undistracted. It is truly difficult, emotionally, to do such a thing, since both of these events hold deep emotional significance. The question is, who should move aside? Who has the right of way?

The sages established the rule: "The coffin yields before a bride." The funeral procession is rerouted to a different path to allow the bride's entourage to proceed unfettered in its joyful celebration.

Beyond relating to this specific case, the sages established a general principle: Joy should be enhanced and strengthened even when sorrow and grief is present. Life must go on, and with joy.

Similarly, with regard to national mourning, the sages taught that when a person paints his house, he should leave a small square unpainted

853. In Moed Katan (19a–b) and *Avel Rabati* (7:1), different opinions are presented as to how long mourning has to be observed before the holiday in order for the holiday to curtail the mourning period. The halakha follows the opinion that even if mourning was observed for a very short time, the festival curtails the mourning; *Tur* and *Shulḥan Arukh, Yoreh De'ah* 399.

opposite the entrance to commemorate the destruction of the Temple. This conveys the same principle – despite our mourning for the Temple, we continue to marry, to build our homes, and to make them beautiful. Amidst all this, one should leave a small corner to remember the Temple's destruction and this should be done in a noticeable spot so that we do not forget. But the principle is to continue our lives and celebrate the establishment of a new house and home.

The distinction between mourning on Shabbat and mourning on holidays was addressed in the introduction to the section on the halakhot of mourning on Shabbat: The holidays express an outpouring of joy: "You shall rejoice in your festival…you shall have nothing but joy." Therefore, the advent of a holiday stops the mourning, and if the burial is on the holiday itself, the mourning is delayed and only begins once the holiday is over.

The obligation to be joyful on the festival overrides mourning. There are two reasons for this: One is because the halakha chooses to give precedence to celebration over sorrow in a case where they clash with one other (as explained above). The other reason is that the mitzva of rejoicing on the holiday is a public, communal mitzva; the halakha puts this ahead of sorrow, which is of a personal nature. A Kabbalistic explanation for the holiday curtailing the shiva and *shloshim* is that the holiday prevents the divine judgment of the soul.[854]

What does "holidays" refer to?

1. "Yom Tov" is a term used in connection with the festivals mentioned in the Torah: The three pilgrimage festivals – Passover, Shavuot, and Sukkot – as well as Rosh HaShana and Yom Kippur, which are treated as festivals in the context of mourning.[855] These are to be distinguished from Ḥanukka and Purim – rabbinic holidays – whose laws are different and will be explained separately.

854. *Responsa Ḥatam Sofer, Yoreh De'ah* 348 (quoted in *Pnei Barukh* 27, note 1); *Tzror HaḤayim*, p. 98.
855. *Shulḥan Arukh, Yoreh De'ah* 399:6.

Holidays as opposed to Shabbat

2. In the context of mourning, a holiday differs from Shabbat in a number of ways:
   - The holiday cuts short and cancels the shiva if the mourners observed the laws of mourning before the holiday. That is to say, if someone buried a relative before the holiday began and managed to observe even some of the laws of mourning, e.g., removing one's shoes, then the festival cuts the shiva short and ends it.
   - The festival cuts short and cancels *shloshim* if the shiva ended before the holiday began.
   - If the relative died on the holiday itself or if the mourners did not manage to observe any laws of mourning before the holiday, the mourning is delayed until after the holiday. In such a case, the days of the holiday are not counted as days of shiva, but they are counted as days of the *shloshim*.[856]

What is considered having "observed mourning"?

3. If the mourners did not manage to observe any of the laws of mourning before the holiday, or if the person died on the holiday – then the holiday does not cancel the shiva. However, mourning is still observed in private matters.[857] The mourners begin counting the shiva after the holiday. This is explained later, see Sec. 49, "Receiving Notice of a Death," halakha 11.
4. Even if the mourner only observed mourning in private, this still cancels the shiva. For example, if one learned of a relative's death on a Shabbat preceding a holiday and observed mourning in private (as ones does on Shabbat).[858]

---

856. *Shulḥan Arukh, Oraḥ Ḥayim* 548:1; *Gesher HaḤayim* 23:1, 1–2.
857. Rabbi Nebenzahl: According to Maimonides, private mourning is not observed on the holiday.
858. *Shulḥan Arukh, Yoreh De'ah* 399:1, 402:10.

5. If the mourner could not observe mourning due to weakness or illness, but knew of the relative's death, the holiday cancels the shiva.[859]
6. If a person begins the Yom Tov early, prior to sunset, and then found out that their relative died and was buried, they may observe mourning for a few moments and then the holiday will cancel the shiva.[860]
7. If someone died on the day before a holiday and the relatives gave the body to gentiles to perform the burial, because they were concerned that they might not be able to do it themselves before the holiday – mourning begins once the body has been taken out of the city and can no longer be seen by the relatives. If this is shortly before the festival and they observe mourning, then the holiday cancels the shiva, even if the burial takes place on the holiday itself.[861]
8. If someone is in Israel and a relative dies and will be buried in the Diaspora (west of Israel), if the person in Israel observed mourning for a short time before the onset of the holiday in Israel, he need not continue to sit shiva despite the fact that the burial did not yet occur.[862] See Sec. 47, "Delayed Burial."

When to stop the mourning

9. In order to allow the mourners to prepare for the holiday, they are permitted to stop observing the customs of mourning a short time before the holiday begins,[863] e.g., the mourner may bathe in hot water before sunset; that is when all the other customs of mourning cease, as well.[864] Some Sephardic Jews wait until dark, unless the holiday falls out on Shabbat in which case they allow bathing before nightfall.

---

859. *Mishna Berura* 548:53.
860. *Yalkut Yosef* 42:3.
861. *Shulḥan Arukh, Yoreh De'ah* 399:14.
862. *Nitei Gavriel,* vol. 1, 133:15.
863. *Mishna Berura* 548:42; *Gesher HaḤayim* 23:3, 1; *Tzror HaḤayim* 228 and 230.
864. *Shulḥan Arukh* and Rema, *Yoreh De'ah* 399:5; *Siftei Cohen* ad loc. 14; *Gesher HaḤayim* 23:3, 1; *Shemirat Shabbat KeHilkhata,* vol. 2, 65:45.

10. All mourning customs are suspended on Passover eve after midday because it is considered a holiday.
11. On Erev Yom Kippur, the mourner may bathe and immerse in the *mikve* close to nightfall, even before praying Minḥa;[865] he can then go to Minḥa in the synagogue.[866] He may also sit on a regular chair to eat the meal before the fast.[867]
12. If no one can build a sukka for the mourner, he may build it himself. The same is true for purchasing the four species (lulav and etrog).[868]

Holidays that are close together

13. If a holiday falls out during the shiva and a second holiday falls out during the *shloshim*, the first holiday cancels shiva and the second holiday curtails *shloshim*.[869] This is explained further in Sec. 37, "Calculating the Shloshim when a Holiday Cancels Shiva." Mourning for all relatives besides parents ends at this point; for a parent, the limitations of the twelve-month mourning period remain.

Shabbat on the day before a holiday

14. If someone dies on Friday, and that Shabbat is the day before a holiday (i.e., the festival begins on Motza'ei Shabbat), some permit the mourner to bathe on Friday before nightfall, in honor of the holiday.[870]
15. For someone mourning for a relative other than a parent, if the *shloshim* is cancelled by a holiday and the mourner did not shave on the day before the holiday, he may not shave

865. *Mishna Berura* 606:25.
866. *Darkei Moshe, Yoreh De'ah* 384:3.
867. *Pitḥei Teshuva* 387:1.
868. *Nitei Gavriel,* vol. 1, 122:2.
869. However, in the *Tur, Yoreh De'ah* 399 he brings opinions that do not allow for applying two leniencies to one mourner, i.e., that one holiday annuls shiva and another annuls the *shloshim*. But the halakhic consensus here is to be lenient; this is the accepted practice, see *Beit Yosef* ad loc.
870. *Siftei Cohen* ad loc. 16.

during Ḥol HaMoed since he could have shaved before the festival began. But if the last day of shiva was on Shabbat and the holiday began on Motza'ei Shabbat, he can shave during Ḥol HaMoed since there was no opportunity for him to shave before the holiday.[871]

Washing clothes

16. When a holiday occurs during the shiva, clothes may be washed during Ḥol HaMoed since they could not have been washed before the holiday, because the person was still in mourning.[872]

Moving up the memorial service

17. For those who have the custom to hold a memorial service on the last night of shiva, and the shiva has been shortened because of the holiday, the memorial service should be moved up and held the night before the end of shiva, i.e., the night before the eve of the holiday.

Fast of the Firstborn

18. During the shiva period, a mourner who is a firstborn should not leave the house to attend a *siyum*, which would exempt him from the Fast of the Firstborn. Rather, he may exempt himself from the fast by giving charity.[873]

Memorial candle

19. If a holiday cancels the shiva, one should still leave a candle burning in memory of the deceased for the full seven days.[874]

---

871. *Shulḥan Arukh, Oraḥ Ḥayim* 548:8; *Gesher HaḤayim* 23:3, 4.
872. *Tzror HaḤayim* 228.
873. *Yalkut Yosef* 43:4. And in *Ḥazon LaMoed* (13:29) he writes that the person doing the *siyum* may come to the mourner's house. Rabbi Nebenzahl: Some say that he should fast.
874. *Mishna Berura* 548:3. Rabbi Nebenzahl: But they should not put the candle where meals will be taking place during the holiday.

SECTION 36: HOLIDAYS AND FESTIVALS – DELAYING MOURNING IF THE DEATH OCCURRED ON A HOLIDAY OR IF NO MOURNING WAS OBSERVED BEFORE IT BEGAN

If a person died on a holiday, or if the mourners did not have a chance to observe mourning before it began, they begin to observe the mourning practices only after the holiday is over.

If someone has died on Yom Tov

1. The halakhot for such a case are largely similar to those that apply when someone has died on Shabbat. See Sec. 5, "Caring for the Dying and Deceased: Shabbat."
   For the laws of *aninut* on Shabbat and Yom Tov, see Sec. 6, "Pre-Burial Phase of Mourning (*Aninut*): Shabbat."

Burial on a holiday

The funeral

2. As a general rule, burials are not performed on Yom Tov.[875]
3. Burial may be performed on Ḥol HaMoed. Before the funeral, mourners change into regular, weekday clothing and perform *kriya* as explained below, and after the burial they change back into holiday clothing.
4. Eulogies are not delivered on Ḥol HaMoed.[876]
5. *Tziduk HaDin* is not recited. The Sephardic custom is to say *Tziduk HaDin*.[877] See Sec. 7, "Arrangements for the Funeral and Burial: *Tziduk HaDin* – Acceptance of God's Judgment."
6. After the funeral, the attendees form two rows as usual, for the mourners to walk in between, but the mourners do not remove their shoes.

---

875. *Shulḥan Arukh, Oraḥ Ḥayim* 526:1. In Israel, although the funeral could be performed by gentiles, this is a rare occurrence. Outside of Israel, one should find out what is customary, as it differs from place to place.
876. *Shulḥan Arukh, Yoreh De'ah* 401:1. Rabbi Nebenzahl: It is permissible to eulogize a scholar in the presence of the deceased, as discussed earlier.
877. *Shulḥan Arukh* and Rema, *Yoreh De'ah* 401:6.

Kriya

7. *Kriya* is not performed on Yom Tov; it is postponed until after Yom Tov. In some communities, the custom is to perform *kriya* on Ḥol HaMoed for all relatives. The custom in Jerusalem is that one does *kriya* on Ḥol HaMoed only for a parent, and for other relatives, *kriya* is delayed until after the holiday.[878]
8. All relatives make the *Dayan HaEmet* blessing on Ḥol HaMoed.

The meal of condolence

9. The *seudat havraah*, meal of condolence, is not eaten on Yom Tov.[879] The Sephardic custom is to have this meal on the night after the holiday since that is when the mourning begins, but the Ashkenazic custom is not to have this meal because the mourning was delayed.[880]
10. On Ḥol HaMoed, the meal of condolence is eaten while sitting on regular chairs.[881] Hard-boiled eggs which are usually eaten at this meal are not eaten. Some say that the custom in Jerusalem is that only those mourning a parent should have the meal of condolence. (See Key Concepts, ***Minhag Yerushalayim* – Customs of Jerusalem.**)

Mourning customs that are observed on holidays

11. On holidays, private mourning is observed; the mourner may not bathe for pleasure nor have marital relations. Some allow a woman who is in mourning to go to the *mikve* if her designated night falls out during Ḥol HaMoed and to have relations before the mourning begins.[882] The Yemenite custom follows

---

878. In *Gesher HaḤayim* (4:24) he brings four opinions on the question of doing *kriya* on Ḥol HaMoed; he writes that in a place where there is no set custom, *kriya* should be done by all relatives. See also *Shulḥan Arukh, Oraḥ Ḥayim* 547:6.

879. *Shulḥan Arukh, Yoreh De'ah* 401:4.

880. *Shulḥan Arukh* and Rema, *Yoreh De'ah* 378:11; *Gesher HaḤayim* 20:2, 11; *Yalkut Yosef* 13:13; *Tzror HaḤayim* 73.

881. *Shulḥan Arukh, Oraḥ Ḥayim* 547:8, 401:4.

882. *Yalkut Yosef* 19:1 and 42:8; based on Maimonides' opinion that mourning is not observed at all during the festival, and this includes private mourning. He permitted this specifically if there is a case of urgency, such as a concern that the husband

Maimonides, who says that laws of mourning are not observed at all during Ḥol HaMoed, even in private, except for the forming of rows after the burial.[883]

12. A *kohen* in mourning should not perform the Priestly Blessing.[884] See Sec. 12, "Prayers in the House of Mourning," halakha 9. Some do go up to make the Priestly Blessing on Shabbat during the shiva. In Jerusalem, it is the custom that some *kohanim* recite the blessing even on weekdays during the shiva.
13. The mourner may learn Torah[885] since there is no greater example of an unrecoverable loss than this, even though there are some who forbid it. On Hoshana Rabba night, mourners may join in the Torah study so as not to appear to be mourning in public.[886]
14. One may bathe in honor of the last day(s) of Yom Tov and change one's undergarments.[887]
15. Work that would otherwise incur a loss and is thus allowed on Ḥol HaMoed, is allowed for mourners.[888]
16. When seven days have passed since the burial, even though the mourning has not finished, work may be performed by others in the mourner's home, even if there is no risk of incurring a loss. The Yemenite custom is to refrain from work for the entire shiva since they did not observe mourning at all during the holiday.[889]

Comforting the mourners

17. Even though mourners do not sit shiva during Ḥol HaMoed, relatives and friends may comfort them.[890]

---

will not be able to control himself and may waste seed. This rule also applies if the husband is the mourner.

883. *Be'er LeḤai Roi* 145 in the name of *Shtilei Eitzim* and the Maharitz, *Beit Moed* and *Nefesh Kol Ḥai.*
884. *Magen Avraham* 128:66.
885. *Gesher HaḤayim* 23:1, 4; *Yalkut Yosef* 42:9.
886. *Tzror HaḤayim* 224; *Yalkut Yosef* ibid. 10, in the name of the rabbis of Jerusalem.
887. *Gilyon HaMaharsha, Yoreh De'ah* 389:1.
888. *Gesher HaḤayim* 23:1, 4; however, *Shemirat Shabbat KeHilkhata* (vol. 2, 65:38) permits the mourner to work only if no one else can do the work on his behalf.
889. *Be'er LeḤai Roi,* ibid.
890. *Shulḥan Arukh, Yoreh De'ah* 399:1; *Tzror HaḤayim,* p. 100.

Prayer services

18. Hallel is recited in the services held at the house of mourning since public mourning is not observed. The mourner recites Hallel, as well.[891]
19. The mourner does not change his place in the synagogue even in places where the custom is to change one's seat on Shabbat.

Memorial candle

20. A memorial candle may be lit on Ḥol HaMoed, even though the mourning only begins after the festival.[892]
21. A memorial candle should not be lit on Yom Tov unless someone will benefit from the light.[893] The sages permitted the use of fire on holidays for the sake of cooking or for some other benefit. A memorial candle does not give pleasure or benefit to a person, and therefore it should not be lit on Yom Tov, unless one derives some type of benefit from it. Thus, if someone forgot to light it before Yom Tov, he may light it somewhere where he is studying or eating, and it will provide more light. It is appropriate to light the candle in the synagogue since there is a mitzva to add more light in the synagogue.[894]

After the holiday

22. When the mourning has been postponed and has begun after the holiday is over, tefillin should be worn on the first day of mourning. This is because the height of the mourner's sadness has already passed over the course of the holiday;[895] the mourner has also observed some of the laws of mourning already, during the holiday. In this case, the first day of mourning is not quite as intense as the usual first day of grieving.[896]

---

891. *Pnei Barukh* 28:20 in the name of *Mishmeret Shalom*.
892. *Gesher HaḤayim* 20:1, 2.
893. *Shulḥan Arukh, Oraḥ Ḥayim* 514:5; *Bei'ur Halakha* ad loc. s.v. "*Ner shel batala.*"
894. *Yalkut Yosef* 40:45.
895. Ibid. 42:17.
896. *Gesher HaḤayim* 18:4, 11.

23. If the last day of Passover is a Friday, and the shiva begins after Passover, then Shabbat is counted as the first day of shiva. The shiva ends the following Friday morning.[897]

Second day of Yom Tov in the Diaspora

24. It has become common custom not to mourn on the second day of Yom Tov (in the Diaspora), even if it is the day of the death and the burial.[898]
25. The second day of Yom Tov is counted as one of the days of shiva even though mourning is not observed.

SECTION 37: CALCULATING THE *SHLOSHIM* WHEN A HOLIDAY CANCELS SHIVA

Principles of calculation

1. If the burial took place during Ḥol HaMoed, the days of Ḥol HaMoed are counted as days of the *shloshim*, even though the shiva began after the festival. The reason being that some of the laws of mourning were observed during the festival, such as limitations on ironing, haircutting, new clothing, celebration, and marital relations.[899]
2. If the shiva concluded before the holiday, then the onset of the holiday cancels the *shloshim*. This is true even when shiva has ended on the day before (i.e., the eve of) the holiday, because part of the day is counted as a whole day – the beginning of that day ends the shiva, and the rest of the day is considered the beginning of the *shloshim*. And thus the holiday cancels the *shloshim*.[900]

Rules of calculation for each holiday

3. If mourners sat shiva before Passover began, however briefly, the time is counted as seven days. This time is counted as

897. *Yalkut Yosef* 42:18.
898. *Shulḥan Arukh, Yoreh De'ah* 399:13; unlike what is written in *Oraḥ Ḥayim* 548:3. *Yalkut Yosef* 42:25. And see the reason in Key Concepts, **Is Mourning a Rabbinic or Torah Commandment?**
899. *Shulḥan Arukh, Yoreh De'ah* 399:1.
900. *Shulḥan Arukh* ibid. 3.

the seven days of shiva since the holiday cuts the shiva short. Together with the seven days of Passover, this comes to fourteen days; these are counted toward the *shloshim*. And so, after Passover, the mourners count another sixteen days until the end of the *shloshim*. (This is true for Israel; in the Diaspora, it would be fifteen days instead of sixteen because of the second day of Yom Tov.) The *shloshim* end on the morning of the seventh of Iyar.[901]

4. Similarly, on Shavuot, after the holiday is over, *shloshim* is observed for another sixteen (or fifteen) days since the time before the holiday is considered seven days and the holiday itself is also counted as seven days. The *shloshim* ends on the morning of the twenty-second of Sivan.
5. If mourning was observed even for a short time before Rosh HaShana, then *shloshim* is only observed until Yom Kippur; Yom Kippur ends the *shloshim*.[902] If the burial was on the third of Tishrei (The Fast of Gedaliah), Yom Kippur also ends the *shloshim* since the last day of shiva (which falls out on Erev Yom Kippur) is also counted as a day of *shloshim*.
6. If the mourners observed any mourning customs before Yom Kippur, however briefly, the *shloshim* ends with the onset of Sukkot.
7. If they observed some mourning customs before Sukkot, then that period of observance is counted as seven days and, together with the days of Sukkot, it is considered fourteen days (in Israel; and fifteen in the Diaspora because of the second day of Yom Tov). Shemini Atzeret is counted as seven days, so together this comes to twenty-one days. After the festival, the mourners need to observe nine more days, and the *shloshim* will end on the morning of the first of Ḥeshvan.

---

901. In the *Shulḥan Arukh* (*Yoreh De'ah* 399:7), he counts according to the Diaspora, where two days of Yom Tov are observed, but in Israel sixteen days are added. *Gesher HaḤayim* 23:2, 7.
902. *Shulḥan Arukh* ibid.; *Gesher HaḤayim* ibid.

8. If the burial was on Ḥol HaMoed Sukkot, Shemini Atzeret does not curtail the mourning. According to the Sephardic custom, Shemini Atzeret is considered one day of the *shloshim*; some of the Ashkenazic authorities count it as seven days of the *shloshim*.[903]

If shiva ended before the holiday

9. If the seven days of shiva have ended before the holiday, even on the morning before the holiday begins, then the holiday cancels all of the customs of *shloshim*. All mourners may bathe in hot water, launder and iron their clothing, and cut their nails.[904] Those mourning a relative other than a parent may get a haircut, shave, and bathe close to the evening, after Minḥa, and in cases of necessity, after midday. On the morning before Passover, it is preferable to shave and/or have one's hair cut before midday.[905]
10. If the last day of shiva was on a Friday and there is a holiday beginning on Motza'ei Shabbat, it is permissible for mourners (other than those mourning a parent) to get a haircut and shave before Shabbat in honor of the holiday. If they did not get a haircut before Shabbat, they may not do so during Ḥol HaMoed, since they had the opportunity to do it before the holiday. But they may get a haircut after the holiday because the *shloshim* has ended.[906]
11. If the seventh day of the shiva is on Shabbat and there is a holiday beginning on Motza'ei Shabbat, the mourner may not get a haircut on Friday. In this case, he is permitted to get a haircut

903. *Shulḥan Arukh, Yoreh De'ah* 399:2; and in *Siftei Cohen* and *Turei Zahav* ad loc. In the *Mishna Berura* (548:4), he writes that Shemini Atzeret is considered one day. And in *Gesher HaḤayim* (23:2, 12) he writes to consider it seven days only in the case of an urgent need. *Yalkut Yosef* 42:19.
904. *Arukh HaShulḥan, Yoreh De'ah* 399:13. And this is according to the Rema, who was strict regarding washing after the shiva (381:1); the *Shulḥan Arukh* (ibid.) always permits washing after the shiva.
905. *Shulḥan Arukh* and Rema, *Yoreh De'ah* 399:3; *Mishna Berura* 148:31.
906. *Shulḥan Arukh, Yoreh De'ah* 399:3; *Gesher HaḤayim* 23:2, 5.

during Ḥol HaMoed, since he could not have cut his hair before the holiday.[907]

12. Someone mourning a parent may not cut his hair or shave until thirty days have passed since the burial. After thirty days, someone must admonish him that he needs to get a haircut and shave. The holiday does not cancel the prohibition on cutting hair, even after *shloshim,* until someone criticizes the mourner's appearance.[908] Some are lenient and allow the mourner to get a haircut after *shloshim* on the day before a holiday, even if no one has criticized his appearance.[909] As explained above, if the mourner has waited long enough for someone to have criticized his appearance, i.e., that his hair is long and disheveled, he may shave and get a haircut even though no one actually criticized him. Some permit shaving a beard when necessary, even during the *shloshim* on the day before the holiday, after someone has criticized the mourner's appearance.[910]
13. If someone is mourning a parent whose *shloshim* ends during Ḥol HaMoed and a friend criticizes the mourner, the person may cut his hair and shave during Ḥol HaMoed.[911]

SECTION 38: THE LAWS FOR THE MOURNER ON JEWISH HOLIDAYS

Rosh HaShana and Yom Kippur

1. During shiva, mourners may not leave their home to recite *Seliḥot* in the synagogue; rather they should say *Seliḥot* on their own home or arrange to have a *minyan* in their house. However, on Erev Rosh HaShana, when many *Seliḥot* are recited, the mourner may leave the house to go to synagogue.[912]

---

907. *Shulḥan Arukh,* ibid.
908. *Shulḥan Arukh, Oraḥ Ḥayim* 548:9, *Yoreh De'ah* 399:4.
909. *Tzror HaḤayim* 180.
910. *Yalkut Yosef* 42:22; the reason is explained in *Yabia Omer,* vol. 1, *Yoreh De'ah* 25.
911. *Yalkut Yosef* 22:23.
912. *Shulḥan Arukh, Oraḥ Ḥayim* 581:1; and *Tzror HaḤayim* (101) permits the mourner to leave the house to recite *Seliḥot* without this distinction.

2. During the *shloshim* or the twelve-month period, a mourner should not blow the shofar or serve as the prayer-leader in the High Holy Day services, unless he has a permanent position, or if no one else can do so.[913] The Yemenite custom is that mourners may blow the shofar or lead services on Shabbat and holidays during the twelve-month mourning period.[914]

Sukkot and Shemini Atzeret

3. The mourner is obligated to sit in the Sukka.[915]
4. According to the Ashkenazic custom, someone within the twelve-month period of mourning a parent (or during *shloshim* for other relatives) should not participate in the *Hakafot* around the synagogue with the lulav on Ḥol HaMoed.[916] This is because it says, "And you shall rejoice before God for seven days" (Lev. 23:40); this refers to the *Hakafot*, encircling the synagogue.[917] The mourner may participate in *Hakafot* on Yom Tov and Hoshana Rabba. There are opinions that say that one can participate in *Hakafot* every day.[918] Some have written that the mourner is obligated to participate in *Hakafot* with his lulav as usual and that there is no distinction made between the Ashkenazic and Sephardic custom.[919]
5. At a *Simḥat Beit HaShoeva* (the Water-Drawing Celebration), the mourner may join in the recitation of *Shir HaMaalot* but not in the dancing.
6. The mourner can participate in Torah study on Hoshana Rabba night as usual, even if his relative died during Sukkot.[920]

---

913. *Gesher HaḤayim* 23:4, 1–2. *Yalkut Yosef* (43, Purim, 3) writes that the Sephardic custom is to be lenient. The mourner may not blow the shofar while having someone else make the *Sheheḥiyanu* blessing, because this would constitute public mourning.
914. *Shulḥan Arukh HaMekutzar, Einei Yitzḥak, Yoreh De'ah* 390:6.
915. *Shulḥan Arukh, Oraḥ Ḥayim* 640:5.
916. Rema, *Oraḥ Ḥayim* 660:2.
917. *Mishna Berura* ad loc. 9.
918. *Gesher HaḤayim* 23:3, 7.
919. *Tzror HaḤayim* 234, unlike the Rema.
920. *Yalkut Yosef* 22:24 in the name of the rabbis of Jerusalem.

7. On Simḥat Torah, according to the Sephardic custom, mourners may join the dancing if seven days have passed since the death. The Ashkenazic custom is that mourners can do *Hakafot* with the Torah scroll but not participate in the dancing.[921]
8. Someone in the twelve-month period of mourning may be honored as *Ḥatan Torah* or *Ḥatan Bereshit.* If he was already designated to receive this honor and his relative died on Sukkot, he can still receive it to avoid showing signs of public mourning.[922] Some have written that if the person became a mourner during Sukkot, he should go to another synagogue and someone should be given the honor instead of him.[923]

Ḥanukka and Purim

9. Ḥanukka and Purim do not cancel mourning, and the days of Ḥanukka and Purim are counted as days of shiva. However, there is a difference between Ḥanukka and Purim, as explained below.

Ḥanukka – The following laws relate to the shiva period.

10. The laws of mourning are observed on Ḥanukka. Mourners may make the *Sheheḥiyanu* blessing on the first night in their home. They may not make the blessing in the synagogue because the blessing said in the synagogue is made in the name of the community; everyone still has a personal obligation to make the blessing at home.
11. A mourner may lead prayer services on Ḥanukka but should not be the prayer-leader for Hallel. Hallel is not recited in the house of mourning. The people praying there should recite it afterwards at home.[924] Some say that the congregation does recite Hallel in the house of mourning and that only the mourner omits it.[925]

921. *Gesher HaḤayim* 23:3, 7; *Tzror HaḤayim* 235.
922. *Yalkut Yosef* 22:23 and 38:27.
923. *Pnei Barukh* 29:11.
924. *Magen Avraham, Oraḥ Ḥayim* 131:10.
925. *Mishna Berura* 683 and *Shaarei Teshuva* ad loc. In *Gesher HaḤayim* (20:3, 7) he quotes opinions that the mourner himself should say Hallel in private.

Purim – The following laws relate to the shiva period.

12. On both days of Purim, mourning is not observed in public, but is observed privately – by refraining from marital relations and bathing.[926] The Yemenite custom is that all of the laws of mourning are observed on Purim.[927]
13. Mourners must fulfill all of the mitzvot of Purim: Megilla-reading, *mishloaḥ manot,* gifts to the poor, and the Purim meal.
14. *Kriya* may be done on Purim, but after the funeral, the mourners change their clothing so as not to engage in public mourning.
15. The meal of condolence (*seudat havraah*) is eaten without hard-boiled eggs.[928]
16. Mourners may wear festive clothing and leather shoes but must limit their celebratory activity.
17. The mourner is obligated to send *mishloaḥ manot*; it is customary to send one simple package in order to fulfill the mitzva.
18. The Ashkenazic custom is for people not to send *mishloaḥ manot* to the mourner, but one may send it to the mourner's spouse and children. If someone sent *mishloaḥ manot* to the mourner, he may send one back, in return.[929] Some permit sending *mishloaḥ manot* to a mourner who has finished the *shloshim,* even within the twelve-month period for a parent.[930] The Sephardic custom is to send *mishloaḥ manot* to the mourner as usual.[931]

---

926. The *Shulḥan Arukh* (*Oraḥ Ḥayim* 696:4) writes that all the laws of mourning are observed on Purim, but in *Yoreh De'ah* (401:7) it is written that only private mourning is observed on Purim. The Rema in *Oraḥ Ḥayim* follows this latter opinion, as does the *Mishna Berura* ad loc., *Gesher HaḤayim* (23:3, 9), and *Tzror HaḤayim* (236).
927. Following the opinion of Maimonides (*Mishneh Torah, Hilkhot Avel* 11:3), *Be'er LeḤai Roi* 157, from the Maharitz and *Beit Moed* and *Shem Tov.*
928. *Yalkut Yosef* (43, Purim, 1) writes that the custom in Jerusalem is only to serve this meal on Purim for someone mourning a parent, like on Ḥol HaMoed.
929. *Tzror HaḤayim* 237.
930. *Gesher HaḤayim* 21:7, 10; based on the Rema, *Yoreh De'ah* 385, that in a place where the custom is to greet mourners on Shabbat, people may send *mishloaḥ manot* to mourners after the *shloshim.* Rabbi Nebenzahl: And some do not have this custom.
931. *Yalkut Yosef* 23:16.

19. If the mourner is poor, it is permissible and commendable to send gifts and charity on Purim.
20. On the night of Purim, it is preferable for mourners to have a *minyan* arranged in their home for praying and hearing the Megilla. If this is not possible, the mourner may go to the synagogue. On Purim day, mourners may go to the synagogue, even if they could have arranged for a *minyan* in their house. However, on Shushan Purim (or on the fourteenth of Adar where Shushan Purim is observed), the mourner may not go to synagogue to pray.
21. The mourner may read the Megilla for the congregation,[932] but someone else should recite the *Sheheḥiyanu* blessing. Some permit the mourner to recite the *Sheheḥiyanu* blessing because the mourner is also obligated in the Megilla and if he was to read it in private, he would have to make the blessing.[933]
22. Even though there is no public mourning on Purim, one may come and comfort the mourners on Purim.[934]
23. The laws concerning *Purim Meshulash* (the "triple Purim") in Jerusalem are explained in the footnote.[935]
24. If Purim falls out on the last day of mourning, mourners may go to the gravesite without having other people join them for a *minyan*.[936]

---

932. *Mishna Berura* 696:12.

933. *Mishna Berura* 692:2; *Pnei Barukh* 29:21, in the note.

934. Since even on a festival it is permissible to comfort them; *Shulḥan Arukh, Yoreh De'ah* 399:1.

935. Where Shushan Purim is observed: When the fifteenth of Adar (Shushan Purim) falls out on Shabbat, since the Megilla cannot be read on Shabbat, it is read on Friday; on Shabbat, the Torah reading is for Purim; the meal and *mishloaḥ manot* are done on Sunday. This is called *Purim Meshulash* (the triple Purim) since the celebration covers three days. According to those who are of the opinion that mourning is not observed on Purim, in a year of *Purim Meshulash* this is the case on Friday. But regarding Sunday, some say it is like Purim itself and there is no public mourning (Rabbi Shlomo Zalman Auerbach) and some say that mourning should be observed (Rabbi Elyashiv and Rabbi Ben Zion Aba Shaul). Some say that the laws of mourning should be observed other than sitting on the ground (Rabbi Grossberg) and some say that mourning is observed for the entire day except for during the meal (Rabbi Moshe Sternbokh). And see *Mikra'ei Kodesh* (Rabbi Moshe Harari) 16:10, 26.

936. *Gesher HaḤayim* 23:3, 9.

25. A musician who is in the twelve-month mourning period for a parent may play music in honor of Purim, or for the *seudat mitzva*.[937]

Passover

26. On the eve of Passover, mourners are not served a meal of condolence after the time that it is prohibited to eat *ḥametz*.
27. The mourner is obligated to lean during the Seder but should try to do so in a way that is different than usual.
28. Mourner say Hallel on Seder night.

Yom HaAtzma'ut

29. All the laws of mourning are observed on Yom HaAtzma'ut.[938]

Shavuot

30. On Shavuot night, a mourner may learn the Tikkun if that is his usual practice.

Tisha B'Av

31. The mourner may leave his house on Tisha B'Av morning to go to the synagogue. If it is after the first three days of shiva, he may also go at night. The mourner does not need to change his seat since everyone is considered a mourner on Tisha B'Av.[939]
32. The mourner may be called to the *haftara* on Tisha B'Av morning since the *haftara* in Shaḥarit involves passages from the woeful prophecies in the Book of Jeremiah, but not at Minḥa. However, in practice, it is better for him not to read it.[940]

---

937. *Yalkut Yosef* 43, *Purim* 8.
938. Rabbi Moshe Maimon, in "*Hilkhot Yom HaAtzma'ut VeYom Yerushalayim*," p. 341.
939. *Shulḥan Arukh, Oraḥ Ḥayim* 559:6 and *Mishna Berura* ad loc. Rabbi Nebenzahl: Sitting on the ground is itself a change of seat. The mourner should change his seat at Minḥa because everyone else sits on regular chairs.
940. *Yalkut Yosef* 22:20–22.

SECTION 39: THE MOURNER AS PRAYER-LEADER ON FESTIVE DAYS

1. It is customary for mourners not to lead prayers on Shabbat or holidays,[941] including Rosh HaShana and Yom Kippur, and even for Minḥa or Maariv or *Pesukei DeZimra*[942] since God's attribute of justice hovers over mourners. However, if there is no one else capable, the mourner is permitted to lead the prayers.[943] The Sephardic custom is that mourners may lead prayers, including on Rosh HaShana and Yom Kippur.[944]
2. If the mourner is the regular cantor, he may lead services on Shabbat, holidays, and High Holy Days, if no one else is capable. This applies even in a situation where the relative died during the holiday and the mourning has been postponed until after the holiday. Some are strict in this case, allowing a mourner to lead the prayers only if the holiday occurred after the shiva and has cancelled the *shloshim*.[945]
3. In this matter, the laws for Ḥol HaMoed are like those of Yom Tov.
4. On Rosh Ḥodesh, Ḥanukka, and Purim:[946] The Ashkenazic custom is that a mourner may lead services at Minḥa and Maariv and may lead Shaḥarit up until Hallel, while someone else leads for Hallel and *Musaf*. The Sephardic custom is that a mourner may also lead the prayers for Hallel.[947] Some prefer that the mourner not lead Shaḥarit services on Rosh Ḥodesh;[948] some prefer that the mourner not lead services on any of these days.[949]

---

941. Rema, *Yoreh De'ah* 376:4; *Shemirat Shabbat KeHilkhata*, vol. 2, 65:27.
942. *Gesher HaḤayim* 23:4, 1.
943. *Magen Avraham, Oraḥ Ḥayim* 581:4; *Mishna Berura* ad loc. 7; *Siftei Cohen, Yoreh De'ah* 376:14.
944. *Yalkut Yosef* 29:5.
945. *Gesher HaḤayim* ibid. 3.
946. Rabbi Nebenzahl: Rabbi Shlomo Zalman Auerbach did not permit mourners to lead services on Purim.
947. *Tzror HaḤayim* 217.
948. *Mishna Berura* 581:7.
949. *Kuntras Maamar Kaddishin*, quoted in *Bei'ur Halakha, Oraḥ Ḥayim* 132.

5. The Ashkenazic custom is that a mourner may lead services for *Seliḥot* even during the shiva. The Sephardic custom is that mourners do not lead services or *Seliḥot* during the shiva, unless no one else is capable.[950] Some wrote that even according to the Ashkenazic custom, the mourner should not lead *Seliḥot* or services on Rosh HaShana, since God's attribute of justice hovers over him and it is not appropriate for him to serve as prayer-leader.[951]
6. A mourner may lead *Seliḥot* after shiva is over.[952]
7. It is customary that a mourner may lead services on days when *Taḥanun* is omitted.[953]
8. If the mourner has the custom to lead services on a relative's Yahrzeit and the Yahrzeit falls out on a Shabbat when he has concluded shiva for a different relative, the person may lead services since there is no public mourning on Shabbat even if the last day of his shiva falls out on that Shabbat.[954]

Yahrzeit, Visiting the Grave, and Memorial Service

SECTION 40: ANNIVERSARY OF THE DEATH – YAHRZEIT

> "A good name is better than precious oil, and the day of death than the day of one's birth." When a person is born, they count until his death; when he dies they count his life. (Ecclesiastes Rabba 7:4)

The date

1. The Yahrzeit is the date of the death and not the date of the burial.[955] Although the laws of mourning are counted from the

---

950. *Tzror HaḤayim* 157.
951. *Pnei Barukh* 29:2 in the name of *Matei Ephrayim*. In a footnote, however, he quotes the *Noda BeYehuda* that there is no source to prevent the mourner from leading the prayers during the Ten Days of Repentance, even during shiva.
952. *Mishna Berura* 581:7.
953. *Kuntras Maamar Kaddishin*, quoted in *Bei'ur Halakha, Oraḥ Ḥayim* 132.
954. *Gesher HaḤayim* 23:4, 8.
955. If the burial was three or more days after the death, some Ashkenazim observe the first Yahrzeit on the date of the burial and in subsequent years, observe the

day of the burial, the Yahrzeit customs (such as holding a memorial service, fasting, and visiting the grave) are observed on the date of the death.

2. In a leap year, the day of the Yahrzeit is still the date of the death, despite the fact that mourning ends after twelve months.
3. If the death occurred during Adar in a non-leap year, the Sephardic and Yemenite custom is that in a leap year, the Yahrzeit is observed in Adar II; the Ashkenazic custom is to observe it in Adar I. Some Ashkenazim observe the Yahrzeit in both Adar I and Adar II.[956] The root of the disagreement is about which one of the two Adars is the one that most people call "Adar" in a leap year. Another reason cited for the Ashkenazic custom of observing the Yahrzeit in the first Adar is so as not to delay the mitzva.[957]
4. The months of Ḥeshvan and Kislev can have twenty-nine or thirty days. Therefore, if the deceased passed away on the thirtieth of Ḥeshvan or the thirtieth of Kislev, the custom is to follow the date on which the first Yahrzeit occurred: If one year after the death, the month was thirty days long, then the date of the Yahrzeit should henceforth be Rosh Ḥodesh (Kislev or Tevet, respectively) and if it was twenty-nine days, the Yahrzeit should henceforth be the twenty-ninth of Ḥeshvan or Kislev, respectively.[958] Some say that it should be observed on the first day of the following month.[959]
5. If the person died in a leap year on the thirtieth day of Adar I, which is Rosh Ḥodesh of Adar II, then during a non-leap year, the Yahrzeit is observed on the thirtieth of Shvat, which is Rosh Ḥodesh Adar, since the second Adar is the "regular" Adar. Some

---

Yahrzeit on the date of the death (*Mishna Berura* 568:44; *Siftei Cohen, Yoreh De'ah* 402:10; *Tzror HaḤayim* 241).

956. *Shulḥan Arukh* and Rema, *Oraḥ Ḥayim* 568:7; Rema, *Yoreh De'ah* 402:12; *Gesher HaḤayim* 32:10.

957. *Mishna Berura,* ad loc. 41.

958. *Gesher HaḤayim* 32:11, like the *Magen Avraham* and *Mishna Berura* ibid. 42.

959. *Responsa Igrot Moshe, Yoreh De'ah,* vol. 3, 159. The reason being that the deceased was still alive on the twenty-ninth, so it should not be set for then; on the first of the month, the person had already died.

say that it should be observed on the first of Nisan.[960] (In a regular Adar there are twenty-nine days.)

6. If there is a doubt regarding the date of the Yahrzeit, for example if the person died at twilight, Kaddish should be recited on both days and the relative should try to lead services on both days. Relatives should visit the grave and hold the memorial service on the first of these days.[961]
7. The Yahrzeit is determined by the location of the deceased, for example, if the person died outside of Israel while in Israel it was already the next day.[962]
8. If the month of death is known, but not the actual date of death, the Yahrzeit should be set for the last day of that month, because we make the assumption that the person was alive the whole month unless we know otherwise. Some say that the Yahrzeit should be on the first day of the month in order to move up the Kaddish and memorial Torah study to before the date of death.[963]
9. If the date of death is unknown, a date should be chosen and observed as the Yahrzeit, like the rabbis established the tenth of Tevet as the day to commemorate the deaths of Holocaust victims whose date of death is unknown.
10. Some say that a relative's Yahrzeit should be observed for fifty years following their death; others say that it should be observed indefinitely.[964]

---

960. *Igrot Moshe*, ibid.
961. *Gesher HaḤayim* 32:12; *Yalkut Yosef* 30:33, and in 40:5 he writes that the first day should be chosen in order to increase merit for the deceased before the date of the death. In *Tzror HaḤayim* (242) he also writes that the Yahrzeit should be on the first day.
962. *Gesher HaḤayim* ibid. 14.
963. *Kaf HaḤayim* (568:78) brings the former opinion in the name of the *Ḥokhmat Adam*, but he agrees with the latter opinion. *Yalkut Yosef* (30:34) also brings both opinions and concludes that the Yahrzeit should be on the first of the month.
964. In *Yalkut Yosef* (40:31), he quotes the Admor of Sanz and the author of *Kehillot Yaakov*, that after half a century, the soul has reached its final resting place and there is no further benefit to visiting the gravesite. According to the Ari, however,

11. One should observe the Yahrzeit at the proper time and not postpone it. The main elements of observing the Yahrzeit are leading services and reciting Kaddish. It is good to visit the grave on that day, as well, but it can be done earlier if necessary.[965]

The Shabbat before

It is written in the name of the Ari that all souls ascend to the Garden of Eden on Shabbat; because the soul is elevated on the Yahrzeit, on the Shabbat before the twelve-month period ends, the soul ascends and does not descend. It is considered auspicious and beneficial for the deceased's son to leads services then, to elevate the deceased's soul.

12. The mourner should be called up to the Torah on the Shabbat preceding the Yahrzeit. The Sephardic custom is that the person should be called up for the seventh *aliya* and recite Kaddish. The Ashkenazic custom is for him to be called up for "*maftir.*"
13. Some have the custom to recite Kaddish after "*Mizmor Shir LeYom HaShabbat*" on the Friday night preceding the Yahrzeit. The Sephardic custom is to begin reciting Kaddish on the Friday night before the Yahrzeit after "*BaMeh Madlikin*" and to continue reciting it in all the prayers until the day of the Yahrzeit itself. If the Yahrzeit is on Shabbat, then one would begin saying Kaddish on the previous Friday night.[966]
14. Some have the custom to lead all of the services on Shabbat. Some have the custom to lead *Musaf* and to recite the Rabbis' Kaddish before *Aleinu.*
15. The mourner leads the prayers for Maariv on Motza'ei Shabbat, which is the time when souls are thought to return to hell after having rested on Shabbat, and so it is a time when the deceased is in need of further merit.[967] According to the Sephardic tradi-

---

there is an elevation of the soul each year, and the Yahrzeit should be observed for even a hundred years.

965. *Tzror HaḤayim* 251.
966. *Yalkut Yosef* 30:9; *Tzror HaḤayim* p. 105, 5.
967. Rabbi Nebenzahl: Some do not, so as not to give the impression that their parents' souls are in hell, God forbid.

tion, some have the custom to continue leading prayers from the Motza'ei Shabbat before the Yahrzeit until the Yahrzeit.[968]

Some of the customs practiced on the Yahrzeit

16. On the Yahrzeit, relatives pray for the soul's elevation. It is a day of judgment for the deceased. According to the Ari, the Kaddish said by the deceased's children over the course of the year is to elevate the parent from hell to the Garden of Eden; on the Yahrzeit, the Kaddish is to elevate the deceased from the Garden of Eden to an even higher level.
17. It is customary for the deceased's son to lead all of the prayers on the Yahrzeit and to recite all the Kaddishes. If one forgot and did not say Kaddish on the Yahrzeit, one should say it as soon as one remembers, since Kaddish and Torah study and any mitzva that the deceased's child performs, at any time, brings gratification to the parent's soul.[969]
18. The deceased's children should not embark on a journey right before the Yahrzeit if they know it will mean that they will be unable to have a *minyan* to say Kaddish – unless not going on the trip would incur a loss and is absolutely necessary.[970] If one is in a place where one cannot join a *minyan*, one should request that another family member say Kaddish; someone can also be hired to do so.
19. The custom is to be called up to the Torah and recite *El Maleh Raḥamim*. If the Yahrzeit is on a day when the Torah is not read, some have the custom to do this in the days preceding the Yahrzeit.[971]
20. It is customary to visit the gravesite and to pray there for the elevation of the deceased's soul. If a relative is unable visit the gravesite, some say that he should go to a nearby cemetery and pray there. The laws of visiting the gravesite are explained in Sec. 41, "Visiting the Gravesite."

968. *Yalkut Yosef* 30:9.
969. Ibid. 40:36.
970. *Pnei Barukh* 39:4 in the name of *Matei Ephrayim* and *Mishmeret Shalom*.
971. *Gesher HaḤayim* 32:1, 2.

21. Some have the custom to fast on the Yahrzeit. This is explained below.
22. It is customary to hold a memorial service on the Yahrzeit. As explained below.
23. Some hold a meal in honor of the deceased on the Yahrzeit, saying words of Torah and making blessings to elevate the deceased's soul. If possible, on the Yahrzeit, the deceased's son or other relative should mark the completion of a tractate of Talmud or Mishna, to elevate the soul. The meal is then considered a *seudat mitzva* and the Great Kaddish is recited at the end of the *siyum*.[972]
24. The Sephardic custom is to hold a meal and memorial service on the night before the Yahrzeit and to recite the *Hashkava* prayer. In the first year following the death, it is customary to do this after eleven months, as well as on the Yahrzeit. In a leap year, some hold another meal after twelve months and thus have three memorial services.[973]
25. These meals are a custom and not an obligation. Therefore, if it is difficult to arrange, it does not need to be done. The most important aspect of the Yahrzeit is reciting Kaddish. One should not spend excessive amounts of money on a large and lavish meal.[974]
26. The meal and Torah study may take place in the synagogue as long as the atmosphere is one of seriousness and decorum.

Lighting a memorial candle

27. Lighting a candle on the anniversary of the death (a "Yahrzeit candle") is an age-old custom. The candle remains lit for the entire day. It should not be extinguished even when the day has ended.

---

972. *Yalkut Yosef* 30:43.

973. *Tzror HaḤayim* 243 based on the *Ben Ish Ḥai*. In *Yalkut Yosef* (30:7) he writes that there is no need to have a third memorial on the day of the death since the first year is calculated by the months and not the year. But even in his opinion, if they have this third meal, it is commendable. He adds that the main memorial is at the end of the twelve months (40:3).

974. *Yalkut Yosef*, Introduction, p. 7, and 40:3.

28. It is preferable to light with olive oil; if not, then with a wax candle; and if that is not possible, then an electric bulb can be used.[975]
29. Some light the candle at home and others light it in the synagogue.
30. If the Yahrzeit falls out on Yom Tov, one should light the candle before Yom Tov begins. If one forgot, the candle can be lit in a place where people are eating so that they will benefit from the light of the candle; it is even better to light it in the synagogue, if possible.[976]
31. One candle may be lit for two deceased people.[977]
32. A woman should not light a candle on the Yahrzeit of her first husband, especially not in the presence of her second husband. Likewise, a husband should not light a candle for his first wife in the presence of his second wife.[978]

Fasting

33. There is a mitzva to fast on the Yahrzeit of one's parent.[979] This is because the day is considered to be inauspicious for the deceased's child. As our sages said, the anniversary of unhappy events attracts additional misfortune. Moreover, the parent is judged on that day each year. The deceased's children can give meaning to the day as one of memory and longing, introspection and thought. Fasting tends to have a purifying effect, allowing one to remove himself somewhat from physical matters and increase his spiritual contemplation.
34. Even though it is important and commendable to fast on one's parent's Yahrzeit, if fasting significantly impedes one's ability to

---

975. *Gesher HaḤayim* 20:1, 1.
976. *Bei'ur Halakha, Oraḥ Ḥayim* 514:5; *Yalkut Yosef* 40:45. In *Gesher HaḤayim* (32:1, 4) he writes to light it at home at night and during the daytime, to only light in the synagogue; the reason is given in Sec. 36, "Holidays and Festivals: Memorial Candle," halakha 20 and in Key Concepts.
977. And this does not constitute performing multiple mitzvot, *Yalkut Yosef* 40:34; *Tzror HaḤayim* 262.
978. *Kol Bo al Aveilut* p. 404.
979. Rema, *Yoreh De'ah* 376:4, 492:12.

function, it is not necessary to fast. If the fast impinges on one's ability to work or serve the community, one need not fast.[980] One who teaches children should not fast so as not to detract from Torah study and God's work.[981]

35. A Torah scholar need not fast if the fasting would upset his Torah study, but he should increase his Torah study on that day. If possible, he should take upon himself a *taanit dibur* (abstaining from speech).[982]
36. An individual who fasts must declare at Minḥa on the preceding day that he is accepting the fast.[983] One who fasts every year is not required to formally accept it upon himself.
37. If the Yahrzeit is on Shabbat or Rosh Ḥodesh, or on a day when *Taḥanun* is not recited, the custom is not to fast,[984] but one should increase one's Torah study, prayer, and charity on that day. If it falls out on Shabbat, some fast the following day but not before;[985] some have written that it is preferable to fast on the Thursday before.[986]
38. If there is a fast day within a week of the Yahrzeit, then one should not fast on the Yahrzeit, but one should increase his Torah study, prayer, and charity.[987]
39. A groom during the seven days of rejoicing after the wedding and a boy who reaches his bar mitzva on the day of the Yahrzeit are exempt from fasting. If there is a *brit mila,* the father of the baby, the mohel, and the *sandak* do not fast. If there is a *pidyon haben,* the father and the *kohen* who is redeeming the baby do not fast.

---

980. *Tzror HaḤayim* 245.
981. *Ben Ish Ḥai,* Second Year, *Ki Tetze,* 23.
982. *Yalkut Yosef* 40:15.
983. *Shulḥan Arukh, Oraḥ Ḥayim* 562:5.
984. Rema, *Yoreh De'ah* 402:12.
985. *Shulḥan Arukh, Oraḥ Ḥayim* 568:9.
986. *Yalkut Yosef* 40:24 based on the Ari. The reason is brought there in the footnotes: in order to increase merit for the deceased before the judgment on the Yahrzeit, to elevate the person's level in the Garden of Eden. If they push it off until Sunday, it would be too late to change the judgment, which has already been made.
987. *Tzror HaḤayim* 247.

40. Many exempt the person from this fast if he completes a unit of Torah study and does a *siyum*.[988] As mentioned above, it is a good practice to do a *siyum* to elevate the deceased's soul. The meal eaten is then a *seudat mitzva* and the blessings recited there elevate the deceased's soul. This *seudat mitzva* exempts one from fasting.
41. If someone fasted on the first Yahrzeit without declaring "*Bli neder*" ("Without making a vow"), it is considered as though he has accepted upon himself to fast every year. If he wants to stop the commitment, he needs an annulment of the vow.[989] For this reason, it is preferable for the person fasting to state that it is without a vow. This is helpful if a circumstance arises that make it hard for him to fast one year, or if the Yahrzeit falls out on Friday and he wants to fast on a different day instead, or if he wants to do a *siyum* instead of fasting.
42. Some are lenient with regard to fasting on the Yahrzeit, especially because nowadays people find it hard to fast. The rabbis established that one should increase one's Torah study, charity, and good deeds. It is customary to serve refreshments after services in the synagogue to make blessings for the elevation of the deceased's soul.[990]

Mourning practices

43. Some do not listen to music on the Yahrzeit.[991]
44. The Ashkenazic custom is not to attend weddings on the day or night of the Yahrzeit.[992] Some hold this stringency only on the first Yahrzeit.[993] The Sephardic practice is not to attend other

---

988. *Gesher HaḤayim* 32:7.
989. Rema, *Yoreh De'ah* 402; and see *Pitḥei Teshuva* ad loc. 8. In *Yalkut Yosef* (40:17) he wrote that if the person fasted three times and wants to stop the custom, he needs an annulment of the vow, but if he wants to skip fasting one time due to illness, this does not require an annulment.
990. *Pnei Barukh* 39:34.
991. *Tzror HaḤayim* 257; *Yalkut Yosef* 40:2.
992. Rema, *Yoreh De'ah* 391; and see *Pitḥei Teshuva* ad loc. 8.
993. *Arukh HaShulḥan, Yoreh De'ah* 391:14, and he brings the *Levush* who writes that he was not familiar with this custom; this is another reason to be lenient when necessary.

celebrations, either; but if it will cause ill will, one may go to a wedding to offer congratulations and give a gift, and then leave.[994] Some say that Sephardim may attend celebrations, but should be strict where possible. If their absence would upset the bride or groom, they may attend.[995]

When the Yahrzeit falls out on Shabbat

45. Visiting the gravesite: Sephardim go before Shabbat and Ashkenazim go after Shabbat.
46. Fasting has been explained above – halakha 37.
47. Being called up to the Torah: The custom is to be called up to the Torah on the Shabbat preceding the Yahrzeit.[996] Some have the custom to also be called up on the Shabbat of the Yahrzeit itself. The Sephardic custom is to be called up last for the seventh *aliya* and to say the Kaddish that follows. The Ashkenazic custom is to be called up for the *maftir*. Some Sephardim also prefer to be called up for the *maftir*. One should, of course, avoid conflict or disagreement, even if it means not being called up at all.[997]
48. Kaddish is said on that Shabbat. Sephardim start saying it from the previous Shabbat.[998]
49. If the Yahrzeit falls out on a holiday or Ḥol HaMoed, see the next chapter, halakha 4.

SECTION 41: VISITING THE GRAVESITE

"He enters into peace, they rest on their beds, each one that walks in his uprightness" (Is. 572). With regard to the bodies of the righteous, it states: "He enters into peace, they rest on their beds." And with regard to their souls, it states: "And the soul of my master will be bound up in the bond of life with the Lord your God" (I Sam. 25:29). (Shabbat 152b)

994. *Tzror HaḤayim* 257.
995. *Yalkut Yosef* 40:2.
996. *Pnei Barukh* 39:1, in order to give merit to the deceased's soul before being judged on the date of the death.
997. *Yalkut Yosef* 40:37–38.
998. *Yalkut Yosef* 30:9; and *Tzror HaḤayim* (258) also wrote that it is good to do so.

The source for visiting the gravesite

We find the first source for visiting graves in the Midrash about Joseph: When he was taken down to Egypt, he prostrated himself on his mother Rachel's tomb, and his mother responded, telling him that God will save him from all misfortune.

Rashi explains the verse about Rachel's tomb – "And I buried her there on the road to Efrat, now Bethlehem" (Gen. 48:7) – as follows: She was buried there according to a divine instruction, which said that she will help her children when they are exiled by Nevuzarden and they pass her tomb. At that point, Rachel will come out and cry, pleading for mercy for them, as it says: "A cry is heard in Ramah – wailing, bitter weeping – Rachel weeping for her children" (Jer. 31:15). God answers her: "For there is a reward for your labor – declares the Lord: They shall return from the enemy's land. And there is hope for your future – declares the Lord: Your children shall return to their country" (ibid., 15–16).

Another example of visiting relatives' graves is in the verse where Caleb ben Yefuneh "came to Hebron" (Num. 13:22). Our sages explain that he left the other spies and went to visit the forefathers' graves, saying: Request mercy for me that I will be saved from the counsel of the spies (Sota 34b).

Barzilai HaGil'adi said, "I will die in my city, with my father's and my mother's tomb" (II Sam. 19:38). It was learned from this that the dead benefit when their children and relatives and close friends visit and pray at their gravesite, because the soul is hovering over the grave (*Maavar Yabok*, "*Siftei Renanot*," ch. 23).

When does one visit the grave?

1. It is customary to visit the graves of family members, especially at the end of the shiva, *shloshim*, or twelve-month mourning period, as well as on the Yahrzeit.
2. If the last day of shiva falls out on Shabbat, then they go to visit the grave on the following day. If the last day of *shloshim* or the twelve months is a Shabbat, Sephardim visit the grave on Thursday; some Ashkenazim visit on Thursday and others do so on Sunday.[999] If Friday or Sunday is Rosh Ḥodesh, it is preferable

999. *Tzror HaḤayim* 186.

to go on a day that is not Rosh Ḥodesh. If the burial took place the day after the death and the Yahrzeit falls out on Shabbat, then they postpone the visit to Sunday.[1000]

3. If the seventh day is during a holiday, then they visit the grave on the day after the holiday.[1001]
4. If the Yahrzeit falls out on Yom Tov or Ḥol HaMoed, the Sephardic custom is to do the visit to the gravesite earlier and the Ashkenazic custom is to delay it.[1002]
5. One is permitted to go to the cemetery a few days before the Yahrzeit if it is better for the family; and, even though it is not the date of the Yahrzeit, if there is a *minyan* present, they should say Kaddish and psalms, as per usual. Kaddish should be said in the synagogue on the Yahrzeit as usual, or from the preceding Shabbat, according to one's custom.[1003]
6. Someone who is elderly, ill, or frail, for whom it is difficult to make the visit to the gravesite, or someone who is learning Torah and is concerned about taking time away from Torah study, does not have to go to the cemetery. The person should say Kaddish and practice the other Yahrzeit customs – saying the *Hashkava* prayer or *El Maleh Raḥamim* and learning Torah to elevate the soul. Going to the gravesite is a custom and not an obligation.[1004]
7. Some have the custom to visit the gravesite on Erev Rosh HaShana, Erev Yom Kippur, and Erev Tisha B'Av. There is a Sephardic custom to visit the gravesite on Erev Rosh Ḥodesh Nissan and Rosh Ḥodesh Elul.

1000. *Gesher HaḤayim* 32:5.

1001. *Gesher HaḤayim* 29:6, and he writes that following Passover or Sukkot, some wait until after the *shloshim*.

1002. *Tzror HaḤayim* 152; and in *Gesher HaḤayim* (ibid. 7) he writes to delay the visit unless it falls out on the first day of Passover or Sukkot, in which case it is moved up.

1003. *Tzror HaḤayim* 251.

1004. *Yalkut Yosef* 40:10; *Nitei Gavriel*, vol. 2, 76:3 in the name of the *Ḥazon Ish*. In *Tzror HaḤayim* (248) he writes that it is important enough to override learning Torah, but if the person teaches Torah and the cemetery is far away, the person may increase Torah learning to elevate the deceased's soul instead of travelling to the cemetery.

8. Some have the custom to go to the graves of relatives and righteous people to pray for the sick or to pray about other matters. See in Key Concepts, **Graves of the Forefathers and Graves of the Righteous.**
9. In the times when communal fast days were decreed, the people would go to the cemetery to convey the message that we are like the dead before God or that the dead should ask for mercy on our behalf (Taanit 16). (See Key Concepts, **Consulting the Dead.**)

Times when one does not go to the cemetery

10. One does not visit graves on Ḥol HaMoed or Purim. If the Yahrzeit is on Ḥol HaMoed, Sephardim go before the holiday and Ashkenazim go after the holiday[1005] and some do not go at all.[1006] The reason for not going to the cemetery on Ḥol HaMoed is to avoid crying and grieving. In view of that, if a number of years have passed since the death and one would like to show relatives or children where a grandparent (or other relative) is buried, they may go on Ḥol HaMoed, if and when there is no concern that it will cause them to cry and be sorrowful.[1007]
11. If the last day of shiva or *shloshim* falls out on Rosh Ḥodesh or Ḥanukka, some postpone visiting the grave until afterwards, and some go and say psalms and Kaddish but not *El Maleh Raḥamim.*[1008] Sephardim do not go to the cemetery on Rosh Ḥodesh or Ḥanukka but go beforehand.[1009]

1005. *Tzror HaḤayim* 252; *Yalkut Yosef* 36:5.
1006. *Gesher HaḤayim* 32:5 and 29:7.
1007. *Yalkut Yosef* 40:25.
1008. *Gesher HaḤayim* 29:5, and see halakha 22, below.
1009. *Tzror HaḤayim* 253; and in *Yalkut Yosef* (35:10) he writes that if the last day of shiva is on Rosh Ḥodesh, one should wait and go after Rosh Ḥodesh since going to the gravesite is likely to cause one to cry and grieve, which should be avoided on Rosh Ḥodesh. But if the mourners will be able to contain themselves and not cry, they may go on Rosh Ḥodesh. If the last day of shiva is on Ḥanukka, they should go after Ḥanukka.

12. It is permissible to go to the grave on Purim or Ḥanukka if the Yahrzeit falls out then since the pain of the deceased is forgotten after twelve months, but it is preferable to go beforehand.[1010]
13. The custom is to refrain from going to the cemetery during the month of Nisan. However, at the end of shiva or *shloshim* or on the Yahrzeit, one can visit the grave during Nisan.[1011] Psalms and Kaddish are recited, but not *El Maleh Raḥamim.*
14. According to the Kabbala, one should not visit the grave to pray for a sick person or for other matters in the first year after the person's death because, at that point, the soul itself is still being judged in the heavenly court. But one may pray to elevate the deceased's soul. Many limits visiting the grave during the first year, even for praying to elevate the soul. If one is going away on a long trip and will not be able to visit the gravesite afterwards, one can visit during the first year. The Sephardic custom is that it is permissible to visit the grave during the first year.[1012]
15. One should not visit the same grave twice in the same day.[1013]
16. There are some who avoid going to cemeteries except for attending funerals. In the Ari's writings it says that one who has had a seminal emission and has not immersed in the *mikve* should avoid going to a cemetery since the impure spirits cleave to him.[1014] This also appears in the Gra's letter to his family. Some do not visit the graves of wicked people. But even according to these opinions, one may go to the graves of the righteous and those of one's parents in order to honor them.[1015]

1010. *Yalkut Yosef* 36:4.
1011. *Gesher HaḤayim* 29:5; *Tzror HaḤayim* 254.
1012. *Tzror HaḤayim* 218.
1013. The source of this is the will of Rabbi Judah the Hasid, paragraph 12. The reason for this, as explained in the *Damesek Eliezer,* is that it would appear as though the deceased did not intercede for them the first time, which is not respectful to the deceased, implying that they were unsympathetic. Therefore, if a new need came up for the person, he may go back even on the same day; or if he planned ahead of time to go twice in one day, he may do so (*Tzror HaḤayim,* page 129). Another reason is so as not to burden or disturb the deceased.
1014. *Magen Avraham, Oraḥ Ḥayim* 559.
1015. *Yalkut Yosef* 10:25.

17. According to the Kabbala, a menstruating woman should not go to the cemetery[1016] but is allowed to go for a memorial service there.[1017] All opinions agree that women may go to graves of the righteous (such as Me'arat HaMakhpela, Rachel's Tomb, Rabbi Shimon bar Yoḥai's grave, etc.) if they are not inside a cemetery.[1018] See in Key Concepts, **Women – Attending a Funeral and Going to the Cemetery**.

The memorial service in the cemetery

18. The custom is to recite seven psalms to elevate the soul: Psalm 33, 16, 17, 72, 91, 104, and 130. These psalms contemplate the life and death of man and the eternity of the soul. For example, "For You will not abandon me to Sheol, or let Your faithful one see the pit"; "Take away their breath, they perish and turn again into dust. Send back Your breath, they are created, and You renew the face of the earth." Psalm 91 expresses man's trust in God, who watches over the person in his lifetime and protects the soul after death.
19. Afterwards, passages from Psalm 119 are recited according to the letters of the deceased's first name and the letters *nun, shin, mem,* and *hei,* spelling out *neshama* (soul). Psalm 119 is written according to the *Aleph-Beit*: Eight verses that start with the letter *aleph,* eight that start with the letter *beit,* etc. The custom is to recite the verses that spell out the person's name, followed by the letters that spell *neshama.* (See Key Concepts, ***Alfa Beita***.)
20. The *Ana* prayer and the Mourner's Kaddish are said. Afterwards, *El Maleh Raḥamim* is recited. Sephardim say *Hashkavot.*

1016. *Pitḥei Teshuva, Yoreh De'ah* 195:19; *Gesher HaḤayim* 29:13, in the name of the Ari. And he wrote that women should not go to the cemetery before going to the *mikve.* *Yalkut Yosef* (10:25) wrote that the issue is specifically when they are menstruating but that it is permitted during the clean days before immersing in the *mikve.*
1017. Rabbi Nebenzahl: Not everyone agrees with this; on the contrary, some do forbid it, even when she is not in *nidda.*
1018. *Tzror HaḤayim* 291.

21. On days when *Taḥanun* is omitted, Ashkenazim do not say *Ana* or *El Maleh Raḥamim* so as not to cause sadness and crying.[1019] Some write that *El Maleh Raḥamim* should be recited during the shiva, i.e., not in the context of the funeral[1020] or on the Yahrzeit.[1021]
22. One should try to gather a *minyan* when visiting the grave. But if there is no *minyan,* one should still go. Some write that there is no need to have a *minyan.*[1022]
23. Kaddish is recited if there is a *minyan.* If there is no *minyan,* Kaddish is not recited. If there is no *minyan,* one may gather with people at the cemetery entrance and say Kaddish.[1023] The psalms, *Ana,* and *El Maleh Raḥamim* can be said by the grave even without a *minyan.*

Customs at the gravesite

24. It is customary to place one's left hand on the grave and say:

    The Lord will guide you always. He will slake your thirst in parched places and give strength to your bones. You shall be like a watered garden, like a spring whose waters do not fail.

    Men from your midst shall rebuild ancient ruins. You shall restore foundations laid long ago. And you shall be called "Repairer of fallen walls, Restorer of lanes for habitation." (Is. 58:11–12).

    Rest in peace until the Comforter comes sounding peace.

25. The custom is to place a small stone or some grass on the grave to show that one was there. Another reason for this custom is that, in the past, there were no headstones, and a pile of stones would be made on the grave as a marker. Over time, these piles

1019. Rema, *Yoreh De'ah* 401:6; *Kol Bo al Aveilut* p. 104.
1020. *Magen Avraham, Oraḥ Ḥayim* 696:5.
1021. *Mishna Berura* 547:8.
1022. *Sefer Hilkhot Avel* 6:36.
1023. *Tzror HaḤayim* 249.

of stones would scatter; because part of visiting the grave involves seeing to it that the grave is well-marked, people would add stones to the pile.

26. Some have the custom to light a memorial candle beside the grave. Sometimes a headstone is constructed with a special spot for a candle to protect the flame from being blown out by the wind.
27. There is a concept that one must refrain from "**mocking the helpless**"; in our context, this refers to the deceased, and there are certain rules that stem from this idea: Because the deceased cannot learn Torah and keep the mitzvot, one is not allowed to learn Torah beside the grave. For the same reason, one may not wear tefillin in the cemetery or leave one's tzitzit sticking out of one's clothing when one is within four cubits of the graves.[1024] Even though one should not learn Torah within four cubits of a grave, one may recite psalms and say words of Torah in honor of the deceased beside the grave, since this is done in honor of the deceased and to elevate his soul.[1025]
28. When one prays at the gravesite, one must not pray to the dead, nor ask anything from them, nor put one's trust in the dead, because one is not supposed to "consult with the dead." Rather, one should pray to God and ask Him to show mercy in the merit of the righteous who have passed away. The belief in one God includes an obligation to pray to God alone, not to pray through "intermediaries"; one may not pray to angels, the righteous, or the deceased for help. Although we pray only to God, people can sometimes earn special merit that enhances the possibility of their prayers being accepted. For example, communal prayer is more readily accepted than private prayer, and prayer during the days when *Seliḥot* are said are more readily accepted than on other days of the year. So too, praying at the graves of righteous people can give merit to the one who prays there. But the belief in one

---

1024. *Shulḥan Arukh, Oraḥ Ḥayim* 23:45; *Yoreh De'ah* 367:2–3. In *Tzror HaḤayim* (50) he adds that one should not walk with holy books in the cemetery or within four cubits of the graves, even if one is not reading the books.

1025. *Shulḥan Arukh, Yoreh De'ah* 344:17, 367:3.

God must be foremost in every case. Ancient paganism began as a result of this type of mistake.[1026] There are, however, some authorities who have permitted asking the dead to be intermediaries and to pray for the living. (See Key Concepts, **Consulting the Dead.**)

29. Some have the custom that if a person did not visit his father's grave for ten years, he should never go back to visit.[1027] Some have written that one need not be concerned about this.[1028]
30. It is not prohibited to kiss the tombstone.[1029]
31. A widow or widower who remarried should not go to visit the grave of the deceased spouse. On the Yahrzeit, only the children and other relatives should go to the grave.[1030] The principle here is that the memory of the past should not hinder the building of the future. Therefore, despite the grief that is present, commemoration of the deceased is set aside so that one can focus on building the new relationship. This of course depends on the particular situation, especially the new spouse's feelings about the matter. Some couples have agreed ahead of time how they will behave in this regard. In general, if there is agreement between the couple, and it does not interfere with their new relationship, there should not be a problem with visiting the grave. However, it must be approached with care and sensitivity, and in cases of doubt, it is better not to push the issue.
32. *Kohanim* may visit the gravesite. However, as mentioned above, when visiting a gravesite, *kohanim* are not allowed to become

---

1026. See Maimonides, *Mishneh Torah, Hilkhot Avoda Zara* 1:1.
1027. This has to do with the obligation to honor one's parents, which applies after the parents' death, as well. It includes such practices as saying Kaddish and performing good deeds after their death in order to bring them merit and elevate the soul. Visiting the grave is considered part of this honor; if one did not go visit the grave, then one has failed to show one's parents honor in this way, and it may have offended the deceased. However, even according to this opinion, if one was not able to go in that time, this does not apply, and one can visit the grave even after many years. *Pnei Barukh* p. 402, note 47, and see *Yalkut Yosef* 40:14 in the footnote.
1028. *Gesher HaḤayim* 29:16; *Kol Bo al Aveilut* p. 180.
1029. *Tzror HaḤayim* 255.
1030. *Tzror HaḤayim* 300; and in *Gesher HaḤayim* (29:8) he writes that if the new spouse agrees to it, one can go visit the grave, but if the spouse objects, one should not go.

impure through contact with the dead. See Sec. 6 "Pre-Burial Phase of Mourning (*Aninut*): Restrictions on *kohanim*."

Washing hands

33. One should wash one's hands before praying at the gravesite and again when leaving the cemetery; some also wash their face.[1031] The reason is brought above, see Sec. 7 "Arrangements for the Fuenral and Burial," halakha 47.

SECTION 42: THE MEMORIAL SERVICE

1. On the thirtieth day (the last day of the *shloshim*) and on the Yahrzeit, it is customary to hold a memorial service for the deceased. The Sephardic custom is to also hold a meal and Torah study on the night before shiva ends, for the elevation of the deceased's soul.
2. The memorial service includes going to visit the grave as explained in the previous chapter.

Studying Mishna

3. It is customary to study sections of Mishna to elevate the deceased's soul. See the explanation in the Key Concepts section, **Learning Mishna.**
4. The custom is to study chapters of Mishna that begin with the letters of the deceased's name. Afterwards, it is customary to learn the last four mishnas of the seventh chapter of Tractate Mikvaot, because they spell out the word *neshama* (soul).
5. If it is difficult to learn Mishna according to the letters of the name, other sections of Mishna can be studied, since all sections have the capacity to elevate the deceased's soul. If the family wishes, other Torah study can be done, either in addition to or instead of the Mishna study.
6. After the learning, the *Ana* prayer is recited – except on days when *Taḥanun* is not omitted (the prayer appears at the back of

1031. *Mishna Berura* 4:42.

this book).[1032] Sephardim say the *Hashkava* prayer. *Hashkava* and its halakhot will be explained in the next chapter.

7. After the Torah study, the following mishna is said:

> Rabbi Ḥananya ben Akashya says, The Holy One, Blessed be He, wanted to give Israel merit; therefore, He multiplied for them Torah and commandments, as it said, "The Lord desired, for the sake of His righteousness, to make the Torah great and glorious" (Is. 42:21). (Avot 6)

This mishna has been explained in many different ways. In this context, we can say that the reason it is customary to say it after Torah study and before the Rabbis' Kaddish is because it includes Aggada content; the Rabbi's Kaddish is meant to be recited after studying a portion of Aggada (it is therefore also called *Kaddish DeAggadata*).

Kaddish

8. The children of the deceased recite the Rabbis' Kaddish, See Sec. 57, "Kaddish." If no children of the deceased are present, it can be recited by other relatives.

Blessings to bring merit to the soul

9. After the Torah study and prayers, it is customary to serve a meal or refreshments so that blessings can be made over the food, with the intention of them being for the merit of the deceased's soul. (See Key Concepts, **Elevating the Soul.**)

Minḥa and Maariv with the mourner leading the service

10. People generally try to hold the memorial in the late afternoon so that they can pray Minḥa and/or Maariv, with the mourner leading the service and saying Kaddish.

1032. *Pnei Barukh* 39:13.

Shabbat and holidays

11. If the last day of shiva or *shloshim* or the Yahrzeit occurs on a Shabbat or Yom Tov, the meal and Torah study may still be held. That is to say, even though we do not visit the grave on Shabbat and holidays, a meal and Torah study can still be held as a memorial.

Close to a holiday

12. The sages decreed not to hold a memorial service in the thirty days before a holiday. This is so as not to reawaken one's grief, which might impinge on the joy of the holiday.[1033] Although one should not plan memorial services in the thirty days before a holiday, if the last day of the *shloshim* or the Yahrzeit occur at this time, it is permitted.[1034]
13. If a holiday cancelled the shiva, the Sephardic custom is that the memorial and Torah study are held on the night before it ends.

Summary of preparations for the memorial

- Set a date and time, after consulting with other family members.
- If the plan is to pray Minḥa before the memorial and to say Maariv after it, consider when sunset will be and how long the Torah study will be.
- When visiting the grave, booklets should be brought with the chapters of Psalms customarily said in the cemetery.
- Determine where the memorial service will be take place. If it will be in the synagogue, this should be coordinated with the *gabbai*.
- Determine who will say the chapters of Mishna and/or teach Torah.
- Arrange for refreshments, drinks, and utensils.
- Inform family members and friends.

1033. Mishna Moed Katan 8:1; *Shulḥan Arukh, Oraḥ Ḥayim* 547:3; *Yoreh De'ah* 347.
1034. *Shulḥan Arukh, Yoreh De'ah* 347:3; *Pnei Barukh* 3:9. Rabbi Nebenzahl: This requires further consideration, in my opinion.

SECTION 43: RECALLING THE SOULS (*HAZKARAT NESHAMOT*), *HASHKAVA*, AND *YIZKOR*

> With regard to the custom of recalling the deceased on Shabbat, there is no doubt that doing so on the day of rest benefits them greatly; they are in a state of rest and are rejuvenated when their name is mentioned because one's name is connected to one's soul… each name is associated with the essence of the person. … When their name is remembered, they are renewed and their soul shines.
>
> The person reciting the deceased's name must do so with intention, since the speech of the lower beings works through the mystical secret of the breath that ascends. This is especially so if it is the deceased's child or relative that says it, and if it is done in the synagogue where the person used to pray, and all the more so if the person built the synagogue or dedicated something within it – all of this helps to give the soul peace and joy on the holy day. Just as God sanctifies the souls of the living righteous, so too the souls of the deceased get joy and rest, especially when their name is mentioned. (*Maavar Yabok*, "*Siftei Renanot*" 23)

The basic idea of recalling the souls (*hazkarat neshamot*) is that the living can bring benefit to the souls of the dead; it has this in common with the recitation of Kaddish. The *Yizkor* prayer includes a promise to give charity, since prayer is one of the set of actions including charity and loving-kindness that causes the deceased's soul to be elevated. As mentioned, it is a Jewish belief that each good deed done to benefit the deceased gives them merit in the world to come.

Recalling the Souls (Hazkarat Neshamot) and *Hashkava*

1. It is customary to mention the names of the deceased in the *El Maleh Raḥamim* prayer on every Shabbat during the first year, and in subsequent years, on the Shabbat before the Yahrzeit.
2. The main benefit is considered to be through giving charity for the merit of the soul. If one pledges to give charity, one must make sure to follow through on this, preferably right away.[1035] It is even better

1035. *Pnei Barukh* 39:17.

to give charity first and then say, "For I gave" ("*ba'avur shenatati*").[1036] If pledging the charity, it is better to say "For the family pledges" and not "promises" (in Hebrew, *nedava* as opposed to *neder*), so that it does not take on the severe halakhic category of a vow. That said, one should still do the *Hashkava* even if one is not pledging charity.[1037]

3. *Hazkarat Neshamot* is not done on days when *Taḥanun* is omitted, nor when there is a groom present or a *brit mila* taking place in the synagogue.
4. *El Maleh Raḥamim* is not said on *Shabbat Mevarkhim* – the Shabbat when the new month is blessed, except if the Yahrzeit falls out that coming week.[1038] Nor is it said on a Shabbat when one of the four special *parshiyot* is read (from Adar to Passover).[1039]
5. The Ashkenazic and Yemenite custom[1040] is to say the name of the deceased and his or her father's name. Sephardim say the deceased's name and father's name for a man, and the deceased's name and mother's name for a woman. Some always say the deceased's name and the mother's name. One may follow the local custom.[1041]
6. One should say the name that most people used for the deceased when he or she was alive. If the person was known by a non-Jewish name, even if he had a Jewish name, that name should be mentioned in the *Hashkava*.[1042]

Therefore, the dead are mentioned on Shabbat, so that they do not return to hell. For it says in the Torah, "Absolve, O Lord, Your people Israel" (Deut. 21:8) – these are the living; "Whom You

1036. *Gesher HaḤayim* 31:2, 3.
1037. *Yalkut Yosef* 32:1.
1038. *Magen Avraham, Oraḥ Ḥayim* 284:7.
1039. *Mishna Berura* 685:18.
1040. *Shulḥan Arukh HaMekutzar, Einei Yitzḥak, Yoreh De'ah* 187:14.
1041. *Gesher HaḤayim* 31:2, 10; *Yalkut Yosef* 32:3. And some wrote that the Sephardic custom is to say both the father's and mother's name (*Sefer Hilkhot Avel* 6:18).
1042. *Yalkut Yosef* ibid. 5. Rabbi Nebenzahl: This requires further consideration, in my opinion. The Jewish people were redeemed from Egypt because they did not change their Jewish names.

redeemed" – these are the deceased. From here we learn that the living redeem the dead. Therefore, we have the custom of mentioning them on Yom Kippur and giving charity in their name. (*Midrash Tanḥuma, Haazinu*)

Yizkor

7. The Ashkenazic custom is to recite *Yizkor* for one's parents and other relatives four times a year: on Yom Kippur, Shemini Atzeret, the last day of Passover, and Shavuot. Sephardim recite *Hashkavot* on Erev Yom Kippur [1043] and in the week before the Yahrzeit.
8. *Yizkor* is also recited during the first year of mourning.[1044]
9. *Yizkor* is also recited on festivals and Yom Kippur when they fall out on Shabbat.
8. It is customary that those whose parents are alive exit the synagogue sanctuary when *Yizkor* is said. The *gabbai* usually announces that it is the time for *Yizkor* so that people can leave the sanctuary.
9. Saying *Yizkor* with a congregation is important, but an individual may say it at home or in the cemetery without a *minyan.*[1045]
12. *Yizkor* may be said for children.[1046]
13. One may say *Yizkor* for one's first wife or first husband even if one has remarried. Although there is an issue with and limitations on visiting the grave or lighting a memorial candle for a first spouse, saying *Yizkor* is different. The first two practices are public in nature; the focus should be on establishing and strengthening the current relationship and household, even if it detracts from remembering the past. *Yizkor*, on the other hand, is said quietly,

---

1043. *Yalkut Yosef* 32:8.

1044. *Gesher HaḤayim* 31:2, 7. Even though some have given reasons why it should not be said during the first year, that custom has been shown to be without basis and without a source; on the contrary, during the first year, it is even more important to say it. *Kol Bo al Aveilut* p. 404.

1045. *Pnei Barukh* 38:16.

1046. *Gesher HaḤayim* 31:2, 8.

privately, between the person and his Creator. It is not likely to impinge on the new marriage or the new household.

14. One may say *Yizkor* in the synagogue for a Druze solider who was killed in the line of duty (in the Israeli army) or for a gentile who saved Jews during the Holocaust.[1047]
15. It is customary to light memorial candles in memory of one's parents or relatives on the four days when *Yizkor* is recited. (For further discussion, see Key Concepts, **Memorial Candle.**)

The text of *Yizkor* is brought in the section with prayers and other texts.

The Cemetery

SECTION 44: THE TOMBSTONE

Rabbi Shimon ben Pazi said: Where is there an allusion in the Torah to the marking of graves? The verse states: "And any see a man's bone, then shall he set up a sign by it," (Ezek. 39:15). (Moed Katan 5a)

Setting the tombstone

Marking graves is an age-old custom.

In Hebrew, this marker has three different names: *Matzeva, Tziyun,* and *Nefesh.*

The name "*matzeva*" (lit. "pillar") appears in the Torah: "Over her grave Jacob set up a *matzeva*; it is the *matzeva* at Rachel's grave to this day" (Gen. 35:20).

The name "*tziyun*" (lit. "marker") appears in the Prophets: "He asked, 'What is the *tziyun* I see there?' And the men of the town replied, 'That is the grave of the man of God who came from Judah'" (II Kings 23:17).

And the name "*nefesh*" (in this context, "gravestone") appears in the Mishna and the Talmud: "Build a *nefesh* on his grave" (Mishna Shekalim 2:5).

There are a number of reasons for setting a tombstone –

1047. *Yalkut Yosef* 30:26–27.

- So that the deceased is remembered. The sages said that one need not make a tombstone for the righteous since their words are their legacy[1048] and Maimonides ruled in accordance with this idea.[1049] But the Ari wrote[1050] that there is a great need for a tombstone and that it is a rectification for the soul; the Rashba wrote[1051] that it is an honor to the deceased. This is the custom nowadays, to set a tombstone for great rabbis, as well.
- To know where the grave is located, so that people can visit and pray there.
- To mark a place of impurity, so that *kohanim* can take note.
- To honor the soul that hovers there.

There is a connection between the three different Hebrew names and these various reasons. The name "*matzeva*" shares its root with the word *yatziv*, meaning steady or established; this relates to the idea that the grave should be known so that people may visit and the deceased not be forgotten. The name "*tziyun*" (a marker) expresses the idea that the grave should be marked to warn *kohanim* of the impurity. And the name "*nefesh*" speaks to the *nefesh* (soul) of the deceased that hovers there, as described in the Zohar.[1052]

Unveiling the tombstone[1053]

1. It is good to unveil the tombstone at the end of the shiva.[1054] Some do so towards the end of the *shloshim*. Others delay it until after the twelve-month period.

1048. Y. Shekalim 2:5.

1049. *Mishneh Torah, Hilkhot Avel* 4:4.

1050. *Shaar HaMitzvot, Parashat Vayeḥi*

1051. *Responsa Rashba* 375.

1052. Based on *Gesher HaḤayim* 28:1, 1.

1053. In Israel, there is no custom to physically unveil the tombstone, and the halakha does not mention this ritual; there is no need for the tombstone to be covered and uncovered (noted by Rabbi Yaakov Ariel in *Darka Shel HaYahadut BeMavet U'BeAveilut* p. 360).

1054. *Gesher HaḤayim* 28:2; *Kuntras HaYeḥieli* p. 55; *Kol Bo al Aveilut* p. 379; *Yalkut Yosef* 50:1; *Pnei Barukh* 36:2. In *Tzror HaḤayim* he writes that the Sephardic custom is

2. If a festival falls out during the *shloshim*, it is preferable to unveil the tombstone before the festival.
3. It is customary to eulogize the deceased at the unveiling of the tombstone. Because of this, some have written that it should only be done on days when one is permitted to eulogize the deceased.[1055]
4. There is significance to setting a tombstone even after many years, e.g., if the family discovered the grave after it had been left unmarked for a long period of time, since the tombstone is for the deceased's soul.[1056]

What is written on the tombstone?

5. The deceased's name is written on the tombstone. Ashkenazim write the name of the deceased and the father's name; Sephardim write the deceased's name and the mother's name.[1057] Nowadays, it is customary to write the names of both parents, and, if they are alive, the letters הי"ו are added, which is short for "*Hashem yishamrem veyeḥyem*," "God shall protect them and keep them alive." If the parents are no longer living, they write "*Zikhronam livrakha*," "Of blessed memory."[1058]
6. One should not engage in exaggerated praise of the deceased.[1059]
7. If the tombstone is replaced, the praises on the new tombstone should not be less than what was written on the previous one.[1060]
8. If someone had a name added during an illness and then recovered and used the new name for thirty days afterwards – this name should be written on the tombstone. But if the person never recovered from the illness, the new name is not written on the tombstone.

---

to set the foundations during the shiva and to unveil the tombstone immediately after the shiva, not to wait until the *shloshim*. But Ashkenazim unveil the tombstone on the thirtieth day.

1055. *Responsa Minḥat Yitzḥak*, vol. 3, 51.

1056. Rabbi Yaakov Ruza in the name of the book *Maavar Yabok*.

1057. *Gesher HaḤayim* 28:3; 1; *Pnei Barukh* 36:3.

1058. *Tzror HaḤayim* 282.

1059. *Yalkut Yosef* 50:3, and he added that if they suffered greatly before they died, then it is appropriate to write that this since suffering atones for their sins.

1060. *Responsa Igrot Moshe, Yoreh De'ah*, vol. 1, 228.

9. The Hebrew date of death is written, not the English date.[1061]
10. In Israel, the tombstone should be written in Hebrew and not in other languages.[1062]
11. At the end of the inscription, it is customary to add תנצב"ה, which stands for "*tehei nishmato betzror haḥayim*," "Let his (or her) soul be bound up in the bond of life."[1063] See Key Concepts, **Bond of Life (*Tzror HaḤayim*)**.
12. If the person who passed away gave instructions not to make a tombstone, these instructions are not followed. But if the person gave instructions not to write praises on the tombstone, one should comply with this wish.[1064]
13. The tombstone should be engraved, and not have raised lettering, because according to the Kabbala, one should be careful not read raised lettering on grave-markers.[1065]
14. The deceased's likeness should not be carved onto the tombstone.[1066]

Style and cost of the tombstone

Initially, the funeral expenditures for the deceased were more taxing for his relatives than his death, until it reached a point where people would abandon the deceased and flee. This continued until

---

1061. *Gesher HaḤayim* 28:3, 4. Some rabbis were of the opinion that writing the English date might be a Torah prohibition because of the verse, "Make no mention of the names of other gods" (Ex. 23:13) (*Responsa Maharam Shik, Yoreh De'ah* 171, and *Ḥoshen Mishpat* 56) or because of the verse, "Nor shall you follow their ways" (Lev. 18:3) (Rabbi Yitzḥak Palacci in his book *Yafeh LaLev*, vol. 5, 178). In *Yalkut Yosef* (50:6–7) he writes not to write the English date even though there is no prohibition against doing so – and if the English date has been written, it should be covered up. In *Kol Bo al Aveilut* (p. 380) he writes that if the custom in a particular place is to write the English date, one should not argue with this since it is not done with bad intentions. If both the Hebrew and English dates are written, that is certainly fine.

1062. *Yalkut Yosef* in the name of Maharam Schick.

1063. Some use periods between the letters, .ת.נ.צ.ב.ה, but from a linguistic perspective this is not correct. It should be written תנצב"ה, because acronyms in Hebrew are written this way, whereas periods are used in English and other languages.

1064. *Yalkut Yosef* 50:7; *Pnei Barukh* 36:10.

1065. *Tzror HaḤayim* 283.

1066. *Tzror HaḤayim* 286.

Rabbi Gamliel came and conducted himself in a self-deprecatory manner; they took him for burial in plain linen garments. And all the people conducted themselves following his example and were taken for burial in plain linen garments. Rav Pappa said: And today, everyone is accustomed to bury the dead in plain garments, even in rough cloth worth one zuz. (Ketubot 8a)

15. Some have written that flat tombstones are preferable to upright ones. However, even according to this opinion, if the other tombstones in the cemetery are upright, there is no prohibition against following that custom.[1067]
16. Some tombstones have a small niche built into them for lighting a candle, to prevent the flame from being blown out by the wind.
17. One should try to have the tombstone be in line with local custom. It should be respectable enough to honor the deceased but should not be lavish nor showy. One should be especially careful not to be wasteful or ostentatious. Commissioning an ordinary tombstone and giving the rest of the money to the needy can give the deceased's soul great satisfaction and merit.

SECTION 45: LAWS RELATING TO THE CEMETERY

Respect for the cemetery

The cemetery is called "The house assigned for all the living" ("*beit moed lekol ḥai,*" based on Job 30:23) and the "eternal house" ("*beit olam,*" based on Eccl. 12:8); the sages called it the "house of eternity" ("*beit almin,*" e.g., in Sanhedrin 19); it is also called the "house of life" (based on the idea of transitioning from one state of life to another).

1. Although people should not spend large amounts of money on an ornate, expensive tombstone, it is important that the cemetery remained orderly and tidy. The graves should be arranged in rows

1067. *Tzror HaḤayim* 287. The reason is not halakhic, but rather that flat tombstones are less expensive, and burial costs should be kept low. Thus, in a new cemetery, where guidelines are being established for the *ḥevra kaddisha,* flat tombstones are preferable.

with paths between them so that visitors can avoid stepping on graves when moving around.

2. Many communities have trees and flowers planted in the cemetery in honor of the dead. The trees should not hang over the graves or over paths outside the cemetery so as not to cause *kohanim* to become ritually impure. (*Kohanim* may not be under the same "roof" as the dead, and overhanging trees form a type of roof.) Care should also be taken that tree roots are not drawing from the graves themselves.[1068]
3. Planting trees is not considered a gentile custom[1069] since the prohibition against imitating gentile customs only applies to customs that were explicitly mentioned in the Talmud.[1070]
4. In the ancient cities of Jerusalem, Safed, Tiberias, and Hebron, there is a custom not to plant trees in the cemetery. This is because of an early custom: When people were especially careful about purity, they did not want trees to hang over the graves, for the sake of *kohanim* or others who were being careful about ritual purity. Another reason was that trees tend to draw people to come and enjoy the landscape, which was neither desirable nor appropriate for the cemetery.[1071] Some have written that there should not be trees and flowers in cemeteries, wherever they are located.[1072]
5. One should not walk in the cemetery while wearing tefillin or with one's tzitzit showing, as this is considered "mocking the helpless" (this idea is explained in the Key Concepts section). One should not learn or pray in the cemetery unless it is to bring merit to the deceased's soul. Some permit praying and learning in the cemetery if one is at least four cubits' distance from the deceased and the other graves.[1073]

1068. *Siftei Cohen, Yoreh De'ah* 368:4.

1069. See Lev. 18:3.

1070. *Responsa Rashba,* vol. 1, 825; and see *Responsa BeMar'eh HaBazak,* vol. 5, 97.

1071. *Responsa Daat Cohen* 212; *Gesher HaḤayim* 27:1, 2.

1072. *Yalkut Yosef* 12:3.

1073. *Shulḥan Arukh, Yoreh De'ah* 367:3 and 6; *Gesher HaḤayim* 27:2, 2. And see *Bei'ur Halakha, Oraḥ Ḥayim* 45, who discussed three ways of defining the places where one should not enter with tefillin. In practice, if one wants to pray at the cemetery,

6. One should not act frivolously in the cemetery, including eating, drinking, or using the area as a shortcut.[1074] One should not smoke there[1075] and one should wear appropriate clothing and cover one's head.
7. It is permissible and commendable to clean and scrub tombstones and to do upkeep or preservation on tombstones, even if this is done only for the sake of documentation and historical research. But one should not dig under tombstones; the soil of the cemetery should be preserved.[1076]

Blessing upon seeing Jewish graves

8. One who sees Jewish graves after having not seen any for thirty days makes the following blessing:[1077]

בָּרוּךְ אַתָּה הי אֱלֹהֵינוּ מֶלֶךְ הָעוֹלָם אֲשֶׁר יָצַר אֶתְכֶם בַּדִּין וְזָן אֶתְכֶם בַּדִּין וְכִלְכֵּל אֶתְכֶם בַּדִּין וְהֵמִית אֶתְכֶם בַּדִּין וְיוֹדֵעַ מִסְפַּר כֻּלְּכֶם וְהוּא עָתִיד לְהַחֲיוֹתְכֶם וּלְקַיֵּם אֶתְכֶם בַּדִּין. בָּרוּךְ אַתָּה הי מְחַיֵּה הַמֵּתִים.

אַתָּה גִּבּוֹר לְעוֹלָם הי מְחַיֵּה מֵתִים אַתָּה רַב לְהוֹשִׁיעַ. מְכַלְכֵּל חַיִּים בְּחֶסֶד מְחַיֵּה מֵתִים בְּרַחֲמִים רַבִּים סוֹמֵךְ נוֹפְלִים וְרוֹפֵא חוֹלִים וּמַתִּיר אֲסוּרִים וּמְקַיֵּם אֱמוּנָתוֹ לִישֵׁנֵי עָפָר מִי כָמוֹךָ בַּעַל גְּבוּרוֹת וּמִי דּוֹמֶה לָּךְ מֶלֶךְ מֵמִית וּמְחַיֶּה וּמַצְמִיחַ יְשׁוּעָה וְנֶאֱמָן אַתָּה לְהַחֲיוֹת מֵתִים.

Blessed are You, the Lord our God, King of the universe, who fashioned you in justice, nourished and sustained you in justice and caused you to die in justice. Who knows your total count in justice and who in the future will revive and keep you alive in justice. Blessed are You, the Lord, who resurrects the dead.

You are eternally mighty, my Lord, You resurrect the dead, You are great in Your ability to save. He who nourishes the living

---

one may do so near the offices, where there are no graves, or at least four cubits from the area dedicated to the graves.

1074. *Shulḥan Arukh, Yoreh De'ah* 368:1.

1075. *Yalkut Yosef* 40:11.

1076. *Responsa BeMar'eh HaBazak*, vol. 3, 74.

1077. *Shulḥan Arukh, Oraḥ Ḥayim* 224:12.

> with kindness, resurrects the dead with great mercy, supports the fallen and heals the sick, frees the imprisoned and maintains His faith to those who sleep in the dust. Who is like You, Master of Might? And who can be compared to You? King, who brings death, and restores life and sprouts salvation. You are faithful to resurrect the dead.

The beginning of the blessing is based on the mishna in Avot (end of Sec. 4, "Visiting the Sick (*Bikur Ḥolim*)":

> Against your will you were created, and against your will you were born, and against your will you live, and against your will you die, and against your will you are destined to give account and reckoning before the King of kings, the Holy One, blessed be He.

The Mishna first expresses God's ultimate control over man:

> To know, to make known, and to become conscious that He is God, He is the Maker, He is the Creator, He is the Understander, He is the Judge, He is the Witness, He is the Litigant, and He is destined to judge.

Such ultimate power can awaken concern in man, about God's attribute of Justice. Therefore, the Mishna goes on to emphasize:

> Blessed be He, who has before Him no wrong, no forgetfulness, no respect of persons, no taking of bribes, for all is His. And know that everything is according to the reckoning.

The Mishna lays the foundations for the blessing said upon seeing graves: The recognition of God's power and complete control over the world, which is the opposite of man's inevitable cycle of birth, life, and death. The Mishna stresses the complete divine justice that enables man to justify God's judgments, despite his inability to fathom its depths.

The continuation of the blessing is based on *birkat hagevurot* (the blessing of powers) in the *Amida*[1078] that concludes with the blessing of reviving the dead. The resurrection of the dead is one of the thirteen principles of faith according to Maimonides; this blessing also expresses faith in the resurrection: "You are faithful to revive the dead." There are many ways to understand the resurrection. One that is relevant here is that, despite man's impermanence, despite the fact that his life will come to an end, ultimately, his soul is eternal; this divine part of man does not die. And it is this part that will cause a revival of the body and give it eternal life.

Even when we are alive, we receive our lives from God in every moment. A greater consciousness would enable us to see that in every moment of life, there is a resurrection that occurs within us. It is why we make the blessing each morning, "The One who restores souls." The blessing raises our awareness of the body's renewal every day and in each moment.

This blessing connects the future resurrection with God's powers – He supports the fallen, heals the sick, and redeems the captive. All of these allow for humanity's continued existence in the world. Our daily resurrection helps us understand the resurrection of the future.

9. The blessing may be made within four cubits of the grave.[1079]
10. The blessing is made even if one sees the graves on Shabbat or a holiday,[1080] since this blessing does not constitute a justification of God's judgment (like *Tziduk HaDin*, which is not said on these days). Rather, it describes God's actions with all of His creations. However, it is inappropriate to enter the cemetery on Shabbat due to the evil spirit that resides there.[1081]
11. An onen should not make this blessing. If an onen did make the blessing, there are opinions he may rely on that allow it.[1082]

1078. According to the Kabbala, this section is said after the funeral in order to ward off the impure spirits through the force of the holy names in the blessing. The explanation appears in the book *Maavar Yabok*, "*Siftei Renanot*" 12.

1079. *Gesher HaḤayim* 29:17.

1080. *Kol Bo al Aveilut* p. 165; *Yalkut Yosef* 10:33.

1081. *Kol Bo*, ibid. in the name of the *Hadrat Kodesh*. Rabbi Yaakov Ruza taught me this reason.

1082. *Yalkut Yosef* 10:34, and see above, Sec. 6, Pre-Burial Phase of Mourning (*Aninut*), halakha 20.

12. Even though this blessing should not be made at a funeral[1083] because during the funeral one is involved in the mitzva of burying the dead and exempt from saying the blessing, the custom is for the *ḥazan* of the *ḥevra kaddisha* to make this blessing at each funeral, even though members of the *ḥevra kaddisha* are likely to have seen graves within the past thirty days. The reason given is that the blessing is made on each new grave.[1084] The *ḥazan* has the intention to fulfill the obligation for others who have not seen graves in the past thirty days and who are obligated to make the blessing.[1085]

Acquiring a burial plot

13. It is good for a person to be buried in a grave bought specifically for him.[1086] Abraham purchased Me'arat HaMakhpela before burying Sarah: "So Ephron's land in Makhpela, near Mamre – the field with its cave and all the trees anywhere within the confines of that field – passed to Abraham as his possession, in the presence of the Hittites, of all whom entered the gate of his town. And then Abraham buried his wife Sarah in the cave of the field of Makhpela, facing Mamre – now Hebron – in the land of Canaan" (Gen. 23:17). Jacob also emphasized the purchase of Me'arat HaMakhpela: "Bury me with my fathers ... in the cave that is in the field of Makhpela, facing Mamre, in the land of Canaan, the field that Abraham bought" (ibid. 49:29–30). It is also mentioned in relation to Joseph's burial: "The bones of Joseph, which the Israelites had brought up from Egypt, were buried at Shekhem, in the piece of ground which Jacob had bought" (Joshua 24:32). It is even permissible to move the deceased from the grave in order to bury him in a grave that was bought specifically for him as explained below.
14. For this reason, many people purchase a burial plot during their lifetime. If a person did not do so, the family purchases the grave for the deceased. It is preferable to do so before the burial. If no

1083. *Gesher HaḤayim* 29:17.
1084. *Kol Bo al Aveilut*, p. 166.
1085. *Yalkut Yosef* 10:36.
1086. *Gesher HaḤayim* 16:1, 4.

one can pay to purchase the burial plot, they should at least pay a symbolic amount so that the grave will belong to the deceased's family. If there is no one to purchase the burial plot, then the community provides the grave to the deceased.[1087]

15. When someone purchases a plot during his lifetime, some will have the grave dug and prepared in advance, and then covered up.
16. When a grave is dug and is not used immediately, one must take care not to leave it open but to make sure that it is covered that same day.[1088] Sometimes the *ḥevra kaddisha* will did the graves partially ahead of time, without completing the digging; in this case, they do not have to be as careful to cover them up; on the day of the burial, they finish digging the grave.[1089] When necessary, the grave can be dug and covered up with boards.[1090]

Family burial plots

17. When possible, a person should be buried with his family.[1091] The Tanakh indicates the importance of being buried with one's family: Abraham bought Me'arat HaMakhpela in Hebron to bury his wife Sarah and he himself was buried there. Isaac and Rebecca were also buried there. Jacob buried Leah there and instructed Joseph, "Bury me in their burial place." According to the Midrash, Jacob apologized to Joseph that he was not able to bury Rachel in Hebron (see Rashi on Gen. 48:7). Elazar, Aaron's son, was buried in Givat Pinḥas with his son (at the end of the Book of Joshua). Gideon was buried in the grave of Yoash his father (Judges 8:32). King Saul's bones were buried together with Jonathan, his son, in the land of

1087. In Israel today, in light of the legal status of land in the State of Israel, the grave does not become the possession of the deceased or the family; rather, they are given permission to use the plot of land. After acquiring this permission, the right to be buried in this plot is reserved for the person as long as he is not buried elsewhere. (This information is based on a letter from the offices of the Ministry of Religious Matters, Yehuda Elram, LL.B.)

1088. Rema, *Yoreh De'ah* 339:1, in the name of Rabbenu Yeruḥam, from the will of Rabbi Judah the Hasid (2).

1089. *Gesher HaḤayim* 27:8, 2.

1090. *Yalkut Yosef* 5:7.

1091. *Shulḥan Arukh, Yoreh De'ah* 366.

Binyamin, in the grave of Kish, Saul's father (II Sam. 21:14). Asahel was buried in his father's grave (II Sam. 2:32). Reḥavam was buried in his father's plot (I Kings 14:31) as were other kings. Nehemiah calls Jerusalem, "The city of my fathers' graves" (Neh. 2:2).

It is comforting for to be buried with one's family. As Barzilai the Giladi said: "Let me die in my own town, near the graves of my father and mother" (II Sam. 19:38)

18. This matter is so important that it is permissible to move the deceased from his grave in order to be buried with his family.[1092]
19. If the father is buried in one place and the mother is buried somewhere else, one should be buried next to one's father.[1093]
20. There is no halakhic obligation for a couple to be buried next to one another, but it is advisable.[1094] If they were divorced, the wife should be buried next to her parents and family.
21. If a woman was married twice, one should try to judge where she would have preferred to be buried. For example, if her children were from only one of the husbands, it is likely she would have wanted to be buried next to him. If she had no children, or she had children with both of them, and we do not know her preference, then she is buried next to her first husband.[1095]
22. A man or woman who bought a plot next to their spouse, but later changed their mind and wanted to be buried elsewhere can be buried according to their preference.[1096]

Burial in the Land of Israel

And when the time approached for Israel to die, he summoned his son Joseph and said to him, "Do me this favor, place your hand under my thigh as a pledge of your steadfast loyalty: Please do not bury me in Egypt. When I lie down with my fathers, take me

1092. Ibid. 363:1.
1093. *Gesher HaḤayim* 27:7, 1.
1094. *Tzror HaḤayim* 289.
1095. *Gesher HaḤayim* ibid., 2.
1096. *Responsa BeMar'eh HaBazak*, vol. 2, p. 137.

up from Egypt and bury me in their burial-place." He replied, "I will do as you have spoken." (Gen. 47:29–30)

23. It is a great merit to be buried in the Land of Israel. Our sages said that anyone who is buried in Israel, it is as though they were buried under the Altar.[1097] Happy is one who merits to be received by the Land of Israel when he is alive and whose soul departs while in that place of purity, opposite the gates of Heaven.[1098] But if a person died outside of Israel, it is a merit to be buried in Israel.

    The sages described the following benefits of being buried in Israel:[1099]

    - Burial in Israel atones, as it says: "Atonement for the soil of his people" (Deut. 32:33).
    - Resurrection in Israel comes without having to roll through the underground tunnels.[1100]
    - The deceased are saved from the pain of burial (see Key Concepts, **Suffering of the Grave**).
    - The deceased do not become putrid and consumed by worms.[1101]
    - The soul ascends through the gates of Heaven directly: It says in the Zohar that all souls pass through Jerusalem. And in another source in the Zohar[1102] it is written that, when the soul leaves this world, it first comes to Me'arat HaMakhpela.

Although the sages criticized those who arrive in Israel to be buried after having died in the Diaspora – linking this practice with a harsh

1097. Ketubot 111a.
1098. Our sages said of this (ad loc.) that being in Israel during one's life is better than just being buried there.
1099. See *Gesher HaḤayim* 27:9, 1.
1100. According to our sages, in the resurrection, the dead outside of Israel will reach Israel by revolving through underground tunnels. The source is in the Talmud (Ketubot 111a).
1101. Rabbi Nebenzahl: In my opinion, this requires further consideration.
1102. *Zohar HaḤadash, Parashat Noaḥ.*

verse: "I call upon them: 'You made My possession abhorrent' – in your lives, 'But you came and defiled My land' – in your deaths"[1103] – they still condoned the custom of being buried in Israel. Perhaps it implies that their criticism was only for those who could have come during their life but did not do so, or that the merit of the Land of Israel atoned for them. Indeed, there were many great sages who gave instructions to be buried in Israel after their death in the Diaspora.

24. As a general rule, the deceased should not be taken from one city to another in order to be buried, out of respect for the dead who were buried in the first city, so as not to insult them by appearing to refuse to be buried with them. This may be done, however, to move the deceased from the Diaspora to Israel, or to be bury the deceased with his family, or if the person left instructions to bury them elsewhere.[1104] In practice, in Israel, it is not customary to be strict about this and the deceased may be transported to a different city; it is not considered a degradation to the dead. Some are careful not to remove the dead from Jerusalem or Hebron because of the special merit of being buried there, and some also had this custom with Safed and Tiberias.[1105]
25. The deceased should not be taken from Israel to the Diaspora, according to the rule "**One May Bring Anyone to the Land of Israel, but One May Not Remove Anyone.**" See an explanation in the Key Concepts section. Israel takes precedence over the Diaspora. Thus, for example, when a couple argues and one spouse wants to stay in Israel but the other wants to leave, the one who wants to stay has the upper hand. So too with someone who lived in the Diaspora and died in Israel versus someone who lived in Israel but died in the Diaspora – one can bring the deceased to Israel, but not take someone who has died in Israel to the Diaspora.[1106]

1103. Y. Kilayim 9:4, on the verse in Jer. 2:7.

1104. *Shulḥan Arukh, Yoreh De'ah* 363:2 and *Siftei Cohen* ad loc.

1105. *Gesher HaḤayim* 27:9, 3.

1106. If a tourist died in Israel and was buried in Israel – the family is not permitted to open the grave and take them to the Diaspora, unless the deceased made his intention clear and asked to be buried outside of Israel. If the family is upset by

26. Outside of Israel, there is a custom to place a bit of earth from Israel in the grave.[1107]
27. A grave may be opened in order to take the body for burial in Israel.

The prohibition against deriving benefit from graves

28. One may not derive benefit from a grave[1108] and therefore one should not step, lean, or stand on graves. It is permissible to step on a grave in order to perform a mitzva (e.g., those who carry the body during the funeral),[1109] and it is customary to ask the deceased for forgiveness when one needs to step on the grave.
29. It is also forbidden to derive benefit from the tombstone or the earth of the grave,[1110] but it is permissible to derive benefit from the dirt that was dug.[1111] Earth cannot be subject to a prohibition on deriving benefit. This halakhic principle appears in other areas of halakha, as well; for example, earth that was used for idol worship is permitted for use, despite the fact that one is forbidden to derive benefit from idolatry itself.
30. If a body has been removed from a grave, someone else may be buried there.[1112] If the grave was reserved for one's parent, who was then buried elsewhere, one should not be buried there out of respect for one's parent. A different person may be buried there.[1113]
31. If the tombstone is replaced, the old tombstone cannot be used, sold, or exchanged. It may be donated to be used for another deceased person, at no cost.[1114]

---

this, one should speak to them sensitively and assure them that it is a merit for their relative to be buried in Israel (*Yalkut Yosef* 52:7).

1107. Rema, *Yoreh De'ah* 363:1.

1108. *Shulḥan Arukh, Yoreh De'ah* 364:1.

1109. *Turei Zahav*, ad loc. 1.

1110. Rema, *Yoreh De'ah* 368:1. There was a custom to take earth from the Mount of Olives and send it to the Diaspora and this was allowed. *Gesher HaḤayim* 27:4, 4.

1111. *Shulḥan Arukh, Yoreh De'ah* 364:1, according to the general rule that appears in the Talmud (Sanhedrin 47b).

1112. *Gesher HaḤayim* 27:3, 11.

1113. *Shulḥan Arukh, Yoreh De'ah* 364:7.

1114. Ibid. 14–15, and regarding using the wall of the cemetery see ibid. 19.

32. In general, one may not derive benefit from a coffin that was used, from which the deceased was removed. This is also the rule regarding other items used for the deceased. Some have written that if a coffin that was used to send a body to Israel, where the person was then buried without a coffin, then the coffin can be used again, especially if not doing so would involve a significant financial loss.[1115]
33. Plants and fruit that have grown on the graves are forbidden, but they may be used or sold by the cemetery.
34. Trees that are planted in the cemetery but do not grow on the graves themselves – their fruit may be gathered and used.[1116]

Establishing a new cemetery

35. When a new cemetery is established or an existing one is expanded, when purchasing the land, one should say "And death shall vanish eternally," so as not to create a bad omen.
36. Some places have the custom that at least ten members (a *minyan*) of the *ḥevra kaddisha* encircle the plot allocated for the cemetery seven times. Beginning in the south-east corner, they go counter-clockwise (east, north, west, and south). Before this ceremony, they recite passages and psalms, among them "*VeYehi Noam*," Psalm 91, the section about the ritual incense (see Part 7, Selected Prayers and Passages: "The Incense," "*Ana Bekoaḥ*." While they circle the area, they again recite "*VeYehi Noam*," Psalm 91, and "*Ana Bekoaḥ*." After the seven times around, they spell out the name of the city using the alphabetical verses in Psalm 119 and the Hebrew letters, קרע שטן.

1115. *Yalkut Yosef* 51:1. The reason is because those who sent the body from the Diaspora were relying on the *ḥevra kaddisha* in Israel for the burial; because burial in Israel is done without a coffin, the coffin is not considered to have been sanctified and therefore not forbidden for other use. Even if those sending the body were not familiar with the custom in Israel, it was a mistake and the coffin is not considered to have been sanctified. He added there that one should check to see what the intentions were of those sending the coffin. If their intention was that the coffin would be buried with the body, then it should not be used.

1116. *Shulḥan Arukh, Yoreh De'ah* 368:2; *Gesher HaḤayim* 27:5, 2; *Pnei Barukh* 37:27.

Some communities add other special prayers and verses.[1117] See in Key Concepts, **Dedicating a Cemetery.**

Method of burial

37. It is customary for the deceased to be buried lying on their back[1118] facing upwards, with the feet pointing towards Israel and, within Israel, with the feet pointing toward Jerusalem. But if this is not the local custom, then the individual should be buried according to the accepted method in the cemetery.[1119]
38. A wicked person should not be buried next to a righteous person, as it says: "Do not sweep me away with sinners" (Ps. 26:9).
39. Two people who hated each other should not be buried next to each other.[1120]
40. Some places have the custom of trying to bury men next to men and women next to women. But even in these places, it is permissible to bury a man and woman next to each other.[1121]

    Regarding different types of burial in the cemetery, see Key Concepts, **Multi-Level Burial.**

The dimensions of and distance between graves

41. The dimensions of the grave should be spacious enough for the deceased to fit comfortably. The dimensions vary from place to place; the grave is usually 6.6 feet (2 meters) long, 2.3 feet (0.7 meters) wide, and 3.9 feet (1.2 meters) deep. (Some would prefer

---

1117. See the list in *Gesher HaḤayim* 27:11. He writes that in Jerusalem and the other ancient cities of Israel, they did not have the custom to encircle the cemetery. See also *Kol Bo al Aveilut* p. 163.
1118. The Yemenite custom is to bury the body on its side with the face turned upwards (*Shulḥan Arukh HaMekutzar, Einei Yitzḥak, Yoreh De'ah* 181:1, in the footnote). The custom in Yemen was to dig a hole along the side of the dug-up grave and to place the deceased there. The hole was then sealed with stones and the grave with earth (ibid., and Rabbi Kapaḥ wrote the same in the book *Halikhot Teiman, Minhagei Kevura VeAveilut*, p. 328).
1119. *Kol Bo al Aveilut*, p. 177–178.
1120. *Shulḥan Arukh, Yoreh De'ah* 362:5–6.
1121. *Kol Bo al Aveilut* p. 179. And Ḥananya Shaḥor, the head of Jerusalem's Kehilat Yerushalayim *ḥevra kaddisha* related this to me in the name of Rabbi Kulitz.

the grave be deeper in accordance with Kabbalistic teachings, even as deep as the height of a person.) A frame of blocks or stones is built inside the grave, around the perimeter, to a height of 15.7 inches (40 centimeters). The deceased is placed inside the frame. A covering of blocks is placed over the frame, leaving a space of 3.1 inches (8 centimeters) above the body.

42. There should be a gap of at least six handbreadths (between 21.7–25.6 inches; 55–65 centimeters) between graves. If there is a rock or a cement divide, then there need only be a twelve-centimeter gap. In some places, due to lack of space, they have this smaller gap even without a rock or barrier between the graves, but it is appropriate to leave a distance of six handbreadths (between 21.7–25.6 inches). This is the custom in many places, but it does vary from place to place.
43. In a family plot, there need only be a 4.7-inch (12-centimeter) gap between the graves.[1122]
44. If the cemetery is full and there is no more space that can be allocated for burial, it is permissible to cover the graves with earth to the height of six handbreadths (23.6 inches; 60 centimeters) and prepare new graves above these.[1123] Today, in Israel, there is a severe shortage of space, and it is customary to bury in levels in accordance with halakhic guidelines, especially in hilly areas, such as in Har HaMenuḥot in Jerusalem. (See Key Concepts, **Multi-Level Burial.**) Some have written that this type of burial should be avoided for burying a man and woman on top of one another, even if they were married.[1124]

1122. *Gesher HaḤayim* 27:7, 2.

1123. *Shulḥan Arukh, Yoreh De'ah* 362:4. However, in the *Beit Yosef* he quotes Naḥmanides in *Torat HaAdam*, that it is enough to leave three handbreadths. Rabbi Akiva Eiger (ad loc.) agrees that this is sufficient; the *Pitḥei Teshuva* (ad loc. 3) also writes that it is enough to have a gap of less than six handbreadths, but the *Gesher HaḤayim* (27:6, 6) writes that one should be stringent to leave a gap of six handbreadths and not to be lenient by leaving less. In *Tzror HaḤayim* (290) he writes that they should leave six handbreadths between the graves, and, if there is no room, they should do multi-level burial.

1124. *BeMar'eh HaBazak*, vol. 2, p. 136, in the name of Rabbi Shaul Yisraeli.

45. In the case of a tragedy, where a large number of people must be buried together, there should be at least a small separation between the bodies.[1125]

SECTION 46: EXHUMING A GRAVE

The reason for the prohibition

1. The prohibition against exhuming the deceased is due to "the degradation of the dead." The concern is that if the body is moved, it may come apart or be exposed in a dishonorable manner. The prohibition is also due to the fear of God's judgment because when handling the body, one disturbs the deceased's rest. This corresponds to what Job said, about his desire to die: "I would be asleep and at rest" (3:13). The prophet Samuel also said, "Why have you disturbed me and brought me up?" (I Sam. 28:15).[1126]

In what circumstances can a grave be moved?

2. As a rule, a dead body should not be exhumed, except in the following circumstances:

- To bury the person with his family
- To move the person from a grave that is not his to one that is
- If the person has been buried among gentiles or next to a gentile
- If the person is buried in a stolen grave, i.e., one that was not actually owned by the owner
- If the grave causes distress to many people, e.g., it if is close to a road
- In order to bring the person to Israel from the Diaspora
- If the grave is somewhere unprotected, at risk of being harmed

1125. *Gesher HaḤayim* 27:6, 4.
1126. *Siftei Cohen, Yoreh De'ah* 363:1.

- If the person was buried in a temporary grave or gave instructions to move his body to a different place

3. It is clearly forbidden to move bones for the sake of research. In cases where one is permitted to remove the deceased's bones from a grave, they should be buried right away in a respectful manner.
4. If the deceased was buried in Israel, he should not be moved in order to be buried in Jerusalem. There is a halakhic principle about Jerusalem that is similar to "One may bring anyone to the Land of Israel." The principle states, "One may bring anyone to Jerusalem, but one may not remove anyone." However, this principle is only applied to the living, not to the deceased. The details of these rules are brought in Key Concepts, **One May Bring Anyone to the Land of Israel, But One May Not Remove Anyone.**
5. According to the halakha, a *met mitzva* – a deceased person who was discovered and has no one to tend to him – should be buried where he was found.[1127] However, this is not the custom nowadays. The person is buried in the cemetery.[1128] (See Key Concepts, ***Met Mitzva.***)
6. If one finds a grave in one's field and does not know whether the person was buried with the previous owner's knowledge, one is permitted to move the remains, and the site is considered pure. But if the person was buried there with the consent of the previous owner, the grave cannot be moved; if it was moved, the site is considered impure and one cannot derive benefit from it.[1129] (See Key Concepts, **Grave That Is Discovered.**)
7. A grave that causes damage to others, e.g., if it is close to a road – even if the burial had the consent of the landowner, the grave

1127. Ibid. 364:3, based on the Talmud, Bava Kamma 81b.
1128. *Ḥazon Ish, Yoreh De'ah* 209:13; *Yalkut Yosef* 14:23.
1129. *Tur, Yoreh De'ah* 364 and in *Shulḥan Arukh,* ibid. 2.

can be moved and the site is considered pure. One is allowed to derive benefit from this ground.[1130]

8. If a grave or a cemetery is in a disgraceful state, it is permissible to move the graves. However, this is only after all efforts have been made to preserve the graves in their original location. A rabbi who is familiar with all the details should be consulted.[1131]

How to move a grave

9. In a case where it is permissible to exhume a body, one must try to wait until the flesh has decomposed and exhume only the bones. If a coffin is being moved, it should not be opened.
10. When moving the body, the earth that was around it must also be taken and buried in the new location, together with body. The amount to be taken is three finger-widths (2.4 inches; 6 centimeters) deep on all sides.
11. The person who transports the bones must do so in the most respectful manner possible, out of sensitivity and respect for this human being who carried God's image. The Talmud (Berakhot 18a) states: "One who transports bones from place to place may not place them in a saddlebag and place them on the donkey's back and ride on them, as in doing so he treats the remains disgracefully. However, if he is afraid of gentiles or highwaymen – he is permitted to do so." That is to say, the way to deal with the bones is determined by the circumstances, and the guiding principle is respect for the deceased.

Customs of mourning when a grave is moved

12. If the person was buried with the intention of moving the body during the shiva, the relatives begin the mourning period only from the time of the second burial.
13. If the deceased was buried with the intention of moving the body after the shiva, the relatives start the shiva immediately after the

1130. *Shulḥan Arukh, Yoreh De'ah* 364:5; *Siftei Cohen* ad loc. 12, according to the Talmud, Sanhedrin 47b, "*Karka olam eina ne'eseret.*"

1131. *Responsa Igrot Moshe, Yoreh De'ah*, vol. 1, 246, and see also *BeMar'eh HaBazak*, vol. 5, 95.

first burial. If the grave was moved during the shiva, they start counting the shiva again from the second burial. If the grave was moved after the shiva, they do not sit shiva again.

14. If the person was buried and there was no intention that it would be moved – if the grave was eventually moved, the relatives do not begin the mourning period again. Rather, they follow the practices of likut *atzamot,* "gathering the bones," as explained below.[1132]

The prohibition against opening a grave

15. After closing the grave, it should not be reopened.[1133]
16. The prohibition is against opening the inner covering, called the "*ohel,*" the "tent." But if necessary, one can dig in the ground above the inner covering, e.g., if something fell into that area. Before the grave is closed up, it is permissible to lift the inner covering if necessary.
17. If, after the grave was closed, they remember that the deceased gave instructions to bury something specific with him, the item should be buried in the ground above the inner covering; the inner covering itself should not be opened.
18. The grave may be opened for the purpose of identifying the deceased, in order to allow the deceased's wife to remarry.[1134]
19. If an infant was buried without having been circumcised, the grave may be opened within the first one or two days in order to perform the circumcision. After that, the grave should not be opened so as not to defile the dead.
20. If they forgot to dress the body in one of the shrouds – if the deceased was a child under the age of thirteen, the grave can be opened within a day or two of burial. But this should not be done if the person was older, out of fear of God's judgment.

1132. *Shulḥan Arukh, Yoreh De'ah* 375:3; *Gesher HaḤayim* 19:4, 9; *Pnei Barukh* 8:2.
1133. *Shulḥan Arukh, Yoreh De'ah* 363:7.
1134. *Yalkut Yosef* 52:9.

21. If the body was not arranged properly or the limbs were not straightened, the grave may be opened within a day or two, even if the deceased was an adult.

Gathering of the bones (*Likut Atzamot*)

In Talmudic times, they would bury the body temporarily in a hole; once the body had decomposed, they would gather the bones and bury them in a different spot. When the bones were gathered, customs of mourning were observed for one day.[1135] Today, this law is only observed in a case where a body is moved to a new grave.

22. When the "gathering of the bones" begins, the relatives observe the customs of mourning – they do *kriya* again, sit on the ground, remove their shoes, and observe mourning until evening. At nightfall, the mourning ceases, even if the bones have not yet been reburied. No mourning is observed the next day, even if the exhumation continues and the reburial takes place on that day. Therefore, the bones should not be exhumed close to nightfall so that it will not create a situation where the relatives did not have the chance to observe mourning over the "gathering of the bones."[1136]
23. Eulogies are not said at the "gathering of the bones," but they praise the deceased and praise God who gives life and takes it away.
24. The customs of mourning apply to a "gathering of the bones" even in a case where the body has not yet decomposed.
25. The laws of *aninut* do not apply to the "gathering of the bones." Therefore it is permitted to eat meat and drink wine.[1137]

1135. *Gesher HaḤayim* 26:4, 8. Before that (in paragraph 5) he writes that, in his opinion, the prohibition not to leave the body overnight does not apply to the bones, only to a body with flesh.
1136. *Shulḥan Arukh, Yoreh De'ah* 403:1. According to the *Ḥazon Ish* (*Yoreh De'ah* 213:4), the mourning begins when the gathering of the bones is finished. Therefore, if they started during the day and completed gathering the bones at night, mourning would be observed the following day for the whole day.
1137. *Shulḥan Arukh*, ibid.

26. If a relative did not observe the laws of mourning on the day of the "gathering of the bones," he should not observe these laws on the following day.
27. The relatives observe the laws of mourning on the day of the "gathering of the bones" even if they were not present to witness the activity but were simply told about it. But if they were informed about it only on the following day, they do not observe the laws of mourning.
28. There is no obligation to inform the relatives about the "gathering of the bones." Some claim that it is preferable not to inform them so that they do not have to mourn again.[1138]
29. The bones that are exhumed should be treated respectfully, carefully preserved, and carried with care, the way a dead body is carried.
30. Bones should not be exhumed during a holiday so as not to arouse sadness.
31. When the bones of two or more bodies are exhumed, those doing so must take care not to mix up the bones. The bodies may be buried in one big grave with each person in a separate coffin.[1139]
32. A child should not exhume his parent's bones on his own. This is especially forbidden when the body is still intact, out of respect for one's parents.
33. If the son is a *kohen*, he may not become defiled for his relative since the body may be incomplete, and *kohanim* are not permitted to become defiled for a body that is incomplete.[1140]
34. If the person was buried in a temporary grave and was moved during the shiva, then the shiva begins again. If it was moved after the shiva, then the mourning is for one day.

1138. In *Yalkut Yosef* (59:2) he wrote that when the bodies of war victims were moved to a permanent grave and resting place, it was appropriate not to inform the family when it would be done so they would not be obligated to mourn again.
1139. *Yalkut Yosef* 52:12.
1140. *Siftei Cohen, Yoreh De'ah* 403:1.

35. The laws of mourning on the day of "gathering of the bones" are only observed once. Even if the body is exhumed again, the laws of mourning are not observed.
36. Moving the body from a coffin into the ground or from the ground into a coffin is considered to be a "gathering of the bones." Moving the coffin in its entirety from one place to another is not considered a "gathering of the bones."[1141]

Special Situations in Mourning

SECTION 47: DELAYED BURIAL

1. If the burial is delayed and, during this time, it is possible and necessary for the relatives to tend to the deceased and the burial, they observe *aninut*.[1142] But if it not possible for them to tend to the deceased, there is no *aninut*.[1143] See Sec. 6, "Pre-Burial Phase of Mourning (*Aninut*): When Does *Aninut* Apply?"
2. If the body was sent to another city and the mourners do not know when it will be buried, then, generally speaking, those who remain behind begin mourning when they come back from accompanying the body.[1144] See Sec. 7, "Arrangements for the Funeral and Burial: The beginning of *aveilut*" and see also, Sec. 48, "Notice of Death After Others Began Sitting Shiva." Those who travel with the body and attend the burial start their mourning

1141. *Gesher HaḤayim* 26:4, 12. *Responsa Yabia Omer*, vol. 9, 48. However, in *Responsa Igrot Moshe* (*Yoreh De'ah*, vol. 1, 260) he wrote that one should be stringent and observe mourning in such a case. See also *Responsa BeMar'eh HaBazak*, vol. 2, p. 139.
1142. *Yad Ephrayim, Hilkhot Onen* 1.
1143. *Kol Bo al Aveilut* p. 118. In his time, there were official laws in certain places according to which a person could not be buried within forty-eight hours after dying. This was to ensure that the person was dead. It raised a question as to the definition of *aninut*. See e.g., ibid., p. 119, for the halakhic discussion of this matter.
1144. Rabbi Nebenzahl: If one maintains contact over the phone or by other means and gives instructions where the deceased should be buried, etc., one still has the status of *aninut*.

after the burial.[1145] See the next chapter for more details and discussion about this halakha.

3. If one received news that a relative died in another city and the burial is delayed – if one is not going to travel to the funeral, then mourning begins only at the time of the burial.[1146] Some say that it begins immediately. If someone in Israel has a relative who has died in the Diaspora and the funeral will be held there on Erev Yom Tov – if one began mourning a short while before the Yom Tov began, one is exempt from the shiva despite the fact that the deceased was not yet buried.[1147]
4. One who began and completed shiva earlier than the other mourners also completes the *shloshim* earlier. But one should not visit the grave until thirty days have passed since the burial.[1148]
5. If the deceased was placed in a coffin but was not buried because the city was under siege, then the mourners begin shiva and *shloshim* immediately, even though they intend to bury the person when the siege is over. In this situation, the closing of the coffin is considered to be the equivalent of burial, and mourning begins immediately.[1149]

1145. *Shulḥan Arukh, Yoreh De'ah* 375:2; *Gesher HaḤayim* 19:4, 8. And see above, page ???, "The beginning of *aveilut*."

1146. *Gesher HaḤayim* 19:4, 10; *Pnei Barukh* 8:11; *BeMar'eh HaBazak*, vol. 2, p. 144. In a case where the body was sent to be buried in another city, the mourners begin shiva immediately since they have completed their involvement with the deceased; but when the mourning is based on having been informed of the death and of the burial being the following day, the mourning starts with the burial. Some have rejected this reasoning and claim that, in this case, as well, mourning begins immediately and they do not have to wait for the burial. Even according to the opinion that they must wait until the burial, *aninut* does not apply since they are not involved in the preparations for the burial (*Pnei Barukh* ibid., note 23).

Rabbi Nebenzahl: Unless the relative is still giving instructions regarding the deceased.

1147. *Nitei Gavriel*, vol. 1, 133:15.

1148. This is what Rabbi Yaakov Ruza taught me. It is because *aveilut* concerns the relatives and is measured by the amount of time that they have observed mourning, while visiting the grave has to do with the state of the soul, which depends on the burial.

1149. *Shulcḥan Arukh, Yoreh De'ah* 375:4.

6. If a Jew is executed by the ruler, and that ruler will not permit the deceased to be buried, the relatives should still observe the shiva and *shloshim*. The period of mourning begins on the day when the relatives give up hope that the deceased will be buried.[1150]
7. If someone began to sit shiva because he thought his relative had been buried, but then found out that the relative had not been buried, he must begin to sit shiva again from the time the deceased was buried, or from the point at which hope of burial was given up.[1151]
8. If the body was sent to another city and one began to sit shiva, but the burial was then delayed for an extended period of time, one does not stop sitting shiva, nor does one need to sit shiva again after the burial.[1152]
9. If there is an unavoidable delay of the burial, the body may be frozen or embalmed, out of respect for the deceased.[1153]

SECTION 48: NOTICE OF DEATH AFTER OTHERS BEGAN SITTING SHIVA

1. If a person did not know that a relative had died, and he arrived at the house of mourning in the middle of the shiva, or if he knew about the death but did not start shiva until he joined the other mourners in the house of mourning – in certain circumstances, this person needs to begin counting shiva for himself, from the beginning; in other circumstances, he will complete shiva together with the other mourners.
2. An important halakhic concept in this area is the "leader of the household." This is the central person in the family, the mourner who makes decisions related to the deceased and the burial. This is not necessarily the eldest person in the family.

1150. Ibid. 5.

1151. Rema, ad loc. 1, *Shulḥan Arukh* ibid., 6.

1152. Rema, *Yoreh De'ah* 375:7; *Pnei Barukh* 8:9.

1153. I heard this from Rabbi Mordekhai Eliyahu. (And this is similar to Rema, *Yoreh De'ah* 363:2. Although the discussion there is about quickening the process, while here it is about delaying it, the common principle is that it may be done out of respect for the deceased.)

3. If the leader of the household is sitting shiva with the rest of the mourners, then the relative who has arrived in the middle of shiva shall join them and complete the shiva with them.
4. The following four conditions must be met in order for the newcomer to complete his shiva together with the other mourners:

   - This person did not know of the death, or knew of it but had not started counting shiva until he came to the house of mourning. If he had begun to count shiva on his own, he may not join the others in their counting.
   - The leader of the household is one of the other mourners.
   - The mourners are sitting shiva in the city where the deceased died or was buried.
   - The relative was no more than a day's journey away at the time of the burial.[1154]

   If these four conditions are not met, the relative counts the seven days of shiva for himself, beginning at the point when he heard about the death.

5. In a case where there is no "leader of the household," for example, if there are several brothers who hold equal status – then the majority of the brothers are counted as the leader of the household. In this case, it is customary to allow the newcomer to join the rest of the mourners in their counting of shiva.
6. Even if the newcomer has arrived on the seventh day of shiva, if the others have not yet gotten up from shiva, the newcomer should sit with them for a short while; he can then get up with

1154. In the *Shulḥan Arukh* (*Yoreh De'ah* 375:8) he ruled that if the person was in a nearby location, defined as the distance that can be traveled in one day, then he may join the other mourners. The later halakhic authorities argued whether today we should take into account the distance that can be traveled by train or by airplane. The opinions are brought in *Yalkut Yosef* 15, note 3, and he adds (ibid. 6) that if it is theoretically possible for the person to arrive within twelve hours, even if it actually took more time because of stops along the way, it is still considered a distance of a day's journey, and he may join the other mourners.

them from shiva and put on tefillin (with the blessing).[1155] If the other mourners have already gotten up from shiva, the newcomer should start counting shiva for himself.

7. If the newcomer joins the other mourners and sits shiva with them, even if he subsequently returns to his own home, he gets up from shiva at the same time as the leader of the household.
8. If the leader of the household himself hears about the death after the other mourners, he does not join them in their counting. Some do allow him to join them.[1156]
9. If the leader of the household began sitting shiva and then went to the location of the other relatives and informed them of the death, the others count for themselves; they do not join him in his counting. Only someone who arrives in the place where other mourners are sitting shiva would join their counting.
10. If the body of the deceased is moved from one city to another, and some of the relatives stay behind while others accompany the deceased – the rule is that those who stay in the first city begin counting shiva after parting from the deceased, and those accompanying the body begin shiva after the burial. However, when the leader of the household accompanies the deceased and will not be returning to the other relatives, they all follow the leader in starting shiva after the burial. But this only applies if the location where the deceased will be buried is no more than three-days' journey away; if it is farther than that, they begin sitting shiva immediately. If the leader of the household will be returning to the house of mourning within seven days, then the other relatives start shiva after they depart from escorting the deceased; those returning from the burial join them and finish shiva together with them.[1157]
11. Someone who hears that a relative has died in another city and does not intend to go to the funeral – if he knows that the funeral will be held that day, he begins shiva from the time the burial

1155. *Yalkut Yosef* 58:14.
1156. Ibid. 15:8.
1157. *Shulḥan Arukh, Yoreh De'ah* 375:2; *Gesher HaḤayim* 19:5, 6; *Ḥokhmat Adam* 162:15.

is over. If the burial will not be held that day, he starts shiva immediately, without waiting for the funeral. If he does not know when the funeral will be held, he should start shiva immediately, from when he is informed of the death.[1158]

12. If someone was informed that a relative died in the Diaspora, he does not put on tefillin that day. He should begin sitting shiva after the burial. Some say that the person can begin mourning immediately if he does not know when the burial will take place. If he began mourning immediately and then found out that the burial was delayed for three days, he does not need to sit an additional three days of shiva.[1159]

SECTION 49: RECEIVING NOTICE OF A DEATH

Prompt report (*Shmua krova*)

The rule in the matter is: The day of hearing a prompt report is like the day of burial. (Maimonides, *Mishneh Torah, Hilkhot Avel* 7:1)

1. If someone hears about the death of a relative within thirty days of the date of the death (including on the thirtieth day) – this is called a prompt report (*shmua krova*).[1160]
2. Upon receiving a prompt report of a relative's death, the mourner does not put on tefillin, does *kriya*, and eats a meal of condolence (*seudat havraah*). The mourner sits shiva and counts *shloshim* from the day he received the news.
3. One makes the blessing "*Dayan HaEmet*" immediately upon hearing the news, even on Shabbat or Yom Tov.[1161]
4. It is possible for the laws of a "prompt report" to apply before the burial. For example, according to the opinion that one begins shiva immediately upon receiving the report, if someone heard

---

1158. *Tzror HaḤayim* 76.
1159. *Yalkut Yosef* 15:10, and in the footnote, he discusses whether there are cases where mourning begins before the funeral.
1160. *Shulḥan Arukh, Yoreh De'ah* 402:1.
1161. *Shemirat Shabbat KeHilkhata*, vol. 2, 65:49.

the news and was not planning to attend the funeral, he would begin sitting shiva upon receipt of the report, even prior to the funeral. And see the previous chapter, halakhot 11–12.

On Shabbat and holidays

5. If one received a prompt report on Shabbat, the shiva begins on Shabbat since one observes mourning in private and it ends on Friday morning.[1162]
6. If the person received a prompt report on the day before a holiday, even if the holiday falls out on Shabbat, the holiday cancels the shiva.[1163]
7. If a person received a prompt report on Yom Tov, he should say the *Dayan HaEmet* blessing. On Motza'ei Yom Tov, if it is not Ḥol HaMoed, one performs *kriya*; but if it is Ḥol HaMoed, no *kriya* is performed since this is after the height of the mourner's grief has passed, and after the moment of hearing the news.[1164] The shiva begins after the holiday, but the days of the holiday are counted towards the *shloshim*.
8. If someone received news after a festival that a relative died before the festival – since he did not observe mourning before the festival began, he begins mourning from the day he heard the news.[1165]
9. The meal of condolence is not eaten on Shabbat or Yom Tov.[1166] But if one received a prompt report on Shabbat or a holiday, then, according to the Sephardic custom, mourners eat a meal of condolence on that Motza'ei Shabbat or Motza'ei Yom Tov, since this is when mourning begins; according to the Ashkenazic custom, the meal is not held then, because the mourning was delayed.[1167]

1162. *Shulḥan Arukh, Yoreh De'ah* 402:7.
1163. Ibid. 399:1, 492:10; *Shemirat Shabbat KeHilkhata* ibid., 50.
1164. *Mishna Berura* 547:11.
1165. *Shulḥan Arukh, Oraḥ Ḥayim* 548:20 and *Yoreh De'ah* 402:8.
1166. *Shulḥan Arukh, Yoreh De'ah* 401:4.
1167. *Shulḥan Arukh* and Rema, *Yoreh De'ah* 378:11; *Gesher HaḤayim* 20:2, 11; *Yalkut Yosef* 13:13.

10. If one received a prompt report on Ḥol HaMoed, the law is the same as if the death occurred on Ḥol HaMoed. But if by the end of the festival, more than thirty days will have passed from the date of death, one performs kriya on Ḥol HaMoed (for any of the seven close relatives).[1168]
11. Even when the news of the death is received days or weeks after the death, the *shloshim* is counted from the day of the death. However, if a holiday falls out after the death and before the receipt of the prompt report, the festival does not shorten the *shloshim*. For example, if a person's relative died on Erev Sukkot, and he heard about it only ten days after Sukkot, we do not calculate the short time before the festival as seven days, nor do we count the festival of Shemini Atzeret as seven days. The holiday does not cancel mourning unless someone has actually observed the customs of mourning before the holiday – which is not the case if the person did not know of the death.[1169]

If one did not observe mourning upon hearing the news

12. If one received a prompt report but did not observe mourning, one is still obligated to sit shiva and observe *shloshim* unless thirty days have passed since the day of receiving the news. This is because the day of receiving the news is considered like the day of the burial, and the mourner is subject to the same rules as those that apply to someone who did not observe mourning and is within the *shloshim* – he is required to sit shiva and observe the complete thirty days. If thirty days have passed since he heard the news, and he did not observe the laws of mourning, then he can no longer sit shiva or observe the *shloshim*.[1170] Some say that if thirty days have passed from the day of the death, then the relative does not need to mourn.[1171]

1168. Even according to the custom that one performs *kriya* only for a parent on Ḥol HaMoed. *Shulḥan Arukh, Yoreh De'ah* 304:32, 401:3; *Gesher HaḤayim* 4:25.
1169. *Shulḥan Arukh, Oraḥ Ḥayim* 548:20 and *Yoreh De'ah* 402:8.
1170. *Gesher HaḤayim* 24:1, 7.
1171. *Nitei Gavriel*, vol. 2, 38:13, in the name of the *Ḥida*.

13. If a bride or groom received a prompt report during the week following their wedding, and after that week, more than thirty days will have passed from the date of death, he or she should observe mourning in private until the week is over; on the night following the end of that week, mourning should be observed for a short time, as one does upon receiving a "delayed report."[1172]

Memorial service marking the end of *shloshim*

14. Even though shiva and *shloshim* are observed from the day of receiving the news, the memorial service marking the end of *shloshim* should be held on the thirtieth day after the burial.[1173]

Delayed report (*Shmua reḥoka*)

But if he heard the news after thirty days, this is a delayed report, and he only observes for one day and does not perform kriya, and the day of receiving the news is like the seventh and the thirtieth day, where part of the day is counted as a whole day. (Maimonides, ibid.)

Timing

15. If a person received news of a relative's death more than thirty days after the death, including on the night that begins the thirty-first day – this is called a "delayed report."
16. In determining whether the news of a death is a delayed report, the number of days is counted from the day of the death, not the day of the burial.[1174]
17. The shortened customs of mourning that are observed in this case may also be observed at night.[1175]

1172. Ibid. 16.

1173. *Yalkut Yosef* 36:6.

1174. *Shulḥan Arukh, Yoreh De'ah* 402:1. Although there are opinions that are stringent and calculate only from the day of the burial, in *Gesher HaḤayim* (24:1, 1) he writes that if one wants to be lenient, there are opinions one can rely on. In *Yalkut Yosef* (58:4) and *Pnei Barukh* (26:3) they are also lenient.

1175. *Shulḥan Arukh, Yoreh De'ah* 395:2. Although there is a difference of opinion as to whether we apply the rule that part of the day is counted as a whole day for shiva

How mourning is observed

18. In the case of a delayed report, mourning is observed for a short time. It is sufficient to perform one act of mourning, e.g., removing one's leather shoes or sitting on a low chair. One can then immediately put one's shoes back on and sit on a regular chair.[1176]
19. If a person was learning Torah, or working, or bathing when he heard a delayed report, he must cease this activity immediately. But if he was wearing tefillin, he does not need to remove them. In any case, one must do some act that is clearly done because of mourning.
20. There is no meal of condolence in the case of a delayed report.[1177]

Dayan HaEmet

21. One must make the blessing "*Dayan HaEmet*" for all of one's relatives. If one did not make the blessing within twenty-four hours of hearing the news, the initial grief has passed and one does not make the blessing.[1178]

Kriya

22. One should tear one's garment only for a parent and not for other relatives. One must perform *kriya* for a parent in all cases, whenever one hears the news,[1179] as explained above in the laws of *kriya* for a parent.
23. If one receives a delayed report of a parent's death on Ḥol HaMoed, one delays performing *kriya* until after the festival;[1180]

---

observed at night, in the case of a delayed report, all agree that mourning at night is counted as mourning for an entire day (*Tur* ad loc.) and ibid. 402:1.

1176. *Shulḥan Arukh, Yoreh De'ah* 402:2.

1177. Ibid. 378:12.

1178. *Gesher HaḤayim* 24:2, 3. Despite the fact that one who is sitting shiva and did not say the blessing may say it within three days, that refers to someone who is actually sitting shiva, where the pain is more tangible.

1179. *Shulḥan Arukh, Yoreh De'ah* 340:18 and 402:4.

1180. *Mishna Berura* 547:14; *Gesher HaḤayim* 4:24.

however, the "*Dayan HaEmet*" blessing should be said immediately, even on Shabbat or Yom Tov.[1181]

Shiva, *shloshim*, and the twelve-month period

24. In a case of a delayed report, after the person has observed mourning for a short period, he does not observe the laws of shiva and *shloshim*. For a parent's death, the laws of the twelve-month period continue to apply; he may not get a haircut until someone criticizes him, wear new clothes, or attend celebrations, etc. (as explained in Sec. 34, "The Twelve-Month Mourning Period"). The twelve months are counted from the day of death, not from when the person received the news, Therefore, if one heard of a parent's death twelve months after the death, one performs *kriya* and observes mourning for a short time, and this is sufficient.[1182]
25. If someone has received a delayed report of a parent's death and observed mourning for a short time – if a holiday falls out within thirty days of the mourning, the person may get a haircut the day before the holiday, in honor of the holiday.[1183]
26. If one heard a delayed report on Shabbat or Yom Tov, one does not observe mourning, not even in private, until Motza'ei Shabbat or Yom Tov; at that point, they observe mourning for a short time, as explained above.[1184]
27. A prompt report that becomes a delayed report: If one hears the news of a relative's death on a Shabbat or Yom Tov that is the thirtieth day after the death, and the following day, the news would become a delayed report – even though one observed mourning in private on the Shabbat or Yom Tov, on Motza'ei

---

1181. Since the blessing was established for occasions of hearing bad news. In *Gesher HaḤayim* (4:26) he writes that those who connect the blessing to the *kriya* delay the blessing until after Shabbat or Yom Tov and then do *kriya*; but if it is a long delay, e.g., from Ḥol HaMoed until after the festival, then one should not wait to make the blessing.
1182. *Shulḥan Arukh, Yoreh De'ah* 402:1; *Gesher HaḤayim* 24:2, 4.
1183. *Yalkut Yosef* 58:3.
1184. *Shulḥan Arukh, Oraḥ Ḥayim* 548:18 and *Yoreh De'ah* 402:6.

Shabbat or Motza'ei Yom Tov it is considered a delayed report.[1185] Some say that the same is true if one hears the news of the relative's death on Purim.[1186]

28. If the recipient of the news is located in a different country than the deceased was, the calculation of days is made according to the location of the recipient of the news. For example, if an Israeli resident receives news of a death in the U.S. at a time when, in the U.S., it is still the thirtieth day after the death, but in Israel it is already the thirty-first day – it is considered a delayed report. And vice versa – if the person died in Israel and it is already the thirty-first day there, but a relative heard about it in the U.S., where it is still the thirtieth day – it is considered a prompt report.[1187]
29. If one is uncertain whether it is a prompt report or a delayed report, one should be lenient and not perform *kriya* for relatives other than one's parents. One should observe mourning for about an hour, and that is sufficient.[1188]
30. If it only becomes known that a scholar has died after twelve months have passed from the time of death, the scholar should not be eulogized.

Hearing news about two relatives

31. If one has simultaneously received news of the death of two relatives – whether the news is a prompt or delayed report – one observes mourning for both of them at the same time.

1185. *Shulḥan Arukh, Yoreh De'ah* 402:5.

1186. *Pnei Barukh* 26:15.

1187. *Yalkut Yosef* 58:10.

1188. There are opinions that say that one is obligated in the laws of mourning because we make the assumption that the deceased was living as long as that might have been possible, and that he only recently died (see *Bayit Ḥadash, Yoreh De'ah* 397). But the *Turei Zahav* disagrees since we do not assume the status of living for someone who has already died; moreover, we are generally lenient when it comes to mourning. *Gesher HaḤayim* 24:2, 7 and *Yalkut Yosef* 58:8 ruled according to this opinion. *Pnei Barukh* (26:4) quotes the *Shevet HaLevi* (*Yoreh De'ah* 213) that nowadays when the information can be easily clarified over the telephone, etc., we should be strict until the details have been clarified.

32. If one heard about the death of one relative and, after a day or more, heard about the death of another relative, one begins mourning anew for the second relative; these days apply for mourning the first relative, as well.[1189] Further explanation appears in Sec. 53, "If Another Relative Dies during the Mourning Period."

Mistakes in counting

33. If someone heard news of a relative's death and assumed it was a delayed report, but thirty days later he discovered that it had been a prompt report – or if someone misled the person, telling him that it was a delayed report when it was actually a prompt report, or if the person himself made a mistake and observed the way one mourns for a delayed report when it was actually a prompt report – he does not need to observe mourning again.[1190]
34. If someone heard that a relative had died and sat shiva, but later learned that the relative had only just died, he must sit shiva again. This is also the case if one sat shiva for a relative and only afterwards learned that it was in fact a different relative who had died; in this case, one must sit shiva again.[1191]

If one did not observe mourning upon hearing the news

35. If one did not observe mourning upon hearing the news, one must do so afterwards.[1192]

SECTION 50: A DOUBT REGARDING A DEATH

If there is uncertainty about whether a death has occurred, the basic rule is as follows: Any testimony that would allow a woman whose husband is missing to remarry, it is relied upon to obligate the relatives to mourn.[1193]

1189. *Shulḥan Arukh, Yoreh De'ah* 402:9.
1190. *Yalkut Yosef* 58:9; *Pnei Barukh* 26:6; and *Gesher HaḤayim* 24:2, 9.
1191. *Pnei Barukh* ibid. 7–8.
1192. *Responsa Tzitz Eliezer*, vol. 7, 49:10.
1193. Naḥmanides, *Torat HaAdam* (p. 239).

The laws about permitting an *aguna* (a woman bound in marriage) to remarry are quite complex. In general, the sages were lenient and relied on testimonies that would not otherwise be relied upon, in order to free the *aguna* and allow her to remarry. They relied on these testimonies because, first of all, they presume that a woman would check very thoroughly before remarrying and would not remarry while there is any lingering doubt as to whether her husband is alive. Furthermore, there is an assumption that witnesses do not lie in matters that will eventually be proven to be true or false.

Although only the second reason applies where mourning is concerned, the halakhic ruling was that, in cases of doubt regarding a death, we rely on various testimonies that would not otherwise be relied upon.

Testimonies that are acceptable to establish the obligation to mourn

1. Mourning is observed based on the testimony of one male or female witness, or that of a witness who heard from someone that the relative has died, or a gentile who relates it in passing.[1194] This last scenario indicates that the gentile did not intend to convey a testimony because, in that case, it could be claimed that he had an ulterior motive, and the testimony would be rejected. Rather, the halakha stipulates that he related the facts in passing, without the intention of giving testimony.
2. If one witness says that the person died and another witness said that the person did not die, or if two said that the person died and two said that the person did not die, then one does not mourn, since we assume that a person is alive until it is clear to us that he is dead. When the testimonies contradict each other, we are left with the assumption that the person is still alive.
3. Shiva and *shloshim* are counted from when the relative has received the news. If someone notified the relatives that

1194. *Shulḥan Arukh, Yoreh De'ah* 397:1. Although some have written that, for the obligation of mourning, we should not rely on a gentile who relates the information in passing (*Turei Zahav* in the name of the *Or Zarua*), in *Gesher HaḤayim* (19:9, 1) he writes that one should act according to the *Shulḥan Arukh* and rely on a gentile who relates the news in passing.

someone has died, and they do not know whether the death occurred within the last thirty days, in which case the news is a prompt report and they need to sit shiva, or whether thirty days have passed and they would need to observe only shortened mourning as is done with a delayed report, there are different opinions; the halakha follows the lenient position in mourning, and they do not need to sit shiva.[1195] The same is true if the relatives were instructed not to mourn and later learned that they had received the news within thirty days of the death. In this case, they do not need to mourn after the thirty days have passed.[1196]

4. If there is a doubt as to whether a married man has died, he should not be mourned nor should Kaddish be said for him until the Beit Din permits his wife to remarry.[1197]

Captives and missing persons

5. If someone was taken captive and it is not known whether he is alive or dead, or if it is known that he is dead, but the body has not been found, the relatives do not mourn for him until they have lost hope of finding the body and burying it.[1198] A rabbi should be consulted if a lot of time has passed and there is little chance that the body will ever be found.

1195. *Turei Zahav* 397:2; *Arukh HaShulḥan, Yoreh De'ah* 397.

1196. *Turei Zaha*v ibid. Although in *Siftei Cohen* he writes that they do need to mourn, in *Gesher HaḤayim* (19:9, 4) he writes not to mourn. (It appears that it is a printing error in the *Siftei Cohen*; he is of the opinion that they should not mourn, according to what is brought in the *Nekudot HaKesef*, ad loc.)

1197. *Shulḥan Arukh, Even HaEzer* 17:5; *Siftei Cohen* on the *Shulḥan Arukh, Yoreh De'ah* 375:7. The source is the responsa of the Rif, quoted by the *Beit Yosef* ad loc. The rule is that as long as the wife is not permitted to remarry, the person is considered alive and should not be mourned. This is out of concern that if they mourn for him without definitive proof, it could lead the wife to mistakenly remarry.

1198. *Shulḥan Arukh, Yoreh De'ah* 375:5. The category of "having given up hope" applies to those who have been actively searching. If the police or army were performing the search, it is determined according to when they have given up searching. In certain cases, the family takes on the responsibility to find their relative. In that case, it is determined by when they have given up hope of finding the body.

6. Relatives begin mourning and saying Kaddish from the time that they have lost hope of finding the person.[1199] The twelve months are counted that time, as well, even if the deceased was subsequently found and buried.[1200]
7. If they had given up hope of finding the person and observed the laws of mourning and sat shiva and then the body was found, they do not need to mourn again. In the case of a parent, one should perform *kriya* based on a delayed report. And if one was present when the body was found, one should observe mourning for that day.[1201]

SECTION 51: A BRIDE AND GROOM

When a bride or groom loses a relative, there is a direct clash between joy and grief. The halakha approaches this the same way it approaches the clash between a holiday and mourning (as explained in Key Concepts, **The Coffin Yields Before a Bride**).

The death of a relative after the wedding

1. For the bride and groom, the seven days following the wedding have the same status as a holiday. Therefore, if one of their relatives dies during the first seven days after the wedding, they begin to observe mourning after the end of that seven-day period.[1202]
2. In fact, the seven days differ from a festival in two respects: On a holiday, mourners observe the prohibitions on marital relations, hair-cutting, and ironing. However, during the seven days following the wedding, only marital relations are forbidden; the other activities are permitted. In addition, if a relative has died on a holiday, the *shloshim* is counted from the burial since they observed some of the laws of mourning; the bride or groom, however, starts counting the *shloshim* only after the seven days following the wedding have ended.

1199. Ibid. 7
1200. *Gesher HaḤayim* 30:9, 11.
1201. *Shulḥan Arukh, Yoreh De'ah* 375:7.
1202. *Gesher HaḤayim* 19:7, 11; and see *Shulḥan Arukh, Yoreh De'ah* 342.

Aninut and impurity

3. The bride and groom do not observe *aninut.*[1203]
4. The groom wears tefillin on the first day and is allowed to eat meat and drink wine.[1204]
5. Some argue that if the groom is a *kohen,* he should not become impure for his relatives, even for his parents;[1205] others say that he is obligated to become impure for his relatives.[1206]

Kriya and the *Dayan HaEmet* blessing

6. Most are of the opinion that the bride and groom do not perform *kriya.*[1207]
7. Even though the bride and groom do not observe mourning, they do make the "*Dayan HaEmet*" blessing.

Participating in the funeral

8. After the funeral, the bride or groom may accompany the deceased a few steps; they should not go to the cemetery so as not to detract from their joy. Sometimes it is preferable to delay informing them of the death. Some say that it is a mitzva for them to go to the funeral.[1208]

1203. *Gesher HaḤayim* 18. In *Yalkut Yosef* (7:50) he writes that *aninut* does apply to a groom and that only the consummation of the marriage, which is a mitzva, is permitted. However, if there are other relatives who can handle the arrangements for the funeral and burial, then the bride and groom do not observe *aninut.* But if no one else can do so, it is their obligation to make the funeral arrangements and they do observe the laws of *aninut.*

1204. *Gesher HaḤayim* 18:4, 12; vol. 2, end of ch. 15.

1205. *Gesher HaḤayim* 19:7, 9; *Kol Bo al Aveilut* p. 70.

1206. *Responsa Minḥat Shlomo Tanina,* 89. But he does not give a halakhic decision and leaves it undecided.

1207. Although there are opinions that say that, for a parent, the bride or grooms should change clothes, performs *kriya* in private, and then puts the wedding garments back on, it is better not to perform *kriya* at all. *Gesher HaḤayim,* page 190;5; *Yalkut Yosef* 15:9.

1208. *Gesher HaḤayim* (19:7, 7) writes that they should not go to the cemetery. In *Yalkut Yosef* (10:9) he writes that it is a mitzva to attend, and in 15:9 he writes that they are permitted to participate in the funeral.

Comforting the mourners

9. Clearly, people should not come to comfort the bride and groom during the seven days following the wedding.[1209] It is certainly appropriate and commendable to visit them and make them happy.
10. The bride and groom may comfort other mourners.

The seven days following the wedding

11. In the seven days following the wedding, the principle of "part of the day is counted as a whole day" does not apply. Seven complete days of celebration are counted.
12. The bride and groom are not permitted to neglect their celebration and observe mourning during these days.[1210]

A holiday that falls out in the seven days following the wedding

13. If a festival occurs during these seven days, it does not cancel the shiva since this rule applies only in the case when one began observing mourning prior to the festival. The bride or groom has not begun mourning in the seven days of celebration and thus the shiva is not cancelled.[1211] However, some halakhic authorities wrote that the holiday does annul their mourning since they observed some of the laws of mourning in private.[1212]

Joining the other mourners

14. If one of the bride or groom's relatives died during the seven days following the wedding, and he or she will begin sitting shiva when the other relatives are in the middle of shiva, the bride or groom shall finish shiva together with them (as explained in Sec. 48, "Receiving Notice of a Death." and in the Key Concepts section, **Leader of the Household (*Gadol HaBayit*)**. Even if the bride or groom is joining on the last day of shiva, he or she

---

1209. *Gesher HaḤayim* 19:7, 5.
1210. *Yalkut Yosef* 15:9.
1211. See *Gesher HaḤayim* 19:7, 2.
1212. *Yalkut Yosef* 44:5; *Kol Bo al Aveilut* p. 66.

still finishes the shiva with the others.[1213] But if the shiva ended before the end of the sevens day of celebration, and so the bride or groom did not join the others, he or she begins counting the shiva alone.

Second marriage

15. In a second marriage for both parties (e.g., a widow marrying a widower), the same principle applies, that the seven days of celebration following the wedding should be completed before observing the customs of mourning.

A wedding during the shiva or after it

16. If one of the bride or groom's seven close relatives died before the wedding, and the wedding is scheduled for a date that falls out during the shiva, the wedding should be postponed. They should first observe shiva and are permitted to get married on the seventh day of the shiva.
17. A bride who is in mourning may bathe and otherwise prepare herself immediately after the shiva so that she can immerse in the *mikve* prior to the wedding.
18. If the wedding was set for after the shiva, then it should not be postponed; it should be conducted as usual with music and dancing.

SECTION 52: ONE WHO DID NOT OBSERVE MOURNING

1. If someone did not observe any of the laws of mourning, inadvertently or willfully, the person is required to sit shiva, as long as thirty days have not passed since the burial.[1214]
2. If one did not sit shiva for seven days, one cannot make up the missing days afterwards.
3. *Kriya* can only be performed during the shiva, except for a parent; one can do *kriya* for a parent at any time.

1213. *Gesher HaḤayim* 19:7, 4.
1214. *Shulḥan Arukh, Yoreh De'ah* 396:1.

4. If one intended to sit shiva but was not able to do so because of illness, the days are counted as shiva, and one does not need to sit shiva again.[1215]
5. If one sat shiva but did not observe the laws of *shloshim*, one does not need to make them up afterwards.[1216]

One who reaches bar or bat mitzva during the shiva

6. A boy or girl who reaches bar or bat mitzva during the shiva is exempt from sitting shiva, since they were not obligated from the beginning.[1217] However, it is customary for him or her to join the shiva from the time of becoming bar or bat mitzva.[1218] If the date of the bar/bat mitzva is after the shiva, he or she does not need to observe mourning because at the time of the death, he or she was completely exempt.[1219] The Yemenite custom is that a child who is old enough to understand the rules of mourning should observe them.[1220]

SECTION 53: IF ANOTHER RELATIVE DIES DURING THE MOURNING PERIOD

The halakhic term for this is "*takhfuhu avelav*," "his bereavements became constant," meaning that they came one after the other. Before concluding the mourning period for one person, one must start a new mourning period for another relative who has died.

1215. *Gesher HaḤayim* 21:15, 4, based on *Arukh HaShulḥan* 396:2. Although in *Pnei Barukh* (25:3) he brings opinions that they must complete the shiva, his conclusion is to be lenient. In *Yalkut Yosef* (page 779) he also wrote to be lenient.
1216. *Kol Bo al Aveilut* p. 351.
1217. *Shulḥan Arukh, Yoreh De'ah* 396:3.
1218. *Gesher HaḤayim* 19:3, 3.
1219. *Tzror HaḤayim* 293. However, some are strict, saying that if they reached bar/bat mitzva during the *shloshim* then they have to observe shiva and *shloshim* (Maharam). Some wrote that they should observe the mourning for twelve months out of respect for their parent (*Ḥokhmat Adam* 168:6). But in *Gesher HaḤayim* (19:3, 3), he writes that one can be lenient, following the *Shulḥan Arukh*.
1220. *Shulḥan Arukh HaMekutzar, Einei Yitzḥak, Yoreh De'ah* 186:13; *Be'er LeḤai Roi* 6–7.

1. If two of the person's relatives died on the same day, he observes one period of mourning for both of them.[1221]
2. If another relative died during the shiva, one must begin counting shiva again from the time of the second death; those days also counts toward the shiva for the first relative.[1222]
3. There are several leniencies that apply to such a case. If one's hair has become long and burdensome, one may get a haircut, but it should be done in an unusual way – with a knife and not with scissors. After the shiva for the first relative, one may wash one's clothes (without detergent) even though one is continuing to sit shiva for the second relative. Similarly, if one has begun mourning in the week leading up to Tisha B'Av, one may bathe in cold water but not in hot water.[1223]
4. As explained above in the halakhot of Kaddish, if one is saying Kaddish for a parent and another relative dies during the twelve-month mourning period, according to the Sephardic custom, one should stop reciting Kaddish for one week at the end of the twelve months and then continue.[1224] Some say that one should continue to lead prayers and say Kaddish and not stop at the end of the twelve months, even for one day.[1225] The Ashkenazic custom is to stop for the first and last day of the twelfth month; some write that one should arrange to have someone else say Kaddish during the twelfth month.[1226]

SECTION 54: SUICIDE

Where can I escape from Your spirit? Where can I flee from Your presence? If I ascend to heaven, You are there; if I descend to Sheol, You are there too. If I take wing with the dawn to come to

1221. *Shulḥan Arukh, Yoreh De'ah* 402:9.
1222. Ibid. 375:10.
1223. Moed Katan 17b; Maimonides, *Mishneh Torah, Hilkhot Avel* 6:13; *Shulḥan Arukh, Oraḥ Ḥayim* 551:15 and *Yoreh De'ah* 389:1 and 390:3.
1224. *Tzror HaḤayim* 264.
1225. *Yalkut Yosef* 30:8, and he writes that this also written in *Halikhot Shlomo* (*Hilkhot Tefilla*, p. 225) in the name of Rabbi Shlomo Zalman Auerbach.
1226. *Gesher HaḤayim* 30:9, 8.

> rest on the western horizon, even there Your hand will be guiding me, Your right hand will be holding me fast. If I say, "Surely darkness will conceal me, night will provide me with cover," darkness is not dark for You; night is as light as day; darkness and light are the same. (Ps. 139)

Jewish law takes a stern approach to someone who took his own life. The Jewish perspective maintains that, because a person's life does not belong to him, one is not permitted to take a life. This is true with regard to the lives of other people – "You shall not murder" – and also with regard to oneself. In this sense, someone who takes his own life is like a murderer.

From a purely theoretical halakhic perspective, someone who has taken his own life has committed a greater sin than someone who has killed somebody else. A person who has taken his own life has expressed, through this act, his denial of the Almighty who gave him his soul and who has sole permission to take it back; he ostensibly removes God's dominion over his soul, denying the basic idea that he – man – did not have a part in his own creation.

Death is considered to atone for man's sins. But when someone takes his own life, his death is not an atonement.

From a moral and social perspective, suicide is an escape from responsibility and a betrayal and abandonment of family and friends. For all these reasons, it is utterly condemned.

The rules governing a suicide are severe. But, from a practical perspective, we go to extreme lengths to ensure that no death is classified as a suicide. The mental and emotional pain that led a person to such an act surely clouded their judgment. As a result, the rules presented below are not applied in practice. This is explained below.

General approach

1. The general approach to a suicide is expressed by the sages in the following sentence: "The rule is that anything that expresses respect for the living should be done, but whatever does not

express respect for the living (but rather for the dead) should not be done by the community."[1227]

Laws regarding a suicide

2. *Aninut* is not observed; some disagree and say that the relatives do observe *aninut*.[1228] There are two reasons for the laws of *aninut*: One is the practical need to deal with the burial and the other is respect for the deceased, so that the relatives will focus their attention on the deceased. In the case of a suicide, the first reason applies since the deceased must be buried, but the second reason does not apply because of the aforementioned general approach to these cases.
3. *Kriya* is not performed. Some halakhic authorities, however, are of the opinion that the relatives should perform *kriya*.
4. The relatives do not make the blessing "*Dayan HaEmet*" since the person took his own life, against God's will, and it is inappropriate to say that God is the judge in this case. Nevertheless, a relative who wants to say the blessing may do so since the blessing is made in response to bad news and sorrow.[1229]
5. No eulogies are delivered and the deceased is not honored.
6. The deceased is buried four cubits away from other graves.
7. A relative who is a *kohen* shall not defile himself for the deceased.[1230]
8. The comforters stand in two rows and comfort the mourners since this is done out of respect for the living.
9. In principle, one does not mourn for the deceased in this case. But since certain halakhic authorities view mourning as honoring the living (not for the honor of the dead), if a family wishes to

---

1227. Smaḥot 2:1.

1228. According to *Gesher HaḤayim* (25:2, 6), they do not observe *aninut*; according to the *Tzitz Eliezer* (vol. 5, *Even HaEzer* 2) they do observe *aninut*. In *Kol Bo al Aveilut* (p. 142) he brings various opinions about this.

1229. *Yalkut Yosef* 56:1.

1230. *Shulḥan Arukh, Yoreh De'ah* 373:8.

sit shiva, they may do so. Thus, in practice, it is customary to sit shiva in the case of a suicide.[1231]

10. Kaddish is said for one who takes his own life. It should be recited for a full twelve months. Kaddish is usually only said for eleven months, since the wicked are judged for twelve months, and we do not want it to appear as if the child is suggesting that his parent was wicked. But in this case, the Kaddish should be recited for twelve whole months to increase merit for the deceased.
11. It is clear and evident that a *baal teshuva* (someone who became observant) is not permitted to take his own life to atone for his sins and that there is a severe prohibition against this. Nevertheless, if he sinned and did so, he should be mourned, because his intention was sincerely religious.[1232]

What is considered a suicide?

There was a case with the son of Gornos in Lod, who ran away from school and his father punished him. He feared his father so much that he drowned himself in a well. They came and asked Rabbi Tarfon and he said – Nothing should be spared from him. (*Avel Rabati* 2:4)

12. In all cases of suicide, we try to avoid classifying the deceased as a suicide.[1233] Therefore, whenever possible, we say that it was an accident, or that someone else was at fault, or that the person was mentally ill or confused, or that the person did the act but regretted his actions. We try to judge him favorably and be lenient and avoid approaching it as a suicide. Even if the person left a note or made his intentions clear, and time had passed before he

1231. *Tzror HaḤayim* 294 writes that in the *Ben Ish Ḥai* he brings seven reasons to mourn for the person and that this should be the accepted practice.

1232. *Yalkut Yosef* 56:3, and see the footnote where he discusses Yakim Ish Tzerurot, who performed the four capital punishments on himself to atone for his sins.

1233. Rabbi Nebenzahl: This requires further consideration, whether we should be lenient or whether it is preferable to be strict in order to deter others from doing the same.

committed the act, we try to claim that the person then changed his mind or regretted his actions.

13. If someone killed himself because he had no other choice, like King Saul, who feared that the Philistines would torture him, or if a small child took his own life – this is not treated as a suicide.
14. Some have suggested that if a person took his own life out of despair over his many misfortunes, is should not be treated as a suicide. Others have rejected this approach since anyone who takes his own life does so in response to misfortune.[1234]

SECTION 55: AN APOSTATE

1. For a *mumar* – a Jew who converts to another religion – even though halakhically he still retains his Jewish status, the halakha stipulates that no *kriya* is done for him and mourning is not observed; the person is not buried in a Jewish cemetery, and the relatives are not responsible for his burial.[1235] However, halakhic authorities have written that, in practice, the relatives are obligated to bury him.[1236]
2. When the person dies, there is no need to perform *kriya* or mourn.
3. Some say that an apostate who was killed by gentiles should be mourned. The same is true for a child who converted from Judaism together with his parents since the child is considered an *anus*, one who acted under duress.[1237]
4. If an apostate repented and decided to return to Judaism, even if he did not manage to do so before he died, he is treated like any other Jew in matters of burial and mourning.[1238]

1234. *Gesher HaḤayim* 25:3, 4 in the name of the *Besamim Rosh*. Rabbi Nebenzahl: Which is known to be an unreliable book. (The book is attributed to the Rosh but is alleged to be a forgery.)
1235. Rema, *Yoreh De'ah* 340:5.
1236. *Responsa Ḥatam Sofer, Yoreh De'ah* 341.
1237. Rema, *Yoreh De'ah* 340:5. Despite the Rema's conclusion that the person should not be mourned, the *Siftei Cohen* (ad loc. 9) writes that he should be mourned since his death at the hands of the gentiles atones for him.
1238. *Responsa BeMar'eh HaBazak*, vol. 4, 123, based on the Rema, *Ḥoshen Mishpat* 34:22.

5. Relatives mourn for an apostate from the time he converts to another religion.[1239] When the family hears that the person has converted, they mourn for one day.[1240] Some wrote that the custom in Jerusalem is to mourn for fourteen days.[1241] *Kriya* should be done, as is the law for hearing bad tidings, and they make the "*Dayan HaEmet*" blessing.

SECTION 56: EXTENUATING CIRCUMSTANCES FOR BURIAL

Ideally, every effort should be made to give all Jews, from anywhere in the world, a Jewish burial. All the customs of purification and the funeral and burial should be observed according to Jewish tradition. Most of the time, this is possible, even if it requires much effort. If it is not possible for all of the Jewish practices to be followed, they should be adhered to as much as possible. The following instructions are intended only for extenuating circumstances, where, after all efforts have been made, it is not possible to bury the deceased according to the rules laid out by Jewish tradition. They were written following consultation with Rabbi Mordekhai Eliyahu.

Purification and shrouds

1. International law in most places requires washing the deceased if the body will be being transported from one country to another.[1242] This means that there is usually a non-Jewish administrative service that performs a process similar to the Jewish ritual purification. All efforts should be made to do *tahara* on the body, and if possible, one can be assisted by the local administrative services.
2. In extenuating circumstances, there is no prohibition against having gentiles help with purifying the body.[1243] Ideally, however, every effort should be made that the body not be touched by

1239. *Gesher HaḤayim* 25:4, 3.

1240. Rabbi Nebenzahl: Some say for seven days, and Rabbenu Gershon Meor HaGola observed fourteen days.

1241. *Responsa Tzitz Eliezer*, vol. 5, *Even HaEzer* 4.

1242. Ḥananya Shaḥor, the head of the Kehilat Yerushalayim *ḥevra kaddisha*, told this to me.

1243. Beitza 6a: "If he dies on the first day of Yom Tov, gentiles should prepare him," and see *Shulchan Arukh, Oraḥ Ḥayim* 526:1.

gentiles, or by Jews who do not observe the Jewish laws of purity.[1244] If gentiles assist in the process, then, after they finish handling the body, a Jew should pour water over the entire body so that the final *tahara* is performed by a Jew.[1245]

3. If *tahara* cannot be performed, the surface of the body should be cleaned with alcohol or another sterilizing or cleansing agent.[1246]
4. If there are no shrouds available, the body should be wrapped in white cloth.

If there is no space in a Jewish cemetery

5. If the Jewish cemetery is completely full, it is permissible to bury the deceased above an existing grave (see Key Concepts, **Multi-Level Burial**) on the following conditions:

   - There is no other place available
   - The graves are separated by six handbreadths (23.6 inches; 60 centimeters) of dirt
   - The family no longer comes to visit the bottom grave
   - If possible, one should photograph the old gravestone and add the name of the person in the lower grave to the new gravestone.

6. In extenuating circumstances, an above-ground burial is possible, meaning that they fill a concrete frame with earth and bury the deceased there.

Burial among gentiles

7. A Jew should not be buried among gentiles. But it is preferable to bury the deceased among gentiles if there is a concern that the body will otherwise be cremated,.

1244. *Gesher HaḤayim* 12:1, 2; based on *Perek Maaseh HaMet* attributed to Hillel the Elder.

1245. *Responsa BeMar'eh HaBazak*, vol. 3, 66.

1246. Response in a letter from Rabbi Mordekhai Eliyahu.

8. If there is no other choice and a Jew is buried in a gentile cemetery:

    - There should be four cubits (around two meters) distance from gentile graves and, if possible, eight cubits.[1247]
    - If a four-cubit distance is not possible, a barrier should be made that is one-meter high, even if it is just a wire fence.
    - If this is not possible, the grave should be deepened by one meter.
    - One should try to purchase the gravesite in perpetuity so that the grave will not be removed in the future.

9. If a Jew must be buried among gentiles, all of the purification, funeral, and burial procedures should still be done by Jews, wherever possible.

Burial in a coffin

10. If a coffin is being used in the burial, it is preferable for there to be holes on the underside of the coffin or at least along the sides. These holes should be at least four-centimeters in diameter. (See Key Concepts, **Coffin**, for a discussion of burial in a coffin.)

Burial on Shabbat or Yom Tov

In practice, these halakhot are only applicable outside of Israel because burials are not performed on Yom Tov in Israel.

11. Burials are not performed on Shabbat or Yom Kippur, even by gentiles.[1248]
12. On Yom Tov, it is permissible for a grave to be dug and prepared by gentiles and for burial to be done by Jews. On the second day of Yom Tov in the Diaspora, and even on the second day of Rosh HaShana, all the preparations may be done by Jews because, with

1247. *Responsa Minḥat Elazar*, quoted in *Kol Bo al Aveilut*, p. 163.
1248. *Shulḥan Arukh, Oraḥ Ḥayim* 526:3.

regard to burial, the sages treated the second day of Yom Tov as a non-holiday.[1249]

13. The deceased may be transported to the cemetery by a gentile on the second day of Yom Tov. A few members of the *ḥevra kaddisha* may accompany the body in order to bury the deceased. If there is no gentile driver available, a Jewish driver may transport the deceased.[1250]
14. If the person died on a Shabbat where the following day is a Yom Tov, and there is a concern that the body will begin to decompose, a few members of the *ḥevra kaddisha* may travel with a non-Jewish driver to bury the deceased, even on the first day of Yom Tov.[1251]
15. The burial of the deceased should not be delayed from the first day of Yom Tov to the second day just so that the burial can be done by Jews.
16. The second day of Yom Tov in the Diaspora is counted towards the shiva, despite the fact that mourning is not observed.[1252]
17. If, against the wishes of the Jewish relatives, the deceased is buried on Shabbat, one should not participate in the funeral since this will certainly entail breaking Shabbat. But one may say Kaddish in the synagogue. In such a case, shiva begins on Shabbat.

Mourning in the case of a civil marriage

18. In matters of shiva and mourning, there is no halakhic significance to civil marriage and divorce. Therefore, those who are married in a civil ceremony are not considered husband and wife by Jewish Law, and need not mourn for one another. Conversely, a married couple who divorced civilly are considered to be still married and must mourn for one another.

1249. *Shulḥan Arukh* ibid., 4. The Rema wrote that the work should ideally be done by gentiles. In *Gesher HaḤayim* (17:2, 2) he wrote that nowadays Sephardim also have the custom to have the grave dug by gentiles on the second day of Rosh HaShana.
1250. *Gesher HaḤayim* 17:2, 4.
1251. Rabbi Tzvi Pesaḥ Frank, quoted in *Gesher HaḤayim* ibid., 5.
1252. *Tur, Yoreh De'ah* 399; *Shulḥan Arukh, Oraḥ Ḥayim* 448:2. In *Gesher HaḤayim* (23:2, 15), he wrote to be lenient with Rosh HaShana, as well.

Part 3

Analysis and Thought

The following sections relate to various important subjects in the area of death and mourning. Although each subject could be discussed in much greater depth and detail, the scope of this book does not allow it.

SECTION 57: KADDISH

Even among those with little Jewish background, Kaddish is well known. It is commonly associated with prayer services, mourning, memorial days, bereavement, and loss. The Kaddish expresses praise for God, along with a request that God's name be exalted in the world. What is, in fact, the connection between Kaddish and mourning?

Translation of Kaddish

Let us first look at a translation of Kaddish in order to understand its basic meaning. See Part 7: Selected Prayers and Passages.

> Glorified and sanctified be God's great name throughout the world, which He has created according to His will. May He establish His kingdom (and cause His salvation to sprout and bring near His Messiah[1]) in your lifetime and during your days, and within the life of the entire House of Israel, speedily and soon; and say, Amen.

1. Only in *nusaḥ Sepharad* and not in *nusaḥ Ashkenaz*. This is also true for the *nusaḥ* of the Kaddish texts that follow.

> May His great name be blessed forever and to all eternity. Blessed and praised, glorified and exalted, extolled and honored, adored and lauded be the name of the Holy One, blessed be He, beyond all the blessings and hymns, praises and consolations that are ever spoken in the world; and say, Amen.
>
> May there be abundant peace from heaven, and life, for us and for all Israel; and say, Amen.
>
> He who creates peace in His celestial heights, may He create peace for us and for all Israel; and say, Amen.

The Source of Kaddish and Its Relationship to Mourning

A simple reading of the Kaddish shows that it involves praising God. And so, we return to our original question: What is the connection between Kaddish and mourning?

In order to answer that question, let us propose certain basic assumptions. The first of these is that the Jewish people have a duty in the world:

> Now then, if you will obey Me faithfully and keep My covenant, you shall be My treasured possession among all the peoples. Indeed, all the earth is Mine, but you shall be to Me a kingdom of *kohanim* and a holy nation. (Ex. 19:5–6)

The Jewish nation was singled out to be a chosen, holy nation. It has tasks and challenges that are unique to it, beyond the tasks given to the rest of humanity. More commandments and ethical requirements were given to the Jewish nation, who has the ability to meet these difficult demands. "The chosen people" is not meant – God forbid – as a concept with connotations of racism, domination, or exploitation. Rather, it refers to a nation that has accepted upon itself not only the Seven Noahide Laws but the 613 commandments, as well as countless invaluable rulings and customs that have been added by the Jewish people over time.

> See, I have imparted to you laws and rules, as the Lord my God has commanded me, for you to abide by in the land that you are

> about to enter and occupy. Observe them faithfully, for that will be proof of your wisdom and discernment to other peoples, who on hearing of all these laws will say, "Surely, that great nation is a wise and discerning people." For what great nation is there that has a god so close at hand as is the Lord our God whenever we call upon Him? Or what great nation has laws and rules as perfect as all this teaching that I set before you this day? (Deut. 4:5–9)

The purpose of the commandments is to increase good, ethical behavior in the world and to inculcate ourselves – and by extension the entire world – with the values of justice, ethics, love, and empathy. This is the special task that God has given us. In order for us to succeed in this great task, we have received detailed guidance from God in the Torah.

"*Segula*," "chosen-ness," is like a jewel that all observe and ponder. Thus, the behavior of the Jewish nation is judged and examined carefully by other nations. If we merit to act properly, we can hope that other nations will learn from our good actions. We are required to act so ethically and with such integrity that the other nations shall come, out of their own will, to learn from us and from our actions that have been guided by God as commanded in the Torah. According to this idea, proper behavior by Jewish people may certainly be considered sanctifying God's holy name; it can serve as a positive model to be emulated by other nations. This is the manner of behavior that God desires for His world.

From this perspective, every Jew represents God on earth. Every Jew is a unique representative for expressing God's divine light in the world. One can do this through good actions, Torah study, and keeping the mitzvot – those between man and others, and those between man and God – and through cultivating the attributes of love and compassion, refinement and purity, truth and integrity, simplicity and humility. The Jewish nation has three characteristics: humility, compassion, and loving-kindness.

"One who is present when the person dies, tears his clothing. What is this like? Like seeing a Torah scroll that is burned" (Moed Katan 25a). Every Jew is like a Torah scroll, representing God's word in this world. The same way that one can learn ethics and good character traits from Torah study, it should also be the case that one can learn these from observing the good deeds of a Jew. Every Torah scroll is somewhat different: Although they all contain the same letters, each Torah scroll is individual and unique. This is true of each Jew, as well; every Jew can reveal God's presence in the world in a way that no one else can.

When a Jew dies, God suffers greatly: "The death of His faithful ones is grievous in the Lord's sight" (Ps. 116:15). Rashi explains: "God shows me that this is difficult in His eyes, to kill His faithful ones," since every Jew is part of the *Shekhina*, the Divine Presence, in the world. When one dies, it is as if a small part of the Divine Presence has left the world – the very part that that Jew could express in the world. It is as thought, when the person dies, there is a disturbance in God's name, as though He is lacking.

The disturbance in the manifestation of God's name is rectified by the recitation of Kaddish. The Kaddish offers an amplification and sanctification of God's name, which has been adversely affected by the person's death; a spiritual vacuum has been created, and the Kaddish comes to balance it out, to add to and rectify it.

The greatness of the Jewish people can be seen in this: Here is a Jew standing heartbroken and grieving, pained by the loss of his loved one, and this person is reciting Kaddish – is involved in increasing the expression of God's name in the world. It is almost as though his own grief is set aside for a moment in order to tend to the grief and constriction of the *Shekhina*. It is an act of wanting to fix the vacuum that has been created in the manifestation of God, to elevate the divine name in the world, to exalt it and beautify it – "Glorified and sanctified be God's great name throughout the world."

When the mourner increases his good deeds in honor of the deceased, whether in mitzvot between man and God or between man and others, and increases the sanctification of God's name through good attributes and integrity – this is part of the same principle expressed by saying Kaddish. Kaddish gives merit to both the deceased and the living and causes the *Shekhina* to reside among the Jewish people.

Increasing merit for the deceased has another element: People's actions are judged according to what they have achieved during their lifetime, but there are actions that result from them and from their deeds even after they die. When such positive actions continue after a person's death, especially through one's children, who are such a direct product of one's life, this increases one's merits even after death.

The earliest source for Kaddish is in an Aramaic translation of the Torah (the *Targum Yerushalmi*)[2] and is attributed to Jacob: When Jacob blessed his sons before his death, he wanted to reveal to them the end of time, and the Divine Presence left him. He said – Could it be, God forbid, that my bed is flawed, like Abraham my grandfather who fathered Ishmael, and Isaac my father who fathered Esau? His sons answered him "Hear O Israel, the Lord our God, the Lord is one." The same way that in your heart is One, so too in our hearts is only One. Jacob answered and said: "May His great name be blessed forever and to all eternity."[3]

> Once Rabbi Akiva was walking in a cemetery and met a man who was naked and black as coal and carrying a huge burden of thorns on his head. Rabbi Akiva thought that he was alive and ran like a horse. Rabbi Akiva told him to stand. He asked – Why is such a man working so hard? If you are a slave and your master works you like this, I will redeem you immediately, and if you are poor and those who owe you money come to get their money I will give you money. He replied – Please do not prevent me, lest those who are over me will be angry with me. He said – What is this and what is your work? He said – That man is dead and every day I am sent to chop wood. He said to him – My son, what was your job in the world that you came from? He replied – I was a tax collector and I favored the rich and killed the poor. He said – Did you not hear from those in charge of you any way to rectify? He said – Please, do not delay me, lest those who do evil will be angry with me, for this man has no rectification. But I heard from them something that is impossible, that if this poor man had a son

2. On Gen. 49:1.
3. The version in the Talmud, Pesaḥim 56a, and in most of the sources in the Midrash is "*Barukh shem kevod malkhuto leOlam va'ed,*" "Blessed is the name of His glorious kingdom forever." However, according to the *Targum Yerushalmi*, Jacob answered with the words of the Kaddish.

> who stood in the congregation and declared, "*Barekhu et Hashem hamevorakh,*" "Bless ye the Lord who is to be blessed," and they would answer, "*Yehe shmei raba mevorakh,*" "May His great name be blessed," immediately they would free him from the punishment. But this man never had a son and when he died his wife was pregnant and I do not know whether she had a boy and if she did who will teach him Torah? For this man has no friend in the world.
>
> Immediately Rabbi Akiva decided to go and find out whether he had a son in order to teach him Torah and stand him before the congregation. He said – What is your name? He replied – Akiva. And your wife's name? – Shoshniva. And the name of your city? Ludkia. Rabbi Akiva was immediately very upset and went to ask about him. When he came to that city he asked about him. They said to him – The bones of that man shall be erased. He asked after his wife. They replied – Her memory shall be blotted from the earth. He asked after his son. He is uncircumcised, they didn't even perform the mitzva of circumcision on him. Immediately Rabbi Akiva circumcised him and sat him before him with a book, and he would not accept the Torah until he had fasted for forty days. A heavenly voice was heard and said – You are fasting for him? He said before Him – Master of the Universe, I did this for You. Immediately, the child opened his heart and he taught him Torah, *Shema*, and Grace after Meals, and he placed him before the community and he said, "*Barekhu,*" "Bless ye," and they answered, "*Barukh hu hamevorakh,*" "Blessed is He who is blessed." That hour, they freed him from the suffering. He immediately came to Rabbi Akiva in a dream and said – May it be God's will that you shall rest in the Garden of Eden, that you saved me from Hell's judgment. Rabbi Akiva declared "O Lord, Your name endures forever, Your fame, O Lord, through all generations" (Ps. 135:13). Therefore, the custom is for an orphan to lead the prayers after Shabbat and to say *Barekhu* or Kaddish. (*Maḥzor Vitry*, 144)

The source for the mourner's recitation of Kaddish for the sake of increasing the deceased's merit can be found in ancient sources. That is where the above story is related, in which Rabbi Akiva (other versions say Rabbi Yoḥanan b. Zakkai) saw a strange man who was suffering greatly. He told Rabbi Akiva that he had died some months before and had sinned during his lifetime, and he was sentenced to severe punishment. Only after Rabbi Akiva taught the dead man's son to say Kaddish was he spared his punishment.[4]

Another reason that Kaddish is said specifically by mourners is that it contains an acceptance of divine judgment. The mourner, in his grief, could be angry with God and with the judgment that has taken away his loved one. When saying Kaddish, the mourner accepts God's will and praises Him that His judgments are fair and true.

Kaddish includes praises of God and requests and prayers for the salvation of the Jewish people. It mentions the major tenets of the Jewish faith – the creation of the world, the Messiah, and the redemption. The Great Kaddish also refers to the resurrection of the dead and the rebuilding of Jerusalem and the Temple.

The Talmud and the Zohar discuss the high spiritual level that one achieves when reciting Kaddish and when answering Amen, and how one must concentrate on the recitation and the response. The Talmud brings the following aggada about Rabbi Yossi ben Ḥalafta who met Elijah in a ruin in Jerusalem. Elijah said to him:

> When Israel enters synagogues and study halls and answers, "May His great name be blessed," the Holy One, Blessed be He, shakes His head and says: Happy is the king who is thus praised in his house.[5]

Whoever answers amen with all his might has many merits:

---

4. *Tanna Devei Eliyahu Zuta*, at the end of ch. 17. Tractate Kalla Rabati 2; *Maḥzor Vitry* 144; see *Gesher HaḤayim* 30:1, where he wrote an explanation of the words and meaning of Kaddish, why the text is in Aramaic, and what intentions one should have. Earlier sources appear in *Tur, Oraḥ Ḥayim* 56 and Rema, *Yoreh De'ah* 376:4. In *Sefer HaKaddish*, Rabbi David Assaf brings numerous sources, explanations, and halakhot. A brief explanation appears in Rabbi Steinsaltz's *HaSiddur VeHaTefilla*, vol. 1, p. 293. Many other books have been written on the subject, but they cannot all be listed here.
5. Berakhot 3a.

> Rabbi Yehoshua ben Levi said: Anyone who answers, "Amen, may His great name be blessed," with all his might, they rip up his sentence. Resh Lakish said: One who answers amen with all his strength, they open the gates of the Garden of Eden before him, as it is stated: "Open the gates, and a righteous nation shall come who keeps the faith" (Is. 26:2). Do not read: Who keeps [*shomer*] the faith [*emunim*], but rather: Who say [*she'omerim*] amen. What is *amen*? Rabbi Ḥanina said: It is an acronym of the words: God, faithful King [*El Melekh ne'eman*].[6]

During the Talmudic period, the custom was to gather together on Shabbat and holidays to hear lectures in the synagogue and beit midrash. Afterwards, they had the custom to recite, "May His great name." The *Amora* Rava explains the supreme importance of this:

> But why does the world exist? By the sanctification that is the order (*Sidra*) and "May His great name" of Aggada. An explanation: What sustains the world's existence? The *Kedusha* of *Sidra* (*Kadosh, Kadosh, Kadosh* that is said after *Uva LeTziyon*) and "May His great name" that is recited after learning Aggada in a group.[7]

Kaddish in Aramaic

The historical reason for Kaddish being recited in Aramaic is that Kaddish was originally said after hearing the public Torah lecture, "And the commoners did not understand Hebrew; therefore, it was established to be said in Aramaic, a language that everyone understood and spoke."[8] Another historical reason: "Because in their days, there was a decree not to say, 'His great name will be blessed' [in Hebrew], and so they had the custom to say it in Aramaic so that their enemies could not understand; and even though the decree was annulled, they did not revert back to

6. Shabbat 119b.
7. Sota 49a.
8. *Tosafot*, Berakhot 3a s.v. "*VeOnin*."

saying it in Hebrew so that they should not forget the miracles and wonders, and in order to publicize this."[9]

Other explanations, based on Kabbalistic teachings, also appear in this context: "Since it is a beautiful prayer and a great praise, it was established in Aramaic so that the angels would not understand and become jealous of us."[10]

The different types of Kaddish and when they are recited during services

All the versions of Kaddish come to sanctify God's name in the world, as discussed above. That is the opening statement in all the versions of Kaddish.

The different versions of Kaddish have different endings and are thus called different names: "Half Kaddish," "Full Kaddish" – also called the "Mourner's Kaddish," "*Kaddish Titkabel*," the "Rabbis' Kaddish" (*Kaddish DeRabbanan*), and a special version called the "Great Kaddish."

Every person and congregation should hear Kaddish at least seven times a day.[11] Four times in Shaḥarit: before "*Yotzer Or*," after the reader's repetition of the *Amida*, after "*Uva LeTziyon*," and after "*Aleinu*"; two at Minḥa: after "*Ashrei*" and after the reader's repetition of the *Amida*; and one in Maariv before the *Amida*. The Kabbalists quote from the Ari that one should hear Kaddish twelve times.[12] Six times in Shaḥarit: the above-mentioned four, plus one before "*Hodu*" and one after "*Pitum HaKetoret*"; and another six in Minḥa and Maariv. (According to the Sephardic custom, there are two in Minḥa and four in Maariv, and according to the Ashkenazic custom, there are three at Minḥa and three at Maariv.) The points at which Kaddish is recited in the service

---

9. *Tanya Rabati* (Italy, 14th cen.) 2:46, quoted in *Or LeAvel* p. 158.
10. *Tosafot*, Berakhot ibid. They also bring another opinion but reject it.

    In Rashi's opinion, the reason that Kaddish opens in Hebrew and continues in Aramaic is, "Because today it is not read as it is written since it is written with the name of God and we cannot read it as it is written; but in the world to come it will be read as it is written, as it says: 'On that day He will be one and His name will be one'" (*Sefer HaPardes* p. 323, quoted in *Sefer HaKaddish*, p. 65). And I have not merited to fully understand Rashi's words.
11. *Beit Yosef, Oraḥ Ḥayim* 55 in the name of *HaAgur* and *Shibolei HaLeket*; see *Gesher HaḤayim* 30:7, 1.
12. *Kaf HaḤayim* 55:19.

are points of transition between various sections of prayer. According to the Kabbalists, having Kaddish said at those points is essential for elevating the mystical worlds:

> The sages established the Kaddish in the morning because prayer is in order to elevate the Four Worlds (*Atzilut* – Emanation, *Beria* – Creation, *Yetzira* – Formation, and *Asiya* – Action). From the beginning of the morning prayer until *Barukh SheAmar* is the world of Action. From there until *Yotzer Or* is the world of Formation. Until the *Shemoneh Esreh* is the world of Creation. And the *Shemoneh Esreh* is the world of Emanation. Afterwards, they descend from high to low... (and the descent is gradual).
>
> Therefore, Kaddish was instituted between each of these worlds, that through Kaddish, which is based on Kabbalistic secrets with a specific number of words and letters, there shall be a complete elevation of the worlds beyond their measure.[13]

We have the custom to recite Kaddish thirteen times each day;[14] Kaddish is also added after the *Shir shel Yom* (Song of the Day), which is not an obligation.

"Half Kaddish" – This is the first half of the Kaddish, until "*Deamiran bealma veimru amen.*" This is the basis of all the other types of Kaddish (except the Great Kaddish); other sections are added on to it.[15] This Kaddish is recited at certain points in the prayer service, as an introduction to sections of prayers within the service and as an ending

---

13. *Ben Ish Ḥai,* first year, *Parashat Vayeḥi,* 1. See also 12 where he discusses the Kaddish before "*Hodu,*" and before "*Yotzer Or,*" and the Kaddish between the *Shemoneh Esreh* and "*Ashrei,*" and before "*Tefilla LeDavid*" (*Kaddish Titkabel* after "*Uva LeTziyon*") and before *Pitum HaKetoret* – that these were instituted for the sake of the worlds. It appears that he means both the elevation of the worlds and the gradual descent, like one who draws near to the king gradually and, when taking his leave after their meeting – the *Shemoneh Esreh,* he does so gradually.
14. *Gesher HaḤayim* 30:7, 1.
15. Rabbi Nebenzahl: This is the true Kaddish. The others have been added through custom.

to the Torah reading. Mourners do not generally recite this Kaddish unless they are leading the service. Some Sephardim recite Half Kaddish at the conclusion of the prayer service.

"Full Kaddish" – "Mourner's Kaddish" – This is the Kaddish that appeared earlier in this chapter.[16] It is the Kaddish generally recited by mourners. It is recited at the end of certain sections of communal prayer, as well as after reciting chapters of Psalms. It is often said by those who have lost a parent or to elevate the souls of the deceased.

"Kaddish Titkabel" – This is the Kaddish recited after the *Amida*; it includes a section that requests that the prayers of the Jewish nation be acceptable before God: "May the prayers and pleas of all Israel be accepted by their Father in heaven. And say, Amen"

In the weekday Shaḥarit service, this Kaddish is recited after *Uva LeTziyon*. On Shabbat and holidays, this Kaddish is said after the Shaḥarit service, before reading the Torah, and once more after the *Musaf* service.

"Rabbis' Kaddish" ("*Kaddish DeRabbanan*") – This is the Kaddish that is said after studying *Torah Shebe'al Peh* (Oral Torah). This Kaddish contains a prayer to honor the sages and their students and a blessing for those who study Torah. The mourners recite this Kaddish after studying Mishna or other texts of *Torah Shebe'al Peh*.

> Upon Israel, and upon our sages, and upon their disciples, and upon all the disciples of their disciples, and upon all those who occupy themselves with the Torah, here or in any other place, upon them and upon you, may there be abundant peace, grace, kindness, compassion, long life, ample sustenance and deliverance, from their Father in heaven; and say, Amen.

"The Great Kaddish" – This is also called the Kaddish of Aggadata.[17] This Kaddish discusses the future resurrection of the dead and the rebuilding of the Temple. It is only said on special occasions – after Tziduk HaDin in the cemetery and when finishing a tractate of Talmud.

16. Also called "Kaddish *Yehe Shlama*."
17. It is mentioned in tractate Soferim 19 and Nahmanides' *Torat HaAdam*, p. 155.

The Yemenite custom is to recite this Kaddish in the house of mourning after studying Oral Torah.

יִתְגַּדַּל וְיִתְקַדַּשׁ שְׁמֵהּ רַבָּא
בְּעָלְמָא דִּי הוּא עָתִיד לְאִתְחַדָּתָא
וּלְאַחֲיָאָה מֵתַיָּא וּלְאַסָּקָא יַתְהוֹן לְחַיֵּי
עָלְמָא וּלְמִבְנָא קַרְתָּא דִּי יְרוּשְׁלֵם
וּלְשַׁכְלְלָא הֵיכָלֵהּ בְּגַוָּהּ
וּלְמֶעֱקַר פּוּלְחָנָא נוּכְרָאָה מִן אַרְעָא
וּלְאָתָבָא פּוּלְחָנָא דִּי שְׁמַיָּא לְאַתְרֵהּ
וְיַמְלִיךְ קוּדְשָׁא בְּרִיךְ הוּא
בְּמַלְכוּתֵהּ וִיקָרֵהּ
בְּחַיֵּיכוֹן וּבְיוֹמֵיכוֹן וּבְחַיֵּי דְכָל בֵּית
יִשְׂרָאֵל בַּעֲגָלָא וּבִזְמַן קָרִיב וְאִמְרוּ אָמֵן
(from this point, Kaddish continues with the regular version)

Exalted and hallowed be His great Name.

In the world which He will create anew, where He will revive the dead, construct His Temple, deliver life, and rebuild the city of Jerusalem, and uproot foreign idol worship from His land, and restore the holy service of Heaven to its place, along with His radiance, splendor and *Shekhina*, and may He bring forth His redemption and hasten the coming of His Messiah.

In your lifetime and in your days and in the lifetime of the entire House of Israel, sword, famine, and death shall cease from us and from the entire Jewish nation, speedily and soon, and say, Amen.

May His great Name be blessed forever and to all eternity. Blessed and praised, glorified, exalted, and extolled, honored, adored and lauded be the Name of the Holy One, blessed be He.

Beyond all the blessings, hymns, praises and consolations that are uttered in the world; and say, Amen.

May there be abundant peace from heaven, and a good life for us and for all Israel; and say, Amen.

He Who makes peace in His heavens, may He make peace for us and for all Israel; and say, Amen.

SECTION 58: ORGAN DONATION AND TRANSPLANTS

Organ donation and organ transplants are an area of significance in the halakhic and medical realms; the topic also serves as an example of an area where medicine and halakha can be integrated. This integration is crucial for the sake of those involved in providing healing, guidance, advice, encouragement, and support, and all those working to improve human life. The possibility of combining halakha with medicine primarily depends upon those who have dedicated their lives to this issue – halakhic authorities and doctors. The Jewish community desires and expects clear statements in this sensitive and important area. This chapter brings the official position of the Israeli Chief Rabbinate, as well as two opposing stances of contemporary *poskim* (halakhic authorities). These differing stances stem from, among other things, insufficient cooperation between the medical and halakhic systems. Fostering dialogue and collaboration between doctors and *poskim* is crucial. This partnership is not a luxury; it is necessary to save lives.

Heart transplants – The Israeli Chief Rabbinate's statement on the matter of heart transplants[18]

Below is the full text of the Israeli Chief Rabbinate's statement on the matter of organ transplants (translated from the original Hebrew):

Today, on the first day of Rosh Ḥodesh Ḥeshvan 5747 (November 3, 1986), the Chief Rabbinate Council unanimously approved the recommendations of the committee on transplants, as detailed below:

1. The [Israeli] Ministry of Health made a request to the Israeli Chief Rabbinate to determine the halakhic stance with regard to heart transplants in Israel. For this purpose, the Chief Rabbinate appointed a joint committee of rabbis and physicians, who

18. It is important to note that that are *poskim* who consider death to be determined by the cardiac activity and not respiration. Their opinion is that it is entirely forbidden to remove an organ from a person who has been shown to have undergone brain death but whose heart is still beating since they consider this person to be alive. In their opinion, performing a heart or liver transplant is not ever a possibility. See the summary of opinions and sources in *Encyclopedia Hilkhatit Refuit*, vol. 2, "*Hashtalat Evarim*," p. 224.

conducted an in-depth study of the medical and halakhic dimensions relevant to this question. The committee was informed by consultations with and opinions from the leading doctors in this field in the Shaarei Tzedek and Hadassah medical centers in Jerusalem.

2. In the early period of heart transplants (seventeen years ago), the esteemed Rabbi Moshe Feinstein *z"tl* and the Chief Rabbi of Israel, Rabbi Isser Yehuda Unterman *z"tl*, made the halakhic ruling to prohibit heart transplants, holding that it constituted a double act of murder, of both the donor and the recipient.

   Over the past decade, the following fundamental changes have occurred in the factual and medical data that concerns heart transplants:

   a) The success rates for recipients of heart transplants have risen: Around 80% of transplant recipients live for a year or more following the transplant, and around 70% of them stay alive for five years following the transplant.
   b) Today it is possible to safely and reliably determine that the cessation of respiration in the deceased is final and irreversible.
   c) We have received testimonies that even Rabbi Moshe Feinstein more recently permitted heart transplants in the United States. We also know of great rabbis who have advised cardiac patients to undergo a heart transplant.

3. Since this is an issue that involves life and death, we feel obligated to announce a decision in a clear and decisive matter.
4. **Relying on principles from the Talmud in Yoma (85) and the ruling by the *Ḥatam Sofer* (*Yoreh De'ah* 338), the halakha determines death by the cessation of respiration (and see *Igrot Moshe, Yoreh De'ah*, vol. 3, 132).** Therefore, is must be established that respiration has ceased completely and irreversibly. This can be determined by evidence of brain death, as the brain is what activates a person's independent respiration.
5. In medical practice, there are five prerequisites required to establish brain death:
   a) Clear knowledge of the cause of injury
   b) Complete cessation of spontaneous breathing

   c) Detailed clinical evidence of destruction of the brainstem
   d) Objective proof of destruction of the brainstem through scientific examinations, such as the BAER test
   e) Proof that the complete cessation of breathing and lack of brainstem activity has lasted for at least twelve hours, **despite full customary care and treatment**

6. After having examined the recommendations for determining death presented by physicians at Hadassah medical center in Jerusalem on the eighth of Tammuz, 5745, and submitted to the Chief Rabbinate on the fifth of Tishrei, 5746, we have found that these recommendations can be accepted halakhically if an addition is made that stipulates the inclusion of an objective scientific test (BAER) for the brainstem.
7. In light of the above, the Israeli Chief Rabbinate is prepared to permit heart transplants (from accident-victims) in the Hadassah medical center in Jerusalem under the following conditions:
   a) Fulfillment of all prerequisites for determining the donor's death, as stated above
   b) Involvement of a representative of the Chief Rabbinate as a full member of the team determining the donor's death. This representative shall be appointed by the [Israeli] Ministry of Health from a list submitted once a year by the Chief Rabbinate to the Ministry of Health.
   c) Prior written consent by the donor or donor's family for the heart donation
   d) The Ministry of Health, in partnership with the Chief Rabbinate, will establish a review committee to examine all heart transplants performed in Israel.
   e) The Ministry of Health will establish national regulations outlining the aforementioned procedures.
8. Until the conditions detailed in paragraph 7 are accepted, no permission has been granted for performing heart transplants in Israel.
9. If permission is given based on compliance with the conditions detailed in paragraph 7, the Chief Rabbinate will establish a review committee, whose role will be to ensure full compliance with these conditions.

A practical halakhic approach to organ donation and to carrying a donor card

Essay on organ donation by Rabbi Yaakov Ariel, Chief Rabbi, Ramat Gan

According to the halakha, it is a mitzva to donate vital organs for organ transplant, whether the donor is living or deceased.

It is well-known that the mitzva of saving a life (*pikuaḥ nefesh*) overrides the entire Torah, including mitzvot pertaining to Shabbat and Yom Kippur, etc. It is therefore permissible and even commendable to use the organs of those who have passed away in order to save a life. However, there are three serious transgressions that are not overridden for the sake of saving life: idolatry, sexual immorality, and murder. Thus, in the present context, it is forbidden to take one person's life in order to save someone else's. Life cannot be measured either quantitatively or qualitatively. Life has an absolute value. For example, one may not save a righteous person at the expense of a wicked one, a healthy person at the expense of someone who is ill, a young person at the expense of an elderly one, etc. Each moment of life has value unto itself. Removing organs from a person's body in order to save someone else's life is therefore only permitted after it has been ascertained, beyond any doubt, that the donor is dead.

Besides there being a biological definition of death, there is also a legal-ethical definition. Death is a process that begins while the person is still considered alive; and some life continues after what we call death. Thus, there is a need to establish a definitive point in the dying process after which a person can no longer be considered alive. This definition is legal and not medical. It needs to take the medical information into account, but must also be exact in determining which moment within this long process is considered death.

This is a problem primarily in cases where certain activity continues to occur in the body; in such a case, should this be considered being alive or not?

The Talmud (Ḥullin 21a) brings a fascinating example: "They beheaded them; even though they quiver – they are impure, like the lizard's tail that quivers." That is to say, the lizard's tail continues to quiver, but this is not life, for the tail is detached from the body. This is the law when the head is removed from the body. A heart beating without a head, is not a living heart. The question is, what is the law regarding brain death?

According to Rabbi Shaul Yisraeli, Rabbi Avraham Shapira, and Rabbi Mordekhai Eliyahu, life is indicated by respiration, as it says: "All in whose nostrils was the merest breath of life" (Gen. 7:22). Therefore, in previous generations, before there were respirators, death was determined by breathing alone (Yoma 85a; Maimonides, *Mishneh Torah, Hilkhot Shabbat* 2:19). However, when there is artificial respiration, and it is clear that the person can no longer breathe independently whatsoever, and there is no chance that he will be able to do so because the areas in the brain responsible for respiration are completely destroyed – the person is considered dead. For if the mechanism for breathing does not exist, there is no more respiration.

Thus, in order to permit the transplanting of organs, several conditions must be met:

1. Detailed clinical evidence that the brain stem is completely destroyed
2. Objective evidence that the brain stem is destroyed, such as a BAER test
3. Evidence that independent breathing has completely ceased and that there has been no change for twelve hours
4. The doctors who determine the death have no direct or indirect connection with the doctors who would perform the transplant in the sick individual
5. A representative of the Chief Rabbinate is part of the committee determining death. This representative can be a doctor who is familiar with the halakha and its considerations and way of thinking (Decisions by the Chief Rabbinate of Israel from 1 Ḥeshvan, 5767, published in "*Barkai*" 4, p. 11).

When all of these conditions are met, the transplant may be done in accordance with halakha and with its sanction and support. Unfortunately, at this point, these conditions have not been met [in Israel] and the halakha can therefore not assist in this essential mitzva of saving life. Cooperation between doctors and rabbis could lead to saving lives and to harmony between medicine and halakha; it could perhaps serve as a good example of correct and harmonious communal life that would be relevant to other areas, as well.

Although many years have passed since the aforementioned decision was passed, the hospitals and the Ministry of Health [in Israel] have not done enough to implement it. (Moreover, the [Israeli] Ministry of Health publicized a policy on 11 Iyar, 5756, providing clear instructions for determining death, whilst ignoring the Rabbinate's conditions: It includes no clear instruction to perform laboratory tests such as the BAER test, except in cases where the clinical results are inconclusive. The policy also reduced the waiting time from six hours to two hours, and there is no mention of a Rabbinate representative on the committee.)

Therefore, the hospitals and the Ministry of Health have the ball in their court, as well as the burden of responsibility for the fact that many transplants are not performed due to a lack of donors.

Those who allow one to carry a donor card – even at such a time when hospitals do not act in accordance with the criteria above – have brought proofs to support their position; these proofs have been well-studied in the halakhic world and have been largely rejected. (The "donor card" referred to here is a card carried by someone who is interested in donating his organs in the case of sudden death. The card testifies to the person's agreement to the organ donation.)

A case that involves preventing the saving of life, or causing a death, should not be compared with actively and directly ending a life.

For example, the *Minḥat Ḥinukh* (Mitzva 296:28) brings a case where gentiles have demanded that a group of Jews turn in one person to be executed, and if they fail to do so, the whole group will be killed. In this case, it is permissible to give over someone who is considered a "*treifa*" (someone suffering from damage to an essential organ that cannot be healed). This case refers to handing someone over to gentiles, not physically killing the person. The *Minḥat Ḥinukh* does not permit actively killing a *treifa* in order to save someone else.

Another example is the famous case in the Talmud (Bava Metzia 62a) about two people in the desert, where only one of them has a jug of water. The halakha follows Rabbi Akiva, whose opinion is that one's own life takes precedence over another person's life. Even so, the halakhic authorities wrote (*Pitḥei Teshuva, Yoreh De'ah* 252:1; *Mishpat Cohen* 144:15) that the person with the water is permitted to give up his own for the good of his friend; this does not constitute actively taking one's life. It is forbidden for someone to physically take his own life in order to save someone else. (Only in a case of doubt did the sages permit a person to enter into a situation where there is a possibility of danger, in order to save his friend from certain danger. See *Sefer Me'irat Einayim, Ḥoshen Mishpat* 426:2; *Pitḥei Teshuva* ad loc. 2; *Responsa Tzitz Eliezer*, vol. 9, 17:5.)

There is also a case in Nedarim (22a) in which Ulla was in a life-threatening situation. His companion had been killed, and Ulla was forced to tell the murderer – Cut his wound deeper, i.e., kill him completely – for if he had not said that, it would have cost him his own life. In that case, too, he only said these words to the murderer; he did not actively do anything himself. (But the *Tiferet Yisrael*, at the end of Yoma, Boaz s.v. "VeN"L," asks whether Ulla would have been permitted to cut his friend's throat in order to save his own life. The *Tiferet Yisrael*'s question, however, does not override the definite opinions of most of the halakhic authorities.)

The only unresolved disagreement is the one between Rabbi Yeshaya Pick and the *Noda BeYehuda* (*Mahadura Tanina, Ḥoshen Mishpat* 59) about a fetus that endangers the mother and is a *treifa*. According to Rabbi Pick, it is preferable to kill the fetus and save the mother, while the *Noda BeYehuda* does not permit this. This argument was not resolved. According to Rabbi Pick, who permits killing the fetus in this case, the connection between doing so and saving the endangered individual is direct. This is not true in with regard to organ transplants: In the case of an organ transplant, there is a critically ill patient who is in need of a vital organ, and there is a dying person whose organs could be used to save the sick person. The threat to the sick individual is not direct. The connection to the donor only exists because of our modern-day knowledge of the information, involving a computer system that is able to locate the two people. But these two cases cannot be equated. (See *Nishmat Avraham, Yoreh De'ah* 252:2 for a summary of this.)

Those who permit the carrying of a donor card agree that they do not consider it permissible for doctors to remove the organs, but they are lessening the severity of the taking of life. In our opinion, this is not a solution to the problem. On the contrary, it makes it more severe because there is currently a lack of trust between families and doctors. Only the acceptance of the Rabbinate's conditions will increase families' willingness to allow an organ to be taken from their loved one, to be transplanted in a sick individual who needs it.

Some doctors oppose the involvement of a Rabbinate representative on the committee that determines death. (As stated above, this representative can be a doctor who is familiar with halakha.) They cannot stomach what they view as "*kashrut* supervision" by the Rabbinate. They see this as a lack of trust, which is not the case. The reason for the stipulation is to ensure that a close connection is maintained between the halakhic decisions and the actual actions. Medicine is dynamic and situations change; halakhic instructions must be applied accordingly, and there must be a symbiosis between the day-to-day norms and the halakhic decisions. A Rabbinate representative would prevent the disconnection between theoretical halakha and its practical applications. For example, a test has been discovered that is more accurate in determining death than the BAER test, which does not require moving the patient (which presents an additional reason for the rabbis to accept it). This information could change the halakhic requirements.

We [in Israel] are dealing with a difficult public issue that has a simple solution: provision of correct instructions to hospitals to act in cooperation with the Rabbinate and in accordance with its guidelines, in order to save Jewish lives.

(From "*Maayanei HaYeshua*," *Tenua LeTarbut Yisrael*, issue 108–109–110.)

It should be noted that most of the rabbis who permit transplants agree with Rabbi Yaakov Ariel's position.

Essay on organ donation by Rabbi Shlomo Aviner – Rabbi of Beit El and *Rosh Yeshiva* of Yeshivat Ateret Yerushalayim

Question: Is organ donation a mitzva? Should one carry a donor card?

Answer: Indeed, there are difficult halakhic issues that arise with regard to organ donation, including the commandment to bury those organs, respect for the deceased, physical degradation of the dead by cutting the flesh, etc.

However, organ donation is *pikuaḥ nefesh* (the saving of life) – literally. It is saving the life of one who is dying, or saving someone from awful suffering, e.g., someone with an artificial kidney. Saving life overrides those prohibitions. There are times when one individual can save seven others: One person receives the heart, another receives a kidney, a third receives a lung, etc. – the individual is greater in his death than in his life. The real, grave difficulty lies in the question of whether the donor is truly dead or is only expiring (*goses*). It is forbidden to kill one person in order to save another, even if the first person is dying, with no hope of recovery.

There are several responses to this:

1. Doctors are not murderers. They are good people who are dedicated to saving the lives of others and would not do such a thing. They are ethical people who would not ignore the guidelines, which are the guidelines of both the Chief Rabbinate and the Ministry of Health.
2. Even if there is an immoral doctor, who, for his own gain, is willing to act this way – there are indeed immoral people in every walk of life and sector of society – this doctor would not dare to take such a risk because, if it were to be discovered, the doctor and the entire hospital would pay dearly, and it would be the end of the doctor's career.
3. If, despite this, a doctor would still do such a thing, against halakha and against the law, this is not a sin on the part of the donor but on the part of the doctor. For example, if a person donates money on Friday to be divided that day, but the recipient drives and divides the money on Shabbat, is this considered a sin on the part of the donor? No, the donor did a mitzva, and it was the person who distributed the money that sinned. Likewise, in our case, if the doctor breaks the law, the donor has still done a mitzva, and it is the doctor that has sinned.

It is truly a disgrace that the medical institutions [in Israel] have not arranged for rabbinic supervision, or supervision by doctors on behalf of rabbis. This prevents many people, both religious and secular, from organ donation. There are many Jews who live secular lives but who do not, in their death, want to do anything that goes against religion.

I personally know of cases where individuals who were killed in a car accident were able to save the lives of many people through organ donation.

It is a great mitzva to carry a donor card and to donate one's organs, including the cornea. I myself carry such a card. We hope that, in the future, appropriate legislation will be made and the number of donors will increase. In the meantime, even in the current situation, it is a great mitzva to donate.

Of course, if a person did not fill out a donor card when he was alive, the family members may donate his organs since it is a great mitzva.

Some are concerned lest the organs be missing when the time comes for the resurrection of the dead. Certainly, the person will have them; those who were sick or injured in war – they too will have their organs.

If someone carries a donor card and lives to be 120 years old, without having had the opportunity to donate his organs – this is a righteous person.

(From "*BeAhava UvEmuna*," the weekly publication of Makhon Meir, issue no. 284.)

SECTIONS 59–61: PHILOSOPHICAL DISCUSSIONS

Sec. 59: Maimonides' discussion on "What is the World to Come?" can be found in *Hilkhot Teshvua*, ch. 8.

Sec. 60: Rabbi Abraham Isaac Kook's perspective on Death and the Resurrection of the Dead can be found in *Orot HaKodesh*, vol 2, in the section entitled "*HaḤayut HaOlamit*" paragraphs 38 -42;

Sec. 61: Discussion on the relationship between ritual purity and impurity. The discussions can be found in the original Hebrew volume of this book.

Part 4

Guidance for Supporting the Bereaved

Rabbi Samlai taught: With regard to the Torah, its beginning is an act of kindness and its end is an act of kindness. Its beginning is an act of kindness, as it is written: "And the Lord God made for Adam and for his wife garments of skin and clothed them" (Gen. 3:21). And its end is an act of kindness, as it is written: "And he was buried in the valley" (Deut. 34:6). (Sota 14a)

SECTION 62: INFORMING A FAMILY OF A TRAGEDY

Jewish tradition has always emphasized the importance of social support. Especially in times of crisis, a supportive and nurturing community has tremendous significance. The network of people surrounding those in mourning often has a definitive impact on how the mourners feel and behave.

It is common that friends and community members want to help the grieving individuals but lack the tools and knowledge of how to do so. This often causes embarrassment or anxiety about getting close to mourners, though it is actually the time when the mourners are most in need of support. The following chapter offers some guidance for those who want to support the bereaved.

This chapter is geared toward people who are part of the mourners' immediate circle and to those who must inform a family of a tragedy or a death. It was written with great assistance from Yehudit Bar Dor, who has been involved in this difficult and sensitive area for years. I want to express my thanks and appreciation to her.

Introduction

A family tragedy, especially a sudden and unforeseen death, is a major shock that is impossible to describe in words. Family members and relatives are suddenly cast into a new reality – one that is challenging, painful, and threatening and fraught with intense emotions. Oftentimes, the family is completely unprepared and lacks the necessary tools for coping. The news of the tragedy disrupts the person's activity in all areas: emotional, physical, mental, and functional. It causes a breakdown of the usual norms; any reaction is possible in the initial stage of shock.

Coping with their new reality demands immense emotional energy from family members, along with practical organization to take necessary steps and make decisions.

Intense emotional challenges tend to demand the greatest reserves of emotional strength; this strength is not always present. For the family, news of a tragedy may incite feelings of exhaustion and devastation, alongside the need to understand what needs to be done, where to begin, who to turn to.

At such a time, the family – both individually and as a unit – require communal or social support. Such support can help them face the tragedy, come to grips with it, and find the strength to cope.

It is also during those most difficult first hours that irreversible decisions must be made: Who should be told the news first, and how should they be told? The place and time of the burial – should they wait or not to wait and for whom? The funeral arrangements – who will participate? (Should children participate? From what age? Who will be with them during the funeral?) Who will speak? What will be said? Identifying the deceased – who will go to do it, who can handle it? Where will shiva take place? These decisions must be made without delay, but they carry significant emotional weight and sometimes involve differences of opinions within the family.

There is sometimes a mistaken notion that, because of the magnitude of the tragedy, the details of how the family is informed and the initial support they receive are not all that important – but this is not the case. Most people remember the exact details of how they were informed of the tragedy: who told them and how, what was said, and how they felt. The way the people around them act and the words they say are very significant for the family. Often, because of their significance, these moments become etched in the person's mind, and the mourner returns to the memory again and again.

Many people express appreciation or, alternatively, criticism for the way they were informed of the bad news. Because of the sensitive and vulnerable nature of the situation, any missteps in how the news is given over are sources of difficulty and pain. Such missteps can increase confusion, anger, and hopelessness, or a sense of alienation; they leave a painful mark. Conversely, the appropriate support is of such great help to the family that it can be difficult to describe in words. In such cases, families are incredibly grateful for the strength and support they received, which enabled them to cope with their crisis.

Therefore, the way tragic news is conveyed to the family is of great importance, as is the support they receive; this is especially the case in the initial phase, when they must face the tragedy after hearing the news. Having the information relayed by a sensitive, responsible individual who is capable of fulfilling this task, eases the family's process of grasping this new information. It also eases the initial acclimation to their devastating new reality.

The risk of developing a pathological response to a relative's death (e.g., pathological grief, depression, and even suicide attempts) can be reduced if the news is delivered in appropriately.

A pathological state is characterized by extended withdrawal; lack of interest in others; an inability to return to routine; an inability to distance oneself from the tragedy; a lack of interest in anything; a lack of joy; a lack of hope or expectations; feelings of meaninglessness; a mechanical, perfunctory attitude towards life.

A sense of guilt can exacerbate the situation. When the bereaved act with bitterness, criticism, and frequent demands or complaints aimed at others, this is likely to cause others to distance themselves, despite the fact that their proximity is so important for the mourning family.

Proper assistance and support, especially in the initial stages, is likely to have a positive impact on the mourners' emotional process. The goal of this process, as mentioned earlier, is a return to normal life, to the degree possible. (The process of mourning was discussed in Sec. 14, "A Conceptual Understanding of the Process of Mourning" and will be discussed further in Sec. 64, "Psychological Aspects of the Mourning Process.")

The goal of supporting and helping the family is to begin a bereavement process that will eventually be complete, one that will allow the mourners to gradually return to their regular life and routine, as much as possible, without becoming paralyzed by the grip of the tragedy. Such a life is one in which one can experience, alongside the pain and grief that remain, a sense of control, interest, joy, and satisfaction.

Below are some guidelines for those accompanying the family in their most difficult hour. However, it must be stressed that these are only brief guidelines. It is vital to exercise sensitivity and thought before every encounter and in each case.[1]

The central role of those informing the family and accompanying them

Humans are social beings who needs meaningful human interaction and connection. Through it, they share their feelings, thoughts, and doubts, get advice when it is needed, and, in hard times, gain support and a helping hand.

When difficult news is being delivered, and in the initial stages that follow, it is imperative that an experienced and suitably capable person be present in addition to the family, relatives, and friends. Whoever delivers the news and supports the family must be prepared both practically and emotionally to face the family in their experience of hearing it. This person must be able to maintain a healthy distance from the situation and remain objective, **while maintaining empathy and expressions of empathy towards the suffering family** (as opposed to a detached, distant attitude). When the person informing the family is able to maintain a proper degree of distance, without becoming emotionally involved, it allows him to observe and understand the family's reactions, to identify their various and shifting needs, and to respond to them with the right timing and manner.

As previously stated, Jewish tradition and law stress the need for social and communal support. It is customary that community figures – the rabbi or others notable figures – come to the home to inform the

1. Rabbi Nebenzahl: It may also be important to have a doctor present should there be, God forbid, a need to administer medication or provide other treatment.

family of the tragedy. The news should be given personally, and whenever possible, in person (unlike places where the information about a fallen soldier is conveyed via telegram).

For years, the IDF has had a network of teams for informing bereaved families, under the auspices of the City Officer. Each team is comprised of reserve soldiers, and, where necessary, soldiers from the City Officer's unit who have taken on this sensitive and difficult task. They undergo training to acquire the tools and knowledge to perform their task in the best way possible.

In Israel, local authorities are also equipped to inform families about tragedies, to accompany the family, and to provide professional assistance where needed, especially in the first twenty-four hours following an incident. There are also other organizations that provide assistance and support to families who have suffered a tragedy, after the initial twenty-fours have passed.

Various roles

The people delivering the news and accompanying the family have several tasks and roles:

- The social role
- The emotional role – "We are with you"
- Consultation about practical matters and help in making decisions

The social role

The person who informs the family represents the society/the organization to which the deceased or the family belong. In coming to give the news, the message is: The deceased and you, the family, are significant to us; your tragedy is our tragedy, your pain is our pain, we care and we are with you.

The emotional role – "We are with you"

Other people's presence, when done well, is of great value and significance to the family. Through their presence, the family receives the message – often without words – that, "We are here with you and here for you."

This idea is expressed in many of the laws and customs of mourning. See the introduction to Sec. 11, "Comforting the Mourners." The presence of others, in and of itself, usually generates a sense of security (to the degree possible under the circumstances). It gives the family the sense that they are held in the face of the emotional turmoil, confusion, and helplessness that they feel. This presence is somewhat of an antidote to feelings of loneliness, or other emotions and thoughts like, "there is no hope" or "everything is over." It is especially important if the mourner lacks social support or a network, or if those in the mourner's environment cannot, for whatever reason, provide support.

Delivering the news also involves the following non-verbal responsibilities. One should:

Lend a listening ear and a warm heart – Allow the family to express their feelings, accept and contain them, without hushing or justifying anything, without judgment or arguing. One must maintain this stance even in response to family members blaming the messenger or the organization that the family belongs to.

Convey warmth – in actions and in words. When necessary, and within the boundaries of the halakha, this may be done in physical gestures, as well – touching the person's hand or giving a hug (not automatically but based on one's impressions and understanding of the person's needs).

Be present, understanding, and empathetic – And if the family needs silence, do this in silence, as Job's companions did:

> When Job's three friends heard about all these calamities that had befallen him, each came from his home – Eliphaz the Temanite, Bildad the Shuhite, and Zophar the Naamathite. They met together to go and console and comfort him. When they saw him from a distance, they could not recognize him, and they broke into loud weeping; each one tore his robe and threw dust into the air onto his head. They sat with him on the ground seven days and seven nights. None spoke a word to him for they saw how very great was his suffering. (Job 2:11–13)

Refrain at this stage from offering words of comfort – as the sages taught, "Do not comfort your friend when his deceased is before him" (Avot 4:23). One should refrain from statements of encouragement (e.g., "You'll get through this"; "It'll be alright").

Consultation about practical matters and help in making decisions

This aspect involves: Providing initial halakhic guidance about guarding the body, leaving it overnight, the definition of *aninut* and its ramifications; providing information about the official documentation process; presenting the various possibilities relevant to the funeral, burial, timing, people who can help the family, etc. These are addressed in Chapter 1, "Arrangements."

In addition to providing information, it is important to guide the family as they make various decisions. In that context, certain points should be emphasized:

Making decisions is not the very first stage. The first stage is receiving the information. It is not possible to make decisions right away; the family must first absorb the difficult news.

The confluence of needing to face the tragedy while also needing to arrange the funeral and burial promptly creates pressure and stress, on top of the emotional turmoil and confusion. Having other people present to share this burden usually alleviates the pressure on the family.

Our task is not to make decisions for the family but rather to present the possibilities in as clear and simple a way as possible, to allow them to make the right decisions that suit their wishes and needs. In making sure that it is the family who makes the decisions, one conveys an unspoken message that, despite the tragedy, the family can continue to function and make choices. This message, even when conveyed at the height of their emotional pain, serves to empower them to some extent.

As the bearers of the news, we must refrain from getting carried away emotionally, and certainly verbally, even if the family has this type of response.

If there is a disagreement within the family, it is not our job to become the judge. We must be very careful not to take on that role. One can and should explain the ramifications of each course of action but with great care, so as not to offend any individual. A good explanation can convince somebody when it is provided in a sensitive and respectful manner, especially if one is able to identify the needs of the person who disagrees and when one tries to address and offer solutions to those needs.

A figure from the family or someone from their regular environment (neighbors or friends who have gathered in the home) can be of service – someone who exhibits self-control and an ability to relate to the different positions within the family with tolerance and sensitivity; someone who can communicate with the different family members and serve, if needed, as a representative of the family in communicating with the team that has informed them of the death.

On the other hand, a little assertiveness is sometimes necessary to shield the family from the many people around them and to allow them to receive information, ask questions, and make decisions. This must be done gently, with a maximum amount of respect and sensitivity.

Advance preparation for the team

After news of a tragedy has arrived, the team of people who will inform the family should meet. Their meeting has several purposes:

1. Emotional and personal preparation for the team (especially if team members knew the deceased or the family personally; in that case, they themselves need to face the tragedy and grasp its implications.)
2. Emotional preparation for meeting the family – The members of the team must prepare themselves for the possibility of being exposed to emotional or intimate states of family members (unusual behavior, family feuds, being woken up or not fully dressed, etc.).
3. Making logistical arrangements for team members (e.g., cancelling other meetings and making family arrangements)
4. Gathering relevant family details as quickly as possible:
   - Family status – Who are the first-degree family members and where are they presently located? Who can accompany them where they are currently located? Have there been previous

tragedies in the family? Are there other notable details such as a divorce or previous deaths?
- Medical state – Pregnancy, illnesses (heart, high blood-pressure, asthma, epilepsy, mental illness, psychological treatment). If there a need for a doctor to be present when certain family members receive the news?
- Religious and/or cultural affiliation, language spoken

In light of the information that they gather, the team should prepare itself in terms of how to deliver the news: Who should be told first? Does the situation require a nurse or doctor to be present? Do they need someone who speaks the family's language to be present? Who will be with family members who are currently somewhere else?

Thinking and preparing ahead of time is imperative, and those informing the family must not rush over to the home without first doing so. At the same time, they should not delay their task, to reduce the chances of the family getting the information through some other channel (rumors, the media, etc.).

In the family home

- It is better to enter the house as a team, not as one person alone. Being together is also helpful for those providing support.
- Upon entering the house, the person informing the family should state his name and job (rabbi, social worker, city/regional/army representative).
- One should make sure that the people in the house are indeed those to whom the news is meant to be given. One should find out who is present in the house apart from family members.
- Refrain from telling them in the doorway of the house. It is best if the family members are seated when they hear the news.
- Relay the information in a direct, clear, succinct manner. At first, it should be done without getting into the details of the event.
- Provide reliable information – without softening, adding, or leaving out important details. Only information that one has received officially should be relayed.

An example of how one might word this:

"Is Mrs. (state the name) home? – We are so sorry, but we have come to tell you something very unfortunate... there has been a tragedy. Mr. (state the name), your husband, has been killed." If she responds: "Did something happened to my husband or my son?" one should confirm: "Yes, unfortunately there has been an accident and Mr. (state the name) was killed in the accident."

- Do not make any promises that you are not absolutely certain you will be able to fulfill.
- Allow for family members' spontaneous reactions. There is no need to intervene or interrupt or give orders. In the initial stages, almost all spontaneous reactions are okay, as long as they do not involve self-degradation or a risk to someone's safety. A discussion of possible reactions and their implications will be brought later in this chapter.

  On the seventh day the child died. David's servants were afraid to tell David that the child was dead; for they said, "We spoke to him when the child was alive and he wouldn't listen to us; how can we tell him that the child is dead? He might do something terrible." (II Sam. 12:18)
- Be alert to situations, circumstances, and behaviors that could be disastrous. Scan the location and stay alert; if there is an open window, keep an eye on it and close it if necessary; notice if there are weapons nearby and move them away. If a family member has left the house in a turbulent state, someone should follow them. Pay attention to children and teenagers.
- If someone becomes emotionally turbulent in a such way that might lead to dangerous, unusual, or self-degrading behavior that the person would later regret (e.g., banging their head against the wall, ripping out their hair, laying on the floor with their clothing tangled and their body exposed) – gently, sensitively, assertively (but NOT aggressively!) stop the behavior.

- If needed, and with due discretion, additional assistance can be summoned (a doctor, paramedic, ambulance, neighbors).
- **Do not overlook any family member**. Find out who has already been informed and who still needs to be informed. It is always preferable to deliver the information in-person and not over the phone. If there are relatives in another city, one can ask professionals in that location to inform the relatives. If that is not possible, one should try to locate a trustworthy, responsible person who can inform the relative directly, or at least be present with the relative when he is informed.

Telling children what has happened

- It is necessary and imperative to tell children what has happened. Children can sense that something has happened, even if they do not show it. If the information is not stated explicitly, the child may become confused and unable to distinguish between fantasy and reality. It is also necessary to inform the child so that he knows he can trust and depend on the adults, knowing that they are telling him the truth and not hiding it from him.
- It is important for children to comprehend the fact of the death – its finality and irreversibility – so that they can mourn and so as to minimize the development of magical thinking, feelings of guilt, or existential anxiety.
- It is best for parents to inform their child. If the parent needs or would like the assistance of a relative, friend, or professional counselor, one should help make sure that the parent gets this help. The professional is not meant to replace the parent in this role. If a professional "takes over," the parent is likely to feel that he or she is unable to cope, while the goal is quite the opposite. The parents will likely feel empowered by being able to fulfill this task, and it can help them feel capable of coping in the time ahead.
- Children should be informed of the death of their loved one and of the circumstances of the death in such a way that they feel held and supported.

Children's attendance at the funeral

There are several factors that should be considered:

- For a child, the funeral and burial present the fact of their loved one's death in a very final manner, to whatever degree the child is capable of grasping it.
- One should consider a child's developmental stage – not simply their age. As a very general guideline, children who are ten-to-twelve years-old and older should participate in the funeral. For children who are younger than six-to-eight years-old, it is preferable that they not attend.
- The child's individual personality should be taken into consideration.
- How close was the child's relationship with the deceased, both in terms of the degree of family relation and the emotional attachment?
- The parent's perspective: They know their child. It is possible that, initially, the parents will want to "protect" the child and prevent the child from attending the funeral. But one must take into account that children who do not attend will sense that everyone is there except for him. Sometimes the experience of missing the funeral can be hard for children, and sometimes what the child imagines is worse than the reality.
- If a child does not want to attend the funeral, one should speak with him about it and try to gently understand the reason he does not want to go. If the child does not want to go, he or she should not be pressured to.
- **No matter what, it is essential that the child be closely accompanied and supported when the funeral is taking place.** If the child stays home, someone who is close to him should stay and take full responsibility for him while his other relatives are at the funeral. If the child attends the funeral, someone must be at his side. It should be someone that the child is attached to; at the same time, though, it should be a person who is emotionally available to be with the child.

- If the child attends the funeral, the person escorting him should explain whatever is happening. There are things that are obvious to adults that may not be clear to a child. The adult should "facilitate" the experience in a quiet, simple, clear, and concise manner.

Possible reactions of family members

> The king was shaken. He went up to the upper chamber of the gateway and wept, moaning these words as he went, "My son Absalom! O my son, my son Absalom! If only I had died instead of you! O Absalom, my son, my son!"
>
> The king covered his face and the king kept crying aloud, "O my son Absalom! O Absalom, my son, my son!" (II Sam. 19:1, 19:5)

When the individuals informing and supporting a bereaved family are knowledgeable about and alert to possible reactions and their implications, this allows them to be prepared, both on a personal-emotional level and in terms of their ability to respond and give support.

Family members' reactions can be quite varied, including very trying and extreme reactions. What their response will be depends on a variety of interrelated factors: The individual's personality, religious faith or general outlook, culture, personal relationship with the deceased, previous tragedies, physical health, mental state, and family status.

There is a wide range of possible reactions that generally fall along a continuum between two extremes: One extreme is that of silence, turning inward, and disconnecting from one's surroundings – in extreme cases, becoming motionless and frozen. At the other end of the continuum are profuse, stormy reactions – explosions of intense emotion, non-stop talking, running around, excessive activity – in extreme cases, self-flagellation, banging one's head against the wall, ripping out one's hair.

Here are some of the extreme reactions that are possible, most of which are **expressions of anger, guilt, and blame**:

- Towards the organization to which the deceased belonged ("They are so negligent about safety there"; "No one there cares.")

- Towards a family member ("You encouraged him to join that dangerous unit!"; "Why did you let him buy a motorcycle?")
- Towards oneself ("I'll never forgive myself for letting him drive on such a dangerous road at night.")
- Towards the person informing them – This can range from a variety of verbal expressions to preventing the person from entering their house, pushing them out of the house, physically attacking the person
- Towards the deceased ("How could you leave me when I'm sick?")
- Ignoring the tragedy, absence of expressions of pain, acting as if everything is normal ("Excuse me, but I have to go on my regular evening walk now"; "I'll just finish up cooking and then join you.")
- Denying the tragedy ("I know that he is still alive"; "It can't be him, he was supposed to be somewhere else.")

As we mentioned above, these reactions are normal in the initial stage, right after receiving the news. They should not be seen as pathological. We have also discussed which cases require intervention out of fear for someone's safety or self-degradation.

The family's reactions have a certain dynamic and significance. Anger is normal and natural in the face of a sudden tragedy. Someone who is very angry to have been suddenly faced with a tragedy will sometimes release the anger onto the person who delivered the news or others directly connected to the tragedy.

Reactions that involve avoiding the tragedy, denying it, or dismissing it are defense mechanisms. These reactions are not a conscious decision or choice but a way to absorb the facts gradually. Grappling with the tragedy directly and immediately is beyond the person's ability in that moment. This type of reaction gives the person a sense (an illusion, really) of control, that one can still change or prevent what has happened.

Pushing away the person who has delivered the news stems from identifying this person with the tragedy. It is irrational thinking in which the person is seen as the source of the tragedy and thus distancing him will distance or even undo the tragedy.

It is very difficult for those informing the family to encounter such reactions, especially if they are extreme or antagonistic. It can bring up feelings of concern, confusion, embarrassment, blame, and anxiety or fear; it can shake a person's confidence and affect his self-control.

Knowing that extreme reactions are natural and are psychologically meaningful, as described above, can help those informing and supporting the family to understand that the reactions should not be taken personally. Hopefully, this can increase their ability to serve as helpful, supportive figures for the family members.

Support for the supporters

Being in the role of informing or supporting relatives in such situations exposes one to very difficult and painful situations. Repeated encounters with death and grief can awaken intense emotions, each time anew.

The role of informing and supporting bereaved families is one that is complex, challenging, and emotionally-charged, for a number of reasons:

- The direct and immediate exposure to someone else's most acute pain
- Encountering death forces one to face an existential reality that we tend to repress: We tend to minimize our thoughts about the possibility of our own death; this denial enables us to continue living our daily lives with strength, hope, and optimism. Encountering death is a reminder of our own mortality.
- The tremendous responsibility that the task involves
- Uncertainty as to what the family's reactions will be – fear that they might collapse, be overcome with emotion or helplessness, or have an outburst or lose control to the point where they might harm themselves
- Uncertainty as to one's own response, as the one informing or providing support (What is the right thing to say? What will happen if I lose control/swallow my words/if my voice shakes/if I burst into tears? Can I handle this situation?)

- The direct encounter with tragedy can awaken memories of one's personal tragedies.

On the other hand, in this role, one might appreciate the sense of providing support and encouragement to others. Those informing and supporting the family may not always be thanked or shown appreciation for their work; at times they may even be faced with hostile responses. Because of this, their work to support and help the family can be considered a truly selfless mitzva.

It is important to have an internal framework for supporting individuals that inform and support bereaved families. Teams who do this regularly must have a supportive framework so that they can continue do their job well.

SECTION 63: INFORMATION FOR *ḤEVRA KADDISHA* VOLUNTEERS

Sometimes in smaller towns, the *ḥevra kaddisha* works on an as-needed, volunteer basis. Volunteers need guidelines and information about how to prepare for and manage the funeral. Below are guidelines from the *ḥevra kaddisha* of the regional council of Binyamin in Israel. Based on years of experience, these guidelines and notes are offered to members of *ḥevra kaddishas*. They should, of course, be adapted as needed in various situations and locations.

Objectives

1) To care of the deceased and bury them honorably, according to the rules set out by the halakha
2) To attend to the family respectfully and sensitively, to assist and guide them
3) To make the appropriate arrangements for the funeral

Advance preparations

There should be **a list of all current members of the *ḥevra kaddisha*,** including their telephone numbers so that they can be contacted and located immediately. The list can be printed out on a compact card so that members can carry a copy of the list with them. The *ḥevra kaddisha* can have a website with the information listed there.

It should be determined who is **the person in charge** and who will substitute for them if that person is absent.

There should be a **map of the cemetery** in the cemetery itself. Each grave should be marked as "Available," "Reserved for (name)," or "Buried (name)."

There should be a **kit for the shiva house** that includes **siddurs, texts with halakhic information, kippot, and memorial candles**. Other items can be included according to the list provided later in this chapter.

Outline of the *Ḥevra Kaddisha*'s activities

The tasks of the *ḥevra kaddisha* up until the funeral can be divided into four main areas:

1) Attending to the deceased, *tahara* (ritual purification), and transportation of the body
2) Official documentation, death certificate, burial permit; in cases of unnatural death, police authorization is also required.
3) Preparing the grave, digging it; great care must be taken with regard to the grave's location.
4) Attending to the family and assisting with halakhic guidance, *kriya*, eulogies

Other steps are necessary after the funeral and they will be detailed later.

Particulars of the *Ḥevra Kaddisha*'s activities

1. **Attending to the deceased:** One must shut the deceased's eyes and mouth. The deceased is left untouched in the bed for twenty minutes. Afterwards, the body is lowered to the ground – not onto a sheet or a carpet – with the feet pointing towards the door. Every time the deceased is moved, one should first ask the deceased for forgiveness. Two candles are lit beside the deceased's head. Psalms 23 and 91 are recited, and the deceased

is covered with a white sheet. The deceased's shoes and clothing are removed, while making sure that the face and groin remained covered. Men tend to a deceased man and women tend to a deceased woman. If those present are emotionally unable to do these things, they should wait for the regular members of the *ḥevra kaddisha* to do them at the funeral home. **A person who was killed** is buried in his clothing. **On Shabbat**, the deceased cannot be moved in the usual manner. If there is an extended delay, the **body must be cooled**, especially in summertime. The deceased must be guarded. In the hospital, a guard may be needed to prevent an autopsy from being done against the family's wishes.

Ritual purification (*Tahara*) – The *tahara* is usually performed by the *ḥevra kaddisha*. A system must be established ahead of time as to how to the *tehara* is performed, where it is done, and who brings the deceased to and from this location.

Transportation of the deceased – There is usually a designated vehicle used for this purpose, but any other appropriate vehicle may be used. There is a **special kind of stretcher** to use for this, but any other stretcher may be used. Care should be taken that the **deceased is covered** during transportation in the vehicle and also throughout the funeral until the burial. Some individuals have had their own **shrouds** prepared ahead of time. The *ḥevra kaddisha* should check whether there are such shrouds, and if so, they should be given to the *ḥevra kaddisha* before the *tahara*.

2. **Official documentation: Death certificate** – this must be signed by a doctor; **burial permit** – in Israel, this is given by the Ministry of Health; in the case of an unnatural death, **documentation from the police** must be obtained before the burial permit can be granted. All of these details appear above in Sec. 1, "Official Documentation."
3. **Preparation of the grave:** There need to be clear instructions about how to dig the grave so that it is done properly and in a timely fashion. The location of the grave must be chosen very carefully. There are sometimes reserved burial plots in

the cemetery. The person in charge should have a map of the cemetery and backup maps that are updated regularly.

The **grave's dimensions** should be as follows: 1.2 meters deep, two meters long, and half-a-meter wide. Inside the grave, there should be a frame made of blocks or stones; it should be forty centimeters high, with the blocks being fifteen centimeters in thickness. One must also see to it that there are **stone slabs for covering** the grave. In Israel, these slabs and blocks can usually be obtained through the local religious council. A local rabbi can be consulted to find out where they can be obtained. Extra stone slabs should be on hand in case one of them breaks or there are not enough. **Four poles**, each two-meters long, should be placed at the four corners of the grave at the end of the burial, before covering it with earth, to mark the place of the grave; this is for the purpose of placing a gravestone there at a later date (unless the graves have been dug in advance and covered with a cement slab).

Generally, the **distance between graves** is around fifty to sixty centimeters (in cities, this is the distance between the graves, while the gravestones are closer to one another). *Kohanim* should be allotted graves on the outer periphery of the cemetery to allow access for their family. There should be at least a three-meter gap between the outer graves and the cemetery fence.

If the **deceased was very tall**, a longer grave should be prepared. The grave-diggers must be informed of this beforehand.

If the **grave is dug in advance**, they must be careful not to leave it open but to cover it up that same day. Sometimes the *ḥevra kaddisha* will prepare graves in advance but dig them incompletely, leaving the digging to be completed on the day of burial. When they do this, they are not particular about covering up the graves. In areas where the ground is hard, it is better to dig and prepare the graves ahead of time and fill them in with sand to make the digging easier when the time comes for it to be used.

4. **Attending to the family**: The family requires social and familial support. They also require immediate halakhic guidance. The guidance will vary from family to family, depending on a number of factors: level of religious observance, ethnicity, and customs, as well as specific questions that come up in unique circumstances. If the local rabbi is not available, other Torah scholars who are close with the family or who live nearby can be consulted.

   ***Kriya*, the "*Dayan HaEmet*" blessing, funeral, eulogies, burial, comforting the mourners** – In these matters, it is preferable that the family be assisted by the *ḥevra kaddisha* or a rabbi.

   Scissors should be on hand for the ***kriya***, and **safety pins** will be needed for women. It is also helpful to have an outer garment available that can be used in case someone's clothing is ripped too much by mistake. Some have the custom to break a piece of **clay** before the funeral; a simple ceramic item can be used for this.

Practical supplies for the funeral

Water must be made available if people are walking some distance to the cemetery for the funeral, especially on hot days and when a significant amount of walking is involved. Water should either be brought along or be available at certain spots along the way. Water should also be available at the exit of the cemetery so that people can wash their hands. **The faucets outside the cemetery should be checked** – someone should turn them on to make sure they work. There should be **tools (hoes and shovels)** for covering the grave. A **sign with the deceased's name** should be prepared. Sometimes it is necessary for an **ambulance** to be on-call nearby with a medical team. A **sound system** will be needed for big funerals.

After the funeral

After the funeral, there should be a meal of condolence (*seudat havraah*) for the relatives. This is the first meal that the mourners eat after the funeral. It is usually prepared by their neighbors. It customarily includes hard-boiled eggs and other round foods.

It is customary to light a **memorial candle** in the house of mourning. It is also customary to cover mirrors, especially if prayer services are held in the house. Pictures need not be covered, but if services are held in the house and those praying will be facing an area with pictures, they should be covered. The seating for shiva should be arranged ahead of time: A place must be prepared for the mourners to sit, customarily **low stools or chairs.** Benches and chairs should be arranged for those coming to offer condolences. Sometimes, if there will be many people coming to comfort the mourners, a tent is put up outside the house to accommodate the visitors. In this case, lighting should be arranged, as well.

Some have the custom to serve **refreshments. Disposable cutlery, cups, and plates** are most convenient in this case. It can also be helpful to have a **hot-water urn** set up.

Some people like to make a **charity box** available in the shiva house, to encourage people to do a mitzva for the elevation of the deceased's soul.

Prayer services in the mourners' home: This is determined according to the family's wishes. It is best to obtain the assistance of the *gabbai'im* of the local synagogue to arrange the services. If services are going to be held in the house, **siddurs and kippot** should be brought there. A ***sefer Torah*** can be brought for the Torah reading. Some communities have a small **portable ark** available for this purpose. A **lectern** for the prayer-leader can be brought. If services will be held in the house on Shabbat, ***Ḥumash* books** will be needed. The **times for prayer services** must be determined. Passages of Mishna or psalms are customarily recited in the shiva house; some people divide up chapters of Mishna to be learned by individuals who come to visit who agree to do the learning for the elevation of the deceased's soul. Books of Psalms can also be brought to the cemetery.

"Death shall vanish eternally and God shall dry the tears from all faces"

SECTION 64: PSYCHOLOGICAL ASPECTS OF THE MOURNING PROCESS

Dr. Meir Perlov, Clinical Psychologist

In modern psychology, the emotional process of grief and bereavement is considered extremely important for a person's mental health. This is in keeping with the perspective that holds that a healthy human psyche is capable of recognizing and expressing emotions, instead of denying, ignoring, or dismissing them. Emotions are considered an important component of the psyche's basic energy; having this energy flow freely is necessary for one's mental health. Bereavement is an emotionally-charged, challenging process for the psyche – a challenge that, if it is withstood, can increase the psyche's resilience and health, and if not, is likely to lead to future psychological struggles.

Many emotions may be experienced during the grieving process. Some emotions are expected and accepted, such as pain, sadness, and longing. But there may also be unexpected emotions or ones that tend to be scorned, such as blame ("Why wasn't it me who died instead of him?"), anger (towards the deceased or towards God), and even joy or relief (especially if the person's deterioration had been long and drawn-out and involved much suffering). During the grieving process, these emotions may be very intense. Mourners require a supportive, accepting framework that will allow them time and space to express and experience these emotions without feeling that they are being judged.

The Jewish laws about sitting shiva and comforting mourners cause the mourners to encounter a variety of people connected to them or to the deceased. These encounters lead to sharing memories about the deceased. The memories are likely to touch on various aspects of the deceased's character and history, and this is a process that can bring up a wide range of emotions. Through this practice, Jewish tradition provides a space for the mourning process, which includes the variety of emotions that arise. All of this is taken into account in the broader message we convey to the mourners, demonstrated by the words that comforters say to them: "May you be comforted from Heaven" or "May God comfort you, etc."

And herein lies another psychological principle central to the process of mourning: While pain and sorrow are recognized and given space, they are emotions that will pass. The mourner's inner life will one day return to a state where he is capable of feeling joy. This is at odds with the mourner's immediate experience, especially in the case of a sudden or tragic death, which is so painful; this often involves the sense that the pain will overtake one's life forevermore (as Jacob said: "Now I will go down mourning to my son in Sheol" [Gen. 37:35]). Sometimes, mourners do not want to hear words of comfort (like Jacob who "refused to be comforted") and feel the desire to continue their mourning as an expression of the emotional intensity they feel, as if to say: If my mourning feels so intense right now, then I will feel this way forever or should feel this way forever. Sometimes feelings of love for the deceased generate a sense that it is one's duty to continue mourning for them, as though it is the only way to prove one's love and dedication. This notion and expressions of it can have their place in the grieving process, as part of the way one expresses one's powerful emotions; we do not need to force the mourner, in that moment, to face the facts of reality, of the future, etc. At times, we must simply accept the mourner's emotional need to express his feelings in an extreme way, as an expression of the intensity of emotion he is struggling with. We do this with the hope that, towards the end of the grieving period, if the person has expressed his emotions to his satisfaction, he will be able to return to his regular functioning, both on a practical and an emotional level. So, along with recognizing the pain, we do indeed expect that mourners will succeed in processing their emotions and will be able to return to their lives. This is the message of, "May you be comforted from Heaven."

Our sages established a series of frameworks for mourning (shiva, *shloshim*, the one-year period) and different degrees of mourning for each of them. Modern psychology research has shown that in extreme cases, the mourning process can also last for more than a year. Sometimes a mourner requires professional psychological help to cope with the mourning, if he is finding it difficult to return to his regular functioning. In most cases, mourning as set out by the halakha allows for the emotional healing process that a person requires in order to return to normal life.

SECTION 65: ASPECTS PARTICULAR TO MOURNING IN CHILDREN

Dr. Forto Ben Harush, Child Psychiatrist, Hadassah Hospital, Mount Scopus Campus

This section does not attempt in any way to cover the subject in its entirety. Rather, it briefly highlights several points particular to children in mourning. Other important aspects of mourning are discussed elsewhere in this book and will not be repeated here.

The first stage of grieving is the most acute and extends over the first few weeks following a death. In this stage, any response is natural. A complete absence of any response could signal an emotional issue.

After this first acute stage, if the response continues without change, it is important to consult with a professional who is experienced in treating children. However, the child should not be treated as someone with a problem or pathology. Only a professional can determine whether there is a need for external intervention, after having gathered sufficient information about the child and the environment.

On the other hand, a child's emotional distress can oftentimes go unnoticed or unidentified because the child seems to be functioning and playing normally.

Sometimes the child intuitively (subconsciously) senses that the adults around him are overwhelmed by emotions. In order to "protect them," the child resists expressing his distress but ends up feeling quite alone.

A child's emotional distress can be manifested in many different ways. For example:

- Difficulty concentrating in school
- Physical complaints such as headaches, "something" bothersome in the throat, exhaustion, stomachaches
- Reduced appetite or increased appetite
- Insomnia, disturbing dreams, bed-wetting
- New fears (even if they are not related directly to death or the specific tragedy) such as fear of the dark or fear of going to the bathroom alone
- Developmental regression (a loss of the abilities already acquired, such as motor skills, speech, independence)
- Social withdrawal
- Over-activity or disturbance in behavior
- Lack of interest in things that previously were of interest

Many people relate to emotions of loss and grieving as things that need to be "gotten out" as quickly as possible. According to this approach, mourning is a type of "illness" and we can prevent negative effects of this "illness" by expressing the difficult emotions until they have been expelled. Those who view grieving in this way speak about "putting it behind us" or "recovery" and of completing the experience within an allocated time-frame.

This approach is often not suited to the actual experience of children and teens in their grieving. They tend to feel that they are undergoing many processes of change, adaptation, and transition. For them it is not simply about "going through some difficult emotions."

Therefore, a more accurate understanding of bereavement for them is one that defines it as a **stage of transition in the life-cycle**. This perspective takes into account the wide array of areas and roles in which the child and parents must cope with change as a result of the loss and its impact on their lives (changing routines or lifestyle, adapting to changes, etc.).

In other words, one must remember that:

- Mourning is predominantly a **stage of change and transition.**
- The natural process is when the child, in the context of his family and friends, **finds his own ways of coping** with the changing situation – ways that work for him.
- In helping the mourning child, the task is to empower and reinforce his ability to find his own ways of coping.

Guidelines for Approaching a Grieving Child

There is no easy prescription to ease the child's pain. However, there are ways that those close to the child and the family can help the mourners feel more capable of coping with the challenges of transitioning into their new life-situation:

1. Many adults ask: "Should we speak to the child about it or not?"

   The answer is that one should **cultivate an atmosphere around the child that allows for honest talking and listening.** The child will either speak about it or not, according to his own needs, and this should be honored.

   Two extremes should be avoided:

   - Pressuring the child to talk
   - Denying or ignoring the subject

2. It is important that every child be **included in the process and family rituals** of mourning (in ways that are appropriate for the child's age and developmental stage, of course).
3. Parents need to learn how to **speak with their child about the deceased**, the circumstances of the death, **their shared pain**, and **how they will, together, build their lives from this point on.**
4. When speaking with a grieving child, one should **listen** to the child's personal story **without telling him how he feels or should feel**. The child should be allowed to express and tell an adult what he actually feels. Some children do not want any special treatment and some do not want to talk. These preferences should be respected.
5. For many children, it is more important to speak about the deceased and **what they have lost with this death**, than to speak about how they feel. It is important for the child to feel that it is **legitimate to relate to the deceased in different ways**; this may include remembering both positive and negative traits of the deceased, looking for ways to continue connecting with the figure of the deceased, etc.
6. One should avoid making generalities and assumptions.
7. It is preferable to avoid giving advice when it has not been requested.
8. Some children need a place to be alone for a while, during the shiva, for example, or at school. Other children may need someone else to draw them into an activity. It is important to be sensitive to the child's expressions of what he needs and when.

Children, like adults, need love and patience. Sometimes adults become too distressed by a child's response or reaction, or they compound or project their own problems onto those of the child. This stress is clearly not beneficial to the child. What is helpful in relating to both children and adults in mourning is conducting oneself in a simple manner that conveys love and support, as well as a sense of safety, patience, and optimism.

SECTION 66: THE FORGOTTEN WISDOM OF CONSOLATION

By Nahi Alon and Prof. Haim Omer[2]

> When Job's three friends heard about all these calamities that had befallen him, each came from his home – Eliphaz the Temanite, Bildad the Shuhite, and Zophar the Naamathite. They met together to go and console and comfort him. When they saw him from a distance, they could not recognize him, and they broke into loud weeping; each one tore his robe and threw dust into the air onto his head. They sat with him on the ground seven days and seven nights. None spoke a word to him for they saw how very great was his suffering. (Job 2:11–13)

Throughout history, consoling a person who is in pain has been considered a mitzva. In the modern world, comforting has lost some of its honor. Modern expressions such as "cheap consolation" reflect its reduced value. Even the traditional expressions of condolence have lost their power in modern times, and if they are said at all, they are usually mumbled awkwardly. Particularly surprising is the fact that the skills of consolation are given little attention in the training of therapists. Perhaps there is an assumption that such skills cannot be learned; perhaps therapists striving for a "cure" see consolation as being secondary in importance; or perhaps therapists do not recognize its importance because they are called in only after the usual attempts at comfort have failed. In any case, many believe that the real emotional healing occurs far beyond the domain of comforting, which is the jurisdiction of the clergy or simple folk. In this way, consolation has become a forgotten wisdom.

---

2. Nahi Alon is a clinical psychologist and Prof. Haim Omer is a lecturer of psychology at Tel Aviv University. This chapter is a translation from a Hebrew essay based on passages from their book, "*HaSatan SheBeinenu*," published by Sefarim Publishers, ch. 5, from p. 153. I want to thank them and the publisher for their willingness and permission to quote from the book. (The book was published in English under the title "The Psychology of Demonization." The present translation has drawn from the English edition.)

Consolation, like its twin sister, acceptance, is a "tragic" virtue. In a society that gives prime importance to control, there is no great value to incomplete solutions. In contrast, the starting point of the tragic perspective is that suffering exists. Where life exists, there is also suffering, and thus there is no complete solution. The tragic view dares to seek modest happiness in a harsh world. Therefore, it tends toward acceptance and finding relief, more than a cure. The hope for a cure has one goal – the disappearance of suffering. Condolence, on the other hand, has two facets: acceptance and encouragement. Acceptance is addressed toward the suffering, whereas encouragement addresses the possibility of limiting the suffering or easing its burden. Suffering and loss do not disappear, but a person can look back at them whilst moving forward. These facets of condolence are related to one another since the willingness to seek acceptance requires abandoning the dream of complete recovery. Thus, consolation is a bittersweet pill: The degree of encouragement it contains is equal to the person's willingness to accept his suffering. There is only one kind of encouragement that does not include acceptance: The kind that comes from the popular version of positive thinking that views any complaint as an attack on the correct, optimistic stance. We, the authors, believe that this type of encouragement is not all that encouraging: In denying the sufferer the right to suffer, it tends to be closer to condemnation than to consolation.

Consolation can be extended; it cannot be forced. An attempt to force the sufferer to be comforted is doomed to fail. The sufferer may show willingness to be comforted and he also may not. It all depends on what he is needing. In the biblical story, Jacob refuses to be comforted for the loss of Joseph. It would be absurd to claim that Jacob is "acting sorry for himself" or displaying "pathological grief." If Jacob had become convinced that he should stop mourning, it is likely that he would have later felt a sense of great self-betrayal. The anger the sufferer sometimes expresses at the consoler is thus rather understandable: Sometimes the comfort hints that the one who is suffering should stop suffering. In the experience of the person who is suffering, this implication is a denial of his right to protest the cruelty of fate that has befallen him. The common mistake of encouraging the sufferer is often made out of a lack of sensitivity and awareness.

Sometimes comforters give the impression that they wish to avoid contact with the sufferer, as though afraid that it is contagious. The late psychologist Marianne Amir, when she was ill with terminal cancer, wrote an article entitled "*Run* for *Your Life!*" describing the effect of this avoidant attitude on the sufferer. One friend would call when she knew she was not home and leave a message saying, "I wanted to know how you are feeling but did not want to disturb you. No need to call back." A different friend left flowers at her door. A third friend would stay for a very short time and would always leave with a cheerful, "Everything will be okay!" Among Marianne's friends, there were those who were critical of her sadness and of her attitude toward her illness, claiming that she was not helping herself get better. This approach was perhaps the most unhelpful to her. The difficulty that friends, colleagues, and doctors face in such situations is understandable; they feel helpless and anxious. However, one cannot effectively console a person when exhibiting this attitude.

When a consoler rushes and conveys impatience, it reflects another aspect of consolation: whether the consoler feels similar to or different from the sufferer. The impatient consoler sends a message of the difference between them: "We are not in the same boat. You are heading your way and I am heading mine!" It is not surprising, then, that the sufferer feels abandoned. A potentially helpful attempt at consolation will convey not only proximity but also a basic similarity: "This could happen to me, too." This message does not need to be said explicitly, of course, but is conveyed in the consoler's attitude.

Consoling thus involves removing the barriers between consoler and consoled. If the consoling is accepted, the giver also becomes a receiver. Consoling, like compassion, emphasizes the basic similarity between the two sides, as well as their inter-connectedness.

SECTION 67: MEMORIAL

The following section is not about halakha; instead, it offers a theoretical and practical discussion of memorializing the deceased. This discussion has been included in light of the emotional and tangible need to memorialize a loved one, something that relatives often feel.

The basic need for memorialization stems from the human need to feel connected to eternity, to feel that death will not erase one from the world. Naturally, after people die, their descendants carry on their memory, both in a biological sense and a spiritual one. The descendants remember the person's life, carry their name, etc.

The need for memorialization is especially felt when a person has died before his time, or without any descendants to carry on his memory. The Torah commands a man to marry his brother's wife if the brother has died childless, so that the brother's name will not be erased (Deut. 25:6); it relates how Judah fulfilled this duty to his daughter-in-law, Tamar (Gen. 38), even before the Torah was given; the Book of Ruth describes how Boaz married Ruth in order to perpetuate the memory of Maḥlon, her first husband: "I am also acquiring Ruth the Moabite, the wife of Maḥlon, as my wife, so as to perpetuate the name of the deceased upon his estate, that the name of the deceased will not disappear from among his kinsmen and from the gate of his home town" (Ruth 4:10). The Bible uses the phrase "redeemer" for one who perpetuates the name of the deceased.

Job also sought to establish a memorial after his sons and daughters died and he remained childless:

> "O that my words were written down. Would they were inscribed in a record, incised on a rock forever with iron stylus and lead! But I know that my redeemer lives; in the end he will testify on earth." (Job 19:23–25)

The childless Job wants his words to be carved forever in a book and in stone. He also uses the expression "my redeemer" for someone who will read his words; this anonymous person who will read his words and know that he lived will redeem Job! It allows Job to be connected to eternity for many years after his death; although whatever is physical is fleeting, his spiritual message can remain forever.

The desire and need for memorialization is still present today, particularly for young people who have died before their time but not only. It expresses a need for spiritual continuity, even after the soul has departed and left the body.

Beyond the relatives' emotional need to relate to the memory of the deceased, it is also significant for them to perform an action, to create something from their place of pain and sorrow. Becoming involved in this type of positive deed can offer some healing to mourners. If a mourner is feeling like he has lost part of his own life, such acts can provide something positive and encouraging. In this context, it is also relevant to note the Jewish idea that every positive and valuable act performed in honor of the deceased increases the deceased's merit in the world to come.

The first step when thinking about memorialization is to assess whether the larger community has a need for a memorial, and whether it will be truly beneficial and meaningful, such that the relatives' efforts and investment will be justified. The cost – both emotional and financial – must be considered. Is the family able and willing to undertake this expense? Are they mistakenly entering into this because of the emotional turmoil following the death and taking on significant costs that they cannot truly bear? The relatives should consult with other families who have been through the process. Families usually try to create a memorial that is in line with who the deceased was. Although the language used below is for the memorialization of one person, a memorial can of course be for a number of people, or even for an entire community. Here we will offer some suggestions and options for memorializing the deceased.

Memorial Booklet

This generally includes a biography of the deceased, together with pictures, letters, and memories. The booklet allows for an immediate, personal encounter with the deceased. It is accessible to readers and can be easily distributed.

Memorial Book

> O that I might dwell in Your tent forever, take refuge under Your protecting wings. *Selah.* (Ps. 61:5)
>
> Did David think that he would live forever? Rather David said before God: Master of the Universe, I shall merit that my words be recited in synagogues and the beit midrash. Shimon ben Nezira said in the name of Rabbi Yitzḥak: Whenever a law is related in the name of a Torah scholar in this

> world, his lips tremble with him in the grave as it says: "Let it flow to my beloved as new wine, gliding over the lips of sleepers" (Song. 7:10). The same way that a bunch of grapes on the vine moves when someone touches it, so too with the lips of the righteous – when a halakha is said in their name, their lips move. (Y. Shekalim 2:5)

A memorial book can be entirely about the deceased. This is usually only done for great Torah scholars or remarkable individuals from whom others can learn, and thus reading about them would be meaningful and inspirational.

Another possibility is a book where the content is partially or primarily about something other than the deceased. A collection of articles can be made into a memorial book, to which personal pieces about the deceased can be added; sometimes, a Torah subject is chosen and Torah scholars are asked to write an article on the subject. One can provide a list of secondary topics connected to the main theme. It is very important to choose a unifying theme for the book; it will make it much more useful to people. If the book is focused on one topic, especially if it something relevant to the public, there is a greater chance that people will read the book for its own sake and will then also read the section that has been included in memory of the deceased.

Both the book and the booklet should **not be made in haste**! It takes time to create a valuable book. This is not always possible in the emotional upheaval immediately following a death. Take the time to choose a topic that is of public interest. It is better to do so and produce a valuable book that has been executed with deliberation and consideration, so that the book or booklet will be read for many years to come because of its quality and value.

Sefer Torah

We have already mentioned that every Jewish person is likened to a Torah scroll. Writing or acquiring a *sefer Torah* in memory of the deceased is an expression of this relationship. For this purpose, a Torah scroll can be purchased or commissioned, and it may be given to the local synagogue or congregation; some people choose to lend it out.

Some prefer to donate the *sefer Torah* to a synagogue that does not own any or enough Torah scrolls, so that the one that has been donated will be read from regularly. It is a significant and costly undertaking to commission or purchase a *sefer Torah*. Many kinds of scrolls and writing are available, and there is a wide range of prices. Professionals or experts in this area should be consulted before coming to a decision.

Some have written that, rather than purchasing a Torah scroll that will remain in the synagogue, it is preferable to donate money to publish a Torah scholar's book on a halakhic or religious topic, or to re-publish an early halakhic work. The reasoning behind this is that, since it is said that God resides in the four cubits of halakha, publishing such as book is a great mitzva that brings merit to the deceased.[3]

Torah study session

An evening or daytime study session can be arranged in memory of the deceased. It customarily focuses on studying a Torah-related topic. The study session should not be too long so as not to become burdensome to those attending. The topics and time-frame should be determined in advance. If the learning goes on for too long and people begin to leave, it can become rather uncomfortable. A focused learning session is best. Personal anecdotes about the deceased can be included. Making use of didactic tools is permissible and sometimes desirable, to engage those attending. When using technical aids such as video or audio clips, there should be a capable person responsible for operating them.

Study group

A group dedicated to Torah study, reciting psalms, or studying Torah with children, etc. can be established or funded in memory of the deceased. Torah study in memory of the deceased is a great merit for the deceased and the family.

Dedication

A common way to memorialize the deceased is by having the deceased's name displayed on a plaque, or dedicating a Torah scroll, synagogue,

---

3. *Yalkut Yosef* 30:12.

yeshiva, or beit midrash, or some item in it, e.g., a Torah ark, the curtain of the ark, furniture for the synagogue, a library or Torah library, an ambulance or medical equipment, scholarships for study, or study materials.

Charity and acts of kindness

One can memorialize the deceased by giving to social projects. Some examples of this are establishing a charitable fund for helping others, or a free-loan society, or one that offers any type of help to those in need. Yad Sarah in Israel, for example, began as a small fund for lending out medical equipment and has become a national institution of assistance and charity. Other examples are volunteering to help the sick, the elderly, struggling students, new immigrants, the disabled, or any other group or individual in need. This type of activity is very important because it has lasting effects and channels the feelings of sadness and pain into positive acts of helping others. In this type of ongoing charitable activity, the deceased is not usually given a lot of attention or glory; oftentimes there is not even a plaque to memorialize them. However, this work is deeply meaningful and important.

Some other examples of activities or projects in memory of the deceased are: a trip or hike in memory of the deceased; building or restoring a site in nature or naming it after the deceased; producing a CD, exhibition, or sporting event. Sometimes the memorial is a one-time event and sometimes it is ongoing or annual. Any act that is in line with Jewish values is a merit to the deceased and their family.

Naming a child after the deceased

Much has been written about naming children after the deceased, and this is not the place to discuss it at length. The brief discussion below is based on the book "*Kor'ei Shemo*," written by my friend Rabbi Mishael Rubin. Those who want to explore the topic further can consult his book or others written on the subject.

There is a Jewish custom to name children after a parent or other relative. The Ashkenazic custom is to name children after someone who has died. The Sephardic custom is to name children after someone who is still alive; it is considered a blessing for a long life.

According to most opinions, the child may be given a name similar to the deceased's name, or a name can be added to the name of the deceased. Some say that one should not name a child after a person who died after the child was born.

According to most opinions, one should not name a child after a person who suffered bad luck, such as someone who died young. Instead, one should change the name slightly[4] or add a name (and use both names). In this case, some make sure to use the deceased's name as a second name.[5] Some say that there is no problem in naming a child after someone who died young.[6] Some say that if the person was killed while sanctifying God's name, the child can be named after the deceased without adding another name.

4. *Responsa Igrot Moshe, Yoreh De'ah*, vol. 2, 122.
5. *Yalkut Yosef, Kibud Av VaEm*, vol. 2, p. 94.
6. Rabbi Haim David HaLevi, *Aseh Lekha Rav*, vol. 6, 69. He brings a case in which the Gaon of Vilna's daughter's sons died in childhood, and her father told her to give the next child the name of the one who died but to add another name as the first name.

Part 5

Wills and Inheritance

Civil law views the deceased as owning his property even after his death, while halakha views the owner as controlling his property only until death. After that point, instructions cannot be given about his estate.

SECTION 68: INHERITANCE LAW ACCORDING TO HALAKHA

By Rabbi Yishai Bukhris

If no will has been written, inheritance law determines who the inheritors of the deceased will be, according to civil law. If someone has drawn up a will that is legally valid, the law will recognize and uphold it. According to the halakha, a will cannot be drawn up the way it is under civil law. Halakha views man's control as binding only when he is alive; after death, one's possessions become the property of one's inheritors, and a person does not have the ability to control his money and property after death.

There is, however, an exception to this rule, namely the will of a critically ill person (*shekhiv meRa*). The sages said that if a person is on his deathbed, his wishes must be accepted, even though the instructions come into effect only after his death. This is done so that the person will not have doubts as to whether his wishes will be honored because such worry could hasten his death. A person who is not in that situation is not permitted to control his possessions after death.[1]

1. There are opinions that say that anyone who gives instructions about his own estate is considered to do so because of his own imminent death and can thus be treated

There is another way that one can halakhically distribute one's possessions: through "the mitzva to uphold the words of the deceased." This means that if a person gave instructions as to how to distribute his estate, there is a mitzva to fulfill these instructions. However, there are a number of conditions that must be in place for this scenario to be halakhically valid, and these conditions can be difficult to execute. The main condition is that the possessions that will be distributed after death are handled by a third party while the person is still alive. Many halakhic authorities also explain that the recipient has no legal right to the gift. The inheritors have an obligation to uphold the deceased's instructions, but if they choose not to do so, they cannot be forced into it.

Despite what has been written above, there is a legal method in line with the halakha that one can use to divide up his estate as he wishes; it will be presented here. Of course, some question this approach since it in some sense bypasses the spirit of the halakha: The halakha has established a certain manner of distribution and using this method means that one's estate is divided up differently. Some wrote that this borders on being strictly prohibited. The *Shulḥan Arukh* (*Ḥoshen Mishpat* 282:1) discusses it as follows:

> Anyone who gives his property to others and does not leave it for his inheritors, even if the inheritors are not behaving properly toward him – the rabbis' spirit is not pleased with him, and others take possession of whatever he gave them. It is the way of the righteous not to testify for a will in which the inheritance is removed from the inheritor, even a son who is misbehaving, to be given to his wise and properly-behaved brother.

In order to overcome this problem, some have suggested setting aside part of the inheritance to be distributed according to the halakha.

The contemporary benefit of and need for writing a will

The following is written in the context of civil law in Israel, but it is largely relevant to civil law in other countries, as well.

---

similarly to the critically ill person, whose will is honored. However, the halakha adopts the other opinion.

The civil laws of inheritance are different from those of the halakha. For this reason, even if one wants the estate to simply be divided according to the halakha without any deviation, one should write a will; if one does not write a will, the estate will be divided in accordance with civil law and not according to halakha. If a person desires a distribution that is even slightly different from that of the law or the halakha, it should be clearly stated and detailed in the will. One should make sure that the will is valid both legally and halakhically.

The Torah's instruction is that daughters do not receive inheritance, but the sages gave them rights that are sometimes even greater than those of sons (e.g., they are sustained from the estate until they get married [Ketubot 108b] and receive a tithing of the property as a dowry for marriage [ibid. 68]). The universal custom, also cited in halakhic works, is to give a portion to daughters, as well, often one that is equivalent to a son's portion. This is defined in the halakha as "*shtar ḥatzi zakhar*," literally "half a male deed," which means that the daughter receives a portion equivalent to that of sons, or half as much – "half a male deed" (Rema, *Even HaEzer* 108; *Gesher HaḤayim* 1:8, 2).

It is good and appropriate to bestow some of the estate to daughters, primarily because this is the widely-accepted custom, and the sages themselves established many decrees for the benefit of daughters. Another reason to do so is to prevent fighting and disagreements among the inheritors, and to prevent a situation wherein some of the inheritors demand that the Torah law be followed, while others demand that the estate be divided according to civil laws that contradict halakha.

Even if the deceased has not left a will, the sons should give the daughters an equal portion for the aforementioned reasons. This is certainly also true with regard to the deceased's wife (*Gesher HaḤayim* ibid).

Principles of a halakhic will

As discussed above, after death, a person is no longer considered owner of his estate and therefore cannot give instructions regarding it. In order to solve this problem, there are two options for halakhic wills:

a. A will based on a gift given by a healthy person – giving the property as a gift while one is alive
b. A will based on a financial agreement for the good of the recipient

Drawbacks of writing a will based on a gift given by a healthy person

Clearly, a person may give gifts as he wishes during his lifetime. However, since the gift is given when the person is alive, there are certain drawbacks to this and some things that need to be taken into consideration:

a. If the giver has transferred ownership of the property, how can he continue to use it until he dies?
b. One can only give a gift from what is in one's possession; future acquisitions after drawing up the will cannot be included.
c. One cannot give a gift to someone who was born after the gift was given. Therefore, if other children were born to the person between the time the will was drawn up and before his death, these children would not be included in the inheritance.
d. There are transactions that are effective for land but not for transferring ownership of objects, and vice versa; there are also transactions that are effective for land and objects, but not for loans and bank deposits. Therefore, one needs to consider the other parts of one's estate for which the transaction is not applicable.

Drawbacks of writing a will based on a financial agreement

There is another method of writing a halakhic will: Making a financial commitment for a particular amount that one would like to bestow on a particular person who is not eligible to receive part of the inheritance according to the halakha. For example, Reuven has a daughter and three sons (none of whom is the firstborn, since the Torah law is that the firstborn receives a portion that is double that of the other brothers). He leaves behind $1000 and wants it to be divided equally among all of his children. In this case, Reuven should make a financial promise of $250 to his daughter, and this ensures an equal division.

Drawbacks of this approach

a. Since the person does not know the exact amount that he will bequeath when he dies, he cannot know the precise amount to promise the recipient.
b. The recipient will receive the amount promised but not an actual part of the estate like other inheritors.
c. If the inheritors sell all of the property without paying the above-mentioned recipient, how can the deceased's debt, the financial promise, be collected?

There are additional drawbacks and ways of addressing them, but the scope of the present text does not allow for a lengthy discussion on the topic. Each of the methods mentioned above has its disadvantages; we have therefore provided a sample text, below, for a will that is both halakhically and legally valid [in Israel] and that addresses most of the potential problems.

Sample text for a will

I, the undersigned, ________, write this will with a sound mind and of my own free will, so that it will be upheld when I die (1).

a. I hereby revoke any and all wills and codicils heretofore made or promised by me and declare this my final will (2).
b. I transfer ownership of all the property owned by me on the day of and shortly before my death, except for an amount equivalent to four dollars for each inheritor that is entitled to inherit from me according to Jewish law; and for the firstborn, a sum equivalent to eight dollars (3). To the following recipients I bequeath according to the following distribution.

    For Reuven, (property) and (amount).

    For Shimon, (property) and (amount).

The remainder of my property that I have not bequeathed, my inheritors shall inherit according to the laws of Torah.

c. I declare that I have bequeathed all of the above-mentioned property in the most effective manner, each item as it is fit (4).

d. If there is something that the transaction is not effective for, this should not interfere with the gift of the other possessions that have been bequeathed (5).

e. For those possessions that were not effectively bequeathed, I hereby declare that I have obligated myself to make a complete gift through "*Kinyan Sudar*" (literally, an acquisition done by a cloth) and "*Kinyan Agav*" (an acquisition of movable property as an adjunct to acquiring real estate) to the following beneficiaries: To __________, __________ percentage of my estate, to __________, __________ percentage of my estate (6).

f. In case of any doubt regarding the intention of this will, the beneficiaries should have the benefit of the doubt, and any halakhic doubt shall be determined by the halakhic authorities who execute this will.

g. I have made a condition with the aforementioned beneficiaries that if I rescind this will or a part thereof by writing another will or a written revocation before halakhically sanctioned witnesses, then this will or the specific part thereof shall be annulled.

h. Every condition in this will is made in accordance with all the conditions of our sages and following the conditions of the children of Gad and the children of Reuven (7).

i. This document was approved by a representative of all the beneficiaries and they made a valid acquisition as though it was done in a religious court.

I have signed my name on the date ____________________, signed, ________________.

We, the undersigned, uphold that the testator _______________, when he was of sound mind, told us to be his witnesses for all that is included in this will and signed it in our presence, and we have made a valid acquisition on behalf of all the benefactors and have acquired from him all that is mentioned above in an effective transaction.

Date: ____________________

Signed ____________________, Witness

Signed____________________, Witness.

Explanations of the sample will

(1) Every will is essentially a commitment and therefore must be made with a competent and sound mind. By the testator declaring that he is of sound mind and the witnesses signing that it is so, there is testimony from the witnesses not only for the will but for the person's soundness of mind.

(2) This clause is intended to avoid the creation of duplicate wills, which is something that could disqualify both wills.

(3) Some are of the opinion that it is forbidden to transfer a portion of inheritance from someone who was meant to inherit it, even though it was done using a halakhically valid will. In order to overcome this, the person leaves a certain amount to be inherited according to the halakha. (In the sample text above, this is a sum equivalent to four dollars for each benefactor and eight dollars for the firstborn.)

(4) Since the method of transferring ownership (*kinyan*) for land is different from that of chattels, which is different from that for loans, this clause states that the gifts have been bequeathed in the most effective way for each type of property.

(5) Some claim that if a document contains something that is invalid, then the whole deed is annulled. This clause intends to address this by stating that if part of the deed is invalid, it does not cause the deed to be invalid.

(6) For a variety of reasons, some things cannot be bequeathed at all. That is why this clause is included, which is effective either because of the declaration or because this itself serves as a special type of gift that is effective in many places where other types of *kinyan* are not effective.

(7) Any condition that a person makes with regard to transferring ownership must be done with specific language (e.g., the

condition must be stated doubly, and a variety of other conditions). This clause includes all such rules that concern those conditions, without detailing them.

SECTION 69: A LEGAL PERSPECTIVE ON MANAGEMENT OF ONE'S ESTATE THROUGH WILL OR SUCCESSION ORDER

By Justice Tzvi Tal

The following section was written with regard to residents of the State of Israel. For information regarding the United States, see the Beth Din of America.[2] Regarding other countries, contact your local rabbi.

Succession Order (*Tzav Yerusha*) or Probate Order (*Tzav Kiyum Tzava'a*)

(For brevity's sake, male pronouns are used here to refer to the deceased, but the same applies to a deceased woman.)

After the shiva, and sometimes even during the shiva itself, family members begin to ask themselves what will be done with the property that the deceased has left behind, i.e., the estate.

In order to divide up the estate among the benefactors, or to do anything else with it, a Succession Order (*Tzav Yerusha*) or, if the deceased has left a will, a Probate Order (*Tzav Kiyum Tzavaa*) must be obtained from the court.

This process can take time – a month, at best. There are sometimes urgent matters in dealing with the estate, such as saving items that could be wasted or destroyed; collecting debts owed to the estate; paying the deceased's debts; withdrawing money from the deceased's bank account for sustenance; preventing others from taking control of property, etc. In such cases, one cannot wait until the official documentation (succession order or probate order) has been received; one must promptly make a request to appoint a **temporary executor** of the estate. This can be one of the family members. The temporary executor has permission to gather and maintain the properties of the estate, to pay immediate debts, and to prevent others from taking possession of the estate.

2. http://bethdin.org/wp-content/uploads/2015/07/HalachicWill.pdf

The official court presiding over these matters is the Family Court, with jurisdiction over the deceased's place of residence (or the location of the property, if the deceased did not reside in that location). The request is made by submitting a request to the registrar of this court, at the nearest office of the Administrator General.

Whether or not a request is made to appoint a temporary executor, the family should check whether the deceased has left a will. Even if they do not know of the existence of a will, it does not necessarily mean that the deceased did not left one. Family members should search the house thoroughly, ask the deceased's lawyer, and inquire at the office of the Administrator General, where there is a record of wills. If a will is found, they should approach the local court mentioned above to request a Probate Order (*Tzav Kiyum Tzava'a*). If there is no will, they should request a Succession Order (*Tzav Yerusha*).

Religious court

Religious courts are also authorized to confirm succession orders and probate orders for upholding a will. (In Israel, religious courts include the rabbinic court, Sharia court, Christian court, and Druze court.) However, their authority depends on obtaining the written agreement of all those involved. (A minor may agree through his legal guardian.) The religious court is authorized to rule according to religious law. For example, in the absence of a will, the religious court can make decisions based on Torah law (i.e., a double portion for the firstborn, no inheritance for daughters if there are also sons, and no inheritance for a widow except for her *ketuba* and alimony from her husband). Nowadays, the courts usually "accept a transfer" from the sons so that their sisters receive a portion, as well, and so that the widow has her rights.

Israeli Succession Law

In the absence of a will, the following are the rules (in layman's terms) that have been outlined by the Israeli Succession Law (of the year 1965):

1. If the deceased is survived only by a spouse – the spouse inherits everything.

2. If the deceased is survived only by children – they inherit everything, and everything is divided equally among them, sons and daughters alike.
3. If the deceased is survived by a spouse and children, the spouse inherits chattel (including vehicles), as well as half of the rest of the estate, and the other half is divided equally among the children.
4. If the deceased is not survived by any children (or descendants) but is survived by a spouse and a parent (or parents), the spouse inherits half and the other half is inherited by the parent (or is divided equally between both parents).
5. If the descendant is survived by a spouse and grandparent(s) or their descendants, the spouse inherits two thirds and the remaining third goes to the grandparents or their descendants.
6. If the deceased is not survived by any of the above-mentioned relatives or descendants – the State of Israel inherits the estate for purposes of education, science, health, or other social needs.

In addition to these rules, it should be noted that:

1) The law regards a legally-adopted child the same way as a biological child.
2) If, at the time of death, the deceased was married to more than one wife, the wives receive the spousal portion together.
3) If the spouse inherits two-thirds (see case 5 above), he or she inherits the entire portion of the testator in their place of residence (only if they were married for three years or more and lived together in the same residence).
4) A man and woman who are in a relationship of common-law marriage (*yeduim baTzibur* – a marriage considered valid by both partners but that has not been formally recorded in a state or religious registry) – the survivor inherits the portion that the spouse is meant to receive (unless the deceased's will has instructed otherwise).

An inheritor who disclaims his portion

An inheritor may disclaim part or all of his portion of the estate through a written declaration to the court. Inheritors cannot disclaim a specific property, rather their percentage of the estate (or a portion thereof). If an inheritor disclaimed his portion but did not stipulate who would receive the portion in his stead, the portion he disclaimed is divided among the other inheritors, and the person is not considered to have been an inheritor at all. But one may bequeath one's portion to the deceased's spouse, child, or sibling, in which case this portion is added to the portion of that beneficiary. The disclaimer is final and cannot be rescinded.

This is of importance under certain circumstances. For example, in a case where a widow has inherited her and her husband's residence together with their children, and the apartment was registered in both spouses' names, each of them owns half of it; when the husband dies, half of his half is transferred to his wife. She now owns three-quarters of the apartment. The remaining quarter goes to the children. If there are three children, each of them thus receives one-twelfth of the apartment. This division is inconvenient; any change that the widow wants to make to the apartment would need written approval from all of the children (or whoever has power of attorney, which could also be the mother herself). Even if the family gets along well and the children comply with the widow's wishes, it becomes complicated, and the widow may find it insulting that she now has to obtain her children's approval for things related to the residence. In such a case, it is preferable for the children to disclaim their portion of the estate for the widow's sake and leave her as sole owner of the residence.

To write a will or not to write a will

If one finds the succession order as set out by the law acceptable – then one need not draw up a will. The estate will be divided according to the inheritance laws, and the inheritors will be spared from unnecessary discussions and proceedings. Even in such a case, this is not a simple matter. Someone must manage the estate until it has been distributed and ensure that all inheritors receive their portion. One may want to ensure that the children will act in the widow's interest, regarding ownership of the home. If one wants specific items to go to certain people, or for part of the estate to go to an organization or person other than the inheritors, then this is also something to address. Such concerns lead people to write a will. Some people are less concerned with the monetary arrangements and more with guiding their children in the way that they see fit or expressing final requests, all of which can be written in the will.

In Judge Cheshin's book *Dmuyot MiBeit HaMishpat* (Masada Publications, 1953), there is an excellent discussion on the matter of wills. He writes:

> There is no greater truth than what is written in a will. This is a person's inner truth, without airs or guile. The person writes what he writes and instructs what he instructs without flattery or ulterior motive. He does not seek anyone's favor, nor to make friend or foe. He is not concerned with any benefit at all for himself because he well knows that when his will is opened and made public, he himself will be gone, and the trappings of this world will no longer please his soul. In this sense, a will has a similar quality to that of a confession – the great and final confession of a person for himself and to himself; without pageantry and without embellishment. The person is not seeking kindnesses and fears no one. Because of this, he feels free to write all that is in this heart: His love for people, his affection, joy, anger, rage, and hatred – all of these are given sharp expression in his will. You can know someone for a long time and believe you know him inside and out, and then the time comes when you read his will and suddenly see a different man before you – wonderful, full of glory and magic. And you wonder: Could this be the same person that I knew? Even cheats and hypocrites are revealed in a different light by their wills; and this light, their hidden light, may indeed be their true light.
>
> A will is not a dull legal document. Nor is it a fossil or a mummy. It speaks, it communicates things. It has form and content that are alive. It reveals the deep inner workings of a person's soul. Sometimes it contains a bit of family history, praising the legacy of Torah scholars in the family's bloodline. Sometimes it contains good advice and helpful guidance, expressions of endearment that the person has used for loved ones, and expressions of admiration for them and others. These

demonstrate the way a person relates to his family and to the world around him.

Wills appear numerous times in Jewish tradition. In the Bible, Jacob gives his children a will (Gen. 49), and David gives his son Solomon a will (I, II Kings). The will document is called *daytiki,* and the halakha discusses various types of will at length. The Talmud describes Rabbi Yehuda HaNasi's will: "The rabbis taught that when Rebbi [Rabbi Yehuda HaNasi] was on his deathbed, he said: I need my sons. His sons entered. He said to them: Take care to respect your mother..." (who was their step-mother). One especially poignant will is that of Rabbi Naphtali Katz, the seventeenth-century author of *Semikhat Ḥakhamim,* who died penniless and in exile. In his will, he implores his wife, in the name of their love, to forgive him for not leaving enough in his estate to pay even what was promised to her in her *ketuba.*

There are those who use the will as a means of revenge or recrimination, lashing out at relatives that one despised. This relative might be excluded from the inheritance or given a pittance to anger him, or the deceased might offer the inheritance on the condition that the inheritor fulfills strange and demeaning stipulations. There are also those who put conditions on the inheritance with good intentions, intending to improve the ways of their benefactors. Such conditions might stipulate, for example, that the beneficiary move to Israel or marry someone Jewish. These types of wills and others like them have been subject to endless debate in the Israeli courts and in courts around the world, which have expressed their perspectives for the public rule.

Writing a will

If a person has decided to write a will, it can be done in one of several ways:

1) **A hand-written will:** This is written entirely by hand by the testator and is dated and signed by the testator.
2) **A will signed by the testator in the presence of two witnesses:** The date is recorded, and the testator declares before two witnesses that this is his will. The two witnesses must

sign and verify that the testator has declared and signed the document.

3) **A will before authorities**: This is an oral declaration of one's will before a judge, registrar, or notary, who records the will in writing. This authorized official then reads it back to the person, who declares that it is his will. The official confirms this in the will itself. The testator may read over the will himself instead of having it read back to him by the official.
4) **An oral will**: Another option is an oral will given by someone who is critically ill or who believes that he is in a situation that warrants preparation for death. This person can make a declaration before two witnesses. The person's words, together with the date and the circumstances, are written down and signed by the witnesses as soon after the declaration as possible; this is then deposited in the court of law. If the person lives for more than a month after the circumstances warranting the declaration have passed, the will is annulled.

Halakhic validity

The types of wills listed above are legally valid. Those who observe mitzvot will also want to ensure that their will is halakhically valid. The Jewish laws of inheritance cannot be made conditional. Therefore, if someone stipulates a benefactor who is not eligible to inherit property according to the Torah – these words are meaningless. However, halakha permits a person to give gifts as desired. Thus, the appropriate language to use in the will for bequeathing something to one's daughter or wife is "**gift**" and not "**inheritance**."

A will drawn up by a healthy person (as opposed to someone who is critically ill) should state that the person gives possession of his estate from that day forward, as a gift, to the benefactors; but he retains the "fruits," i.e., use of the property, until shortly before his death. A halakhic problem that arises here is that such a will does not include subsequent acquisitions. In order to include these, the person should declare in the will that the beneficiaries shall receive whatever is in the estate right before he dies. Another problem that needs to be addressed is that, in order for the gift to be valid, it must be public, while a will is often not publicized until after one's death.

All of these issues have been addressed by lawyers who are well-acquainted with the halakha, who have drawn up versions of wills that are both legally and halakhically valid.[3]

Changing or annulling a will

A will can be changed or annulled by the testator at any time. The will can be annulled by physically destroying the document or can be addressed through the method that was used to create the will. Changes or additions can be made through one of the ways of creating a will. When there is a discrepancy between different wills, the latest directive annuls the previous one(s).

A word of advice

Even though any person may create a will for himself in one of the aforementioned ways, it is worthwhile to consult a lawyer with expertise in this area. How much ink has been spilled and how many thousands of litigations have been conducted about wills and inheritance; no one wants their family to become entangled in that kind of a mess. A proficient lawyer will take certain precautions to prevent litigation by someone who feels that he has not been given his due in the will. The lawyer will ensure that the witnesses are bona fide and are not benefitting from the will in any way. The lawyer will also take precautions to counteract potential arguments regarding the person's soundness of mind, or allegations that the deceased had been pressured or forced into something (e.g., by having the process filmed). If the person was hospitalized when making the will, the lawyer will take care to obtain medical records demonstrating that the person was of sound mind and sufficiently capable of making a will. The lawyer will suggest that the testator appoint someone to execute the will and will cover a variety of possible scenarios that one would not normally think of. An lawyer with expertise in the area can also answer questions, such as:

3. A sample format is brought in the previous chapter.

- Can one give an inheritance to one person and only afterwards to a different person? (Yes, it is possible. The first person can do what they want with the property, including using it or selling it, and pass on what remains to the second person. However, the first person cannot disinherit the second person from what remains of the estate that he received.)
- Can one promise a certain individual that one will include certain clauses in the will? (No, one may not do so.)
- Can one leave the decision-making up to the executor of the will as to how to divide up the estate? (No, one may not do so.)
- Is the amount to which a woman is entitled based on her *ketuba* deducted from her portion of the estate? (Yes.)
- Are the wife and children eligible to receive a livelihood from the estate before other benefactors of the will? (Yes, in certain circumstances.)
- Is a child who was born after the person's death considered an inheritor? (Yes, if the child was born within three hundred days after the death. If the child was born afterwards, he or she is not related to the deceased. Today, it is possible for a woman to become pregnant using frozen sperm long after the man's death; the courts must consider whether this child would be considered an inheritor, even if he was born more than three hundred days after the death. The legislative branches of government should also give their input on the matter.)

Another piece of advice: Our sages frowned upon dispossessing an inheritor from his portion of the inheritance. The sage Shmuel told his student Rabbi Judah: My learned student, do not be involved in transferring an inheritance! Even from a bad son to a good son!

The will should not be used as retribution, nor should it be used for discrimination and favoritism among one's children.

Part 6

Key Concepts

LIST OF TERMS (in alphabetical order)

The explanation of terms presented here is intended to make it easier to understand and recognize certain concepts, whether in the context of this book or outside of it. The Key Concepts sections has several purposes: to explain the concepts; to present select terms that have not appeared elsewhere in the book; as a reference point for the laws of mourning that have been presented in the book; and to provide the reader with references and resources for further study. Some of the explanations in this section repeat things that were mentioned elsewhere in the book; some of them offer greater detail and additional sources. A few of the terms in this listing are Kabbalistic concepts. Although it is not our place to delve into these mystical secrets, in order to orient the reader to these concepts, abridged descriptions and select quotes have been brought from Kabbalistic works.

Though one could write entire books on some of the terms discussed here, the explanations have been kept relatively short; this is certainly not an attempt to cover all aspects of each concept. The Key Concepts section should be seen as an opening – a brief and incomplete beginning. Most of the entries include references for further study and exploration.

The references that have been provided here generally point the reader to major, accepted halakhic texts. These include: The *Mishneh Torah* by Maimonides – Rabbi Moses ben Maimon (Spain, North Africa, and Egypt) who lived some 850 years ago. This work contains fourteen books covering all areas of Torah, including laws that are not observed today, such as laws about sacrifices and ritual purity. The references here to Maimonides' writings are mostly from the *Hilkhot Avel* (*Laws of Mourning*) section in the volume *Shoftim*. Additionally, the references include *Tur* – the book *Arba Turim* ("four pillars") was written by Rabbi Jacob ben Asher around six hundred years ago (the author was born in the Ashkenaz region and traveled with his father, the Rosh, to Spain). The *Tur* is divided into four sections: *Oraḥ Ḥayim* is about prayer, blessings, Shabbat, and holidays; *Yoreh De'ah* is about what is permitted and what is forbidden; *Even HaEzer* is about laws pertaining to a husband and wife; and *Ḥoshen Mishpat* is about civil and monetary law. Rabbi Joseph Karo (exiled from Spain, and from Turkey and Safed) wrote a scholarly work on the Tur called *Beit Yosef*. He later shortened this work into the more well-known *Shulḥan Arukh*, which was accepted as the major halakhic work by Sephardic Jews. Because of the book's prominence and value, Rabbi Moshe Isserlis (known as the Rema) wrote notes on it, adding Ashkenazic customs to the work. The *Shulḥan Arukh* was thus accepted as the central halakhic text for all Jews. The chapters and sub-sections of the *Tur* and the *Shulḥan Arukh* correspond to one another. The references in this section from these two works are mostly from the *Yoreh De'ah* section.

A Child Brings Merit to the Father (*Bara Mezakei Aba*)

This is an Aramaic aphorism stating that one can bring merit to the deceased and especially to one's parent by doing good deeds and mitzvot in their honor and memory, to elevate the soul. In this way, the child honors the parents even after their death.

> From Barzilai the Gileadi who said, "Let me die in my own town" (II Sam. 19:38) it appears that the dead benefit when their family and friends visit their graves to pray for them. A child's prayers for a parent who taught him Torah, or a student's prayers for his teacher, or Torah scholars' prayers for each other, are even more desired and will give even greater pleasure than the prayers of others... and if the parents instructed their children to do something after their death, when the children do so it is as if the parents did it, for "a son gives merit to his father," since it is because of the

father that the son merited to do what he did. (*Maavar Yabok*, "*Siftei Renanot*," ch. 23)

See also **Elevating the Soul; Kaddish; Moving the Lips of the Sleeping.**

A Deceased Person with No Mourners to Be Comforted

When a deceased person has no mourners who must be comforted, ten upright men from the community at large come and sit in his place throughout the seven days of mourning. Others gather around them. If there are not ten fixed people who remain throughout the seven days, then each day, ten other people are selected and they sit in his place. (Maimonides, *Mishneh Torah, Hilkhot Teshuva* 13:4; *Shulḥan Arukh, Yoreh De'ah* 376:3. However, the Rema (ad loc.) writes that he did not see this law being observed despite it being the proper thing to do.)

The source for this is in the Talmud (Shabbat 152a–b). A story is related about a person who died who lived near Rabbi Judah, and there was no one to mourn for him. Rabbi Judah gathered ten people and sat shiva for the man. After the shiva, the man appeared to Rabbi Judah in a dream and said – "Put your mind to rest, for you have put my mind to rest."

A Staff in the Hand of the Deceased

Rabbi Jeremiah instructed before his death – Dress me in white shrouds and place shoes on my feet and my staff in my hand and lie me on my side so that I will be ready to awaken and stand up when the Messiah comes. (Y. Kilayim 9:3)

Some have the custom to place a piece of wood (called a *gaflikh*) in the deceased's hand at the burial; some say this custom should be discontinued. The *Pitḥei Teshuva* (*Yoreh De'ah*, 352) writes of this custom and says that it should be discontinued because it makes the deceased's fingers be spread out instead of clenched shut. In the *Responsa Ḥatam Sofer* (*Yoreh De'ah* 327) he writes that the custom should not be discontinued because it would have not come to be practiced for no reason. Some bring proof for its validity from Rabbi Jeremiah's instructions to place a staff in his hand (although we do not abide his other instructions – to place shoes on the deceased's feet and lay them on their side). See *Nitei Gavriel*, vol. 1, 76:14.

A Widow Who Remarries

A widow must wait ninety days after the death of her husband before she can remarry, not including the day of his death or the day of the second marriage. This is so that it can be clear whether or not she is pregnant and to be able to clearly distinguish between the offspring of the first husband versus that of the second husband. This rule applies to all women, even an older woman or one who cannot get pregnant (*Shulḥan Arukh, Even HaEzer* 13:1). According to the Kabbalists, there is a special prayer to be recited for the elevation of the first husband's soul before the woman marries the second husband. The text is brought in the name of the *Ben Ish Ḥai* – Rabbi Yosef Ḥayim of Bagdad (*Lashon Ḥakhamim*, vol. 2). See also *Responsa Tzitz Eliezer*, vol. 7, 49:5.

A Widower Who Remarries

A widower should wait for a cycle of three festivals to pass from the time his wife died, before remarrying (Moed Katan 23a). This is to allow him to recover from the death of his first wife so that he will be able to rejoice with his new wife; the joy of the three festivals helps with this process. That is why it is specifically the three festivals; Rosh HaShana and Yom Kippur are not included as festivals in this regard because they are not considered days of joy (*Beit Yosef, Yoreh De'ah* 392, in the name of Rabbenu Asher and Nahmanides). If the man has no children, he is permitted to remarry immediately following the shiva. If he has small children or some other pressing need, he may remarry after the *shloshim* (*Shulḥan Arukh, Yoreh De'ah* 392:2; *Yalkut Yosef* 38:14).

Acronyms

In Hebrew, *Rashei Tevot*. There are many acronyms used in the context of mourning, and for gravestones and memorials. Some of the phrases explained below are also used in contexts other than mourning.

- **גחש"א** – *Gemilut Ḥesed Shel Emet*, True kindness – A name for the *ḥevra kaddisha*. See **Ḥesed Shel Emet (True Kindness)**.

- **הכ"מ** – *Hareini Kaparat Mishkavo* – I am the atonement for his death. See **Hareini Kaparat Mishkavo/Mishkava (I Am the Atonement for His/Her Death)**.
- **המלוב"ן** – *HaMelumad BeNisim,* Well-versed in miracles – An expression for well-known righteous individuals who wrought miracles and wonders. The Talmud calls Rabbi Shimon Bar Yoḥai (Me'ila 17b) and Naḥum Ish Gamzo (Taanit 21a; Sanhedrin 109a) people who were well-versed in miracles.
- **הי"ד** – *Hashem Yikom Damo,* God shall avenge his blood.
- **זיע"א** – *Zekhuto Yagen Aleinu, Amen,* His merit will protect us, Amen – This is a phrase used when mentioning a righteous person who died.
- **ז"ל** – *Zikhrono Livrakha,* May his memory be a blessing – The source for this expression is in the Talmud (Kiddushin 31b): "The Sages taught: One honors him in his life and honors him in his death. How in his life?... How in his death? If he gives over something that he heard from his [father's] mouth, he should not say: 'So said Father.' Rather, 'So said Father, my teacher, may I be an atonement for his resting [soul].' And this he should say during the twelve months. From this time onward, he says: May his memory be a blessing, for the life of the world to come."
- **זללה"ה** – "*Zikhrono liVrakha leḤayei haOlam haBa,*" "May his memory be a blessing, for the life of the world to come" – This expression is also taken from the passage in Tractate Kiddushin (ibid.).
- **זצוק"ל** – *Zekher tzadik veKadosh liVrakha,* May the memory of the righteous, holy person be a blessing – This is based on the verse (Prov. 10:7): "The memory of the righteous is invoked in blessing (*zekher tzadik liVrakha*), but the fame of the wicked rots."
- **זצוקללה"ה** – *Zekher tzadik veKadosh liVrakha leḤayei haOlam haBa,* May the memory of the righteous, holy person be a blessing for the life of the world to come – This is based on the passage from Tractate Kiddushin (ibid.) and the verse in Proverbs (ibid.).
- **זצ"ל** – *Zekher tzadik liVrakha,* May the memory of the righteous person be a blessing.
- **יבדל"א** – *Yibadel leḤayim arukim,* May he be designated for long life – This expression is used when mentioning a living person in

the same sentence or context as a person who has died, so as not to link the living with the dead. (Another variation is יבדל"חטא – *Yibadel leḤayim tovim, Amen,* May he be designated for a good life, Amen.)

- לע"נ – *LeIlui nishmat,* For the elevation of the soul of – See **Elevating the Soul.**
- נבג"מ – *Nishmato beGinzei maromim,* His soul is in the treasure-house on High.
- נלב"ע – *Nilkaḥ leBeit Olamo,* He has been taken to his eternal abode – Based on the verse, "Man sets out for his eternal abode" (Eccl. 12:5).
- ע"ה – *Alav HaShalom,* Peace be upon him – This is based on the rabbinic saying that connects the righteous with peace: "Rabbi Meir would say: Peace is great; God created no better characteristic than peace, which was given to the righteous. When they die, three groups of ministering angels come to greet them with peace. The first says, 'Come in peace'" (*Sifrei Zuta, Naso* 26). See **Peace Be upon Him (*Alav HaShalom*).**
- פ"נ – *Po nikbar,* Here is buried – Often written on gravestones.
- צים"ע – *Tzadik yesod olam,* The righteous person, everlasting foundation – Based on a verse in Proverbs (10:25). An appellation for the righteous in whose merit the world is upheld (see Yoma 38b; Ḥagiga 12b).
- ר"ל – *Raḥmana litzlan,* God help us – An Aramaic saying from Tractate Shabbat (84b).
- תנצב"ה – *Tehe nishmato/nishmata tzrura beTzror haḤayim,* May his/her soul be bound up in the bond of life – Often written on gravestones. (Some write the acronym ת.נ.צ.ב.ה., but linguistically it is preferable to write it the first way because in Hebrew, acronyms are not separated by periods.) See **Bond of Life (*Tzror HaḤayim*).**

Adding to *Kriya*

In the case of someone who, after tearing his garment for one relative, was informed of another relative's death – if the second death occurred during the shiva for the first relative, the mourner tears a second time; if it was after the shiva, the mourner extends the original tear a little. If a third relative died more than seven days after the second one, he extends the tear a little (Moed Katan 26b; *Shulḥan Arukh, Yoreh De'ah* 340:21).

See also ***Kriya***.

Alpha Beita

Psalm 119 is based on the Hebrew alphabet. It contains eight verses that begin with the letter *aleph*, then eight verses that begin with *beit*, and so on. In total, there are 176 verses (eight times twenty-two letters). It is customary to pray for a sick person by spelling out their name with the verses that correspond to the letters of their name. Also, when visiting the grave, there is a custom to recite verses that spell out the deceased's name, followed by the letters *nun*, *shin*, *mem*, and *heh*, which spell out "*neshama*," "soul."

In Genesis (2:20) it is written that Adam gave names to all the animals. Giving a name is a statement about the essence of something. The physical entity is seen on the outside, but this does not reflect the inner essence. A name is somewhat like the soul, an expression of the essence of the being; a person's name is their essence, their inner self. After death, the body, the outward and temporary facet of the person, is buried and disintegrates; but the person's essence remains and is expressed by the soul. This eternal element is communicated when reciting the letters of the name followed by the letters of the word *neshama*.

There are a number of psalms that are arranged alphabetically, but only Psalm 119 contains eight verses for each letter. In Judaism, the number eight represents the dimension beyond nature (the number seven represents nature and the number eight, beyond nature. See Maharal, *Tiferet Yisrael*, ch. 2). Reciting these verses to elevate the soul expresses the belief that the soul belongs to the eternal dimension, beyond the natural one.

The paragraphs from Psalm 119 that spell out "*neshama*" appear in Part 7, "*Neshama*."

In line with this principle, there is also a custom to study mishnas beginning with the letters of the deceased's name, for the elevation of the deceased's soul. See Part 7, "*Mishnayot* Studied in the Merit of the Soul," for a list of *mishnayot* arranged according to the *Aleph-Bet*.

See also **Elevating the Soul**.

Aninut

This refers to the period of time between a relative's death and burial. The word *aninut* comes from the linguistic root that means sorrow and sadness. As a commandment from the Torah, *aninut* is observed only until evening, during which time one is prohibited from eating sacrifices (Lev. 10:19) and second tithes (Deut. 26:14). The sages expanded the period of *aninut* to continue up until the burial (Berakhot 16b). It is a set period that precedes *aveilut* (mourning). During *aninut,* the mourner is not supposed to occupy himself with anything other than the needs of the deceased and the burial.

Aninut exempts a person from all positive Torah commandments. There are two reasons for this: First, out of respect for the deceased – the *onen* (one who is in *aninut*) demonstrates that he is completely focused on his grief over the relative's death. Second, there is a practical need to take care of the arrangements for the funeral and burial as quickly and efficiently as possible.

The *onen* is called "someone whose dead lies before him" (Berakhot 17b). That is to say, if the *onen* can attend to the deceased, he is obliged to do so. For this reason, if a relative is not able to attend to the needs of the deceased, e.g., if the deceased's body is being held by the authorities, or if the transportation of the body from one country to another has been delayed, or if the body has already been handed over to the *ḥevra kaddisha* who are going to bury it elsewhere – then he does not have the halakhic status of *onen.*

Ashes of One Who Was Burned

If the deceased died in a fire and all that is left of his body is ashes, the ashes are buried in the ground, even though there is no mitzva to bury ashes, nor do ashes cause ritual impurity (Ohalot 2:2). The reasons for burying ashes are: so as not to derive benefit from the dead; because the ashes of the dead are likened to the ashes of the sacrifices, which require burial; and because the ashes contain the "*luz,*" the small bone that is considered indestructible and represents the eternality from which a person will be revived at the resurrection of the dead.

The ashes may be buried in the ground inside a vessel, but it is preferable to bury them directly inside the ground.

There is no obligation to hold a funeral for burying ashes nor to erect a tombstone. The comforters do not form two columns, and the blessing for the mourners is not recited. Mourning begins from when the person died and not from the burial of the ashes (*Gesher HaḤayim* 16:8–9).

See also ***Luz.***

Asking Forgiveness from the Deceased

> If a person wronged his fellow and the latter died before he could ask him for forgiveness, he should take ten people and say the following while they are standing before the fellow's grave: "I sinned against God, the Lord of Israel, and against this person by doing the following to him...." If he owed him money, he should return it to his heirs. (Maimonides, *Mishneh Torah, Hilkhot Teshuva* 2:11)

If a person insulted someone after the person died, he does not need not go to the grave but should ask for forgiveness in the place where he insulted him (*Magen Avraham, Oraḥ Ḥayim* 606:7). However, the *Kaf HaHayim* (ad loc. 35) writes that even in this case, he must go to the grave.

A member of the *ḥevra kaddisha* also asks the deceased for forgiveness, towards the end of the burial:

> I, (name of the person speaking), in the name of the *ḥevra kaddisha,* in the name of the members who prepared you, in the name of your family and friends, I ask you for forgiveness and absolution, for any harm we may have inflicted, God forbid, during the purification and the carrying and burial.
>
> Forgive us, for it was unintentional. Everything we did was for your honor, in accordance with the customs of the *ḥevra kaddisha.*
>
> We exempt you from being a member of any group or collective.

> Go in peace and rest in peace and arise at the end of days. Be a good advocate on behalf of your family and friends. And may there be life and peace for us and for all of Israel.

See also **The Dead Do Not Know Anything**.

Autopsy

Autopsies are generally prohibited, out of respect for the deceased and the prohibition against deriving benefit from the dead. The sages likened a Jew to a *sefer Torah*; even if a Torah scroll is no longer usable, one is prohibited from cutting it up or destroying it. Likewise, the deceased's body, which was a vessel for the soul and a part of the Divine, may not be destroyed or degraded.

It is therefore prohibited to perform an autopsy for training purposes. The halakhic literature has discussed, at length, the argument that autopsies for medical training or research may save future lives. This claim is generally accepted by halakhic authorities since saving life overrides the mitzvot, but there are different approaches as to when this can be applied. There are opinions that accept this claim only in a case where there are two people with the same illness, and one of them dies, and the doctors say that the other person may be saved if they perform an autopsy and learn about the disease. (The halakhic term for this is "*ḥoleh lefaneinu*," "a sick person at hand.") There are more lenient opinions that take into account that nowadays, due to the ongoing communication between medical researchers and practitioners, the halakhic category of "*ḥoleh lefaneinu*" is always applicable because a medical finding in one place can bring immediate benefit to a sick person located somewhere else. Accordingly, former Chief Rabbi of Israel Rabbi Herzog wrote:

> A board of three expert doctors should consist of the head of the department in the specific hospital, a representative of the local rabbinate, and a representative of the family of the deceased. If they decide that there is a chance that the autopsy will shed light on the disease that caused the person to die…based on their written decision and signature, the autopsy may be permitted, on the condition that they perform only essential procedures

and that anything removed will be given to the *ḥevra kaddisha* afterwards for burial.

A letter from Rabbi Yeḥiel Yaakov Weinberg to Rabbi Kalman Kahana, who was the Deputy Minister of Education at the time, was published in *Teḥumin* (vol. 12, p. 382). The letter referred to the issue of autopsies, and he gave his opinion that, today, every case is considered "*ḥoleh lefaneinu*," "a sick person at hand," because information can be rapidly communicated between locations. Rabbi Kahana himself published a bibliography of articles on halakha and autopsies in the journal *HaMaayan* (see the article in *Teḥumin*, ibid., note 1).

Halakhically, there is no weight given to a person's instructions to leave his body to science. The Jewish perspective holds that a person does not own his body, rather that one's body is on loan from the Creator for a limited time. For this reason, a person may not harm his body, commit suicide, or leave his body to science. And clearly the family and heirs have no such authority, either.

Legally, an autopsy cannot be performed without the family's consent or a court order. In special cases, a rabbi should be consulted.

(For further reading, see *Responsa Noda BeYehuda*, Tinyana edition, *Yoreh De'ah*, responsa 210; *Ḥatam Sofer, Yoreh De'ah* 336; *Gesher HaḤayim* 5:6; Rabbi Herzog's letter from 4 Iyar 5714 is brought in *Pesakim U'Mikhtavim shel HaRav Herzog*, vol. 5, 155.)

***Av HaRaḥamim* Prayer**

This is a prayer recited to remember the souls of communities and individuals who were killed in God's name, to pray for them and ask God to avenge their deaths. It is only found in the Ashkenazic tradition, having been composed in memory of those killed during the First Crusade in 1096.

See also ***El Male Raḥamim***; ***Hashkava***; **Recalling the Souls (*Hazkarat Neshamot*)**; ***Yizkor***.

Avel Rabati

This is a tractate that deals with mourning. The tractate is also euphemistically referred to as Tractate Smaḥot (meaning "rejoicing"). The tractate is included among the minor tractates, a collection of *baraitot* (rabbinic teachings external to the Mishna) found in the Babylonian Talmud. The minor tractates are usually printed at the end of the order of Nezikin. The topic of mourning appears many times throughout the Talmud but is mainly concentrated in Tractate Moed Katan, which deals with the laws of Ḥol HaMoed (the intermediate days of the festivals of Sukkot and Passover). In discussing the laws of mourning on Ḥol HaMoed, Tractate Moed Katan also discusses the subject of mourning more generally.

Ban (*Ḥerem*) – "His Seed Will Not Follow Him"

According to the Kabbala, when the soul leaves the body, a kind of spiritual vacuum is formed. There are negative forces that seek to rest and dwell in such a body, a body that has been emptied of its soul and has not yet been buried. And the burial should be performed promptly, to avoid unnecessary suffering for the deceased.

Particularly distressing for the deceased is any wasted semen that he saw in his lifetime. Such semen could have been used to form new life, but it was wasted. The spiritual vacuum created by this can be especially disruptive to the deceased's rest, claiming that he failed to fulfill his task in the world. In order to prevent the deceased from becoming distressed by these spiritual beings who were not actualized, the *ḥevra kaddisha* issue a mystical "ban" [*ḥerem*] preventing the deceased's seed from accompanying him to the grave (some invoke the name Yehoshua bin Nun in the ban).

Because of this ban, the deceased's children and descendants – who are also the person's seed – should also not follow the body to the grave. This is why in certain places there is a custom that the deceased's children and descendants do not attend the burial, so as not to follow after the deceased. In cases where the descendants still want to be present at the burial, it is customary to tell them to arrive at the gravesite before the body arrives so as to come before the deceased and not follow behind him.

This ban clearly applies only to a deceased male. If the descendants nevertheless want to follow behind the deceased, they either do not make the ban or they specify "His unworthy seed shall not follow him," thus excepting his actual children from the ban (*Gesher HaḤayim* 12:3). The ban should be made as close as possible to when the death occurred.

In Israel, this custom is observed mainly in Jerusalem and is less common in other Israeli cities. Outside of Israel, the custom is for all mourners to attend and participate in the funeral. If someone has the custom that the descendants do not follow the deceased, he should not rebuke those who want to follow their custom of accompanying the deceased father, even in Jerusalem. But if they are Torah-observant and keen on listening to the rabbis, they should be encouraged not to deviate from the local custom, out of respect for the deceased. If they disagree, and it seems that the matter will result in arguments, they should be allowed to follow their own custom. In other places in Israel, they should be told to follow the custom of Jerusalem (*Yalkut Yosef* 10:7).

See also Rema, *Yoreh De'ah* 358:3; *Gesher HaḤayim* 12:3; and *Tzror HaḤayim* 47, who is adamant that the children should not follow the body at the funeral. The text of the *ḥerem* appears in the book *HaḤayim VeHaShalom*, p. 23, from the *Sdei Ḥemed*'s will.

See also **Leaving the Body Overnight (*Halanat HaMet*); *Hakafot;* Suffering of the Grave.**

Being Cut Off (*Karet*)

This is a severe divine punishment mentioned many times in the Torah: "That soul shall surely be cut off." The Mishna (Keritot 1:1) lists thirty-six sins for which the punishment is *karet*.

What is the punishment of *karet*? Rashi (Shabbat 25b) explains that it means that the person's days are cut off and that he dies childless and before his time. The Talmud (Moed Katan 28a) brings a *baraita*: "If one dies when he is fifty years old, this is death through *karet*." And Rabba says: "From fifty to sixty, this is death through *karet*." Rabbi Joseph made a celebration when he turned sixty, saying that he had passed the age of *karet*.

In the Ibn Ezra's commentary on the Torah (Gen. 17:14), he quotes the opinion that *karet* means that the person's name will be cut off through the death of their seed, because whoever has children, it is as though he is alive and his name is not erased, as brought in the Talmud (Yevamot 55a): If he has sons – he buries them, if he has no sons – he goes childless.

Maimonides (*Mishneh Torah, Hilkhot Teshuva* 8:5) writes that *karet* means that the person's soul is cut off and will not merit the world to come. Nahmanides (in his commentary on Lev. 18:29) disagrees with Maimonides and differentiates between three types of *karet*: The one about which it is written, "The man shall be cut off" ("*veNikhrat haIsh*") – If they are righteous and have much merit but are overcome by their desires and committed a sin that is punishable through *karet*, their days are shortened, and they will die by the age of sixty; but they will have a portion in the next world. The second type of *karet* is the one about which is says, "The soul shall be cut off" ("*veNikhreta haNefesh*") – If, in addition to the sin that carries a punishment of *karet*, they have more sins than merit, the *karet* that they will suffer is that their soul will be removed from their body and will be cut off from the world of souls. But this is not a *karet* of the body; the person may live a long life, while their soul will be cut off from the next world. For the third type, which is written about in relation to idolatry and blasphemy, the verse uses a double expression: "*Hikaret tikaret haNefesh haHee*," ("That person will be cut off") – "*Hikaret*" refers to this world, and "*tikaret*" refers to the next world. The body will be cut off from this world and the soul will be cut off from the next world. Such a person will die young and his soul is cut off from the next world.

Benefit from the Dead

The basic Jewish approach is that a person does not own his body or soul. This belief is manifested in certain halakhic principles: A person may not harm or damage his body and may certainly not take his own life. Likewise, one may not derive benefit from a corpse; one should honor it and bury it appropriately.

Maimonides (*Mishneh Torah, Hilkhot Avel* 14:21–24) defines the main rules regarding this principle:

- It is forbidden to benefit from a corpse. Similarly, it is forbidden to benefit from the coffin and the shrouds. There is no prohibition against benefiting from garments prepared to be used as shrouds. Even if one knitted a garment intending it to be used for a corpse, it is not forbidden to benefit from it until it reaches the deceased since the intention that an article be used for a corpse does not cause it to be forbidden.

- It is forbidden to benefit from the garments thrown upon the deceased, lest they be mistaken for shrouds.
- If a person's father or mother were throwing garments on the deceased in their grief, it is a mitzva to retrieve them. If the items came in contact with the bier that is buried with the corpse, we do not retrieve them.
- We teach a person that he should not recklessly destroy property and throw it to oblivion. It is better to give it to the poor than to throw it to the maggots and worms. Whoever casts many articles upon a deceased person violates the commandment against destroying property.

According to Maimonides, one may derive benefit from a dead person's hair. But the *Shulḥan Arukh* (*Yoreh De'ah* 349:2) writes that one may not use items that were connected to the deceased's body, such as a wig, and that, like the corpse itself, these are forbidden. But if the item was not physically connected to the deceased, it can be used. For this reason, one may use rings that belonged to the deceased. According to most opinions, the above is a Torah prohibition. Some permit using the deceased's cornea since this is not considered for one's enjoyment (*Responsa Yabia Omer*, vol. 3, 21:9; *Yalkut Yosef* 53:2).

It is also forbidden to derive benefit from the skin of a dead person, though there are opinions that permit it (*Tosafot*, Zevaḥim 71b; Nidda 55a). The halakha follows the majority opinion that one may not derive benefit from the skin (*Yabia Omer* ibid. 8). This question was raised in the context of a skin bank to be used in emergency situations for treating burn victims. Rabbi Yisraeli discusses this topic at length (*Teḥumin*, vol. 1, p. 237) and concludes that it is permitted if the deceased, before he died, gave permission to use his skin for medical purposes. Also see the article by Rabbi Chalom Messas on the topic (*Teḥumin*, vol. 7, p. 193) and Rabbi Yisraeli's response to it (ibid. p. 206).

With regard to pacemakers, some opinions permit a pacemaker to be removed from the deceased's body so that it can be used by someone else who needs it; there are lenient opinions that one can rely on in that situation. It is preferable that the hospital give the pacemaker on loan and that the recipient give his written permission for it to be removed after his death, to be given to someone else (*Yalkut Yosef* 53:5).

If the deceased had false teeth or gold teeth – if the teeth were connected to the body and only removed occasionally, they may not be used. But if the person did not use them when eating, and had them more for aesthetic reasons so as not to appear toothless, and would remove them at night – then they are considered similar to jewelry and may be used (*Kol Bo al Aveilut*, p. 57 in the name of *Responsa Binyan Tziyon* 114).

One may not derive benefit from a gentile corpse (*Shulḥan Arukh, Yoreh De'ah* 349). Some claim that there is no prohibition against deriving benefit from a gentile corpse; some are of the opinion that there is a Torah prohibition against deriving benefit from a Jewish corpse and a rabbinic prohibition against deriving benefit from a gentile corpse (*Responsa Even Shoham*, brought in the *Pitḥei Teshuva*, ibid.). According to this, it would be permitted to use the cornea from a gentile corpse for a transplant (*Yabia Omer*, ibid. 20, answer from Rabbi Ben Zion Abba Shaul. We have mentioned above that Rabbi Ovadia Yossef permitted using a Jew's cornea).

See also **Ways of the Amorite; The Deceased's Possessions; Cremation**. See Sec. 45 "Laws Relating to the Cemetery: Regarding the prohibition against deriving benefit from graves."

Blessing Over an Inheritance

If one's mother or father died, one recites the blessing "*Dayan HaEmet.*" If the parents left an inheritance to their only child, the person also makes the blessing "*Sheheḥiyanu.*" If the person has siblings, all the children make the blessing "*HaTov VeHametiv*" (*Shulḥan Arukh, Oraḥ Ḥayim* 223:2 based on Berakhot 59b). Even though the child would want the parent to have lived longer, he still makes the blessing; this is because reciting the *Sheheḥiyanu* is not based on whether a person feels joy, but on the occasion of experiencing a certain benefit, even though it is mixed with sadness (*Mishna Berura* ad loc., based on the Rashba).

The Rema points out that many people do not make this blessing. Some hold that one should not make the blessing because it is not the accepted custom, and it appears cruel and degrading to the parent, as if one was happy that one's parent had died. Furthermore, how could one recite the continuation of the *Sheheḥiyanu* blessing – "Who has granted us life and enabled us to reach this occasion" – at such a bitter time? (See *Nitei Gavriel,* vol. 1, 38, note 7.) Rabbi Shlomo Zalman Auerbach also wrote that many God-fearing people do not have the custom of reciting a blessing over the inheritance and that only a few special individuals do so (*Halikhot Shlomo* 23, note 33). Some advise making the blessing only if the parent who died was quite elderly and had lived a long life, because in such cases, the sorrow is generally more subdued (*Nitei Gavriel* ibid. and *Piskei Teshuvot,* ad loc.).

See also **One Should Be as Thankful for the Bad as One Is for the Good – and Accept It with Joy.**

Blood of the Soul (*Dam HaNefesh*)

This refers to blood that exits the body at the moment of death. There is an obligation to bury this "blood of the soul." Therefore, if someone was killed, and this blood may have been absorbed into his clothing, he is buried in his clothes. Dirt or garments that absorbed the blood are also buried together with the person. Blood that was shed before the person died is not considered "blood of the soul" and does not need to be buried.

Bond of Life (*Tzror HaḤayim*)

This expression comes from the words of Abigail, wife of Naval the Carmelite, to David: "The life of my lord will be bound up in the bond of life" (I Sam. 25:29). The phrase signifies connection and association, like a bundle or package that ties things together. The bond of life is the continuity of life and the eternal connection with God, which continues even after death; the soul is eternal and continues to be connected to its Maker. One who disconnects from God is called wicked; the wicked are called dead even when they are alive, while the righteous are called alive even in death.

The expression also appears in the Talmud with the same connotation (Shabbat 152b):

> Thus too, with the Holy One, Blessed be He. Concerning the bodies of the righteous, He says: "He enters into peace, they rest on their beds, each one that walks in his uprightness" (Is. 57:2). And with regard to their souls, it states: "And the soul of my lord shall be bound in the bond of life with the Lord your God" (I Sam. 25:29). … It was taught that Rabbi Eliezer says: The souls of the righteous are stored beneath the Throne of Glory, as it states: "And the soul of my lord shall be bound in the bond of life" (I Sam. 25:29).

Maimonides interpreted the "bond of life" to refer to eternal life:

> Since this life is not accompanied by death – for death is an event associated with the body alone and, in that realm, there is no body – it is called "the bond of life," as it states (I Sam. 25:29): "The life of my lord will be bound up in the bond of life." This is the reward, above which there is no higher reward and the good beyond which there can be no [other] good. This was [the good] desired by all the prophets. (*Mishneh Torah, Hilkhot Teshuva* 8:3)

The verse, "Their hallowed are all in Your hand" (Deut. 33:3), was interpreted to mean the souls of the righteous because these are in His treasury, as it says: "The life of my lord will be bound up in the bond of life" (*Sifrei, Devarim* 344). *Tzror haḤayim* is the treasure-house for all souls.

See also **El Maleh Raḥamim**; **Soul (*Neshama*)**.

Breaking Clay

There is a custom that, as the deceased is brought out before the funeral begins, a piece of clay is broken and the relatives say, "The trap broke and we escaped" (Ps. 124:7). Various reasons have been given for this custom:

- Breaking symbolizes grief over the death and the loss of the deceased (similar to breaking a glass at a wedding in memory of the destruction of Jerusalem).
- The broken clay represents the breaking of the body through death, which is like clay that has been broken and cannot be fixed. In *Kuntras HaYeḥieli* (*Beit Olamim*, ch. 9), he writes the

opposite: Just as clay can be remade when it is taken to the artisan, who fixes it and puts it back in the furnace, so too the deceased will be revived by God after death. See **Resurrection.**

- A clay pot that becomes impure is purified by being broken; so too, when a Jewish person dies, his death atones for his sins. See **Suffering Atones.**

Reciting the verse, "The trap broke and we escaped," conveys the wish that nothing bad should happen to the family, as if to transfer the family's heartbreak to the broken clay – the clay shall break and this family shall continue to enjoy a good, long life. (This is similar to the *Kapparot* done on Erev Yom Kippur, where one says, "This chicken shall die and we shall go on to a good, long life and to peace.")

Burial

Burial is the placing of the deceased in the ground or in a crypt intended for this purpose. Burial is alluded to in the punishment given to Adam when he ate from the Tree of Knowledge: "Until you return to the ground – for from it you were taken. For dust you are, and to dust you shall return" (Gen. 3:19).

In the Bible, not being buried is considered a curse: "Your carcasses shall become food for all the birds of the sky and all the beasts of the earth, with none to frighten them off" (Deut. 28:26). Jeremiah uses similar language in his prophecy about the calamity to befall his generation (16:4).

It is a positive commandment to bury someone killed by the courts on the day of their death, as it says: "You must bury him that same day" (Deut. 21:23). From here, the sages deduced that there is a mitzva to bury every person on the day of his death (Maimonides, *Sefer HaMitzvot*, Positive Commandments 231).

There is a Torah prohibition not to leave a dead body hanging from a tree or gallows, as it says: "You must not let his corpse remain on the stake overnight" (Deut. ibid.; Sanhedrin 46b; Maimonides, *Mishneh Torah, Hilkhot Sanhedrin* 15:8). They were particularly careful not to leave the dead overnight in Jerusalem (Bava Kamma 82b; *Tosefta*, Nega'im 6:2).

Burial must be in the ground – "Because each person has impurity from the impurity of the snake, and through death and returning to the dust, the impurity returns to the earth and cleaves to it; for the snake eats dust, and the person remains pure" (*Menaḥem Aveilim,* letters *Mem, "Met – Taam HaMita"*).

One who inters a body in a coffin but does not bury the coffin in the earth violates a Torah prohibition, because he keeps the dead unburied overnight (*Shulḥan Arukh, Yoreh De'ah* 362:1).

The Talmud debates whether burial serves as atonement for the deceased or is done to prevent degradation of the dead body.

The burial must be performed by Jews. Only if this is not possible (e.g., if the burial will take place on Yom Tov in a place where burials are done on Yom Tov) can the deceased be buried by gentiles. This is because it is considered a good omen for the deceased to be buried by Jews and a mitzva for those who bury the dead (*Gesher HaḤayim* 16:1, 5).

A son is obligated to bury his parents (*Shulḥan Arukh, Yoreh De'ah* 348:2). A husband is obligated to bury his wife (*Shulḥan Arukh, Even HaEzer* 89).

The wicked should not be buried next to the righteous. But one who became observant (*baal teshuva*) may be buried next to the righteous. Two people who hated each other when they were alive should not be buried next to each other.

The deceased is buried lying on his back, facing upwards (*Shulḥan Arukh, Yoreh De'ah* 362:2). The custom is to bury the body with the feet pointing in the direction of Jerusalem.

See also **Coffin; Honor of the Living, Honor of the Deceased; Whosoever Sleeps with Him during His Lifetime May be Buried with Him When He Dies.**

Burial Caves

In ancient time, people would bury the dead in caves. The most famous example of such a burial is Me'arat HaMakhpela, purchased by Abraham for the burial of his wife Sarah. And this became the burial site for our forefathers and foremothers, Abraham, Isaac, Jacob, and Sarah, Rebecca, and Leah. Adam and Eve are also thought to be buried there, and this is one of the reasons that the location is called "*Kiryat Arba,*"

("Town of Four") after the four couples buried there. See also **Me'arat HaMakhpela**.

The Mishna and Talmud, while discussing the sale and purchase of fields, provide detailed descriptions of cave burials (Bava Batra, Ch. 6).

Burial in the Land of Israel

The Land of Israel has been called the "Land of the living" (Ezek. 26:20) and the "Lands of Life" (Ps. 116:9). The Talmud (Ketubbot 111a) quotes Rabbi Elazar, who said: "The dead outside of the Land of Israel will not come alive, as it is stated: 'And I will set glory [*tzvi*] in the land of the living' (Ezek. 26:20). A land which contains My desire [*tzivyoni*], its dead will come alive; that which does not contain My desire, [i.e., outside of the Land of Israel], its dead will not come alive." The Talmud then asks whether he thinks that the righteous in the Diaspora do not come alive? The Talmud gives two possible answers: They either come alive through rolling or through the tunnels.

Even though burial in Israel is considered very special and is likened to being buried under the holy Altar, it is preferable to move to Israel when one is alive – as opposed to having one's body brought after death.

The Zohar (*Aḥarei Mot* 72b) conveys a stern perspective about those who die outside of Israel and are brought to Israel for burial:

> A merit to he who lived in the Holy Land, for whoever merits this, merits to a heavenly dew that comes to the land. And whoever merits to connect with the Holy Land during his lifetime merits to connect with the higher Holy place.
>
> Whoever did not merit this during his lifetime and is brought to Israel to be buried, about him it says: "And you made my possession abhorrent" (Jer. 2:7). His spirit departed [when he was] in a different, foreign domain; his body arrives in the domain of the Holy Land. It makes the holy profane and the profane holy, so to speak.
>
> Whoever merits to die in the Holy Land, this atones for him and he merits to reside under the wings of the *Shekhina*, as it says: "Atonement for the soil of his people."

Nevertheless, it is considered a mitzva to bring the dead for burial in Israel, and a body may be removed from a grave outside of Israel for this purpose (*Shulḥan Arukh, Yoreh De'ah* 363). If the deceased cannot be buried in Israel, it is customary to place some soil from the Land of Israel inside the grave (Rema ad loc.).

See also **Earth from the Land of Israel; Exhuming a Grave**.

Burial of a Torah Scroll

See **Geniza.**

Burial of Limbs

All parts of a dead body should be buried along with the deceased, because of the prohibition on deriving benefit from the dead and also because it causes impurity for *kohanim*. Moreover, we treat the person's body similar to the way we treat a *sefer Torah*: The Torah scroll is a vessel with which to receive God's divine message to the Jewish people, and we therefore honor it and treat it with sanctity. Similarly, the body is a receptacle for the divine soul and should therefore be treated with the utmost respect. Just as each letter and segment of the Torah has sanctity, even though it is only one part of the scroll, each limb of the body has sanctity. Therefore, a limb that was amputated in an operation or in an accident must be buried. The custom is to wash and clean the limb, wrap it in linen cloth, and bury it. If the person is alive but owns a burial plot, the limb should be buried in this plot, where the person will eventually be buried (*Gesher HaḤayim* 16:2, 2).

In *Responsa Shvut Yaakov,* he replies to a question about a person whose leg was amputated – does the leg needs to be buried or not? He replied that even though the Talmud (Ketubbot 20b) suggests that it must be buried, there is no obligation to do so, and if there is a danger involved in performing the burial, it need not be done. However, the limb should be placed in a room where there is no chance for *kohanim* to inadvertently enter and thus become impure (because a limb causes impurity) (*Pitḥei Teshuva, Yoreh De'ah* 362:1). The *Noda BeYehuda* also ruled this way (*Tinyana, Yoreh De'ah* 209).

Rabbi Moshe Feinstein (*Igrot Moshe, Yoreh De'ah,* Vol. 1, 232; Vol. 3, 141) wrote that there is an obligation to bury the limb of a living person but not their flesh. Hence there is an obligation to bury a limb only if it contains tendons and bone but not, for example, intestines or a placenta.

In *Responsa Tzitz Eliezer* (vol. 10, 25:8) he writes that there is no obligation to bury a limb from a living person but that it is customary is to bury it, and the custom should be followed. When necessary, he permits placing it in a special room. One may derive benefit from a limb; doctors may study it and dissect it, but when they are finished, it should not be treated casually or disrespectfully; it should be put away or buried. See *Nishmat Avraham*, vol. 2, *Yoreh De'ah* 362:1.

Burying a Miscarried Fetus

A miscarried fetus is buried in the ground for three reasons: So as not to derive benefit from the deceased, out of concern for *kohanim'* impurity, and so that the baby will be able to take part in the resurrection. Because of this last reason, the custom is to give the fetus a name before the burial. Circumcision is performed on a male fetus or a male infant who died before being circumcised (*Responsa Rabbi Naḥshon Gaon,* quoted in *Torah HaAdam,* p. 87; *Tur* and *Shulḥan Arukh, Yoreh De'ah* 353:6). It is not customary to bury a placenta.

Mourning practices are not observed after a miscarriage, nor for an infant who dies within thirty days of birth, since at that point, the infant is still classified as unviable ("*nefel*").

If an infant was born prematurely and was in an incubator for more than a month, and then he died – some say that we count thirty days from the birth and therefore the laws of mourning are observed; others say that the laws of mourning are not observed since it was clear from the start that the baby was not viable. The halakha follows this latter opinion (*Yalkut Yosef* 14:8).

A miscarried fetus is normally buried by the *ḥevra kaddisha* in a discreet manner, usually without the participation of family members:

> A baby under thirty days old is taken out in one's bosom to the cemetery and not in a coffin. From thirty [days] to a year, on a wide plank carried in the arms. From twelve months, he is taken out in a coffin. (Moed Katan 24)

Cemetery

This is a designated place for burying the dead. It is also called "the house assigned for all the living" ("*beit moed leKol ḥai,*" based on Job 30:23) and the "eternal home" ("*beit olam,*" based on Eccl. 12:8), and the sages called it the "house of eternity" ("*beit almin,*" e.g., in Sanhedrin 19). It is also called the "house of life" ("*beit haḤayim*") based on the idea of transitioning from one state of life to another.

There are rules about where cemeteries should be located and about how to conduct oneself in a cemetery. In the past, cemeteries would be located fifty cubits away from the city (Bava Batra 2:9; *Shulḥan Arukh, Yoreh De'ah* 365:2). One must act respectfully in a cemetery (*Shulḥan Arukh, Yoreh De'ah* 368). One should not walk in a cemetery while wearing tefillin or carrying a Torah scroll, since this is considered "mocking the poor" (*Shulḥan Arukh,* ibid. 367:2–3). Somebody who has not been in a cemetery within the previous thirty days should, upon entering, make the blessing, "Who fashioned you in justice." There is ritual impurity in the cemetery, and therefore *kohanim* may not enter except for the sake of their seven relatives. In the past, when public communal fast days were declared, the custom was to go en masse to the cemetery to declare that the people are like the dead before God, or to ask that the dead intercede on their behalf (Taanit 16). When asking the deceased to intercede on one's behalf, one must very careful not to engage in "consulting the dead." (See **Consulting the Dead.**)

It is customary to visit and pray at the graves of one's ancestors. It is customary to visit the cemetery on Tisha B'Av, and during the month of Elul and the Ten Days of Repentance, especially on Erev Rosh HaShana and Erev Yom Kippur. It is customary to pray there and give charity to the poor.

See also **The Blessing "Who Fashioned You in Justice"; Ritual Impurity of the Deceased; Mocking the Poor; Graves of the Forefathers and Graves of the Righteous.**

Changing and Adding a Name for a Sick Person

Changing a person's name is meant to reflect a change in the person; it is first found in the context of our forefathers, where it indicated a significant change in their life.

In the times of the Talmud, they would change a sick person's name to try to increase his chances of recovery (Rosh HaShana 16b). The idea is that, now that the person has a different name, he is a different person and should therefore have a different fate than the person who had the previous name.

When changing the person's name, the custom is to give charity for the merit of the sick person's and to recite the *Mi Sheberakh* prayer and add: "Even if Your court decreed death, that he will die from this illness, our holy sages declared that three things can change a person's decree, and one of them is changing his name. We are fulfilling their words and his name is changed; he is a different person. And if the decree was made for (insert the previous name), upon (insert the new name) this was not decreed. For he is a different person and is not called by that first name. And in the same way that his name is changed, so should his fate be changed from judgment to mercy, from death to life, from sickness to complete recovery for (insert new name), and he should live a long and pleasant life and enjoy the rest of his days with strength and peace from now until forever, Amen."

Maimonides (*Mishneh Torah, Hilkhot Teshuva* 2:4) mentions changing one's name as one of the ways of repenting: "And one who changes his name, it is as if to say, 'I am another; I am not the same person who did those things.'"

Changing One's Seat in the Synagogue

Mourners change their usual seat in the synagogue. This can be understood as a type of symbolic, temporary exile in which the person leaves his familiar, habitual place, moving to a new one. It is considered an additional sign of mourning; mourners behave differently in order to express their sadness and draw attention to the fact that they are in mourning. The source for this is the mishna that describes how mourners would go in the direction opposite to others (Middot 2:2):

> All who would enter the Temple Mount entered toward the right and would encircle it and exit through the left.
>
> Aside for one to which something has occurred [that he is a mourner], that he would encircle it towards the left.

"Why are you encircling towards the left?"

"Because I am a mourner."

"He who rests in this house should comfort you."

When the Head of the Beit Din dies, it customary to change one's place in the beit midrash as a sign of mourning. Those who sit in the north section should sit in the south, and those who sit in the south section should move to the north. This is found in Moed Katan (22b–23a) and in the halakha (*Shulḥan Arukh, Yoreh De'ah* 393:2, 4).

Charity

It is customary to give charity to elevate the soul of the deceased, especially during the funeral. All good deeds that the mourners or other people do as a result of the mourning and to elevate the deceased's soul bring merit to the deceased. Those who receive the charity should pray for the dead or for the people who gave the charity. Those giving the charity should pray for God to present them with deserving individuals to whom to give the charity. One who is rich should give charity in secret. The charity will be especially beneficial to the deceased if it had been the person's custom to give charity when he was alive. And this is certainly so for someone who dedicated a third of his money to charity while he was still alive; he will gain merit; and about this it is written that we are obligated to fulfill the deceased's wishes. (See *Maavar Yabok*, "*Siftei Renanot*," ch. 21–23).

See also **Elevating the Soul**.

Closing the Deceased's Eyes and Covering the Eyes with Earth

When someone's mother or father dies, one puts a small amount of soil on the parent's eyes; one then closes the eyes while saying, "For dust you are and to dust you will return" (Gen. 3:19) and then, "And Joseph's hand shall close your eyes" (Gen. 46:4). The source for closing the eyes appears in the Zohar (*Shelaḥ* 169), where it says that people can only see in the higher world after their eyes have been closed from this world. Elsewhere in the Zohar (*Vayeḥi* 226) it is written that one cannot see God's glory when one is alive but only after one dies. For this reason, the deceased's eyes must be closed. (See *Maavar Yabok*, "*Siftei Renanot*," ch. 9.)

The following aggada from the Talmud (Tamid 32b) may also offer an explanation for placing soil on the deceased's eyelids:

> Alexander of Macedon returned from a place in Africa. On his journey, he sat beside a spring and ate bread and salted fish. When the fish were being washed, they gave off a sweet odor. He said: This shows that this well comes from the Garden of Eden. He followed the water until he came to the door of the Garden of Eden. He cried out, "Open the door for me." They replied: This is the gate of the Lord, [the righteous shall enter into it]. He replied: I too am a king; I am also of some account, give me something. They gave him an eyeball. He went and weighed all his silver and gold against it, and it was not equal to it. He said to the sages: How is this? They replied: It is the eyeball of a human being, which is never satisfied. (Prov. 27:20)

Coffin

Burying the dead in a coffin was the custom in ancient times and is mentioned in the Torah in relation to Joseph: "And he was placed in a coffin in Egypt" (Gen. 50:26). Some Jewish sages were buried in coffins, such as Akkavya b. Mehalalel (Eduyot 5:6), Rabbi Yehuda HaNasi (Y. Kilayim 9:3), and others.

The Torah obligation is to bury the deceased in the ground. Therefore, one who places the body in a coffin without burying it in the ground transgresses the prohibition against not burying the dead. If the coffin is buried in the ground, it does not transgress the prohibition. However, it is still commendable to bury the body directly in the ground, even in the Diaspora, as the verse says: "For dust you are and to dust you will return" (Gen. 3:19). For this reason, Rabbi Yehuda HaNasi gave instructions to make holes in his coffin ("Rebbi's Will" in Y. Kilayim 9:3 and Y. Ketubbot 12:3). Nahmanides (*Torat HaAdam*, p. 117) ruled that this is the halakha, as did the *Shulḥan Arukh* (*Yoreh De'ah* 362:1).

Pirkei DeRabbi Eliezer (ch. 34) teaches that there is significance to being buried directly in the ground and that the connection between the body and the earth is meaningful: "Rabbi Shimon says: All corpses touch the ground until they decompose and mix together with the earth like leaven into dough – it enhances, increases, and raises up the entire body, unblemished, the way that leaven enhances, increases, and makes the dough rise." The Zohar (*Teruma*, p. 151) also discusses the advantage of being buried in the ground: "How good it is for them, the righteous or the wicked, to have their bodies cleave to the ground and to be absorbed into the earth." Burial in caves and niches, which was customary during the period of the Mishna and the Talmud, was done with coffins that were placed in the niches. These coffins were made of wood, stone, metal, or clay. They would initially bury the body in the ground; after the body had decomposed, they would gather the bones and bury them in a coffin. In Persia, they would bury the deceased in coffins but would put dirt on the face and on the eyes (*Responsa Rabbi Natronai Gaon*, brought in Nahmanides' *Torat HaAdam*, p. 116). Today, wooden coffins should be used (Maimonides, *Mishneh Torah, Hilkhot Avel* 4:4, also quoted in the *Beit Yosef, Yoreh De'ah* 362).

In some places it was customary for *kohanim* and firstborns to be buried in coffins as a mark of honor, but the sages disapproved of this custom because the commandment is to bury the deceased in the ground (*Ḥokhmat Adam*, Rule 158:1). The Zohar (*Vayeḥi*, p. 251) also wrote that people should not be buried in coffins and that only a righteous person should, as in the case of Joseph, who maintained sanctity in sexual matters. But other people should be buried in the ground. (See *Kuntras HaYeḥieli, Beit Olamim*, ch. 8.)

Gesher HaḤayim (vol. 2, ch. 7) discusses at length the difference between a coffin and a burial bier. He concludes that it is better to be carried on a bier and buried in the ground without a coffin. He demonstrates that the original custom was always to carry the body on a bier; the coffin was only used to bury the person inside the grave, or to carry the body over a long distance, like with Jacob and Joseph. (The author of *Gesher HaḤayim* wanted to prevent a situation where people would spend more and more money on ornate coffins, and it might begin to resemble the state of affairs that was described in Moed Katan, where the poor were embarrassed.)

Kuntras HaYeḥieli (*Beit Olamim*, ch. 7) also demonstrated that in the time of the Talmud, the coffin was used only to transport the deceased from one place to another:

> We see from what has been said that they would carry their dead on biers and not in coffins, even outside of Israel... and in Israel they did not use coffins at all, except when they needed to move the deceased from one city to another, and for the most part it was after the body had decomposed. And they buried directly in the ground so that the flesh would decompose quickly and the pain and judgment would cease, as mentioned in the Zohar (*Mishpatim*) that the whole time the flesh remains, God's attribute of justice hovers over them.

In certain circumstances, placing the deceased in the coffin may be counted as the beginning of mourning:

> If they placed the corpse in the coffin and put it in a different room and did not bury it because the city was under siege, they start counting the shiva and *shloshim* immediately, even though they intend to later bury the person in the cemetery, after the siege. In this case, sealing the coffin is considered like the burial and the laws of mourning apply immediately. (*Shulḥan Arukh, Yoreh De'ah* 375:4)

When the body is placed in the coffin, special verses are recited:

> But let them not go inside and witness the dismantling of the sanctuary, lest they die. (Num. 4:20)

> I see a lampstand all of gold, with a bowl above it. The lamps on it are seven in number, and the lamps above it have seven pipes. (Zech. 4:2)

> Whoever you are, O great mountain in the path of Zerubbabel, turn into level ground! For he shall produce that excellent stone; it shall be greeted with shouts of "Beautiful! Beautiful!" (Ibid. 7)

> Therefore, I pray, let my Lord's forbearance be great, as You have declared, saying, "The Lord! Slow to anger and abounding in kindness; forgiving iniquity and transgression; yet not remitting all punishment, but visiting the iniquity of fathers upon children, upon the third and fourth generations." Pardon, I pray, the iniquity of this people according to Your great kindness, as You have forgiven this people ever since Egypt. And the Lord said: I pardon, as you have asked. Nevertheless, I live and the Lord's presence fills the whole world. (Numbers 14:17–21)

There are special Kabbalistic intentions associated with these verses, brought in the book *Maavar Yabok* ("*Siftei Renanot*" 14), that compare placing the body in the coffin to Noah entering the ark.

The accepted custom in Israel is to bury the body directly in the ground, without a coffin. Outside of Israel, it is customary in most places to bury the deceased in a coffin.

When a body is transported from the Diaspora to Israel nowadays, it is transported in a coffin; they then open the coffin and bury the body in the ground. If someone wants the body to be buried in the coffin in Israel, this is considered disrespectful to the deceased, and it also goes against the local custom. For these reasons, it should not be done (*Yalkut Yosef* 45:1).

With regard to whether a coffin may be used for someone else after the deceased has been removed from it: Where the local custom is not to bury the deceased in a coffin, but a coffin was used to transport the body from one place to another, the coffin may be used once the body has been removed, because the body was put there with the intention of removing it. However, if the deceased was brought in a coffin from the Diaspora from a place where the local custom is to bury in a coffin, and it can be assumed that they placed the body in the coffin with the intention that it would be buried that way – then the coffin has been designated for the deceased; it is thus forbidden to derive benefit from the coffin (*Gesher HaḤayim* 8:11–12). The same is true of a tallit: In Israel, the local custom is not to bury the deceased in a tallit, and thus a tallit that has been used for a short time to cover the deceased can be used again. But if the body was sent from outside of Israel with a tallit wrapped around it, from a place where the local custom is to bury the body in a tallit, then tallit has been designated for the deceased; one may not derive benefit from it. In practice, the tallit is buried above the body in the grave (*Gesher HaḤayim* 10:5).

See also **Benefit from the Dead; Burial.**

Comforting the Mourners

In Hebrew, *Niḥum Avelim*. Consoling mourners is an age-old custom. Isaac was comforted when his mother died (Gen. 27:67). Jacob thought that Joseph died and so he "rent his clothes, put sackcloth on his loins, and observed mourning for his son for many days. All his sons and daughters sought to comfort him" (ibid. 37:34–35). The Talmud (Sota 14a) writes that God Himself comforts mourners, based on an understanding of the verse, "After the death of Abraham, God blessed his son Isaac" (Gen. 25:11); Rashi explains that God comforted him and blessed him with the mourner's blessing. God also comforted Jacob after his mother died (see Rashi, Gen. 35:8–9).

In the rabbinic literature, there is much discussion about the act of comforting mourners as one of loving-kindness. There is also much discussion about how customs of comforting mourners can vary depending on the mourners, their status, the place and time, and specific circumstances.

> The Sages taught: Initially the mourners would stand, and all the people would pass by. And there were two families in Jerusalem who would fight with each other, as this one would say: We pass by first; and that one would say: We pass by first. They decreed that the people should stand and the mourners pass by. (Sanhedrin 19a)

> Solomon saw that the observance of loving-kindness was great before the Holy One, blessed be He. When he built the Temple, he erected two gates – one for the bridegrooms and the other

for the mourners and the excommunicated. On Sabbaths, the Israelites went and sat between those two gates. They knew that anyone who entered through the gate of the bridegrooms was a bridegroom, and they said to him, "May He who dwells in this house cause thee to rejoice with sons and daughters." If one entered through the gate of the mourners with his upper lip covered, then they knew that he was a mourner, and they would say to him, "May He who dwells in this house comfort thee."

When the Temple was destroyed, the sages instituted that the bridegrooms and mourners should go to the synagogues and to the houses of study. The men of the place see the bridegroom and rejoice with him, and they see the mourner and sit with him upon the earth, so that all the Israelites may discharge their duty in the service of loving-kindness. With reference to them he says: Blessed art Thou, who giveth a good reward to those who show loving-kindness. (*Pirkei DeRabbi Eliezer*, ch. 17, quoted in the *Tur, Yoreh De'ah* 393)

When the High Priest comforts other [mourners], it is the custom that all the people pass by one by one, and the appointed one interposes himself between [the High Priest] and the people. When he is being comforted by others, all the people say to him, "We are your atonement," and he says to them, "From heaven shall you be blessed." (Sanhedrin 2:1)

All who would enter the Temple Mount entered toward the right and would encircle it and exit through the left. Aside for one to which something has occurred [that he is a mourner], and he would encircle it towards the left. "Why are you encircling towards the left?" "Because I am a mourner." "He who rests in this house should comfort you." (Middot 2:2)

Rabbi Natan ben Joseph said – Comforting the mourners, visiting the sick, and doing loving-kindness bring good to the world. (*Avot DeRabbi Natan*, ch. 30)

> The custom today is that after the burial, the people form two rows and the mourners pass between them. Those standing in the rows say – "May God comfort you among the other mourners of Zion and Jerusalem." And they also go to comfort the mourners during the shiva. (*Otzar Dinim U'Minhagim, Niḥum Aveilim*)
>
> Before dark on the Friday during shiva, the mourner goes to the synagogue for *Kabbalat Shabbat* and waits outside until the congregation recites "*Bo'i kalla*" ("Come, O bride"), and the rabbi or a member of the congregation calls to the mourner to come in; when they finish "*Bo'i kalla*," they say to the mourner – "May God comfort you, etc." (ibid.)

Another important part of comforting the mourners is the meal of condolence, which is the first meal that the mourners are given after the burial.

The customary words said by consolers to mourners: The Sephardic custom is to say, "*Min haShamayim tenuḥamu*," "From heaven may you be comforted." The Yemenite custom is to say, "*Tenuḥamu min haShamayim*," "May you be comforted from heaven." The Ashkenazic custom is to say: "*HaMakom yenaḥem etḥem betokh shaar avlei Zion veYerushalayim* (*veLo tosifu ledaava od*)," "May God comfort you among the other mourners of Zion and Jerusalem (and may you know no more sorrow). In Israel, it is common to say, "*SheLo ted'u od tsaar*," "May you know no more sorrow," but this custom has no source; it is preferable to say the traditional Jewish words of comfort that include the mention of God. Sometimes the words are displayed in the shiva house; this way, visitors who do not know the exact words can read them, and thus avoid any embarrassment.

When the time comes for Grace after Meals, one says: "*Nevarekh Menaḥem aveilim sheAkhalnu miShelo*," "We will bless the Comforter of mourners from whom we have eaten"; the reply is, "*Barukh Menaḥem aveilim sheAkhalnu miShelo uBetuvo ḥayinu*," "Blessed is the Comforter of mourners from whom we have eaten and from whose goodness we have eaten." Mourners add a special blessing in the Grace After Meals after the blessing "*Boneh Yerushalayim*," "Builder of Jerusalem." The blessing appears in ch. 10, "Customs in the House of Mourning," "Grace After Meals."

Confession (*Viduy*)

Viduy, the confessional prayer, involves acknowledging and verbalizing one's sins.

> It is a positive commandment, that a sinner should repent from his sins before God and confess. If a person transgresses any of the mitzvot of the Torah, whether a positive commandment or a negative commandment – whether willingly or inadvertently – when he repents, and returns from his sin, he must confess before God, as [Num. 5:6–7] states: "If a man or a woman commits any of the sins of man… they must confess the sin that they committed." This refers to a verbal confession. This confession is a positive commandment. How does one confess? One states: "I implore You, God, I sinned, I transgressed, I committed iniquity before You by doing the following. Behold, I regret and am embarrassed for my deeds. I promise never to repeat this act again." These are the essential elements of the confessional prayer. Whoever confesses profusely and elaborates on these matters is worthy of praise. Those who bring sin offerings or guilt offerings must also [confess their sins] when they bring their sacrifices for their inadvertent or willful transgressions. Their sacrifices will not atone for their sins until they repent and make a verbal confession as [Lev. 5:5] states: "He shall confess the sin he has committed upon it." Similarly, those obligated to be executed or lashed by the court do not attain atonement through their death or lashing unless they repent and confess. Similarly, someone who injures a colleague or damages his property, does not attain atonement, even though he pays him what he owes, until he confesses and makes a commitment never to do such a thing again, as implied by the phrase, "Any of the sins of man." (Maimonides, *Mishneh Torah, Hilkhot Teshuva* 1:1[1])

Joshua said to Akhan, "My son, pay honor to the Lord, the God of Israel, and make confession to Him. Tell me what you have done" (Josh. 7:19). The main part of *Viduy* is verbal admission of one's sins. The midrash

1. Eliyahu Touger's translation from Chabad.org.

Soḥer Tov (Prov. 18:21) comments on the verse, "Death and life are in the hands of the tongue": A person's tongue can bring him to the next world. Who caused David to enter the world to come? His tongue, which said, "I sinned." In the Zohar (*Pinḥas*) it says, "Those who declare their sins, the Beit Din leaves them alone."

> One who is critically ill, they say to him – Confess. (Shabbat 32a)

> The custom in certain communities was that when a person was ill, on the third day of the illness, *gabbai'im* of the society for *bikur ḥolim* (visiting the sick) or other individuals would go to visit them and say – "You know that this is the custom with all sick individuals and therefore it should not worry you, but make a will regarding your wishes, what you owe, and what others owe you." And they also say – "Confess, for anyone who confesses his sins is forgiven." Since this was customary in those communities, it would not cause the sick person to worry; this should be the custom in every city. But in places where this is not the custom, it should not be said to the sick person, so as not to worry him about his possible death. (*Ḥokhmat Adam* 151:11)

> Even so, when visitors see that the sick person is dying, they talk with him in a roundabout manner, saying, "Confess and do not fear, for many have confessed and did not die, and many who did not confess died. The reward of your confessing will be that you live; anyone who confesses has a place in the world to come." If the person cannot confess verbally, he may confess in his heart. (Nahmanides, *Torat HaAdam, Shaar HaViduy*, p. 46)

The short form of *Viduy* is: "If I die, let my death be an atonement for all my sins." Various additions have resulted in there being different versions of the *Viduy*. Some use the *Viduy* text that is recited on Yom Kippur.

It has become rare for people nowadays to say *Viduy* on their deathbed. Some say that the reason for this is that most people die in the hospital and it is not always possible, in that situation, to fulfill the mitzva of *Viduy*. Some say that the reason is because the *Viduy* may harm the sick person by causing them severe distress (*Encyclopedia Hilkhatit Refuit, "Viduy"*).

See also **Person Who is Dying (*Goses*)**.

Consecutive Bereavements

In Hebrew, "*Takhfuhu Avelav*," "his bereavements were constant." This is a halakhic term meaning that two or more mourning periods overlap. Before concluding the shiva for the first relative, one has to begin a new mourning period for a second relative who died. In such a case, the person begins counting seven days for the second relative, and those days are also counted toward the shiva for the first relative (*Shulḥan Arukh, Yoreh De'ah* 375:11). There are certain halakhic leniencies in such a case: One may trim one's hair if it is burdensome, but in a way that is different from the usual way, such as with a knife and not scissors. Once the first shiva ends, one may wash clothing without detergent, even though the shiva is continuing for the second relative. The law is similar when mourning is close to the week leading up to Tisha B'Av – the person may bathe in cold water, not hot water (Moed Katan 17b; Smaḥot 4:9; Maimonides, *Mishneh Torah, Hilkhot Avel* 6:13; *Shulḥan Arukh, Oraḥ Ḥayim* 551:15 and *Yoreh De'ah* 389:1, 390:3).

Consulting the Dead

This refers to the prohibition against trying to reveal the future or other mysteries by consulting with the dead. It is derived from the verse, "Let no one be found among you... one who consults ghosts or familiar spirits, or one who inquires of the dead" (Deut. 18:10–11).

> Who is one who seeks [information] from the dead? A person who starves himself and goes to sleep in a cemetery so that a deceased person will come to him in a dream and reply to his questions. There are others who wear special clothes, recite incantations, burn a particular type of incense, and sleep alone so that a deceased person will come to them and speak to them in a dream. To summarize: Anyone who performs a deed in order that a deceased person should come to him and give him information

> is [liable for] lashes, as [Deut. 18:10] states: "Let no one be found among you … who inquires of the dead." (Maimonides, *Mishneh Torah, Hilkhot Avodat Kokhavim* 11:13)

> Those who go to visit graves of their ancestors or the righteous should not pray to the dead buried there, so that it does not appear as though that they are consulting the dead. Rather they should pray only to God, in a place where their prayers will be heard, and ask God to show them compassion on the merit of the righteous people buried there. (*Mishna Berura*, 581)

Some later authorities are of the opinion that there is no prohibition against consulting the dead, even asking them to pray on behalf of the living. Proof is brought from the Talmud (Taanit 16a), where is describes how, on public fast days when the community would pray for rain, the people would go to the cemetery to ask the dead to pray that God have mercy on them. Another proof is that Caleb ben Yefuneh went and bowed down on the graves of the forefathers and said, "My forefathers, pray for mercy for me so that I will be saved from the counsel of the spies" (Sota 34b). In the Zohar (*Vayikra* 71:2) it states explicitly that there is no prohibition against consulting the dead. And *Yalkut Yosef* (40:10) ruled that this is the halakha. See *Gesher HaḤayim* 29:9; and in greater depth, ibid., vol. 2, ch. 26.

See also **Necromancy (*Ov*); Graves of the Forefathers and Graves of the Righteous.**

Converts and Mourning

According to the original halakha, a convert does not have to mourn for relatives. This is because conversion is considered to be like a re-birth where the convert becomes a completely new being, and the biological ties are not considered binding (Yevamot 97b; *Shulḥan Arukh, Yoreh De'ah* 374:5). Still, it is customary for converts to mourn their relatives. But they may study Torah and do not make the "*Dayan HaEmet*" blessing (*Tzror HaḤayim*, 5). Rabbi Nebenzahl notes: In my opinion, if they are grieving, they may make the blessing.

Cremation

There is a grave prohibition against cremation. One who has his relative cremated fails to fulfill the commandment to bury the dead. Cremation is a mistreatment and desecration of the deceased; failure to bury the dead is considered a curse in the Bible (e.g., Jer. 8:2, 14:16, 16:4, 6). Cremation is considered a sin: "For three transgressions of Moab, for four, I will not revoke it: Because he burned the bones of the king of Edom to lime" (Amos 2:1).

The Talmud (Gittin 56b) relates that Titus commanded that his body be cremated and his ashes spread over the seven seas so that the God of the Jews would not be able to find him.

If a person gave instructions to cremate his body, we do not heed this request. If the body was cremated, the ashes are not buried in a Jewish cemetery. The explanation for this is that, for a person who spurned the mitzva of burial and rejected the concept of the resurrection while he was alive, burial will not enable him to merit the resurrection – God's image has left this person and the ashes have no sanctity (*Gesher HaḤayim* 16:9).

Although the Bible mentions the burning of kings who died, that burning does not refer to their bodies, but rather to the burning of their possessions. This was done out of respect for them after death, based on the notion that no one else should use the kings' possessions:

> The king must be treated with great honor. We must implant awe and fear of him in the hearts of all men. The command, "Appoint a king," implies the obligation to be in awe of him (Deut. 17:15). We may not ride on his horse, nor sit on his throne, use his scepter, wear his crown, or use any of his personal possessions. When he dies, they should all be burned before his bier. (Maimonides, *Mishneh Torah, Hilkhot Melakhim* 2:1)

For example, Jeremiah said to Tzidkiyahu: "You will die a peaceful death; and as they burned for your ancestors, the earlier kings who preceded you, so they will burn for you, and they will lament for you, 'Ah, lord!'" (Jer. 34:5). Regarding Jehoram, son of Jehoshaphat, it says: "His people did not make a fire for him like the fire for his fathers" (II Chron. 21:19).

There is a clearer description of the practice in the verses about Asa, King of Judah: "And he was buried in the grave that he had made for himself in the City of David. He was laid in his resting place, which was filled with spices of all kinds, expertly blended; a very great fire was made in his honor" (ibid. 16:14). The burning for kings was done in their honor; it did not involve the bodies being burned.

They also used to light a fire for kings and princes in the Mishnaic period, as the Talmud describes (Avoda Zara 11a; Smaḥot, ch. 8):

> One lights a fire for kings, and this is not prohibited as following the ways of the Amorite. And just as one burns items of kings, so too one burns items of a *nasi*. And what do they burn upon the death of kings? Their beds and their personal possessions. And there was an incident in which Rabban Gamliel the Elder died, and upon his death, Onkelos the convert burned [property worth] seven thousand dinars in Tyrian coinage.

The *Shulḥan Arukh* (*Yoreh De'ah* 348:1) writes: "They burn for kings or for a *nasi*, their beds and articles which they used, but for commoners it is forbidden [to do so]."

In ancient times, gentiles would also light fires for kings as part of idolatrous ceremonies, and the day of the burning was considered a festival. The sages said: "Any death accompanied by burning [of articles] is considered idolatry, but where there is not such burning there is no idolatry" (Avoda Zara 8a). This was also established as the halakha (Maimonides, Mishneh Torah, Hilkhot Avodat Kokhavim 9:5). The Talmud raises the question whether burning the possessions of the deceased should be considered a gentile custom, and thus forbidden due to the commandment, "Nor shall you follow their ways" (Lev. 18:3). It answers that, because the burning is mentioned in the Bible before it became a gentile custom, it does not violate the prohibition of "following in their ways," since the custom was not adopted from the gentiles.

Maimonides (*Mishneh Torah, Hilkhot Avel* 14:22–26) writes that:

- It is forbidden to benefit from the garments thrown upon the deceased, on the bier which is buried with him.

- If the deceased's parent threw garments toward the bier in their extreme grief, it is a mitzva to retrieve them. If they reached the bier on which the dead person lies, it is forbidden to retrieve them.
- We teach a person not to recklessly destroy property. It is better to give it to the poor than to throw it to maggots and worms. Whoever casts items on a deceased person violates the commandment against destroying property.
- When a king or *nasi* dies, one may burn his bed and all his personal utensils. This is not considered an Amorite practice or wasteful destruction. For it states: "You will die a peaceful death; and as they burned for your ancestors, the earlier kings who preceded you, so they will burn for you" (Jer. 34:5).

This is also the halakha, as it appears in the *Shulḥan Arukh* (ibid. 3–4).

See *Gesher HaḤayim* (vol. 2, ch. 13) on the differences between burial and burning.

See also **Ashes of One Who Was Burned; Benefit from the Dead; Burial; Ways of the Amorite.**

Customs of Jerusalem (*Minhag Yerushalayim*)

In addition to the halakhot that have been established about mourning, there are many customs and practices associated with it. There are certain customs that are practiced in Jerusalem. They are listed below:

- The custom in Jerusalem is to bury the deceased on the day of the death and not to wait until the next day, even if it would be done out of respect for the deceased. This is the custom in the Old City of Jerusalem. Rabbi Nebenzahl notes: The halakha (and not only the common practice) forbids leaving the deceased to lie overnight within the Old City walls (except for on Shabbat).
- In Jerusalem, the deceased is carried on a bier constructed of two poles with eighteen rungs. This has been the custom in Jerusalem and Safed for many years (*Gesher HaḤayim*, vol. 2, 7:1).
- The custom in Jerusalem, based on the Kabbala, is that a deceased man's children and descendants do not follow the

body. Some even have the custom that they do not to go to the gravesite. Others have the descendants arrive at the grave before the deceased. See **Ban (*Ḥerem*) – His Seed Will Not Follow Him**.

- It is the custom in Jerusalem and among Hasidim to do "*hakafot*" – to walk in a circle around the body before the burial. The idea is to protect the body and the soul from impure forces that might cleave to the deceased. See also ***Hakafot***.
- The custom in Jerusalem and among Sephardim is for *kohanim* to make the priestly blessing in the house of mourning. However, mourners themselves only give the blessing on Shabbat (not during the week), so as not to engage in public mourning (*Gesher HaḤayim* 20:3, 5; *Tzror HaḤayim* 151). Rabbi Nebenzahl notes: Some have the custom that even the mourners themselves make the blessing during the week.
- Mourners may say Kaddish before the burial (*Gesher HaḤayim* 18:2, 3). Although in *Tzror HaḤayim* (17) he writes that Kaddish should not be recited before the burial, the custom in Jerusalem is to say Kaddish before the burial (ibid. Introduction to ch. 5). See also ***Aninut***.
- If a woman dies in childbirth, the custom in Jerusalem is to dress her in shrouds. If her clothes are soaked in blood, they are buried with her (*Gesher HaḤayim* 11:6). See also **Blood of the Soul (*Dam HaNefesh*)**.
- *Tziduk HaDin* – Sephardim say it both at night and during the day. Those who follow the custom of the *Ben Ish Ḥai* do not recite it at night. The Ashkenazic custom is not to say *Tziduk HaDin* at night or on festive days when *Taḥanun* is omitted. The custom in Jerusalem is not say it on the day preceding a day when *Taḥanun* is not recited (e.g., Erev Rosh Ḥodesh).
- *Kriya* is not done on Shabbat or Yom Tov. There are different customs regarding Ḥol HaMoed; in a place where there is no set custom, *kriya* should be done. The custom in Jerusalem is to do *kriya* during Ḥol HaMoed only for a parent, but for other relatives, the *kriya* should be done after the festival, when they begin the shiva (*Yalkut Yosef* 9:25). See also ***Kriya***.

- The custom in Jerusalem is to serve a meal of condolence for the *ḥevra kaddisha* after the burial, to emphasize that those in charge of the burial are forbidden to eat a full meal before the burial (*Gesher HaḤayim* 33:2, 2).
- On Ḥol HaMoed, the meal of condolence should consist of coffee and cake and not eggs and lentils. The mourners should sit on regular chairs and not on the floor or low chairs. The custom in Jerusalem is that only those mourning for a parent eat the meal of condolence, not those mourning other relatives (*Yalkut Yosef* 13:10; *Pnei Barukh* 28:11). In *Gesher HaḤayim* (20:2, 10), however, he mentions this custom in the name of the book *Mizbeaḥ Adama* and says that this custom is not clear and does not appear to have a source. (In *Yalkut Yosef* 43, Purim, 1, he brings a custom that on Purim and Ḥol HaMoed, one brings a meal of condolence only for someone mourning a parent. This appears to contradict what he wrote in 13:7, where he did not distinguish between mourning a parent and other relatives.)
- The custom in Jerusalem is not to dry one's hands after washing them upon leaving the cemetery (*Gesher HaḤayim* 14:21). Rabbi Nebenzahl notes: Rabbi Shlomo Zalman Auerbach taught that they can dry their hands if they did the ritual hand-washing two times.
- If the person was buried on the day following the death, the custom in Jerusalem is that on the first day of shiva, the mourner wears tefillin in private without reciting the blessing. But if the relative died on Shabbat and was buried on Motza'ei Shabbat, the mourner does not wear tefillin on Sunday (*Yalkut Yosef* 7:25; *Tzror HaḤayim* 125). See also **Tefillin on the First Day**.
- The *Brakha Me'ein Sheva* – the "*Magen Avraham*" passage said during Maariv on Friday night – is not recited on the house of mourning (*Shulḥan Arukh, Oraḥ Ḥayim* 268:10). Some wrote that the custom in Jerusalem is to say the blessing (*Yalkut Yosef* 29:16).
- The custom in Jerusalem is to say "*Shabbat Shalom*" to mourners, following Maimonides' opinion, in order not to engage in public mourning (*Yalkut Yosef* 23:6).

- The Sephardic custom is that Hallel is recited on Rosh Ḥodesh in the house of mourning but that mourners themselves should not recite it (*Yalkut Yosef* 29:14). The custom in Jerusalem is that if they are praying where the person died, the congregation should go to a different room to recite Hallel and then return. If the person died in a hospital or in a different house, they do not need to go out.
- A dead body cannot be brought inside the walls of the Old City of Jerusalem. The source for this is the Mishna: "And they may carry around a corpse therein as far as necessary, but once it is taken out, they may not bring it back" (Kelim 1:7). This is because of the sanctity of Jerusalem. (The borders and details are brought in *Gesher HaḤayim* 14:4 and, in great detail, in *Ir HaKodesh VeHaMikdash* (vol. 2, ch. 12) by Rabbi Tuchinsky.)

Day of Collective Kaddish

In Hebrew, *Yom HaKaddish haKlali.* This day was instituted by the Chief Rabbis of Israel, Rabbi Yitzḥak Isaac HaLevi Herzog and Rabbi Yitzḥak Nissim, as a day to recite Kaddish and commemorate those murdered in the Holocaust whose date of death is unknown.

They instituted that this date would be the tenth of Tevet, which has been a fast day since the time of the destruction of the First Temple. The tenth of Tevet is mentioned in Ezekiel (24:2): "O mortal, record this date, this exact day; for this very day the king of Babylon has laid siege to Jerusalem." It was the day that the siege of Jerusalem began. It led to the fall of the city, at the hands of the Babylonians, and the destruction of the Temple.

In a pamphlet published by the Israeli Chief Rabbinate in 1956, they wrote:

> We have instituted the tenth of Tevet for now and for future generations, as a memorial day for the holy communities, and men, women, and children who were brutally murdered by the Nazis in Europe, and whose bodies and date of death were covered over by the smoke of the crematoria in which they were burned.

> For these millions of martyrs, whose date of death cannot be known – this day is dedicated to commemorating and elevating their pure souls. This day, the tenth of Tevet, shall serve as the date of death [Yahrzeit] for their children and relatives, to recite Kaddish, study Mishna, and light memorial candles.

See also ***Av HaRaḥamim*****;** ***El Maleh Raḥamim*****; Yahrzeit;** ***Yizkor*****.**

Dayan HaEmet

This is a blessing made upon hearing bad news. It is said by mourners when they tear their garments. The blessing appears in the Mishna (Berakhot 9:2). Despite its association with tragedy, the blessing is considered one of praise; our sages taught that one must accept bad news lovingly, in the same way that one accepts good news.

This blessing holds deep significance, precisely because it is said in moments of great pain and sorrow. In making the blessing, the person is proclaiming his awareness that everything comes from God: "I form light and create darkness, I make peace and create woe – I the Lord do all these things" (Is. 45:7). Rav Kook's perspective on this blessing is brought in Sec. 7, "Arrangements for the Funeral and Burial: Explanation of the *Dayan HaEmet* blessing."

See also **One Should Be as Thankful for the Bad as One Is for the Good – and Accept It with Joy**.

Death and Adam

Humans were sentenced to die a mortal death as a result of Adam's sin.

> Rabbi Meir would say: Adam, the first man, was very pious. When he saw that death was imposed as a punishment because of him, he observed a fast for 130 years, and he separated from his wife for 130 years. (Eruvin 18b)

Why was he punished with death? Some opinions do not relate the existence of death with Adam, in particular, but with the human race, in general:

> Rabbi Ḥama the son of Rabbi Ḥanina said: Adam should not have tasted death, but why was he punished with death? God saw that Nebuchadnezzar and Hiram would eventually deify themselves, and so He brought death, as it says, "You were in Eden, the garden of God" (Ezek. 28:13). But was Hiram in Eden?! Rather he said to him: You were the one who caused the one who was in Eden to die. (Genesis Rabba 9)

According to this explanation, humanity was punished with death due to the concern that man would deify himself, as indeed occurred several times over the course of human history. In this view, Adam was punished with death because of his descendants' sins.

There are opinions that do link the existence of death with Adam in particular, because he did not follow God's instructions:

> If the Jewish people had waited for Moses and not made the Golden Calf, the exiles would not have occurred, and the Angel of Death would have no jurisdiction over them. As the verse states (Ex. 32): "The writing was the writing of God, carved (*ḥarut*) on the tablets." Rabbi Judah said: Free (*ḥerut*) of the exiles. Rabbi Neḥemiah said: Free from the Angel of Death. When the Jewish people declared, "All that the Lord has spoken we will faithfully do," God said: I commanded Adam one commandment and I compared him to the angels, as it says, "The man has become like one of us" (Gen. 3); these who keep 613 commandments, should they not live forever? But when they said, "This is your god, O Israel" (Ex. 32:4) [about the Golden Calf], death came upon them. God said: You followed the ways of Adam, who did not withstand the test for three hours and was punished in the ninth hour with the decree of death. "I had taken you for divine beings," and you followed in Adam's ways – "Indeed you shall die like Adam." (Exodus Rabba (Vilna), *Parasha* 32, s.v. "*Hineh Anokhi*")

Much has been written about the connection between death and Adam's sin. Below is one source on this topic:

> Because he ate from the Tree of Knowledge on that day, he was cut down and was then given food that is difficult to digest… and Adam was meant to continue with that eating and arrive with his body and soul in Eden, where there is no food and drink but only pleasure from the rays of the *Shekhina*. But after the sin, digestion occurred every day, and the food is not sufficient – all the more so because one works hard to eat for one hour. Until one becomes a corpse at the end of his life to end iniquity and sin. (Rabbi Menaḥem Azariah of Fano, *Asara Maamarot*, "*Ḥikur HaDin*," vol. 2, ch. 6)

According to this, Adam should have lived forever, but since he sinned, his food was corrupted and his body could not survive. It can be said that a person begins dying from the moment he is born and that the process of dying ends with death. The following verse could be explained in that light: "A good name is better than precious oil and the day of death than the day of one's birth" (Eccl. 7:1). Rav Kook described it in a similar manner: "Death is an illusion; its impurity is its falsehood. What people call death is only an increase and an intensification of life" (*Orot HaKodesh*, vol. 2, 40).

And see Rabbi Ovadia Sforno in his introduction to Genesis.

See also ***Karet*****; Kiss of Death; Me'arat HaMakhpela; Life Expectancy.**

Deceased Gentile

> The sages taught – One sustains poor gentiles along with poor Jews, and one visits sick gentiles along with sick Jews, and one buries dead gentiles along with dead Jews, on account of the ways of peace. (Gittin 61a)

Thus, even though the Torah's commandment to "Love your neighbor as yourself" (Lev. 19:18) refers to one's fellow Jews, the sages decreed that one must show kindness toward everyone, including gentiles. The trait of kindness is the trait of our forefather Abraham, who showed loving-kindness to all people. It is important for the Jewish people to continue practicing the admirable values of our forefathers.

Rashi explains that this does not mean that gentiles should be buried in a Jewish cemetery but that we must ensure that they are buried, just as we see to it that Jews are buried.

And this was established as the halakha: "One buries the dead of the gentiles and comforts their mourners and visits their sick on account of the ways of peace" (Maimonides, *Mishneh Torah, Hilkhot Avel* 14:12; *Shulḥan Arukh, Yoreh De'ah* 367:1).

One may attend a gentile's funeral if it is not a religious ceremony. But if it is held in a church or involves a religious ceremony, one should not attend. (This was taught to me by Rabbi Yaakov Ruza.)

See also **Ways of Peace (*Darkei Shalom*)**.

Dedicating a Cemetery

In Hebrew, *Ḥanukat Beit HaKvarot*. This refers to designating a field as a new cemetery or as an addition to an existing cemetery. The ceremony for dedicating a cemetery addresses the concern that establishing the cemetery could be seen as inviting further deaths, God forbid. Therefore, certain symbolic acts are performed for protection, and prayers and psalms are recited. Sometimes, people involved in the dedication will fast and say *Seliḥot* prayers, stirring themselves to repentance, in order to bring merit upon the inhabitants of the city. This will be explained below. *Maavar Yabok* brings a custom, in the name of Rabbi Judah the Hasid, that it is good to bury a rooster (called *gever*) in an empty grave. The idea is that this will perhaps serve to weaken the attribute of justice and avoid provoking the wrath of the angel Gabriel (also called *gever*), who influences the attribute of justice. The custom is that when they bury the first person in a cemetery, they slaughter a rooster without making a blessing and bury it by the person's feet. There is no need to be concerned that this is "the ways of the Amorite," i.e., idolatrous (*Yalkut Yosef* 45:11).

The steps involved in the dedication of a cemetery are as follows: When purchasing the lot, those doing so state that they are performing burial so that "death shall vanish eternally." Some have the custom for the *ḥevra kaddisha* to fast on that day until midday and add *Seliḥot* in their morning prayers. They go to the cemetery and say Psalm 91 – "O you who dwell in the shelter of the Most High" – which describes God's protection over man. Afterwards, they say *Pitum HaKetoret*; according to the Kabbala, this text offers protection against impure spirits. They read three verses from the Torah from *Parashat Koraḥ* (Num. 17:11–13). Some add other special prayers. They recite Psalms 102 and 103, which describe man's limitations in contrast with God's eternality and divine loving-kindness.

Some have the custom of walking around the cemetery seven times, while reciting holy words: "*Vayehi Noam*," Psalm 91, "*Ana Bekoaḥ*," Psalm 104, and verses from Isaiah (42:1–21) that praise God's works in the world and the circle of life.

After going around seven times, they spell the name of the city using the verses from Psalm 119 and the letters K"RA S"TN ("Satan should be torn up"), and they conclude with the prayer, "May it be Your will that You remove from us and from all of Israel all types of illness, destruction, and evil decrees, and death shall vanish eternally." They then say *El Maleh Raḥamim* for the dead and ask their forgiveness and give charity to the poor.

See also **Cemetery; *Hakafot*; Ways of the Amorite.**

Degradation of the Dead

In Hebrew, "*Nivul haMet*." This concept refers to the shaming or disgracing of the deceased; one must be careful not to cause degradation to the dead. One of the reasons that we avoid exhuming the dead from the grave, opening the grave, or performing an autopsy is to avoid causing such degradation. However, these things may be permitted if there is a genuine need. For example, if an organ transplant can be done to save another person's life, some opinions permit taking organs from Jews. When necessary, the lenient opinion can be relied upon, such as in a case where the organs cannot be obtained from a gentile (*Yalkut Yosef* 53:2, based on Bava Batra 154a; Ḥullin 11b; *Shulḥan Arukh, Yoreh De'ah* 363:7)

See also **Exhuming a Grave; Honoring the Deceased.**

Desecrating the Dead

This prohibition appears in the Yerushalmi Talmud (Moed Katan 3:1): "One who mocks the elderly, even after their death, should be excommunicated." In the Midrash Tanhuma (Va'ethanan 6) it appears that it is more severe to desecrate the dead than to mock the living: Moses was punished for saying, "And now you, a breed of sinful men, have replaced your fathers" (Num. 32:14). God said to him: "Were Abraham, Isaac, and Jacob sinners that you have said this to their children?" Moses answered: "I learned from You, that You said, 'The fire pans of those who have sinned in their souls' (Num. 17:3)." God said to him: "I said in their souls (*beNafshotam*) not in their fathers (*beAvotam*)." However, a basic reading of the Yerushalmi suggests that mocking the living is a graver act because it says, "Even after their death." That is the Ra'avya's explanation there. (See *Gesher HaḤayim* 5:3, who explains the discrepancy between these two sources.)

The *Shulḥan Arukh* (*Oraḥ Ḥayim* 426:3) writes: "It is an ancient decree to excommunicate one who speaks badly of the dead." The *Kaf HaḤayim* (ad loc. 46) writes that although Moses was not censured with excommunication, the sages before us treated this severely, even requiring excommunication.

> Whoever speaks badly of the dead must take upon himself fasting and repentance and be fined as the Beit Din sees fit. If the grave is nearby, he should go to the person's grave and ask for forgiveness, and if the grave is far away, he should send a messenger there. (Rema, *Ḥoshen Mishpat* 420:38)

If someone left instructions to desecrate his body after death as atonement, this should be obeyed, since whatever is done for the good of the deceased is not considered degrading (*Kol Bo al Aveilut*, p. 59). King Ḥizkiyahu desecrated his father, King Aḥaz, after his death as an atonement (Pesaḥim 56a).

If someone has desecrated the dead or spoken badly of them, they must ask for forgiveness.

See also **Asking Forgiveness from the Deceased; Honoring the Deceased.**

Earth from the Land of Israel

Many Jewish people residing outside of Israel try to acquire a small amount of soil from the Land of Israel (especially from the Mount of Olives), to be scattered inside the grave (Rema, *Yoreh De'ah* 363:1) under the deceased. Some scatter earth under the tallit or on the person's face (forehead, eyes, eyebrows) and on the place of circumcision (*Gesher HaḤayim* 27:10, quoting from *Maavar Yabok, "Sefat Emet,"* ch. 27).

The source for this is the Yerushalmi Talmud (Kilayim 9:4): "When they get to the Land of Israel, they take earth and place it on the coffin, as it says: 'Atonement for the soil of his people.'" And although the discussion there it about someone who is brought to be buried in Israel, the earth itself has sanctity and a special quality. *Gesher HaḤayim* (27:10) writes that this will prove beneficial at the time of the resurrection for several reasons: Because of the dirt itself; because the deceased has the desire to fulfill the verse, "Your servants take delight in its stones and cherish its dust" (Ps. 102:15); and because of the rule that everything returns to its source and place. A person is formed from the earth and returns to it. Adam was created from the earth of the Land of Israel, from the Foundation Stone, located where the Holy of Holies was, inside the Temple (Maimonides, *Mishneh Torah, Hilkhot Beit HaBekhira* 2:1, based on Y. Nazir). We are all descendants of Adam; the Foundation Stone from which he was created is the place from which all humanity came. When a small amount of earth from the Land of Israel is placed in the grave, we figuratively close the circle.

See also **Burial in the Land of Israel; One May Bring Anyone to the Land of Israel, But One May Not Remove Anyone**.

El Maleh Raḥamim

A prayer said by the grave after the burial or memorial service, on days when people go to the gravesite. The prayer asks God to accept the deceased's soul, to give it eternal life, and to let it rest in the Garden of Eden.

El Maleh Raḥamim ("O God, full of compassion") is recited in the cemetery and in the synagogue after the Torah reading. The prayer-leader who recites *El Maleh Raḥamim* holds the Torah scroll in his right hand. This is because it is customary to pledge charity (*tzedaka*) and the verse states, "Justice (*tzedek*) fills Your right hand" (Ps. 48:11). Another reason is that the Torah was given from the right side: "Lightening flashing at them from His right" (Deut. 33:2). The prayer-leader also holds the Torah so that he will feel the awe of Torah and pray for the deceased with great concentration.

The words of the prayer should be: "O God, full of compassion, who dwells on high, grant true rest upon the wings of the *Shekhina.*" It is important to say "upon the wings" ("*al kanfei haShekhina*") and not "under the wings" ("*taḥat kanfei haShekhina*") (*Yalkut Yosef* 32:2, citing the book *Shnei Luḥot HaBrit*).

El Maleh Raḥamim is recited by the prayer-leader, unlike *Yizkor,* which is recited by individuals for their relatives (*Gesher HaḤayim* 31:2, 3). *Yizkor* is only recited four times a year (on the three festivals and Yom Kippur), while *El Maleh Raḥamim* is also said when people go to the gravesite and at memorial services.

The prayer appears to have been composed during the pogroms of 1648–1649 by Rabbi Yeḥiel Michel from Nemirov in Poland, or in his memory. In the past, there were other versions of *El Maleh Raḥamim,* most of which concluded with the most significant phrase of the prayer: "May his soul be bound in the bond of life" (*Gesher HaḤayim* 31:2, 1. In the footnote, he mentions the date the twentieth of Sivan, which was chosen as the day to commemorate the destruction of the Polish communities, as mentioned in the *Mishna Berura* (580 and 566:10). In the *Shoneh Halakhot* (580:3), he brings additional sources. Also see *Or LaAvel,* p. 146).

The custom is not to say *El Maleh Raḥamim* on days when *Taḥanun* is not recited, to avoid arousing grief and crying. *El Maleh Raḥamim* may be said even when there is no *minyan* present.

See also ***Av HaRaḥaman* Prayer; Bond of Life (*Tzror HaḤayim*); *Hashkava*; Recalling the Souls (*Hazkarat Neshamot*); *Yizkor*.**

Elevating the Soul

The Jewish perspective holds that every good deed performed because of the deceased or in his honor brings him merit. Kaddish is the most well-known example of this; in Kaddish, God's name is sanctified in order to give merit to the deceased. It is customary to recite psalms or study Mishna (the word "Mishna" consists of the same letters as "*neshama,*" soul) for the merit of the deceased. Some try to arrange for the study of all six orders of the Mishna, by dividing up the tractates among various people, to be completed by the end of the *shloshim* or the end of the year. It is customary to give charity or to donate books that will be learned for the merit of the deceased, and it is customary to light a candle in their honor (see *Yalkut Yosef* 30:31).

There is also a custom to make blessings over food or drink for the elevation of the deceased's soul. A person usually eats out of hunger or a desire to eat. And, although Jewish people make a blessing before eating, expressing gratitude and gaining permission to eat the food – eating is still primarily about human need and desire. However, when blessings are made to elevate the deceased's soul, the opposite is true: The reason for eating is to bless God. In this case, we eat because it gives us an opportunity to bless God, in contrast to the normal scenario where eating is the main purpose and the blessing is what enables it.

Since the goal here is not the eating itself, but rather to allow the people to make blessings, the eating is largely symbolic. For example, a person might eat one raisin in order to make the "*Boreh pri haEtz*" blessing, and one peanut to make the "*Boreh pri haAdama*" blessing. The purpose of the eating is not the single raisin or the peanut but to bless the Master of the Universe. These blessings bring merit to the deceased.

In order to make as many blessings as possible, there is a specified order to the blessings. When refreshments are served in the shiva house but bread is not eaten, the order is as follows: *mezonot* (for grain products), *hagafen* (for wine), *haetz* (for tree fruit), *haadama* (produce other than tree fruits), and *shehakol* (miscellaneous foods – animal products, drinks, or candy, etc.).

Sometimes a sign will be put in a visible spot in the shiva house, stating that the blessings are to elevate the soul of (the deceased's name, son/daughter of mother's/father's name).

See also **A Child Brings Merit to the Father (*Bara Mezakei Aba*); Acronyms; *Alpha Beita*; Charity; Elevating the Soul; Kaddish; Memorial (or Yahrzeit) Candle (*Ner Neshama*); Studying Mishna.**

Embalming

In Hebrew, *Ḥanita*. This is the use of special materials to preserve the body of the deceased from decomposing and emitting a bad odor. The word "*ḥanita*" shares its root with the word used for a good smell, as in the verse: "The figs gave a good smell (*ḥanta*)" (Song. 2:13). The Egyptians used to embalm their dead using a variety of methods.

The process of embalming is described in relation to Jacob and Joseph. The sages disagreed as to whether Joseph acted appropriately when he embalmed his father:

> Why did Joseph die before his brothers? Rebbi said: Because he embalmed his father. God said to him – Was I incapable of preserving my righteous person? Did I not say to him "Do not fear the worm of Jacob" (Is. 41:14)? The sages said: He commanded him to embalm him, as it says, "His sons did so as he had commanded them" (Gen. 50:12). (Genesis Rabba 100:4)

There is a difference of opinion about how Jacob and Joseph were embalmed. According to the Zohar (*Vayeḥi*), embalming did not include dissecting the body but using oils externally; the oils were absorbed into the body. Some wrote that they would cut open the abdomen and remove the intestines (so they would not start emitting an odor), and they would then spread persimmon oil over the entire body, inside and out, and fill it with herbs that would help dry out the body. The herbs needed to be switched daily until the body dried out and hardened, and would thus not rot and become foul-smelling. Even though this method involved cutting the abdomen, it is not considered to cause pain or desecration to the deceased since it is done to honor and care for them (*Responsa Rashba,* vol. 1, 369; *Responsa Ridbaz,* vol. 1, 484). Some are of the opinion that it is prohibited to embalm the dead by making an abdominal incision and removing the intestines, because they consider it to be damaging and desecrating of the dead; another reason they prohibit it is because it prevents the burial of those body parts, but one is permitted to inject or insert preservatives into the body (*Responsa Tzafnat Paneaḥ,* vol. 1, 21; *Responsa Maharitz, Ḥayot* 6). Some do not permit any kind of embalming, even without making an incision or removing internal organs. Firstly, because one who puts the body in a coffin without burying it transgresses the negative commandment not to delay burial and, secondly, because the decomposition of the flesh is considered part of the deceased's atonement; embalming prevents the decomposition of the flesh and therefore delays the atonement (*Responsa Igrot Moshe, Yoreh De'ah,* vol. 3, 143–144).

In Israel, it is not customary to preserve the body in any way. But if the body is going to be transported to a distant location, it is customary to preserve the body by injecting preservatives through the nostrils. When circumstances require it, such as if the body will be transported long distances, it is customary to inject preservatives into the blood. The blood and liquid removed from the body should be collected and sent with the body to be buried with it. Internal organs should not be removed from the body.

See also *Responsa Emek Halakha*, vol. 1, 49; *Encyclopedia Hilkhatit Refuit* "*Ḥanita*"; *Gesher HaḤayim* 5:7; *Kol Bo al Aveilut*, p. 51–53. See *Darka Shel Yahadut BeMavet U'BeAveilut*, p. 36, for the theoretical position that opposes all kinds of embalming.

Eternality of the Soul

My God –
The soul You have given me is pure.
You created it, You formed it,
You breathed it into me,
You guard it within me.
You will, in the future, take it from me,
And restore it to me at a future time. (From the morning blessings, based on Berakhot 60b)

This is a basic tenet in the Jewish faith. All of God's Torah and mitzvot – and the rewards and punishments pertaining to them – are based on the principle of the soul's existence during one's life and the future good. And not only does the soul endure, it will also be revived.

Many verses convey the notion of the eternality of the soul's. For examples: "The life of my lord will be bound up in the bond of life in the care of the Lord" (I Sam. 25:29); "But God will redeem my life from the clutches of Sheol, for He will take me. *Selah*" (Ps. 49:16); "And the lifebreath returns to God Who bestowed it" (Eccl. 12:7).

The idea behind the punishment of *karet* (literally, being "cut off") is based on the principle that the soul endures and is eternal. If someone is "cut off," this means that his soul is cut off from eternity.

Thus, death is a change in form, from a physical to a spiritual existence. "As the soul is dressed in this world, it is also dressed in splendor in the next world" (Zohar, *Noaḥ* 67; see *Gesher HaḤayim*, vol. 3, 6).

> In my opinion, the term "holy nation" is a promise that the soul will remain before God: You are a holy nation and chosen by God and He will not leave any soul, and so you should not afflict yourselves and cut yourselves off in grief, even for a person who died young. The verses do not prohibit crying, for it is natural to cry at the loss of a loved one, but the sages learned (Moed Katan 27b) that one must not cry excessively for a soul. (Nahmanides on the Torah, Deut. 14:1)

> It is written in the *Orḥot Ḥayim*: If the mother died before the circumcision, one should say – The mother will rejoice in the Garden of Eden. And if the father died, one should say – The father will rejoice in the Garden of Eden. For we find that there is joy after death, as in the phrases: Abraham rejoices, Isaac will be happy, Moses will rejoice. And this expresses the belief in the eternality of the soul and in the resurrection of the dead. (*Beit Yosef, Yoreh De'ah* 265:1)

We find examples of the everlasting nature of the soul in both the Tanakh and the words of the sages: Samuel the prophet spoke with King Saul after he died (I Sam. 28); there are various stories in the Talmud of people hearing souls speak after their death, for example, the tale of someone who slept in a graveyard and heard two girls speaking after they had died (Berakhot 18b); Rabbi Naḥman spoke to Aḥai bar Yoshiya after he died (Shabbat 152b); and Rabbi Elazar b. Rabbi Shimon would give responses after he had died (Bava Metzia 84b).

The ideas regarding the soul's eternality are deep and complex. Nahmanides discusses the topic at length in his book *Torat HaAdam, Shaar HaGemul*. See also *Kuntras Hishaarut HaNefesh* in the book *Aseh Lekha Rav* (Rabbi Haim David HaLevi), vol. 2.

See also **Being Cut Off (*Karet*); *Neshama* (Soul); Resurrection; The World to Come.**

Eulogy

Eulogies are speeches delivered in honor of the deceased; they are intended to recall the person's goodness and good deeds, express sorrow and sadness over the death, and elicit the audience's grief. Eulogies are delivered at the funeral. Some people continue to eulogize the deceased for the entire first year. Today this is called an *azkara* (memorial).

In the Tanakh, we see that Abraham eulogized his wife Sarah (Gen. 23:2) and that Jacob was eulogized by his sons and all of Egypt (Gen. 50:10). When Samuel the prophet died, all of Israel eulogized him (II Sam. 25:1).

It is a great mitzva to deliver eulogies in a way that befits the deceased. In ancient times, they would hire professional eulogizers who were paid generously. A story is told of one woman who gave the eulogizer all the money that her husband had collected for making a pilgrimage to Jerusalem, and he was therefore not able to go to Jerusalem (Moed Katan 8a). The higher the payment, the greater was the praise of the deceased. Our sages said: "Just as the deceased are punished, so too are the eulogizers" (Berakhot 62a) – if they say untrue things. Thus, people should not add unnecessary praise in their eulogies. Someone who speaks about good traits that the person did not in fact possess, or exaggerates the praise, causes harm to himself and to the deceased. On the other hand, deserving individuals and Torah scholars must be properly eulogized. Our sages said: "Anyone who sheds tears over an upright person – the Holy One, Blessed be He, counts his tears and places them in His treasury. Anyone who is lazy in eulogizing a Torah scholar, it is fitting to bury him alive, and he does not live a long life." They derived this from the verses related to Joshua ben Nun who was not eulogized properly (Shabbat 105b), and when the Jewish people were punished because they did not eulogize King Saul as they should have (II Sam. 21:1). This idea also appears in the following: "An eclipse occurs for four reasons… because of the head of the Beit Din who died and was not properly eulogized" (Sukka 29a).

If an outstanding scholar has died, his body is brought into the beit midrash where he would teach and he is eulogized there (*Shulḥan Arukh, Yoreh De'ah* 344:20; and see *Responsa Yabia Omer*, vol. 9, *Yoreh De'ah* 46).

The Talmud (Sanhedrin 46b) discusses whether eulogies are for the honor of the living or the honor of the dead. If the deceased gave instructions not to eulogize him, this instruction is obeyed and the person is not eulogized (*Shulḥan Arukh*, ibid. 344:10), like Rabbi Yehuda HaNasi, who instructed: "Do not eulogize me in the towns" (Ketubbot 103b). But even if a great Torah scholar gave instructions not to eulogize him, it is permissible to do so in order to awaken the community to repent (*Pitḥei Teshuva* ad loc. 344:1; see also the footnotes in *Yalkut Yosef* 11:6).

There are certain days on which eulogies are not delivered because they are festive days. These days are listed in *Megillat Taanit*, which is an ancient tannaitic text written in Aramaic.

A person should not eulogize the deceased in the thirty days prior to a festival. (In present times, this means that a memorial service should not be scheduled during this period.) The reason for this is that it causes one to remember the deceased and the sorrow and grief associated with the loss; this remains with the person for thirty days. However, if someone died within thirty days of a festival, he may be eulogized during the shiva, even on the eve of a holiday. This is because the sorrow is already present and it is not elicited by the eulogy (Moed Katan 8:1; *Shulḥan Arukh, Oraḥ Ḥayim* 547:3 and *Yoreh De'ah* 347). If the *shloshim* or Yahrzeit fall out during this period, a memorial service may be held (*Shulḥan Arukh, Oraḥ Ḥayim* 547:5; *Pnei Barukh* 3:9).

In addition to its halakhic significance, eulogies hold social significance:

The eulogy provides a measure of comfort to the mourners by demonstrating respect and appreciation for the deceased and his actions. The eulogy can also alleviate feelings of guilt that the mourner may feel towards the deceased, that perhaps one did not do enough for them or offended them. Eulogizing and showing the appropriate respect to the deceased can help compensate for and alleviate some of these feelings.

The pain of facing a relative's death can be eased by gentle words and idioms. Eulogies can also help mourners internalize the fact of their relative's death, by hearing their loved one spoken about as no longer in the world.

Important social values are often emphasized in eulogies, linking these values to the deceased. It may serve to strengthen people's identification with the values and with the deceased, increasing a sense of unity and bringing them together; this feeling can help people cope with the death (based on "*Ketz HaḤayim,*" Nisan Rubin, p. 205).

See also **Honor of the Living, Honor of the Deceased; Honoring the Deceased.**

Exhuming a Grave

It is forbidden to dig up a dead body, so as not to cause degradation to the deceased; the body might fall apart when it is moved or might otherwise be seen in an undignified manner. The prohibition also stems from the "fear of judgment," namely that, when handling the body, one disturbs the deceased from his rest.

As a rule, a dead body should not be exhumed, except in the following circumstances:

- To bury the person with his family
- To move the person from a grave that is not his to one that is
- If the person is buried among gentiles or next to a gentile
- If the person is buried in a stolen grave, i.e., one that was not actually owned by the owner
- If the grave is a nuisance to many people, such as if it is close to a road
- In order to bury the person in Israel
- If the person is buried somewhere unprotected and there is a concern that the grave might be vandalized
- If the person was buried in a temporary grave or gave instructions to move his body to a different place

In a case where it is permissible to exhume a body, one must try to wait until the flesh has decomposed and to exhume only the bones. If a coffin is being moved, it should not be opened. When moving the body, the earth that was around the body must also be moved and buried in the new location, together with body. The amount of dirt that should be taken from the grave together with the body is three finger-widths (six centimeters) in depth on all sides (Mishna Nazir 9:3; Ohalot 16:3). The laws regarding exhuming a grave can be found in the *Shulḥan Arukh, Yoreh De'ah* 363 and in this book in Sec. 46, "Exhuming a Grave."

See also **Degradation of the Dead; Fear of Judgment; Grave That is a Public Nuisance; Grave That Is Discovered.**

Family Grave

In Hebrew, "*Kever Mishpaḥti.*" If possible, people should be buried together with their family. The Bible mentions a number of examples of people making efforts to be buried in a family plot: Abraham bought Me'arat HaMakhpela in Hebron for Sarah's burial, and he was also buried there, as were Isaac and Rebecca; Jacob buried Leah there and instructed Joseph, "Bury me in their burial place." According to the Midrash, Jacob apologized to Joseph that he was not able to bury his mother Rachel in the grave of the forefathers in Hebron.

Aaron's son, Elazar the Cohen, was buried on the hill of his son Pinḥas (at end of the Book of Joshua). Gideon was buried in the burial place of his father, Yoash (Judges 8:32). The bones of King Saul and his son Jonathan were buried in the territory of Benjamin, in the burial place of Saul's father, Kish (II Sam. 21:14). Asahel was buried in his father's burial place (II Sam. 2:32). Reḥavam was buried in his father's plot (I Kings 14:31) as were other kings. Nehemiah calls Jerusalem, "The city of my fathers' graves" (Neh. 2:2).

It is comforting for a person to be buried with his family. As Barzilai the Giladi said: "Let me die in my own town, near the graves of my father and mother" (II Sam. 19:38).

Being buried with one's family is considered so important that one is allowed to exhume a body from the grave in order to bury the deceased with their family (*Shulḥan Arukh, Yoreh De'ah* 363).

See also **Graves of the Forefathers and Graves of the Righteous.**

Fear of Judgment

According to Judaism, the dead are judged and they fear judgment just as living people do. Samuel said to Saul, "Why have you disturbed me and brought me up?" (I Sam. 28:15). The Talmud (Ḥagiga 4b) explains that Samuel feared judgment and brought Moses up with him to add to his merit. One of the reasons that, according to the halakha, a corpse should not be removed from the grave is so as not to agitate the dead from their resting place (*Siftei Cohen, Shulḥan Arukh, Yoreh De'ah* 363:1). Yom Kippur is called *Yom Kippurim* (in the plural) because the dead also receive atonement on Yom Kippur (*Shulḥan Arukh, Oraḥ Ḥayim* 622:6). On Rosh HaShana, the books of life and death are opened before God in judgment. This is usually understood as referring only to the living – who will live, and who will die. But in light of the explanation above, it can also be understood more literally – that both the living and the dead are judged.

See also **Exhuming a Grave; The Dead Do Not Know Anything**.

Funeral

It is a great mitzva to escort the dead, and it is considered a fulfillment of the commandment to love one's neighbor as oneself.

One who sees a body [taken to be buried] and does not escort it thereby transgresses, "He who mocks the poor" (Prov. 17:5), and he should be placed under a ban; and one should escort the body at least four cubits (*Shulḥan Arukh, Yoreh De'ah* 361). The custom is to accompany the dead four cubits or more and then to wait until the body can no longer be seen. This is alluded to in the Ḥizkuni's explanation of the verse at the end of *Parashat Shoftim*, "And our eyes did not see" – from here we learn that someone who is escorting the deceased must stand in place until he can no longer see the deceased (*Yalkut Yosef* 10:2).

Attending a funeral mandates interrupting one's Torah study. If the deceased was someone who taught Torah to others, everyone should stop their Torah study to attend the funeral, even if there are already thousands of others attending. For a funeral of one who did not teach Torah, if there are ten people attending so that Kaddish can be recited, then others do not need to interrupt their Torah study to attend. If there are not ten people, then the people in the town must cease their work to escort the deceased.

When the body is moved, it is customary to recite, "When the Tabernacle is to set out, the Levites shall take it down, and when the Tabernacle is to be pitched, the Levites shall set it up" (Num. 1:51); "When the Ark was to set out, Moses would say: Advance, O Lord! May Your enemies be scattered, and may Your foes flee before You!" (ibid. 10:35). These verses are said because a Jewish person is likened to a Torah scroll. A Torah scroll is the symbol of positive and appropriate behavior, which ideally characterizes a Jew, as well. The aforementioned verses speak of the Tabernacle and the Ark; just as the *Shekhina* dwelt in them though they were physical objects, so too, a person's physical body is the vessel for the soul, a part of God.

The Kabbalistic perspective adds other elements of significance to our understanding of the funeral:

> Carrying a deceased righteous person on one's shoulder is like the Tabernacle that they brought to Moses; and when the Tabernacle travelled – this is the soul, which dwells in this world against its will… and when the Tabernacle rested during its journey to its resting place, it was escorted by countless angels, as it is written: "The stranger who draws close shall die." The stranger who draws close to this soul shall be consumed to clear a path to ascend to God: "Clear a road to God!" And so those who escort the dead become a vessel for the higher beings that accompany them, and just as they escort the body with their bodies, they should have the intention to escort the soul with their own soul. For the deceased's soul and spirit accompany the body to the grave. It was not for nothing that our sages warned us to honor the dead and escort them. They said that whoever sees the dead and does not escort them transgresses the prohibition against mocking the poor, etc.; and they certainly did not limit this honor to the deceased's body.
>
> The order that Jacob established for his sons in carrying his bier, as the Midrash describes: Since Jacob was about to die, he called his sons and instructed them and encouraged them in God's ways, and they accepted upon themselves the kingdom of Heaven. When he finished, he told them – When you carry me, do so with awe and respect, and no one else should touch my coffin. And it is learned from Rabbi Yehuda HaNasi's instructions and those of Rabbi Shimon bar Yoḥai, that the righteous are comforted when they are properly attended to after death.

> The bride and groom are brought into the *ḥuppa* by great individuals; likewise, the soul and the body, when they are laid to rest, should be treated with respect by great individuals. Rabbi Shimon bar Yoḥai said that burial is a Torah commandment from the verse, "One must bury him the same day." And the Yerushalmi Talmud explained that a funeral takes precedence over Torah study. The Mishna views this as a great merit, saying (Sota 1:9): Joseph merited to bury his father, and none of his brothers were greater than he, as it says, "And Joseph went up (to Israel) to bury his father... and chariots and cavalry went up with him" (Gen 50:7 and 50:9). Who among us was greater than Joseph, that only Moses was permitted to attend to him? Moses merited [carrying] Joseph's bones [to Israel], and none of Israel is greater than him, as it says, "And Moses took the bones of Joseph with him" (Ex. 13:19). Who among us was greater than Moses, that only God merited attending to him, as it says, "And He buried him in the valley" (Deut. 34:6). When they escort the deceased, they should have the intention to escort the sanctity within the person by means of the power of the soul's sparks within each of them. For sanctity resides in all [members] of Israel, as it says: "And I will be sanctified among the children of Israel." Whoever knows the mystical secret of escorting into life will understand from it the need to escort the dead and will add other intentions when escorting the dead. Some of the intentions for the funeral are alluded to in the Zohar (*Parashat Vayera*, 126). And it is not without reason that the funeral can override Torah study; and for someone who taught others, there is no limitation. (*Maavar Yabok*, "*Siftei Renanot*," ch. 15)

See also **Coffin; *Ḥevra Kaddisha*; *Ḥesed shel Emet* (True Kindness); Mocking the Poor.**

Funeral Home

Usually, this is where the *tahara* takes place. After receiving permission from the authorities, the body is prepared through the ritual *tahara* (purification) by the *ḥevra kaddisha*. If it has not been prepared in the funeral home, it is then brought there. After the funeral, the body is brought to the cemetery.

See also **Cemetery**.

Gathering of Bones

In Hebrew, *Likut Atzamot*. In Talmudic times, they would initially bury the body in a hole or cave until the flesh had decomposed. They would then gather the bones and bury them in a different spot. When the bones were gathered, the customs of mourning were observed for one day. The gathering of the bones was usually done in the afternoon, close to nightfall, to reduce the mourning time (Tractate Smaḥot, sec. 12).

The laws are explained in *Shulḥan Arukh, Yoreh De'ah* 403, and above in Sec. 46, "Exhuming a Grave."

Geniza

There is an obligation to bury holy items – Torah scrolls, tefillin, *mezuzot*, and books that contain God's name or holy subject matter. These items may not be destroyed or discarded.

The custom is to have a receptacle for these items, called a *geniza* or *shemot*, generally somewhere in the synagogue, where people can place worn holy books or pages containing God's name. When the receptacle fills up, the contents are taken and buried in the cemetery, like a *met mitzva*. A Torah scroll that can no longer be used is buried in a clay vessel in the grave of a Torah scholar (Megilla 26b; Bava Batra 20b; *Shulḥan Arukh, Oraḥ Ḥayim* 154:5 and *Yoreh De'ah* 282:10).

Go in Peace

> Rabbi Avin HaLevi said: One who takes leave from another should not say to him: Go in peace, but rather: Go to peace. As we see, Yitro said to Moses: "Go to peace" (Ex 4:18), and Moses ascended and was successful. While David said to his son, Absalom: "Go in peace" (II Sam. 15:9), and Absalom went and was hanged. Rabbi Avin HaLevi also said: One who takes leave from a dead person should not say to him: Go to peace, but rather: Go in peace, as it is stated: "But you shall go to your fathers in peace" (Gen. 15:15). (Berakhot 64a. And see

> the halakha in Maimonides, *Mishneh Torah, Hilkhot Avel* 4:4; *Magen Avraham* 110:9)

The relationship between peace and the deceased is explained in the Talmud and Midrash (Shabbat 152b; *Yalkut Shimoni, Parashat Naso* 711):

> Peace is great that it was given to the righteous. When they die, three groups of ministering angels greet them. The first says, "He shall come to peace." The second says, "They rest on their beds." The third says, "Who walked straightforward" (Is. 57:2). And it is not enough for the righteous, for their death is with honor, as it says, "Your Vindicator shall march before you, the Presence of the Lord shall be your rear guard" (ibid. 58:8). And they further praise them and say, "He shall come to peace, they rest on their beds, who walked straightforward." Peace is great that it is withheld from the wicked, that when they die, three groups of ministering angels greet them. The first says "There is no peace." The second says, "Said my God, for the wicked" (ibid. 57:21). And the third says, "You shall lie down in pain" (ibid. 50:11). This is not sufficient for the wicked, rather their death is in the hands of the destroyers, as it says, "He comes close to the Pit, His life [verges] on death" (Job 33:22); "He is thrust from light to darkness, Driven from the world" (ibid. 18:18); "Let them be as chaff in the wind, the Lord's angel driving them on" (Ps. 35:5). And they are also rebuked, saying, "There is no peace – said my God – for the wicked," "You shall lie down in pain."

The Maharal explains the reason for this (*Netivot Olam, Netiv HaShalom*, ch. 1):

> Peace is given to the righteous when they pass on from this world, since it is then considered that they have attained completion. The living cannot achieve total completion since they can always achieve further completion. Therefore, one who takes leave of the living should not say, "Go in peace," which sounds

> as though they should go in completion (*hashlama*), having already achieved completion; [but] the living can always progress further. Rather, they should say "Go to peace" – be connected to peace and always increase in peace. But whoever takes leave of the dead should say "Go in peace," since they have achieved their final completion.

See also **Peace Be upon Him (*Alav HaShalom*).**

Grave That Is a Public Nuisance

> A grave that is a public nuisance, e.g., it is close to the road – even if the body was buried there with the knowledge of the owner of the field – it may be cleared; but the site of the grave is prohibited for use, [provided] the grave was there first. But if the road was there first, the site is permitted for use. (*Tur* and *Shulḥan Arukh, Yoreh De'ah* 364:5)

When the text discusses whether the site of the grave is prohibited for use, this refers to a tomb. The ground itself is not prohibited for use (Sanhedrin 47b; *Shulḥan Arukh*, ibid. 1).

See also **Exhuming a Grave; Grave That Is Discovered.**

Grave That Is Discovered

This is a grave that was discovered somewhere other than in a cemetery.

> If one discovers a grave in a field, and one does not know whether the person was buried with the previous owner's knowledge, one is permitted to move it, and the place is considered pure. But if the person was buried there with the agreement of the previous owner, the grave cannot be moved; and if it was moved, the place is considered impure and one cannot derive benefit from it. (*Tur, Yoreh De'ah* 364; *Shulḥan Arukh, Yoreh De'ah* 364:2)

This is based on the Talmud (Sanhedrin 47b). Such a grave may be removed if the burial was done without the owner of the field's permission. It appears from Rashi (ad loc.) that this only applies if the burial was done against the owner's wishes. But the *Tur* and *Shulḥan Arukh* permit removing the grave unless it is clear that the owner granted permission for the burial, in which case it would be forbidden.

An exception to this rule is the *met mitzva*, who takes possession of the site where he lies. His grave cannot be removed even if the owner did not consent (*Shulḥan Arukh*, ibid., based on Bava Kamma 81b). Today, the custom is to move this type of grave to a cemetery.

See also **Exhuming a Grave; *Met Mitzva*; Neighborhood of Graves.**

Graves of the Forefathers and Graves of the Righteous

> This passage [about Sarah's burial in Me'arat HaMakhpela] was written… to inform us where the forefathers were buried, since we are obligated to honor the burial place of our holy forefathers. (Nahmanides, Commentary on the Torah, Gen. 23:19)

Many people have a powerful inner desire to connect with the souls of our forefathers and righteous individuals. This is part of what brings people to visit their graves; when there, people ask that the merit of the righteous person(s) who is buried there shall strengthen their connection to God, and remove the barriers between them and God, barriers that too easily arise by virtue of human beings' shortcomings. When people want to come closer to God, it can be helpful for them to connect to their desire to emulate the righteous and to be influenced by them. We do this for example, when we invoke the forefathers, Abraham, Isaac, and Jacob, at the beginning of the *Amida* prayer. This is done both in order to invoke the merits of the forefathers and also out of an internal sense of identification with the ethical model they provide.

Kohanim may not visit the graves of the righteous, even Me'arat HaMakhpela and Rachel's Tomb. However, Rabbi Ido Elbah wrote in his book "*Taharat Sde HaMakhpela*" that, in his opinion, *kohanim* may enter the building above Me'arat HaMakhpela. Rabbi Nebenzahl notes: Further consideration is required as to whether or not *kohanim* may enter Rachel's Tomb, because the grave is from a time before the Torah was given.

When people pray beside a grave, they should pray for God's compassion and loving-kindness, by virtue of the merit of the righteous. It is forbidden to pray to the dead themselves (Rema, *Oraḥ Ḥayim* 605).

See *Gesher HaḤayim*, vol. 2, 26.

See also **Consulting the Dead; Family Grave.**

Guarding the Deceased

The deceased must be guarded night and day, even if there is no concern that the body will be harmed.

The custom to guard the deceased stems from several reasons: One is to show respect for the deceased; if left alone, it would appear as though the deceased had been abandoned and neglected, like a disregarded vessel (Y. Berakhot, ch. 3; Rema, *Yoreh De'ah* 373:5). The second reason for guarding the deceased is that, because the body is a holy sheath that has been emptied of the soul, the spirits of impurity are then drawn to enter it (according to Kabbalistic texts). It is compared to a barrel that has been emptied of honey, and bugs now rush to enter it. As the Zohar writes (*Emor* 88b): "The whole time that the body is not buried... an impure spirit rests upon it and contaminates that body."

This is even more of a concern if the body is located somewhere where it is at risk of being damaged or disrespected, such as a place with mice, rats, or dogs, a public place, or a place that could catch fire. The body must be protected from damage and disrespect and should be brought to a safe location.

See also **Honor of the Dead.**

Guarding the Mourner

In Hebrew, *Shemira LaAvel*. In Judaism, mourners are considered people who have recently been subject to God's attribute of justice. As such, the mourner is considered vulnerable and easily susceptible to harm. Therefore, there is an interest in protecting mourners, to prevent them from suffering further harm.

> Rabbi Judah said: Three need protection and they are: a sick person, a bride, and a groom. The Mishna taught: a sick person,

> a woman who gave birth, a bride, and a groom. And some say a mourner, as well. (Berakhot 54b; *Magen Avraham* 339:7)

The sages discussed this in a Midrash describing how God's attribute of judgment hovers over the mourners, conveying the message that mourners must be extra careful and protect themselves, and that the process of returning to normal must be gradual:

> For the entire seven days a sword is drawn, up to the thirty days it is loose, after twelve months it returns to its scabbard. What is this like? Like an arch of stones, if one is removed, they all shake. (Y. Moed Katan 3:3)

And another version:

> The [first] three days the mourner should perceive as if there is a sword resting between his shoulders; from three to seven [days] as though it is across from him in a corner; from seven to thirty [days] as though it passes before him in the marketplace. (Moed Katan 27b)
>
> And for the first year, the attribute of judgment is spread before the family, and if a baby boy is born – the entire family is healed. (Y. Moed Katan 3:7; *Shulḥan Arukh, Yoreh De'ah* 394:4)

See also **Breaking the Clay**.

Hakafot

Walking around the deceased, *hakafot,* is a custom held by the Hasidim, the Yemenite community, and the Jerusalem custom. It is done before the burial, to protect the body and the soul from impure forces that can cleave to it. This custom is specifically for a dead male – because a man needs extra protection (see also **Ban (*Ḥerem*) – "His Seed Will Not Follow Him"**). It is only done during the day, not at night, since the night is the time when the impure forces have power and cannot be overcome. It is only done on days when *Taḥanun* is recited, since on joyful days (when *Taḥanun* is omitted), the sanctity of the day overcomes the impure forces. The people who walk around the body take each other's hands, forming a circle, and walk around the body seven times, each time reciting Psalm 91, from "O you who dwell in the shelter of the Most High" until "Because you the Lord, my refuge," adding a passage from "*Ana BeKoaḥ*" and a request for mercy for the deceased. One of the *ḥevra kaddisha* leads the procession. He takes seven coins or broken pieces of money, and each time he goes around, he throws down one coin while saying the verse, "But to Abraham's sons by concubines, Abraham gave gifts while he was still living, and he sent them away from his son Isaac eastward, to the land of the East." Before lowering the body into the grave, they say:

> God, Sovereign who sits on a throne of mercy, acting with unbounded grace, forgiving the sins of Your people, one by one, as each comes before You, generously forgiving sinners and pardoning transgressors, acting charitably with every living thing: Do not repay them for their misdeeds. God, You taught us how to recite the thirteen attributes of your name; remember the promise implied in these thirteen attributes, which You first revealed to Moses, the humble one, so it is written: God descended in a cloud and stood beside him, and he called the name Adonai.

When the body is lowered into the grave they say:

> And God passed before him and he said, The Lord! The Lord! A God compassionate and gracious, slow to anger, abounding in kindness and faithfulness, extending kindness to the thousandth generation, forgiving iniquity, transgression, and sin. Forgive us our sins and iniquities.

Afterwards, they continue the regular sequence of the burial – *Tziduk HaDin* and the Great Kaddish.

According to the Kabbala, the *hakafot* protect the deceased; the circle they create is called the "*or hamekif*," the "encompassing light." The deceased requires protection, especially between death and the burial. Furthermore, throwing the coins is like an offering to the evil spirits, who take the coins and leave the soul in peace. Each time they go around, one or several coins are thrown, and the rest of the coins are given to charity. The book *Maavar Yabok* ("*Siftei Tzedek*," p. 115) attributes this practice to Hillel the Elder. (See also *Gesher HaḤayim* 15:1.)

The Yemenite custom is to walk around seven times and to recite an absolution in the name of the heavenly court, etc. At the conclusion, everyone says three times, "Everything is forgiven and absolved." They then say the verse, "But to Abraham's sons by concubines, Abraham gave gifts, etc." (*Halikhot Teiman, Minhagei Kevura VeAveilut,* p. 328; *Shulḥan Arukh HaMekutzar, Einei Yitzḥak, Yoreh De'ah* 180:16).

See also the **Suffering of the Grave; Ban (*Ḥerem*) – "His Seed Will Not Follow Him."**

Hashkava

This comes from the Aramaic word for eulogy, "*ashkavta,*" e.g., "*ashkavtiha deRebbi,*" "eulogy for Rebbi" (Ketubbot 103b). Nowadays, it refers to a prayer said by Sephardim for the deceased's soul, asking for true rest, forgiveness, atonement, and life in the world to come. It is generally recited at the funeral, and also when visiting the grave and on the Yahrzeit.

> Therefore, it is appropriate and is an obligation to pray for the deceased for thirty days, day and night, to remember them before God for the good and to recall the memory of their soul at least every Shabbat. This is the custom of the Sephardim, and the halakhic authorities praised this practice. It should be recited at least once a day during the *shloshim* – especially if the deceased was a Torah scholar, or had a place dedicated to Torah study, or supported a yeshiva – by their children or grandchildren or the prayer-leader (if the others are unable) for this undoubtedly gives joy to the soul. And this should be done at the end of the month and at the end of the year. The verses with the special psalms are fitting for requesting mercy for the deceased. (*Maavar Yabok,* "*Sefat Emet,*" ch. 21)

It is recommended that during the *Hashkava,* one should state the name of the deceased and his father's name (for a man) or mother's name (for a woman); some always use the mother's name. The local custom can be followed, and one should diverge from the local practice (*Yalkut Yosef* 32:3).

The deceased's name should include the name that most people called him when he was alive. If the person had a Jewish name but was known by a non-Jewish name, the latter name should also be mentioned in the *Hashkava* (*Yalkut Yosef*, ibid. 5).

It is not customary to recite the *Hashkava* for someone who died before reaching the age of thirteen; this is the Yemenite custom, as well. This is because the young person was not liable for punishment, and so we do not need to soften the judgment for the deceased.

See also ***El Maleh Raḥamim*; Recalling the Souls (*Hazkarat Neshamot*); *Yizkor*.**

Ḥevra Kaddisha

This is a group dedicated to preparing the deceased for burial. The name *ḥevra kaddisha* literally means "holy group." It is said about those who tend to the deceased that "they are the holy in the world" (Menaḥot 53:1). Another reason for this name is that they dedicate (*makdishim)* themselves to the deceased and their needs. On the other hand, the name "*kaddisha,*" "holy," is a euphemism since these individuals become impure by coming into contact with dead bodies.

The source for the idea of having a *ḥevra kaddisha* appears in the Talmud (Moed Katan 27b):

> When a person dies in a city, all of the residents of that city are prohibited from performing work. Rav Hamnuna once happened to come to a place called Darumata. He heard the sound of a shofar announcing that a person had died in the town. When he saw some people doing work he said to them: Let these people be under a ban. Is there not a dead person in town? They said to him: There are groups in the town, [responsible for dealing with the dead]. He said to them: If so, it is permitted.

The halakha ruled:

> [As long as there is] a dead person in town [awaiting burial], all the townspeople are forbidden [to engage] in work. And whosoever sees a corpse and does not attend to all its [burial] needs is subject to be placed under a ban. However, if there are associations in the town, each one of which attends to [the burial needs of] the dead on its [particular] day, it is permissible [for the others who are not required to attend to the burial needs, to engage in work] on the day which is not [appointed] for it [the association]. (*Shulhan Arukh, Yoreh De'ah* 343, and similarly in 361:2)

The *ḥevra kaddisha* thus enables everyone else to continue working and going about their regular lives, because its members tend to the needs of the deceased and the burial.

Members of the *ḥevra kaddisha* are not permitted to eat a meal before burying the dead (*Mishna Berura* 526:52).

Section 63 provides information and guidance for *ḥevra kaddisha* volunteers.

Ḥezkat Ḥayim

This refers to a person who is missing but was known to be alive – we presume that he is still alive, even though he is missing. He retains the status of one who is alive, even for an indefinite period of time. Unless new information is received, this presumption may not be changed.

This has significant ramifications. For example, if two witnesses testify that a person died and two others testify that the person is still alive, the person is not be mourned because he is presumed to still be living.

The Talmud discusses whether someone who has reached the age of eighty years old is still included under this assumption.

A *goses* is not subject to this presumption, because most terminally ill people will die. But one can presume that a sick person is alive, since most sick people live (Gittin 28a).

See also **Identifying the Body**.

Honor of the Living, Honor of the Deceased

This is translated from the Aramaic term, *"yikra deḤayey, yikra deShekhavey."* There is a debate in the Talmud regarding eulogies at a funeral: Are they for the honor of the deceased or the honor of the living? In other words, is the main purpose of the eulogy to show respect for the person who died or to give comfort to the mourners? The halakhic relevance of this question arises, for example, in a case where someone left instructions not to be eulogized. If eulogies are for the honor of the living, then the person should be eulogized. But if it is for the honor of the deceased, then the person's wish should be honored. The same is true with regard to the question of delaying the funeral so that the eulogies can be better prepared and more polished; if the eulogy is for the honor of the deceased, the burial should be delayed, but if it is for the honor of the living, it should not be delayed for this reason. The Talmud (Sanhedrin 46–47) concludes that eulogies are in honor of the deceased. And so, if someone left instructions not to be eulogized, the instructions should be followed. However, if someone gave instructions not to be buried, this is not followed, because burial is a mitzva, and failing to bury someone degrades the living, as well (Maimonides, *Mishneh Torah, Hilkhot Avel* 12:1; *Shulḥan Arukh, Yoreh De'ah* 348:2–3).

See also **Burial; Eulogy; Honoring the Deceased; Mitzva to Fulfill the Deceased's Wishes.**

Honoring the Deceased

The deceased's body, before he died, was a vessel for the soul; since the soul is part of the Divine, the body should be treated with respect.

The sages compared a Jewish person to a Torah scroll. Both represent a physical manifestation of the *Shekhina*. Thus, when someone is present when a Jew dies, he is obligated to tear his garment as though he has witnessed a Torah scroll being burned (Moed Katan 25a). We handle the body of a Jew, whose soul has left his body, in the same way that a Torah scroll is handled once it can no longer be used. Even the most insignificant body parts of the deceased are treated with respect, as are the parts of a Torah scroll.

There are many laws related to honoring the deceased: guarding, washing, and purifying the body; dressing the deceased in shrouds;

and the practices of the funeral and burial. It is forbidden to act in a frivolous manner in the presence of a dead body or in a cemetery. One should also refrain from eating or drinking in the presence of the dead body.

See also **Asking Forgiveness from the Deceased; Embalming; Guarding the Deceased; Honor of the Living, Honor of the Deceased; Mocking the Poor; The Coffin Yields Before a Bride.**

I Am the Atonement for His/Her Death (*Hareini Kaparat Mishkavo/ Mishkava*)

This is a phrase said if one is mourning for a parent, or one's rabbi, during the twelve months of mourning following the death. The person says it whenever mentioning the deceased or his memory.

The source for the phrase is in the Talmud (Kiddushin 31b):

> The Sages taught: One honors [his father] in his life and honors him in his death. How in his life?… How in his death? If he says a matter he heard from his [father's] mouth, he should not say: "So said Father." Rather, "So said Father, my teacher, may I be an atonement for his death." And this *halakha* applies within the twelve months. From this time onward, he says: "May his memory be for a blessing, for the life of the world to come."

And this is the halakha (*Shulḥan Arukh, Yoreh De'ah* 240:9, 242:28). For a parent, one says this phrase when one refers to or quotes the parent. *Yalkut Yosef* (39:1) explains why this obligation is specifically relevant to instances of quoting halakhic teachings in one's parent's name; if the son or daughter made a mistake and said a wrong halakha, the phrase indicates that punishment for this mistake shall be borne by the child and not the parent.

During the twelve-month period, one may also say "*Zikhrono/ zikhrona livrakha,*" "May his/her memory be a blessing" about a parent. But after the first year, one should not say "I am the atonement for his death," because the wicked are judged for only twelve months (*Siftei Cohen* 240:13).

In general, mourning practices for one's parents are more stringent than mourning for other relatives. A primary example of this is that mourning for other relatives lasts for thirty days and is stopped if there is a holiday, while mourning for a parent lasts for twelve months. This is out of the obligation to honor one's father and mother, an obligation that applies not only during their lifetime but also after their death.

The phrase, "I am atonement for his/her death," is an expression of dedication to one's parents, as Rashi explains (ad loc.): "All evil that was meant to befall them should befall me."

This phrase has become a general expression of affection for those for whom one is willing to give one's life. Thus, for example, Rabbi Yishmael said about the Jewish people, "The children of Israel – I am their atonement!" (Mishna Nega'im 2:1).

Identifying the Body

The Mishna (Yevamot 16:3) defines the parameters for identifying the dead: "One may only testify [that somebody has died on the basis] of the face, including the nose, even if there are [identifying] signs on his body and his clothes." Identification is done by sight by someone who knew the deceased and would recognize him, or by clear signs on his body (not by his clothes). The Talmud and halakhic literature include extensive discussions of these rules. Identifying the dead is very important, both for establishing the facts and also because of its halakhic implications, namely to permit the wife of the deceased to remarry and to know whether to sit shiva. The laws appear in Maimonides, *Mishneh Torah, Hilkhot Gerushin* 13:21 and *Shulḥan Arukh, Even HaEzer* 17:24.

See also ***Ḥezkat Ḥayim.***

Immediate Burial

The verse, "Miriam died there and was buried there" (Num. 20:1) teaches that burial should take place as soon after the death as possible, especially in the case of a woman (Moed Katan 28a). This is the halakha (*Shulḥan Arukh, Yoreh De'ah* 357). Therefore, all efforts should be made not to delay the funeral.

See also **Leaving the Body Overnight (*Halanat HaMet*).**

Impurity of a *Kohen*

A *kohen* is forbidden from becoming ritually impure through contact with a corpse, except for his seven relatives, for whom he is commanded to become impure: his father, mother, son, daughter, brother, unmarried sister (paternal siblings, not maternal siblings), and wife (Lev. 21:1–3; Yevamot 60a). For other relatives (such as maternal siblings or a married sister), even though he cannot become ritually impure, he does mourn for them. The principle here is that the *kohen* is obligated to become ritually impure to tend to the needs of the deceased and the burial, but for a married sister or half-siblings, the Torah places this obligation on the other relatives and not the *kohen*.

A *kohen* is obligated to become ritually impure for a dead person who has no one to bury him – a *met mitzva*. The obligation and permission to become impure applies up until the grave has covered. But it is forbidden for him to become impure during the shiva or when there is a visit to the grave.

Kohanim may not enter a tomb built over the grave of a righteous person. Although the Midrash (*Yalkut Shimoni*, Prov., 544) writes that the righteous do not cause ritual impurity when they die, we do not rely on this idea. The *Tosafot* (Bava Metzia 114b s.v. "*Mahu*") wrote that Elijah the prophet, who was a *kohen* buried Rabbi Akiva and became impure because no one else was able to bury him, not because the righteous do not cause ritual impurity. A female from a priestly family is not prohibited from becoming ritually impure since it says, "Aaron's sons," not his daughters. A *kohen*'s wife who is pregnant is permitted to enter a tomb over a grave (*Siftei Cohen, Yoreh De'ah* 371:1).

According to Maimonides, the *kohen*'s prohibition against contact with the ritually impure is bypassed with regard to his relatives but is not released entirely (*Mishneh Torah, Hilkhot Avel* 2:6, 15). According to Nahmanides, however, the prohibition is completely lifted when a relative must be buried, since the relative could not be buried without the *kohen* coming into contact with the ritually impure, and so the Torah had to make the prohibition entirely permissible (*Torat HaAdam*).

These laws are elaborated in *Shulḥan Arukh, Yoreh De'ah* 369–374.

See also **Cemetery; Ritual Impurity of the Deceased**.

Is Mourning a Rabbinic or a Torah Commandment?

There are different opinions as to whether mourning is from the Torah (*deOraita*) or rabbinic (*DeRabbanan*):

Some say that mourning is primarily a Torah obligation (Y. Moed Katan 3:5). This is derived from Joseph, about whom it says, "And he mourned his father for seven days" (Gen. 50:10) and from Moses, who commanded Aaron and his sons: "You shall remain at the entrance to the Tent of Meeting day and night for seven days, keeping the Lord's charge" (Lev. 8:35). Just as with regard to Nadav and Avihu (the sons of Aaron who died on the eighth day), God kept His world for seven days, so shall you observe seven days for your brothers. In the Yerushalmi Talmud (ibid.), some derived it from a verse that precedes the beginning of the flood: "And on the seventh day" (Gen. 7:10); this refers to seven days of mourning for Methuselah, because of whom the flood was postponed. (This idea is mentioned in Sanhedrin 108b and *Avot DeRabbi Natan* 32.)

According to most opinions (*Geonim*, Maimonides, the Rif, Nahmanides, and the Raavad), only the first day of mourning – usually the day of death and burial – is a Torah commandment, while the other days are not; it is said that Moses established seven days of mourning. This is true regarding the relatives explicitly mentioned in the Torah (Lev. 21); but mourning for relatives that were added by the sages is a rabbinic commandment and not a Torah one, including on the first day (*Shulḥan Arukh, Yoreh De'ah* 398). See also **Seven Relatives**.

There are opinions that even the first day of mourning is not a Torah commandment, rather that *aninut* is from the Torah and mourning is rabbinic (Rabbenu Tam and the Rosh). One practical implication of this difference of opinion is whether mourning should be observed on the second day of Yom Tov in the Diaspora: The second day of Yom Tov is a rabbinic commandment; if mourning is a Torah obligation, it would take precedence over the rabbinic commandment to rejoice on the second day of Yom Tov. But if mourning is rabbinic, then it does not override the second day of Yom Tov, and one should not mourn on that day.

The *Shulḥan Arukh* (*Yoreh De'ah* 398, 399:13) ruled that the principle of mourning is from the Torah, and therefore one should mourn on the second day of Yom Tov (the *Shulḥan Arukh* also rules this way in *Oraḥ Ḥayim* 548:3). However, the *Shulḥan Arukh* also writes that the accepted custom is not to mourn for anyone on the second day of Yom Tov, even if it is the day of death and burial. The Rema writes this, as well – that this is the basic custom, and it should not be changed.

(Further explanation and discussion of this is brought in *Gesher HaḤayim*, Vol. 2, ch. 15.)

Judgment on the Day of One's Death

> "He is just and righteous." This teaches that when a person dies, all his deeds are enumerated before him and he is told: You did such and such, in such and such a place, on such and such a day, and he says: Yes. And they say to him: Sign, and he signs, as it is stated: "He makes the hand of every man sign" (Job 37:7). And not only that, he declares the judgment just and says to them: You have judged me well, to fulfill that which is stated: "That You may be justified when You speak and be right when You judge" (Ps. 51:6). (Taanit 11a)
>
> Just as a person's merits and sins are weighed at the time of his death, so, too, the sins of every inhabitant of the world together with his merits are weighed on the festival of Rosh HaShana. (Maimonides, *Mishneh Torah, Hilkhot Teshuva* 3:3)
>
> We now need to explain the judgment that a person is judged; our sages said that a person is judged when he dies, as it says in the first chapter of Taanit (11a), that all a person's deeds are enumerated before him and he is told: You did such and such, in such and such a place, on such and such a day, and he says: Yes, etc.…. And not only that, he declares that the judgment is just, and says to them: You have judged me well, etc. And it appears in many other places, as well. If we say that a person is judged on Rosh HaShana and the judgment is sealed on Yom Kippur, then the judgment at the time of death is only for things they did from the last Rosh HaShana until the death – but our sages explicitly stated that all a person's actions are enumerated before him. Our sages also mentioned that the day of judgment is in the future, at the time of the resurrection of the dead, as it is stated (Sanhedrin 107b): The generation of the flood have no

share in the world to come and will not stand in judgment.... The people of Sodom have no share in the world to come... but they will stand in judgment. And in the Midrash, this judgment day is called the Great Day of Judgment.

Rather, the idea is the following: On Rosh HaShana, everyone in the world is judged, individually, about worldly matters, if they will merit to receive life, peace, wealth, and honor, or whether they will die in the coming year, or suffer pain or poverty. But the soul is not judged on whether it will merit the Garden of Eden and eternal life in the next world, or suffer hell and destruction in the next world.... And thus in the Talmud it says: They said that three books are opened on Rosh HaShana, the utterly righteous are immediately inscribed and sealed for life, completely evil individuals are immediately inscribed and sealed for death. They mentioned life and death here, but not hell or eternal life in the world to come.... The rule here is that Rosh HaShana is the judgment day for this world, and at the time of death, it is the soul's judgment day for the next world and the world of souls. At that point, all of one's actions are enumerated before God, whether one's soul merits to the highest level of the Garden of Eden or the lower level, or whatever level one has reached, or whether the soul will go to hell and suffer greatly. Hence, we learn that there is a judgment day for the body and a different judgment day for the soul.

There is another judgment day that is a day of judgment for both body and soul, described by the prophets: "That day is at hand, burning like an oven. All the arrogant and all the doers of evil shall be straw, and the day that is coming" (Mal. 3:19). And it says, "Lo, I will send the prophet Elijah to you before the coming of the awesome, fearful day of the Lord" (ibid. 23). That day refers to the resurrection of the dead which is called the Great Day of Judgment, and all people from the beginning of creation will be judged in both body and soul, if they are worthy of resurrection and joy of the body and soul for all the time ahead, or whether they will not live and will remain in hell or be punished even more severely. This is as mentioned in the

Mishna (Sanhedrin 107b) that there are those who do not stand trial and those that do stand trial, and as mentioned in the Talmud (Rosh HaShana 16b) regarding the three groups on judgment day: The completely righteous are immediately inscribed and sealed for eternal life in the world to come; the completely wicked are immediately inscribed and sealed for hell, and the verse says: "Many of those who sleep in the ground will awake for eternal life" (Dan. 12:2). Maimonides wrote the following in [*Mishneh Torah,*] *Hilkhot Teshuva*: "Just as a person's merits and sins are weighed at the time of his death, so, too, the sins of every inhabitant of the world together with his merits are weighed on Rosh HaShana." And the *baraita* also wrote about the three groups on judgment day with regard to the judgment of Rosh HaShana, and it appears from his words that he did not make a distinction. (Nahmanides' discourse for Rosh HaShana, brought in *Kitvei HaRamban,* Vol. 1, p. 221)

See also **Resurrection of the Dead.**

Kaddish

Kaddish is a prayer of praise to God. The text is in Aramaic, which made Kaddish more accessible to ordinary people in the Talmudic period, when the prayer was first introduced; at the time, the average person was not conversant in Hebrew. In the Talmud, Kaddish is called "*Yehe Shmei Raba Mevorakh,*" "May His great name be blessed," which is the central praise in Kaddish.

There are ten distinct expressions of praise in the Kaddish: *yitgadal veYitkadash,* exalted and hallowed; *yitbarakh veYishtabaḥ veYitpaar veYitromem veYitnaseh veYithadar veYit'aleh veYithalal,* blessed, praised, glorified, exalted, extolled, honored, adored, and lauded. The ten expressions correspond to the ten statements through which God created the world. Some identify five more praises in the Kaddish text: *Veyamlikh,* He will restore reign; *birkhata veshirata tushbeḥata veneḥemata,* blessings, hymns, praises, and consolations. When these five are added to the first ten praises, the number corresponds to the fifteen psalms of the Song of Ascents in the Book of Psalms.

In the Kaddish, the congregation answers, "May His great name be blessed forever and to all eternity." In the Aramaic ("*Yehe shmei raba mevorakh leolam uleolmei almaya*"), there are seven words and twenty-eight letters; these numbers correspond to the number of words and letters in the first verse in Genesis. Based on this idea, it is said that one who answers, "May His great name be blessed forever and to all eternity" – is like a partner to God in the act of Creation.

See Sec. 57, "Kaddish" for more about the connection between Kaddish and mourning and the different types of Kaddish – Half Kaddish, Full Kaddish, Mourner's Kaddish, *Kaddish Titkabel*, Rabbis' Kaddish, Great Kaddish. There are many explanations for the different types of Kaddish and the different versions (See, for example, *Sefer HaKaddish*; *Gesher HaḤayim*, Ch 30; "*HaSiddur VeHaTefilla*" by Rabbi Steinsaltz, etc.).

Kiss of Death

This phrase has two meanings. One is an expression that describes a painless death:

> Nine hundred and three types of death were created in the world... The most difficult of all is croup [*askara*], the easiest is the kiss [of death]. Croup is like a thorn in wool fleece, which, when pulled out backwards [tears the wool]. Some say that croup is like ropes at the entrance to the esophagus, [which would be nearly impossible to insert and excruciating to remove]. The kiss of death is like drawing a hair from milk. (Berakhot 8a)

The second meaning of this phrase is a reference to the deaths of lofty righteous individuals who died in an exalted manner – not at the hands of the Angel of Death, but directly by God:

> The Sages taught: There were six people over whom the Angel of Death had no sway, and they are: Abraham, Isaac, and Jacob, Moses, Aaron, and Miriam. Abraham, Isaac, and Jacob, as it is written with regard to them, [respectively]: "With everything,"

> "From everything," "Everything"; Moses, Aaron, and Miriam, as it is written with regard to them: "By the mouth of the Lord" (Num. 33:38; Deut. 34:5). But with regard to Miriam it is not written: "By the mouth of the Lord." Rabbi Elazar says: Miriam also died with a kiss. (Bava Batra 17a)

Rashi explained, "Over whom the Angel of Death had no sway": They died from the *Shekhina*'s kiss.

The result of this, according to the Zohar, is that the bodies of the righteous do not become impure:

> Rabbi Elazar said: Anyone who studies Torah with the right intentions does not die by the evil inclination, the snake, or the Angel of Death. Rather, they die with a kiss. And therefore, the bodies of the righteous who study Torah do not become impure. They are pure, like Elijah who stood in the entrance of graves even though he was a *kohen*, since the righteous do not become impure when they die; a spirit of impurity does not dwell upon them. (Zohar, *Vayishlaḥ* 168:1)

Nahmanides in his commentary on the Torah (Num. 19:1) wrote: "The reason for the impurity of death is the snake, because those who die by a kiss do not become impure, as it says – the righteous do not make others impure."

Nahmanides' words are clarified by Recanati:

> The reason for the impurity of death is the Angel of Death, who placed toxicity and impurity inside the person. But whoever dies through the kiss of death dies because of God's word, and impurity does not reside in his death. And therefore, the air does not become lacking since they kept their souls and were not led astray by their evil inclination, and they remained pure and clean as when God gave them breathe. (Notes of Rabbi Cheval, ad loc., *Mosad HaRav Kook* edition)

The book *Maavar Yabok* explains this, as well:

> The Angel of Death does not wield power over those who learn Torah for its own sake, rather they die directly by God. And this is a kiss – their soul cleaves to the *Shekhina*. Hence the righteous do not cause impurity when they die, as it says: "On the day that Rebbi died, the priesthood was cancelled," meaning that the *kohanim* dealt with his body because the spirit of impurity did not reside over him. ("*Siftei Renanot*," ch. 3)

Rabbi Nebenzahl notes: We do not rely on this idea for the practical halakha.

Kissing the Deceased

The topic of kissing the deceased is not a halakhic matter, but one that is discussed in the hidden mystical teachings of Kabbala. We believe it is relevant to offer a passage from the book *Maavar Yabok* (a book that addresses Kabbalistic aspects of death) because mourners often wonder about this. We must highlight the fact not all rabbis accept these Kabbalistic elements. As the Talmud (Pesaḥim 110b) states: "Whoever is particular is particular and whoever is not particular is not particular, but one must be cautious." That is to say, one who is concerned about these matters should be careful about them. But if one is not concerned about these matters, Heaven is also not exacting about them with him.

> One who had a son or daughter who died should not kiss him or her, even though we find that a son kisses his father – that Joseph kissed Jacob; and also in the Midrash (Genesis Rabba 65:18) on the verse: "Come here and I will kiss you, my son," Isaac said to Jacob – Kiss me in my burial and no one else should kiss me. It is written in the book *Tzror HaMor* that we learn from here about the departing kiss, a person should kiss his deceased when he leaves him. Nevertheless, a child is a different matter; a mother should also not kiss her child who has died, as this may shorten the lives of her other children.
>
> And one should not say to his deceased that one will come after them, nor hold their hand that they should lead them – for

> one must never open one's mouth to Satan. (*Maavar Yabok, "Sefat Emet,"* ch. 11.)

It thus appears that one should not kiss one's deceased children but that one may kiss other relatives who have died (*Shulḥan Arukh HaMekutzar, Einei Yitzḥak, Yoreh De'ah* 179:7, quoting from *Sefer Ḥasidim* and the will of Rabbi Judah the Hasid). However, the *Or HaḤayim* addresses this in his commentary on the Torah, on the verse, "Joseph flung himself upon his father's face and wept over him and kissed him" (Gen 50:1); he explains: "He kissed him, but one should not do so for another dead person, for the corpse is filled with impurity, and this impurity rises up to the heavens and will adversely affect the soul of the person who kissed him; but Joseph could kiss Jacob since he was still alive and only looked as though he were dead." Therefore, one should not kiss any dead person, and this is the halakha according to *Nitei Gavriel*, Vol. 1, 4:17.

Leader of the Household (*Gadol HaBayit*)

This refers to the family member who leads the rest of the family in issues related to mourning when a relative has died. It is the mourner who makes decisions about the deceased and the burial, not necessarily the eldest member of the family.

If someone did not know that a relative had died and arrived during the shiva at the house of mourning – if the leader of the household was there, sitting shiva, then the newcomer joins the others in sitting shiva. The newcomer finishes shiva when the others do, even if he only joined them on the seventh day, as long as they had not yet gotten up from shiva. If they had already gotten up from shiva, the newcomer must start counting the seven days of shiva for himself.

Four conditions must be met in order for this relative to join the other mourners in their shiva:

- He did not know about the death or did not start sitting shiva until coming there.
- The leader of the household is among the other mourners (even if the leader of the household had sat shiva and left the house).

- The mourners are sitting shiva in the same city where the deceased died or was buried.
- The newcomer had been no more than one day's journey away at the time of the burial.

If all four of these conditions are not met, the newcomer counts the seven days of shiva from the time he learned of the death.

If the body is moved from one city to another and some of the relatives are staying in the first city while others accompany the deceased to the other city, the rule is as follows: Those that remain in the first city begin counting shiva after parting from the deceased, and those continuing to escort the body start shiva after the burial. But if the leader of the household is continuing to escort the deceased and will not be returning to the other relatives, they all follow the leader of the household and start shiva after the burial. This is only the case if the place of burial is no more than three-days' journey away.

(*Tur* and *Shulḥan Arukh, Yoreh De'ah* 375; *Gesher HaḤayim* 19:5; *Encyclopedia Talmudit, "Gadol HaBayit"*; and see above, Sec. 48, "Notice of Death After Others Began Sitting Shiva.")

Learning Mishna

It is customary to study Mishna to elevate the deceased's soul.

Human beings are comprised of both a soul – a spiritual, eternal dimension – and a physical, temporary dimension. Studying timeless ideas stands in complete contrast to the physical body of the deceased, which has now begun to decompose and fade away. By engaging in Torah study, we attempt to transcend the temporal physical realm and move closer to the eternal spiritual one. The letters of the word "Mishna" can be rearranged to spell the word "*neshama*," soul. In Judaism, it is considered a merit for the deceased when the living engage in studying Torah; if a person's death and the study that it leads to cause people to improve their ways, it is also considered a merit for the deceased.

Any mishna and any Torah study can be learned to elevate the deceased's soul. The common practice, however, is to study the mishnas that spell out the letters of the deceased's name (based on the letter that begins the specific mishna); or passages of Mishna from *Pirkei*

Avot (Ethics of the Fathers), a tractate that deals with ethics and good behavior; or passages of Mishna from Tractate Mikvaot, which concerns matters of purification. Though the dead body causes impurity, studying this tractate is seen as a sort of rectification for the deceased's departure. See Part 7, "*Neshama*," for passages of Mishna that spell out "*neshama*" and those that conclude with the word "*tahara*," purity.

Some have the custom that, on every Motza'ei Shabbat of the twelve-month mourning period, they study chapter twenty-four of Tractate Kelim; each mishna in this chapter concludes with the word "*tahara*." Some people divide up the tractates of Mishna among different people so that all six orders of the Mishna will be completed by the end of *shloshim* or the end of the year.

See also **Elevating the Soul.**

Leaving the Body Overnight (*Halanat HaMet*)

This concept prohibits leaving the body overnight; it should be buried on the day of the death. This is deduced from the verse, "You must not let his corpse remain on the stake overnight but must bury him the same day" (Deut. 21:23). Even though the verse refers to a person put to death by hanging, this principle was applied to all.

> It is a positive commandment to bury the body of an executed person on the day of his execution, as it says: "But must bury him the same day." And from here, the sages deduced that for all people of Israel, it is a mitzva to bury them on the day they die. (Maimonides, *Sefer HaMitzvot*, Mitzva 231)

The Talmud (Sanhedrin 47a; Tractate Smaḥot, sec. 11) taught that the prohibition against leaving the body applies when it is degrading to the dead, like when it is hanging from a tree. But if it was done for the deceased's honor, then it is permitted. And this is the halakha (*Shulḥan Arukh, Yoreh De'ah* 357:1). In Jerusalem, the custom is to be stringent about not letting the body lie overnight (Bava Kamma 82b; *Tosefta* Nega'im 6:2).

The reason for this prohibition is respect for the dead, because letting the body lie would be disrespectful. This is related to the following verse containing a phrase that shares the root of the word "*halanat*": "Man does not abide (*bal yalin*) honor; he is like the beasts that perish" (Ps. 49:13). The body of a human being, the most honorable of creatures, should not be left out; if it would be left out, the person would be akin to an animal (Zohar, *Naso*).

This principle requires that there be a prompt burial, and this has a positive psychological benefit to it: Before the deceased has been buried, the family carries a great burden. When the body is brought to its resting place, there is psychological relief for the family (*Darka Shel HaYahadut BeMavet U'BeAveilut*, p. 40).

There is a distinction made between one's parents and other relatives in terms of this principle: "For all other relatives, the quicker they are buried, the more commendable; but for a parent, this is shameful, unless it was Erev Shabbat or Erev Yom Tov, or if rain was pouring down on the body" (Smaḥot, ch. 9). This is the halakha in the *Shulḥan Arukh* (*Yoreh De'ah* 357:2). The *Siftei Cohen* explains this distinction: "Since it is not common to eulogize at length for one's other relatives, it is more respectful to bury them promptly, rather than have the deceased left out for a long time without being eulogized. But for one's mother and father, whom one is obligated to eulogize and bewail, it is shameful to bury them quickly." Today, the custom is to bury everyone as quickly as possible and not to distinguish between parents and other relatives (*Pnei Barukh* 4:10, in the name of the book *Beit Hillel*).

Out of respect, a woman's bier is not set down in the open street since it may lead to her being degraded (*Shulḥan Arukh, Yoreh De'ah* 355).

See also **Burial; Honoring the Dead; Immediate Burial.**

Letting the Hair Grow

This refers to the prohibition on mourners not to have their hair cut. It is deduced from the warning given to Aaron's sons: "Do not let your hair become unkempt" (Lev. 10:6). Aaron's sons were instructed not to observe practices of mourning – not to let their hair grow unkempt, but rather to cut their hair – because their mourning occurred during the dedication of the Tabernacle; the instructions they were given describe the exception to the rule. It was deduced from here that all other mourners do not cut their hair but let it grow unkempt (*Tur* and *Shulḥan Arukh, Yoreh De'ah* 390).

Life Expectancy

The sages debated the question of whether a person's life expectancy is predetermined or not.

The verse, "I am one hundred and twenty years old today" (Deut. 31:2) is explained by the Talmud (Rosh HaShana 11a) as follows: "Today my days and years are complete. To teach you that the Holy One, Blessed be He, sits and fulfills the years of the righteous from day to day and from month to month, as it is stated: 'The number of your days I will fulfill' (Ex. 23:26)." For on that day, Moses reached the age of 120. Similarly, it is said that great righteous people are born and die on the same date.

> I will now discuss the end of man's days, and I say that the Creator allotted a certain amount of time, as it says: "The number of your days I will fulfill." And He said to the master of the prophets [Moses], "The time is drawing near for you to die" (Deut. 31:14). And to one of the righteous [King David], He said, "When your days are done and you lie with your fathers" (II Sam. 7:12). I say that He adds and subtracts from this allocation and He knows how much time He will leave the soul and the body. His knowledge is not different from the truth, but that allotment that is increased or decreased is the amount of time that the body is given strength for its existence. From the beginning of one's creation, it is clear that one has limited forces, some more and some less, and the amount of time that these continue to exist is the amount of time a person lives. He can add to them, and they will exist with the seventy [years] thirty more and He can weaken them and they will disintegrate at forty.... For the body's foundation is built for seventy [years], and He adds thirty or removes thirty.
>
> How do I know that He can add or subtract? From the verse, "The fear of the Lord prolongs life, while the years of the wicked will be shortened" (Prov. 10:27); and it says of one

> of the righteous [Ḥizkiyahu]: "I will add fifteen years to your days" (II Kings 20:6). And many of the rewards are described saying, "That your days may be long" (Ex. 20:11; Deut. 5:16, 6:2, 25:15) and the like; and regarding some of the wicked, it says: "The Lord struck down all the first-born in the land of Egypt" (Ex. 12:29), "Those who died of the plague" (Num. 25:9), etc. If they had died according to their allocated time, the plague would not have occurred due to their sins, and Pinḥas would not have been able to accomplish anything [in stopping the plague]. The prophet showed that the plague befalls someone instead of him living out until the end of his days: "His time will come and he will die, or he will go down to battle and perish" (I Sam. 26:10, David said this about Saul).
>
> I say that not every righteous person receives more days and not every wicked person loses days, but only according to the Creator's will and according to the righteous person. Those righteous people who did not receive more days will receive a reward in the next world; and the wicked who were not cut off will receive their punishment in the end of days, as is written, "For there is a time for every experience and for every happening" (Eccl. 3:17). (Rabbi Saadia Gaon's *HaNivḥar BeEmunot VeDeot*, Article 6, ch. 6)

See also the introduction to Rabbi Ovadia Sforno's commentary on Genesis. See also **Angel of Death; Death and Adam.**

Luz

The *luz* bone is considered to be a "spiritual bone" in a person's spine. It is the primordial source of life from which the person was formed and is the place from which he will be recreated at the resurrection of the dead. The *luz* is a concentrated kernel of life that is impossible to destroy.

> "The Lord said: I will blot out man" (Gen. 6:7), even the *luz* in the spine from which God forms man, in the future will be destroyed (in the flood).

Adrinus asked Rabbi Joshua ben Ḥananya – From where does God grow a person in the future? He replied – From the *luz* of the spine. He said – How do you know? He replied – Bring it to me and I will show you. They ground it in a millstone and it did not become ground, they burned it in fire and it did not burn, they put it in water and it did not disintegrate, they pounded it with a hammer and the hammer split, but nothing happened to [the *luz*]. (Genesis Rabba 28:3; Leviticus Rabba 18:1)

A part of the body called "*naskoy*" is a bone within a person that does not benefit from food, except for on Motza'ei Shabbat. (*Beit Yosef, Oraḥ Ḥayim* 300, quoted in the *Mishna Berura* and the *Arukh HaShulḥan*).

The Kabbalists wrote that a person has a bone that does not benefit from food apart from the meal on Motza'ei Shabbat, and this bone remains in the grave and does not decompose; it is called "*luz*," or "*naskoy*" or "*Betuel*." The body is formed from this bone in the resurrection, specifically for Jews, as it says: "While you, who held fast to the Lord your God, are all alive today" (Deut. 4:4). (*Ben Ish Ḥai, Parashat Vayishlaḥ*, Second Year, Halakha 27)

Our sages said that a person has a bone called the *luz*, and death has no control over it; from this bone, a person will be formed at the resurrection, for all the bones decompose except for this one. This is the explanation of the verse, "Keeping all his bones intact, one of them is not broken" (Ps. 34:21). [A simple reading of the second half of this line would be translated, "Not one of them being broken."] God preserves all of one's bones for the future resurrection of the dead from "one of them," which is the *luz*, which "is not broken" at any time; all the bones will be formed from it.

The reason that death does not affect this bone is because it did not benefit from the fruit that Adam ate. All of one's organs and limbs benefit from whatever Adam ate during the six days of the week except for that bone, which only benefited from what he ate on Motza'ei Shabbat. Adam ate from the tree on the sixth day of creation, and so this bone did not benefit from the fruit; therefore death has no control over it. (*Menaḥem Aveilim*, the letter *Tet*, "*Teḥiyat HaMetim*")

See also **Resurrection.**

Maavar Yabok

The literal meaning of this Kabbalistic expression is the crossing of Yabok. It is based on a phrase that appears in the verses about Jacob's passage when he returned from Ḥaran to the Land of Canaan. It says about Jacob: "He crossed the ford of the Yabok. Jacob was left alone. And a man wrestled with him until the break of dawn" (Gen. 32:22–24). In this passage, Jacob had to battle with an angel until dawn. In the Kabbala, the phrase denotes a difficult transition. There is light at the end of the difficult transition, as with Jacob who fought all night long: "The sun rose upon him as he passed Penuel." The idea is relevant in various contexts, for example, at the entrance to a house; this is a vulnerable spot that can at times presents challenge, and so there is a mitzva to affix a mezuza there. The merit of the mitzva is meant to provide support and protection as people transition from inside the home, where it is safe, to the outside. It is also meant to protect the house itself from the threat of external forces.

Birth is another example of this since it involves a precarious, difficult transition for both mother and baby. The Mishna (Shabbat 2:6) writes that women die in childbirth for three transgressions: If they are not careful with the laws of menstruation; if they are not careful to separate some dough when baking bread to give to the *kohen*; and if they are not careful with the lighting of the Shabbat candles. These three mitzvot occur at significant points of transition: The laws of menstruation involve important transitions for a couple, from purity to impurity and from impurity to purity. Separating the dough marks the transition of grain in its raw form, which is the food of animals, to bread, a food that is basic to human nourishment and represents man's capacity to create his food. Lighting the Shabbat candles is the transition from the six days of the week to Shabbat – from the days of work and labor, to the spiritual, holy time. Each of these transitions involves a mitzva that imbues our human efforts with spiritual significance and divinity. The merit of the mitzva provides protection and safety. If we consider the positive implication of the Mishna's statement, we might say that the care a woman takes in these mitzvot, which represent difficult transitions, affords her protection when she herself is in the birth process – a difficult and potentially dangerous life-giving transition.

Like in birth, at the moment of death, there soul needs support in its transition from one state to the next. Some of the customs around death and the funeral and burial, especially those customs based on the Kabbala, are related to helping the deceased and the soul through this transition.

The Kabbala explains that the combination of the letters of God's names add up to make the letters KYB. These can be rearranged as YaBoK. "And the holy name of Yabok is also alluded to [by the first letters] in the verse '*Ya'anenu BeYom Koreinu*' ('He will answer us on the day we cry out to Him'" (*Maavar Yabok*, "*Siftei Renanot*," ch. 5).

See also **Ban (*Ḥerem*) – His Seed Will Not Follow Him; Fear of Judgment; *Hakafot*; Song of Afflictions; Standing and Sitting (*Maamad* and *Moshav*).**

May God Comfort You Among the Other Mourners of Zion and Jerusalem (and May You Know No More Sorrow)

In Hebrew: "*HaMakom yenaḥem etḥem betokh shaar avlei Zion veYerushalayim.*" In the Ashkenazic tradition, these are the words of comfort that people say to the mourners when departing from them. In Hebrew, the custom is to add: "*velo tosifu ledaava od*" – "And may you know no more sorrow."

There is an enduring connection between individual Jews and the larger community. At the height of a bride and groom's personal joy, we declare, "If I forget you, O Jerusalem, let my right hand wither; let my tongue stick to my palate if I cease to think of you, if I do not keep Jerusalem in memory even at my happiest hour" (Ps. 137:5); a glass is broken to remember the destruction of the Temple. When it comes to people's personal mourning, as well, we remember Jerusalem: "May God comfort you among the other mourners of Zion and Jerusalem."

There is a deep symbolic principle expressed in the connection between the national and the individual: Every personal milestone, such as the *ḥuppa* and *kiddushin* at a wedding, is seen as part of the realization of constructing the national home; it is part of the redemption and the ingathering of the exiles. Accordingly, the sages said that anyone who causes the bride and groom to rejoice, it is as if he has restored one of the ruins of Jerusalem. The Talmud (Berakhot 6a) based this on the verses in Jeremiah (33:10–13):

> Thus said the Lord: Again there shall be heard in this place, which you say is ruined, without man or beast – in the towns of Judah and the streets of Jerusalem that are desolate, without man, without inhabitants, without beast – the sound of mirth and gladness, the voice of bridegroom and bride, the voice of those who cry, "Give thanks to the Lord of Hosts, for the Lord is good, for His kindness is everlasting!" as they bring thanksgiving offerings to the House of the Lord. For I will restore the fortunes of the land as of old – said the Lord.

These verses and, in keeping with them, our sages, connect the individual building with the national building.

This relationship is not only present in times of joy but also in times of mourning and sorrow. Every individual's mourning is part of the national mourning, and therefore the mourner is comforted with the words, "May God comfort you among the other mourners of Zion and Jerusalem."

See also **Comforting the Mourners.**

May You Be Comforted from Heaven

In Hebrew: "*Min haShamayim tenuḥamu.*" In the Sephardic tradition, these are the words said when taking leave of the mourners.

See also **Comforting the Mourners; May God Comfort You Among the Other Mourners of Zion and Jerusalem.**

Meal of Condolence

In Hebrew, *Seudat Havraah.* The meal of condolence is the first meal that is served to the mourners when they return from the funeral. The

Tanakh mentions that the people brought a meal to King David after Avner ben Ner was killed (II Sam. 3:35). From the case of the prophet Ezekiel, who was told not to mourn when his wife died, the sages derived that it is forbidden for mourners to eat their own food on the first day. Ezekiel was told, "Do not eat the bread of comforters" (Ezek. 24:17), i.e., that he should not eat the comforting meal. Ezekiel was an exception to the rule, and thus it teaches that a mourner usually eats a meal brought by other people (Moed Katan 27b).

This is a time when the mourners are too upset to eat, distraught over the relative's death. We therefore emphasize their most basic need – eating – at the beginning of the mourning. Another aspect of the meal of condolence is that the mourners' community participates in preparing it. The meal is an opportunity for community members to offer a type of condolence. Some have given another reason for this meal, one that implies the opposite: Our sages said that whoever eats from the table of others', his world is darkened; this is the situation of the mourner.

The halakhot regarding the meal of condolence can be found in *Shulḥan Arukh, Yoreh De'ah* 378 and in this book in ch. 9, "Meal of Condolence (*Seudat Havraah*)."

The custom in Jerusalem is to hold a meal for the *ḥevra kaddisha* after they finish the burial, to emphasize that those in charge of the burial may not eat a full meal before the burial (*Gesher HaḤayim* 33:2, 2).

Me'arat HaMakhpela

Also known as Tomb of the Patriarchs, this is the burial cave where Adam and Eve and the forefathers and foremothers – Abraham and Sarah, Isaac and Rebecca, and Jacob and Leah – are buried. In the Kabbala, Me'arat HaMakhpela is considered the entrance to the Garden of Eden and the place where souls transition from this world to the next. Though we cannot claim to fully grasp these deep mysteries, we can cautiously offer a small taste of what has already been printed in the holy books.

The first person to discover Me'arat HaMakhpela was Adam:

> God removed Adam up above all the lands, into the universe, where the Land of Israel was, in Hebron. He carved a grave for

> him there and made a cave in front of the cave adjacent to the Garden of Eden. And that was where he was buried, as were Abraham, Isaac, Jacob and the mothers. Rabbi Kisma said – Me'arat HaMakhpela is close to the entrance of the Garden of Eden. When Eve died, Adam buried her there and smelled the fragrance of the Garden of Eden. He wanted to dig more; a heavenly voice was heard and said – Enough! He did not dig anymore and he was buried there. (*Zohar HaḤadash*, Ruth, 79d, Sulam edition 414)

After many years, the location was forgotten and covered over, but it was revealed to Abraham:

> And none knew about it until Abraham came and entered and saw it and smelled the fragrance of the Garden of Eden and heard the angels saying: Adam is buried here, and Abraham, Isaac, and Jacob should be buried here. He saw the candle burning and exited. He immediately desired that place.
>
> Rabbi Huna said: Before Abraham came, many wanted to be buried there, and the angels protected the place; the burning candle would be seen there and they could not enter, until Abraham entered and purchased it. (*Zohar HaḤadash*, Ruth, ibid., Sulam edition 415–416)

Me'arat HaMakhpela, the entrance to the Garden of Eden, is the place where souls ascend to the higher realm:

> When souls leave this world, they come to Me'arat HaMakhpela, which is the entrance to the Garden of Eden, and they meet Adam and the forefathers who are there. If the soul is worthy, then they rejoice with it and open the doors, and the soul enters. If not, the soul is pushed out. If it is worthy, the soul enters the Garden of Eden. When it enters, it dwells there and wears a garment like that which it wore in this world. (*Targum Zohar, Lekh Lekha* 95)

> There are seven entryways for the souls of the righteous to enter the highest level, and there are guards at each entrance. The first entrance is where the soul enters Me'arat HaMakhpela, which is adjacent to the Garden of Eden. And Adam guards it. If the soul merits it, he announces: Clear a path, come in peace! (*Zohar Ḥadash, Midrash HaNe'elam, Noaḥ* 21:1)

Naturally this view of Me'arat HaMakhpela cannot be taken at face value; it is an allusion, an allegory, a deep mystical secret. What is the meaning of the "entrance to the Garden of Eden"? How can a physical place, the field and cave, be the entrance to the Garden of Eden, which is a spiritual place where souls are refined? The Kabbalists have explored and explained this point. We offer some brief lines on the subject:

> The intention is not that the Garden of Eden is under the earth's ground – God forbid one should believe so. But one can, through the physical medium of the Cave, be slowly purified until one cleaves to the spiritual, and the spiritual cleaving can be found there. (Rabbi Moshe Cordovero, *Or HaḤokhma* on Zohar, *Parashat Bereshit* 127b)

> Even though they ascribed a place to the Garden, that it was in the East – as it says, "In the Garden of Eden from the East" – this is only a parable; the Garden is spread across the entire world, and one side of it comes close to this world. And there is its essence – which binds the body to the soul, and from there it spreads to the entire world, even facing our world. Me'arat HaMakhpela is the entrance through which the souls enter. But it is not that the Garden is under the ground, rather from there the physical enters the spiritual. (Rabbi Abraham Azulai, *Ḥesed LeAvraham, Maayan HaḤamishi,* 44)

> Hebron is called by this name because of the connection (*hitḥabrut*) of the Cave with the higher world, as we know, since

it is the entrance to the Garden of Eden. (Rabbi Moshe Alshikh, *Parashat Ḥayei Sarah*)

According to this, the Garden of Eden is the place where souls are refined as they pass from the physical to the spiritual, and Hebron is the place of connection between the physical and the spiritual. Moreover, according to this, Me'arat HaMakhpela represents the duality of the world. (The word *Makhpela* shares its root with the word *kaful*, meaning double or dual.) It is where the physical and the spiritual are linked. And this, of course, is a very deep and lofty concept.

See the booklet "Emek Ḥevron – Me'arat HaMakhpela VeZekhut Avot BeMidrashei Ḥazal," published by Midreshet Ḥevron; and Maavar Yabok, "Imrei Noam," ch. 27.

See also **Burial Caves; Death and Adam.**

Memorial

The basic need for memorialization stems from the human need to feel connected to eternity, to feel that death will not erase us from the world. Naturally, when a person dies, their descendants carry on their memory, both in a biological sense and a spiritual one. The descendants remember the person's life, carry their name, etc.

The need for memorialization is especially felt when a person has died before his time, or without any descendants to carry on his memory. The Torah commands a man to marry his brother's wife if the brother has died childless, so that the brother's name will not be erased (Deut. 25:6). The Torah relates how Judah fulfilled this duty to his daughter-in-law, Tamar (Gen. 38), even before the Torah was given. The Book of Ruth describes how Boaz married Ruth in order to perpetuate the memory of Maḥlon, her first husband: "I am also acquiring Ruth the Moabite, the wife of Maḥlon, as my wife, so as to perpetuate the name of the deceased upon his estate, that the name of the deceased will not disappear from among his kinsmen and from the gate of his home town" (Ruth 4:10). The Bible uses the phrase "redeemer" for one who perpetuates the name of the deceased.

Job also sought to establish a memorial after his sons and daughters died and he remained childless: "O that my words were written down. Would they were inscribed in a record, incised on a rock forever with iron stylus and lead! But I know that my redeemer lives; in the end he will testify on earth" (Job 19:23–25).

The childless Job wants his words to be carved forever in a book and in stone. He also uses the expression "my redeemer" for someone who will read his words. The anonymous person reading Job's words, who knows that he lived, will redeem Job! It allows Job to be connected to eternity for many years after his death; although whatever is physical is fleeting, his spiritual message can remain forever.

Nowadays, we still often feel a desire and a need for memorialization, particularly when a young person has died before their time, but not only. It expresses a need for spiritual continuity, even after the soul has departed and left the body.

Beyond the relatives' emotional need for memory and memorial, it is also meaningful for them to perform an action, to create something from their place of pain and sorrow. Becoming involved in this type of positive deed can offer some healing to mourners. If a mourner is feeling like he has lost part of his own life, such acts can provide something positive and encouraging. In this context, it is also relevant to note the Jewish idea that every positive and valuable act performed in honor of the deceased increases the person's merits in the world to come.

For a further discussion of memorialization, see Sec. 67, "Memorial."

See also **Naming a Child After the Deceased**.

Memorial (or Yahrzeit) Candle (*Ner Neshama*)

This is a candle that is lit for the elevation of the deceased's soul. Before his death, Rabbi Yehuda HaNasi instructed: "A candle shall be lit in my place" (Ketubbot 103a). It is customary to have a memorial candle lit throughout the shiva. Some have the custom of lighting it throughout the *shloshim*; some do so for the entire twelve months.

It is also customary to light a memorial candle on the Yahrzeit and to have it lit for the entire day, for twenty-four hours. For this purpose, people use candles that stay lit for twenty-four hours.

There is an Ashkenazic custom to light a memorial candle at the four times of the year that *Yizkor* is recited: Yom Kippur, Shemini Atzeret, the last day of Passover, and Shavuot.

There was also a custom of lighting memorial candles for the deceased in the synagogue, which would serve as the *ner tamid* – the "eternal light" that burns perpetually in the sanctuary. Lighting the candle is connected to the custom of studying Torah to elevate the deceased's soul, and so the candle is lit to provide light for those studying Torah in the synagogue. It later became customary to light a candle where shiva was taking place and to study there to elevate the deceased's soul. There are also spiritual reasons for this custom, as will be explained below.

In some communities, it is customary that whoever is leading the prayers on the Yahrzeit lights a candle. Some have the custom to light two candles; some light five candles, corresponding to the five levels of the soul (*nefesh, ruaḥ, neshama, ḥaya, yeḥida*).

The preferred option is to light with olive oil, and if that is not available, then with a wax candle. If a wax candle is not available, then gas is used. If that is not possible, then an electric bulb can be used.

In Judaism, the candle represents the soul: "The life-breath of man is the lamp of the Lord" (Prov. 20:27). The sages used this image to honor the soul of the deceased. "Light" symbolizes several things in the Bible:

- God as the source of light – "The Lord is my light and my help" (Ps. 27:1)
- The presence of the *Shekhina* – "May the Lord make His face shine on you and be gracious to you" (Num. 6:25)
- Light as likened to life – "Like babies who never saw the light" (Job 3:16)
- The Torah – "The commandment is a lamp, and the Torah is a light" (Prov. 6:13)

All of these images are the opposite of death and darkness. The sages called the soul, which is eternal, a candle or a lamp (*ner*) – "The soul which I placed in you is called a lamp" (Shabbat 32a).

There is another resemblance between the two: The candle or lamp is comprised of the physical combustible material and the flame itself. The flame is the essence, the most important part of the candle, though it has no weight or mass. Similarly, humans possess the physical the body, but their essence is the spiritual soul; it cannot be defined in physical terms, and it is the most significant part of man.

The light of the candle is drawn upwards, even though the combustible material comes from below it. One might say that the soul, similarly, is connected to the physical body but strives for lofty heights. When a person passes on to the next world, his spirit returns to God, to the higher worlds. The human candle returns to the source of light.

In Kabbala, the candle takes on additional significance:

> The Jewish custom is to light candles in the presence of someone who is dying because the candle can dispel the evil forces, even at night, when the evil forces wield power. For this reason, removing *ḥametz* (which is a symbol of evil and impure forces) is performed by the light of a candle; for the candle will dampen the light of the wicked. And it will be of even greater help in the daytime, to break the evil and dispel it. Because the flame of the candle symbolizes the Higher Unity, and that is why the verse states, "The life-breath of man is the lamp of the Lord." (*Maavar Yabok, "Sefat Emet,"* ch. 15)

Shabbat candles – Some women have the custom to light Shabbat candles according to the number of people in the household. If this was a woman's custom, and one of her family members has died, she should continue to light the same number of candles that she lit beforehand (*Tzror HaḤayim* 292).

If someone has died during a festival, even though the shiva commences only once the festival is over, a memorial candle is lit right away. Memorial candles should not be lit on Yom Tov itself unless benefit will be derived from it on Yom Tov. The lighting of fire on holidays was permitted for the sake of cooking, or for some other practical use. A memorial candle does not generally provide any benefit, and therefore one may not light a candle on Yom Tov unless one will derive some benefit from it. In order to derive benefit from it, one can light the candle in a place where one is learning or eating, in order to provide more light. However, when necessary, lighting the candle can be permitted, because it can be considered a candle lit for the sake of a mitzva, i.e., the mitzva of honoring one's parents or relatives (*Bei'ur Halakha* 514 s.v. "*Ner shel batala*").

See also **Elevating the Soul; Ways of the Amorite**.

Memorial Day for Fallen Soldiers of the IDF (*Yom HaZikaron*)

This day is observed on the fourth of Iyar. The date for *Yom HaZikaron* was set in 1951; it is the day that precedes *Yom HaAtzma'ut*.

Yom HaZikaron ceremonies in Israel begin with a siren at eight o'clock in the evening. From the time of Jerusalem's liberation, the central ceremony has been held in the square by the Western Wall. On *Yom HaZikaron* day, people recite prayers, psalms, and *Yizkor* and light candles in honor of the fallen. A siren is sounded at eleven o'clock in the morning. Public ceremonies are held in military cemeteries, schools, army bases, and other public spaces.

In recent years, *Yom HaZikaron* has also been dedicated to commemorating those murdered in terror attacks.

There is also a day dedicated to the memory of soldiers whose burial place is unknown. See **Seventh of Adar**.

Memorials Are Not Made for the Righteous

The source of this is the Yerushalmi Talmud (Shekalim 2:5). The phrase concludes, "Their words are their memorial." The simple explanation of this idea is that we do not need to erect headstones for the righteous because, "Their words are their memorial"; righteous individuals are not memorialized with a grand tomb but in the legacy of their good words and deeds. Maimonides made a ruling in accordance with this concept (*Mishneh Torah, Hilkhot Avel* 4:4), but the Ari (*Shaar HaMitzvot, Vayeḥi*) wrote that a gravestone is necessary and that it contains a rectification for the soul. The Rashba (*Responsa HaRashba* 375) also wrote that gravestones should be erected to honor the dead. The custom nowadays is to make gravestones even for the great rabbis.

Another explanation of this saying has to do with the fact that, in the past, it was not customary to write the name of the deceased on the gravestone. One reason for having grave-markers is as a warning to *kohanim* that there are dead bodies there; for that purpose, there is no need to write the deceased's name. Indeed, in the ancient cemetery in Hebron, it was not customary to write names on the headstones. Those coming to visit a specific grave would use a map drawn by the local *ḥevra kaddisha* (*Gesher HaḤayim* 28:3, 2). However, for the other reasons – to know the grave's location in order to visit and pray there, etc. – the name of the deceased should be carved on the stone. This is the custom today.

See also **Tombstone.**

Met Mitzva

A *met mitzva* is a deceased individual who has no relatives or friends to tend to his burial. In such a case, anyone who is able to deal with the body and ensure that it receives a proper burial is obligated to do so.

> Who is a *met mitzva*? One who cries and no one in the city hears him. But if the people in the city hear him, he is not a *met mitzva*. He is considered a *met mitzva* until there are enough people to transport and bury him. (Smaḥot 4:29–30)

Since burying the deceased is a great mitzva, when it happens that someone has died and there is no one to bury him, it becomes the obligation of every Jew to see to it that the person is buried. Even the High Priest and the nazarite, who are forbidden from becoming ritually impure, are obligated to become impure in order to tend to a *met mitzva*. Burying a *met mitzva* takes precedence over many mitzvot, including the reading of *Megillat Ester*, provided that one is able to read it afterwards. Some say that even if it is not possible to hear the reading afterwards, the *met mitzva* takes precedence (Megilla 3b; *Shulḥan Arukh, Oraḥ Ḥayim* 687:2; *Mishna Berura* ad loc.).

One of the ten principles that Joshua bin Nun established is that a *met mitzva* takes possession of the place where he lies and is thus buried where the body is found – if it was outside of the city. But if the body was found inside the city limits, it is buried in the cemetery.

The status of "*met mitzva*" only applies when the head and most of the body has been found (Bava Batra 81a–b; *Shulḥan Arukh, Yoreh De'ah* 364:3 and 374:1–3).

> Rabbi Akiva said: That was the beginning of my studying from the sages; I awoke early and found a dead body and was dealing with him (from a distance of) three *teḥumei Shabbat* [the amount one is allowed to travel on foot on Shabbat] until I brought him to a burial

> place and buried him. And when I came and explained to the sages what I had done, they said that every step you took, it is as though you were spilling blood. And I judged that if I intended for the good and sinned, how much more so if I had had less meritorious intentions. And when they would mention this to Rabbi Akiva, he would say: This was the beginning of my merit. (Smaḥot, end of ch. 4)

The *Tosafot* (Ketubbot 17a) wrote that Rabbi Akiva was rebuked because a *met mitzva* takes possession of the place he is found. Another explanation in *Tosafot* is that Rabbi Akiva was rebuked because he did not attend to the sages; this is the version brought the Yerushalmi Talmud (Nazir 7:1): "At that time I did not stop waiting upon the Torah scholars. He used to say: One who does not wait upon the sages – is liable to capital punishment."

Today, we do not hold the law that a *met mitzva* takes possession of the place he is found. Rather, the body must be taken to the cemetery. This is because grave-markers outside of a cemetery cannot be properly maintained, and in Israel, burial in established cemeteries protects the purity of the Land of Israel. The family would also probably prefer burial in a cemetery rather than in a desolate place. Another reason for doing this is to prevent situations where a *kohen* might mistakenly become impure (*Ḥazon Ish, Yoreh De'ah* 209:13).

See also **Exhuming Grave; *Geniza*; Impurity of the *Kohen*; Grave that Is Discovered.**

Mitzva to Fulfill the Deceased's Wishes

This is a general halakhic rule that appears in the Talmud and in the writings of halakhic authorities in a variety of contexts. In terms of mourning, the general approach is that one complies with instructions in which the deceased wishes to waive certain honors. But we do not comply with the deceased's wishes if they contradict an obligation or practice that is for the honor of the mourners.

For example, a eulogy is given to show honor to the deceased. Therefore, if the deceased requested that he not be eulogized, we comply with the request. If, however, he requested that he not be buried, we do not agree to this because burial is a mitzva, as it says (Deut. 21:22): "You must bury him the same day" (Maimonides, *Mishneh Torah, Hilkhot Avel* 12:1; *Shulḥan Arukh, Yoreh De'ah* 348:2–3).

> If one of the greats of the generation died and instructed that he should not be eulogized, some wrote to be lenient and to eulogize him against his wishes. (*Pitḥei Teshuva* 344:1)

> One who instructed that his family not observe shiva and *shloshim* is not heeded. But if a parent instructed his children not to mourn for the twelve-month period, this is heeded because the twelve-month period is to show respect for the deceased, unlike shiva and *shloshim* where it is not clear whether it is out of respect for the deceased or the living. (Rema, *Yoreh De'ah* 344:10, based on *Responsa Mahari Weil*)

Some have written that if a person instructed his child not recite Kaddish for him, this is heeded (*Pitḥei Teshuva* ibid.). However, in *Yalkut Yossef* (41:3) he writes that they are required to say Kaddish. He explains that this is because if the deceased had known the benefit of reciting Kaddish, he would never have instructed his children not to say it; and now that he is dead, it would be pleasing to him that Kaddish be recited.

> One who gave instructions not to place a tombstone by his grave is not obeyed. But if he instructed that praises not be written on the tombstone, this is obeyed. If he was not insistent regarding his own honor and gave instruction not to mourn during the twelve months, this is obeyed. (*Yalkut Yosef* ibid.)

> If the deceased instructed his relatives not to perform *kriya*, some are of the opinion that we comply with this, while others wrote not to because *kriya* is a mitzva and the deceased's request cannot overrule it. (*Pitḥei Teshuva* ibid. 2)

> A person who gave instructions that one of his children handle the burial and not the others, this is obeyed; but all of the children are considered to be in *aninut*. (*Yalkut Yosef* 41:5)

> If a parent instructed his children to do something in his honor after he died, but it is costly to do so, some say that the children are obligated to comply with the parent's wish and spend the money from the inheritance. (The halakhic rule in this matter is: "The children are obligated to pay their parents' debts." Ketubbot 91b; Bava Batra 157a; a discussion of this and the opinion of various *Rishonim* is brought in *Yalkut Yosef* 41:4.)

See also **Charity; Honoring the Deceased; Will.**

Mocking the Poor

"Rav Yehuda said: One who sees the deceased and does not escort him has committed a transgression due to [the verse]: 'He who mocks the poor blasphemes his Creator.' (Prov. 17:5)" (Berakhot 18a). Anyone who mocks the poor, in this case, the dead, poor because they cannot perform the commandments, adversely affects God, Master of the world. This is the halakha (*Shulḥan Arukh, Yoreh De'ah* 361:3); one must escort the deceased four cubits.

There are other rules related to this principle: A person should not study Torah near a dead person or in a grave or cemetery, because one is performing a mitzva in the presence of the deceased who cannot do so themselves. Because the dead are unable to study Torah or perform mitzvot, it appears as though one is mocking them. For this reason, it is also forbidden to wear tefillin or have one's tzitzit hanging out of one's clothing in a cemetery or within four cubits of a grave (*Shulḥan Arukh, Oraḥ Ḥayim* 45:1; *Yoreh De'ah* 367:2–6). It is permitted when one is more than four cubits away. However, if there is a dead body in a house, the whole house is treated as though it is within four cubits of the deceased. This law applies with regard to deceased minors as well. It does not apply for deceased females because women are exempt from tefillin and tzitzit (*Mishna Berura* 23:5).

Even though one should not study Torah within four cubits of a grave, one is allowed to recite verses or psalms during the *tahara* and to say words of Torah in honor of the deceased, because these are done to honor the deceased and elevate the soul (*Shulḥan Arukh, Yoreh De'ah* 344:17).

One may make the relevant blessings, such as *Dayan HaEmet* and "Who fashioned you in justice," upon entering a cemetery since they are about the dead and about accepting God's judgment.

See also **Cemetery; Funeral; Honoring the Deceased.**

Mourning Follows the Lenient Opinion

This is a halakhic principle that appears in the Talmud (Eruvin 46a; Moed Katan 18a, etc.). The principle dictates that in Talmudic disputes about mourning customs where the majority is strict and one sage is lenient – the halakha follows the lenient minority opinion. This is unusual, since generally when there is a dispute between a majority and an individual, the halakha follows the majority.

There are certain limitations to this rule: It only applies to disputes in the Talmud and not to disputes among later halakhic authorities (*Gesher HaḤayim* 19:8, 1); some say that it does apply to later halakhic authorities (*Kol Bo al Aveilut*, p. 257). There is a discussion as to whether this principle applies also to *aninut* and *kriya*; the halakha is that it does not apply to *kriya* (Moed Katan 26b – "*Aveilut leḥud veKriya leḥud*"). See *Gesher HaḤayim* 19:8. If a law or custom has become widely accepted and one person dissents, this principle does not apply (*Kol Bo al Aveilut*, p. 258).

Yalkut Yosef (p. 801) summarizes the rules as follows:

- The halakha follows the lenient opinion in mourning, including in differences of opinions among the halakhic authorities.
- The halakha follows the lenient opinion even when it is against the majority.
- The halakha follows the lenient opinion in mourning even with one opinion against many, but this applies to mourning (*aveilut*) and not *aninut*.
- The principle that the halakha follows the lenient opinion in mourning does not apply against the opinion of the *Shulḥan Arukh*. But if it is a case where it was customary to be lenient or if it is about to Torah study, we are lenient even if it goes against the opinion of the *Shulḥan Arukh*.
- If the custom was to be strict, then the principle does not apply.

- Even on the first day of mourning, the halakha follows the lenient opinion, including with regard to haircutting.

Moving the Lips of the Sleeping

This is an expression based on a verse in Song of Songs (7:10) that is interpreted as referring to the dead: They are like people sleeping, but their words of Torah, which remain in the world and continue to be studied, provide them an element of eternity.

> Rabbi Yohanan said in the name of Rabbi Shimon b. Yohai: Any Torah scholar in whose name a matter of halakha is said in this world, his lips mouth the words in the grave. Rabbi Yitzhak ben Ze'eira said, and some say this was stated by Shimon the Nazirite: What is the verse? "And the roof of your mouth is like the best wine that glides down smoothly for my beloved, moving gently the lips of those who are asleep" (Song. 7:10). This is like a pile of grapes: Just as a pile of grapes, when a person places his finger on it, immediately it moves, so too with Torah scholars: When a teaching is said in their name in this world, their lips mouth the words in the grave. (Yevamot 97a; Sanhedrin 90b; Bekhorot 31b)

> This is true kindness that one can do for the righteous, to learn their words; and their merit shall protect them… this obligation falls especially on the descendants of one who authored a book learned over generations – to learn the books of their ancestors and to respond to the questions they pose… and they will protect them and advocate on their behalf. (*Pele Yoetz*, "*Dovev Siftei Yeshenim*")

See also **A Child Brings Merit to the Father (*Bara Mezakei Aba*)**.

Multi-Level Burial

Two coffins should not be buried one over the other. If they were placed in this position, the owner of the upper one should remove it. If there are six handbreadths of earth between the coffins, it is permissible (*Shulḥan*

Arukh, Yoreh De'ah 362:4). The *Beit Yosef* quotes Nahmanides, who says that three cubits is sufficient; Rabbi Akiva Eiger also writes that three is enough. The *Pitḥei Teshuva* (ad loc. 3) quotes the *Shvut Yaakov* who wrote that, even though the graves must be separated, in his day, they would bury bodies close together and even on top of each other, because space was quite limited; he writes that the laws of separating between graves only apply where there is an abundance of space but should be observed wherever possible. The Gesher HaHayim (27:6, 6) writes that the separation should be no less than six cubits. In *BeMar'eh HaBazak* (vol. 4, 114) there is a detailed responsa on this subject, which quotes the Israeli Chief Rabbinate's ruling that permitted multi-level burial.

Naming a Child After the Deceased

There is a Jewish custom to name children after a parent or other relative. The Ashkenazic custom is to name children after someone who has died. The Sephardic custom is to name children after someone who is still alive; it is considered a blessing for a long life.

According to most opinions, the child may be given a name similar to the deceased's name, or a name can be added to the name of the deceased. Some say that one should not name a child after a person who died after the child was born.

According to most opinions, one should not name a child after someone who suffered bad luck, such as someone who died young. One should instead change the name slightly (*Igrot Moshe, Yoreh De'ah*, Vo. 2, 122) or add a name (and use both names). In this case, some make sure to use the deceased's name as a second name (*Yalkut Yosef, Kibud Av VaEm*, vol. 2, 94). Some say that it is not problematic to give a child the name of someone who died young (Rabbi Haim David HaLevi, *Aseh Lekha Rav*, vol. 6, 69. He brings a case in which the Gaon of Vilna's daughter's sons died in childhood, and her father told her to give the next child the name of the one who died but to add another name as the first name.) Some say that if someone was killed while sanctifying God's name, a child can be named after the deceased without adding another name.

Much has been written about naming children after a loved one, and this is not the place to discuss it at length. The brief discussion above is based on the book "*Kor'ei Shemo*," written by my friend Rabbi Mishael Rubin. Those who want to explore the topic further can consult this book or others written on the subject.

See also **Memorial**.

Necromancy (*Ov*)

This refers to a type of magic meant to reveal the future to those who seek it out.

There are different types of necromancy:

> A necromancer is a *pitom* from whose armpit [the deceased] speaks. A necromancer is one who speaks from between the joints and between the fingers. A necromancer includes both one who raises [the dead] with his sorcery and one who inquires from a skull. (Sanhedrin 65a – b)

There definitions are explained in different ways. According to Rashi, "*pitom*" is the name of the sorcerer, who raises the dead from the ground and places him in his armpit, and the dead speaks from the armpit of the sorcerer.

Maimonides writes:

> What do the deeds associated with an *ov* involve? A person stands up and offers an incense offering of known content. He holds a wand of myrtle in his hand and waves it while whispering a known incantation in a hushed tone. [This continues] until the person making the inquiry hears a voice, as if another person is speaking to him and replying to his questions. It appears as if the words are coming from below the earth in a very low tone, to the extent that it cannot be perceived by the ear but only sensed by thought. Similarly, among the deeds associated with an *ov* is taking the skull of a corpse, offering incense, and chanting incantations until one hears a voice in a very low tone emanating from his armpits and replying [to his questions]. All these are deeds associated with an *ov*. (*Mishneh Torah, Hilkhot Avodat Kokhavim* 6:1)

Other explanations are brought in the *Encyclopedia Talmudit*, "*Ov*."

Some are of the opinion that nothing connected to the *ov* is genuine. The necromancer is misleading others so that it seems like he is hearing and seeing things. The *Geonim* held differing opinions about the female necromancer who raised Samuel the prophet after he died (I Sam. 28) – whether hers was a false vision and that she tricked Saul, or whether God truly revived Samuel to make his words known to Saul. But the necromancer himself is certainly not capable of reviving the dead. (See *Otzar HaGeonim, Ḥagiga,* 4–6; Responsa of Rabbi Abraham Maimonides, Frieman Edition, 27; and Radak, I Sam, 1:28.)

Beyond the general prohibition on sorcery, the Torah specifically warned against the *ov*, as it says: "Do not turn to necromancers... I the Lord am your God" (Lev. 19:31). If a person used necromancy intentionally, he is liable to *karet* (lit. to be cut off): "If any person turns to necromancers and familiar spirits and goes astray after them, I will set My face against him and cut him off from among his people" (Lev. 20:6). If there was a warning and witnesses, then the transgression is punishable by stoning (Mishna Sanhedrin 53:1). One who consulted with a necromancer, even though he did not do the sorcery himself, transgresses a negative commandment from the Torah. (See "*Minyan HaMitzvot*" in the beginning of Maimonides' *Mishneh Torah, Hilkhot Avodat Kokhavim.*) Some of the *Rishonim* derive a unique commandment about this from the verse "Be of perfect faith with God, your Lord" (Deut. 18:13), saying that it is an admonition to dedicate our hearts wholeheartedly to God; all those involved in sorcery and trying to see the future, with the *ov* among them, transgress this obligation (Nahmanides' commentary on *Sefer HaMitzvot*, Mitzva 8; *Yere'im HaShalem*, Mitzva 431). Some are of the opinion that this is not a separate mitzva but rather a reason for the prohibition of magic:

> All the above matters are falsehood and lies, with which the original idolaters deceived the gentile nations in order to lead them after them. It is not fitting for the Jews who are wise sages to be drawn into such emptiness, nor to consider that they have any value as [implied by Num. 23:23]: "No black magic can be found

among Jacob, or occult arts within Israel." Similarly, [Deut. 18:14] states: "These nations which you are driving out listen to astrologers and diviners. This is not [what God has granted] you." Whoever believes in [occult arts] of this nature and, in his heart, thinks that they are true and words of wisdom but are forbidden by the Torah, is foolish and feebleminded. He is considered like women and children who have underdeveloped intellects. The masters of wisdom and those of perfect knowledge know with clear proof that all these crafts which the Torah forbade are not reflections of wisdom, but rather emptiness and vanity that attracted the feebleminded and caused them to abandon all the paths of truth. For these reasons, when the Torah warned against all these empty matters, it advised [Deut. 18:13]: "Be of perfect faith with God, your Lord." (Maimonides, *Mishneh Torah, Hilkhot Avodat Kokhavim* 11:16)

See also **Consulting the Dead; Eternality the Soul; Fear of Judgment; Ways of the Amorite.**

Neighborhood of Graves

This is a halakhic classification for a place where graves are found close to one other and we therefore consider it likely that there would be additional, unidentified graves in the vicinity. There is greater concern about impurity in such a place than when a single grave is found:

> One who initially finds [one] corpse buried normally, he [may] move it and its surrounding dirt [*tevusato*]. [If] he found two, he [may] move them along with their surrounding dirt. [If] he found three: If there are four to eight cubits from one to the next, this is a neighborhood of graves. From it, he checks twenty cubits outward. [If] he found one [corpse] twenty cubits away, he checks from this one twenty cubits outward. This matter has what to stand upon, even though, had he found this one first, he [could] move it and its surrounding dirt. (Nazir 9:3 and Ohalot 16:3)

"*Tevusato*," "the surrounding dirt," means the earth that absorbed the blood or the earth surrounding the dead body. The language is similar to the phrase "*mitboseset beDamayikh*," "wallowing in your blood" (Ezek. 16:6). Some say that the word is "*tefusato*" from the word for catching – that the earth has caught the dead.

When people are digging somewhere or are involved in an excavation, they sometimes find bones, and the question arises whether there might be other bones in the vicinity and whether it might be an ancient cemetery. (See e.g., the answer of *Ḥavot Yair*, quoted in the *Pitḥei Teshuva, Yoreh De'ah* 364:4.)

See also; **Grave That Is Discovered; Impurity of the *Kohen*.**

No Training for Mourning

Education (*ḥinukh*) is "familiarizing a person or a vessel with the task that they will uphold in the future." That is how Rashi explains the verse, "He mustered his disciples (*ḥanikhav*)" (Gen. 14:14). Therefore, we must "train a lad in the way he ought to go; he will not swerve from it, even in old age" (Prov. 22:6). The idea is to place the child on the good and correct path so that he will continue to follow it through old age. In this vein, the Dedication of (*Ḥanukat*) the Altar (Num. 7) and Dedication of (*Ḥanukat*) the Temple (Ps. 30) involve initiating the Altar and the Temple into their roles.

In the education of people, and children in particular, the idea is to begin practicing behavioral patterns that are good and proper. The goal is for the student to continue on the righteous path that has been impressed upon him through his education. The sages established the rule that one does not train for mourning, meaning that we do not wish to initiate a child, who is not yet obligated in mitzvot, on a path of learning and acquiring the behaviors appropriate for mourning.

The underlying perspective here is that death and mourning are not a permanent part of life. They are an outcome of man's sins and not a divine creation. Despite the fact that nowadays no one can escape death, the principle remains that, when man was created in the Garden of Eden, death was not an inevitable part of reality. In the end of days, humans and the world at large will be free of death.

The rule that there is no obligation to train for mourning also includes old mourning, i.e., the fast days and grief over the destruction of the Temple and Jerusalem. This, too, is an expression of the belief that the Temple was not supposed to have been destroyed at all but that it was a result of the Jewish people's sins. According to this perspective, sin is temporary and circumstantial, and not essential or inevitable. Sin is an unfortunate, temporary phenomenon in a world that is meant to achieve perfection. In its perfect state, the world has no room for sin, just like an illness is not an essential part of man. Despite illness being a common phenomenon that one cannot escape, the normal state is for a person to be healthy in body and soul. So too, death and mourning are abnormal states that the world is meant to strive to eradicate. In this vein, one might say that medicine, which seeks to overcome illness and lengthen human life, contains a dimension of resurrecting the dead.

Another idea expressed in this rule is that it is theoretically conceivable that, by the time the child matures, the world will have reached its perfect state: Jerusalem and the Temple will be built, the dead will be resurrected, and in any case, there will be no significance to knowing about mourning.

See also **Resurrection of the Dead.**

Old Mourning and New Mourning

Old mourning is the Jewish people's national mourning for the destruction of the Temple. New mourning is a person's individual mourning when a relative has died. There is a certain similarity between the practical halakhot of these two kinds of mourning. See Sec. 14, "A Conceptual Understanding of the Process of Mourning," for an explanation and comparison of the two.

One May Bring Anyone to the Land of Israel, but One May Not Remove Anyone

This is a halakhic principle that appears in the Mishna (Ketubbot 110b) that gives preference to residence in the Land of Israel over other countries. For example, in a dispute between a husband and wife in which one of them wants to remain in Israel and the other does not, the person who wants to remain in Israel has priority. See Maimonides (*Mishneh Torah, Hilkhot Ishut* 13:19–20) and the *Shulḥan Arukh* (*Even HaEzer* 75:3–4).

In accordance with this principle, we do not transport the deceased from Israel to other countries. Thus, if someone has died in Israel, he should be buried in Israel, even if he was a tourist and had a family plot outside of Israel; if the person died in Israel, he should be buried there (*Gesher HaḤayim* 27:9, 2). Conversely, if someone died outside of Israel, the body may be taken to Israel. Rabbi Ovadia Yossef ruled in line with this principle (*Yalkut Yosef* 52:7): If a tourist dies and is buried in Israel, and the family wants to return the body to their family plot in the Diaspora, the body should not be taken there after the person has merited to be buried in Israel – even if the person had expressed a wish to be buried in the family plot. If the family feels resentful or upset about this, one should console them and explain that this was from God, for the good of the deceased, who has merited to be buried in the Land of Israel.

If someone was buried in Israel, the body may not be removed from the grave in order to be buried in Jerusalem. Although there is a halakhic principle that says that "one may bring anyone to Jerusalem, but one may not remove anyone," this applies only during one's lifetime and not after death. Therefore, although a body can be removed from a grave outside of Israel to be brought to Israel, a body may not be removed from a grave in Israel to be brought to Jerusalem.

See also **Burial in the Land of Israel; Earth from the Land of Israel.**

One Should Be as Thankful for the Bad as One Is for the Good – and Accept It with Joy

The Talmud (Berakhot 60b) brings four sources for this principle:

> Rav Aḥa said in the name of Rabbi Levi: What is the verse that alludes to this? "I will sing of loving-kindness and justice; unto You, O Lord, will I sing praises" (Ps. 101:1). If it is loving-kindness, I will sing, and if it is justice, I will sing.
>
> Rabbi Shmuel bar Naḥmani said: From here: "In God, I will praise His word; in the Lord, I will praise His word" (Ps. 56:11). "In God, I will praise His word" – that is God's attribute of benevolence, while "In the Lord, I will praise His word" – that is the attribute of suffering; [the name of God is considered

> to refer to mercy, as opposed to the name "*Elohim*" which is considered to refer to the attribute of judgment].
>
> Rabbi Tanḥum said: From here: "I will lift up the cup of salvation and call upon the name of the Lord" (Ps. 116:13), and, "I found trouble and sorrow, but I called upon the name of the Lord" (Ps. 116:3–4).
>
> And the Rabbis said: From here: "The Lord has given and the Lord has taken away; blessed be the name of the Lord" (Job 1:21).

The *Shulḥan Arukh* (*Oraḥ Ḥayim* 222:2) writes:

> A person should be as thankful for the bad, with complete conviction and sincere desire, as he is for the good, because for servants of God, the bad is their happiness and goodness. Since he has accepted out of love what God has decreed, he finds that by accepting this bad he is serving God, which brings him happiness.

Rav Kook in his Siddur, *Olat Raaya* (p. 403), relates to this in his characteristically poetic language:

> Elimination of emotion, to the point where one cannot distinguish between good and evil and one does not value the individual self at all, is not the highest level of a soul; this is not the correct approach for a lofty person. Rather the intelligent person should become familiar with good and evil – the beauty of life's good and the harm of evil's void, including in one's own life; and one should assign them their appropriate value.

That is to say, the principle of making a blessing over the bad as we do over the good should not cause a person to blur the differences between good and evil, or between joy and sadness. On the contrary, the intelligent person must distinguish between the two and know the value of good and beauty, in contrast with evil.

The question may still be asked, however: How can a person make a blessing over the bad with the same feeling as a blessing over the good?

> One should know that the Divine good and the complete justness of Higher Providence are infinitely beyond this; one should give oneself over to it with one's entire heart and soul. Therefore, with all of a person's knowledge of and feelings towards life and its value, he should happily accept everything that is given to him from God's love and through His ways, which are filled with justice and integrity. And although the blessings over events must be in attunement with the emotions that the soul experiences at the time – and they are certainly different when there is good versus when there is evil – the perfect wisdom will rise above and encompass all of these with justice and deliberation, to accept them with joy.

That is to say, a person must know that the Divine good and the justice of the Higher Providence are infinitely greater than limited human perceptions and emotions. One can arrive at this understanding from a place of love for God and a recognition that all of God's works are just and merciful. This is what enables a person to make a blessing over the bad, from a place of acceptance and even joy – as if one were blessing the good.

The book *Maavar Yabok* ("*Siftei Renanot*," ch. 19) writes about this in the context of those who come to comfort the mourners:

> Consolation is mainly about God's decree becoming justified in the mourner's heart, to the point where he thanks the God of justice and blesses the bad just he blesses the good. Then he will merit what the prophet promised: "For she has received at the hand of the Lord double for all her sins" (Is. 40:2). Israel will be comforted double their sins – once for their doing repentance out of love and once for accepting the suffering with love. Thus the mourner should do, and the comforters should keep this in mind.

See also **Comforting the Mourners; *Tziduk HaDin*.**

One Who Is Frantic About the Corpse

This describes a state in which a person is so concerned for a deceased relative that we fear he might come to transgress the halakha. It is a general halakhic concept that appears in the Talmud (Shabbat 43b; Yoma 85a). The sages were lenient and allowed for the violation of a minor rabbinic prohibition, so that a corpse caught in a fire on Shabbat could be moved in certain ways to rescue it from the fire. They ruled this way despite the corpse being considered *muktzeh* (set aside, not to be used or touched on Shabbat); one would normally be prohibited from moving it. The concern was that if one was not permitted to move the body – a rabbinic prohibition – one might come to extinguish the fire on Shabbat – a Torah prohibition – out of frantic concern for the corpse. Other leniencies about moving a corpse have also been adopted, out of a desire to honor the deceased. Details about how the body can be moved and various opinions on the matter can be found in *Shulḥan Arukh, Oraḥ Ḥayim* 311.

Overturning One's Bed

This was a sign of mourning in Talmudic times.

The mourner was obligated to overturn his bed. This act symbolizes the mourners' experience of shock and instability following the death of their loved one. The sages gave the following reason for it: Because, "I have placed the likeness of My image [*deyokan*] within humans, as they were created in My image, and owing to their sins I have overturned it; and when this person died, the Divine image in him was removed. Therefore, you must also overturn your beds on account of this (Moed Katan 15a–b; Y. Moed Katan 3:5). That is to say, this overturning is a call for contemplation – for the mourners to experience a reckoning and consider their priorities; what does is mean that human beings are made in God's image? Is one conscious of one's divine image, is one acting accordingly? The act of overturning the bed is a magnified emotional expression; the sense of loss and emptiness may lead a person to contemplate his values.

One should overturn not only one's own bed, but all the beds in the house. "Nowadays, it is not the common practice to overturn the beds because the gentiles will say that it is [a kind] of sorcery. Moreover, our beds are not made like their beds were such that overturning would be discernible [as it was in former days]" (*Tosafot,* ad loc.; *Shulḥan Arukh, Yoreh De'ah* 387:2). Thus, today, this is not practiced.

Part of the Day Is Counted as a Whole Day

This principle is applied to the beginning and end of shiva. If the burial takes place close to sunset, or after sunset but before dark (the exact rules are brought in Sec. 7, "Arrangements for the Burial and Funeral," halakha 51), if the mourners manage to observe mourning practices, however briefly, that day is counted as the first day of the shiva. The same is true at the end of the shiva: The mourners sit for a short while after the morning prayer services and then conclude the shiva. According to the *Shulḥan Arukh*, mourning ends when the sun comes up; but the Rema says that the mourners should wait until the last comforter has left (*Shulḥan Arukh, Yoreh De'ah* 395:1).

The rule also applies to the *shloshim*. On the last day of the *shloshim*, mourning ends after sunrise. A situation can occur where part of the day would be counted toward the shiva and the rest of the day toward the *shloshim*: For example, when shiva ends on the eve of a festival, the first part of the day is counted as the entire day and thus ends the shiva; the rest of the day is counted as part of the *shloshim*, and when the festival begins, it cancels the rest of *shloshim* (*Shulḥan Arukh* ibid. 399:3).

This rule can also apply on the third day of mourning – part of the third day can be counted as a whole day (Rema, ibid. 393:1; *Gesher HaḤayim* 21:1, 70). But it does not apply for the end of the twelve-month mourning period (*Shulḥan Arukh*, 395:3). The reason for this distinction is that the rule is relevant when days are being counted, as in the shiva and *shloshim*. The twelve-month period, on the other hand, is counted by months, and one may not say that part of the month is counted as an entire month (*Turei Zahav* ad loc. 2).

We also say that part of the day is counted as a whole day with regard to marital relations (*Turei Zahav, Oraḥ Ḥayim* 555; *Arukh HaShulḥan, Yoreh De'ah* 395:3; *Turei Zahav* 402:5). Some forbid relations until the night (*Pnei Barukh* 24:5).

Some are of the opinion that, when there is a genuine need, the rule can be applied to the night preceding the seventh day: Part of the day (in this case, the beginning of the night) may be counted as a whole day. The *Tur* (395) quotes Nahmanides (*Torat HaAdam*, p. 215) saying that part of the night is counted as a whole day. He permits washing and marital relations on the seventh night. However, the *Shulḥan Arukh*

(*Yoreh De'ah* 395:1) follows the ruling of the Maharam of Rotenburg, that the night is not considered part of the day for shiva. In the case of a delayed report, all opinions agree that the night is counted as a whole day.

Some permit marital relations and Torah study on the seventh night since these are mitzvot (*Pitḥei Teshuva,* ad loc., in the name of the Ridbaz; *Yalkut Yosef* 22:25), but one should wait until later than usual in the night so that part of the night can be counted as a whole day. This view may be relied on in times of a genuine need, for example if the husband must travel on the seventh day, provided his intentions are pure (*Sdei Hemed, Aveilut* 25). *Gesher HaḤayim* (21:14, 3) also wrote to be lenient in terms of private matters on the night preceding the seventh day, and in *Kol Bo Al Aveilut* (p. 295) it says to be lenient if the husband is travelling the next day. See a longer discussion in *Pnei Barukh* 25, note 10.

Peace Be upon Him (*Alav HaShalom*)

This is an expression of respect used when mentioning the name of someone who died. For example: "Abraham our father, peace be upon him" (Avot 5:3). The expression is based on the verse, "He enters into peace, they rest on their beds, each one that walks in his uprightness" (Is. 57:2).

The Talmud and Midrash include discussions about the connection between righteous people who have died and peace. Regarding the divine promise to Abraham, the Midrash says:

> Peace is so great that even the dead need peace, as it says (Gen. 15:15): "You shall go to your fathers in peace." (Sifrei, *Bemidbar* 42, s.v. "*VaYasem lekha*")

And in relation to Moses's death, it is written:

> Groups of angels came in groups before Moses' coffin and said, "He enters into peace, they rest on their beds each one that walks in his uprightness." (*Avot DeRabbi Natan,* ch. 25)

And in relation to the death of Rabbi Yehuda HaNasi's death, the Talmud relates:

> At the time of the death of Rabbi Yehuda HaNasi, he raised his ten fingers toward Heaven and said: Master of the Universe, it is revealed and known before You that I toiled with my ten fingers in the Torah, and I have not derived any benefit even with my small finger. May it be Your will that there be peace in my repose. A divine voice emerged and said: "He enters into peace, they rest on their beds" (Is. 57:2). ... A supporting [opinion of] Rabbi Ḥiyya bar Gamda. As Rabbi Ḥiyya bar Gamda said Rabbi Yossi ben Shaul said: At the time when a righteous individual departs from the world, the ministering angels say before the Holy One, Blessed be He: Master of the Universe, the righteous [individual] so-and-so is coming. He says to them: The righteous should come and they should go out toward him. And they say to him: He enters into peace, they rest on their beds. Rabbi Elazar said: At the time when a righteous individual departs from the world, three contingents of ministering angels go out toward him. One says to him: Enter in peace; and one says: That walks in his uprightness; and one says to him: He enters into peace, they rest on their beds. At the time when a wicked person perishes from the world, three contingents of angels of destruction go out toward him. One says to him: "There is no peace, says the Lord concerning the wicked" (Is. 48:22); and one says to him: "You shall lie down in sorrow" (Is. 50:11); and one says to him: "Go down, and be laid with the uncircumcised" (Ez. 32:19). (Ketubbot 104b)

The Maharal (*Netivot Olam, Netiv HaShalom*, ch. 1) explains why:

> Peace is given to the righteous when they pass on from this world, since it is then considered that they have attained completion. The living cannot achieve total completion since they can always achieve further completion.... Therefore, he says that peace is given to the righteous; when they die, peace is given to them because they have achieved completion.

There is another mention of peace (based on the verse in Isaiah) in the Sephardic version of the *Hashkavot* prayers, recited for distinguished individuals: "Peace shall accompany him and there shall be peace upon his death. As it is written: 'He enters into peace, they rest on their beds, each one that walks in his uprightness.'"

See also **Acronyms; Go in Peace**.

Person Who Is Dying (*Goses*)

In halakha, a "*goses*" refers to someone who is about to die due to an illness or injury. The *goses* is still alive; one is not permitted to harm him or do anything that may shorten his life. It is prohibited to touch or move a *goses*, and anyone who touches him is considered to have taken a life. There are halakhic discussions regarding the removal of impediments to allow for death (Rema, *Shulḥan Arukh, Yoreh De'ah* 339:1). Even though most people in this condition will die, one is not allowed to testify that the person is dead until he has actually died. Since the person is still alive, if there is any hope that he will live, one is obligated to care for him, and one may violate Shabbat to do so. An extensive discussion of various halakhic issues related to the *goses* appears in the *Encyclopedia Hilkhatit Refuit*, vol. 4, "*Goses*."

See also **Confession (*Viduy*)**.

Pouring Out the Water

There was a custom to pour out the water in the deceased's house and in the adjacent area. This was in order to publicize that someone had died in the neighborhood and that a funeral would be taking place. By doing this, one would avoid having to announce the death (*Shulḥan Arukh, Yoreh De'ah* 402:12). One should not relate bad news if one can avoid doing so. The general orientation in Judaism is to avoid announcing bad news. (See e.g., II Sam. 18:19–27).

> Some say that the reason for this custom is that the Angel of Death puts a drop of the poison of death into the water; since he has been given permission, he is emboldened to turn the forces of kindness into anger and judgment. Because of this, we pour the water onto the ground where it came from, where it will not become impure. Through this, we arouse and disseminate the forces of kindness in the world, like the righteous

> and kind people who pour water on days of prayer and fasting (see, e.g., I Sam. 7:6). The pouring of the water shall also be a sign to man to dismiss the things of this world. Because even water, which is purifying and is essential for all of man's needs, is not considered important in comparison to the world after death. For the end of life is like water being poured out on to the ground; all is lost and over. Only the souls of His righteous remain forever. Another reason to pour out the water onto the ground is that it announces that one day God will mix the earth with the heavenly dew and it will come to us abundantly like rain on the land [an allusion to the resurrection of the dead and the dew that will awaken the dead]. (*Maavar Yabok, "Sefat Emet,"* ch. 23)

Another reason for pouring out the water was to warn the *kohanim* of impurity from the dead body. This was also established as halakha (*Shulḥan Arukh,* ibid. 339:5).

This only applies in a private home, not in a hospital. Water is not poured out on Shabbat or Yom Tov. Water in bottles need not be poured out. There are different opinions regarding hot water. Water in large barrels is not poured out, but the faucet should be opened, allowing the water to run out for a short time, and then shut (*Tzror HaḤayim* 296; *Yalkut Yosef* 6:3). Some wrote that today this custom is not observed in the neighboring homes, and it need not even be done in the deceased's house; it is enough to open the faucets and let a small amount of water run out (*Yalkut Yosef* ibid.; *Ḥayim VeḤesed* 1:20). Some have written than one may be very lenient with this custom (*Shulḥan Arukh, Yoreh De'ah* 339:9).

Prompt Report and Delayed Report

A prompt report (*shmua krova*) refers to a person who was not informed of a relative's death at the time of the death but was informed within thirty days of the person's passing. In the case of a prompt report, the mourner is obligated to observe mourning for the seven-day and thirty-day periods, starting from the day that he was informed of the death.

A delayed report (*shmua reḥoka*) refers to a person who was notified of a relative's death more than thirty days after the death, including on the night of the thirty-first day. In the case of a delayed report, the person observes mourning only for a short time, and does not observe all of the mourning practices. It is sufficient for him to perform one act of mourning, such as taking off his shoes or sitting on the ground; he can put his shoes back on, or stand up, right away.

The laws are elaborated in Sec. 49, "Receiving Notice of a Death."

Property of the Deceased

One may use the deceased's belongings, even during the shiva; however, it is customary not to use the deceased's shoes (*Gesher HaḤayim* 8:7; *Tzror HaḤayim*, p. 123; the source is *Sefer Ḥasidim* 454). Some say that this only includes the shoes that the deceased was wearing when he died while other shoes that the deceased owned and wore during his lifetime may be used. If nobody wants to use the shoes, they should be given to the needy, who should be informed of their source (*Yalkut Yosef* 21:11). The *Gesher HaḤayim* (ibid., note 2) cites the Talmud (Berakhot 57b) and writes that this only includes shoes worn during the final illness or at the time of death, but that there is no reason to be concerned about using shoes worn when the person was healthy, especially if they had not been worn for thirty days.

Children may wear their deceased parent's clothing, besides for their shoes (*Yalkut Yosef* ibid. and 53:8).

It appears that there was once a custom among Jews to put shoes on the deceased. The Talmud (Yevamot 104a) mentions shoes that are made in honor of an elderly person and Rashi explains that these shoes were for the burial shrouds. The Yerushalmi Talmud (Kilayim 9:3) mentions that Rabbi Jeremiah gave instructions to be buried in shoes. Some point to this as the source for the custom of not using the deceased's shoes, in case the shoes were intended to be part of the burial shrouds; if that were the case, it would be forbidden to derive benefit from them (*Kol Bo al Aveilut*, p. 91, in the footnote). Perhaps the stringency about shoes also stemmed from a desire to avoid having the living figuratively "step into the shoes" of the deceased. This is what happens, for example, when a man marries his deceased brother's wife, "replacing" him. See Sec. 21, "Wearing Leather Shoes."

See also **Benefit from the Dead; Shrouds.**

Psalms for a Sick Person and for Elevating the Soul

There is a Jewish custom to say psalms over any misfortune, especially when someone is ill, or to bring merit to the soul of the deceased. The Book of Psalms gives expression to a wide range of human emotions and experiences – joy and sadness, good times and bad. Because of this, it became the Jewish book of prayer and thanks; everyone can use psalms to express their feelings. Large portions of the siddur are based on Psalms, and the Levites would sing psalms in the Temple.

> There is nothing greater than the Book of Psalms, which includes everything: Many praises of God, psalms that awaken us to repent, ones asking for forgiveness and atonement – all written through the hand of God. King David authored them with divine inspiration. One who recites psalms is like someone praying and also like someone studying Torah. David requested that whoever reads psalms shall receive reward as though he has studied Torah. (*Otzar Dinim U'Minhagim*, "*Tehillim*," in the name of the Shelah from the book *Amud HaTeshuva*)

Reasons for Mourning

Mourning (*Aveilut*), in halakhic terms, refers to the laws and customs observed when one of one's seven close relatives has died. A central reason for mourning has to do with repentance: Maimonides (*Mishneh Torah, Hilkhot Avel* 13:12) writes that the mourner should engage in contemplation of his deeds and repent. Nahmanides (Introduction to *Torat HaAdam*) writes similarly, as does *Sefer HaḤinukh* (Mitzva 264): "For God does not willfully bring grief or affliction to man (based on the verse in Lam. 3:33) rather due to man's sin; and when one considers this during mourning, he will consider repentance and improve his actions as much as he is able."

Another reason for mourning is to emphasize the importance and significance of human life. Every human's life is one of will and choice, through which one can achieve a meaningful existence, differentiating a spiritual life from a base, animalistic existence. However, the main reason for mourning is so that people set aside their work for one week, to honor the deceased and remember them. Another aspect of this is that the living shall take heart and see that this is the end of man, and they may contemplate their actions. If people would continue going about their regular work and activities after their relative had died, they might fail to think about the deceased and the bitter news. For this reason, the Torah permitted *kohanim* to mourn for their relatives and to become ritually impure by burying them (*Otzar Dinim U'Minhagim* in the name of *Yalkut Yitzḥak*, Mitzva 264).

Recalling the Souls (*Hazkarat Neshamot*)

This refers to the custom of praying for the souls of the departed and pledging charity in their memory. *Av HaRaḥamim* is a general version of this, recited to recall the souls who died in sanctifying God's name.

The source for this custom is the Yerushalmi Talmud (Bava Kamma 1:5) on the mishna, "One should not awaken the dead or eulogize them": What is awakening? Mentioning them among the other dead. *Midrash Tanḥuma* (*Haazinu*) says: "This is why we have the habit of mentioning the dead on Shabbat, so that they will not return to hell. As it says in the verse: 'Absolve, O Lord, Your people Israel' – these are the living, 'Whom You redeemed' – these are the dead. From here we learn that the living can redeem the dead. For this reason, it is customary to mention the dead on Yom Kippur and to give charity in their name." This is also the halakha as written in the *Shulḥan Arukh* (*Oraḥ Ḥayim* 621:6).

The *Gesher HaḤayim* (31:2) specifies that *"hazkarat neshamot"* generally refers to the *"El Maleh Raḥamim"* prayer recited by the prayer-leader on Shabbat and on Mondays and Thursdays after the Torah reading. *"Yizkor"* is the prayer said four times a year by individuals for their departed relatives. It is said on Yom Kippur and on the three festivals.

> With regard to the custom of recalling the deceased on Shabbat, there is no doubt that doing so on the day of rest benefits them greatly since they are in a state of rest and are rejuvenated when their name is mentioned, because one's name is connected to one's soul… each name is associated with the essence of the

> person.... When their name is remembered, they are renewed and their soul shines.
>
> The person reciting the deceased's name must do so with intention, because the speech of the lower beings works through the mystical secret of the breath that ascends. This is especially so if it is the deceased's child or relative that says it and it is done in the synagogue where the person used to pray, and all the more so if the person built the synagogue or dedicated something within it – all of this helps to give the soul peace and joy on the holy day. Just as God sanctifies the souls of the living righteous, so too the souls of the deceased get joy and rest, especially when their names are mentioned. (*Maavar Yabok*, "*Siftei Renanot*," ch. 23)

See also ***Av HaRaḥamim*; *El Maleh Raḥamim*; *Yizkor*.**

Reincarnation (*Gilgul Neshamot*)

This is the Kabbalistic concept about the soul of the deceased returning to the world in another body. This means that the soul has been given another chance to repair itself. (The Hebrew word for baby, "*tinok*," contains the same letters as the word for repair, "*tikkun*.") It allows for the purification of that core soul; the soul comes back to repair whatever it did not manage to fix in its previous manifestation.

For example, the following is a Kabbalistic explanation of the verse, "One generation comes, another one goes" (Eccl. 1:4): The generation that passed is the same generation that comes. Like a tree that rots or is burned and disintegrates and, from it, a new tree grows in a different form, so too the soul comes back in a new form, in another body. It is also taught that the word *gilgul* comes from the word *gilui*, revelation – that the soul is revealed in a new form, which allows for rectification in a new way.

According to the Ari (Rabbi Isaac Luria, 1524–1572), there are various levels of rectification. Initially, one repairs the lower levels, and then progresses to higher levels. One first repairs the level called *nefesh* (life-force), then the *ruaḥ* (spirit), and then the *neshama* (soul). What has been repaired in one incarnation does not need to be fixed again.

There were Jewish scholars who completely refuted this concept. See, for example, Rabbi Saadia Gaon in his book, *HaNivḥar BeEmunot VeDeot* (Section 6, ch. 8, from p. 214 in the Rabbi Kapaḥ edition). However, after the Ari's time, the idea became widespread among Jews.

See also ***Luz*; Resurrection of the Dead; Soul (*Neshama*).**

Reserving a Grave While One Is Alive

A person ought to be buried in a grave bought specifically for him. Abraham made a special effort to purchase Me'arat HaMakhpela before burying Sarah: "So Ephron's land in Makhpela, near Mamre – the field with its cave and all the trees anywhere within the confines of that field – passed to Abraham as his possession, in the presence of the Hittites, who all entered the gate of his town. And then Abraham buried his wife Sarah in the cave of the field of Makhpela, facing Mamre – now Hebron – in the land of Canaan" (Gen. 23:17–20). Jacob also emphasized the purchase of Me'arat HaMakhpela: "Bury me with my fathers... in the cave which is in the field of Makhpela, facing Mamre, in the land of Canaan, the field that Abraham bought" (ibid. 49:29–30). In relation to Joseph's grave it also states: "The bones of Joseph, which the Israelites had brought up from Egypt, were buried at Shekhem, in the piece of ground that Jacob had bought" (Joshua 24:32).

Many people purchase a burial plot while they are still alive. If not, the family members purchase the grave; it is preferable to do this before the burial. In Israel nowadays, in light of the legal status of land in the State of Israel, the grave does not become the possession of the deceased or the family; rather, they are given permission to use this plot of land. After receiving the authorization, the right to be buried in that plot is reserved for the specific person, as long as the person is not buried elsewhere. (This information is based on a letter from the legal office of the Ministry of Religious Affairs in Israel, Yehuda Elram, LL.B.)

Resurrection

> Thus said the Lord God: I am going to open your graves and lift you out of the graves, O My people, and bring you to the land of Israel. You shall know, O My people, that I am the Lord, when I have opened your graves and lifted you out of

> your graves. I will put My breath into you and you shall live again, and I will set you upon your own soil. Then you shall know that I the Lord have spoken and have acted – declares the Lord. (Ezek. 37:12–14)

> You sustain the living with loving kindness, You revive the dead to life with great mercy... and preserve Your faith with those asleep in the dust. Who is like You, Master of mighty deeds? Who can be compared to You, O King Who causes death and restores life and causes Your salvation to sprout. You are faithful to restore the dead to life. Blessed are You, O Lord, who brings life to the dead. (The *Amida* prayer)

Resurrection of the dead is one of Maimonides' Thirteen Principles of Faith, which the Jewish people accepted their tenets. It is the belief that the resurrection, when the dead will arise from their graves, will occur at the time that God determines (Introduction to *Perek Ḥelek*).

Maimonides dedicated an entire essay to this topic, called "Treatise on the Resurrection of the Dead." In it, he writes that, although the Torah does not explicitly mention the resurrection, there are allusions to it in the text. In Hanna's Song (I Sam. 2:6) it says: "The Lord deals death and gives life, casts down into Sheol and raises up." It is implied by Ezekiel's vision of the dry bones, quoted above. In Isaiah (26:19) it says: "Oh, let Your dead revive! Let corpses arise! Awake and shout for joy, you who dwell in the dust! – For Your dew is like the dew on fresh growth; You make the land of the shades come to life." It is particularly highlighted in the Book of Daniel (12:2): "Many of those that sleep in the dust of the earth will awake, some to eternal life, others to reproaches, to everlasting abhorrence"; the book ends with the verse: "But you, go on to the end; you shall rest and arise to your destiny at the end of the days."

This fundamental principle of faith appears in the *Amida* prayer, as the epitome of God's might.

Only the righteous will be resurrected. Hence, Daniel is told: "Many of those that sleep in the dust of the earth will awake," but not all. Even among those who will rise, "Some to eternal life, others to reproaches, to everlasting abhorrence." Isaiah (26:14) also says: "They are dead, they can never live; Shades, they can never rise; of a truth, You have dealt with them and wiped them out, have put an end to all mention of them."

There is a phenomenon in the Tanakh of prophets resurrecting the dead: Elijah revived the widow's son (I Kings 17:17–24) and Elisha revived the Shunamite woman's son (II Kings 4:32–37). When a corpse was thrown into Elisha's grave and its bones touched Elisha's bones, the person was revived (ibid. 13:21).

Job uttered expressions that the sages (see Bava Batra 16a) categorized as a heretical rejection of resurrection:

> As a cloud fades away, so whoever goes down to Sheol does not come up. (Job 7:9)

> There is hope for a tree. If it is cut down, it will renew itself; its shoots will not cease. If its roots are old in the earth and its stump dies in the ground, at the scent of water it will bud and produce branches like a sapling. But mortals languish and die; man expires; where is he? The waters of the sea fail, and the river dries up and is parched. So man lies down never to rise; he will awake only when the heavens are no more, only then be aroused from his sleep. O that You would hide me in Sheol, conceal me until Your anger passes, set me a fixed time to attend to me. If a man dies, can he live again? All the time of my service I wait until my replacement comes. (ibid. 14:7–14)

The Talmud (Sanhedrin 90b-91a) brings additional proofs of the resurrection from the Bible. The sages in the Talmud debate whether the resurrection will include non-Jews.

There is a fundamental disagreement about the final status of those resurrected in the end of days. Maimonides claimed that after the resurrection, all of the people will die again. He is of the opinion that the body cannot be eternal since it is physical, and the physical cannot be eternal. The ultimate perfect state will be that of a disembodied soul. Rabbi Saadia Gaon, Nahmanides, and Rabbi Moshe Haim Luzzatto take a different approach, which follows the Kabbala; namely that, although the body decomposes after death, in the future resurrection, the body will achieve eternal life. Eternity will be for the soul and the body together. Nahmanides (at the end of *Torat HaAdam*) discusses Maimonides' opinion respectfully and at length, despite disagreeing with it. Nahmanides concludes: "Everyone agrees that there will be a resurrection… but Maimonides has a different opinion from my own and limits the resurrection and returns everything to the World of Souls. We think that the people in the resurrection will exist for eternity, from the time of the resurrection until the world to come which is never-ending." (See also Rabbi Moshe Haim Luzzatto's *Way of God,* Section 1, ch. 3, and *The Knowing Heart,* 67–75.) The Raavad also disagrees with Maimonides and brings proofs from the Talmud that the resurrection is for the body and not only the soul (*Hilkhot Teshuva* 8:2).

Although there was an opinion that the resurrection mentioned in the Bible is a parable for the resurrection of the Jewish people, and should not to be taken literally, Rabbi Saadia Gaon provided a thorough explanation as to why the verses must be understood as referring to a literal resurrection of the dead in this world. He brings proof from the verses in the Book of Ezekiel and the Book of Daniel. Rabbi Saadia Gaon discusses issues related to the resurrection: Who will come back to life and how; will they eat and drink and marry; if there is no death after the resurrection, how will they pass on to the next world; will people recognize each other; how will there be enough space for everyone; will people still sin; and will they receive reward or punishment for their deeds? A discussion of these important questions is beyond the scope of this book. Interested readers can refer to the original text (Rabbi Saadia Gaon, *HaNivḥar BeEmunot VeDeot,* Article 7).

One of the reasons given for burying the deceased is to strengthen the belief in the resurrection:

> Burial is esteemed for two reasons… And the second reason, which is a stronger reason, is that it is necessary for our belief in the resurrection of the dead. For if we were to dispose of the body like a dead animal, people would think that we are like beasts; they would not accept the belief in the resurrection, as they can when they see the burial, and that we build a house for them and

> dress them in garments and bury the dead with their family and forefathers, since they will eventually rise up together with their family. And to reinforce this essential belief, the Torah writes about burial, "And I will lie down with my fathers" (Gen. 47:30). And my teachers wrote about this: Why did the fathers want to be buried in the Land of Israel? One rabbi said "I will walk before God in the land of life" (Ps. 116:9), referring to the belief in the resurrection, to strengthen this belief. They said that the righteous will rise in their clothing, and this is said about the righteous and not about everyone; thus there is great care taken to honor the bodies of the dead. (*Kol Bo* 114)

The book *Pnei Barukh* includes a chapter on resurrection.

See also **Soul (*Neshama*)**.

Ritual Impurity of the Deceased

This is the most severe type of ritual impurity and is called the "source of all impurity," "*avi avot haTum'a.*" This impurity, as well as the other types of ritual impurity, are discussed throughout the Talmud, and particularly in the Order of Teharot.

In general, ritual impurity is a distinctive concept in the Torah. It is not a matter of hygiene; it is considered one of the divine statutes that have no explanation.

Sealing the Grave

In Hebrew, *stimat hagolel.* The "*golel*" is the stone, usually round, which in the Talmudic period covered the grave or the body. When burial was done in caves, people would roll a round stone in front of the cave's entrance. They would then take a stone called the "*dofek,*" which was shaped like a wedge, and would insert one end under the *golel.* The *dofek* stone prevented the round stone from rolling away. In Israel, where the body is buried in the ground without a coffin, a frame is built around the body and is then covered with flat stones. The framework is called the *dofek* and the cover is called the *golel.*

Mourning begins after *stimat hagolel,* i.e., when the grave has been sealed, or dirt covers the grave, marking the end of the burial (Moed

Katan 27a). There are some opinions (Nahmanides) that the sealing of the grave is when a coffin is sealed with nails; some (*Tosafot,* Ketubbot 4b) say it is when a marker is placed on the grave. Today, the sealing of the grave is considered to be when the grave is covered over with stones, even before it is filled with dirt (*Yalkut Yosef* 15:1).

Seven Days of Mourning

Moses established seven days of mourning even though the Torah only stipulated one day of mourning (Y. Ketubbot 1). The seven days of mourning are alluded to in the Torah in the following verse about Joseph: "And he observed mourning for seven days for his father" (Gen. 50:10). Another verse is understood to allude to seven days of mourning, as well: "And on the seventh day, the waters of the flood came upon the earth" (Gen. 7:10). Commentators interpreted this as referring to seven days of mourning for the righteous man Metushelaḥ; during those seven days, God waited and did not bring the flood, which teaches us that eulogizing the righteous delays calamities (Sanhedrin 98b). Another allusion is found in the verse, "I will turn your festivals into mourning" (Amos 8:10); just as the festivals last for seven days, mourning lasts for seven days (Moed Katan 20a). With regard to the verse, "You shall not go outside the entrance of the Tent of Meeting for seven days" (Lev. 8:33), the Midrash (*Tanḥuma,* beginning of ch. 8) explains that Moses said to Aaron and his sons: Mourn for seven days until it does not reach you.

The main reason for the seven days of mourning is so that people set aside their work for one week, to honor the deceased and remember them. Another aspect of this is that the living shall take heart and see that this is the end of man, and they may contemplate their actions. If people would continue going about their regular work and activities after their relative had died, they might fail to think about the deceased and the bitter news. For this reason, the Torah permitted *kohanim* to mourn for their relatives and to become ritually impure by burying them (*Otzar Dinim U'Minhagim, "Aveilut"* p.4, in the name of *Yalkut Yitzḥak,* Mitzva 264; Kabbalistic reasons for mourning appear in *Maavar Yabok, "Sefat Emet,"* ch. 19).

See also **The Soul's Journey Upon Leaving the Body.**

Seven Days of Mourning and the Seven Days of Feasting

Moses our teacher ordained for the Jewish people the seven days of mourning and the seven days of the wedding celebration. (Maimonides, *Mishneh Torah, Hilkhot Avel* 1:1)

There are many similarities between the seven days of mourning and the seven days of feasting and celebration following a wedding. Besides the parallel of the seven-day period, there are parallels between the wedding celebrations and the thirty-day and twelve-month periods of mourning: The bride maintains a special status for thirty days after the wedding; for example, during this period, she is permitted to wash her face on Yom Kippur (Mishna Yoma 73a). The twelve-month mourning period for a parent is parallel to the first year of marriage, during which the groom is commanded to make his wife happy (Deut. 24:5). Maimonides (*Mishneh Torah, Hilkhot Berakhot* 5:5) writes that, in the thirty days after a wedding, a phrase is added in Grace after Meals: "The joy is in His sanctuary"; if a festive meal is held because of the marriage, this can and should be said for the first twelve months.

A groom reclines at the head of the table and so does the mourner (Moed Katan 28b). The groom is like a king and is shown respect, and the mourner is also shown respect: "Everyone is obligated to stand in front of a *nasi* (important leader), except for a mourner and sick person" (Maimonides, *Mishneh Torah, Hilkhot Avel* 13:5).

The custom of circling around the grave seven times (see ***Hakafot***) parallels the custom of the bride walking around the groom seven times under the *ḥuppa*.

A glass is broken under the *ḥuppa* to remember the destruction of Jerusalem. There is a custom to break clay at the beginning of the funeral.

The Talmud (Ketubbot 8b) mentions the ancient custom of drinking ten cups of wine in the house of mourning (see Maimonides, *Mishneh Torah, Hilkhot Avel* 13:8). This is supported by the verse, "Give strong drink to him that is ready to perish and wine to the bitter of soul" (Prov. 31:6). This reminds us of the festive wine-drinking that takes place in the seven days of celebration following a wedding.

The Talmud (ibid. 8a–b) compares the blessing of the groom to the blessing of the mourner: They are both said in the presence of ten people. Nahmanides (*Torat HaAdam*, p. 154–5) wrote that they continue to make the mourner's blessing for seven days if new people appear, similar to the practice of having new people attend the celebrations of the seven days of feasting.

The custom in Talmudic times was to bring dirge-singers and instruments to a funeral (Ketubbot 4:4), which calls to mind the musical instruments at a wedding, even though the purpose of the music has the opposite goal – to awaken joy as opposed to sorrow.

The halakha links the commandments of burial and comforting mourners with the commandment to make a bride and groom happy:

> It is a positive commandment of rabbinic origin to visit the sick, comfort mourners, to prepare for a funeral, prepare a bride, accompany guests, attend to all the needs of a burial, carry a corpse on one's shoulders, walk before the bier, mourn, dig a grave, and bury the dead, and also to bring joy to a bride and groom and help them with all their needs. These are deeds of kindness that one carries out with his person that have no limit. Although all these mitzvot are of rabbinic origin, they are included in the scriptural commandment (Lev. 19:18): "Love your neighbor as yourself." That charge implies that whatever you would like other people to do for you, you should do for your comrade in the Torah and mitzvot. (Maimonides, *Mishneh Torah, Hilkhot Avel* 14:1)

Having reviewed the parallels between mourning and wedding celebrations, we can try to provide some explanation for the puzzling link between them. In order to compare the two periods of time, shiva and the seven days of feasting, we focus on the word "process." These two periods of time mark the most significant events in a person's life, and they bring about some of the most significant changes of a person's lifetime. Although marriage involves intense joy, the complete opposite of the grief and sorrow following a death, there is a common denominator in terms of the gradual process involved in adapting to one's new reality. The different periods of times – shiva, *shloshim,* and one year – can be explained as part of this adjustment period.

In terms of the honor shown to mourners and to brides and grooms: Jewish law dictates that these individuals must be escorted. They are honored for different reasons, but in both cases, there is a recognition that they – the bride and groom and the mourners – hold a special status. This is also expressed by their sitting at the head of the table.

Both mourners and the bride and groom may feel anxious about their new situation, perhaps fearing the unknown future. For the mourner, this is caused by the shock following the relative's death. Brides and grooms may also experience this anxiety, having left the safety and familiarity of their parents' home and taken on the responsibility of building their own home. Thus, there is a mitzva to make a bride and groom happy and, as different as it may be, to comfort mourners. The importance given to communal recognition of their experience is instructive; it teaches us the importance of sharing in others' feelings, providing them with support and encouragement.

The encircling movement of the *hakafot,* done at the burial and under the *ḥuppa,* is a symbolic gesture of protection. For the deceased, one's aim is to protect them from the impure forces that cleave to them during the very sensitive time of burial. The same is true at the *ḥuppa*: The sages say that a man who has no wife is without joy, blessing, goodness, Torah, protection, and peace (Yevamot 62b). Marriage protects the couple from life's common mistakes and temptations. Mourning and a marriage are both life transitions at sensitive stages that require protection.

Regarding the special blessings: The blessings remind us of God and teach us to accept the processes of the lifecycle, whether they be happy or sad. "I will lift up the cup of salvation and call upon the name of the Lord" (Ps. 116:13). This is paralleled by the verse: "I found trouble and sorrow, but I called upon the name of the Lord" (Ps. 116:3–4). In all situations, we call upon God.

See also **One Should Be as Thankful for the Bad as One Is for the Good – and Accept It with Joy.**

Seven Relatives

> The Lord said to Moses: Speak to the *kohanim*, the sons of Aaron, and say to them: None shall defile himself for any [dead] person among his kin, except for the relatives that are closest to him: his mother, his father, his son, his daughter, and his brother; also for a virgin sister, close to him because she has not married, for her he may defile himself. (Lev. 21:1–3)

The relatives for whom one has to mourn are one's father, mother, brother, sister, son, daughter, and spouse.

The relatives mentioned in the Torah (Lev. 21:2) are: father, mother, son, daughter, and paternal brother and sister. To this list, the rabbis added a spouse as well as maternal siblings (Maimonides, *Mishneh Torah, Hilkhot Avel* 2:1). For further discussion, see Sec. 16, "Who Mourns and for Whom?"

See **Whomever He Mourns For, He Also Mourns With**.

Seventh of Adar

This is the date of Moses' death. God Himself buried Moses, as it says: "He buried him in the valley" (Deut. 34:6). This date was chosen as a special day for *ḥevra kaddishas*; indeed, Moses himself was involved in the holy work of caring for the dead, having taken Joseph's bones from Egypt for burial in Israel.

On the seventh of Adar, members of the *ḥevra kaddisha* fast and visit the cemetery and ask the dead for forgiveness lest they did not honor them properly when performing their work. At the cemetery, they pray and the rabbi speaks about the *ḥevra kaddisha*'s responsibilities to the deceased, and they tend to the needs of the deceased and the cemetery. Afterwards, they say Maariv and have a festive meal together, which fortifies them for the work ahead and fosters a sense of comradery (*Gesher HaḤayim* 33).

In Israel, the seventh of Adar was selected as a memorial day for fallen IDF soldiers whose graves are unknown, just as the location of Moses's grave is unknown: "And no one knows his burial place to this day" (Deut. ibid.).

See also *Ḥevra Kaddisha*; **Memorial Day for Fallen Soldiers of the IDF (*Yom HaZikaron*).**

Shekhiv MeRa

This expression refers to someone who is critically ill and is usually used in the context of legal matters. The sages established a rule: "Whatever the critically-ill person says, it is as though it has been written and given over." This is to avoid causing the person to become agitated, upset by the knowledge that his wishes will not be fulfilled. It is why the sages ruled that the person's oral will is valid. See **Will.**

It is customary that when a person is in critical condition, he blesses his children, as Isaac and Jacob blessed their children before they died.

See also **Confession (*Viduy*); Person Who is Dying (*Goses*); Will.**

Shrouds

In Hebrew, *Takhrikhim*. These are garments made for the deceased in which the body is buried. In Aramaic they are called "*zevadeta*" (Moed Katan 27b). This word parallels the Hebrew word "*zivud*," meaning outfit or equipment. In this context, it conveys the meaning of equipment for the deceased's journey (Rashi, Avoda Zara 17a).

Originally, shrouds were made of expensive cloth to show honor to the deceased, but the custom became problematic:

> Initially, the funeral expenditures for the deceased were more taxing for his relatives than his death, until it reached a point where people would abandon the deceased and flee. This continued until Rabbi Gamliel demonstrated humility, and instructed that he be buried in plain linen garments. And then the people followed his example and were taken for burial in plain linen garments. (Moed Katan ibid.; Ketubbot 10b)

Indeed, a case is described where a poor man had to bury his daughter in a straw mat (Berakhot 18b). Since Rabban Gamliel's death, the custom is to bury the dead in white linen shrouds sewn with white linen thread. Maimonides (*Mishneh Torah, Hilkhot Avel* 4:1) writes: "They are dressed in shrouds sewn with threads of white linen and they should not be costly." White clothing represents simplicity and purity. The Kabbalists compared this to the *kohanim*'s clothing and to the white robes of the High Priest on Yom Kippur. According to the Kabbala, it is important to wear only white linen garments, with no other cloth, so that the deceased will be protected from the impure forces (*Maavar Yabok, "Sefat Emet,"* ch. 23; *Kuntras HaYeḥieli, Beit Olamim,* ch. 2).

> Know that there is a great mystical secret in wearing linen shrouds; every person who dies and wears linen shrouds, even if he died outside of Israel, the accuser becomes an advocate. (*Yalkut HaReuveni, Miketz,* brought in *Pitḥei Teshuva* 352:2)

> The people should hear and the righteous person should prepare pure linen shrouds during his lifetime, without any other kind of fibers. The money used to purchase the shrouds should be from what the person earned and must not include money that was gained unethically, God forbid. (*Menaḥem Avel,* Letter *Tet, "Takhrikhim,"* in the name of Rabbi Moshe Cordovero)

Rabbi Moshe Cordovero first stresses the importance of a technical point: not mixing the flax with other fibers. Afterwards, he discusses an essential point, that one should not use money that is "not kosher," gained dishonestly, for purchasing shrouds. The purity of the clothing is reflected in the purity of the deed.

If there is no linen available or if it is too expensive, the shrouds can be made from simple and cheap cloth (this is the custom in most places, unless someone specifically requests linen). If a wealthy person has given instructions to bury him in expensive clothing, we do not comply with his wish:

> It is forbidden to bury the dead, even a *nasi* among the Jewish people, in silk shrouds or clothes embroidered with gold, for this is an expression of haughtiness, the wasteful destruction of

> property, and the emulation of gentile practices. (Maimonides, *Mishneh Torah, Hilkhot Avel* 4:2)

The *Shulhan Arukh* (*Yoreh De'ah* 352:1) agrees: "The dead are not buried in expensive shrouds, even a *nasi* among the Jewish people."

> Rabbi Natan said: The clothing in which the deceased is buried is the clothing that will rise up with him in the future, as it says: "It changes like clay under the seal until [its hues] are fixed like those of a garment" (Job 38:14). (Smaḥot, ch. 9)

> Rabbi Yanai told his children: My sons, do not bury me in white garments nor in black garments. Not in white, lest I not be acquitted, and I will be like a groom among mourners. And not in black, lest I be acquitted, and I will be like a mourner among grooms. (Shabbat 114a)

Nahmanides (*Torat HaAdam*) quoted Rabbi Yanai's words and wrote that the custom is to use white shrouds and that it is proper to do so. This is the halakha as it appears in the *Tur* and the *Shulḥan Arukh* (*Yoreh De'ah* 353:2).

The Kabbalists explained that the shrouds should be white because white is associated with celestial mercy and atonement, as it says: "Be your sins like crimson, they can turn snow-white" (Is. 1:18). And since death also atones, the shrouds allude to this atonement. (In *Kuntras HaYeḥieli*, ch. 3, seven reasons are brought for using white shrouds; he writes at length in sec. 12 about why the shrouds should not be black, because it is associated with God's attribute of justice.)

It is customary for the shrouds to be hand-sewn by women (since the first woman, Eve, brought about the existence of death in the world). The sewing is done by older women, who no longer need to immerse in the *mikve*.

The shrouds should be clean, without any stains or dirt on them. They are made without a hem and without pockets (to show that the dead cannot take anything with them to the grave). The garment is not closed with knots; it is tied with a bow to show that the clothing is temporary until the resurrection. Shrouds for men and women are the same. Small children are not buried in shrouds but in a white sheet (*Gesher HaḤayim* 12:6, 2).

They are eight pieces of clothing (and for a *kohen,* one more is added), and this is the order of dressing them: 1. Hat 2. Belt, called "*Tallit Katan*" 3. Pants 4. Tunic 5. Jacket 6. *Sovev,* which is a long, wide sheet that is wrapped around the deceased and tied in bows in three places. At this stage, the children of the deceased place a small amount of soil on the eyes while saying, "And Joseph's hand shall close your eyes" (Gen. 46:4). If the person has no children, then one of the members of the *ḥevra kaddisha* does this and says, "For dust you are and to dust you will return" (Gen. 3:19). 7. A veil for covering the face 8. A square cloth that is placed on the head and the eyes, called a "*Tallit Gadol.*" For a *kohen,* gloves are put on the hands, and when putting on the gloves, they say the verses of the Priestly Blessing.

> All the garments that he is dressed in are like the priestly garments; only a sash is not used because the sash must be belted and tied, and shrouds are not tied. The reason for this is that, during one's lifetime, the soul and spirit are bound and connected, but when one dies, the spirit and soul separate and go their separate ways. (*Kuntras HaYeḥieli, Beit Olamim,* ch. 5. Here he discusses the significance of each of the garments.)

While dressing the body, they recite verses: "Nard and saffron, fragrant reed and cinnamon, with all aromatic woods, myrrh and aloes – all the choice perfumes" (Song. 4:14). When putting on the covering called "*Tallit Gadol,*" they say: "I greatly rejoice in the Lord, my whole being exults in my God. For He has clothed me with garments of triumph, wrapped me in a robe of victory, like a bridegroom adorned with a turban, like a bride bedecked with her finery" (Is. 61:10); "Then he gave the order, 'Let a pure diadem be placed on his head.' And they placed the pure diadem on his head and clothed him in garments, as the angel of the Lord stood by" (Zech. 3:5); "For as the earth brings forth her growth and a garden makes the seed shoot up, so the Lord God will make victory and renown shoot up in the presence of all the nations" (Is. 61:11); "The Lord will guide you always; He will slake your thirst in parched places and give strength to your bones. You shall be like a watered garden, like a spring whose waters do not fail" (Is. 58:11). The book *Maavar Yabok* describes the mystical, Kabbalistic intentions that the *ḥevra kaddisha* should have in mind during this process ("*Siftei Renanot*," ch. 12–14; *Gesher HaḤayim* 10:4).

In some places, three myrtles branches are placed between the shrouds; some use hyssop in the shrouds or during the washing of the body (*Kuntras HaYeḥieli, Beit Olamim*, 15:15, 19).

For a deceased man, after they dress him in shrouds, they cover him with a tallit with tzitzit. This is left on until the burial and is then removed. The body is not buried in the tallit. A woman is wrapped in a white sheet.

If a person was killed and his clothes are soaked with blood, the clothes are buried with the body. Someone who was murdered is buried in his clothes, and the shrouds are placed over the clothes. This is done to arouse God's wrath and retribution.

The Yemenite custom is to dress the person in his finest clothing, those that he would wear on Shabbat and Yom Tov. This is meant to convey the belief in the resurrection; but the garments should not be too expensive. Simple white shrouds are put over this clothing (*Be'er LeḤai Roi* 63, based on *Anaf Etz Avot*, p. 697).

Some people prepare their shrouds while they are alive, in order to keep in mind the day of death and be inspired to repent. As the verse states: "Let your clothes always be white" (Eccl. 9:8), and as the sages taught, "Repent the day before you die."

It was once customary among Jews to dress the deceased in shoes. In the Talmud (Yevamot 104a), there is a mention of shoes made for the honor of an elderly person. Rashi explains that the shoes were for shrouds. The Yerushalmi Talmud (Kilayim 9:3) mentions that Rabbi Jeremiah gave instructions to be buried in shoes. (It is difficult to draw conclusions from Rabbi Jeremiah's instruction, however, because he also said to bury him on his side, which differs from the traditional Jewish custom to bury the deceased lying on their back; he also gave instructions that his staff be placed in his hand, and this is not the custom.

The *Ḥatam Sofer*, in a responsa (*Yoreh De'ah* 175), derived the custom of putting scepters in the deceased's hand (called *gaflikh*) from Rabbi Jeremiah's instructions. This is not customary today.) Some wanted to point to this as the source for the custom not to use the deceased's shoes, lest they were intended as part of the deceased's shrouds; if that were the case, it would be forbidden to derive benefit from them (*Kol Bo al Aveilut*, p. 91 in the footnote).

See also **Property of the Deceased; Resurrection; *Tahara*; Tzitzit on the Burial Shrouds.**

Song of Afflictions

This refers to Psalm 91. The psalm is called "Song of Afflictions" because it describes man's salvation from various afflictions that may befall him and his faith that God will save him. There is a custom to recite this psalm at the funeral, to protect the soul of the deceased from impure forces and evil angels (*Maavar Yabok, "Siftei Renanot,"* ch. 20).

The Talmud (Shavuot 15b) calls this psalm "song of afflictions (*pegaim*)" or "song of plagues (*nega'im*)." The psalm is traditionally attributed to Moses, who is believed to have said it at the dedication of the Tabernacle (Rashi ad loc.).

Maimonides (Guide to the Perplexed, vol. 3, ch. 51) uses this psalm to describe the divine protection that a completely righteous person merits to receive.

See also ***Hakafot; Maavar Yabok.***

Soul (*Neshama*)

The soul is an eternal spiritual entity that resides in one's body throughout one's lifetime. When a person dies, the soul leaves the body and passes into eternal life in the "world of truth," the world to come.

> Thus too, with the Holy One, Blessed be He. Concerning the bodies of the righteous, He says: "He enters into peace, they rest on their beds, each one that walks in his uprightness" (Is. 57:2). And with regard to their souls, it states: "And the soul of my lord shall be bound in the bond of life with the Lord your God" (I Sam. 25:29). And with regard to the bodies of

the wicked, it states: "There is no peace, says the Lord, for the wicked" (Is. 57:21). And with regard to their souls, it states: "And the souls of your enemies He shall sling out in the hollow of a sling" (I Sam. 25:29.).

It was taught that Rabbi Eliezer says: The souls of the righteous are stored beneath the Throne of Glory, as it is stated: "And the soul of my lord shall be bound in the bond of life" (I Sam. 25:29). And the souls of the wicked continuously wander; one angel stands at one end of the world and another angel stands at the other end of the world and they sling the souls to one another, as it is stated: "And the souls of your enemies He shall sling out in the hollow of a sling." (Shabbat 152b)

What is the soul's state after it leaves the body? It is preserved until the time comes for it to be rewarded, as it says: "He who watches over your life will know it, And He will pay each man as he deserves" (Prov. 24:12). And their merits are stored on high and their sins below... as the sages said: "The souls of the righteous are stored beneath the Throne of Glory and those of the wicked roam throughout the world."

At the beginning of the separation, there is a restless time until the body disintegrates and its parts decompose. The soul suffers during this time, knowing what is happening to the body by means of maggots and worms, in the same way that a person would suffer if he knew that his house was being destroyed and becoming overgrown with thorns and brambles. And the suffering of the soul will be more or less intense depending on what it deserves, and therefore our sages say, "Maggots are as excruciating to the dead as the stab of a needle to the flesh of the living" (Berakhot 18b). And this corresponds with what is written: "He feels only the pain of his flesh, and his spirit mourns in him" (Job 14:22). And this is what I know of what is called *ḥibut haKever,* the suffering of the grave. (Rabbi Saadia Gaon, *HaNivḥar BeEmunot VeDeot,* sixth article, ch. 7)

See also **Suffering of the Grave; Resurrection.**

Suffering Atones

> Rabbi Shimon ben Lakish said: The word covenant is used with regard to salt, and the word covenant is used with regard to afflictions. Covenant is used with regard to salt, as it is written: "The salt of the covenant should not be excluded" (Lev. 2:13). And covenant is used with regard to afflictions, as it is written: "These are the words of the covenant" (Deut. 28:69). Just as the covenant mentioned with regard to salt – and the salt sweetens the meat, so too the covenant mentioned with regard to suffering – and the suffering cleanses a person's transgressions. (Berakhot 5a)

Salt draws blood from the meat. When the salt is washed off, the blood is also washed away. Similarly, suffering draws out a person's negative traits and when the suffering goes away, the person is left cleansed. King Solomon wrote: "If folly settles in the heart of a lad, the rod of discipline will remove it" (Prov. 22:15). Therefore, a person should not reject his suffering. He should pray that suffering will not befall him, but if it does nonetheless, he should contemplate how he might be helped by it. (See e.g., Rabbi J. B. Soloveitchik's essay, "*Kol Dodi Dofek*.")

> Rabbi Yehuda said – The early hasidim used to suffer stomach pains ten or twenty days before their death in order to cleanse everything, so that they should enter the next world meritorious, as it says (Prov. 27:21): "For silver – the crucible, for gold – the furnace, and a man is tested by his praise" (Smaḥot, ch. 3:10). The same way the furnace purifies silver and gold from all impurities, so does God refine the righteous in this world so that they shall enter the next world cleansed and pure. (Commentary of *Naḥalat Yaakov* ibid.)

Some individuals tell the *ḥevra kaddisha* that, when they die, the *ḥevra kaddisha* should perform a version of the four capital punishments on them. These instructions should be obeyed; i.e., the members of *the ḥevra kaddisha* raise up the body and let it fall to the ground, which is similar to stoning; drip wax into the mouth which is like burning, etc.

(*Yalkut Yosef* 9:16). See the will of Rabbi Alexander Zeskind, printed at the end of his book *Yesod VeShoresh HaAvoda*, where he instructed the *ḥevra kaddisha* to perform the four capital punishments on him after death.

See also **One Should Be as Thankful for the Bad as One Is for the Good – and Accept it with Joy; *Tziduk HaDin*.**

Suffering of the Grave

This is a Kabbalistic concept, *ḥibut haKever*, that refers to the suffering of the soul after the body dies.

The reason for the suffering of the grave is that bad traits adhere to the soul as a sort of spiritual infection (the Kabbalistic term for this is "*klipot*") and these need to be removed, which causes the soul pain. The more *klipot* there are, the more severe the pain will be. It can be likened to a dirty garment that needs to be cleaned; the thicker and heavier the dirt is, and the more embedded filth, the harsher the cleansing is.

There is a related concept describing someone who does not remember his own name on the day of his death. It is said that this happens because the *klipot* cause the person to forget. "*Shiḥakha*," forgetfulness, contains the same letters as "*ḥashekha*," darkness; the *klipot* block out the "light," which symbolizes knowledge and memory. On a spiritual plane, there is no forgetfulness, and so someone who does not know his own name has forgotten his essence. The *klipot*, the negative traits, have caused him to detach from his true self. Part of the idea of the suffering of the grave is that the suffering shakes a person in order to rid him of these negative traits, so that he can know himself and his essence. When a person has forgotten his own name, the suffering of the grave is harsh and intense, because one has forgotten one's essence. But when a person knows his name, the pain is minimal.

One who was buried on Erev Shabbat is said not to undergo suffering of the grave because of the sanctity of Shabbat (*Kuntras HaYeḥieli, Beit Olamim*, 15:39; he writes that the holiness of Shabbat begins from the fifth hour on Friday). But it is forbidden to delay the burial in order to perform it on Friday afternoon. See also *Maavar Yabok*, "*Siftei Renanot*," ch. 42.

Suffering also atones for the living:

> A person truly merits with his suffering when he tolerates it good-naturedly, as though he were meriting to do a mitzva. This is because suffering weakens the body, which is the force of impurity, and the soul becomes refined from its impurity and remains pure and cleansed and ready to be cloaked in the garment of light that it wore in the Garden of Eden. (*Maavar Yabok, Siftei Tzedek*, ch. 20)

According to this explanation, suffering is somewhat like an antibiotic; it is meant to weaken the bacteria to enable the body to overcome them. If less negative traits are present and require removal, the person will endure less suffering. One whose "body" is spiritually strong does not require suffering.

This idea is explained somewhat differently by Rabbi Saadia Gaon.

See also ***Hakafot*; Soul (*Neshama*); Suffering Atones.**

Suicide

Jewish law has a stern approach when it comes to the death of someone who took his own life. The Jewish perspective maintains that, because a person's life does not belong to him, one is not permitted to extinguish life. This is true with regard to other people – "You shall not murder" – and also with regard to oneself. In this way, someone who takes his own life is in the same category as a murderer.

From a theoretical halakhic perspective, someone who has taken his own life has committed a greater sin than someone who has killed somebody else. A person who has taken his own life has emphasized, through this act, his denial of the Almighty who gave him his soul and who has sole permission to take it back; he ostensibly removes God's dominion over his soul, denying the basic idea that he – man – did not have a part in his own creation.

Death is considered to atone for man's sins. But when someone takes his own life, his death is not an atonement. On the contrary, it is a sin as grave as murder.

Moreover, one who commits suicide is denying the belief in the soul's eternal nature. Suicide expresses an escape from life, but Judaism believes that the soul is eternal and that one cannot escape from God; man will need to give an accounting for his deeds after death.

Despite this philosophical rejection of suicide, on a practical level, our sages adopted a lenient approach to actual cases of someone who took his own life. Attempts are made to avoid classifying the death as a suicide. For example, they will consider whether the death can be seen as an accident or as caused by somebody else, or whether the person was perhaps suffering a mental breakdown. If the person was not mentally sound, this is considered to be a case of *anoos* (one who is coerced) and does not constitute a suicide. A minor is also never considered to have committed suicide. If a person had no other choice, like King Saul who feared that he would fall into the hands of the enemy, this not considered a case of a suicide (Smaḥot, ch. 2; *Tur* and *Shulḥan Arukh, Yoreh De'ah* 345). There are halakhic debates concerning the case of someone who was extremely intoxicated. "The rule is that for someone who commits suicide, we try to attribute it to something such as fear or pain or insanity, or to say that the person assumed it was permitted and not a sin, etc., because it is truly rare for a person to do something so despicable with a sound mind" (*Arukh HaShulḥan, Yoreh De'ah* 345:5).

The halakhic definition of suicide includes three main conditions: The person made a clear verbal declaration stating that he was going to kill himself; he immediately did what he said he would do; and he did so in anger. The halakhic authorities added another condition: They consider that the person may have regretted their act after doing it. Even if the person left a suicide note that reflected that he was of sound mind – it is possible that after writing it, he changed his mind. Some wrote that it is only considered a suicide if the person killed himself after being warned not to do so. If someone took his own life as atonement for his sins or from the desire to resist his inclination to sin, even though this is forbidden, the case is not regarded as a suicide (*Gesher HaḤayim* 25:3, 4).

In the case of a suicide, the halakhic principle for the practices of mourning is that anything done for the honor of the living should be done, while any practices done for the honor of the deceased should not be done (Smaḥot 2:1; Maimonides, *Mishneh Torah, Hilkhot Avel* 1:11; *Shulḥan Arukh*, ibid.).

There are commandments for which a person is obliged to die rather than transgress – idolatry, sexual immorality, and murder (Sanhedrin 74). There have been cases where Jews took their own lives out of fear that they would be forced to commit these or other sins.

See also **Being Cut Off (*Karet*); Eternality of the Soul.**

Tahara

Tahara literally means "purification." The deceased undergo ritual purification by the *ḥevra kaddisha* before burial. *Tahara* involves washing the body and dressing it in shrouds before the burial. Men prepare men and women prepare women. *Tahara* is done with respect for the deceased – respect for both their body and soul.

The *tahara* ritual is performed in the funeral home in a designated room. The members of the *ḥevra kaddisha* wash their hands and say a special prayer before beginning the *tahara* (brought in *Gesher HaḤayim* 9:1 from *Maavar Yabok*; the source for the prayer is quite ancient, attributed to Hillel the Elder). During *tahara,* they say certain verses related to washing and purification, such as: "I will sprinkle clean water upon you, and you shall be clean: I will cleanse you from all your uncleanness and from all your fetishes" (Ezek. 36:25). The reason for reciting these verses is twofold: because the verses discuss the purification ceremony and because reciting the verses prevents the people doing the *tahara* from engaging in idle chatter and mundane matters. See *Maavar Yabok, "Siftei Renanot,"* ch. 4–6 and 12; psalms that are recited and Kabbalistic intentions for washing and dressing the body appear there. *Gesher HaḤayim* (9:1–2) brings verses that are said when washing each limb of the body.

The washing is performed while the deceased is lying on his back facing upwards and covered by a sheet, for purposes of respect and modesty. The washing includes scrubbing with soap and a sponge. This includes cleaning inside the rectum until the water comes out clear and clean. Afterwards, the deceased's fingernails and toenails are cleaned.

The central part of the *tahara* is the pouring of nine *kabin* (about twenty liters) of water over the deceased (as explained in *Gesher HaḤayim* 9:4).

Some have the custom of immersing a deceased male in a *mikve* after washing him, before dressing him in the shrouds.

He should be washed to remove the dirt, so that the people do not refrain from carrying him. (*Kol Bo,* quoted in the *Beit Yosef* 352)

The reason for washing the body – because one might ask, what is actually the benefit of the washing? For even if all the water in the world would be poured over the body, they could not remove its impurity, since it is the ultimate source of impurity. It is because we, the Jewish people, await the resurrection of the dead; and also, because the person feared the Angel of Death, he sees spilled seed. He should therefore be washed of this impurity to be pure for the resurrection of the dead. (*Sefer Menaḥem Aveilim*)

The reason the body is washed is that the shrouds are like the priestly clothing; regarding the *kohen,* it states: "He shall bathe his body in water and then put them on" (Lev. 16:4). Hence it is also the custom to wash the deceased's body before wearing them. Another reason is that, just as people are washed when they are born, they are likewise washed when they leave this world. And the reason it is customary to clean them of any feces inside… is to clean the food from the intestines, to be clean and pure like angels. As it says in *Avot DeRabbi Natan* (1): Rabbi Natan said – Why did Moses wait for six days before ascending to Mount Sinai and the voice of God did not come upon him? So he could be cleansed of food and drink from his insides, so that he could be holy like the angels. Thus, the custom is to clean a person's insides so that he should be clean and worthy for the next world and merit to hear the divine word. And his orifices are closed up, as it says in the Talmud (Yoma 85; Sukka 45; Nidda 30): When a person is in the womb, the mouth is closed and the navel is open, and when the person comes into the world, what is closed opens up and what is open closes up, etc. When he leaves this world, what is open closes up and what is closed opens up. And that is why when he leaves the world his orifices are closed up. (*Kuntras HaYeḥieli, Beit Olamim,* ch. 4)

After being washed, the deceased is dressed in simple white shrouds. Linen shrouds are preferable. According to the Kabbala, it is important that the shrouds be of linen and not other materials, in order to protect the deceased from impure forces (*Menaḥem Aveilim*, in the name of Rabbi Moshe Cordovero; *Kuntras HaYeḥieli, Beit Olamim*, ch. 2). Linen is derived from a plant and is thus connected to the ground, unlike wool which comes from animals. The land also is able to absorb spiritual forces that could harm the dead person (similar to the way the land can absorb electric waves). This is one of the reasons we bury the deceased in the ground, and linen is associated with the ground. People who are meticulous in their observance will choose to be buried in linen shrouds because they offer extra protection for the body.

There is a custom to wrap a man in a tallit during the funeral but not to bury him in the tallit. In the *Tur* and *Shulḥan Arukh, Yoreh De'ah* 531 there is a discussion as to whether the tallit used for the deceased should be kosher and valid for use. See also **Tzitzit on the Burial Shrouds**.

One should not participate or be present at one's parent's *tahara* out of respect for the parent, nor at the *tahara* of one's parent-in-law, step-parent, or sister's husband. But a parent may be present at his child's or son- or daughter-in-law's *tahara*. If someone died of a contagious disease, *tahara* should be performed but on the condition that the members of the *ḥevra kaddisha* take the necessary precautions to maintain cleanliness and sterile conditions so that they are not infected. Someone who was killed does not undergo *tahara*, but is instead buried in his clothes.

See also **Shrouds.**

Tearing One's Garment (*Kriya*)

Tearing a garment is a sign of pain and mourning. We see this in the example of Jacob, who tore his clothing when he heard that his son Joseph was dead. Tearing garments appears as a sign of mourning several times in the Tanakh – David for Saul and Jonathan, David for Avner, Yiftaḥ for his daughter, Elisha upon Elijah's departure, Job for his sons. There are many other examples of tearing one's clothing as an expression of sadness and upon hearing bad news.

The Talmud (Moed Katan 24a) teaches: "A mourner who did not grow wild and did not rend [his garment] is liable to the death penalty." This implies that *kriya* is a Torah obligation. Most opinions, however, hold that it is a rabbinic obligation (*Gesher HaḤayim* 4:1).

In terms of the reasons for *kriya*, some wrote that tearing the clothing comes to awaken sorrow, while others wrote the opposite – that *kriya* serves to distract the mourner somewhat from the loss of his relative by having his thoughts turn to the loss of the garment. Put simply, *kriya* symbolizes the rending of the mourner's heart. The prophet even uses this image to rebuke the people: "Rend your hearts and not your garments" (Joel 2:13). In the book *Maavar Yabok* ("*Imrei Noam*," ch. 31–32), he brings a Kabbalistic explanation for *kriya* and the halakhot pertaining to it. Further details can be found in Sec. 8, "Tearing of Garments (*Kriya*)."

According to the original practice, *kriya* was performed at the moment of death, even for the death of a non-relative. Nowadays, in practice, it is customary to do *kriya* at the beginning of the funeral (according to the Ashkenazic custom) or after the burial (according to the Sephardic custom).

The garment itself must be torn; it is unacceptable to instead tear a piece of cloth that has been attached to the clothing: "This new custom is deplorable… that before *kriya,* they attach a piece of black silk to the mourners' clothing and make a tear in this cloth. This does not fulfill their obligation" (*Kol Bo al Aveilut,* p. 13).

Those mourning someone other than a parent may mend the tear when the mourning period is over. But someone mourning for a parent may never mend the tear. There are circumstances in which a person should do *kriya* the same way one does it for a parent (a tear that is never mended): upon the death of one's rabbi who taught him Torah or the Head of the Sanhedrin or religious court; upon hearing bad news; if someone blasphemed God's name; for a Torah scroll that was burned; and over the destruction of the Temple and the cities of Judah and Jerusalem.

Someone who sees a Torah scroll being burnt must tear two times – once for the parchment and once for the writing. This is derived from the verse in Jeremiah (36:24) where King Yehoyakim burnt the scroll that Jeremiah wrote; it says there about the leaders of Judah,

"They showed no fear and did not rend their garments." The Talmud understands from this that they acted inappropriately and should have torn their garments. Therefore, the halakha is: "One who sees a Torah scroll that is burned or tefillin or even a scroll of the books of Prophets or Writings, tears twice, provided only that it is burnt by force and only in the same manner as it once happened" (Moed Katan 26a; Smaḥot 9; Maimonides, *Mishneh Torah, Hilkhot Avel* 9:2; *Shulḥan Arukh, Oraḥ Ḥayim* 561 and *Yoreh De'ah* 340:36–38).

See *Yalkut Yosef, Aveilut* 9:28, regarding a Torah scroll that was burned because of an electrical mishap in the synagogue, and about a Torah scroll that was destroyed by Arabs in Me'arat HaMakhpela.

Tefillin on the First Day

The mourner is not permitted to wear tefillin on the first day of mourning.

The prohibition is derived from the prophet Ezekiel, who was told, "Wear your splendor upon you" (24:17). This is understood as a specific one-time instruction to Ezekiel, while all other mourners may not wear tefillin (called "splendor") (Moed Katan 15a). There are several explanations for this: First, to demonstrate respect for the tefillin – because the mourner's grieving does not befit the splendor of tefillin (Rashi, Ketubbot 6a). Another reason is that, when one glorifies oneself by wearing tefillin, it appears that one is not mourning (Rashi, Sukka 25a), because tefillin represent glory and beauty, which are the complete opposite of the pain and sorrow that engulf those in the beginning of their mourning. Our sages expound on the difference between "*pe'er*" (splendor) and "*efer*" (ashes), which are comprised of the same letters but are opposites of each other. Tefillin are splendor, unlike mourning, symbolized by ashes. This is seen in the verse in Isaiah (61:3): "To provide for the mourners in Zion – To give them splendor instead of ashes, the festive ointment instead of mourning, a garment of splendor instead of a drooping spirit." Some say that the reason the mourner may not wear tefillin on the first day is that he is unable to concentrate on the mitzva of tefillin since he is immersed in his grief, and one may not wear tefillin when one is unable to concentrate. At the same time, he is not supposed to concentrate on the tefillin since it is his obligation to mourn (*Melo HaRoim*).

The Angel of Death

This is the angel appointed to take a human's soul away.

> Resh Lakish says: Satan, the evil inclination, and the Angel of Death are one. In the Mishna it taught: He descends and leads astray, he ascends and aggravates, he is given permission and takes a soul. (Bava Batra 16a)

Maimonides discusses these concepts extensively in his Guide to the Perplexed (3:22).

> They said that the Angel of Death is full of eyes. When the sick person is on his deathbed, he stands above the person's head with his sword drawn in his hand and a drop of bitterness hanging from it. When the sick person sees him, he is shaken and opens his mouth and he tosses it into the person's mouth. From it he dies, from it he smells putrid, from it his face becomes green. (Avoda Zara 20b)

> Rav Yosef would cry when he reached this verse: "But there are those swept away without justice" (Prov. 13:23). He said: Is there one who goes before his time? Yes, like this incident of Rav Beivai bar Abaye, who would be frequented by the Angel of Death. He said to his agent: Go and bring me Miriam the raiser, [i.e., braider] of women's hair. He went but instead brought him Miriam, the raiser of babies. The Angel of Death said to him: I told you to bring Miriam, the raiser of women's hair. He said to him: If so, return her to life. He said to him: Since you have already brought her, let her be counted [toward the number of deceased people]. But how were you able to kill her? He said, she was holding a shovel in her hand and with it she was lighting and sweeping the oven. She took it and set it on her foot; she was scalded and her luck suffered, and I brought her. Rav Beivai bar Abaye said to him: Do you have the right to act this way? He replied: And is it not written: "But there are those swept away without justice" (Prov. 13:23)? Rav Beivai said to him: And isn't

it written: "One generation passes away, and another generation comes" (Eccl. 1:14) [which indicates that there is a predetermined amount of time for the life of every generation]. He said to him: I shepherd them, until the years of the generation are completed, and then I pass them on to the angel Duma who oversees the souls of the dead. Rav Beivai said to him: Ultimately, what do you do with his extra years? The Angel of Death said to him: If there is a Torah scholar who disregards his matters, I add those years to him and he becomes the replacement. (Ḥagiga 5a)

"David looked up and saw the angel of the Lord standing between heaven and earth, with a drawn sword in his hand directed against Jerusalem" (I Chron. 21:16). What did the angel do? He took his sword and wiped it on David's cloak. David saw the Angel of Death's sword and he was frightened in all his limbs for the rest of his life, as it says (ibid. 21:30): "And David was unable to go to it to worship God because he was terrified by the sword of the angel of the Lord." (*Pirkei DeRebbi Eliezer*, ch. 43)

Our ancestors taught that the angel sent by God to separate between them is revealed to man in the form of green fire that is full of fire-blue eyes, and in his hand is a drawn sword pointing toward him; when they see it, they are frightened of it, and the soul leaves the body. When I looked in the verses, I saw this scenario that they described, as stated in the time of the plague: "David looked up and saw the angel of the Lord standing between heaven and earth, with a drawn sword in his hand directed against Jerusalem" (I Chron. 21:30). And when he prayed and offered sacrifices it is said, "The Lord ordered the angel to return the sword to its sheath" (ibid. 27). I learned from this that the angel's body is of green fire, as it says: "Such then was the appearance of the creatures. With them was something that looked like burning coals of fire" (Ezek. 1:13). And they are all filled with eyes: "Their entire bodies – backs, hands, and wings – and the wheels were covered all over with eyes" (ibid. 10:12). We already know that our forefathers almost died upon seeing the huge fire, "Let us not die" (Deut.

5:22), how much more so if it was an angel with an outstretched sword. And we know that when David saw the Angel of Death, even though it was not directly pointed toward him, he was frightened and shaken (Chron. I 21:30): "Because he was terrified by the sword of the angel of the Lord." And he did not stop shaking from that day until he died: "And though they covered him with bedclothes, he never felt warm" (I Kings 1:1). And how much more so for someone for whom it was pointing at him. (Rabbi Saadia Gaon's *HaNivḥar BeEmunot VeDeot*, article 6, ch. 7)

I found something to support the Jewish custom of not standing beside the foot of the bed of a dying person: since the Angel of Death is before them and wields his sword, as the sages taught, and so one should not draw near. It is written in the Zohar (*Pinḥas*, 134b) that whoever visits a sick person should not sit next to his head since the *Shekhina* is next to the head, and also not by his feet since the Angel of Death is next to his feet. (*Maavar Yabok, "Siftei Renanot,"* ch. 6)

See also **Kiss of Death.**

The Blessing "Who Fashioned You in Justice"

This blessing is said when someone visits a cemetery after not having seen one for thirty days. In some cemeteries, the blessing is displayed at the entrance. The blessing and an explanation can be found in Sec. 45, "Laws Relating to the Cemetery."

The Coffin Yields Before a Bride

This is a general halakhic rule brought in the Talmud (Ketubbot 17a) and established as the halakha (*Shulḥan Arukh, Yoreh De'ah* 360). The sages wanted to illustrate a principle and did so by giving an example of a funeral procession coming down a road from one direction at the same time that a bride and her entourage are coming from the other direction, on the same road. The two processions must not intermingle because it would be inappropriate to have the two emotional extremes confront each other – the depths of pain and sorrow on the one hand,

and the height of joy on the other. One of these processions must step aside and let the other pass, undistracted. It is truly difficult, emotionally, to do such a thing, since both of these events hold deep emotional significance. The question is, who should move aside? Who has the right of way?

The sages established the rule, "The coffin yields before a bride." The funeral procession is rerouted to a different path to allow the bride's entourage to proceed unfettered in its joyful celebration.

Beyond relating to this specific case, the sages established a general principle: Joy should be enhanced and strengthened even when sorrow and grief is present. Life must go on, and with joy.

Similarly, with regard to national mourning, the sages taught that when a person paints his house, he should leave a small square unpainted opposite the entrance to commemorate the destruction of the Temple. This conveys the same principle – despite our mourning for the Temple, we continue to marry, to build our homes, and to make them beautiful. Amidst all this, one should leave a small corner to remember the Temple's destruction and this should be done in a noticeable spot so that we do not forget. But the principle is to continue our lives and celebrate the establishment of a new house and home

The halakhic principle is complex and appears to contradict itself:

> When a person is faced with either tending to a dead person or a bride, he should leave the bride and tend to the deceased. Thus (Eccl. 7:4) states: "The heart of the wise is in a house of mourning, whereas the heart of the fools is in a house of joy." (Maimonides, *Mishneh Torah, Hilkhot Avel* 14:8)

On the other hand:

> When a dead person and a bride confront each other on a road, the coffin yields before the bride (ibid.)

The source for giving preference to the deceased appears in Smaḥot: "If there is a house of mourning and a house of rejoicing, the house of mourning comes first." There a few explanations that attempt to reconcile the two statements. According to Nahmanides (*Torat HaAdam*, p. 109), the bride takes precedence at the time of the *ḥuppa*, but the meal of the mourner takes precedence over the meal that follows the wedding. Some wrote that the honor of the bride takes precedence since the honor of the living takes priority over the honor of the dead. But when someone needs to engage in one of the two mitzvot, it is preferable for him to attend to the burial. However, this is only the case when someone else is able to attend to the wedding. If one must choose between the two, however, the honor of the living takes precedence, and thus the bride is given precedence over the deceased (*Leḥem Mishneh*, ad loc.; *Shulḥan Arukh*, ibid. 360; *Yalkut Yosef* 10:8). But on the individual level, a person must help with burial, as it says in Smaḥot (ch. 12): "But the early righteous people used to go to the cemetery first, as it says: 'It is better to go to a house of mourning than to a house of feasting; for that is the end of every man, and the living should take heart'" (Eccl. 7:2).

See also **Honoring the Deceased.**

The Dead Do Not Know Anything

This comes from a verse in Ecclesiastes (9:5). The Talmud (Berakhot 18b) discusses whether or not the dead know things about the world of the living. A story is told about the children of Rabbi Ḥiya, that they forgot what they had learned and were distressed by this and wanted to recall their Torah knowledge. They debated amongst themselves whether their deceased father knew of their distress, as it is written: "He feels only the pain of his flesh, and his spirit mourns in him" (Job 14:22); or whether he did not know, as it says: "His sons attain honor and he does not know it" (ibid. 21). The Talmud continues discussing this question, bringing stories about spirits of the deceased who were heard speaking to one another, or who knew things that would happen in the future, or who hid things from the living. It also tells of deceased individuals who spoke with the living and answered their questions.

Later, the Talmud writes: "Anyone who speaks after the deceased, it is as if he speaks after the stone." Some say that this is because the dead do not know, and some say that they know but do not care that they are spoken of.

In another source, the Talmud (Shabbat 152b) brings a saying in the name of Rabbi Abahu that the dead hear and know that which is said in their presence, until the grave is covered up; others say that they know until the body decomposes. It is brought in the Yerushalmi Talmud that the dead are aware of and hear their own eulogies and everything said before them as if in a dream, until the grave is closed (quoted in the *Turei Zahav* on *Shulḥan Arukh, Yoreh De'ah* 344:1).

The Talmud brings stories about sages who were aware and spoke after their death. It is told that Rabbi Elazar Ben Rabbi Shimon was not buried but was left in an attic for eighteen or twenty-two years, and people would bring him their court cases. They would present their claim and a heavenly voice was heard and would say, "You are guilty, you are innocent" (Bava Metzia 84b). It says of Rabbi Yehuda HaNasi that he would come to visit his home each Friday after he died (Ketubbot 103a).

> We find that the dead pray for the living. For example, Caleb ben Yefuneh prostrated himself at the graves of the forefathers; Rabbi Abba (quoted in the Zohar, *Shemot* 16b) asked the dead: Do you know the pain of the living? And the Angel of the Grave answered: If they would not pray for us we would not survive for even half a day. And it is known that the dead pray for the living when they have troubles, from when the Torah scholars bring a Torah scroll to the cemetery (as brought in Zohar, *Vayeḥi* 225 and *Aḥarei Mot* 71). But it entails great repentance and preparation and a valid Torah scroll. Also, on Hoshana Raba night, which is when people are inscribed for life – for on the eighth day they are inscribed in matters of livelihood – on that night, the souls come out and pray for the living, and they wander around to hear the judgments and sometimes inform the living in their dreams. And cases of this are brought in *Sefer Hasidim* (422).

> The Zohar (*Teruma* 141) writes that while the flesh is absorbed into the ground, the soul is in the grave, and it travels around the world amongst the living and knows their pain and prays for them. (*Maavar Yabok*, "Siftei Renanot," ch. 24)

See also **Eternality of the Soul**.

The Death of the Righteous Atones

The sages deduced this idea from the Torah's juxtaposition of certain passages:

> Why was [the Torah portion that describes the] death of Miriam juxtaposed to the portion of the red heifer? To tell you: Just as the red heifer atones, so too, the death of the righteous atones. Rabbi Elazar said: Why was [the Torah portion that describes the] death of Aaron juxtaposed to the priestly garments? Just as the priestly garments atone, so too, the death of the righteous atones. (Moed Katan 28a)

The Midrash taught:

> Why is the death of Aaron's sons mentioned on Yom Kippur? It teaches: Just as Yom Kippur atones, so too, the death of the righteous atones. How do we know that Yom Kippur atones? As it says: "For on this day, atonement shall be made" (Lev. 16:30). How do we know that the death of the righteous atones? As it says: "And they buried the bones of Saul and of his son Jonathan in Tzela, in the territory of Benjamin, in the tomb of his father Kish. And when all that the king had commanded was done, God responded to the plea of the land thereafter" (II Sam. 21:14). (*Yalkut Shimoni,* Leviticus 525)

Rashi explains:

> When the Holy One, blessed be He, executes judgment upon the righteous, He becomes feared and exalted and praised. If this is so in the case of these [righteous] how much more so in the case of the wicked [i.e., when He punishes the wicked]! And in a similar sense, it says (Ps. 68:36): "Thou art feared, O god, *mimikdashekha.*" Read not *mimikdashekha,* "From out of Thy sanctuaries," but *mimekudashekha,* "Because of Thy sanctified ones."

In terms of the meaning of the expression – this is one of the mystical secrets of the Divine and of the world. On a basic level, we can explain it as follows: The death of the righteous causes one grief and sorrow, and this suffering is something that brings atonement; God views suffering as part of atonement. The sadness also motivates a person to contemplate repentance. This can lead a person to improve his actions and can be considered atonement. Thus the death of the righteous can motivate people to improve themselves.

The following could serve as another explanation: A person is judged in relation to the environment that he grew up in. When a righteous person is present, those in his environment are subject to a greater spiritual standard. This can be seen in the case of the woman who rebuked Elijah, when he came to recall her sins (Kings I 17:18). She said that until Elijah came, she was considered righteous, and when he arrived she was judged in his shadow and thus held to a higher standard. The spiritual level decreases when a righteous person dies, and the environment is considered spiritually orphaned; people are therefore forgiven to a certain degree.

(In Isaiah 57:1: "The righteous man perishes, and no one considers; pious men are taken away, and no one gives thought that because of evil the righteous was taken away"; this relates to the death of the righteous in a different way.)

See also **"Through Those Near Me I Will Be Sanctified"** (***BeKrovai Akadesh***).

The Deceased's Feet in the Direction of the Door

The custom is to lay the corpse with the feet pointing towards the room's entrance (*Gesher HaḤayim* 3:2, 1). Some have written that this is done to indicate that the deceased will be removed through that specific entry-way. By doing so, one avoids having other entryways become impure (*Maavar Yabok*): When the deceased lies in a room, all entry-ways are impure because the body might be taken out through any of them. But if only one entry-way is left open, that one is impure because the deceased will be removed through that designated door; the other entry-ways remain pure since it has been made clear that the deceased will not pass through them (Ohalot 7:3, quoted in Beitza 10a). This is likely also the reason why the body is carried with the feet pointing forward, in the direction that the pallbearers are walking. The Yemenite custom, however, is to carry the deceased with the head leading, and not the feet (*Shulḥan Arukh HaMekutzar, Einei Yitzḥak, Yoreh De'ah* 179:6).

The Festival Delays Mourning and Is Not Counted

This is a general halakhic rule regarding mourning on festivals; the festival curtails mourning if the mourners have observed some practices of mourning, however briefly, before the festival began. In such a case, the mourners stop sitting shiva shortly before the holiday begins, and they do not complete the shiva when the holiday ends. If the mourners did not begin observing mourning practices before the festival began, or if the relative died during the festival, the days of the festival are not counted towards the shiva. Shiva begins after the festival has ended. This scenario and the laws pertaining to it are detailed in Chapters 35 and 36.

The *Shekhina* is Above the Sick Person's Head

This is an expression from the Talmud (Shabbat 12b) that is derived from the verse, "The Lord will sustain him on his deathbed" (Ps. 41:4). When Joseph went to visit his father, Jacob, when Jacob was ill, the verse states: "Then Israel bowed at the head of the bed" (Gen. 47:31). The Talmud states that this alludes to the *Shekhina* hovering above the sick person's head.

What does this expression mean? Why does the *Shekhina* hover over the sick person, and why specifically above the head?

These questions can perhaps be answered by looking at the response of Elihu, one of Job's companions, to Job (ch. 32). Job initially argued with his friends about why he suffered so greatly. His friends claimed that Job was being punished for his sins, but Job claimed that he had not sinned and that the suffering was unwarranted. They argued heatedly for a long time, until Job's friends stopped arguing with him because Job saw himself as righteous. As this point, when the argument had reached a standstill, Elihu stepped in and offered his remarks to Job and the others.

Elihu's response is complex and can be interpreted in a variety of ways. It could be argued that Elihu was presenting an alternative, a completely different explanation for Job's suffering – different from the explanation that incriminated Job and different from Job's claim, which maintained his own innocence and that his actions had nothing to do with his sorrows. What, then, is Elihu's opinion? Why did Job suffer so?

> For God speaks time and again – though man does not perceive it – in a dream, a night vision, when deep sleep falls on men, while they slumber on their beds. Then He opens men's understanding and by disciplining them leaves His signature… He is reproved by pains on his bed, and the trembling in his bones is constant… He comes close to the Pit, His life [verges] on death. If he has a representative, one advocate against a thousand to declare the man's uprightness, then He has mercy on him and decrees, "Redeem him from descending to the Pit, for I have obtained his ransom; let his flesh be healthier than in his youth; let him return to his younger days." He prays to God and is accepted by Him; he enters His presence with shouts of joy, for He requites a man for his righteousness. (Job 33:13–26)

For the sake of our present discussion, we shall learn one main idea from these verses: God speaks to man in two ways: One way is "in a dream, a night vision, when deep sleep falls on men, while they slumber on their beds," and the other way is through suffering – "He is reproved by pains on his bed." Suffering comes to convey a message; it comes to urge a person to act, to awaken him from the slumber of his routine life, to shake him into contemplation and taking action. Suffering is powerful in the way it interferes with the habitual rules and norms. This is a call to build better rules and greater vessels, for greater and more meaningful actions. Although daily routines are a great blessing in that they allow people to experience slow, gradual processes that can achieve good results over time, sometimes a person needs to be shaken up. It may cause him to step up all at once, to do something that would have been very hard for him to do from within the calm of his daily, routine life.

In light of this understanding, we return to the expression, "The *Shekhina* is above a sick person's head." We can understand it as conveying that the *Shekhina* communicates with the sick person through his suffering. Elihu's words lead us to see that this revelation can be compared to having a vision in a dream. Just as a having a vision can stir one to act, so can suffering. And so, a person must not ignore his suffering. The sages said that whoever sees that suffering has come upon him should examine his deeds and ways. (See Rabbi Soloveitchik's essay "*Kol Dodi Dofek.*")

Nevertheless, in our daily prayers, we ask God to protect us from trials and degradations. To the question, "Is suffering dear to you?," Rabbi Eliezer answered, "Not them nor their reward" (Berakhot 5b). We do not seek to suffer or experience extreme difficulty. This is both because of the difficulty involved and for fear that one might not be up to the task, and this is why we ask not to face such challenges. But man is not asked whether he would like to suffer; and trials and tribulations do indeed occur. They can lead a person to discover his own buried strength, strength that he was not previously aware of.

Besides for the actions that a person must do, he must also pray that his actions will be worthy and effective: "He prays to God and is accepted by Him; he enters His presence with shouts of joy, for He requites a man for his righteousness."

See also **Suffering Atones.**

The Soul's Journey Upon Leaving the Body

According to the Kabbala, the soul's departure from the body consists of seven journeys, corresponding to seven judgments with which a person is judged when he leaves the world. These periods of time parallel the gradual stages of mourning outlined by the halakha. The gradual separation of the soul is reflected in the practices observed in the stages of mourning.

(The following section discusses Kabbalistic teachings and I was uncertain as to whether they, and other, similar sections in the book, should be included because they contain mystical teachings that are not our main concern here. Nevertheless, because people are often curious and ask questions about this topic, we offer a passage from *Gesher*

HaḤayim (vol. 2, ch. 27), in order to provide readers with a small taste of the general idea):

1. Thirty days prior to the death, the soul begins a partial departure, and the divine image leaves him (Zohar, *Vayeḥi* 227).
2. In his final hours, the person loses his divine image (a person has two kinds of images) and he sees the Angel of Death. The bound limbs are loosened and the loose limbs are bound (Zohar, *Emor* 85).
3. The soul departs. A person only leaves this world after he has seen the *Shekhina*, and his soul cleaves to its light like a magnet, and it leaves this world. That is the main day of *aninut*.
4. Three days after the death, the soul abandons the body: "For three days, the soul hovers over the body, thinking that it may return to it. Since it sees (after three days) that its countenance has changed, it departs and goes" (Y. Moed Katan 3:5). The first three days are the ones of most intense mourning. The Talmud (Moed Katan 27b) mentions "three days for wailing." Identifying the body may be done within the first three days (Yevamot 120a). See **Three Days for Wailing.**
5. After the shiva, there is another separation: "For the entire seven days, the soul goes from the home to the grave, from the grave to the home.... After seven days, the soul goes to the place from where it will ascend" (Zohar, *Vayeḥi* 219). Corresponding to this, the main part of mourning is the shiva.
6. After thirty days, the soul pulls further away and ascends further. "For these thirty days, the soul and the body are judged together. Afterwards, the soul ascends and the body decomposes in the earth" (Zohar, *Vayak'hel* 199). Corresponding to this, some of the laws of mourning are observed for a period of thirty days.
7. After twelve months, the soul completely separates from anything physical and ascends to a higher realm; it cannot connect with the physical. As the Talmud (Shabbat 152b) relates: "For a full twelve months, the body remains and the soul ascends and descends. After twelve months, the body ceases and his soul ascends, and it

does not descend anymore." The twelve-month mourning period for a parent corresponds to this.

The Surplus of the Deceased

In Hebrew, *Motar haMet*. This refers to a scenario where there was someone who died without sufficient funds for burial, and the community raised money for his sake but there was a surplus. If, when they collected the money, it was done for the needs of a particular deceased individual, the surplus should be given to his heirs. But if it was not collected specifically for this person, the surplus should be used for the burial needs of other poor people (*Tur* and *Shulḥan Arukh, Yoreh De'ah* 356). This is because if the money was gathered for a particular person, that person's name is already associated with the contribution. As such, we follow the person's presumed preference to give the money to his children. However, if money was collected for deceased poor people, in general, even if their main intention was for a particular person – if money was left over, it should be used for the burial needs of other poor people (Nahmanides, *Torat HaAdam*, p. 97)

See also **Property of the Deceased.**

The World to Come

In Hebrew, *Olam HaBa*. This refers to life after death. The Mishna (Sanhedrin, ch. 11) states that all Jews have a portion in the next world except for those who have forfeited their portion: One who claims that the resurrection of the dead is not from the Torah; one who claims that the Torah is not divine; and the *epikoros* (heretic).

See also **Being Cut Off (*Karet*); Eternality of the Soul; Resurrection; Soul (*Neshama*).**

They Gave Him to the Pallbearers

This is a halakhic term that arises in the context of the laws of *aninut*. It refers to transferring responsibility for the deceased from the relatives to the *ḥevra kaddisha*. The relatives have the status of *aninut* while they are the ones responsible for the deceased; they may not eat meat or drink wine, and they are exempt from positive commandments. But when they give the deceased over to the *ḥevra kaddisha*, the responsibility for the body and the burial shifts to the *ḥevra kaddisha*. At this point, the halakhic discussion about the relatives' status changes. From that point on, the relatives are permitted to eat meat and drink wine and resume being obligated in the mitzvot (*Shulḥan Arukh, Yoreh De'ah* 341:3). Rabbi Nebenzahl notes: This is the case unless they are still planning who will be saying eulogies, whom to inform, what to say in the eulogy, etc.

See also ***Aninut*; *Ḥevra Kaddisha*.**

Those Executed by the Authorities (*Harugei Malkhut*)

"*Harugei malkhut*" means "those executed by the authorities," but the phrase often refers specifically to the Ten Martyrs – the ten great sages who were killed by the Roman Empire. Our sages connect these deaths with the sin of Joseph's ten brothers who sold him: "Rabbi Joshua ben Levi said – The ten martyrs were killed because of the sin of selling Joseph" (*Midrash Mishlei* 1:13).

The phrase "*harugei malkhut*" has been expanded to include anyone who was murdered by gentiles during a time of persecution:

> What does it mean "He did not forget the cry of the poor"? He does not forget the blood of Jews at the hand of non-Jews, and not only the blood of the righteous, but anyone who was killed; and the blood of the ten martyrs: Rabbi Shimon ben Gamliel, Rabbi Yishmael ben Elisha the High Priest, Rabbi Yishvav the scribe, Rabbi Ḥutzpit the translator, Rabbi Yose, Rabbi Yehuda ben Bava, Rabbi Yehuda the baker, Rabbi Shimon ben Azai, Rabbi Ḥanina ben Tradiyon, and Rabbi Akiva. For them it is said, "For He demands blood, which He remembers." (*Midrash Tehillim* (Buber edition) 9, s.v. "*Ki doresh damim*")

Similarly, it is related that Rabbi Joseph the son of Rabbi Joshua ben Levi was very ill, and his soul ascended to heaven and he almost died. Afterwards, his soul returned and he recovered. He related what he saw and heard in heaven, including the following:

> No person can stand near the martyrs. And who are they? If we say it is Rabbi Akiva and his friends, is their only merit that they were martyrs? Rather the murdered of Lod. (Bava Batra 10b)

Rashi explains (based on Taanit 18b) that the murdered of Lod refers to two brothers, Lulinus and Papus who were killed when the king's daughter was found dead and the Jews were accused of killing her. The king made a declaration against the Jews and these two brothers stood and claimed that they had killed her. They were put to death and, in so doing, saved the rest of the Jews (Pesaḥim 50a; Bava Batra 10b).

Three Days for Wailing

This is the main time of sorrow. Our sages said: "Three days for wailing, seven for elegies, thirty [to refrain from] ironing and haircuts" (Moed Katan 27b). Bar Kapara said in the Yerushalmi Talmud: "The intensity of mourning is only for three days" (Y. Moed Katan 3:5).

> For three days, the soul hovers over the body, thinking that it may return to it. Since it sees [after three days] that its countenance changes, it departs and goes. As the verse states, "He feels only the pain of his flesh, and his spirit mourns in him" (Job 14:22).
>
> The [first] three days, the mourner should view himself as if there is a sword resting between his shoulders, from three to seven [days] as though it is across from him in a corner, from seven to thirty [days] as though it passes before him in the marketplace. (Moed Katan 3:7; *Shulḥan Arukh, Yoreh De'ah* 394:4)

The Zohar (*Vayak'hel* 199) compares the three days that Jonah spent in the belly of the fish to the first three days of a person being in the grave. The first three days of mourning also have stricter rules than the rest of shiva (with regard to work, leaving the house, and comforting the mourners).

See also **The Soul's Journey Upon Leaving the Body**.

"Through Those Near Me I Will Be Sanctified" (*BeKrovai Akadesh*)

This is a phrase that teaches that the death of the righteous is an atonement. The source of the phrase is Moses' words to his older brother, Aaron, spoken in God's name after Aaron's two sons, Nadav and Avihu, died while offering a "strange fire" before God (Lev. 10:3). Nadav and Avihu entered the Holy of Holies without permission, going against the rules of the Temple, and they died. Apart from being Aaron's sons, Nadav and Avihu were also Moses' prized students. They were considered two of the greatest Torah scholars of their generation and were candidates to become the next High Priest. The commentators discuss their actions, sin, and death at length.

They died at the height of a tremendous national celebration, namely the dedication of the Tabernacle and the Altar and celebration of God's presence dwelling among the Jewish people. The people of Israel experienced, at the same time, an outpouring of joy because of their connection with God – "All the people saw and shouted and fell on their faces" (Lev. 9:24) – and the sadness of seeing a great tragedy befall the central figure of the celebration, Aaron. This incongruous experience caused sorrow and grief and much confusion, which demanded that Moses guide the people as to how to react to this complex situation. Moses instructed Aaron and his other sons not to observe mourning because of the sanctity of the occasion and their significant public role. Their private mourning was superseded by the communal joy.

Moses said to Aaron: "This is what the Lord meant when He said: Through those near Me I will be sanctified." Rashi explains: When did God say this? "And there I will meet with the Israelites, and it shall be sanctified by My glory" (Ex. 29:43). Do not read it "in My glory" ("*biKhvodi*"), rather "in those who glorify Me" ("*beMekhubadai*"). Moses said to Aaron – Aaron my brother, I knew that the Sanctuary would be sanctified with someone close to God and I assumed that it would be either me or you. I now see that they were greater than me and you. On the same verse, Nahmanides writes: "'Through those near Me I will be sanctified' – that they should not destroy My sanctuary, and 'gain glory before all the people' – they should behave respectfully in My Temple."

The revelation of God demands a higher standard from man. Drawing close to the king puts greater responsibility upon His subjects;

the closer one is, the greater and deeper is the responsibility to act properly. A person must act with exceptional care when standing before the king. Nadav and Avihu were very holy individuals, but they took initiative to do something that was not appropriate. Their death was a grave blow to the Jewish people; it also taught a lesson: The concept of being the "chosen" people carries with it tremendous responsibility. The position of standing before God is not one of wielding power. Rather, it requires flawless behavior that is ethical, proper, and just.

An analogy: An electrician who works with high voltage must be extremely careful – much more so than someone working with a standard electric circuit. The high voltage has the ability to provide great benefit, but a person cannot approach it without the proper training. The Jewish people, as they stand before God, are facing "high spiritual voltage." The greater the individual's level, the greater the spiritual demands. Every small mistake by a great individual is significant, unlike someone whose spiritual level is lower. This is why the sages said that God is demanding of the righteous. Having God dwell among the Jewish people and within the individual is the highest human purpose and spiritual goal that man can achieve. From the deaths of Nadav and Avihu, the Jewish people learned that God can dwell among us but that there are rules about proper behavior to which they must adhere.

See also **The Death of the Righteous Atones.**

Tombstone

Marking graves is an age-old custom. In Hebrew, this marker has three different names: *Matzeva, Tziyun,* and *Nefesh.*

The name "*matzeva*" (lit. "pillar") appears in the Torah: "Over her grave Jacob set up a *matzeva*; it is the *matzeva* at Rachel's grave to this day" (Gen. 35:20).

The name "*tziyun*" (lit. "marker") appears in the Prophets: "He asked, 'What is the *tziyun* I see there?' And the men of the town replied, 'That is the grave of the man of God who came from Judah'" (II Kings 23:17).

And the name "*nefesh*" (in this context, "gravestone") appears in the Mishna and the Talmud: "Build a *nefesh* on his grave" (Mishna Shekalim 2:5).

There are a number of reasons for setting a tombstone –

- So that the deceased is remembered. The sages said that one need not make a tombstone for the righteous since their words are their legacy (Y. Shekalim 2, 5), and Maimonides ruled in accordance with this idea (*Mishneh Torah, Hilkhot Avel* 4:4). But the Ari wrote (*Shaar HaMitzvot, Parashat Vayeḥi*) that there is a great need for a tombstone and that it is a rectification for the soul; the Rashba wrote that it is an honor to the deceased (*Responsa HaRashba*, 175). This is the custom nowadays, to set a tombstone for great rabbis, as well.
- To know where the grave is located, so that people can visit and pray there.
- To mark a place of impurity, so that *kohanim* can take note.
- To honor the soul that hovers there.

There is a connection between the three different Hebrew names and these various reasons. The name "*matzeva*" shares its root with the word *yatziv*, meaning steady or established; this relates to the idea that the grave should be known so that people may visit and the deceased not be forgotten. The name "*tziyun*" (a marker) expresses the idea that the grave should be marked to warn *kohanim* of the impurity. And the name "*nefesh*" speaks to the *nefesh* (soul) of the deceased that hovers there, as described in the Zohar (according to the *Gesher HaḤayim*, ch. 28).

If someone gave instructions not to erect a tombstone by their grave, we do not comply with his wish. But if one asked not to have praises written on the tombstone, the relatives should comply with this (*Yalkut Yosef* 41:3).

See also **Mitzva to Fulfill the Deceased's Wishes.**

True Kindness (*Ḥesed Shel Emet*)

> "And you will have done for me kindness and truth" (Gen. 47:29) – Is there false kindness, such that that he needs to stress "kindness and truth"? He said to him – If you do me kindness after my death, this is true kindness. (Genesis Rabba 96:5)

Escorting the dead is considered to be true kindness, based on Jacob's statement to his son: "And you will have done for me kindness and truth: Please do not bury me in Egypt. When I lie down with my fathers, take me up from Egypt and bury me in their burial-place." Kindness toward the dead is true kindness since the dead cannot return the favor. Another reason that this is referred to as "true kindness" is that these actions bring the deceased to the world to come, which is the true, eternal world. Some have said that the letters of the word *emet* (truth) – *aleph, mem, taf* – can be an acronym for *aron* (the coffin, beginning with *aleph*), *mitah* (the bier, beginning with *mem*), and *takhrikhim* (shrouds, beginning with *taf*) – items used for burial.

See also ***Ḥevra Kaddisha.***

Tziduk HaDin

This is a special blessing and prayer recited at the funeral in which the mourners affirm the justice of God's judgment. It is based on the Talmud (Avoda Zara 18a):

> When Rabbi Ḥanina ben Tardyon, his wife, and his daughter were taken out to be put to death, they accepted the judgment. He said: "The Rock, His work is perfect; for all His ways are justice" (Deut. 32:4). And his wife said: "A God of faithfulness and without iniquity" (ibid.). His daughter said: "Great in counsel and mighty in work; whose eyes are open upon all the ways of the sons of men, to give every one according to his ways" (Jer. 32:19). Rebbi said: How great are these righteous people, that these three verses of acceptance of judgment occurred to them at the time of accepting the judgment.

After Minḥa on Shabbat, we say "*Tzidkatkha Tzedek,*" "Your justice is just," which consists of three verses from Psalms (119:142, 71:19, 36:7). These verses are a kind of *Tziduk HaDin* for three great people who died at that same hour: Joseph, Moses, and David.

Tziduk HaDin is not recited on days when *Taḥanun* is omitted, nor is it recited on Friday afternoon or Erev Yom Tov. The custom in Jerusalem is not to recite *Tziduk HaDin* on Erev Rosh Ḥodesh.

The mourner should justify God's ways, as it says in Sanhedrin and in the Yerushalmi Talmud that when Rabbi Abahu's young child died, he said to those around him: If the following is said about the lower world, in which there is falsehood and corruption: "The relatives come and inquire after the welfare of judges and witnesses, as if saying: We hold nothing against you, you judged a true judgment" (Sanhedrin 46a) – how much more so in the higher realm, where there is no falsehood and no preferential treatment and no bribery and He lives and has total control over all of the worlds; they are obliged to accept the judgment upon themselves. (*Maavar Yabok, "Siftei Renanot,"* ch. 21)

Consolation is mainly about God's decree becoming justified in the mourner's heart, to the point where he thanks the God of justice, and blesses the bad just he blesses the good. Then he will merit what the prophet promised: "For she has received at the hand of the Lord double for all her sins" (Is. 40:2). Israel will be comforted double their sins, once for their doing repentance out of love and once for accepting the suffering with love. And thus the mourner should do, and the comforters should keep this in mind. Therefore, it is written that the Babylonians' comforting is cursing. [As told in Bava Kamma 38a that when R. Samuel b. Judah lost a daughter, the sages said to Ulla: "Let us go in and console him." But he answered them: "What have I to do with the consolation of the Babylonians, which is [almost tantamount to] blasphemy? For they say, 'What could have been done,' which implies that were it possible to do anything they would have done it."] Because they did not try to get the mourner to accept God's judgment. (*Maavar Yabok, "Siftei Renanot,"* ch. 19)

See also **One Should Be as Thankful for the Bad as One Is for the Good – and Accept it with Joy.**

Tzitzit on the Burial Shrouds

There is a discussion among the halakhic authorities as to whether burial shrouds require tzitzit or not.

The reason to require tzitzit on shrouds would be out of concern for "mocking the poor": Those carrying the deceased should not be wearing tzitzit if the deceased himself cannot. On the other hand, the deceased is exempt from all commandments, as it says: "Free among the dead" (Ps. 88:6). Furthermore, tzitzit are tied on a garment "with which you cover yourself" (Deut. 22:12), and the shrouds are not meant as a covering but for burial. Some halakhic authorities wrote that a person who was careful about wearing tzitzit during his lifetime should be buried in them when he dies, but a person who was not careful about wearing them during his lifetime should not be buried in them because, in this case, wearing tzitzit would be like "mocking the poor" – highlighting the fact that the person is only wearing tzitzit after he has died and is no longer obligated in the mitzvot. Thus, one should make the tzitzit invalid or tie them.

The halakhic discussion appears in Nahmanides' *Torat HaAdam* (p. 98–100) and in *Shulḥan Arukh, Yoreh De'ah* 351. The *Shulḥan Arukh* ruled that a man should be buried in tzitzit. The Rema wrote there that there is no need to do so but that the custom is to bury him in tzitzit that are unfit for use or that have one of the corners tied up. The *Gesher HaḤayim* (10:5) writes that the custom is to cover the body of a man in a tallit with tzitzit up until the burial but to bury him without the tallit.

See also **Mocking the Poor; Shrouds.**

Ways of Peace (*Darkei Shalom*)

This refers to customs and actions that are done to keep peace among people, whether between Jews or between Jews and gentiles. The text below describes practices of "*darkei shalom*" in the area of burial and mourning, although the expression and the practices associated with it are relevant in other areas, as well.

> The sages taught – One provides for poor gentiles along with poor Jews, and one visits sick gentiles along with sick Jews, and one buries dead gentiles as well as dead Jews, on account of the ways of peace. (Gittin 61a)

Rashi explains that this does not mean that gentiles should be buried in Jewish cemeteries, but that we must make sure that a gentile is buried just as we ensure that Jews are buried.

The *Shulḥan Arukh* (*Yoreh De'ah* 367:1) also ruled this way: "One buries the dead of the gentiles and comforts their mourners on account of the ways of peace."

See also **Deceased Gentile**.

Ways of the Amorite

This is a phrase used to refer to superstitious customs of idolatrous nations. Some of these customs are related to death and burial.

Jews are prohibited from following the ways of the Amorite or other nations, as it says: "You shall not practice divination." For example, someone who says, because my piece of bread fell out of my mouth, or my staff fell from my hand, I will not travel to such-and-such place today; or, because a fox passed on my right side, I will not go beyond my doorway today, since if I were to go out I would meet a deceiver (Sanhedrin 65b; Maimonides, *Mishneh Torah, Hilkhot Avodat Kokhavim* 11:4). This is related to the prohibition against consulting the dead or a necromancer.

> All the above matters are falsehood and lies with which the original idolaters deceived the gentile nations in order to lead them after them. It is not fitting for the Jews, who are wise sages, to be drawn into such emptiness, nor to consider that they have any value. (Maimonides, *Mishneh Torah, Hilkhot Avodat Kokhavim* 11:16)

The sages described the practices that are not considered the ways of the Amorite and are therefore allowed:

> One may untie the hair of [dead] brides and uncover the faces of [dead] grooms, and one may place ink and a pen at his [the dead person's] side, and one need not be concerned that these are ways of the Amorite. One may hang the dead person's key and writing-tablet on his coffin because of the grief of the soul, and one may set up canopies for [dead] brides and grooms, and one

> may hang upon them only that which is inedible. The rule in the matter is that it is forbidden to derive benefit from anything that is used for the canopy of the dead. For this reason, anything that is edible is prohibited [to be hung thereon] since food should not be made prohibited nor wasted unnecessarily. (*Tur* and *Shulḥan Arukh, Yoreh De'ah* 350, based on Smaḥot 7)

Halakhic authorities in our time have also needed to address these types of questions:

> Some have the custom that, when someone dies, they place a bowl full of water on the ground and burn a candle next to it for the entire shiva. Those who do so should not be rebuked, for there is a reason for this. And some have already written that this is not considered the ways of the Amorite. The reason is that the candle (*ner*) represents the soul: "The life-breath of man is the lamp (*ner*) of the Lord." The water represents the physical being that has been lost, as it says: "We all must die, we are like water that is poured out on the ground" (II Sam. 14:14); this verse compares physical death to water that is poured out. (*Yalkut Yosef* 28:5)

Some have spoken out against this custom, and it is therefore preferable not to do it (*Nitei Gavriel*, vol. 1, 92:4).

See also **Consulting the Dead; Cremation; Necromancy (*Ov*)**.

Wearing Black

In ancient times, black clothing symbolized death and mourning. The Talmud (Yoma 39a) writes:

> The year in which Shimon HaTzadik died, he said to them: In this year, he will die [euphemistically referring to himself]. They said to him: How do you know? He said to them: On every Yom Kippur, I was met by an old man who was dressed in white and wrapped up in white; and he would enter with me, and he would leave with me. But today, I was met by an old man who was dressed in black and wrapped up in black; and he entered

> with me, but he did not leave with me. After the festival, he was ill for seven days and died.

And Rabbi Yanai requested:

> My sons, do not bury me in white garments nor in black garments. Not in white, lest I not be acquitted, and I will be like a groom among mourners. And not in black, lest I be acquitted, and I will be like a mourner among grooms. (Shabbat 114a)

From here we can deduce that mourners wore black.

With regard to people who leave the community and are not mourned for, it says (Smaḥot 2:8): "Their siblings and relatives wear white and eat and drink and rejoice." In this case, the relatives act differently from the norm, which is expressed by their rejoicing and wearing white. Here, too, we can deduce that mourners usually wore black.

It was also customary at the end of the geonic period to wear black, as brought in the name of Rabbi Yitzḥak ben Giat (*Orḥot Ḥayim, Hilkhot Avel,* vol. 2, p. 563):

> From here you learn that the relatives of the deceased wore black, and grooms wore white. And thus we find in the Midrash that Moses said to Joshua – Wear black for me. And each place shall follow its own custom. (Brought in Nahmanides, *Torah HaAdam,* p. 85)

Rabbenu Asher wrote that a person may dress in black for one's mother- or father-in-law when they die and that one who wants to be strict to mourn or wear black for a relative should not be prevented from doing so (*Responsa Rosh,* 27:9). The Rema (*Yoreh De'ah* 374:6) agrees with this opinion.

When German Jews began imitating gentile customs and wearing new black garments, Rabbi Zvi Hirsch Kaidanover and Rabbi Yaakov Emden rebuked them for this but did not object to wearing old black garments.

In Egypt, it became popular to wear black after the shiva, for twelve months. Rabbi Ovadia Yossef was asked about wearing a black arm band or a black tie during the mourning period – whether this is considered to be following gentile customs. He replied that wearing black is an ancient custom based mainly on the Oral Torah and Midrash. Wearing black is a symbol of sadness and subservience. He disagreed with those who wanted to forbid it, saying that those who wear black do not do so to be like the gentiles but out of grief over the deceased.

He concluded that it is preferable not to wear a black arm band or tie and to dress normally, as is customary in Israel; he wrote that the *ḥevra kaddisha* should not wear special black uniforms, even though this is not prohibited by the Torah (*Responsa Yabia Omer*, vol. 3, 25).

Gesher HaḤayim writes that, today, the custom is not to wear black during mourning because it is considered a gentile custom; he writes that this has become the accepted custom in Israel. In *Tzror HaḤayim* (297) he writes that black should not be worn during mourning. (See also *Kuntras HaYeḥieli, Beit Ȯlamim*, ch. 12, who writes that outside of Israel one may wear black, whereas in Israel, one should avoid wearing black. His reasoning is based on the Kabbala.)

See also **Ways of the Amorite**.

Whomever He Mourns For, He Also Mourns With

This is a general halakhic rule that appears in the Talmud (Moed Katan 20b) and was established as the halakha (Maimonides, *Mishna Torah, Hilkhot Avel* 2:4–5; Nahmanides, *Torat HaAdam* 141–144; *Shulḥan Arukh, Yoreh De'ah* 374:6).

The principle is that a person should also practice mourning when one of his seven close relatives (for whom one mourns if they die) are in mourning, out of respect for them. For example, if a grandchild dies, the grandparent is not legally obligated to mourn for him, but the grandparent should still tear his garment and mourn in the mourners' presence. But when not in the mourner's presence, one does not observe shiva. When a man's wife is sitting shiva for her parent, he should observe mourning in her presence out of respect for his parent-in-law, but should not do so if she is mourning a different relative. The same is true for a woman whose husband is sitting shiva for a parent.

The Rema (ad loc.) points out that the contemporary custom is to be lenient with this type of mourning because it is only done to honor the mourners, and mourners nowadays tend to be forgiving about this. Nonetheless, the relatives of the person sitting shiva demonstrate some signs of mourning from the time of the burial until the first Shabbat: they do not bathe or change their clothes or attend festive meals, even mitzva celebrations (*Bayit Ḥadash,* ad loc.). If someone wants to be strict and observe mourning, this is not criticized; it is a matter where one's custom can be followed (*Siftei Cohen,* ad loc. 7). It has also been written that this type of mourning appears not to be observed at all nowadays, though it is written there that it is unclear whether this is only the case in Jerusalem, or in other places, as well (*Pnei Barukh* 9, note 26 in the name of Rabbi Tzvi Pesaḥ Frank).

See also **Seven Relatives.**

Whosoever Sleeps with Him during His Lifetime May be Buried with Him When He Dies

This is a general halakhic rule: Two bodies are not buried alongside one another, unless an intervening wall separates them. However, a man may be buried with his minor daughter and a woman with her minor son, or her son's minor son (Smaḥot 13; *Shulḥan Arukh, Yoreh De'ah* 362:3). That is to say, there are halakhic rules delineating with whom one is permitted or forbidden to share a bed. These halakhot are also applied in the laws for burial. The basic principle is that small children may be buried with their parents or with a grandparent.

This is generally not practiced today, except in the case of a woman who died together with her baby during childbirth; they are buried together, with the baby in her right arm (*Ḥayim VeḤesed* 6:16).

Will

This refers to the wishes or instructions that a person leaves for his children or companions, to be fulfilled after his death. There can be a written will or an oral will.

When a will is written by a healthy individual, it is considered a legal document; according to Torah law, however, it must include a formal act of *kinyan* (transfer of ownership). (If one is drawing up a will with a lawyer and one would like it to be halakhically valid, the will should note that a transfer of ownership has been performed in accordance with Torah law.) Sometimes a will is made by a dying person (*"shekhiv meRa"*); in such a case, the sages determined that an oral declaration by the person is sufficient because all things said by a dying person are considered like something that has been written. See also ***Shekhiv MeRa***.

Even though the Torah contains rules of inheritance that cannot be altered – for example, "When he wills his property to his sons, he may not treat as firstborn the son of the loved one in disregard of the son of the unloved one who is older" (Deut. 21:16) – people may still divide up their possessions as they wish, provided that the possessions are given as gifts and not as an inheritance.

It is appropriate for a person to write a will to give instructions as to how to divide up his estate after he dies, to prevent arguments among his heirs. One should instruct one's family and one's sons and daughters to behave towards each other with love and respect and thus leave them in peace and tranquility. Some have written that one should write a will when one reaches the age of fifty (*Ḥayim VeḤesed*, ch. 25).

> If a person is concerned that his children will argue about the inheritance, he should divide up his possessions before he dies to prevent arguments. Woe to the parent who, through his actions, causes arguments among his children, for he will not rest in peace. And if he is wise and can see what will happen and so does what he can, then about him it is said, "The righteous man finds security in his death" (Prov. 14:32). And if the children act peacefully and appropriately because of the will, this is pleasing to his soul and he will rest without fear. (*Maavar Yabok*, "*Siftei Tzedek*," ch. 8)

Aside from the legal aspects of the will with regard to bequeathing one's the estate, a person may also leave an ethical will, particularly for one's children – about life's purpose, and correct behavior between man and others and between man and God.

A detailed discussion about writing wills in accordance with both halakha and civil law appears in Chs. 68 and 69.

See also **Mitzva to Fulfill the Deceased's Wishes**; ***Shekhiv MeRa.***

Women – Attending a Funeral and Going to the Cemetery

The Talmud (Sanhedrin 20a) writes: "In a place where women were accustomed to follow the bier, they would go, [and if the women were accustomed to walk] in front of the bier, they would go." The *Shulḥan Arukh* (*Yoreh De'ah* 359:1) writes: "Now it is customary for them only to follow the bier, and one should not deviate from this." The Yerushalmi Talmud (Sanhedrin 2:4; and *Tosafot*, ad loc.) explains that the reason why women walked ahead of the deceased was because the original cause of death was woman (i.e., Eve). The reason for the custom of women following the bier was to preserve the honor of Jewish women, since it was considered degrading for them to be walking where others will look at them.

The *Shulḥan Arukh* (ibid. 2) adds: "Women should be prevented from following the bier to the cemetery." Even though they are permitted to walk behind the deceased, it is preferable for them not to do so at all. The source for this is in the Talmud (Berakhot 51a): "The Angel of Death told me three things ... do not stand before the women when they return from the burial of the deceased because I dance and come before them and my sword is in hand, and I have license to destroy." Another source appears in the Zohar (*Vayak'hel* 196). The book *Maavar Yabok* ("*Siftei Renanot*," ch. 10) also warns against this. There is a custom in Israel to announce that the men will go first to the cemetery. And upon leaving, they announce that the men will leave first to form rows to comfort the mourners. This is what should be done. And if one cannot prevent others from doing otherwise, there are lenient opinions that can be relied upon (*BeMar'eh HaBazak*, vol. 3, 73, quoting from the *Responsa Divrei Ḥakhamim*).

Some rule that one should not prevent women from going to the cemetery when escorting the body and that even according to the Zohar the problem is only about returning from the burial. If, at the funeral, the men walk in front of the bier and the women walk behind it, this is not a problem (*Beit Leḥem Yehuda, Shulḥan Arukh, Yoreh De'ah* 359).

The Rema (*Darkei Moshe* ad loc.) mentions the custom that women would walk behind the body at a funeral and return first from the funeral.

Men and women should sit or stand separately during the eulogies, as in the verse, "The land shall wail, each family by itself: The family of the House of David by themselves, and the womenfolk by themselves… and all the other families, every family by itself, with their womenfolk by themselves" (Zech. 12:12–14; Sukka 52a).

The Kabbalists wrote that it is preferable that when women have their period, they should maintain a distance of four cubits from the graves (*Tzror HaḤayim* 129). In *Gesher HaḤayim* (29:13) he quotes the Ari, that women should not go to the cemetery until they have immersed in the *mikve*. In *Yalkut Yosef* (29:13) he writes that the problem is when a woman is menstruating, but that she may go to the cemetery during the seven clean days before she has been to the *mikve*.

The Ashkenazic custom is that pregnant women do not go to the cemetery; the source for the custom is unknown. (*Responsa Minḥat Yitzḥak* (vol. 10, 42) suggests that during the Second Temple period, pregnant women were more careful to avoid becoming ritually impure so that their children would be able to participate in preparing the ashes of the Red Heifer. This is a possible source for the custom.) Perhaps there is a concern that the emotional strain and potentially crowded environment might have a detrimental effect on her health. But if a woman is in the beginning of her pregnancy and does not want to publicize it, she may enter a cemetery when necessary (as taught by Rabbi Yaakov Ruza). In *Nitei Gavriel* (vol. 1, 67:7) he writes that although some have the custom that pregnant women do not attend funerals, Jewish law permits it.

Wrapping the Head

In the Talmudic period, this was one of the signs of mourning that a mourner was instructed to perform (Moed Katan 15a). It is deduced from Ezekiel, who was told: "And cover not your upper lip" (24:17) – but all other mourners are obligated to cover their heads. The head-covering also covers part of the mouth, as it says: "And he shall cover over his upper lip" (Lev. 13:45); Onkelos translates this as, "like a mourner" (Maimonides, *Mishneh Torah, Hilkhot Avel* 5:9). The mourner should cover his nose; but when people come to comfort him, he should uncover his head out of respect for them (*Shulḥan Arukh, Yoreh De'ah* 386). The Rema (ibid.) writes that this is no longer the accepted practice. Rabbis of later generations wrote that the custom was abandoned because it would be mocked by gentiles. That said, one should perform the custom in some symbolic matter, such as by pulling one's hat down over one's eyes.

Still today, the Yemenite custom is to attend the funeral and sit shiva with a wrapping around their heads and part of the body (*Shulḥan Arukh HaMekutzar, Einei Yitzḥak, Yoreh De'ah* 180:9, 190:3).

Yahrzeit

This Yiddish term refers to the anniversary of someone's death. In Yiddish, the word means "time of year."

There are many customs associated with honoring the Yahrzeit of a relative or righteous person. On a relative's Yahrzeit, one should recite Kaddish and, if possible, lead prayer services. On the Shabbat prior to the Yahrzeit, the relative can read the *haftara*, or lead *Musaf*. It is also customary to lead the prayers on the Motza'ei Shabbat prior to the Yahrzeit. Rabbi Nebenzahl notes: Some prefer not to lead the service on the Motza'ei Shabbat prior to the Yahrzeit so as not to suggest that his parent was wicked.

According to the Ari, the soul merits to ascend to a higher level on the Yahrzeit (see also *Gesher HaḤayim* 32:1). Therefore, one should pray and pledge charity on this day to bring merit to the soul. It is also an ancient custom to fast on the Yahrzeit of one's mother or father; it is mentioned in the Talmud (Nedarim 12a) and the *Shulḥan Arukh* (*Oraḥ Ḥayim* 568:8, etc.). The Ari writes that the reason for fasting is so that a person will examine his actions and repent, and that this will raise the parent to a higher level in heaven. The Hasidic custom is not to fast but rather to bring food and drink to the synagogue and, after services, people make blessings over the food and drink, for the elevation of the deceased's soul. This is called "*tikkun*," a repair. Rabbi Nebenzahl notes: The Gaon of Vilna wrote not to fast, because the Talmud only discussed doing so in the first year after one's parent's or rabbi's death.

See also **Elevating the Soul.**

Yizkor

The custom of saying *Yizkor* involves recalling the souls of the departed and pledging charity in their memory to bring merit to the souls of the deceased. *Yizkor* is customarily said in memory of one's parents and other relatives four times a year: Yom Kippur, Shemini Atzeret, the last day of Passover, and Shavuot. Whereas the *El Maleh Raḥamim* prayer is recited by the prayer-leader, *Yizkor* is a prayer for the individual to remember his own relatives. Because of this, *Yizkor* is said in the singular while *El Maleh Raḥamim* is in the plural (*Gesher HaḤayim* 31:2–3).

Giving charity (and doing other mitzvot) in memory of the deceased links the good deeds of the living with those of the deceased. Since the charity is given in memory of the deceased, this brings merit to the them.

Yizkor begins with the words: "May God remember the soul of my (father, mother, other relative), (mention the person's Hebrew name and that of his/her father/mother) who has gone to the next world, because I will donate charity for his/her sake." And it ends with *Av HaRaḥamim*.

The Ashkenazic custom is that those whose parents are still alive exit the synagogue sanctuary when *Yizkor* is recited. There are various reasons for this. One is to avoid a situation where only part of the congregation is praying, while the rest are silent. Others say that it is to avoid the evil eye.

Yizkor is taken very seriously in Ashkenazic communities. Even people who do not usually come to synagogue often come for *Yizkor*, out of respect for the deceased.

Yizkor was composed after the pogroms of 1096 (*Gesher HaḤayim* ibid., 1; *Or LaAvel*, p. 145).

See also ***Av HaRaḥamim*; *El Maleh Raḥamim*.**

You Shall Not Gash

In Hebrew this means *Lo Titgodedu*. *Gedida* is a deep cut or gash in the skin made with an instrument. "Scratching (*srita*) and gashing (*gedida*) are one and the same, but scratching is by hand and gashing is with an instrument" (Makkot 21a). *Karḥa* refers to pulling out one's hair out of grief.

Gashing and pulling out one's hair out of grief were gentile customs. There is a Torah prohibition not to gash or scratch one's flesh for idol worship or over the deceased and not to shave one's hair. "You are children of the Lord your God. You shall not gash yourselves or shave the front of your heads because of the dead" (Deut. 19:28).

> The root of this mitzva is that we should not do anything that resembles idolatry. We are prevented from cutting ourselves over the dead because it is inappropriate for the chosen nation, who possesses the Torah's precious wisdom, to be so aggrieved by God's actions, only for what He has commanded us to grieve. If we destroy our bodies and maim ourselves like fools, it is not good for us, and it is not the way of wise and intelligent people. Nahmanides wrote – this supports the teaching of our sages not to mourn excessively over the deceased (according to *Sefer HaḤinukh*).

> Whoever cuts himself for a dead person is liable to receive lashes, and it is forbidden to hit oneself until one bleeds. One may not tear out one's hair for the dead; one should justify the divine judgment in silence. (*Yalkut Yosef* 27:9)

See Yevamot 13b; Makkot 20a; *Sefer HaḤinukh,* Mitzva 467, 468; Maimonides, *Mishneh Torah, Hilkhot Avodat Kokhavim* 12:12; *Shulḥan Arukh, Yoreh De'ah* 180.

See also **Ways of the Amorite.**

Part 7

Selected Prayers and Passages

Mourner's Kaddish

The following prayer, said by mourners, requires a *minyan*.

Ashkenazic *Nusaḥ*:

אבל:

יִתְגַּדַּל וְיִתְקַדַּשׁ שְׁמֵהּ רַבָּא (קהל: אָמֵן)
בְּעָלְמָא דִּי בְרָא כִרְעוּתֵהּ, וְיַמְלִיךְ מַלְכוּתֵהּ
(וְיַצְמַח פֻּרְקָנֵהּ וִיקָרֵב מְשִׁיחֵהּ)
בְּחַיֵּיכוֹן וּבְיוֹמֵיכוֹן וּבְחַיֵּי דְכָל בֵּית יִשְׂרָאֵל
בַּעֲגָלָא וּבִזְמַן קָרִיב, וְאִמְרוּ אָמֵן. (קהל: אָמֵן)

קהל ואבל:

יְהֵא שְׁמֵהּ רַבָּא מְבָרַךְ לְעָלַם וּלְעָלְמֵי עָלְמַיָּא.

אבל:

יִתְבָּרַךְ וְיִשְׁתַּבַּח וְיִתְפָּאַר
וְיִתְרוֹמַם וְיִתְנַשֵּׂא וְיִתְהַדָּר וְיִתְעַלֶּה וְיִתְהַלָּל
שְׁמֵהּ דְּקֻדְשָׁא, בְּרִיךְ הוּא. (קהל: בְּרִיךְ הוּא)
לְעֵלָּא מִן כָּל בִּרְכָתָא
/בעשרת ימי תשובה: לְעֵלָּא לְעֵלָּא מִכָּל בִּרְכָתָא/
וְשִׁירָתָא, תֻּשְׁבְּחָתָא וְנֶחֱמָתָא
דַּאֲמִירָן בְּעָלְמָא, וְאִמְרוּ אָמֵן. (קהל: אָמֵן)

יְהֵא שְׁלָמָא רַבָּא מִן שְׁמַיָּא
וְחַיִּים טוֹבִים עָלֵינוּ וְעַל כָּל יִשְׂרָאֵל, וְאִמְרוּ אָמֵן. (קהל: אָמֵן)

Bow, take three steps back, as if taking leave of the Divine Presence, then bow, first left, then right, then center, while saying:

עוֹשֶׂה שָׁלוֹם/ בעשרת ימי תשובה: הַשָּׁלוֹם/ בִּמְרוֹמָיו
הוּא יַעֲשֶׂה שָׁלוֹם עָלֵינוּ וְעַל כָּל יִשְׂרָאֵל
וְאִמְרוּ אָמֵן. (קהל: אָמֵן)

Mourner:
Yitgadal veyitkadash shemeh raba. (*Cong.:* Amen)
Be'alema di vera khiruteh, veyamlikh malkhuteh,
(veyatzmaḥ purkaneh vikarev meshiḥeh)
beḥayeikhon, uvyomeikhon, uvḥayei dekhol beit Yisrael, baagala uvizman kariv, veimru Amen. (*Cong.:* Amen)

All:
Yeheh shemeh raba mevarakh le'alam ulalemei alemaya.

Mourner:
Yitbarakh veyishtabaḥ veyitpa'ar
veyitromam veyitnaseh veyithadar veyitaleh veyithallal
shemeh dekudsha, berikh hu. (*Cong:* berikh hu)
Le'ela min kol birkhata
/*Between Rosh HaShana & Yom Kippur:* Le'ela le'ela mikol birkhata/
veshirata tushbeḥata v'neḥemata,
daamiran be'alema, ve'imru, Amen. (*Cong.:* Amen)
Yeheh shelama raba min shemaya
veḥayim (tovim) aleinu ve'al kol Yisrael,
ve'imru Amen. (*Cong.:* Amen)

Bow, take three steps back, as if taking leave of the Divine Presence, then bow, first left, then right, then center, while saying:
Oseh shalom /*Between Rosh HaShana & Yom Kippur:* hashalom/ bimromav,
hu ya'aseh shalom aleinu, ve'al kol Yisrael,
ve'imru Amen. (*Cong.:* Amen)

Sephardic *Nusaḥ*:

אבל:

יִתְגַּדַּל וְיִתְקַדַּשׁ שְׁמֵהּ רַבָּא (קהל: אָמֵן)
בְּעָלְמָא דִּי בְרָא כִרְעוּתֵהּ
וְיַמְלִיךְ מַלְכוּתֵהּ וְיַצְמַח פֻּרְקָנֵהּ וִיקָרֵב מְשִׁיחֵהּ (קהל: אָמֵן)
בְּחַיֵּיכוֹן וּבְיוֹמֵיכוֹן וּבְחַיֵּי דְכָל בֵּית יִשְׂרָאֵל
בַּעֲגָלָא וּבִזְמַן קָרִיב, וְאִמְרוּ אָמֵן. (קהל: אָמֵן)

קהל ואבל:

יְהֵא שְׁמֵהּ רַבָּא מְבָרַךְ לְעָלַם וּלְעָלְמֵי עָלְמַיָּא.

אבל:

יִתְבָּרַךְ וְיִשְׁתַּבַּח וְיִתְפָּאַר
וְיִתְרוֹמַם וְיִתְנַשֵּׂא וְיִתְהַדָּר וְיִתְעַלֶּה וְיִתְהַלָּל
שְׁמֵהּ דְּקֻדְשָׁא, בְּרִיךְ הוּא. (קהל: אָמֵן)
לְעֵלָּא מִן כָּל בִּרְכָתָא
/בעשרת ימי תשובה: לְעֵלָּא לְעֵלָּא מִכָּל בִּרְכָתָא/
וְשִׁירָתָא, תֻּשְׁבְּחָתָא וְנֶחֱמָתָא
דַּאֲמִירָן בְּעָלְמָא, וְאִמְרוּ אָמֵן. (קהל: אָמֵן)

יְהֵא שְׁלָמָא רַבָּא מִן שְׁמַיָּא
חַיִּים וְשָׂבָע וִישׁוּעָה וְנֶחָמָה וְשֵׁיזָבָא וּרְפוּאָה וּגְאֻלָּה וּסְלִיחָה
וְכַפָּרָה וְרֵוַח וְהַצָּלָה, לָנוּ וּלְכָל עַמּוֹ יִשְׂרָאֵל, וְאִמְרוּ אָמֵן.
(קהל: אָמֵן)

Bow, take three steps back, as if taking leave of the Divine Presence, then bow, first left, then right, then center, while saying:

עוֹשֶׂה שָׁלוֹם /בעשרת ימי תשובה: הַשָּׁלוֹם/ בִּמְרוֹמָיו
הוּא בְּרַחֲמָיו יַעֲשֶׂה שָׁלוֹם עָלֵינוּ וְעַל כָּל יִשְׂרָאֵל
וְאִמְרוּ אָמֵן. (קהל: אָמֵן)

Mourner:
Yitgadal veyitkadash shemeh raba. (*Cong.:* Amen)
Be'alema di vera khiruteh,
veyamlikh malkhuteh, veyatzmaḥ purkaneh vikarev meshiḥeh (*Cong:* Amen)
beḥayyeikhon, uvyomeikhon, uvḥayyei dekhol beit Yisrael,
baagala uvizman kariv, ve'imru Amen. (*Cong.:* Amen)

All:
Yeheh shemeh raba mevarakh le'alam ulalemei alemaya.

Mourner:
Yitbarakh veyishtabaḥ veyitpaar
veyitromam veyitnaseh veyithadar veyitaleh veyithallal
shemeh dekudsha, berikh hu. (*Cong.:* berikh hu)
Le'ela min kol birkhata
/*Between Rosh HaShana & Yom Kippur:* Le-ela le-ela mi-kol birkhata/
veshirata tushbeḥata v'neḥemata,
daamiran be'alema, ve'imru, Amen. (*Cong.:* Amen)

Yeheh shelama raba min shemaya
ḥayyim vesava
vishuah veneḥama vesheizava urefuah ugeulla useliḥah vekhaparah
fereivaḥ vehatzalah, lanu, ulekhol amo Yisrael,
ve'imru Amen. (*Cong:* Amen)

Bow, take three steps back, as if taking leave of the Divine Presence, then bow, first left, then right, then center, while saying:
Oseh shalom /*Between Rosh HaShana & Yom Kippur:* hashalom/ bimromav,
hu *beraḥamav* yaaseh shalom aleinu, ve'al kol Yisrael,
ve'imru Amen. (*Cong.:* Amen)

Prayer for the Sick Person; Changing or Adding a Name

For a man:

מִי שֶׁבֵּרַךְ אֲבוֹתֵינוּ אַבְרָהָם יִצְחָק וְיַעֲקֹב, מֹשֶׁה וְאַהֲרֹן דָּוִד
וּשְׁלֹמֹה, שָׂרָה רִבְקָה רָחֵל וְלֵאָה, הוּא יְבָרֵךְ וִירַפֵּא אֶת הַחוֹלֶה
(פלוני בן פלוני), בַּעֲבוּר שֶׁ(פלוני בן פלוני) יִתֵּן צְדָקָה בְּלִי נֶדֶר בַּעֲבוּרוֹ.
בִּשְׂכַר זֶה הַקָּדוֹשׁ בָּרוּךְ הוּא יִמָּלֵא רַחֲמִים עָלָיו לְהַחֲלִימוֹ
וּלְרַפְּאתוֹ, וּלְהַחֲזִיקוֹ וּלְהַחֲיוֹתוֹ, וְיִשְׁלַח לוֹ מְהֵרָה רְפוּאָה שְׁלֵמָה
מִן הַשָּׁמַיִם לְכָל אֵבָרָיו וּלְכָל גִּידָיו בְּתוֹךְ שְׁאָר חוֹלֵי יִשְׂרָאֵל,
רְפוּאַת הַנֶּפֶשׁ וּרְפוּאַת הַגּוּף. [בשבת - שַׁבָּת הִיא מִלִּזְעוֹק וּרְפוּאָה
קְרוֹבָה לָבוֹא.] [ביום טוב - יוֹם טוֹב הוּא מִלִּזְעוֹק וּרְפוּאָה קְרוֹבָה
לָבוֹא.] הַשְׁתָּא בַּעֲגָלָא וּבִזְמַן קָרִיב וְנֹאמַר אָמֵן.

When a new name is added, these thirty-seven psalms are recited first: 20, 6, 9, 13, 16, 17, 18, 22, 23, 25, 30, 31, 32, 33, 36, 37, 38, 39, 41, 49, 55, 56, 69, 86, 88, 89, 90, 91, 102, 103, 104, 107, 116, 118, 142, 143, 128. One then recites the verses from psalm 119 that begin with the letters of the sick person's name, and then the verses beginning with the letters קר״ע שט״ן. Adding a name should ideally be done in the presence of ten people.

וְאַף אִם נִגְזַר עָלָיו בְּבֵית דִּינְךָ הַצֶּדֶק שֶׁיָּמוּת מֵחָלְיוֹ זֶה, הִנֵּה
רַבּוֹתֵינוּ הַקְּדוֹשִׁים אָמְרוּ שְׁלֹשָׁה דְּבָרִים קוֹרְעִים גְּזַר דִּינוֹ שֶׁל
אָדָם, וְאֶחָד מֵהֶם שִׁנּוּי הַשֵּׁם שֶׁיְּשַׁנּוּ הַשֵּׁם שֶׁל הַחוֹלֶה. וְקִיַּמְנוּ
דִּבְרֵיהֶם וְנִשְׁתַּנָּה שְׁמוֹ כִּי אַחֵר הוּא. וְאִם עַל (פלוני בן פלוני -
השם הישן) נִגְזַר הַדִּין, עַל (פלוני בן פלוני - השם החדש) לֹא נִגְזַר, לָכֵן
אַחֵר הוּא וְאֵינוֹ הוּא הַנִּקְרָא בַּשֵּׁם הָרִאשׁוֹן. וּכְשֵׁם שֶׁנִּשְׁתַּנָּה
שְׁמוֹ, כֵּן יִשְׁתַּנֶּה גְּזַר הַדִּין מֵעָלָיו, מִדִּין לְרַחֲמִים, וּמִמִּיתָה

לְחַיִּים, וּמִמַּחֲלָה לִרְפוּאָה שְׁלֵמָה לְ(פלוני בן פלוני - השם החדש), בְּשֵׁם כָּל הַשֵּׁמוֹת הַכְּתוּבִים בְּסֵפֶר תּוֹרָה זֶה, וּבְשֵׁם כָּל הַמַּלְאָכִים הַמְּמוּנִים עַל כָּל הָרְפוּאוֹת וְהַהַצָּלוֹת תִּשְׁלַח מְהֵרָה רְפוּאָה שְׁלֵמָה לְ(פלוני בן פלוני - השם החדש), וְתַאֲרִיךְ יָמָיו וּשְׁנוֹתָיו בַּנְּעִימִים, וִיבַלֶּה בְּטוֹב יָמָיו בְּרֹב עֹז וְשָׁלוֹם מֵעַתָּה וְעַד עוֹלָם, אָמֵן סֶלָה.

For a woman:

מִי שֶׁבֵּרַךְ אֲבוֹתֵינוּ אַבְרָהָם יִצְחָק וְיַעֲקֹב, מֹשֶׁה וְאַהֲרֹן דָּוִד וּשְׁלֹמֹה, שָׂרָה רִבְקָה רָחֵל וְלֵאָה, הוּא יְבָרֵךְ וִירַפֵּא אֶת הַחוֹלָה (פלונית בת פלונית), בַּעֲבוּר שֶׁ(פלוני בן פלוני) יִתֵּן צְדָקָה בְּלִי נֶדֶר בַּעֲבוּרָהּ. בִּשְׂכַר זֶה הַקָּדוֹשׁ בָּרוּךְ הוּא יִמָּלֵא רַחֲמִים עָלֶיהָ לְהַחֲלִימָהּ וּלְרַפְּאֹתָהּ, וּלְהַחֲזִיקָהּ וּלְהַחֲיוֹתָהּ, וְיִשְׁלַח לָהּ מְהֵרָה רְפוּאָה שְׁלֵמָה מִן הַשָּׁמַיִם לְכָל אֵבָרֶיהָ וּלְכָל גִּידֶיהָ בְּתוֹךְ שְׁאָר חוֹלֵי יִשְׂרָאֵל, רְפוּאַת הַנֶּפֶשׁ וּרְפוּאַת הַגּוּף. [בשבת - שַׁבָּת הִיא מִלִּזְעוֹק וּרְפוּאָה קְרוֹבָה לָבוֹא.] [ביום טוב – יוֹם טוֹב הוּא מִלִּזְעוֹק וּרְפוּאָה קְרוֹבָה לָבוֹא.] הַשְׁתָּא בַּעֲגָלָא וּבִזְמַן קָרִיב וְנֹאמַר אָמֵן.

When a name is added, the psalms listed above are recited, and then the following is said:

וְאַף אִם נִגְזַר עָלֶיהָ בְּבֵית דִּינְךָ הַצֶּדֶק שֶׁתָּמוּת מֵחָלְיִ זֶה, הִנֵּה רַבּוֹתֵינוּ הַקְּדוֹשִׁים אָמְרוּ שְׁלֹשָׁה דְבָרִים קוֹרְעִים גְּזַר דִּינוֹ שֶׁל אָדָם, וְאֶחָד מֵהֶם שִׁנּוּי הַשֵּׁם שֶׁיֶּשְׁנוֹ הַשֵּׁם שֶׁל הַחוֹלֶה. וְקִיַּמְנוּ דִּבְרֵיהֶם וְנִשְׁתַּנָּה שְׁמָהּ כִּי אַחֵר הוּא. וְאִם עַל (פלונית בת פלונית - השם הישן) נִגְזַר הַדִּין, עַל (פלונית בת פלונית - השם החדש) לֹא נִגְזַר, לָכֵן אַחֶרֶת הִיא וְאֵינָהּ הִיא הַנִּקְרֵאת בַּשֵּׁם הָרִאשׁוֹן. וּכְשֵׁם שֶׁנִּשְׁתַּנָּה שְׁמָהּ, כֵּן יִשְׁתַּנֶּה גְּזַר הַדִּין מֵעָלֶיהָ, מִדִּין לְרַחֲמִים, וּמִמִּיתָה לְחַיִּים,

וּמִמַּחֲלָה לִרְפוּאָה שְׁלֵמָה ל(פלונית בת פלונית - השם החדש), בְּשֵׁם כָּל
הַשֵּׁמוֹת הַכְּתוּבִים בְּסֵפֶר תּוֹרָה זֶה, וּבְשֵׁם כָּל הַמַּלְאָכִים הַמְּמֻנִּים
עַל כָּל הָרְפוּאוֹת וְהַהַצָּלוֹת תִּשְׁלַח מְהֵרָה רְפוּאָה שְׁלֵמָה ל(פלונית
בת פלונית - השם החדש), וְתַאֲרִיךְ יָמֶיהָ וּשְׁנוֹתֶיהָ בַּנְּעִימִים, וּתְבַלֶּה
בְּטוֹב יָמֶיהָ בְּרֹב עֹז וְשָׁלוֹם מֵעַתָּה וְעַד עוֹלָם, אָמֵן סֶלָה.

Prayers Said Before Death

The following psalms and prayers are customarily recited before and while the soul departs from the body. This is a particularly sensitive time, due to the strong emotions experienced by the one passing away and the loved ones who are present.

Psalm 29

מִזְמוֹר לְדָוִד הָבוּ לַה׳ בְּנֵי אֵלִים הָבוּ לַה׳ כָּבוֹד וָעֹז: הָבוּ לַה׳
כְּבוֹד שְׁמוֹ הִשְׁתַּחֲווּ לַה׳ בְּהַדְרַת קֹדֶשׁ: קוֹל ה׳ עַל הַמָּיִם אֵל
הַכָּבוֹד הִרְעִים ה׳ עַל מַיִם רַבִּים: קוֹל ה׳ בַּכֹּחַ קוֹל ה׳ בֶּהָדָר:
קוֹל ה׳ שֹׁבֵר אֲרָזִים וַיְשַׁבֵּר ה׳ אֶת אַרְזֵי הַלְּבָנוֹן: וַיַּרְקִידֵם כְּמוֹ
עֵגֶל לְבָנוֹן וְשִׂרְיֹן כְּמוֹ בֶן רְאֵמִים: קוֹל ה׳ חֹצֵב לַהֲבוֹת אֵשׁ:
קוֹל ה׳ יָחִיל מִדְבָּר יָחִיל ה׳ מִדְבַּר קָדֵשׁ: קוֹל ה׳ יְחוֹלֵל אַיָּלוֹת
וַיֶּחֱשֹׂף יְעָרוֹת וּבְהֵיכָלוֹ כֻּלּוֹ אֹמֵר כָּבוֹד: ה׳ לַמַּבּוּל יָשָׁב וַיֵּשֶׁב
ה׳ מֶלֶךְ לְעוֹלָם: ה׳ עֹז לְעַמּוֹ יִתֵּן ה׳ יְבָרֵךְ אֶת עַמּוֹ בַשָּׁלוֹם:

Nishmat Kol Ḥai

נִשְׁמַת כָּל חַי תְּבָרֵךְ אֶת שִׁמְךָ ה׳ אֱלֹהֵינוּ. וְרוּחַ כָּל בָּשָׂר תְּפָאֵר
וּתְרוֹמֵם זִכְרְךָ מַלְכֵּנוּ תָּמִיד. מִן הָעוֹלָם וְעַד הָעוֹלָם אַתָּה אֵל.
וּמִבַּלְעָדֶיךָ אֵין לָנוּ מֶלֶךְ גּוֹאֵל וּמוֹשִׁיעַ. פּוֹדֶה וּמַצִּיל וּמְפַרְנֵס
וְעוֹנֶה וּמְרַחֵם בְּכָל עֵת צָרָה וְצוּקָה. אֵין לָנוּ מֶלֶךְ עוֹזֵר וְסוֹמֵךְ
אֶלָּא אָתָּה. אֱלֹהֵי הָרִאשׁוֹנִים וְהָאַחֲרוֹנִים. אֱלוֹהַּ כָּל בְּרִיּוֹת.

אֲדוֹן כָּל תּוֹלָדוֹת. הַמְהֻלָּל בְּכָל (בְּרוֹב) הַתִּשְׁבָּחוֹת. הַמְנַהֵג עוֹלָמוֹ בְּחֶסֶד וּבְרִיּוֹתָיו בְּרַחֲמִים. וַה׳ עֵר. הִנֵּה לֹא יָנוּם וְלֹא יִישָׁן. הַמְעוֹרֵר יְשֵׁנִים. וְהַמֵּקִיץ נִרְדָּמִים. (מְחַיֵּה מֵתִים וְרוֹפֵא חוֹלִים פּוֹקֵחַ עִוְרִים וְזוֹקֵף כְּפוּפִים) וְהַמֵּשִׂיחַ אִלְּמִים. וְהַמַּתִּיר אֲסוּרִים. וְהַסּוֹמֵךְ נוֹפְלִים. וְהַזּוֹקֵף כְּפוּפִים. וְהַמְפַעְנֵחַ נֶעֱלָמִים. וּלְךָ לְבַדְּךָ אֲנַחְנוּ מוֹדִים. וְאִלּוּ פִינוּ מָלֵא שִׁירָה כַּיָּם. וּלְשׁוֹנֵנוּ רִנָּה כַּהֲמוֹן גַּלָּיו. וְשִׂפְתוֹתֵינוּ שֶׁבַח כְּמֶרְחֲבֵי רָקִיעַ. וְעֵינֵינוּ מְאִירוֹת כַּשֶּׁמֶשׁ וְכַיָּרֵחַ. וְיָדֵינוּ פְרוּשׂוֹת כְּנִשְׁרֵי שָׁמָיִם. וְרַגְלֵינוּ קַלּוֹת כָּאַיָּלוֹת. אֵין אֲנַחְנוּ מַסְפִּיקִים לְהוֹדוֹת לְךָ ה׳ אֱלֹהֵינוּ וֵאלֹהֵי אֲבוֹתֵינוּ. וּלְבָרֵךְ אֶת שִׁמְךָ מַלְכֵּנוּ. עַל אַחַת מֵאָלֶף אֶלֶף אַלְפֵי אֲלָפִים וְרִבֵּי רְבָבוֹת פְּעָמִים. הַטּוֹבוֹת נִסִּים וְנִפְלָאוֹת שֶׁעָשִׂיתָ עִם אֲבוֹתֵינוּ וְעִמָּנוּ. מִלְּפָנִים מִמִּצְרַיִם גְּאַלְתָּנוּ ה׳ אֱלֹהֵינוּ. וּמִבֵּית עֲבָדִים פְּדִיתָנוּ. בְּרָעָב זַנְתָּנוּ. וּבְשָׂבָע כִּלְכַּלְתָּנוּ. מֵחֶרֶב הִצַּלְתָּנוּ. וּמִדֶּבֶר מִלַּטְתָּנוּ. וּמֵחֳלָיִם רָעִים וְרַבִּים וְנֶאֱמָנִים דִּלִּיתָנוּ. עַד הֵנָּה עֲזָרוּנוּ רַחֲמֶיךָ. וְלֹא עֲזָבוּנוּ חֲסָדֶיךָ ה׳ אֱלֹהֵינוּ. וְאַל תִּטְּשֵׁנוּ ה׳ אֱלֹהֵינוּ לָנֶצַח. עַל כֵּן אֵבָרִים שֶׁפִּלַּגְתָּ בָּנוּ. וְרוּחַ וּנְשָׁמָה שֶׁנָּפַחְתָּ בְּאַפֵּינוּ. וְלָשׁוֹן אֲשֶׁר שַׂמְתָּ בְּפִינוּ. הֵן הֵם יוֹדוּ וִיבָרְכוּ וִישַׁבְּחוּ וִיפָאֲרוּ וִישׁוֹרְרוּ וִירוֹמְמוּ וְיַעֲרִיצוּ וְיַקְדִּישׁוּ וְיַמְלִיכוּ אֶת שִׁמְךָ מַלְכֵּנוּ תָּמִיד. כִּי כָל פֶּה לְךָ יוֹדֶה. וְכָל לָשׁוֹן לְךָ תִשָּׁבַע. וְכָל עַיִן לְךָ תְצַפֶּה. וְכָל בֶּרֶךְ לְךָ תִכְרַע. וְכָל קוֹמָה לְפָנֶיךָ תִשְׁתַּחֲוֶה. וְכָל הַלְּבָבוֹת יִירָאוּךָ. וְכָל קֶרֶב וּכְלָיוֹת יְזַמְּרוּ לִשְׁמֶךָ. כַּדָּבָר שֶׁכָּתוּב. כָּל עַצְמוֹתַי תֹּאמַרְנָה ה׳ מִי כָמוֹךָ. מַצִּיל עָנִי מֵחָזָק מִמֶּנּוּ. וְעָנִי וְאֶבְיוֹן מִגּוֹזְלוֹ. שַׁוְעַת עֲנִיִּים אַתָּה תִשְׁמַע. צַעֲקַת הַדַּל תַּקְשִׁיב וְתוֹשִׁיעַ. מִי יִדְמֶה לָּךְ. וּמִי יִשְׁוֶה לָּךְ. וּמִי יַעֲרָךְ לָךְ. הָאֵל הַגָּדוֹל הַגִּבּוֹר וְהַנּוֹרָא אֵל עֶלְיוֹן. קוֹנֵה שָׁמַיִם וָאָרֶץ. נְהַלֶּלְךָ וּנְשַׁבֵּחֲךָ וּנְפָאֶרְךָ וּנְבָרֵךְ אֶת שֵׁם קָדְשֶׁךָ. כָּאָמוּר. לְדָוִד. בָּרְכִי נַפְשִׁי אֶת ה׳. וְכָל קְרָבַי אֶת שֵׁם קָדְשׁוֹ.

הָאֵל בְּתַעֲצֻמוֹת עֻזֶּךָ. הַגָּדוֹל בִּכְבוֹד שְׁמֶךָ. הַגִּבּוֹר לָנֶצַח וְהַנּוֹרָא בְּנוֹרְאוֹתֶיךָ. הַמֶּלֶךְ הַיּוֹשֵׁב עַל כִּסֵּא רָם וְנִשָּׂא. שׁוֹכֵן עַד מָרוֹם וְקָדוֹשׁ שְׁמוֹ. וְכָתוּב רַנְּנוּ צַדִּיקִים בַּה׳. לַיְשָׁרִים נָאוָה תְהִלָּה.

בְּפִי יְשָׁרִים תִּתְרוֹמָם.

וּבְשִׂפְתֵי צַדִּיקִים תִּתְבָּרַךְ.

וּבִלְשׁוֹן חֲסִידִים תִּתְקַדָּשׁ.

וּבְקֶרֶב קְדוֹשִׁים תִּתְהַלָּל.

וּבְמַקְהֲלוֹת רִבְבוֹת עַמְּךָ בֵּית יִשְׂרָאֵל. בְּרִנָּה יִתְפָּאַר שִׁמְךָ מַלְכֵּנוּ בְּכָל דּוֹר וָדוֹר. שֶׁכֵּן חוֹבַת כָּל הַיְצוּרִים. לְפָנֶיךָ ה׳ אֱלֹהֵינוּ וֵאלֹהֵי אֲבוֹתֵינוּ. לְהוֹדוֹת לְהַלֵּל לְשַׁבֵּחַ לְפָאֵר לְרוֹמֵם לְהַדֵּר וּלְנַצֵּחַ לְבָרֵךְ לְעַלֵּה וּלְקַלֵּס. עַל כָּל דִּבְרֵי שִׁירוֹת וְתִשְׁבְּחוֹת דָּוִד בֶּן יִשַׁי עַבְדְּךָ מְשִׁיחֶךָ.

וּבְכֵן יִשְׁתַּבַּח שִׁמְךָ לָעַד מַלְכֵּנוּ. הָאֵל הַמֶּלֶךְ הַגָּדוֹל וְהַקָּדוֹשׁ בַּשָּׁמַיִם וּבָאָרֶץ. כִּי לְךָ נָאֶה ה׳ אֱלֹהֵינוּ וֵאלֹהֵי אֲבוֹתֵינוּ. שִׁיר וּשְׁבָחָה. הַלֵּל וְזִמְרָה. עֹז וּמֶמְשָׁלָה. נֶצַח גְּדֻלָּה וּגְבוּרָה. תְּהִלָּה וְתִפְאֶרֶת. קְדֻשָּׁה וּמַלְכוּת. בְּרָכוֹת וְהוֹדָאוֹת לְשִׁמְךָ הַגָּדוֹל וְהַקָּדוֹשׁ. וּמֵעוֹלָם וְעַד עוֹלָם אַתָּה אֵל.

בָּרוּךְ אַתָּה ה׳. אֵל מֶלֶךְ גָּדוֹל וּמְהֻלָּל בַּתִּשְׁבָּחוֹת. אֵל הַהוֹדָאוֹת. אֲדוֹן הַנִּפְלָאוֹת. בּוֹרֵא כָּל הַנְּשָׁמוֹת. רִבּוֹן כָּל הַמַּעֲשִׂים. הַבּוֹחֵר בְּשִׁירֵי זִמְרָה. מֶלֶךְ יָחִיד אֵל חֵי הָעוֹלָמִים.

Elokai Neshama

אֱלֹהַי, נְשָׁמָה שֶׁנָּתַתָּ בִּי טְהוֹרָה הִיא. אַתָּה בְרָאתָהּ. אַתָּה יְצַרְתָּהּ. אַתָּה נְפַחְתָּהּ בִּי. וְאַתָּה מְשַׁמְּרָהּ בְּקִרְבִּי. וְאַתָּה עָתִיד לִטְּלָהּ מִמֶּנִּי. וּלְהַחֲזִירָהּ בִּי לֶעָתִיד לָבוֹא. כָּל זְמַן שֶׁהַנְּשָׁמָה בְּקִרְבִּי מוֹדֶה אֲנִי לְפָנֶיךָ ה׳ אֱלֹהַי וֵאלֹהֵי אֲבוֹתַי. רִבּוֹן כָּל הַמַּעֲשִׂים אֲדוֹן כָּל הַנְּשָׁמוֹת. בָּרוּךְ אַתָּה ה׳ הַמַּחֲזִיר נְשָׁמוֹת לִפְגָרִים מֵתִים.

אַתָּה גִּבּוֹר לְעוֹלָם אֲדֹנָי. מְחַיֵּה מֵתִים אַתָּה רַב לְהוֹשִׁיעַ. מְכַלְכֵּל חַיִּים בְּחֶסֶד. מְחַיֵּה מֵתִים בְּרַחֲמִים רַבִּים. סוֹמֵךְ נוֹפְלִים. וְרוֹפֵא חוֹלִים וּמַתִּיר אֲסוּרִים. וּמְקַיֵּם אֱמוּנָתוֹ לִישֵׁנֵי עָפָר. מִי כָמוֹךָ בַּעַל גְּבוּרוֹת וּמִי דוֹמֶה לָּךְ. מֶלֶךְ מֵמִית וּמְחַיֶּה וּמַצְמִיחַ יְשׁוּעָה. וְנֶאֱמָן אַתָּה לְהַחֲיוֹת מֵתִים.

The Incense

אַתָּה הוּא ה׳ אֱלֹהֵינוּ שֶׁהִקְטִירוּ אֲבוֹתֵינוּ לְפָנֶיךָ אֶת קְטֹרֶת הַסַּמִּים בִּזְמַן שֶׁבֵּית הַמִּקְדָּשׁ קַיָּם כַּאֲשֶׁר צִוִּיתָ אוֹתָם עַל יַד מֹשֶׁה נְבִיאָךְ כַּכָּתוּב בְּתוֹרָתָךְ:

וַיֹּאמֶר ה׳ אֶל מֹשֶׁה קַח לְךָ סַמִּים נָטָף וּשְׁחֵלֶת וְחֶלְבְּנָה סַמִּים וּלְבֹנָה זַכָּה. בַּד בְּבַד יִהְיֶה: וְעָשִׂיתָ אֹתָהּ קְטֹרֶת רֹקַח מַעֲשֵׂה רוֹקֵחַ. מְמֻלָּח טָהוֹר קֹדֶשׁ: וְשָׁחַקְתָּ מִמֶּנָּה הָדֵק וְנָתַתָּה מִמֶּנָּה לִפְנֵי הָעֵדֻת בְּאֹהֶל מוֹעֵד אֲשֶׁר אִוָּעֵד לְךָ שָׁמָּה. קֹדֶשׁ קָדָשִׁים תִּהְיֶה לָכֶם: וְנֶאֱמַר וְהִקְטִיר עָלָיו אַהֲרֹן קְטֹרֶת סַמִּים. בַּבֹּקֶר בַּבֹּקֶר בְּהֵיטִיבוֹ אֶת הַנֵּרֹת יַקְטִירֶנָּה: וּבְהַעֲלֹת אַהֲרֹן אֶת הַנֵּרֹת בֵּין הָעַרְבַּיִם יַקְטִירֶנָּה. קְטֹרֶת תָּמִיד לִפְנֵי ה׳ לְדֹרֹתֵיכֶם:

תָּנוּ רַבָּנָן פִּטּוּם הַקְּטֹרֶת כֵּיצַד. שְׁלֹשׁ מֵאוֹת וְשִׁשִּׁים וּשְׁמוֹנָה מָנִים הָיוּ בָהּ. שְׁלֹשׁ מֵאוֹת וְשִׁשִּׁים וַחֲמִשָּׁה כְּמִנְיַן יְמוֹת הַחַמָּה מָנֶה בְּכָל יוֹם. מַחֲצִיתוֹ בַּבֹּקֶר וּמַחֲצִיתוֹ בָּעֶרֶב. וּשְׁלֹשָׁה מָנִים יְתֵרִים שֶׁמֵּהֶם מַכְנִיס כֹּהֵן גָּדוֹל וְנוֹטֵל מֵהֶם מְלֹא חָפְנָיו בְּיוֹם הַכִּפּוּרִים. וּמַחֲזִירָן לְמַכְתֶּשֶׁת בְּעֶרֶב יוֹם הַכִּפּוּרִים כְּדֵי לְקַיֵּם מִצְוַת דַּקָּה מִן הַדַּקָּה. וְאַחַד עָשָׂר סַמָּנִים הָיוּ בָהּ. וְאֵלּוּ הֵן (טוב למנותם באצבעותיו) (א) הַצֳּרִי. (ב) וְהַצִּפֹּרֶן. (ג) וְהַחֶלְבְּנָה. (ד) וְהַלְּבוֹנָה. מִשְׁקַל שִׁבְעִים שִׁבְעִים מָנֶה. (ה) מוֹר. (ו) וּקְצִיעָה. (ז) וְשִׁבֹּלֶת נֵרְדְּ. (ח) וְכַרְכֹּם. מִשְׁקַל שִׁשָּׁה עָשָׂר שִׁשָּׁה עָשָׂר מָנֶה. (ט) הַקֹּשְׁטְ שְׁנֵים עָשָׂר. (י) וְקִלּוּפָה שְׁלֹשָׁה. (יא) וְקִנָּמוֹן תִּשְׁעָה. בּוֹרִית כַּרְשִׁינָא תִּשְׁעָה קַבִּין. יֵין קַפְרִיסִין סְאִין תְּלָת וְקַבִּין תְּלָתָא. וְאִם לֹא מָצָא יֵין קַפְרִיסִין מֵבִיא חֲמַר חִיוָרִין עַתִּיק. מֶלַח סְדוֹמִית רוֹבַע. מַעֲלֶה עָשָׁן כָּל שֶׁהוּא. רַבִּי נָתָן הַבַּבְלִי אוֹמֵר אַף כִּפַּת הַיַּרְדֵּן כָּל שֶׁהִיא. אִם נָתַן בָּהּ דְּבַשׁ פְּסָלָהּ. וְאִם חִסַּר אַחַת מִכָּל סַמָּנֶיהָ חַיָּב מִיתָה:

רַבָּן שִׁמְעוֹן בֶּן גַּמְלִיאֵל אוֹמֵר הַצֳּרִי אֵינוֹ אֶלָּא שְׂרָף הַנּוֹטֵף מֵעֲצֵי הַקְּטָף. בּוֹרִית כַּרְשִׁינָא לְמָה הִיא בָאָה כְּדֵי לְשַׁפּוֹת בָּהּ אֶת הַצִּפֹּרֶן כְּדֵי שֶׁתְּהֵא נָאָה. יֵין קַפְרִיסִין לְמָה הוּא בָא כְּדֵי לִשְׁרוֹת בּוֹ אֶת הַצִּפֹּרֶן כְּדֵי שֶׁתְּהֵא עַזָּה. וַהֲלֹא מֵי רַגְלַיִם יָפִין לָהּ אֶלָּא שֶׁאֵין מַכְנִיסִין מֵי רַגְלַיִם בַּמִּקְדָּשׁ מִפְּנֵי הַכָּבוֹד:

תַּנְיָא רַבִּי נָתָן אוֹמֵר כְּשֶׁהוּא שׁוֹחֵק אוֹמֵר הָדֵק הֵיטֵב. הֵיטֵב הָדֵק. מִפְּנֵי שֶׁהַקּוֹל יָפֶה לַבְּשָׂמִים. פִּטְּמָהּ לַחֲצָאִין כְּשֵׁרָה. לִשְׁלִישׁ וְלִרְבִיעַ לֹא שָׁמַעְנוּ. אָמַר רַבִּי יְהוּדָה זֶה הַכְּלָל אִם כְּמִדָּתָהּ כְּשֵׁרָה לַחֲצָאִין. וְאִם חִסַּר אַחַת מִכָּל סַמָּנֶיהָ חַיָּב מִיתָה:

תָּנֵי בַּר קַפָּרָא אַחַת לְשִׁשִּׁים אוֹ לְשִׁבְעִים שָׁנָה הָיְתָה בָּאָה שֶׁל שִׁירַיִם לַחֲצָאִין. וְעוֹד תָּנֵי בַּר קַפָּרָא אִלּוּ הָיָה נוֹתֵן בָּהּ קָרְטוֹב שֶׁל דְּבַשׁ אֵין אָדָם יָכוֹל לַעֲמוֹד מִפְּנֵי רֵיחָהּ. וְלָמָּה אֵין מְעָרְבִין בָּהּ דְּבַשׁ מִפְּנֵי שֶׁהַתּוֹרָה אָמְרָה כִּי כָל שְׂאֹר וְכָל דְּבַשׁ לֹא תַקְטִירוּ מִמֶּנּוּ אִשֶּׁה לַה׳:

ה׳ צְבָאוֹת עִמָּנוּ. מִשְׂגָּב לָנוּ אֱלֹהֵי יַעֲקֹב סֶלָה: ה׳ צְבָאוֹת. אַשְׁרֵי אָדָם בֹּטֵחַ בָּךְ: ה׳ הוֹשִׁיעָה. הַמֶּלֶךְ יַעֲנֵנוּ בְיוֹם קָרְאֵנוּ: וְעָרְבָה לַה׳ מִנְחַת יְהוּדָה וִירוּשָׁלָיִם. כִּימֵי עוֹלָם וּכְשָׁנִים קַדְמֹנִיּוֹת:

תָּנָא דְבֵי אֵלִיָּהוּ. כָּל הַשּׁוֹנֶה הֲלָכוֹת בְּכָל יוֹם מֻבְטָח לוֹ שֶׁהוּא בֶּן הָעוֹלָם הַבָּא. שֶׁנֶּאֱמַר הֲלִיכוֹת עוֹלָם לוֹ. אַל תִּקְרֵי הֲלִיכוֹת אֶלָּא הֲלָכוֹת:

אָמַר רַבִּי אֶלְעָזָר אָמַר רַבִּי חֲנִינָא תַּלְמִידֵי חֲכָמִים מַרְבִּים שָׁלוֹם בָּעוֹלָם שֶׁנֶּאֱמַר וְכָל בָּנַיִךְ לִמּוּדֵי ה׳ וְרַב שְׁלוֹם בָּנָיִךְ. אַל תִּקְרֵי בָּנַיִךְ אֶלָּא בּוֹנָיִךְ:

יְהִי שָׁלוֹם בְּחֵילֵךְ שַׁלְוָה בְּאַרְמְנוֹתָיִךְ: לְמַעַן אַחַי וְרֵעָי אֲדַבְּרָה נָּא שָׁלוֹם בָּךְ: לְמַעַן בֵּית ה׳ אֱלֹהֵינוּ אֲבַקְשָׁה טוֹב לָךְ: וּרְאֵה בָנִים לְבָנֶיךָ שָׁלוֹם עַל יִשְׂרָאֵל: שָׁלוֹם רָב לְאֹהֲבֵי תוֹרָתֶךָ וְאֵין לָמוֹ מִכְשׁוֹל: ה׳ עֹז לְעַמּוֹ יִתֵּן. ה׳ יְבָרֵךְ אֶת עַמּוֹ בַשָּׁלוֹם:

In the last hour, if possible, the following should be said by the sick person:

מִי אֵל כָּמוֹךָ נֹשֵׂא עָוֹן וְעֹבֵר עַל פֶּשַׁע לִשְׁאֵרִית נַחֲלָתוֹ לֹא הֶחֱזִיק לָעַד אַפּוֹ כִּי חָפֵץ חֶסֶד הוּא: יָשׁוּב יְרַחֲמֵנוּ יִכְבֹּשׁ

עֲוֹנֹתֵינוּ וְתַשְׁלִיךְ בִּמְצֻלוֹת יָם כָּל חַטֹּאותָם: בְּיָדְךָ אַפְקִיד רוּחִי פָּדִיתָה אוֹתִי ה׳ אֵל אֱמֶת:

Priestly Blessings

יְבָרֶכְךָ ה׳ וְיִשְׁמְרֶךָ
יָאֵר ה׳ פָּנָיו אֵלֶיךָ וִיחֻנֶּךָּ
יִשָּׂא ה׳ פָּנָיו אֵלֶיךָ וְיָשֵׂם לְךָ שָׁלוֹם:
לִישׁוּעָתְךָ קִוִּיתִי ה׳:
ה׳ אֵל אֱמֶת:
מֹשֶׁה אֱמֶת וְתוֹרָתוֹ אֱמֶת.

Shema

שְׁמַע יִשְׂרָאֵל ה׳ אֱלֹהֵינוּ ה׳ אֶחָד
בָּרוּךְ שֵׁם כְּבוֹד מַלְכוּתוֹ לְעוֹלָם וָעֶד

The sick person should then recite the confession. If he is unable to do so, a family member can do so for him.

מוֹדֶה אֲנִי לְפָנֶיךָ ה׳ אֱלֹהַי וֵאלֹהֵי אֲבוֹתַי שֶׁרְפוּאָתִי וּמִיתָתִי בְּיָדְךָ עַל כָּל הַחַיִּים וְצָרְכֵי הַחַיִּים שֶׁנָּתַתָּ לִי. יְהִי רָצוֹן מִלְּפָנֶיךָ שֶׁתְּרַפְּאֵנִי רְפוּאָה שְׁלֵמָה, וְאִם אָמוּת חַס וְשָׁלוֹם תְּהֵא מִיתָתִי כַּפָּרָה עַל כָּל חֲטָאִים וַעֲוֹנוֹת וּפְשָׁעִים שֶׁחָטָאתִי וְשֶׁעָוִיתִי וְשֶׁפָּשַׁעְתִּי לְפָנֶיךָ. וְתֵן חֶלְקִי בְּגַן עֵדֶן וְזַכֵּנִי לָעוֹלָם הַבָּא הַצָּפוּן לַצַּדִּיקִים. אֵל נָא רְפָא נָא לִי.

Also add:

אֲנִי מַאֲמִין בֶּאֱמוּנָה שְׁלֵמָה בַּה׳ אֱלֹהִים אֱמֶת וּשְׁמוֹ אֱמֶת וּבִשְׁלֹשָׁה עָשָׂר הָעִקָּרִים.

One should grant forgiveness to everyone and ask forgiveness from everyone.

A short version of the confession:

אִם אָמוּת, תְּהֵא מִיתָתִי כַּפָּרָה עַל כָּל עֲוֹנוֹתַי

Mesirat Modaa

One may expand upon this confession and say the version recited on Yom Kippur that appears in the *mahzor*. According to some opinions, one should recite the *Mesirat Modaa* (Statement of Disclaimer) with the sick person while the sick person is of sound mind, so that if, God forbid, he is later tempted by the Satan to transgress one of the principles of faith, one of God's commandments, or even a rabbinic commandment, this would be nullified.

שִׁמְעוּ רַבּוֹתַי, הֲרֵי אֲנִי מוֹסֵר מוֹדָעָה בִּפְנֵיכֶם, בְּאִם יָבוֹא הַשָּׂטָן אוֹ כַּת דִּילֵיהּ לְהַסִּית אוֹתִי לַעֲבוֹר עַל אַחַת מִמִּצְוֹת ה׳, הֵן מִצְוֹת עֲשֵׂה וְהֵן מִצְוֹת לֹא תַעֲשֶׂה, הֵן מִצְוֹת שֶׁחַיָּבִים עֲלֵיהֶן כָּרֵתוֹת אוֹ מִיתוֹת בֵּית דִּין, אוֹ נְדָרִים אוֹ סְיָגִים, אוֹ עַל הַכְּלָל כֻּלּוֹ חַס וְשָׁלוֹם, וּבִפְרָט אִם יָבוֹא עֵת פְּקוּדָתִי לְהָשִׁיב הַפִּקָּדוֹן אֲשֶׁר הָפְקַד אִתִּי, יַסִּית וְיַדִּיחַ אוֹתִי, וּמֵחֲמַת אֵימָה וְרַעַד וְטֵרוּף וּבִלְבּוּל הַדַּעַת, אוֹדֶה לוֹ חָלִילָה וְחָלִילָה, הֵן בְּמַחֲשָׁבָה אוֹ בְּדִבּוּר, אוֹ בְּכָל מַה שֶׁהַפֶּה יוּכַל לְדַבֵּר וְלֵב לַחֲשׁוֹב, אַף עַל

פִּי שֶׁאָמְרוּ חֲכָמִים אֵין אָדָם נִתְפָּס עַל צַעֲרוֹ, אִם אֵינוֹ עוֹשֶׂה
כְּלָהּ - עוֹשֶׂה מְחִיצָה בֵּינוֹ לְבֵין אָבִיו שֶׁבַּשָּׁמַיִם. בְּכֵן אֲנִי מוֹסֵר
מוֹדָעָה בִּפְנֵיכֶם שֶׁיִּהְיֶה אוֹתוֹ דִּבּוּר אוֹ מַחֲשָׁבָה, בָּטֵל וּמְבֻטָּל
כְּחֶרֶס הַנִּשְׁבָּר, וְלֹא יִהְיֶה מַמָּשׁ בְּדִבּוּרִי אוֹ בְּמַחֲשַׁבְתִּי אוֹ
בִּרְמִיזָתִי, כִּי אֲנִי מַאֲמִין בְּשִׁמְךָ הַגָּדוֹל שֶׁאַתָּה אֱמֶת וּמֹשֶׁה
עַבְדְּךָ אֱמֶת וְתוֹרָתוֹ אֱמֶת, וְאַתָּה יָחִיד וּמְיֻחָד וְאֵין יְחִידוּת
כָּמוֹךָ בְּשׁוּם פָּנִים, הָיָה הוֹוֶה וְיִהְיֶה, ה׳ מֶלֶךְ ה׳ מָלָךְ ה׳ יִמְלֹךְ
לְעוֹלָם וָעֶד, בַּיּוֹם הַהוּא יִהְיֶה ה׳ אֶחָד וּשְׁמוֹ אֶחָד, כִּי אֵין כָּמוֹךָ
בָּאֱלֹהִים בַּשָּׁמַיִם מִמַּעַל וְעַל הָאָרֶץ מִתַּחַת אֵין עוֹד, בָּרוּךְ
הוּא וּבָרוּךְ שְׁמוֹ לָעַד, בָּרוּךְ שֵׁם כְּבוֹד מַלְכוּתוֹ לְעוֹלָם וָעֶד.

Those who are seated stand and say:

בְּצֵרוּף קֻדְשָׁא בְּרִיךְ הוּא וּשְׁכִינְתֵּהּ, קִבַּלְנוּ מְסִירַת הַמּוֹדָעָה
אֲשֶׁר מָסַר (פלוני בן פלוני) גּוּפוֹ נַפְשׁוֹ רוּחוֹ וְנִשְׁמָתוֹ לְעִלַּת כָּל
הָעִלּוֹת וְסִבַּת כָּל הַסִּבּוֹת, וְכָל מַה שֶּׁיֵּעָשֶׂה מֵהַיּוֹם נֶגֶד מְסִירַת
הַמּוֹדָעָה הַזֹּאת הֵן בְּמַעֲשֶׂה הֵן בְּדִבּוּר וְהֵן בְּמַחֲשָׁבָה, אֲנַחְנוּ
מְבַטְּלִים אוֹתוֹ הַמַּעֲשֶׂה בְּצֵרוּף קֻדְשָׁא בְּרִיךְ הוּא וּשְׁכִינְתֵּהּ,
וְלֹא יֵעָשֶׂה שׁוּם רֹשֶׁם כְּלָל.

Thirteen Principles of Faith

יִגְדַּל אֱלֹהִים חַי וְיִשְׁתַּבַּח, נִמְצָא, וְאֵין עֵת אֶל מְצִיאוּתוֹ:
אֶחָד וְאֵין יָחִיד כְּיִחוּדוֹ, נֶעְלָם, וְגַם אֵין סוֹף לְאַחְדּוּתוֹ: אֵין לוֹ
דְּמוּת הַגּוּף וְאֵינוֹ גּוּף, לֹא נַעֲרוֹךְ אֵלָיו קְדֻשָּׁתוֹ: קַדְמוֹן לְכָל
דָּבָר אֲשֶׁר נִבְרָא, רִאשׁוֹן וְאֵין רֵאשִׁית לְרֵאשִׁיתוֹ: הִנּוֹ אֲדוֹן
עוֹלָם, לְכָל נוֹצָר. יוֹרֶה גְדֻלָּתוֹ וּמַלְכוּתוֹ: שֶׁפַע נְבוּאָתוֹ נְתָנוֹ,
אֶל אַנְשֵׁי סְגֻלָּתוֹ וְתִפְאַרְתּוֹ: לֹא קָם בְּיִשְׂרָאֵל כְּמֹשֶׁה עוֹד,

נָבִיא וּמַבִּיט אֶת תְּמוּנָתוֹ: תּוֹרַת אֱמֶת נָתַן לְעַמּוֹ, אֵל, עַל יַד נְבִיאוֹ נֶאֱמַן בֵּיתוֹ: לֹא יַחֲלִיף הָאֵל וְלֹא יָמִיר דָּתוֹ. לְעוֹלָמִים, לְזוּלָתוֹ: צוֹפֶה וְיוֹדֵעַ סְתָרֵינוּ, מַבִּיט לְסוֹף דָּבָר בְּקַדְמָתוֹ: גּוֹמֵל לְאִישׁ חֶסֶד כְּמִפְעָלוֹ, נוֹתֵן לְרָשָׁע רָע כְּרִשְׁעָתוֹ: יִשְׁלַח לְקֵץ הַיָּמִין מְשִׁיחֵנוּ, לִפְדּוֹת מְחַכֵּי קֵץ יְשׁוּעָתוֹ: מֵתִים יְחַיֶּה אֵל בְּרוֹב חַסְדּוֹ, בָּרוּךְ עֲדֵי עַד שֵׁם תְּהִלָּתוֹ:

אֲדוֹן עוֹלָם אֲשֶׁר מָלַךְ, בְּטֶרֶם כָּל יְצִיר נִבְרָא. לְעֵת נַעֲשָׂה בְחֶפְצוֹ כֹּל, אֲזַי מֶלֶךְ שְׁמוֹ נִקְרָא. וְאַחֲרֵי כִּכְלוֹת הַכֹּל, לְבַדּוֹ יִמְלוֹךְ נוֹרָא. וְהוּא הָיָה, וְהוּא הֹוֶה, וְהוּא יִהְיֶה, בְּתִפְאָרָה. וְהוּא אֶחָד וְאֵין שֵׁנִי, לְהַמְשִׁיל לוֹ לְהַחְבִּירָה. בְּלִי רֵאשִׁית בְּלִי תַכְלִית, וְלוֹ הָעֹז וְהַמִּשְׂרָה. וְהוּא אֵלִי וְחַי גֹּאֲלִי, וְצוּר חֶבְלִי בְּעֵת צָרָה. וְהוּא נִסִּי וּמָנוֹס לִי מְנָת כּוֹסִי בְּיוֹם אֶקְרָא. בְּיָדוֹ אַפְקִיד רוּחִי, בְּעֵת אִישַׁן וְאָעִירָה. וְעִם רוּחִי גְּוִיָּתִי, יְיָ לִי וְלֹא אִירָא.

Ana BeKoaḥ

אָנָּא בְּכֹחַ גְּדֻלַּת יְמִינְךָ תַּתִּיר צְרוּרָה.
קַבֵּל רִנַּת עַמְּךָ שַׂגְּבֵנוּ טַהֲרֵנוּ נוֹרָא.
נָא גִבּוֹר דּוֹרְשֵׁי יִחוּדְךָ כְּבָבַת שָׁמְרֵם.
בָּרְכֵם טַהֲרֵם רַחֲמֵם צִדְקָתְךָ תָּמִיד גָּמְלֵם.
חֲסִין קָדוֹשׁ בְּרוֹב טוּבְךָ נַהֵל עֲדָתֶךָ:
יָחִיד גֵּאֶה לְעַמְּךָ פְּנֵה זוֹכְרֵי קְדֻשָּׁתֶךָ.
שַׁוְעָתֵנוּ קַבֵּל וּשְׁמַע צַעֲקָתֵנוּ יוֹדֵעַ תַּעֲלֻמוֹת.
בָּרוּךְ שֵׁם כְּבוֹד מַלְכוּתוֹ לְעוֹלָם וָעֶד.

עַל כֵּן נְקַוֶּה לְּךָ יְיָ אֱלֹהֵינוּ, לִרְאוֹת מְהֵרָה בְּתִפְאֶרֶת עֻזֶּךָ,
לְהַעֲבִיר גִּלּוּלִים מִן הָאָרֶץ וְהָאֱלִילִים כָּרוֹת יִכָּרֵתוּן. לְתַקֵּן
עוֹלָם בְּמַלְכוּת שַׁדַּי, וְכָל בְּנֵי בָשָׂר יִקְרְאוּ בִשְׁמֶךָ. לְהַפְנוֹת
אֵלֶיךָ כָּל רִשְׁעֵי אָרֶץ. יַכִּירוּ וְיֵדְעוּ כָּל יוֹשְׁבֵי תֵבֵל, כִּי לְךָ תִּכְרַע
כָּל בֶּרֶךְ, תִּשָּׁבַע כָּל לָשׁוֹן: לְפָנֶיךָ יְיָ אֱלֹהֵינוּ יִכְרְעוּ וְיִפֹּלוּ. וְלִכְבוֹד
שִׁמְךָ יְקָר יִתֵּנוּ. וִיקַבְּלוּ כֻלָּם אֶת עוֹל מַלְכוּתֶךָ. וְתִמְלֹךְ עֲלֵיהֶם
מְהֵרָה לְעוֹלָם וָעֶד. כִּי הַמַּלְכוּת שֶׁלְּךָ הִיא, וּלְעוֹלְמֵי עַד תִּמְלוֹךְ
בְּכָבוֹד: כַּכָּתוּב בְּתוֹרָתֶךָ, יְיָ יִמְלֹךְ לְעֹלָם וָעֶד: וְנֶאֱמַר, וְהָיָה
יְיָ לְמֶלֶךְ עַל כָּל הָאָרֶץ, בַּיּוֹם הַהוּא יִהְיֶה יְיָ אֶחָד, וּשְׁמוֹ אֶחָד:

The following solemn psalms are recited:

Psalm 121

שִׁיר לַמַּעֲלוֹת אֶשָּׂא עֵינַי אֶל הֶהָרִים מֵאַיִן יָבֹא עֶזְרִי: עֶזְרִי מֵעִם
ה׳ עֹשֵׂה שָׁמַיִם וָאָרֶץ: אַל יִתֵּן לַמּוֹט רַגְלֶךָ אַל יָנוּם שֹׁמְרֶךָ:
הִנֵּה לֹא יָנוּם וְלֹא יִישָׁן שׁוֹמֵר יִשְׂרָאֵל: ה׳ שֹׁמְרֶךָ ה׳ צִלְּךָ עַל
יַד יְמִינֶךָ: יוֹמָם הַשֶּׁמֶשׁ לֹא יַכֶּכָּה וְיָרֵחַ בַּלָּיְלָה: ה׳ יִשְׁמָרְךָ מִכָּל
רָע יִשְׁמֹר אֶת נַפְשֶׁךָ: ה׳ יִשְׁמָר צֵאתְךָ וּבוֹאֶךָ מֵעַתָּה וְעַד עוֹלָם:

Psalm 130

שִׁיר הַמַּעֲלוֹת מִמַּעֲמַקִּים קְרָאתִיךָ ה׳: אֲדֹנָי שִׁמְעָה בְקוֹלִי
תִּהְיֶינָה אָזְנֶיךָ קַשֻּׁבוֹת לְקוֹל תַּחֲנוּנָי: אִם עֲוֹנוֹת תִּשְׁמָר יָהּ
אֲדֹנָי מִי יַעֲמֹד: כִּי עִמְּךָ הַסְּלִיחָה לְמַעַן תִּוָּרֵא: קִוִּיתִי ה׳ קִוְּתָה
נַפְשִׁי וְלִדְבָרוֹ הוֹחָלְתִּי: נַפְשִׁי לַאדֹנָי מִשֹּׁמְרִים לַבֹּקֶר שֹׁמְרִים
לַבֹּקֶר: יַחֵל יִשְׂרָאֵל אֶל ה׳ כִּי עִם ה׳ הַחֶסֶד וְהַרְבֵּה עִמּוֹ פְדוּת:
וְהוּא יִפְדֶּה אֶת יִשְׂרָאֵל מִכֹּל עֲוֹנֹתָיו:

Psalm 91

יֹשֵׁב בְּסֵתֶר עֶלְיוֹן בְּצֵל שַׁדַּי יִתְלוֹנָן: אֹמַר לַה׳ מַחְסִי וּמְצוּדָתִי
אֱלֹהַי אֶבְטַח בּוֹ: כִּי הוּא יַצִּילְךָ מִפַּח יָקוּשׁ מִדֶּבֶר הַוּוֹת: בְּאֶבְרָתוֹ
יָסֶךְ לָךְ וְתַחַת כְּנָפָיו תֶּחְסֶה צִנָּה וְסֹחֵרָה אֲמִתּוֹ: לֹא תִירָא
מִפַּחַד לָיְלָה מֵחֵץ יָעוּף יוֹמָם: מִדֶּבֶר בָּאֹפֶל יַהֲלֹךְ מִקֶּטֶב יָשׁוּד
צָהֳרָיִם: יִפֹּל מִצִּדְּךָ אֶלֶף וּרְבָבָה מִימִינֶךָ אֵלֶיךָ לֹא יִגָּשׁ: רַק
בְּעֵינֶיךָ תַבִּיט וְשִׁלֻּמַת רְשָׁעִים תִּרְאֶה: כִּי אַתָּה ה׳ מַחְסִי עֶלְיוֹן
שַׂמְתָּ מְעוֹנֶךָ: לֹא תְאֻנֶּה אֵלֶיךָ רָעָה וְנֶגַע לֹא יִקְרַב בְּאָהֳלֶךָ:
כִּי מַלְאָכָיו יְצַוֶּה לָּךְ לִשְׁמָרְךָ בְּכָל דְּרָכֶיךָ: עַל כַּפַּיִם יִשָּׂאוּנְךָ
פֶּן תִּגֹּף בָּאֶבֶן רַגְלֶךָ: עַל שַׁחַל וָפֶתֶן תִּדְרֹךְ תִּרְמֹס כְּפִיר וְתַנִּין:
כִּי בִי חָשַׁק וַאֲפַלְּטֵהוּ אֲשַׂגְּבֵהוּ כִּי יָדַע שְׁמִי: יִקְרָאֵנִי וְאֶעֱנֵהוּ
עִמּוֹ אָנֹכִי בְצָרָה אֲחַלְּצֵהוּ וַאֲכַבְּדֵהוּ: אֹרֶךְ יָמִים אַשְׂבִּיעֵהוּ
וְאַרְאֵהוּ בִּישׁוּעָתִי:

One may recite other psalms as well.

Verses Spelling Out Neshama

It is customary to recite the sets of verses from Psalm 119 whose first letters spell out the word *neshama,* Hebrew for "soul."

(קה) נֵר לְרַגְלִי דְבָרֶךָ וְאוֹר לִנְתִיבָתִי:

(קו) נִשְׁבַּעְתִּי וָאֲקַיֵּמָה לִשְׁמֹר מִשְׁפְּטֵי צִדְקֶךָ:

(קז) נַעֲנֵיתִי עַד מְאֹד ה׳ חַיֵּנִי כִדְבָרֶךָ:

(קח) נִדְבוֹת פִּי רְצֵה נָא ה׳ וּמִשְׁפָּטֶיךָ לַמְּדֵנִי:

(קט) נַפְשִׁי בְכַפִּי תָמִיד וְתוֹרָתְךָ לֹא שָׁכָחְתִּי:

(קי) נָתְנוּ רְשָׁעִים פַּח לִי וּמִפִּקּוּדֶיךָ לֹא תָעִיתִי:

(קיא) נָחַלְתִּי עֵדְוֹתֶיךָ לְעוֹלָם כִּי שְׂשׂוֹן לִבִּי הֵמָּה:

(קיב) נָטִיתִי לִבִּי לַעֲשׂוֹת חֻקֶּיךָ לְעוֹלָם עֵקֶב:

(קסא) שָׂרִים רְדָפוּנִי חִנָּם וּמִדְּבָרְךָ פָּחַד לִבִּי:
(קסב) שָׂשׂ אָנֹכִי עַל אִמְרָתֶךָ כְּמוֹצֵא שָׁלָל רָב:
(קסג) שֶׁקֶר שָׂנֵאתִי וַאֲתַעֵבָה תּוֹרָתְךָ אָהָבְתִּי:
(קסד) שֶׁבַע בַּיּוֹם הִלַּלְתִּיךָ עַל מִשְׁפְּטֵי צִדְקֶךָ:
(קסה) שָׁלוֹם רָב לְאֹהֲבֵי תוֹרָתֶךָ וְאֵין לָמוֹ מִכְשׁוֹל:
(קסו) שִׂבַּרְתִּי לִישׁוּעָתְךָ ה׳ וּמִצְוֹתֶיךָ עָשִׂיתִי:
(קסז) שָׁמְרָה נַפְשִׁי עֵדֹתֶיךָ וָאֹהֲבֵם מְאֹד:
(קסח) שָׁמַרְתִּי פִקּוּדֶיךָ וְעֵדֹתֶיךָ כִּי כָל דְּרָכַי נֶגְדֶּךָ:

(צז) מָה אָהַבְתִּי תוֹרָתֶךָ כָּל הַיּוֹם הִיא שִׂיחָתִי:
(צח) מֵאֹיְבַי תְּחַכְּמֵנִי מִצְוֺתֶךָ כִּי לְעוֹלָם הִיא לִי:
(צט) מִכָּל מְלַמְּדַי הִשְׂכַּלְתִּי כִּי עֵדְוֺתֶיךָ שִׂיחָה לִי:
(ק) מִזְּקֵנִים אֶתְבּוֹנָן כִּי פִקּוּדֶיךָ נָצָרְתִּי:
(קא) מִכָּל אֹרַח רָע כָּלִאתִי רַגְלָי לְמַעַן אֶשְׁמֹר דְּבָרֶךָ:
(קב) מִמִּשְׁפָּטֶיךָ לֹא סָרְתִּי כִּי אַתָּה הוֹרֵתָנִי:
(קג) מַה נִּמְלְצוּ לְחִכִּי אִמְרָתֶךָ מִדְּבַשׁ לְפִי:
(קד) מִפִּקּוּדֶיךָ אֶתְבּוֹנָן עַל כֵּן שָׂנֵאתִי כָּל אֹרַח שָׁקֶר:

(לג) הוֹרֵנִי ה׳ דֶּרֶךְ חֻקֶּיךָ וְאֶצְּרֶנָּה עֵקֶב:
(לד) הֲבִינֵנִי וְאֶצְּרָה תוֹרָתֶךָ וְאֶשְׁמְרֶנָּה בְכָל לֵב:
(לה) הַדְרִיכֵנִי בִּנְתִיב מִצְוֺתֶיךָ כִּי בוֹ חָפָצְתִּי:
(לו) הַט לִבִּי אֶל עֵדְוֺתֶיךָ וְאַל אֶל בָּצַע:
(לז) הַעֲבֵר עֵינַי מֵרְאוֹת שָׁוְא בִּדְרָכֶךָ חַיֵּנִי:
(לח) הָקֵם לְעַבְדְּךָ אִמְרָתֶךָ אֲשֶׁר לְיִרְאָתֶךָ:
(לט) הַעֲבֵר חֶרְפָּתִי אֲשֶׁר יָגֹרְתִּי כִּי מִשְׁפָּטֶיךָ טוֹבִים:
(מ) הִנֵּה תָּאַבְתִּי לְפִקֻּדֶיךָ בְּצִדְקָתְךָ חַיֵּנִי:

Mishnayot Studied in the Merit of the Soul

It is customary to study *mishnayot* in merit of the soul (*neshama*) of the deceased. Man has both a temporary physical existence and an eternal soul. The study of eternal, spiritual ideas marks a contrast to the physical body, which decays into dust. This study is an attempt to rise above the temporal nature of human existence to a higher spiritual plane. According to Jewish tradition, study and spiritual endeavors are considered a merit to the soul of the deceased. This is symbolized by the letters of the Hebrew word משנה, which can be rearranged to form the word נשמה, soul. If the person's passing and their loved ones' consequent study cause them to perform good deeds, these too are in the merit of the deceased person's soul. In principle, one may study any *mishnayot* or Torah in merit of the deceased, but it is customary to study *mishnayot* that begin with the letters of the person's name (one *mishna* beginning with each letter of the name, in order). Some study the *mishnayot* of tractate *Avot,* which discuss proper behavior and good character, or tractate *Mikvaot,* which appears below.

The passing of the deceased from this world is related to impurity; tractate *Mikvaot* deals with purity. The study of topics related to purity is therefore a spiritually reparative response to death. The following are a series of *mishnayot* from tractate *Mikvaot,* ordered so that the first letter of each spells the word נשמה. The study concludes with words of purification.

Mishnayot studied in the merit of the soul – Masekhet Mikvaot chap. 7, *mishnayot* 4–7.

Mishna 4

נָפַל לְתוֹכוֹ יַיִן אוֹ מֹחַל וְשִׁנּוּ מִקְצָת מַרְאָיו, אִם אֵין בּוֹ מַרְאֵה מַיִם אַרְבָּעִים סְאָה, הֲרֵי זֶה לֹא יִטְבֹּול בּוֹ:

Mishna 5

שְׁלֹשָׁה לֻגִּין מַיִם, וְנָפַל לְתוֹכָן קָרְטוֹב יַיִן, וַהֲרֵי מַרְאֵיהֶן כְּמַרְאֵה הַיַּיִן, וְנָפְלוּ לַמִּקְוֶה, לֹא פְסָלוּהוּ. שְׁלֹשָׁה לֻגִּין מַיִם חָסֵר קָרְטוֹב, וְנָפַל לְתוֹכָן קָרְטוֹב חָלָב, וַהֲרֵי מַרְאֵיהֶן כְּמַרְאֵה הַמַּיִם, וְנָפְלוּ לַמִּקְוֶה, לֹא פְסָלוּהוּ. רַבִּי יוֹחָנָן בֶּן נוּרִי אוֹמֵר, הַכֹּל הוֹלֵךְ אַחַר הַמַּרְאֶה:

Mishna 6

מִקְוֶה שֶׁיֶּשׁ בּוֹ אַרְבָּעִים סְאָה מְכֻוָּנוֹת, יָרְדוּ שְׁנַיִם וְטָבְלוּ זֶה אַחַר זֶה, הָרִאשׁוֹן טָהוֹר וְהַשֵּׁנִי טָמֵא. רַבִּי יְהוּדָה אוֹמֵר, אִם הָיוּ רַגְלָיו שֶׁל רִאשׁוֹן נוֹגְעוֹת בַּמַּיִם, אַף הַשֵּׁנִי טָהוֹר. הִטְבִּיל בּוֹ אֶת הַסָּגוֹס וְהֶעֱלָהוּ, מִקְצָתוֹ נוֹגֵעַ בַּמַּיִם, טָהוֹר. הַכַּר וְהַכֶּסֶת שֶׁל עוֹר, כֵּיוָן שֶׁהִגְבִּיהַּ שִׂפְתוֹתֵיהֶם מִן הַמַּיִם, הַמַּיִם שֶׁבְּתוֹכָן שְׁאוּבִין. כֵּיצַד יַעֲשֶׂה, מַטְבִּילָן וּמַעֲלֶה אוֹתָם דֶּרֶךְ שׁוּלֵיהֶם:

Mishna 7

הִטְבִּיל בּוֹ אֶת הַמִּטָּה, אַף עַל פִּי שֶׁרַגְלֶיהָ שׁוֹקְעוֹת בַּטִּיט הֶעָבֶה, טְהוֹרָה, מִפְּנֵי שֶׁהַמַּיִם מְקַדְּמִין. מִקְוֶה שֶׁמֵּימָיו מְרֻדָּדִין, כּוֹבֵשׁ אֲפִלּוּ חֲבִילֵי עֵצִים, אֲפִלּוּ חֲבִילֵי קָנִים, כְּדֵי שֶׁיִּתְפְּחוּ הַמַּיִם, וְיוֹרֵד וְטוֹבֵל. מַחַט שֶׁהִיא נְתוּנָה עַל מַעֲלוֹת הַמְּעָרָה, הָיָה מוֹלִיךְ וּמֵבִיא בַּמַּיִם, כֵּיוָן שֶׁעָבַר עָלֶיהָ הַגַּל, טְהוֹרָה:

אֶרֶץ יִשְׂרָאֵל טְהוֹרָה, וּמִקְוָאוֹתֶיהָ טְהוֹרִים.

List of *Mishnayot* according to the Hebrew Alphabet

The following is a list of chapters of *mishna* that begin with each letter of the Hebrew alphabet. If two or more chapters are listed for a single tractate, all begin with the same Hebrew letter.

א ברכות ה, ח. פאה א. שבת ט, טו. בבא קמא א. פסחים א. ביצה ג. יומא ג.

ב פאה ו. שבת ב, ד, ה, ו. כתובות א. יומא ז. ביצה א. אבות ד, ה. מגילה ג.

ג פאה ה. בבא בתרא י. חולין ז. נגעים ו.

ד סנהדרין א, ג. זבחים יא. כריתות ה. נידה ז.

ה ברכות ב, ט. פאה ד. שבת ח, י, יא, יב. קידושין א, ב, ג. סוכה ה. בבא קמא ט, י.

ו דמאי ב. נדרים ב, יא. סנהדרין ט. מכות ג. מועד קטן ג.

ז טהרות ט. מכשירין ב. עוקצים ב.

ח שבת כב. עירובין ז. יבמות א, יד. חגיגה ג. בבא בתרא ב. חלה א.

ט יומא ד. זבחים יב. כלים יב.

י ביכורים א. שבת א. יומא ח. ביצה ב. ראש השנה ד. בבא בתרא ח. יבמות ט.

כ ברכות ו. פאה ז. שבת ג, ז, טז, יז. פסחים ב, ז. בבא קמא ב. סנהדרין ב, י.

ל מעשר שני ג. סוכה ג, ד. בבא בתרא ב. עבודה זרה א. תמיד ד.

מ ברכות א, ג. פאה ג, ח. שבת יח, כד. פסחים ד, ט. תענית א. מגילה א. אבות א.

נ שבת כא. יבמות יא. כתובות ד. נדרים י. סנהדרין ו. ידיים ב.

ס תרומות ה. סוכה א. תענית ב, ג. כריתות ד. אהלות טו.

ע אבות ג. עירובין ב. פסחים י. קידושין ד. סוטה ט. שביעית א, ב.

פ חלה ב. זבחים יד. מדות ד. פרה ד.

צ פרה ט, יא.

ק כלאים ד. נדרים ח. זבחים ו. מעילה א, ד. קינים ב.

ר שבת יג, יט, כ. ראש השנה ג. יבמות ה. נדרים ט. עדיות ב, ה, ו. אבות ב.

ש ברכות ז. שביעית ו, י. שבת יד, כג. יומא א, ו. כתובות יא. אבות ו. שבועות א, ג, ד.

ת ברכות ד. פסחים ה. כלים ה. אהלות ה. נידה י.

Some have the custom of studying the twenty-fourth chapter of tractate *Kelim* every Saturday night at the conclusion of Shabbat for twelve months, as all of the *mishnayot* in this chapter conclude with purity. Afterward they study the seventh chapter of tractate *Mikvaot,* as appears above.

For *El Maleh Raḥamim,* turn to page. 107.

The fonts used in this book are from the Arno family

Maggid Books
The best of contemporary Jewish thought from
Koren Publishers Jerusalem Ltd.